Practical Internet Groupware

Practical Internet Groupware

Jon Udell

Foreword by Tim O'Reilly

O'REILLY®

Beijing · Cambridge · Farnham · Köln · Paris · Sebastopol · Taipei · Tokyo

Practical Internet Groupware
by Jon Udell

Copyright © 1999 O'Reilly & Associates, Inc. All rights reserved.
Printed in the United States of America.

Published by O'Reilly & Associates, Inc., 101 Morris Street, Sebastopol, CA 95472.

Editor: Tim O'Reilly

Production Editor: Jeffrey Liggett

Printing History:

October 1999:   First Edition.

This book is printed on acid-free paper with 85% recycled content, 15% post-consumer waste. O'Reilly & Associates is committed to using paper with the highest recycled content available consistent with high quality.

ISBN: 1-56592-537-8

Table of Contents

Foreword

At O'Reilly & Associates, we have a history of being ahead of the curve. In the mid-'80s, we started publishing books about many of the free software programs that had been incorporated into the Unix operating system. The books we wrote and published were an important element in the spread and use of Perl, send-mail, the X Window System, and many of the programs that have now been collected under the banner of Linux.

In 1992, we published *The Whole Internet User's Guide and Catalog*, the book that first brought the Internet into the public consciousness. In 1993, we launched GNN, the first ever Internet portal, and were the first company to sell advertising on the Web.

In 1997, we convened the meeting of free software developers that led to the widespread adoption of the term Open Source software. All of a sudden, the world realized that some of the most important innovations in the computer industry hadn't come from big companies, but rather from a loose confederation of independent developers sharing their code over the Internet.

In each case, we've managed to expose the discrepancy between what the industry press and pundits were telling us and what the real programmers, administrators, and power users who make up the leading edge of the industry were actually doing. And in each case, once we blew the whistle, the mainstream wasn't far behind.

I like to think that O'Reilly & Associates has functioned as something like the Paul Revere of the Internet revolution.

I tell you these things not to brag, but to make sure you take me seriously when I tell you that I've got another big fish on the line.

Every once in a while a book comes along that makes me wake up and say, "Wow!" Jon Udell's *Practical Internet Groupware* is such a book.

There are several things that go into making this such a remarkable book.

First, there is the explicit subject: how to build tools for collaborative knowledge management. As we get over the first flush of excitement about the Internet, we want it to work better for us. We're overwhelmed by email, our web searches baffle us by returning tens of thousands of documents and only rarely the ones we want, and our hard disks bulge with documents that we've saved but don't know how to share with other people who might need them.

Jon's book provides practical guidance on how to solve some of these problems by using the overlooked features in modern web browsers that allow us to integrate web pages with the more chaotic flow of conversation that goes on in email and conferencing applications. While much of the book is aimed at developers, virtually anyone who uses the Internet in a business setting can benefit from the perspectives Jon provides in his opening chapters.

How to build effective applications for conferencing and other forms of Internet-enabled collaboration is one of the most important questions developers are wrestling with today. Anyone who wants to build an effective intranet, or to better manage their company's interactions with customers, or to build new kinds of applications that bring people together, will never think about these things in the same way after reading this book.

Second, more than anyone else I know, Jon has thrown off the shackles of the desktop computing paradigm that has shaped our thinking for better part of the last two decades. He works in a world in which the Net, rather than any particular operating system, is truly the application development platform.

All too often, people wear their technology affiliations on their sleeve (or perhaps on their T-shirts), much as people did with chariot racing in ancient Rome. Whether you use NT or Linux, whether you program in Perl or Java or Visual Basic—these are marks of difference and the basis for suspicion. Jon stands above this fragmented world like a giant. He has only one software religion: what works. He moves freely between Windows and Linux, Netscape and Internet Explorer, Perl, Java, and JavaScript, and ties it all together with the understanding that it is the shared Internet protocols that matter.

Any developer worth his salary in tomorrow's market is going to need a cross-platform toolbox much like the one Jon applies in this book.

Third, and perhaps most importantly, Jon has laid his finger on the most important change in the computer industry since the introduction of the Web.

Especially in the later chapters of the book, he lays out a vision in which web sites themselves can be considered as reusable software components. The implications of this paradigm shift are truly astonishing. I confidently predict that in the years ahead, the methodologies Jon demonstrates in this book will be the foundation of multibillion dollar businesses and whole new schools of software development.

As Bob Dylan said, "Something is happening here, but you don't know what it is, do you, Mister Jones?" Well, Jon Udell does know, and if you'd like to know as well, I can't suggest a better place to start.

—Tim O'Reilly
President and CEO
O'Reilly & Associates, Inc.

Preface

A few years ago, as a senior editor at *BYTE Magazine*, I reviewed software and wrote about technologies and industry trends. Everything changed in the spring of 1995 when I became *BYTE*'s executive editor for new media. My charter was to do what every high-tech magazine felt compelled to do in 1995: jump on the Web bandwagon. It was a dream assignment that I tackled with gusto. At first I focused on clever and efficient ways to transform *BYTE* into an electronic publication. But a funny thing happened on the way to the Web. Just weeks into the job, it dawned on me that our content online wasn't just a publication. I began to see that it was fast becoming a suite of Internet-based groupware applications. And I began to see myself as primarily a developer of such applications.

What's Internet groupware? I define it as four interrelated disciplines:

- A way of using standard Internet (web, mail, and news) clients, servers, and protocols

- A way of building web-, mail-, and news-based applications to create, transform, organize, transmit, search, and publish electronic documents

- A way of managing sets of documents that contain semistructured data representing much of the intellectual capital of an enterprise

- A way of deploying web, mail, and news services in support of these activities

I spent three years combining and recombining these disciplines in order to create a wide variety of groupware solutions. Some helped my own department—a team of three—collaborate more effectively. Others helped bind together the whole staff of *BYTE Magazine*, a distributed company that had primary offices in New Hampshire, Massachusetts, and California. Still others linked *BYTE*'s staff to an online population of several million and enabled these online users to collaborate among themselves.

I'd dreamed of, but never thought I'd be able to build, applications that could:

- Be used by 10,000 people a day

- Span multiple zones of privacy

- Connect clients in any location to servers in any location

- Extend HyperText Markup Language (HTML) authoring capability to naive users

- Manage structured and semistructured information

- Run on any client or server platform (Unix, NT)

- Tap into distributed backend services

- Scale across clusters of servers

- Be written in any language (C, Perl, Java™, Unix shell, Visual Basic)

And I'd certainly never have guessed that these applications would turn out to be relatively easy to build. Why is this so? Not because I'm the world's most clever guy. If that were true, this story would be far less compelling. Instead, the answer lies at the heart of the Internet itself. Its applications and data structures rely on simple ideas and protocols. That's why the Internet flourished beyond what many savvy trendsetters—including, most notably, Microsoft—ever thought possible. You can make this simplicity work for you, too. This book explains how.

Who Should Read This Book

This book in its entirety best serves an eclectic toolsmith and information architect who wants to create group-oriented information-management solutions for users. It's full of programming examples, many in Perl and a few in Java, and assumes strong knowledge of these languages and their associated environments. For example, I'll often augment Perl using a Comprehensive Perl Archive Network (CPAN) module, and when I do I'll assume that you know (or can readily learn) how to do that. I'll also assume that you're familiar with:

- Windows NT and Unix/Linux

- HTML (and, to a lesser degree, Extensible Markup Language (XML))

- Cascading Style Sheets (CSS)

- JavaScript (or, more properly, ECMAscript)

- Basic web server setup and administration (both Microsoft IIS and Apache)

- Common Gateway Interface (CGI) scripts and Java servlets

- Web-to-SQL-database integration

- The HyperText Transfer Protocol (HTTP) (and, to a lesser extent, the Network News Transfer Protocol (NNTP))

That's a steep ante, I'll admit, but you don't need to bring all these chips to the table. Just bring a flexible mind. Groupware is slippery stuff, and successful implementation requires a witches' brew of social and technical strategies. The former will outlive the latter, because the technical underpinnings of this book—web document databases, NNTP newsgroups—are about to undergo yet another paradigm shift.

I'll show you ways to get people working together more effectively, and I'll demonstrate using specific examples based on current Internet technologies. I realize, though, that emerging technologies—including web distributed authoring and versioning (WebDAV), and Extensible Stylesheet Language (XSL)—may eclipse some of the solutions shown in this book. I wrestled with this problem and concluded that I had to focus on the here and now, the existing installed base of Internet clients and servers. I base some examples on XML, which matured sufficiently as this book was in progress and which can be used in ways compatible with current clients and servers, but I don't demonstrate WebDAV or XSL, which don't yet meet these requirements.

I know these solutions work, because I've used them successfully. They won't hold up forever, because the infrastructure is evolving. Whatever comes down the pike, though, we'll still need to create, adapt, and use collaborative tools, and we'll likely need an eclectic assortment of strategies to do these things well. Some of this book deals with social engineering, and those principles will have a long shelf-life. Much of the book presents technical strategies whose specifics will change—perhaps quite soon. I've nevertheless grounded the book in specific examples, aiming to deliver a broad vision of how things ought to fit together in groupware systems based on Internet principles, and useful insight into ways to identify and assemble the parts.

Although I use the term Internet groupware, many of the ideas in this book arise from my intranet experiences. I remember looking, one day, for a driver update that I knew was somewhere on my LAN. After wasting half an hour trolling for the file, I searched the Web, found the driver, and downloaded what was probably a newer version than the one I couldn't find on my own network. How, I wondered, could the Web, vast and disorganized, outperform my LAN? And why weren't the Internet technologies we were beginning to use in-house as compellingly useful as the Internet itself?

It's mostly a matter of scale. Internet services such as the Usenet and the Web search engines have critical mass. With millions of contributors and billions of documents, there's lots of action going on and plenty of value to be mined—though you do need to dig for it. Intranets arose when people saw that the Internet's tools could also be useful at narrower scopes: a company, a department. Internet-style collaboration can work well here too, but the dynamics are very different. Far fewer people create far fewer documents; there's not enough fuel for spontaneous combustion. Nevertheless, although there may be only tens or hundreds of us on an intranet, we're working in tightly knit project teams toward common goals. There's a more focused opportunity to use collaborative tools and a greater incentive to do so. This book explores ways to adapt modes of Internet-based collaboration, and the tools that support it, to the smaller and more task-oriented intranet.

Organization of This Book

This book divides into four parts. Part I, *Using Internet Groupware*, is for everyone: you (the aforementioned toolsmith/architect), your bosses, and your users. It introduces two major document-sharing modes: Usenet-style discussion and web document databases. It explains how these modes embody groupware principles, why it's important to apply those principles, how that helps everyone better manage information, and how every user can further that lofty goal by making better use of existing standard Internet client software.

The remaining three parts are a geek-fest. Don't show them to your boss or your users; as with law and sausages, they likely won't want to see groupware being made. These chapters sling Perl scripts right and left, wallow in primordial data structures, deploy Java servlets, run XML parsers, transform documents, automate processes, and explore nooks and crannies of web-server, news-server, and search-engine configuration. Why? In my experience, these are the ways you get things done. Groupware toolkits—commercial ones like Notes and Exchange, as well as the Internet alternatives I explore in this book—only scratch the surface of the problem. Ultimately you have to customize the stuff, because teams and business processes need support that you can't stamp out with a cookie cutter. You have to be willing to use every trick in the book—and a few that aren't.

Part I: Using Internet Groupware

We live and breathe Simple Mail Transfer Protocol (SMTP) email, but its close cousin, NNTP conferencing, isn't something that most people routinely use to collaborate. In this part we'll explore what NNTP conferencing is, why it's such a valuable groupware tool, and how it complements email. We'll discuss why certain kinds of messaging should inhabit shared rather than interpersonal spaces, and how to organize and work within and among those shared spaces, both on public sites and on the intranet. We'll see how a discussion server is a knowledge repository and explore ways to make the best use of it.

Chapter 1: The Conferencing Dimension

Why conferencing is the essential groupware application; the uses and limits of email; definitions of conferencing; how conferencing and email work together; varieties of discussion tools.

Chapter 2: Public Online Communities

How the Usenet came to be; advent of the promiscuous newsreader and site-specific newsgroups; building and managing public online communities; hybrid web/NNTP discussions.

Chapter 3: Intranet Collaboration Using HTML and NNTP

Conferencing and email; principles of information exchange; sharing and privacy; read/write web servers; the art of content aggregation; HTML authoring strategies; reaching your audience.

Chapter 4: Information-Management Strategies for Groupware Users

Scoped zones of discussion; giving information to receive information; inviting colleagues into discussions; packaging and layering messages; using discussion hierarchy; routing and managing email; message-driven data entry.

Part II: Groupware Docbases

A discussion server creates a kind of document database, or *docbase*, that can store a wealth of semistructured information. But Internet messaging tools—mailreaders and newsreaders—use fixed-function message templates. In this part we explore how to build web docbases that aren't bound by fixed templates. We'll see how to activate the groupware features latent in web docbases, and we'll develop a complete system to create, publish, and search them.

Chapter 5: Docbases and Groupware Applications

Principles of Internet software; definition of a docbase; varieties of docbases; translating a repository format into a delivery format; expressing groupware bindings through docbases.

Chapter 6: Docbase Input Techniques

The Docbase system; data-collection strategies; templatized data entry; dynamically configured forms; input validation; previewing records; storing records; managing metadata; message-based assignment forms.

Chapter 7: Docbase Navigation

Sequential indexes; HTML tabbed indexes; docbase maintenance strategies; building a metadata-driven navigational system; dynamic and static versions of the navigational system.

Chapter 8: Organizing Search Results

Docbase web Application Program Interfaces (APIs); Uniform Resource Locator (URL) namespace engineering; search-engine web APIs; multiple search engines and multiple docbases; using URL namespaces and doctitles; an abstract search-results structure; SWISH-E and Microsoft Index Server; field indexing with metadata; Mappers and Classifiers.

Part III: Groupware Applications and Services

Internet services are, by their very nature, scriptable components that can be combined in novel ways. This part shows how to build custom groupware solutions—a collaborative document-review system, a helpdesk, a group calendar, a subscriber-oriented docbase notification system—based on HTTP, NNTP, SMTP, and Lightweight Directory Access Protocol (LDAP) services. Discussion plays a key role in several of these solutions, and this part concludes with a tutorial on setting up and using NNTP discussion servers.

Chapter 9: Conferencing Applications

A reviewable docbase; transforming XML into HTML; a transitional HTML/CSS approach to XML; instrumenting a docbase for collaborative review; XML::Parser case study; using the NNTP API; an alternate email-driven solution; a conferencing-enabled HelpDesk application; advanced newsgroup scripting.

Chapter 10: Groupware Servlets

Why server-side Java matters; Java object storage; servlet efficiency; the Polls servlet; the GroupCal servlet; GroupCal as a provider of a web API; GroupCal as a consumer of a web API; injecting a task monitor into GroupCal.

Chapter 11: Group Membership Services

Internet directory services; the LDAP consensus; a docbase notification system for subscribers; the hybrid push/pull technique; a simple directory; data prototyping; attribute-based subscription; NT-based directories; LDAP directories.

Chapter 12: Authenticating and Authorizing Users

HTTP basic authentication; Apache and IIS; protecting scripts; attribute-based access; scripted authentication; a pass-through Internet Server Application Program Interface (ISAPI) authentication filter; authenticating against Netscape Directory Server; an authorizing docbase viewer; using cookies to authorize access.

Chapter 13: Deploying NNTP Discussion Servers

A model deployment scenario; setting up InterNet News (*INN*) on Linux; setting up Microsoft NNTP service; securing MS NNTP with Secure Sockets Layer (SSL); indexing and searching MS NNTP newsgroups; setting up Netscape Collabra; securing Collabra; indexing and searching Collabra; setting up the MS Exchange 5.5 NNTP service; Internet Message Access Protocol (IMAP) public folders and NNTP newsgroups.

Part IV: Advanced Internet Groupware

Today's Internet tools and services can support groupware activities more effectively than most people realize. But they also promise more than they deliver. This part explores how to use the ideas underlying all Internet software—simple protocols, pipelined components, structured text—to solve advanced groupware problems. We'll see how to automate the testing of web-based groupware and how to aggregate services on behalf of groups. In the final chapter we'll explore ways that scripted HTTP services, distributed to users' workstations, can tackle problems such as offline use of applications and data replication.

Chapter 14: Automating Internet Components

The object Web and Internet groupware; web APIs as automation interfaces; pipelining the Web; web interfaces versus GUI interfaces; XML-RPC; using web APIs to monitor groupware; aggregating and repackaging Internet services; a technology news metasearcher; an LDAP directory metasearcher.

Chapter 15: Distributed HTTP

The peer-to-peer Web; local HTTP servers; the *dhttp* system; connecting *dhttp* to Structured Query Language (SQL) data; persistent database connections; data-bound widgets and namespace completion; polymorphic HTML widgets; event bubbling; networked *dhttp*; data replication; code replication; *dhttp* in the Windows environment.

Chapter 16: Epilogue

Today's Internet groupware opportunities; next-generation Internet groupware; a modest proposal.

Appendixes

Appendix A, *Example Software*, is a guide to the software components created for this book and is available on my web site (*http://udell.roninhouse.com/*). Appendix B, *Internet RFCs: A Groupware Perspective*, traces the groupware technologies discussed in this book to their roots in the Internet Engineering Task Force's Request for Comment (RFC) series of documents.

Appendix A: Example Software

Polls; the docbase modules; the search modules; the ReviewableDocbase kit; the HelpDesk kit; the GroupCal servlet; the directory modules; authorization scripts; test scripts; metasearchers; *dhttp*.

Appendix B: Internet RFCs: A Groupware Perspective

RFCs by category: email (core infrastructure, managing messages, semistructured content, encryption and authentication); news infrastructure; Web (core infrastructure, HTML, and URL schemes); calendaring/scheduling; chat; security; public key infrastructure; directory services; metadata and resource discovery.

Conventions Used in this Book

The many different kinds of software discussed in this book made it a real struggle to come up with consistent typographical conventions. Here are the rules I've tried to follow:

Constant Width
> Used for generic, HTML, SQL, and XML code. Also used for message headers.

Constant Width Bold
> Used for user input.

`Constant Width Italic`

Used for replaceable elements, including markers and abstract markers.

Italic

Used for commands, filenames, functions, GUI labels, modules, newgroups, script names, URLs, and URL fragments. Also used to introduce new terms and for emphasis.

Comments and Questions

Please address comments and questions concerning this book to the publisher:

O'Reilly & Associates
101 Morris Street
Sebastopol, CA 95472
800-998-9938 (in the U.S. or Canada)
707-829-0515 (international or local)
707-829-0104 (FAX)

You can also send us messages electronically. To be put on our mailing list or to request a catalog, send email to:

info@oreilly.com

To ask technical questions or comment on the book, send email to:

bookquestions@oreilly.com

Acknowledgments

As this is book about groupware, I'd like to thank some of the groups that supported the project. They include:

My family

My parents gave me the basic tools. My dear wife, Luann, shared in the challenges of an unusual year that saw us each launch our own businesses. Our children, Robin and Doug, dealt cheerfully with two parents who were always around, but always busy.

O'Reilly and Associates

Mark Bracewell, Andy Oram, John Posner, and Mark Stone all helped shape this book. Then Tim O'Reilly rolled up his sleeves and did the heavy lifting. The final product owes much to his instinctive grasp of what this book was about, and remarkable talent for demonstrating how to get the job done. Tools wizard Chris Maden kindly tolerated my XML experimentation. Katie Gardner and Jeffrey Liggett shepherded the book through production.

Reviewers

Others whose comments helped shape the book include Rael Dornfest, Margaret Levine, John Montgomery, Dave Rowell, and Andrew Schulman.

Former BYTE colleagues

The new media team, Joy Blake and Dave Rowell, indulged my endless groupware experimentation, as did the editorial and production crews. Ben Smith was my Internet service provider and my friend during a tough transitional year.

The BYTE newsgroups

This collective brain trust, now relocated back to *BYTE.com* after a series of migrations, was a touchstone throughout the project, and continues to demonstrate the most important ideas in this book.

I

Using Internet Groupware

We live and breathe SMTP email, but its close cousin, NNTP conferencing, isn't something that most people routinely use to collaborate. In this part we'll explore what NNTP conferencing is, why it's such a valuable groupware tool, and how it complements email. We'll discuss why certain kinds of messaging should inhabit shared rather than interpersonal spaces, and how to organize and work within and among those shared spaces, both on public sites and on the intranet. We'll see how a discussion server is a knowledge repository and explore ways to make the best use of it.

1

The Conferencing Dimension

Almost every day of my working life brings a fresh demonstration of the power and utility of Usenet-style conferencing. Here's a typical example. While logged in to a client's Solaris box, I triggered this unfamiliar error message: "IO object version 1.20 does not match $1.15." What that meant, in general, was that something was wrong with a Perl module that I needed for an application I was building. What it meant specifically was a puzzle. I'm no Solaris expert, and Perl wasn't exhibiting this behavior on my own NT and Linux boxes. I faced the usual choices: fix the problem, or work around it. But which? And in either case, how?

For the last few years, the planetary knowledge base known as the Usenet has been my first line of defense in these situations. Sure enough, plugging the error message into the Deja.com search engine immediately yielded a posting rich with vital clues:

- A Canadian developer named Oleg had run into the same problem.

- Oleg's problem was also on a Solaris system.

- Oleg was using the same slightly outdated version of Perl that my client's system had.

Nobody ever answered Oleg's plea for help. It's tempting to regard his solitary Usenet posting as a futile act of communication. In fact, it was extremely helpful to me (and possibly to others as well). Oleg's message enabled me to:

- Confirm that the problem wasn't specific to my client's system

- Strengthen a hypothesis that a Perl upgrade might fix the problem

- Contact Oleg by email and suggest the hypothesis to him

- Learn that he had already tested and rejected it

- Learn that he had contacted the module's authors and failed to solve the problem

Armed with this knowledge, I was able to spare my client the time and effort required to do an upgrade that wouldn't have helped me get my job done. I concluded that while the problem was likely fixable (most things are, eventually) the path of least resistance lay in the direction of a workaround. So I used CPAN—the Comprehensive Perl Archive Network—to find another Perl module that did what I needed without nasty side effects on Solaris.

What Is Internet Groupware?

I define groupware in a very general way as any technology that links human minds into collaborative relationships. Since we'll have to wait a few years for direct mind hookups, current groupware systems rely on the exchange of documents that record what we do and say.

What's Internet groupware? It arises from three distinct—yet interrelated—modes of document exchange: the Web, email, and Usenet conferencing. The confluence of these modes makes the Internet the mother of all groupware applications. I found Oleg on the Usenet, by way of a browser, and then we communicated using email. During this process an ad hoc group formed, including me and Oleg primarily, but also indirectly some Perl module authors and some of my client's technical staff. Unbounded by time, geography, or corporate affiliation, this group briefly focused attention on a problem, pooled knowledge about it, then disbanded. This is Internet groupware in action.

Shared Versus Annotated Data Stores

At its most minimal, groupware is just software that can read and write a shared data store. But wait a minute; doesn't a simple Novell NetWare file-sharing network qualify as groupware according to this definition? Yes, it does. Who among us hasn't played out the following dialogue?

> You: "Where's the schedule?"

> Me: "It's on drive T:, july98.xls."

More of us do more of our business this way than we care to admit. We realize that it's a flawed mechanism, but we tend not to analyze why it's flawed. There are two reasons. First, the file-sharing approach relies on an *unannotated data store*. A tree of filenames can describe only so much about its contents. Things got much better when long filenames became standard, but a bare hierarchical namespace remains an impoverished way to describe a data store that houses the intellectual capital of an enterprise.

The second flaw with the file-sharing approach is that it isn't, in and of itself, a mode of communication. After you copy *july98.xls* to drive T:, you have to tell someone—maybe everyone—that it's there. Hollering "It's on drive T:" over your cubicle wall to everyone within earshot was the time-honored way. But now that everyone is either working at home, or traveling, or in a satellite office on the other side of the continent, we need to project our voices through digital networks. Enter email.

Email appears to solve both of the problems with file-sharing. It does annotate the data store, in the sense that messages can richly describe and comment on attachments. And it is, obviously, a mode of communication. But do you see what's been lost? We defined groupware as software that can read and write a shared data store. Email doesn't do that; typically it reads and writes personal data stores.

Email can be used to annotate file systems, and in fact it tends to supersede them. We like to use mailboxes to manage documents, because there the documents are surrounded by useful context. We know who wrote them (usually not obvious in a raw file system), when (file systems do know this too), and most crucially, for whom and why. The name *july98.xls* doesn't distinguish between "the version that includes Bob's changes, as requested by Sally, but uses last week's numbers" and "the nearly final version, subject to formatting tweaks by Richard and financial review by Ellen." We're addicted to email, and rightly so, because it helps us relate business documents to business processes.

What's Wrong with Email?

Email isn't really broken, it's just misunderstood and often forced to operate outside its domain of competence. It's the original (and still most effective) push technology. If Bob wants Ellen to review *july98.xls*, it's appropriate that he email her a copy, just as in the pre-electronic era he would have dropped a paper copy on her desk with a yellow sticky note requesting her attention.

Unfortunately things are never quite so simple. At the same time that Ellen needs to review the numbers, Richard wants to spruce up the spreadsheet's appearance. So Bob cc's *july98.xls* to Richard as well. Now when Ellen replies to Bob with a financial clarification, Richard gets an unnecessary and distracting email. Likewise when Richard replies to Bob, Ellen gets junk mail.

Things deteriorate from here. Bob and Ellen begin a dialogue that generates a series of back-and-forth messages, each containing an ever-more-confusing tail of quoted responses. Along the way they recruit George and Susan, by cc'ing them some version of the evolving discussion. George and Susan struggle to get up to speed. They don't have the entire transcript, which is distributed between Bob's mailbox and Ellen's, so they have to read between the lines in order to join the discussion midstream. Meanwhile all these messages keep hitting Richard's mailbox. As a member of the team, Richard should be at least peripherally aware of these goings on. But this chatter should be confined to a lower-priority communication channel.

Sally, whose request to Bob set all this in motion, hasn't heard a thing, because Bob forgot to cc her on his original note to Richard and Ellen. And now, as fate would have it, Sally leaves the company. How will Peter, her successor, learn about the status—or even the existence—of Bob's project? There's plenty of documentation, but it's scattered across a half-dozen mailboxes. All are inaccessible to Peter. None contains a complete transcript. Each holds one view of a group discussion, along with quoted bits of some other views. In theory you could join all these views to reconstruct the complete transcript; in practice nobody has the time, skill, or motivation to stitch the whole quilt together. It goes without saying that there's no way to perform a full-text search across the set of documents related to the project.

Groupware Nirvana and Reality

For years, groupware vendors have touted structured solutions to these communication problems. Often these solutions do leverage email but harness it to software that:

- Coordinates the flow of messages according to some model of a business process
- Relates messages to roles and activities defined within that model
- Stores messages in a central database

These are great ideas, and in certain situations they can be usefully applied. What characterizes those situations? Well-defined workflow, clearly understood roles, agreed-upon milestones, and fully specified deliverables are what pave the way for successful business process automation. Every enterprise has at least a few mainline business processes that qualify. And then there's everything else—the ad hoc, amorphous, fast-paced buzz of communication that weaves in and around the mainline processes. Teams form and split, plans change, training occurs, documents evolve, communication flows across the corporate border to and from vendors, subcontractors, and partners. All this stuff, happening all the time in real time, is what really defines the daily reality of a modern knowledge worker. It's messy and highly idiosyncratic. Software systems that impose order on this chaos just don't exist. Could they? Yes, but to support a corporate culture with a groupware system deeply attuned to that culture requires serious customization. In Part III, *Groupware Applications and Services*, we'll explore ways to customize and extend the standard Internet communication tools. Here in Part I, we'll focus on how to use them more effectively.

The Conferencing Dimension

Is there a middle ground between the flood of email and the drought of structured groupware systems? Yes. That middle ground is *conferencing*, a term that is unfortunately so overloaded that it's crucial to explain, for the purposes of this book, what conferencing is and is not. Here are some examples of what I mean by conferencing:

- A Usenet or private newsgroup, accessed by way of an Network News Transfer Protocol (NNTP) newsreader

- A Lotus Notes discussion database, accessed directly using the Notes client or indirectly through a Domino server by way of a web browser

- A Microsoft Exchange public folder, accessed using the Exchange client

- An Internet Message Access Protocol (IMAP) public folder, accessed using an IMAP email client

- A web-based discussion system, accessed using a web browser

These modes of conferencing share the following characteristics:

- Documents accumulate in a central data store visible to all participants.

- The primary medium of discussion is written text.

- Discussion is typically threaded, exhibiting a treelike structure of statements and responses.

- Text messages may be augmented with binary attachments—spreadsheets, programs, images.

- Participation is asynchronous. I might post a message at noon today; you might read it at midnight; you might then reply at noon tomorrow.

- The stored documents can be scanned along key dimensions: date, author, subject.

- The entire transcript can, ideally, be searched.

Now here are some examples of what I do not mean by conferencing:

Chat

In this mode, participants exchange written messages in real time. It's a popular social pastime. In business settings, it can provide a useful communications backchannel. The O'Reilly software support team, for example, keeps an internal chat line going so that support staffers can confer that way with one another without having to put telephone callers on hold. Chat can support file transfer and can produce a searchable transcript.

A telephone audioconference

> The audioconference is an indispensable business tool. However, it doesn't produce a written transcript, it doesn't provide a medium for file transfer, and it doesn't work asynchronously.

A videoconference

> Most of us lack the facilities to use videoconferencing effectively. When we can, it typically does support file transfer and a very powerful mode called application sharing, in which participants can remotely view and even operate software applications. The business benefit of videoconferencing varies dramatically, depending on the quality of the system and of the network that supports it. Videoconferencing produces no written transcript and doesn't work asynchronously.

Conferencing, as I define it, is email's unknown or misunderstood cousin. Like email, it is a medium for the exchange of written texts with attachments; like email, it works asynchronously. Unlike email, conferencing creates and uses a central data store. What about email archives and IMAP public folders? It's true that, in these cases, email *can* read and write a central data store. But then, I argue, it's acting more like a conferencing system than like email.

It's crucial to separate the two roles. Much of the email abuse that plagues us results from our desire to realize the benefits of conferencing. When we lack a true conferencing system—as most companies do—we seize upon the nearest thing at hand, namely email. So there are two compelling reasons to deploy and use conferencing. First, we require its intrinsic benefits. Second, we need to return email to its domain of competence.

Why Conferencing Matters

The Web was invented so that people could use computer networks to collaborate—that is, exchange documents, discuss them, learn from one another, and create new documents that express the collective knowledge that emerges from this collaboration. It was, in other words, supposed to be a groupware application.

Despite the astonishing popularity of the Web, it has yet to fulfill that original mission. Today's Web is more like a combination of electronic publishing and broadcast television than it is like groupware. The Usenet is, for better and worse, the Internet's most compelling groupware application.

A central theme of this book is that we can, and should, draw a sharp distinction between the *idea* of online communities involved in threaded discussions and its most familiar *implementation*—the Usenet. That institution, at once a crowning achievement of our species and a sprawling mess, will evolve (or not) according to its own rules, in its own way. My message here isn't that we should reinvent the

Usenet (although I think we should), but that its model of collaboration—and its existing, proven tools and technologies—can also serve other vital purposes. On public web sites, on extranets, and on intranets, NNTP conferencing today can support just the kinds of collaboration that the Web has, thus far, failed to deliver.

What we collectively know, in organizations, is expressed in the documents that we write and exchange. Although a new protocol called WebDAV promises to turn the Web into an authoring environment (I'll say more about this in Chapter 3, *Intranet Collaboration with NNTP and HTML*), we're not there yet. The Web, for the vast majority of users, is a library in which we read, not a bulletin board on which we scribble. The Internet application that we do use for scribbling—endlessly, prolifically—is email. But as we've seen, email alone can't do everything we need. It operates in interpersonal spaces, not in group spaces. The value of conferencing is that it enables us to write documents as easily as we can with email and to share them in group spaces as effectively as does the Web.

Lotus Notes, Web Bulletin Boards, and NNTP Newsgroups

You can create a pool of shared documents by using any of the kinds of conferencing I've defined. For example, what Lotus Notes does best, right out of the box, is conferencing. The original and still most essential Notes application is the discussion database. Like NNTP newsgroups, Notes discussion databases are threaded sets of messages with attachments. A Notes discussion can also present views other than NNTP's `Author:`, `Subject:`, and `Date:` views. Notes users can easily tweak the discussion template, adding new fields to the underlying database and corresponding new ways to view the discussion. Notes deeply integrates email and conferencing, using a single data store for both activities. That integration solidifies Notes' position as the premier solution for users who frequently work offline and must synchronize between local and central data stores.

Notes has a whole lot going for it. I rate it as the Cadillac of conferencing systems. Why, then, don't I use Notes? Well, I don't drive a Cadillac either; I drive a Honda Civic. I regard NNTP-based systems as the Honda Civics of the conferencing world. They're cheap, they're widely available, they're less complicated and more reliable than you may think, and they do the basic job well.

What about purely web-based conferencing systems? There are lots of them; see David Woolley's summary page at *http://www.thinkofit.com/* for a current list. In the long run, I think today's standalone mail- and newsreaders will likely become browser-based applications. But that presumes a generation of browsers with richer user interfaces, and much more robust local data stores, than are available to today's browsers. It's true that some users, even corporate users, are beginning to adopt "thin" web-based email. Most, though, still prefer "fat" email programs that exploit native Win32/Mac/Unix graphical interfaces and local storage mechanisms. These programs are faster and more capable than browser-based alternatives and are likely to remain so for a year or two.

As with mailreaders, so with newsreaders. Microsoft's Outlook Express and Netscape's Collabra* are sophisticated conferencing applications. They are faster and more featureful than any browser-based alternative (using currently universal HyperText Markup Language (HTML) standards) can be. And these newsreaders are natural companions to their counterpart mailreaders, sharing the same viewers, sent-message folders, and message composers. One of my challenges in this book is to document NNTP's undiscovered value. Another challenge is to locate NNTP within the larger context of Internet groupware. NNTP is by no means the whole story. But it does deserve more play than it typically gets.

In my work at *BYTE Magazine*, I used NNTP conferencing to support rich collaboration on various levels—within my own department, companywide among three far-flung offices, and worldwide in public newsgroups frequented by *BYTE*'s staff and readership. Lotus Notes or Microsoft Exchange could have done all this, but not (in my estimation) as easily or as cheaply. For best results within the company, we'd have wanted to roll out the Notes or Outlook clients to everyone. That would have required an investment in software, in many cases a supporting hardware upgrade, and training. To reach our readers we'd have needed to use Domino or Exchange to export the public discussions out to web browsers or newsreaders. I'm sure I could have made all this work, but I didn't go that route. Why not? I had observed the following:

- Everyone on staff already had an installed and functional Internet client, either Netscape Navigator or Microsoft Internet Explorer.

- Many of our readers were using one of those two clients.

- Our company email system was in transition from LAN- and dialup-based cc:Mail to an Internet-style Post Office Protocol 3/Simple Mail Transfer Protocol (POP3/SMTP) system. People were using the mail clients bundled with the Netscape and Microsoft browsers.† Those skills were transferable to the NNTP domain, because each mailer shares common components with the corresponding newsreader.

---

* Netscape Collabra is, confusingly, two different products: an NNTP server, Collabra Server, and an NNTP newsreader, which I'll usually call simply Collabra, or else "the Netscape newsreader."

† Netscape Communicator's mailreader is called Messenger, a companion product to the Collabra newsreader. Microsoft's Outlook Express, however, is a single product that includes both a mailreader and a newsreader.

- The Netscape and Microsoft newsreaders were highly functional. With the advent of Version 4 of the products, both newsreaders could operate over Secure Sockets Layer (SSL)-secured channels and display the same rich HTML content that their corresponding browsers could. Both had also augmented their message-composition tools with basic HTML authoring capability.

All that we lacked was our own dedicated news server. When I installed one—and eventually, several assigned to different roles—we began to learn what can be done with a dedicated NNTP conferencing system that operates apart from the worldwide network of replicating Usenet servers. Conferencing servers are tremendous assets. In Chapter 3 and Chapter 4, *Information-Management Strategies for Groupware Users*, I'll show some of the ways to use them, and in Chapter 13, *Deploying NNTP Discussion Servers*, I'll show how to install and configure them. But first, let me anticipate the question you should probably be asking now: "If NNTP servers are so darned useful, how come hardly anybody seems to use them?" Thereby hangs a tale.

2

Public Online Communities

The Network News Transfer Protocol (NNTP) was zipping messages around the Internet long before the Hypertext Transfer Protocol (HTTP) arrived on the scene. The NNTP-based Usenet that still thrives today predates the Web and is built on a very different foundation. Circa 1985 there were relatively few full-time Internet nodes. A store-and-forward technology, Unix-to-Unix Copy (UUCP), enabled intermittently connected nodes to access the Internet. The first incarnation of the Usenet was therefore, of necessity, a discussion system based on data replication. News servers would form pairwise connections, feed each other batches of articles, then disconnect. A complex topology of interconnections created the illusion of a network that was simultaneously accessible to far more nodes than could actually connect in real time to the Internet.

A decade later the World Wide Web catapulted the Internet into the mainstream. But it was a very different kind of Internet. Now end users, from their home PCs, for $20 a month, could access growing numbers of web sites *in real time*. A user in Tel Aviv could connect directly to a web site in Boston, or anywhere else, at any time. There was no need—and given the Web's explosive growth, there would have been no practical way—to mirror the Web onto servers local to that user in Tel Aviv. It's true that caching web servers mirror parts of the Web. But the Web never had to rely on replication to move data.

Meanwhile, the Usenet, now riding the coattails of the Web phenomenon, continued to grow. People who signed up for ISP accounts found that their Netscape client included a thing called a newsreader. They learned that the newsreader could connect to the ISP's news server, which nightly was fed thousands of newsgroups from the Usenet. They began to participate in virtual communities that operated independently of time and space and were defined solely in terms of shared interest: *rec.crafts.rubberstamping, rec.photo.equipment.35mm.* They glimpsed, many for the first time, the extraordinary power of computer-based conferencing.

The Usenet wasn't an unqualified blessing, though. The obvious problems included spam and the hostility of longtime Usenet veterans toward the teeming multitudes of newcomers. But the real problem was subtler and deeper, arising from the very architecture of the Usenet. On the Web, sites grow and evolve, they put down deep roots, and they're lovingly nurtured in order to yield an optimal mix of esthetic and functional value. On the Usenet, newsgroups travel everywhere but have no real homes.

On any given Usenet server, collaboration can occur only within a small, fast-moving window of opportunity—the few days or weeks between the arrival of one newsfeed and its displacement by the next. The remarkable Deja.com service (*http://www.deja.com/*) enlarges that window to several years. It enables full-text search of vast quantities of Usenet data and creates the illusion of a singular, unified Usenet. But under the covers it's still the same old Usenet, based on massive replication of disposable newsfeeds. The communities that create and use the Usenet's newsgroups deserve better. They deserve collaborative spaces that can grow and flourish just as web sites do. Such spaces can exist; some already do. Ironically there's no new technology required. It's only necessary to apply some old tools in a new way.

Advent of the Promiscuous Newsreader

Since Version 2, Netscape Navigator has included a newsreader that could access not only a default news server (typically, your ISP's) but others as well. Moreover, it could keep track of your interactions with multiple news servers, remembering for each which groups you subscribed to, and which messages you read. To show why this matters, Netscape deployed its own news server as a standalone that did not mirror the Usenet. On that server, Netscape's newsgroup hierarchy, which would have taken forever to develop if it had to follow the social and political rules that govern Usenet newsgroup formation, appeared overnight. The Netscape news servers soon supported a huge online community of technical people committed to using and extending Netscape's client and server products. To these folks, *secnews.netscape.com,* and later, *news.mozilla.org,* became unique destinations on the Net, bookmarked in the same way that AltaVista and Lycos were. On its news site, Netscape built mind share, enabled users to provide one another with technical support, and conducted a massive ongoing focus group.

The Dynamics of Site-Specific Public Newsgroups

Following Netscape's lead, other high-tech companies began hosting site-specific newsgroups. One of these was *BYTE*, where I launched a news server that enabled *BYTE's* widely dispersed staff to meet and converse with its even more widely dispersed readership. That server, which was the standard InterNet News (*INN*) 1.4 included with my Caldera Linux kit (see the following tip), immediately paid us a huge dividend. I was planning a cover story for the magazine, a process that for me typically involved weeks of telephone interviews with vendors and users whose perspectives would shape the story. The real challenge had always been simply to find the right people to interview. This is a classic networking problem, in the social sense of networking. We use the people we do know to find the people we don't know. But isn't the Internet the ultimate power tool for social networking? To test that proposition, I started a thread in one of my newsgroups, outlining my plan for the cover story and inviting discussion of it. Then I advertised the thread on our home page.

Setting up your own news server is a lot like setting up a web server—install the software, configure some settings, create a directory structure, and turn it on. See Chapter 13, *Deploying NNTP Discussion Servers*, for details on doing this with various kinds of NNTP servers, on both Linux and NT.

The latest servers from Microsoft and Netscape come with GUI administration tools that turn most of this stuff into a point-and-click exercise. Why don't more people know this? Traditionally, news servers have been used solely as Usenet nodes, and setting up the server-to-server newsfeeds was a complex and arcane chore. When you run a site-specific NNTP server that doesn't replicate with the Usenet, though, you eliminate almost all the hard stuff. The rest is, as I've said, no more difficult than setting up a web server.

In the discussion that ensued, a NASA software engineer mentioned his work using Java to distribute data visualization across an intranet. This was exactly the sort of real-world example that the story required. We conversed online, then by telephone, and what I learned became the centerpiece of the story. What's most remarkable is that my traditional research method never would have found this person, but with the help of Internet groupware, he found me. It was a transforming experience for a journalist, and I think the focus-group technique can apply in other fields as well. The purpose of a corporate web site is not to entertain your customers and business partners but to engage them. Newsgroups or other forms of Internet-based discussion, properly deployed, will help you do that.

Online Focus Groups in Action

Let's look at how this works today at Microsoft's site. Suppose you're interested in Extensible Markup Language (XML), and you land on Microsoft's XML home page (Figure 2-1).

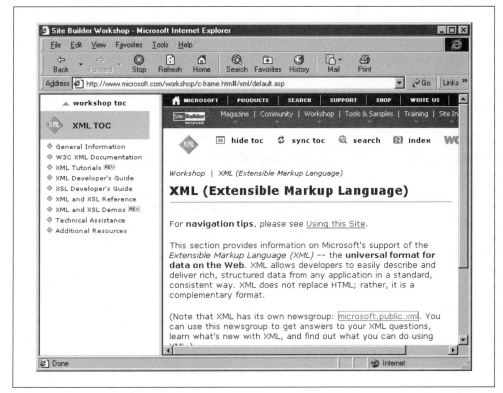

Figure 2-1. Microsoft's XML home page

Note how the third paragraph in the right hand frame includes a link labeled *microsoft.public.xml*. Although it looks like a normal http:// link that leads to a web page, it isn't. Instead it's a news:// link that leads to an NNTP newsgroup hosted on Microsoft's news server, *msnews.microsoft.com*. When you click the link, your newsreader starts up.* If you've never visited this news server before, it's automatically added to the list of servers tracked by your newsreader, and you're automatically subscribed to the newsgroup whose name was encoded in the link's

---

* Which newsreader? In the case of web browsers, when both Microsoft's and Netscape's are installed, one or the other is registered with your system as the default. It's the same with newsreaders: the default newsreader (usually Netscape's, for me) launches when you click a news:// Uniform Resource Locator (URL).

address. As we'll see again in Chapter 13, this shortcut is a terrific way to catapult visitors into the midst of a discussion. The alternative procedure, which involves manually attaching to the news server, viewing its list of available groups, and subscribing to one or more groups, is cumbersome and hard to explain to visitors not already familiar with NNTP conferencing.

What is a newsreader? It's a client application that connects to news servers, retrieves lists of newsgroups, reads and posts articles (messages), and displays messages in several ways. Like the mail and web components of the standard Internet client, the newsreader talks to its own kind of server using its own protocol. But in the Netscape and Microsoft implementations, the newsreader appears to the user as a facet of the email client. See Figure 2-2, which shows my Netscape messaging environment.

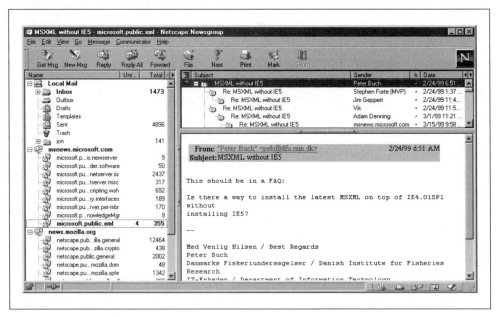

Figure 2-2. Microsoft's XML newsgroup

Along with my email inbox, and its subfolders, we can see two different NNTP servers—one at Microsoft, one at Netscape. Because I clicked on a web link whose address was *news://msnews.microsoft.com/microsoft.public.xml*, that newsgroup is the current selection. Messages are listed in the top right hand pane, and shown in the bottom right hand pane. If I click on an email folder, these viewing panes will instead display email messages. Although mail and news use different protocols and talk to different kinds of servers, they share a common user interface and behave similarly. (See the following tip.)

If you use Post Office Protocol (POP) to fetch your email, entire messages are stored on your client. With NNTP, usually, only message headers are stored there. You have to fetch message bodies from the server each time you view them. However, the reverse is possible in both cases. If you connect to an IMAP mail server, you can opt to retrieve only headers, not entire messages. And because both the Netscape and Microsoft newsreaders support offline use, you can also configure your newsreader to store entire messages locally.

What's going on in this XML newsgroup? In the fragment we can see, someone's asking how to install Microsoft's XML parser as a standalone component not tied to Internet Explorer. If you were to read further, you'd see an interesting dialogue taking place involving third-party developers and the Microsoft employee designated to monitor this newsgroup. The developers were disappointed to hear from a Microsoft representative that, at the release of Microsoft Internet Explorer 5 (MSIE 5), the XML parser would not be redistributable or separately installable, though it would be made so "at a later date." When might that date arrive? That will partly depend on the number and intensity of requests directed to this newsgroup. All sorts of useful things are happening here. A community of XML-oriented developers, given a place to gather, compare notes, and learn from one another, builds a pool of knowledge that it can tap to its own benefit. Microsoft gains a focus group that enables it to monitor the pulse of that community, and a channel it can use to talk directly to the community.

Managing Online Discussions

Big companies like Microsoft and Netscape don't have to try very hard to reap the rewards of maintaining online discussions. Their developer populations are large; critical mass is virtually ensured. What if you want the same dynamic to work for your smaller company? It's often not enough just to create a newsgroup (or a web-based bulletin board), throw open the doors, and wait for a vibrant community to form. In this game, critical mass is, well, critical. Experienced discussion operators know that for everyone who posts, there may be a hundred or more who lurk.

This doesn't mean your site can't attract a community of users interested in your company's products or services. It just means you have to work the process a little differently. One of the best strategies is to use web pages as portals into your discussions. You want to do more than just keep a record of those discussions; you want to enhance them. The key point is that every online discussion, whether NNTP- or web-based, generates a raw document database, or *docbase*, to which you can (and should) add value.

What's a docbase? Mail folders, newsgroups, and web archives are all examples of docbases. That is, they're collections of files, stored in directories, containing text that's structured according to some rules. For mail and news messages, the rules are preordained and specify a set of colon-delimited headers (e.g., `Subject: Tuesday meeting`) followed by a message body that's just more text (which may exhibit internal structure, such as attachments encoded using MIME, or Multipurpose Internet Mail Extensions). For web archives, you need to invent the rules. HTML pages don't require headers, for example, but applications can easily create and use them; Part II is full of examples that show how and why to do that.

A discussion docbase, no matter what its underlying format, provides various ways to navigate its messages—for example, by thread or author or date. But it can't create views that summarize the discussion, or rearrange it, or guide it. Users of the discussion tool confront a raw message stream; it's up to them to separate the wheat from the chaff.

As the operator of a discussion group, though, you can and should summarize, rearrange, and guide the discussion. How? Figure 2-3 shows how a web page can act as a portal into a discussion.

This page, which appeared on the WebBuilder site (*http://www.webbuildermag. com/*), is an example of the Web interface to a set of NNTP newsgroups I ran there. In this fragment, we were discussing the capabilities of the Win32 version of an application suite called StarOffice. The quoted bits are just part of an underlying message stream that contained more chatter about StarOffice and about all sorts of other things. The page selects a few cogent postings about StarOffice for Win32, highlights them, and provides links back into the discussion at those points.

Why do this? Web sites are always hungry for fresh content. Here's an easy and effective way to recycle user-contributed messages into pages that have a thematic focus. These summary pages—which may be posted or perhaps summarized in email bulletins to subscribers—help make your site appear as busy and active as, in fact, it probably is. But they work harder than that. The discussion links multiply the ways in which people can find, join, and contribute to the discussions, which helps you get to critical mass. More subtly, they can be used to reward your outstanding contributors. In every online community there are a few people whose knowledge, and generosity with it, are exemplary. Acknowledge them! Call out their most salient postings in pages that you feature prominently on the site. Close the feedback loop, and you'll amplify the power of your discussions. The success of *slashdot.org*, and of what the media are now calling *weblogs*—sites that aggregate personalized views of the Web—has shown this approach to be one of the most effective drivers of online traffic.

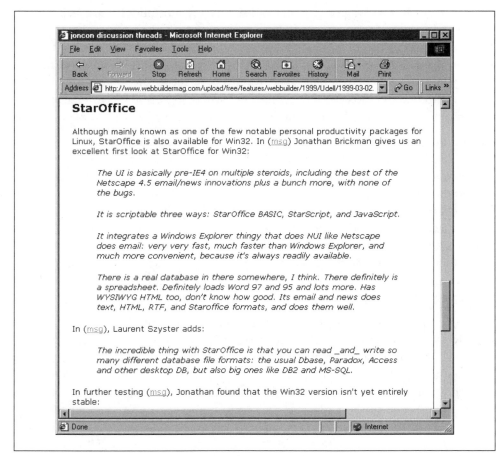

Figure 2-3. Web page as portal to a discussion

Making the Most of Discussions

The Web naturally tends toward aggregation; sites encapsulate other sites, which encapsulate still others. To be an effective user of Internet groupware, you need to understand and exploit this principle of aggregation and apply it to the content that you and others create. To do this doesn't require the kinds of applications we'll build in Part II and Part III. Mostly it's just a matter of working smarter. For example, the vendor of StarOffice, Star Division GmbH, does run NNTP news-groups for its users. But like many such discussion areas, that one doesn't serve its proprietor as well as it could. The Web part of the site links to the newsgroups but doesn't do anything more with them. In addition to advertising the newsgroups and generating fresh web content, richer interconnections between the Web and news domains could help the site gather raw information. Consider FAQs. Discussions often raise the kinds of questions that go into FAQs, and often produce answers as well. A newsgroup in and of itself isn't a substitute for an FAQ, so like most vendors, Star Division consolidates the raw information into a set of formal FAQs expressed as web pages. But why not link from those FAQs back to their roots in the discussion? This technique works two ways. First, it connects readers of the FAQ to source materials—and these connections are otherwise far from obvious. Second, it leads readers of the FAQ who can contribute further clarification to a place where such contributions can appropriately be received.

Getting the most value out of discussions also requires that you index them and make them available for search. Oddly many sites, including Netscape's, Microsoft's, and Star Division's, don't bother to do this. How do you index newsgroups? Some servers, such as Netscape Collabra Server, Microsoft's NNTP service, and NetWin's DNEWS, come with built-in indexers. But newsgroups are just sets of text files. You can index them using any file-oriented indexer, and you should. If you take the trouble to invite people to pool their knowledge, you owe it to them (and to yourself) to make that knowledge as accessible as it can be. Chapter 8, *Organizing Search Results*, has more on indexing newsgroups and organizing search results.

Although I've focused here on NNTP newsgroups, everything I've said applies equally to web discussions. O'Reilly & Associates' WebBoard, Lundeen's Web-Crossing, and many other products support HTML-based threaded discussions. It's tempting to conclude that such discussions, because they manifest as HTML, must integrate more naturally into a web site than NNTP newsgroups can. Yes and no. It's true that nontechnical audiences may feel more comfortable viewing and posting by way of the familiar browser, rather than the less familiar newsreader. But HTML discussions are as likely to become isolated ghettos as NNTP newsgroups are. Connections between discussions and the rest of your site only happen when you make them happen. And the method in both cases is the same: editorial selection, URL-based content aggregation.

Hybrid Web/NNTP Discussion Systems

Newsgroups are nifty, and people who appreciate their value tend to prefer them to web-based alternatives. But there's no point in being a newsgroup snob, either. Many people really would rather converse using a browser. Fortunately this doesn't have to be an either/or choice. Make everyone happy, and run a discussion system that plays to both audiences at the same time. I did that with my *BYTE* newsgroups, mirroring news messages into a parallel web archive. Some commercial news servers, such as NetWin's DNEWS, include web gateways that do the same thing. Conversely some commercial web-conferencing systems, including WebCrossing and WebBoard, offer NNTP interfaces so newsreaders can hook into them.

This hybrid approach isn't so important in an intranet setting, where it's easier to expect everyone to use a single method of access. But public newsgroups should reach out to the widest possible audience, excluding no one unnecessarily. Remember: it's all about getting to critical mass. Don't turn away anyone who can help you get there. Note that for some people, a web interface isn't merely a preference, it's the only possible mode of access. Not all corporate firewalls allow users to attach to external news servers. For these users, the Web may be the only way to use your discussions.

There's another very important reason to create an HTML interface to your public discussions, regardless of whether the underlying engine is web- or NNTP-based. When expressed as HTML, the discussion docbase can be indexed by AltaVista, Excite, and other search engines. That boosts the Web's awareness of your company's products or services, and—here's that feedback loop again—it draws more people into your online community. Some search engines can index NNTP servers directly, but most can't or won't. So even if all your users prefer newsreader-style conferencing (and that's unlikely), it's still a good idea to present the discussions as HTML too.

Public Discussions in Perspective

Every business's customers have something in common: they all use the products or services provided by that business. For example, I bought a bread machine a few years ago. When I lost the recipe book that came with it, I was happy to be able to download a new one from the company's web site. But Internet groupware opens up new realms of possibility. Other owners of the same model of bread machine have doubtless come up with all sorts of recipes that aren't in that book. And they've also, collectively, learned a lot about how to use and maintain the machine. Why not create a home online for that collective knowledge?

Think of online discussion as a resource. Managed properly, it delivers all sorts of benefits. A Net-savvy consumer, faced with a choice between two otherwise comparable products, will tend to prefer the one that's supported by a vibrant online community. A Net-savvy company that successfully creates that community can enable customers to support one another, monitor customer satisfaction, solicit feedback on planned improvements, boost its web mindshare, and generate content that helps keep its web site lively.

3

Intranet Collaboration with NNTP and HTML

Using public newsgroups as described in the last chapter, you can augment a corporate web site with Usenet-style discussion. These site-specific newsgroups work a bit differently from their Usenet counterparts. They can store messages much longer than Usenet newsgroups do—even indefinitely. That persistence creates opportunities to manage the message store as a pool of content that can be advantageously linked into a web site. But this is still a public mode of collaboration, one that ought to appeal to the widest possible audience. It's inappropriate here, as it is inappropriate on the Usenet, to use the full set of capabilities built into the Microsoft/Netscape newsreaders. Public newsgroups necessarily cater to the lowest common denominator: plain ASCII text messages.

On the intranet, it's a different story. Here you're not dealing with the public, only with your own staff. That means you can allow, and should encourage, the most effective use of Internet communication tools—that is, newsreaders and mailers. They can do much more than many people realize. For example, most people know that the Microsoft and Netscape newsreaders can post plain-text messages to newsgroups and can also attach MIME-encoded binary files. But relatively few people have used them to:

- Compose and display HTML messages

- Communicate securely over SSL

- Authenticate using name/password credentials or client certificates (digital IDs)

- Do full-text search of an indexed newsgroup (Netscape Collabra and Collabra Server only)

- Exploit powerful synergies between email and newsgroups

When people discover and use these capabilities, intranet-based discussion can become even more powerful than Internet-based discussion. Why does this rarely happen? There are two reasons, one technical and one cultural. The technical reason is that although every intranet offers web and email service, few provide NNTP service. So there usually isn't a local environment in which to explore and master the kinds of rich collaboration that NNTP can enable. This obstacle, as we'll see here and in more detail in Chapter 13, *Deploying NNTP Discussion Servers*, is easily overcome.

The cultural problem is far more difficult. The methods I'll present in the next few chapters assume that groups really want to collaborate—that is, share documents, move communication from interpersonal to group spaces, pool knowledge. "Our people are our only real asset," corporate executives like to say, and they mean it. They understand that their success depends mainly on what their people know, not just individually but collectively. A Lotus executive once claimed that there is an infinite return on an investment in Lotus Notes. Infinite! That sounds like brash computer-industry hyperbole. In fact it's arguably true when Notes captures organizational knowledge as it was designed to do and is capable of doing. But mostly that doesn't happen, for lots of reasons. People tend to focus only on their own tasks and associate only within their own workgroups. People don't want to document everything they do. People don't want to think carefully about how they communicate, with whom, for what purposes, with what results. People don't want to share what they know, if they believe that doing so will threaten their own security.

There's no magic-bullet solution. Internet groupware succeeds as well as it does, on the large scale of the Internet, because of that large scale. There is critical mass. Thousands of people may know some crucial fact. The vast majority won't be inclined to plug it into the planetary knowledge base. When even one person does, everyone else benefits. On the intranet, though, Internet-style groupware faces the same challenges as Notes does. Critical mass is very hard to achieve. Many companies and workgroups, frankly, won't get there. But your company or workgroup might, and if you succeed, you'll enjoy a huge advantage.

Effective use of Notes (or of Microsoft Exchange) requires commitment and learned discipline. Likewise Internet groupware. It has one big advantage, though: the standard Internet client is ubiquitous. People spend an awful lot of time using it to browse, and read and write email. When an intranet culture encourages people to collaborate more effectively, the same already-installed client can help them do so. I'll say more about why it makes sense to engage in this kind of collaboration and show how you can exploit some little-known and poorly understood features of NNTP conferencing to make it happen. But since not many people have ever set up or used local newsgroups, let's look briefly at how that works.

Using Local Newsgroups: An Overview

At *BYTE* we created a set of intranet newsgroups in which our distributed staff could privately converse, exchange the manuscripts and images that were the raw material of our product, and manage the flow of other documents. There were company wide newsgroups with names like *bytestaff.operations* and *bytestaff. issueplanning*, and departmental newsgroups with names like *newmedia. operations* and *newmedia.design*. Originally the NNTP server that hosted these groups was Microsoft's Internet News Server (INS).* Later we used Netscape's Collabra Server. Chapter 13 is a basic tutorial on setting up and running these news servers and also the standard Unix *INN*.

Why didn't we run our local newsgroups on *INN*? We could have, but modern derivatives of *INN*, including both the Microsoft and Netscape products, are easier to use and more featureful. It's true ease of use, like beauty, is in the eye of the beholder. If you're good at command-line administration, you may feel that the GUI point-and-click interfaces to the newer servers are more trouble than they're worth. Nevertheless, these interfaces vastly enlarge the potential reach of NNTP. A Windows NT LAN administrator who may know nothing of Unix (never mind *INN*, whose quirks and crankiness are legendary) will find the Microsoft or Netscape news servers straightforward and familiar. It takes about an hour to install either of these servers, create some newsgroups, and begin hosting intranet discussions.

Eventually, I'll admit, I spent much more than an hour on setup. As we expanded our use of local newsgroups we needed better structure and more security. The structure that evolved was a system of what I'll call scoped newsgroups. Rather than present everyone in the company with a long list of newsgroups, we made the top level of the newsgroup tree visible to everybody and assigned subtrees to departments and project teams. We'll see later in this chapter, and in Chapter 4, *Information-Management Strategies for Groupware Users*, why this kind of structure is important. And in Chapter 13 we'll see how to create it.

The security issue arose when I moved the news server from our intranet to our Internet-visible DMZ (that's the demilitarized zone between an external firewall and an internal firewall). Originally the news server ran on a corporate intranet, accessible from office PCs around the country but not from home or road PCs. But collaboration isn't just a nine-to-five activity in the modern organization. People need to be able to collaborate anywhere, anytime, so I put the news server out in the DMZ along with our public web server. That meant we had to encrypt all data flowing to and from the news server. You can't do that with *INN*, but you can do it with both the Microsoft and Netscape news servers.

---

* INS was originally a freely available product, then later became part of the Microsoft Commercial Internet Services (MCIS), which was sold exclusively to ISPs and not generally available. However a variant of INS became the NNTP service bundled with the NT 4 Option Pack, which is freely available.

If you've only used NNTP to connect to the Usenet, you may not realize that it supports a name/password protocol similar to HTTP's basic authentication (see the following tip). Like the HTTP version, NNTP authentication involves a simple name/password challenge. Now that use of packet sniffers has become a recreational sport, these unencrypted authentication schemes offer only a weak form of security. As with a password-protected web server that holds confidential data, an extranet-based conference server that hosts private discussions should encrypt not only login credentials but also all message traffic. The Microsoft and Netscape news servers do this in the same way that web servers do. As I'll show in Chapter 13, you can install a digital ID on a news server and run it in Secure Sockets Layer (SSL) mode. The Microsoft and Netscape newsreaders can both communicate securely with either brand of server. The exchange of name/password credentials is encrypted; so are other commands and all message data.

In HTTP authentication, a request for a protected page causes a server to send your browser the HTTP Authorization header. Your browser responds by prompting you, with a dialog box, for a name and password. Then it retries the request, using the supplied name and password. If your credentials are accepted, the server shows you the page originally requested—subject to permissions on your account.

In NNTP authentication, a request to list the contents of a protected newsgroup provokes a response like 480 Authentication required for command. Your newsreader responds by prompting you, with a dialog box, for a name and password. Then it transmits the *authinfo* command twice, first to send a username, then the password. If your credentials are accepted, the news server allows you to list, read, and post messages—subject to permissions on your account.

With a secure private news server in place, editors and writers could collaborate from their offices, their homes, or any other points of attachment to the Internet. In this environment we began to do things that we couldn't do in our public *INN*-based newsgroups. In some cases, the limitations had been *INN*'s. It doesn't support integrated full-text search, for example. That's an NNTP extension that Netscape added to Collabra Server and that works only in conjunction with the Collabra client.

In other cases the limitations weren't *INN* shortcomings. Rather, they were imposed by the culture of the Usenet. For example, the Netscape/Microsoft newsreaders can compose and display HTML documents. This is pretty exciting stuff. It invites users to go beyond the age-old Usenet tradition of line-oriented ASCII text and enrich their online collaboration with rich text, tables, lists, inline images, and hyperlinks.

You might think that you need a modern NNTP server to handle HTML-enriched newsgroups. Actually you don't. HTML news messages, like conventional line-oriented ASCII news messages, are just clumps of headers followed by more text. Venerable old *INN* handles this stuff in the same way that its modern derivatives do. Rich messaging—that is, the ability to compose and view HTML-formatted documents—arises entirely from the new breed of mail/news clients.

The Usenet continues to play to the lowest-common-denominator plain-text-oriented newsreader, as indeed it should. If you create your own public newsgroups, they should probably obey the same rule. But on your intranet or extranet, you can fully exploit all the rich features built into modern newsreaders. Lacking a local news server, not many users of Netscape Collabra or Microsoft Outlook Express have had a chance to discover an amazing fact about these newsreaders. They are arguably the most effective tools now available for creating intranet content. What's that? I think an intranet's mission is to document what is collectively known in a company. Much of that knowledge exists in the form of messages. Conferencing tools are an effective way to move message data into shared spaces, thereby manufacturing intranet content. Before we explore how that process can work, though, let's look more closely at the relationship between two modes of messaging: conferencing and email.

Conferencing and Email

Conferencing has been an essential tool for much of my working life. I used an early version of Notes when I worked as a software developer for Lotus years ago. When I joined *BYTE*, I found myself in the midst of a group of writers and editors who collaborated extensively on BIX*. We conducted a huge amount of editorial business in our private BIX conferences: trading contacts, hashing out story ideas, reviewing drafts, exchanging news items. Across continents and time zones, BIX was our virtual office before the term became fashionable. Clunky by today's standards, it nevertheless embodied many of the virtues of Internet groupware. It was accessible from anywhere, requiring only a modem and freely available software—in the case of BIX, just a terminal emulator. It combined email with conferencing. It was searchable. It could create multiple zones of discussion for sometimes overlapping, sometimes disjoint groups of users. It could admit a transient collaborator—for example, a freelance writer or editor—to one of these groups for a project of limited duration.

Although BIX conferencing was a deeply ingrained part of our corporate culture, by 1996 we could no longer ignore the call of Internet groupware. We switched

---

* BIX stands for the *BYTE* Information Exchange. It's a text-mode message board that derives from the University of Guelph's text-mode CoSY conferencing system. Originally a *BYTE*/McGraw-Hill service, BIX is now owned and operated by Delphi Internet Services Corporation.

from BIX conferences to NNTP newsgroups, retaining nearly all the benefits of BIX while adding a number of new capabilities, which we'll explore in this chapter.

For a long time I thought everybody depended on conferencing the way I did. Eventually I realized that, in many organizations, email was the only collaborative tool in use and that the differing nature and uses of email and conferencing were not widely known or understood. So let's try to spell them out. Put simply, a conferencing system creates a sort of hive-mind. It's a great foundation for teamwork. To understand why that's so, consider these axioms about the flow of information, and the creation of knowledge, in corporate settings.

You May Not Need What I Send You

In email environments, this axiom governs the dreaded FYI (for your information) syndrome. A scrap of information reaches Bob's desk. He forwards it by email to Richard and Ellen, guessing rightly that Richard needs it, guessing wrongly that Ellen will care, and forgetting to include Sally, who for reasons unknown to Richard has just developed a vital interest in the matter. In a conferencing environment, Bob posts his message to a newsgroup that the whole team visits regularly. Richard briefly scans the message; Ellen skips it; Sally seizes it and puts it to immediate use.

When you offer information to a group, the push method (email) obliges you to identify the right set of recipients. The pull method (conferencing) allows recipients to self-select. But it imposes a different obligation on the sender. It's Bob's responsibility to post to an appropriate newsgroup, using an appropriate subject header, so everyone can rapidly evaluate the purpose and significance of the message relative to their needs.

What I Send You Now, You May Not Need Until Later

In an email-only scenario, Bob's correct identification of Richard as an appropriate receiver may still go to waste. Why? Richard didn't need the information at the time Bob sent it; his need arose months later. With luck, Richard will remember Bob's message and will be able to find it in his mailbox. But it might have been purged; it might not be locatable using full-text search; it might never have been downloaded to the laptop Richard's using at the moment. In these cases Richard might prefer that Bob had posted the message to a newsgroup, so access to it would not depend on the state of Richard's email client. Private newsgroups, like Notes discussion databases and Exchange public folders, are server-based data stores that can remember things more effectively than many email clients can.

When You Do Need What I Sent, You May Have Forgotten That I Sent It

When Bob emails Richard a message for which Richard has no immediate use, Bob may still have performed a useful service. Assuming that the information will become useful to Richard at a later time, Bob has a) transmitted it and b) alerted Richard to its existence. When Richard does need what Bob sent, he may remember that Bob sent it. But what if Richard doesn't? What if Bob doesn't either? Nobody else knows about this messaging event, so nobody else can help. Had Bob posted the message to the team's newsgroup, the following dialogue might then occur:

Richard: "I'm researching LDAP and I can't find a description of the LDIF file format."

Sally: "Did you search our newsgroups for LDIF?"

Richard: "Yeah, nothing there."

Sally: "Hmm. Still, I seem to remember Bob posting something about LDIF a few months back. Maybe it was just a URL, not the whole spec, so your LDIF search didn't turn up any hits."

Richard: click, scan, click, sort, "Aha."

Group Spaces and Interpersonal Spaces Work Differently

You can see the power of the hive-mind at work. But isn't there a downside to all this wonderful information sharing? Not everything merits the attention of the group. Overloading the conferencing system with endless chatter will pollute it in the same way that email systems often are. Later I'll show how scoped conferences can help you optimize discussions and cut down on information overload. Here, though, I want to raise the crucial issue of privacy. No matter how a conferencing system is organized, much vital collaboration will need to occur privately between individuals or among ad hoc groups. In these cases the mode of choice is clearly email. It's no accident that the Netscape/Microsoft newsreaders use the same tools to view and compose messages as do their respective mail clients. Fundamental to the idea of Internet groupware is the synergy between these two modes.

To show how email and conferencing work together, let's suppose that Bob and Sally decide to start a new project. They begin developing the idea face-to-face, but since Sally is often on the road, it evolves through a series of phone calls and email messages. Some of these messages are cc'd to Ellen, whom Bob and Sally recruit as an informal project advisor. When the idea gels sufficiently, they post an announcement to the whole group. The anouncement serves three purposes:

• It alerts the group to the existence of the project.

• It invites discussion about the project.

• It invites potential contributors to join the project.

In the ensuing discussion, George raises an issue that Bob and Sally wish they had clarified before taking their idea public. Bob therefore responds not with a posting to the newsgroup, but privately to George and Sally using email. Because the mail and news clients share the same messaging tool, the switch from public to private discourse is seamless. Instead of replying to the newsgroup, Bob replies to George with a Cc: to Sally. He also uses Bcc: (blind carbon copy) to Ellen, to quietly keep the project advisor in the loop. (See the following tip.) Alternatively, George himself could have taken the matter offline with Bob and Sally before posting, and next time he will. In either case, public discussion can resume after an interlude of negotiation and compromise. For users of Internet groupware, the membrane that separates group from interpersonal spaces is selectively permeable. The tools enable you to cross back and forth as needed. Doing that effectively requires skill in the operational mechanics of email and conferencing, and equal skill in the social arts of computer-mediated discourse.

The reply buttons in the Netscape and Microsoft newsreaders mean two different things. In Netscape's Collabra, neither of those is quite right for this purpose. *Reply* means "Post a reply to the newsgroup." *Reply All* means "Post a reply to the newsgroup, and mail it to the person who posted the message." Since Bob wants to drop out of the newsgroup for some private communication, he'll have to eliminate the `Group:` header from the quoted message produced by either of these two buttons, then add `To:`, `Cc:`, and `Bcc:` headers, along with appropriate addresses. (In the case of *Reply All*, the `To:` field will already be there and will contain George's email address.)

Microsoft's Outlook Express handles the transition from conferencing mode to email mode more gracefully. Its *Reply* button means "Reply by email to the person who posted this message." The quoted message it produces will have a *To:* header with George's email address; *Cc:* and *Bcc:* will still have to be supplied. To post a reply to the group in Outlook Express, use the *Reply Group* button.

Groups Need Privacy Too

In one sense a newsgroup is a public space. A message posted there addresses nobody in particular but rather all current—*and future*—members of a group. In groupware lingo, we could say that that this form of communication is "role-oriented." That suggests newsgroup structures ought to mirror organizational structures. For example, you might want to create one set of newsgroups for the engineering division and, within that, subtrees for project teams. I'll talk more about why to scope discussion areas in the next chapter and show how to do it in Chapter 13. Here let's just note an important fact about these kinds of scoped newsgroups: they can be made inaccessible, and even invisible, to nonmembers. Such a newsgroup is both public, because it stores messages that group members would otherwise exchange as email, and private, because only group members are present in the newsgroup.

A good basic design puts a few companywide groups at the tip of the iceberg and a larger substructure of departmental and team groups below the waterline. The companywide groups can carry broadcast announcements. These will typically be emailed too, but a newsgroup can store those emails centrally and make them available to people who weren't on board when the announcements first went out. (See the following tip.) Can't an email archive do the same thing? Yes, it can. There are, for example, innumerable ways to convert sets of email messages (or newsgroup messages, which are nearly the same thing) into web-based archives.

 A newsgroup can be a natural and convenient way to archive email messages. In both the Netscape and Microsoft newsreaders, you can simultaneously post a message to a newsgroup and send it to an email address. This opportunity presents itself when you invoke the message composer in a newsgroup context—that is, when a newsgroup rather than an email folder is the current selection in the triple-pane window in which both applications present mail and news. In this situation, the Outlook Express button labeled *New Post* leads to a message composer that prefills the `Newsgroups:` header and provides an empty `Cc:` header where you can write the address of your email list. Collabra's *New Msg* button likewise prefills the `Newsgroups:` header (which it labels `Group:`), and provides a drop-down list that you can use to address the message to other newsgroups (that is, to cross-post the message) or to email recipients.

Companywide newsgroups aren't just for announcements. They can also serve as a key rendezvous point for teams that usually collaborate in more private spaces. Sometimes a departmental issue needs to bubble up to the surface, gather broad-spectrum input, then return to a more private realm for detailed discussion and implementation. Companywide newsgroups are an excellent way to achieve that effect. In Chapter 4 we'll see other examples of how and why discussions migrate among newsgroup scopes.

Although some people will speak up in public (sometimes too much!), others won't. Departmental or team newsgroups that are too broadly visible will intimidate shy people. Sometimes these people will participate more actively in a more private setting. Do everything you can to make them comfortable. The more communication people are willing to share, department by department and team by team, the more likely it is that the system as a whole will reach critical mass.

If I Put It There, I'll Be Able to Find It Later

When you ask industry analysts why groupware systems fail to reach critical mass, they usually point out—correctly—that there's a kind of "tragedy of the commons" dilemma. Everybody benefits from the ability to tap into a store of pooled knowledge. But contributors aren't rewarded. "Free riders" who never contribute enjoy an equal benefit, so where's the incentive to add to the pool of knowledge?

The "anywhere, anytime" aspect of news, vis à vis email, depends on the degree to which your email system is client-centric or server-centric. The standard Internet client now supports both modes. The POP protocol is client-centric. If you access your mail from multiple machines—your office PC, road PC, and home PC—it's almost impossible to keep those three different local message stores in sync. The IMAP protocol, on the other hand, is server-centric. You can use it to maintain a common message store on a mail server, as well as a common structure of folders and subfolders within the message store, which (as is also true for NNTP) can replicate to any PC you happen to be using. Finally, some IMAP servers support public folders, which work very much like newsgroups. When IMAP's full capability is deployed, an NNTP newsgroup is no more effective as a shared central repository than an IMAP public folder. But IMAP arrived on the scene later than POP did, and although both the Netscape and Microsoft mailreaders support it, many of the mail servers deployed in organizations do not. In this situation, a newsgroup can be a useful repository.

You can appeal to the greater good, arguing that effective communication creates a competitive advantage for a company and yields benefits that trickle down to everybody. But trickle-down rewards are notoriously poor motivators. Why not appeal instead to enlightened self-interest? If I store my project-related documents in a newsgroup that serves as a central repository, I can realize purely selfish benefits. Just as with email, I can find those documents later by scanning the newsgroup along its dimensions of subject, author, and date. But unlike my client-centric email, this server-based newsgroup can be available to me anywhere, anytime, from any computer (see the earlier tip). When newsgroups are indexed for full-text search (we'll see examples of how to do this in Chapters 8 and 13), the case is even more compelling. It's ironic but true that relatively few local filesystems can be searched as effectively as can the Web. We can often find things "out there" more easily than we can find them on our own hard disks. If I might want to find something later, I have an incentive to put it someplace where it will get indexed automatically.

For example, I ran a development team for several years that not only discussed ongoing work in team newsgroups, but also routinely posted project-related documents there. These included email messages received from elsewhere in the company or from outside, web pages we found while researching hardware, software, and networking issues, and records of all the changes we made to our servers, the commercial software we ran on them, and the custom software we built ourselves. We could have used a combination of email and our local filesystems to store all this stuff. As we got into the habit of posting documents to our newsgroups, though, we found this was no more difficult than the email or "File Save As..." methods of saving the stuff. Since we all tended to work from multiple machines and multiple locations, the central and searchable newsgroup paid big dividends. If you know you'll have "anywhere, anytime" access to a document, you're more likely to take the trouble to file it properly. That's enlightened self-interest at work.

I Don't Have Time to File Things Properly

Knowledge workers deal with a relentless flood of information. Even when people want to categorize, file, and share the most important documents that they create, receive, and find every day, they're operating under brutal time constraints. If it takes more than a couple of seconds to move a document into a shared repository, it's just not going to happen. Here's where the close integration between the news, mail, and web clients really shines. A newsgroup isn't just a place for discussion. It can also be a convenient repository for email, and for web pages, that are of interest to a group. It's true that a newsgroup doesn't enable you to define custom fields—things like `ProjectName`, `Category`, `CompletionDate`, or `Summary`, for example. Sometimes, though, less is more. Customized docbases are great for certain uses, and Part II is full of examples showing how to build and manage them. But these are really for line-of-business applications: status reports, trouble tickets, and other sorts of documents that people are required to create. Many more documents can be usefully shared in a team repository—for example, an email from a vendor about a software bug, or the web page on the vendor's site describing the workaround. These kinds of documents are, in aggregate, a vital information resource. Yet there's never time to build forms to catalog them, and even if you did, nobody would have time to fill out those forms. But it's a two-second operation to route an email or a web page into a project newsgroup. You can do it from your mailreader, or your web browser, with virtually no disruption or loss of context. It's as easy as mailing the email or web page to your team but better for a number of reasons.

It's nonintrusive.

News is a lower-priority channel than email, and this is low-priority communi-cation. You just want to alert people to the existence of these documents so they'll know about them and perhaps be able to look them up later. These kinds of communications don't normally need a reply. Sending lots of them as email, on the FYI principle, is an abuse of the higher-priority email channel.

It's centralized.

In environments where email is client-centric, a newsgroup is a more reliable form of "anywhere, anytime" access.

It's historical.

Unless email is archived, new members of a team won't have access to older documents distributed as email. A newsgroup that never expires is automati-cally an archive.

It's searchable.

Users of AltaVista and Deja.com know that these search engines can pick out relevant documents from among millions, when search terms are sufficiently discriminatory. No intranet newsgroup will ever approach this scale, so if you can remember anything at all about a document that you or someone else posted to an indexed local newsgroup, it's likely you'll be able to search for it and find it.

How do you route an email into a newsgroup archive? Netscape Collabra can for-ward a message from the mail domain to the newsgroup domain. While reading an email message in the mailreader, use the *Forward* button to launch an instance of the message composer that contains a copy of the message you were reading. By default the composer presents a `To:` header that invites you to type an email address. Use the dropdown list of headers to instead select a `Group:` header, which invites you to specify a newsgroup. Then type the name of an appropriate local newsgroup—this might be something like *webteam.mailarchive*. Note that this newsgroup name implicitly refers to the default news server specified in Com-municator's preferences—that is, Preferences → Mail & Newsgroups → Newsgroup Servers. When you use local newsgroups as described in this chapter, you can also maintain connections to external news servers (e.g., *msnews.microsoft.com*), but your local NNTP server will be most effective when it's the default server.

In Outlook Express, the *Forward* button works only in the email domain. The message composer that it invokes won't let you specify a `Newsgroups:` header. Fortunately there's another—and arguably better—way to get the job done. You can drag the message from the inbox and drop it onto a local newsgroup! This action launches a message composer with a copy of the email message. And unlike Collabra, which requires that you type the name of a local newsgroup, Out-look Express automatically fills in the `Newsgroups:` header.

You should always try to write a descriptive `Subject:` header for newsgroup postings. In this case, Collabra prepends "Fwd:" to the existing message title, while Outlook Express leaves this field blank. Neither method is adequate. When you route email into a newsgroup, you're consuming a scarce resource—the attention of the people who monitor that newsgroup. Write a `Subject:` header that tells readers of the newsgroup specifically what this message contains. My email inbox, for example, currently contains several dozen messages labeled `Subject: re: server-side performance`. That title tells me nothing about the fact that the server in question is a web server or that the performance issue at stake has to do with Perl's XML parser. Only a few of these messages are keepers. Were I to forward one such message to a local newsgroup, I'd retitle it "Perl-XML performance: Nathan Kurz's benchmark results."

This rule about rewriting `Subject:` headers applies to responses as well as to new postings. If you take the trouble to respond to a posting, it's presumably because you're contributing something new to the discussion. Say so in your message's title! Some people think that the default title—e.g., "re: Perl-XML performance: Nathan Kurz's benchmark results"—must be retained in order to preserve thread hierarchy. Not so. In some email environments, threading may depend on pattern-matching in message titles. But newsreaders don't use titles for threading; they use NNTP message IDs in the `References:` header. There's no reason not to write a fresh, descriptive title for every message that you post to a newsgroup. When you do write fresh titles, you help everyone scan the newsgroup more effectively.

The Quest for a Read/Write Web Server

The inventors of the World Wide Web were scientists who wanted a better way to collaborate with far-flung colleagues. They intended HTTP to work as a read/write protocol. Users of the Web wouldn't just consume hypertextual content; they would also contribute and aggregate it. As the Web went mainstream, though, it became more like television than groupware. The HTTP *PUT* method, a part of the protocol that enables browsers to upload documents and revisions, was rarely implemented in web servers.

Despite the Web's emergence as a mass medium, there remains an intense need for something like a read/write web server. As this book was being finished in the summer of 1999, a solution was in view. Web-based Distributed Authoring and Versioning (WebDAV, RFC 2518) extends HTTP/1.1 so that multiple WebDAV clients can annotate a shared document on a WebDAV server. The protocol also provides support for moving and copying collections of files. WebDAV requests and responses are expressed as Extensible Markup Language (XML) structures. Transporting XML over HTTP or HTTPS in this way is rapidly emerging as the standard

Internet approach to distributed computing, and WebDAV is riding the crest of that wave.

Early WebDAV-enabled clients included MSIE 5 and Office 2000; servers include *PyDAV*, a Python-based WebDAV server, and *mod_dav*, an Apache module. What will WebDAV mean to the future of Internet-based collaboration? Prognosticators suggest that it could replace many current mechanisms, including FTP for file transfer, Concurrent Versions System (CVS) for source-code control, IMAP for server-based message management, and NNTP for conferencing. At the moment, though, nobody really knows whether, or when, or to what extent these predictions will come true. So I've chosen to focus this book on the current installed base of Internet browsers, mailreaders, and newsreaders and to explore their still-untapped collaborative potential.

A large installed base is both a blessing and a curse, as Microsoft learned when many users demanded support for Windows 3.1 long after Microsoft had hoped they would have dumped it for Windows 95. Similarly, in the Internet realm, the inertia created by the installed base of 3.x/4.x browsers is very strong. Many of the specific techniques described in this book assume that it will remain so for a year or two at least. That said, there are also general issues and techniques here that transcend the tools I use to illustrate them. Whether it's based on NNTP or IMAP or WebDAV, a system for pooling knowledge-rich documents in an organization must still achieve critical mass, provide properly scoped zones of privacy, support effective navigation and search, deliver rich authoring capabilities, support and encourage the use of hypertext, and integrate with messaging applications and the Web. This book shows how to meet these challenges with today's tools.

The HTML-aware Newsreader

One such tool is the HTML-capable newsreader. When the Microsoft and Netscape newsreaders gained this capability, first in the 3.x versions and then more powerfully in the 4.x versions, local news servers suddenly became a lot more interesting. An existing HTML document posted to a local newsgroup, or a new HTML document written using the message composers included with either of these newsreaders and then posted to a local newsgroup, could behave much like a web page. It had its own unique URL, albeit of the news:// flavor rather than the http:// flavor. It could display rich text, images, and active hyperlinks. It could even contain scripted behavior. Although not widely noticed or appreciated, the HTML-capable newsreaders could transform an NNTP server into a kind of read/write web server. Where local newsgroups are an established medium of communication, this dramatically lowers the activation threshold that users must otherwise cross in order to publish to an intranet web server. HTML-enriched NNTP conferencing can be, in fact, what most intranets today sorely lack: a simple, user-friendly, single-click mechanism for web publishing.

When I began to explore the possibilities inherent in this idea, and to encourage coworkers to do so, I soon realized that I faced a challenge. Although everyone's a prolific consumer of HTML content, relatively few of us produce it. And we tend to regard what we do produce as published work for public consumption. The HTML features of the Microsoft and Netscape messaging clients invite us to use HTML not only for conventional web publishing, but also as a means to enrich routine correspondence. Some people argue that this is a gratuitous use of HTML and that simple ASCII text is quite sufficient for simple business communication. Perhaps so, yet we routinely send and receive richly formatted Microsoft Word documents. Our messaging tools are now natively capable of all the same effects. What's more, they enable us to use hypertext and to aggregate content in the same ways that the Web does.

Today relatively few people do that kind of aggregation, and they wear a "Web author" hat while they're doing it. But web authors are only doing what we all must do when we collaborate: create and collect useful content and arrange it effectively. The remainder of this chapter explores ways to do that in the context of HTML-enriched local newsgroups. It covers strategies for aggregating external web content by reference and by inclusion, aggregating local or remote news content, attaching files, composing HTML messages, and using images and hyperlinks effectively.

Even the most Net-savvy users seldom exploit the full power of HTML messaging on a dedicated NNTP server. If you're an administrator, you'll find it's not enough to just turn on local newsgroups and point users at them. You'll also need to show your users what kinds of things can be done and how to do them. Happily you can use the conferencing environment itself to deliver much of the necessary training and demonstration.

If you're a user invited to participate in local newsgroups, you can play a key role in exploring and applying the techniques I'll describe. Hypertext authoring and content aggregation are quite new skills that have yet to make their mark on ordinary business communication and won't until we all start to exercise them routinely.

Aggregating Web Content in Newsgroups

When the Microsoft and Netscape messaging clients display plain ASCII messages, they automatically activate URLs found in those messages. If I compose such a message, using a messaging client that's set to text mode (see the following tip), I need only mention the site *http://udell.roninhouse.com/* in a message that I post to a newsgroup or email to you. Your message reader will render the URL's text as a clickable hyperlink. By merely reproducing a correctly spelled URL, we become— in a limited but important sense—hypertext authors. In the text-mode messaging environment, nobody has to know that the HTML representation of that link is `<a href="http://udell.roninhouse.com/">http://udell.roninhouse.com</a>`. You can just type a URL, or better yet, cut and paste one into your message.

The Microsoft and Netscape messaging clients can compose either in text mode or in HTML mode. People are most familiar with text mode. It produces messages whose bodies are just lines of ASCII text, typically not longer than 65 or 70 characters. Alternatively these clients can operate in HTML mode. In Outlook Express, you turn on HTML mode using Tools → Options → Send → Mail Sending Format (or → News Sending Format); the choices are HTML and Plain Text. In Collabra, you use Edit → Preferences → Mail & Newsgroups → Formatting; the choices are "Use the HTML editor" and "Use the plain text editor."

It's true that results aren't always perfect. Long URLs, especially CGI-style URLs containing characters such as the question mark and the ampersand, often run afoul of the message reader's line-wrapping algorithm and fail to render as clickable links (see the following tip). Still, this method of URL autoactivation has made a huge impact on the world. Text mode is the lowest common denominator of Internet messaging. Millions of authors of simple ASCII email messages and newsgroup postings now routinely use live citations to other texts. To a literate person from an earlier era, or even to all of us just a decade ago, this would have seemed miraculous. Indeed it is. As we communicate in the context of the Web, we can create new views of it.

RFC 1738 suggests that *<URL:http://udell.roninhouse.com/>* should signal to a messaging client that the indicated URL should be rendered as a single unbroken entity. In fact URLs written this way don't always work reliably in messaging clients. Outlook Express, for example, won't autoactivate them. Many people instead use the style *<http://udell.roninhouse.com/>* to delimit a URL. This style of bracketed URL does tend to survive the line-oriented ASCII environment much better than the unbracketed style.

Neither approach works reliably in all messaging clients all the time. What to do? Remember, this is only a problem in text mode. In HTML mode, you can produce shorter, more descriptive URLs that will always work reliably when viewed by HTML-aware messaging clients.

A great many web pages do nothing but aggregate other web pages. Thanks to URL autoactivation, even plain ASCII email messages and newsgroup postings can do the same. When you dash off a message that includes a handful of URL citations, you're constructing a unique view of the Web to support your message. In many Usenet newsgroups this happens on a grander scale. An FAQ maintainer will periodically repost a message that documents some area of knowledge and, in so doing, aggregate relevant web content. These documents behave like published bookmark files.

Newsgroups as Shared, Annotated Bookmark Files

In local newsgroups you can take this notion of a published bookmark file a few steps further. Remember that message Bob posted, citing a URL for some Lightweight Directory Access Protocol (LDAP)-related documentation? Let's suppose that Bob's team owns a newsgroup called *webteam.bookmarks*. In this newsgroup, every top-level posting works like a bookmark folder and contains a set of online resources for subjects like LDAP, SSL, Pretty Good Privacy (PGP), and so on. Like Usenet FAQs but unlike browser bookmarks, these postings can annotate the URLs they record. A project team that consolidates its online research in this way can do more than centralize the gathering of bookmarks. It can also pool its knowledge about the nature and value of those bookmarks. Team members can, for example, build a consensus as to which sources are most valuable and why. Critical evaluation of the quality of online resources is the price we all pay for easy access to so many of them. That analysis takes an investment of effort; groupware should help us maximize our return on that investment.

Because Usenet FAQs expire, their authors periodically repost them. This recycling mechanism creates natural opportunities to update these documents. But how should updates be handled in a local newsgroup where messages live forever? One approach is to cancel the message and post an update. Because newsreaders let you cancel only your own messages, this method assumes that the original author of the message is also its maintainer. Another approach is to post updates as responses to the original message. That way, anyone can contribute an update. The set of responses to a message creates an audit trail that documents who posted updates and when.

I prefer the second approach, because anyone can add new material or comment on what's already there. Admittedly it's not perfect. In a hypothetical WebDAV-based conferencing system, for example, regions of a document will be locked and edited *in situ*. And an audit trail will be captured more subtly than as a set of response messages. What will we do until that technically superior solution arrives? If a team is committed to pooling the Web resources it collects—a very big if, to be sure—the technique I've described here can be a simpler and easier alternative to intranet web pages that serve the same purpose.

Including Web content in Newsgroups

The technique of aggregation by reference—that is, assembling URLs that refer to web pages—isn't flawless. A remote server may not be available when you need it. If it is, the page you want may no longer be there. More importantly, although your annotations will be searchable if your newsgroup is searchable, the referenced content won't integrate with your local search engine. It can therefore be useful to add remote documents to your local site's collection. In Collabra's message composer, called Composer, the File → Attach → Web Page option enables you to enter a URL whose content will be attached to your message. You can type the URL, but it's better to surf to the page to ensure that it exists, then copy the URL from the browser's Location: window to the Clipboard and paste it into Composer's attachment dialog box. Easiest of all, if you're browsing a web page that contains your target URL in hyperlink form, you can drag that link into Composer's attachment pane. This little-known procedure is extremely handy!

For Outlook Express users, the procedure is more cumbersome. You have to save a web page as a file, then attach the file using Edit → Insert → File Attachment. If you drag a link from the browser and drop it into the message composer, Outlook Express appears to attach the page. But that attachment is actually just the URL itself, not the page pointed to by the URL.

Web pages aren't the only kinds of documents you might want to move into your local collection. Sometimes it makes sense to do the same thing with downloadable files. For example, it's always a challenge to keep up with the current versions of system-software components, applications, drivers, and related documentation. Vendors often make these available for download from their sites, but an aggregated and annotated view of the items that matter to your group can save time and effort. In Collabra, the File → Attach → Web Page technique will, in a single action, download a remote binary file and add it as an attachment to your posting. In Outlook Express, it's a two-stroke operation. First you download the file to your local disk, then you attach it. In this scenario, the newsgroup provides more than a richly annotated alternative to the LAN file system. It combines a means to aggregate these files with a means to discuss them. If you're going to install a driver, you'd like to know what someone else learned while doing so. Newsgroups encourage informal discussion that can weave in and around an annotated data store.

In this context, local means file-system-accessible rather than web-accessible, and the scope of the file system includes both your local drive and all visible network drives. A file in any of these places can be uploaded as an attachment to a newsgroup posting. Netscape users: File → Attach → File. Microsoft users: Insert → File Attachment.

Sometimes it makes sense to transform a document that you include in a posting. Consider a Microsoft Word file that documents a new driver release. If you attach it (or refer to it), the reader of your posting will be presented with a link that, when clicked, invites that person to save the file for later use in Word or else open it directly in Word. Anyone who doesn't have Word (and the right version of Word!) is out of luck. Even when Word is installed, it may not be running. In this case you force the reader of your posting to wait for Word to launch, then load the attached file.

Alternatively you could use Word's Save As HTML feature to convert the *.DOC* file to a *.HTML* file and then attach that. The obvious benefit is that the content will be instantly available to everyone, requiring no viewer except the newsreader itself. (Nothing prevents you from also attaching the *.DOC*, for those users who prefer Word or to ensure faithful transmission of features of the document that may not survive conversion to HTML.) There is also a subtler benefit to this approach. When you attach a binary file to a newsgroup (or, for that matter, to an email message), it will be encoded (technically: base64-encoded or MIME-encoded) as a stream of apparently meaningless ASCII text. Text in the original document won't be recognizable in the encoded version. This makes full-text indexing and search futile, even when indexers can work with non-ASCII formats such as Word's *.DOC* or Acrobat's *.PDF*. So, in search-enabled newsgroups, it's a good idea to convert binary word-processor file formats to HTML in order to expose the content to the indexer.

Referring to Newsgroup Messages

When news servers don't expire messages, they persist indefinitely. Each posting produces a news URL—something like *news://udell.roninhouse.com/358C707B.ED39B9C1@monad.net*—that's unique and that can be used to retrieve the message months or even years later. Why do news hyperlinks matter? For starters, they're a better way to quote prior messages. Wholesale quoting of a message into a reply to that message is a much abused practice that carries over from the Usenet to private conferencing. It's often useful to intersperse commentary with quoted bits of a prior message when that commentary applies specifically to the cited material. When a response merely refers to a prior message in its entirety, though, there is no need to quote the whole antecedent. Let the response hierarchy show how your message relates to its antecedent. Or if that relationship is distant, cite the news:// URL of the antecedent. These kinds of hyperlinks can add a new dimension to corporate knowledge management. Users can not only contribute documents to a shared archive, but also weave interconnections among those documents.

How do you cite one news message when composing another? Collabra solves this problem handily. You can drag the icon representing the message you want to cite into the message composer's window. If the composer is set to text mode, the raw link address (e.g., *news://udell.roninhouse.com/358C707B.ED39B9C1@monad. net*) will appear. URL autoactivation will make it active when viewed in a newsreader. If instead the composer is set to HTML mode, a link label (e.g., *LDIF specification*) will appear. This label, which echoes the `Subject:` header of the cited message, becomes the visible part of a hyperlink that encodes the raw link address as its `HREF` attribute. The newly composed HTML message will, when viewed in an HTML-aware newsreader, display the label as a clickable link, just as it might appear on a web page.

Collabra's drag-and-drop hyperlink authoring capability is remarkable, though scarcely known. Just about anything represented by a URL—including web pages and newsgroup messages on any server—can be cited in a news (or email) message with very little effort. In a local newsgroup setting, this greatly enhances the ability of the newsgroup to function like a web server. At one point, for example, I posted to a staffwide newsgroup a long memo describing how users could manage their own accounts on a mail server I maintained. Weeks later, people needing that information were asking—in the newsgroup and by email—how to find it. I answered those questions by referring to the original posting. Without a hyperlink, that would have been cumbersome: "Scan bytestaff.operations, sometime in March, look for a message from me titled Email Account Info." But Collabra's hyperlink authoring feature made it a snap. I dragged that message onto my desktop for instant access and could then simply drop it (that is, drop its URL) into my responses. The same method would have been available if I'd put the document on our intranet web server. But it was even easier to post it to the staff newsgroup, and doing that killed two birds with one stone. It announced the memo to the group and created a linkable document for future reference.

In Outlook Express, it's much harder to use hyperlinks to refer to news content. You can drag a message icon or a message hyperlink into the composer's window, but doing that doesn't create a hyperlink. Instead it attaches the dropped URL to the newly composed message. To compose a link, you have to use the *Create a Hyperlink* button that appears on the Composer's toolbar when it's in HTML mode. It asks for a link type (e.g., http:, news:, ftp:) and a link address. Then you need to plug in the address. Many users will understand how to do that for a web page: visit the page, copy its URL, and paste it in as the link address. But few will ever discover how to do the same for a news message. Why? A news:// URL is formed from an NNTP message ID. Outlook Express deems these IDs unfriendly and hides them from the user. It is possible to expose a message's ID and copy it as the address of a newly composed hyperlink. But the procedure is arcane and cumbersome. Virtually no one will discover it, and even those who do won't be able to use it quickly or easily. If you're curious, here's the drill: right-click a message icon to reveal its context menu. Select Properties → Details. Select the angle-bracketed text following the `Message-ID:` header. Use the keyboard copying method (e.g., CTRL-C in Windows) to transfer the message ID to the Clipboard. Then select the link address input box, and use the keyboard paste method (e.g., CTRL-V in Windows) to paste the message ID as the address of the link.

Following Newsgroup Hyperlinks

Collabra's more aggressive approach to hypertext authoring means that Netscape users are best equipped to cross-link content archived to local newsgroups. Once a news:// hyperlink is created, though, both Collabra and Outlook Express can follow it. In Collabra, clicking such a link replaces the source message that contains the link with the target message specified by the link's address. To restore the source message, use Go → Back. All this occurs in the context of a single message-reading window. In Outlook Express, clicking a message link launches a new message-reading window and displays the target message in it.

You can also include news:// URLs in web pages. Why do that? As we saw in the last chapter, a newsgroup can function as the raw material for a more formal document, such as an FAQ. Using news hyperlinks, an FAQ published on your intranet can both summarize and connect to a supporting newsgroup.

The behavior of a news:// URL on a web page varies by client. When you click on such a URL in either Navigator or Internet Explorer, the mail/news message reader will launch and display the message. In Communicator this transition from web space to news space is flawed. You can read the message but not reply to it. Outlook Express, as of MSIE 4.01, gets this right—you can reply to a message that you jump to by way of a news:// URL. However, both products fail to achieve the next level of web/news integration. Ideally, a news:// URL accessed from a web page should not only display the individual message, but also establish a newsreader context surrounding that message—for example, by launching the newsreader, locating the newsgroup, and highlighting the message in the message-list pane. Lacking this feature, both products fail to maximize the potential synergy between the Web and news domains.

HTML Authoring Strategies

When a news server supports a user population guaranteed to be running HTML-aware newsreaders, everyone's a potential HTML author. This doesn't mean you're going to bring in hip, ponytailed web consultants to design your internal discussion pages. It does mean that you can use rich text, tables, images, lists, and color—where appropriate—to communicate more effectively. It means that you can use descriptive labels rather than raw URLs to refer to web pages or news messages. In the special case where the focus of discussion is an evolving web site, you can try out sets of alternative page designs using the newsgroup as a scratchpad web server that also happens to support conferencing. More generally, any product made of words and pictures—a book, a report, a newsletter—can benefit by exposing its raw materials to the production team in a conferencing environment.

The Collabra and Outlook Express message composers both come with integrated HTML authoring tools. In Netscape-only environments, you can also produce a standalone HTML file using another tool, such as FrontPage, HotMetal, or Home-Site, and upload that file as an attachment to a news message. However, the Microsoft newsreader won't display these HTML attachments inline, as the Netscape newsreader will. In any case, the problem with this approach may be that this class of authoring tool is overkill. You don't want to invite users to waste too much time on formatting and layout. Unless the matter under discussion really is a complex web page intended for a production site, it's best to keep things simple. The newsreaders' HTML composers are well suited for their intended use—quick and easy enrichment of discussion content that merits no fancier treatment. With that in mind, here are some guidelines for effective use of HTML in the NNTP environment.

Using Images

There are three ways to use images in a conference message: by reference, by attachment, or by inclusion.

Using images by reference

When you compose a message, you can refer to any image in web space by naming its URL. This typically generates an `<a href>` tag. The reader of your message doesn't see the image displayed in the newsreader; only the link appears. This is usually the best way to handle a large image that, if shown inline, would overwhelm the message's text. In Netscape's composer, it's also possible (using Insert → HTML Tag) to refer to an image using an `<img src>` tag, in which case the image will appear inline.

When you refer to images in either of these two ways, you need to be aware of not only the web space that is accessible to you when you create the message, but also the web space that will be accessible to readers of the message. When might those views differ? It happened to me when I moved *BYTE's* private news server to the DMZ. There, it was visible from both sides of the corporate firewall. That meant that references to Internet-based images were accessible to newsreaders running either inside or outside the firewall. But references to intranet-based content were accessible only to inside newsreaders. When NNTP collaboration crosses the firewall, it's usually better to attach or include images rather than refer to them.

Using images by attachment

You can attach any kind of image to a news message, but newsreaders (like browsers) will natively display only *.GIF* and *.JPG* formats. It's always preferable to convert other formats to one of these. To convert to and from other bitmapped formats, such as Windows *.BMP*, I use JASC's PaintShop Pro; you may favor another image editor and file-format converter. Communicator users who lack a GIF-capable graphics tool—as many people do, since the standard Windows kit doesn't include one—can use Composer do a *.BMP*-to-*.GIF* conversion. Use Insert → Image to import a *.BMP* file onto the canvas, then right-click the image and use Save Image As to save it as a *.GIF* file.

Many vector graphics applications, such as Freehand and Visio, can export to *.GIF* files. Unlike bitmap-to-bitmap conversion, however, vector-to-bitmap conversion results in irreversible loss of editing capability. As in the case of an attached word processor document, you need to consider the purpose of the attachment. If it only needs to be viewed, a *.GIF* version is probably best, because viewing requires no additional software. If it needs to be edited, you'll have to attach the native version. For a mixed audience, it may make sense to attach both versions.

If you use Communicator's message composer, you can attach an image in a variety of ways:

- Use File → Attach → Web Page and specify a URL to attach directly from the Web.

- Use File → Attach → File and specify a path and filename to attach from a local or network drive.

- Drag a URL that points to an image from a web page into Composer's attachment pane.

If you use the Outlook Express message composer, there are two methods:

- Use Insert → File Attachment and specify a file on a local or network drive.

- Drag an image from a browser window and drop it onto the composer.

Note that while Netscape's composer can also accept an image dragged from a browser, the result is not an attached image but an included image.

Using images by inclusion

You can also include images in HTML news (or mail) messages. Unlike attached images, which are enumerated at the end of messages, included images appear inline. They can have titles and captions; they can be centered; they can appear in table cells; text can wrap around them.

If you use Communicator's message composer, there are three ways to include an image:

- Drag it from a browser window and drop it onto Composer's canvas.

- Use the image tool on the toolbar's *Insert Object* dropdown, then specify or navigate to the image file.

- Copy image data to the Clipboard, and paste it into Composer (results vary depending on the format of the pasted bitmap).

If you use the Outlook Express composer, there is only one method: use the toolbar's *Insert Picture* function, then specify or navigate to the image file.

How do you decide whether to include or attach? Include when you need to present the image in a surrounding context—near related text, or with a title and caption, or in a cell of a table. Attach when the image is too large to work well in context. You should also attach when there is no relevant context and the main reason for attaching is to transfer the image data as a file. Why? Both newsreaders can save an included image as a file, but the semantics of saving attachments are more familiar to people.

Note that a news message that displays included images works quite differently from a news message (or web page) that displays images by reference. A message with included images is a kind of self-contained compound document. View the source of such a message (as you can do in the Netscape newsreader) and you'll see that it's a multipart MIME message containing a region of base64-encoded text for each included or attached image.

This aggregation of text and image data into a single package can be very useful. If you use conventional web technology to collaborate on a document made of words and pictures, you have to create an HTML file that refers to separate image files. Then you have to collect all the parts, perhaps into a Zip archive, and transmit the archive to others who in turn must unpack it in order to use what you sent. In this respect, HTML-enriched mail and news clients marry the convenience of HTML with the compound-document features of Microsoft Word.

Using Hyperlinks

Hypertext composition isn't routine or automatic for most people. And most of those who do write web pages are still new to the idea of using hypertext for quick, informal business communication. Here are some guidelines for using links in HTML-aware conferences and in private messages sent to HTML-aware mailreaders.

Composing hyperlinks

We've seen how URLs that you cite in a plain-text news message will become active—that is, clickable—to readers of your message. The same holds true in HTML mode. Both the Netscape and Microsoft composers will convert the text of a URL into a link. By default, the link's label and its address are the same. So if I write "http://udell.roninhouse.com/", the resulting HTML message contains `<a href="http://udell.roninhouse.com/">http://udell.roninhouse. com/</a>`.

URLs always break if misspelled. Avoid typing them. There's no time to do so anyway. The value of providing a link in a routine conference message may not be worth the time it takes to write it. So cut and paste URLs whenever possible; don't retype them. What about complex CGI-style URLs? In a text-mode message, these sometimes line-wrap and fail to render as clickable links. That's not a problem in HTML mode, though.

The easiest way to compose a link is to drag one from a browser, mailer, or newsreader window and drop it onto a message you are composing. This method also yields a link that is labeled rather than raw—for example, *Jon's home page* instead of *http://udell.roninhouse.com/*. Use of such a link requires an HTML-aware viewer, but I'm assuming here that you are operating in a group that unanimously meets that requirement. Remember, though, that this link-dragging method works best in Collabra. When you drag a link into the Outlook Express composer, it turns the text of the link into an attachment to your message.

Relabel links when appropriate

You don't have to accept the label that comes with a link. In both the Netscape and Microsoft composers, the label is an editable property of the link. Why change it? The existing label may poorly describe the link's target or may poorly represent your intended use of it. Is it worth the time it takes to rewrite the label? If you're writing a message that will be seen by a few people and then forgotten, don't bother. If you're writing for a larger audience, or you're producing a document that will be bookmarked or mentioned on a web page, then you may want to beef up the quality of your link descriptions just as you would put more effort into layout and content.

Don't obsess about broken links

Even when you correctly cite a URL, you can't guarantee that it will always work. Servers sometimes go down; pages sometimes move. This inability to control outcomes makes some people reluctant to use links in their messages. Don't worry. Links break all the time on real web sites; it's not the end of the world. When you do post a broken link to your departmental newsgroup, nobody's going to hold it against you.

If you happen to notice the problem yourself, you can cancel and repost the message with a corrected URL. What if the message has grown a subtree of responses? In that case you probably don't want to cancel it, because that will orphan the responses. What you'd really like to do is just edit the message in place. NNTP servers don't allow that, but if you're curious, it can be done—see Chapter 9, *Conferencing Applications* for details.

Reaching your Audience

Creators of web sites constantly seek the right balance point in their use of HTML. Some sites take a lowest-common-denominator approach to ensure equal access even to users of Lynx, a text-mode browser. Others adventurously exploit dynamic HTML, catering to users of the latest browsers from Netscape or Microsoft (but not both at the same time!). The most advanced sites deploy browser-detection scripts that adapt to the capabilities of each client. It's hard enough for professional webmasters to stay on top of this complex and fluid situation. Authors of informal newsgroup postings can't afford to spend time thinking about this stuff. Here are some guidelines to help you use HTML in the most inclusive way:

The Lowest Common Denominator Is Pretty Good

Even if you set the bar fairly low—say at the level of the 3.x Netscape or Microsoft browsers—your postings can communicate far more effectively than if you reject HTML entirely and stick with line-oriented text. The lowest common denominator includes labeled hyperlinks, tables, font control, and attached images. In practice almost all the benefit of HTML messaging flows from the ability to use just these core features.

Pick a Standard Browser

On some intranets, either Netscape's or Microsoft's browser is considered the standard. It's not necessary to choose one, especially if you stick to the lowest common denominator. But it can be helpful. HTML authoring is new to many people. With a standard newsreader/composer—and from this perspective it doesn't matter which kit you choose—everyone learns how to do the same things in the same ways.

Use a Test Newsgroup for Experimentation

It's embarrassing to make mistakes in public, and you're going to make mistakes until you get familiar with HTML messaging. Make liberal use of the scratch newsgroup—usually called *test* or *junk*—that most news servers provide for experimentation. If you want to, you can even cancel your trial postings after you've viewed them.

Specify the Audience

Both the Netscape and Microsoft address books enable you to specify the HTML preference of each recipient, as well as the default mode—HTML or plain text—used for mail messages. You can likewise set the default mode for the newsreaders, although here Collabra permits a more granular specificity. In Outlook Express, the Tools → Options → Send pane controls whether postings default to HTML or plain text. The application warns you, when the default is HTML, that people using non-HTML-capable newsreaders may find your HTML message confusing or rude. But in a multi-news-server environment, where some newsgroups may be designated by group consensus as HTML-friendly and others as plain-text-required, it's up to you to keep track of which is which.

When might you find yourself operating in this kind of mixed environment? It happened to me at *BYTE*. To promote the widest participation in our public newsgroups, I discouraged use of HTML in all but one group earmarked for that purpose. In our private groups, though, HTML was the standard. Collabra goes the extra mile to support these mixed preferences. In a newsgroup's Properties pane (highlight a group in the Message Center and then right-click → Discussion Group Properties) you can designate a newsgroup as HTML-friendly. Then, if HTML messaging is your default mode (Edit → Preferences → Mail & Groups → By default, send HTML messages), Collabra will silently transmit HTML messages to HTML-friendly newsgroups (and mail recipients) and will warn you only when you try to post HTML to a legacy newsgroup.

If a newsgroup is HTML-friendly but any mail recipient isn't, or vice versa, you'll be warned. In these cases, you can opt to send a compound message that includes a plain-text part and an HTML part. How gracefully the HTML degrades to plain text depends on the message. Running text that loses headline, font, and link labeling will usually survive as a useful plain-text message. Tables that get flattened into plain text, though, may turn into gibberish.

It's hard to fault the Netscape and Microsoft implementations. Their mail and news clients are by far the most universal way to exchange rich-text messages; they're bundled with the most widely deployed applications in the history of software; they interoperate rather well in terms of the core features that matter most. The real issue is cultural, not technical. The Internet's roots as a line-oriented ASCII text medium run very deep, and its vast scale imbues that tradition with tremendous inertia. As users of word processors and spreadsheets, we have for years taken rich text for granted. Nevertheless, it's a profound change in the realm of Internet-based communication, and it won't happen overnight. Should you stake out this new territory now? Yes, when there's a reason to do so. The last thing anyone needs is yet another silly web page bursting with gratuitous special effects. But when we collaborate online, we can all benefit from judicious use of HTML to organize and clarify the information we exchange.

4

Information-Management Strategies for Groupware Users

When we collaborate online, we find, receive, and create documents, we store them, we reorganize them, we communicate them to individuals and groups. From a groupware perspective, we need to ask ourselves: Who will benefit from my storage or transmission of this document? Does it merit the attention of individuals or a group? If it should be directed to a group, then which one? From an information-management perspective, we need to ask a different set of questions: In what form should I gather documents? Where do I store them? How should document collections be organized?

We collaborate most effectively when we ask and answer all these questions. Admittedly that requires an open and interdisciplinary mindset. This chapter explores ways to add value to the kinds of things we do every day—participating in discussions, sending email, gathering feedback. These routine activities produce all sorts of documents that, collectively, represent a lot of what we know. Organizing that knowledge into useful forms is an enormous task that can never be fully accomplished. But we can make progress in the right direction by developing good habits. The techniques shown here exemplify what I mean by good habits. They cluster into three categories: understanding and using scoped zones of discussion, effective packaging of messages and threads, and strategies for collecting feedback.

Understanding and Using Scoped Zones of Discussion

Object-oriented programmers spend a lot of time thinking about the right ways to package the parts of the systems they design. This packaging discipline combines functions with the data they create and use. It also defines interfaces that show what packages contain and how they can be used, while at the same time hiding the functions and data that don't have to be visible. The inherent contradiction between showing and hiding, which can never be perfectly resolved, mirrors the contradictory need to both share and withhold information in business organizations. To do our jobs well, we need to transmit and receive the right flows of information. Too much withholding makes people dangerously ignorant and resentful. Too much sharing erodes our ability to focus and prioritize. When we communicate in groupware environments, we make constant demands on one another's attention. A little thought given to the scope of such communication can go a long way toward helping groups work better.

Figure 4-1 illustrates the set of collaborative scopes that was available to editors at *BYTE*.

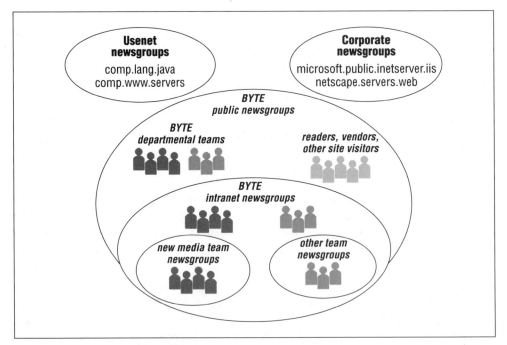

Figure 4-1. Multiple collaborative scopes

As a member of the new media team, I could discuss things with my own team (in the new media newsgroups), with the whole editorial staff (in the *BYTE* intranet newsgroups), with readers, vendors, and other site visitors (in the *BYTE* public newsgroups), with Netscape- or Microsoft-oriented developers (in those companies' corporate newsgroups), and with everyone on the Usenet. How to create and manage layered discussions on an intranet is a question I answer in Chapter 13, *Deploying NNTP Discussion Servers*. At issue here is why and how to use this kind of layered discussion environment and how it relates to other collaborative spaces such as public corporate newsgroups and the Usenet.

Let's start with why. If I am seeking or sharing information, why do I need to be able to address a group of 3 (my team), or 300 (my company), or 300,000 (my company's customers), or 300 million (the Usenet)? At each level, I encounter a group that is larger and more diffuse. Moving up the ladder, I trade off tight affinity with the concerns of my department, or my company, for access to larger hive-minds. But there doesn't really have to be a trade-off, because these realms aren't mutually exclusive. You can, and often should, operate at many levels.

To make this concrete, let's see how one project of mine played out in this environment. My task was to create a subscriber-access version of the *BYTE* web site. A crucial subtask was to apply HTTP basic authentication in an unusual way. I began by summarizing my view of how authentication works, and sketching out my proposed implementation, in a document that I posted to my departmental newsgroup. Why there? Partly to alert my team to the existence and status of this project, and partly just to store this research document in a central, searchable repository.

Although I could have posted it to the entire editorial staff, I chose not to. Why not? I knew that while some of my colleagues might find the summary useful, that didn't warrant placing a demand on the attention of the whole group. Had there been a companywide scope, I'd have skipped that one too. A matter too technical to discuss with the editorial staff would have been inappropriate in a company-wide forum that included sales and marketing people.

But the outer layer of my own site's onion was crucial. Here I could reach people who were my counterparts in other companies, who might find my summary useful, and who might in turn comment usefully on my plan. As it turned out, several did. Other places to find such people include the Netscape newsgroups (e.g., *news://secnews.netscape.com/netscape.servers.web*), the Microsoft newsgroups (e.g., *news://msnews.microsoft.com/public/inetserver/iis*), and the Usenet (e.g., *comp.www.servers*). Since I was lucky enough to have a critical mass of savvy developers in my own newsgroups, I usually went there first. Otherwise, I'd have targeted this kind of message to one of these other communities.

Giving in Order to Receive

It's always tempting to post a message that asks: "Does anybody know how HTTP authentication works?" But you owe your intranet colleagues (and yourself) more consideration than that. And in wider contexts, this kind of naive plea will be ignored, if not actively ridiculed. Instead, summarize what you know already, cite supporting evidence, clearly frame the issues at stake, and ask specific questions. Here's an example of what I mean.

"I've been researching HTTP authentication in order to solve the following problem: <PROBLEM>. Along the way, I've learned some useful things: <LIST>. Based on this information, it seems to me that this plan will work: <PLAN>. Comments and clarifications are welcome and appreciated."

There is of course no guarantee that qualified people will respond helpfully. Nevertheless, people often do when they're interested in the issue you raise and especially when your posting adds to their store of knowledge on the subject even as it seeks to further your own knowledge.

What if nobody responds? If nothing else, the act of writing a thoughtful posting is intrinsically valuable. It helps you to think things through more carefully. But there can be subtler secondary effects too. When I posted this message in our public newsgroup, I alerted several different audiences to the status of my project—colleagues in other parts of my company and potential collaborators outside my company. Anyone who followed that newsgroup learned about my problem and my plan to solve it. As I've said, several outside collaborators did respond immediately and helpfully. But even if they hadn't, the posting planted a seed that might germinate at any time. Weeks later, a staff colleague or an outside collaborator might have run across an idea, or a person, or a tool relevant to my project. Knowing of my interest in the matter creates the possibility of connecting me to that idea, person, or tool. These connections may seem serendipitous, but really they aren't. People make connections to you based on what they know about your interests and activities. Conferencing can expand the number of people who know what you're up to, and increase the likelihood that people can help you.

When you're trying to solve a problem, you never know who might be able to help you solve it. Broadcasting to a discussion medium (newsgroup, listserv, etc.) is an appropriate way to seek help, provided you do so in a thoughtful and informative manner. It's also appropriate, very often, to address this kind of message to specific people who might be able to help or who should be informed about the matter. And sometimes it's appropriate to hold a meeting to discuss the matter. In this situation, it can be useful to launch a discussion thread and then invite selected colleagues to join that thread.

Inviting People into Discussions

In the last chapter we saw how to address individuals and groups at the same time by using a mixture of email and conferencing modes. There, we focused on using the newsgroup as a kind of email archive. Here, we'll focus on achieving a different result—drawing an email recipient into a newsgroup discussion. The technique is the same. You simultaneously post a message to a newsgroup and address it to an email recipient. Both newsreaders—Netscape Collabra and Microsoft Outlook Express—can do this. Collabra is more flexible, enabling you to specify multiple email addresses using `To:`, `Cc:`, or `Bcc:` headers. Outlook Express permits just a single `Cc:` header.

From the perspective of the email recipient, the resulting hybrid mail/news message works as a newsgroup invitation only in the Netscape mailreader, Messenger, not in the Microsoft mailreader, Outlook Express. The reason is that Messenger presents both newsgroup headers (e.g., `Newsgroups: webteam. planning`) and email headers (e.g., `Bcc: Jon Udell <udell@monad.net>`). What's more, when you read this kind of hybrid message in Messenger, the `Newsgroups:` header is not only visible, but clickable. It's wired to a news:// URL that launches the newsreader and focuses it on the indicated newsgroup. That's what I mean when I say that a message of this type can invite people to join a discussion.

Outlook Express unfortunately doesn't work quite the same way. When you use it to view this kind of hybrid message, it ignores the `Newsgroups:` header. So an email recipient can read the message that was posted to the newsgroup but can't use the message as a springboard into the discussion.

Subtle issues arise when you use Collabra to mix email and conferencing modes in this way. For example, although I can invite my extradepartmental colleagues into one of the staffwide discussions on our intranet server, I can't invite them to join my own department's newsgroup if it's configured—as it should be—to admit only members of my team. Nothing prevents me from trying to do this. When I post the message to my project newsgroup, I can cc an extradepartmental colleague. That person will receive the hybrid email/news message and can read it. The email thus successfully notifies the recipient about the contents of the message. But in this situation it's inappropriate to have invited someone lacking access to my project newsgroup to join in a discussion there.

What happens if I do issue this kind of invitation? If my project newsgroup is properly configured to refuse access to nonmembers, clicking the newsgroup name in the message's `Newsgroups:` header will produce an NNTP authentication dialog box. Lacking access to the newsgroup, my extradepartmental colleague will be confused and frustrated by this. But something else happens here that shouldn't. The existence of my project team's newsgroup, which we've said proper scoping should hide from the rest of the company, is revealed.

What if I cc this posting to someone outside my company? In that case, I reveal the existence not only of this newsgroup, but also of the server itself. The fact that my company may be running a private, Internet-accessible discussion server is nobody else's business. However, the `Newsgroups:` header is not a fully qualified news:// URL. It contains only the name of the newsgroup (e.g., *news:webteam. planning*) and not the address of the server that hosts that newsgroup (e.g., *news: //udell.roninhouse.com/webteam.planning*). So if I inadvertently send an email with an intranet newsgroup's name in a `Group:` header, I'll reveal the existence—but not the name or IP address—of my intranet news server. That's not disastrous, but it's not good either. Operating in multiple scopes is powerful, and as always, the flip side of powerful is dangerous.

Here's the upshot: under certain circumstances, Collabra enables you to use `Newsgroups:` headers in email messages to achieve a simultaneous push/pull effect. For example, I might want to alert someone in the company, perhaps outside my department, to a thread that I'm starting in a staffwide newsgroup. If everyone follows that newsgroup regularly, there's no reason to do this. But people won't always be following all the intranet newsgroups you think they are or at any rate not as regularly as you expect. So it's useful to be able to focus attention on a thread by means of an email invitation.

This technique can work across multiple scopes on an intranet server. If I want to raise an issue of interest to my team, but also of interest to extradepartmental colleagues, I can post to a staffwide newsgroup and cc the colleagues whom I'd like to invite. What I can't do, though, is reach even wider scopes using this technique. Suppose I start a thread on my company's public news server. There's nothing secret about that server or the messages on it, so security isn't an issue. But though it's tempting to do so, I can't use this simultaneous push/pull technique to send a hybrid news/email message that both starts a thread and invites selected attendees to join. There are two reasons why not. First, even if Netscape's messaging client were the standard email program in my company, it's not likely that everyone outside my company will be using it. Second, the news:// URL is not fully qualified. It assumes that my company's news server is the default news server, and that won't be true for anyone outside my company.

URL-based invitations to newsgroups

Suppose I've started a thread on my company's public news server. I can alert outsiders to it by placing the following fragment on a web page, in an email message, or even in another news message:

> I'm researching a problem related to HTTP basic authentication. If you want to learn more or can help, see the thread at <news://udell.roninhouse.com/public. webteam> that begins with a message entitled "HTTP basic authentication techniques."

Note that a news:// URL of this form leads people to the newsgroup, not to the individual message. In theory you should be able to do better than that. The recipient of your message shouldn't have to scan the newsgroup to find the thread you've announced. You can cite the news:// URL of the thread's initial posting in your message, and this ought to join the recipient directly to that thread. Unfortunately, although the current newsreaders enable us to try this interesting maneuver, they can't yet quite deliver on its promise. Like the transition from web space to news space, the transition from email space to news space isn't as smooth as it needs to be.

Will these kinks be smoothed out in the next generation of Internet mail/news clients? I'd like to think they will, but at the moment (summer 1999) the future of these tools is unclear. Netscape's vision of Internet groupware produced, in Communicator, a profound integration of mail, news, and the Web. But few people ever discovered the full extent of that integration, and Netscape never adequately explained what had been accomplished or why it mattered. Will next-generation Internet groupware continue to weave the SMTP, NNTP, and HTTP strands more tightly? Or will a single uber-protocol (e.g., WebDAV) subsume them, as advanced browser technology (e.g., dynamic HTML) renders today's standalone mailreaders and newsreaders obselete? I wish I knew, but my crystal ball is cloudy.

Inviting people into web forums

No matter which way the wind blows, today's tools offer us another way to implement this push/pull mechanism. As we saw in the last chapter, discussions can (and should) present a web interface, whether or not the underlying engine is NNTP-based or HTTP-based. When that's the case, an emailed invitation to join a thread can work more reliably. To do this requires a web-based discussion system that uses fully qualified http:// URLs to represent messages. Here are some examples of web discussion URLs:

Deja.com

> *http://x11.deja.com/getdoc.xp?AN=413067781&CONTEXT=911452316.*
> *55902299&hitnum=0*

Allaire Forums

> *http://forums.allaire.com/devconf/Index.*
> *cfm?CFID=266264&CFTOKEN=53509297&&Message_ID=256760*

WebCrossing

> *http://cmpweb-media0.web.cerf.net/scripts/WebX?cmpnet-13@^13165@.*
> *ee6d43a*

The DejaNews URL shown in the previous list is particularly interesting. This http:// URL is stabler than the equivalent news:// URL. If my company receives a newsfeed that includes the newsgroup in which that message was posted (*comp.groupware*) and yours does too, then I could direct you to that thread by emailing you the URL *news:3651AB74.71070E54@top.monad.net*. It's not a fully qualified URL, but if both of our local servers receive *comp.groupware*, then it will mean the same thing to both of our newsreaders. But not for long! The message will expire soon, and that makes transmitting news:// URLs that refer to Usenet postings a quixotic effort. In the DejaNews realm, though, the equivalent http:// URL will remain useful for a year or more.

This creates an interesting opportunity to rendezvous with other people on the Usenet. The DejaNews "Mail a Friend" service encourages you to do just that. If you start a Usenet thread and then use this service to invite people to join you in that thread, the link at the bottom of the email message those people will receive works quite cleverly. It refers not merely to your posting but to the entire thread— which might include your original posting and one or more replies.

Collaboration and Competition

If you're working on a problem, odds are that someone else is working on the same or a similar problem. That person might work in your department, elsewhere in your company, or in a department like yours in another company halfway around the world. Vital collaboration can happen within any of these scopes. A public discussion space for users of your company's products or services is an excellent way to build a brain trust. Usenet newsgroups and email lists can also gather valuable brain trusts.

There are, of course, limits to what you can say in public forums. Nobody should give up a competitive advantage by sharing the wrong kind of information. Nevertheless, collaboration among competitors is not a bizarre or unrealistic idea. Clearly you don't want to divulge company secrets, but not all information is competitively advantageous. You and I might both be working on proprietary applications that exploit certain features of HTTP basic authentication. We needn't reveal details about our respective projects in order to clarify our mutual understanding of how authentication works.

Nor need we collaborate altruistically. As in the case of open-source software, the guiding principle can be enlightened self-interest. The benefit of sharing information, measured in terms of the value of information received in turn, can outweigh the cost of sharing, measured in terms of the effort of collaboration and any competitive exposure that it entails.

Some people think that a culture of collaboration was one of the driving factors in the success of Silicon Valley. In a recent televised documentary, several high-tech executives noted that in the San Francisco Bay area, unlike Boston's Route 128, engineers from different companies tended to congregate after hours to drink, socialize, and compare notes. Thanks to this collaboration, these executives theorized, Silicon Valley functioned more optimally than Route 128. Companies learned enough about each other's successes and failures to avoid charting collision courses and to minimize redundant and wasteful effort. This assertion can probably never be proved, but it's certainly provocative.

Finally, note that you can limit competitive exposure by forming another kind of scope. Consider a transcorporate discussion zone that is private, secure, and accessible by invitation only. Here a coalition can meet without revealing that it exists or what it discusses. In this era of merger mania, Internet groupware can be a simple, low-overhead way to build a temporary virtual community that can complement face-to-face visits during a courtship phase.

Effective Packaging of Messages and Threads

When we create and use scoped discussion zones, we're dealing with the information architecture of the conferencing environment as a whole. Now let's switch lenses and focus more narrowly on information architecture as it relates to individual messages and threads. This may strike you as odd, but if you think in engineering terms, a message is really a kind of object that stores some data and presents an interface that gives users access to that data. Many of us are comfortable with the idea that software objects should properly package their data. But we rarely stop to think that message objects should too.

The techniques for packaging messages aren't difficult, but neither are they automatic. Our messaging tools don't force us to write effective titles, compartmentalize messages, choose appropriate scopes, or layer the information we present. Why should you develop these habits, then? Again I invoke the principle of enlightened self-interest. Quite often a document that I mail or post is also intended for my own future reference. It's to my own advantage to package it in a way that will aid retrieval. Of course, the document is also an effort of communication, invested in hope of some kind of return—a useful reply, a request honored, or simply good will. You can regard good packaging as nothing more, and nothing less, than a calculated bid to maximize your return on an investment of communication effort. Here are some guidelines for packaging mail and news messages.

Write Effective Titles

Subject headers are the titles of mail and news messages. When you scan the contents of an inbox folder or a newsgroup, or when you scan the results of a search of an email archive or a newsgroup, message titles are your best clues about what messages contain. For example, my Sent mail folder at this moment contains a number of months-old messages between me and Mark Stone, an editor at O'Reilly. When I need to refer to the one in which I raised an issue about my contract for this book, I want to see a title like "contract issues" rather than one like "re: re: re: more stuff."

If I raised the issue myself, it was my responsibility to write that title. But if Mark raised the issue, perhaps as part of a larger message bearing the catch-all title "more stuff," I can still seize the packaging initiative by quoting the contract-related material in a reply that I entitle "contract issues." Note that when either party upgrades the quality of a message header, both benefit—because both are now more likely to be able to find that document in their local message stores.

The same principle governs the discussion realm. A posting that launches a new thread should carry a title that accurately describes the message. A response, likewise, should carry a title that accurately describes what it adds to the discussion. In practice, that often won't happen. The path of least resistance will often lead to a cascade of "re: re: re: re:" responses. But anyone, at any point, can add value to the discussion by writing a meaningful message title. Such a message advertises itself, and its surrounding thread context, more effectively to anyone who is scanning or searching the newsgroup. There's another subtle benefit too. A discussion thread is, after all, an online meeting. Agendas drift in online meetings just as they do in face-to-face meetings. Writing an effective title can help clarify the agenda.

Compartmentalize Messages

A message that raises two unrelated issues might be better packaged as two distinct messages. Programmers will recognize this strategy right away. A set of small, single-purpose, descriptively named functions is more useful, and not much harder to produce, than a monolithic do-everything routine. Yet few programmers—never mind civilians—carry this discipline into the messaging domain. There are good reasons to do so. This book divides into sections and subsections because each part fulfills a purpose suggested by its title. You would find an undifferentiated stream of text vastly less useful. The same principle can and should apply to mail and news messages.

Won't two mail messages double the demand you are making on my attention? Not at all. It takes hardly any longer to absorb the same quantity of text when it comes in two packages instead of one. The effort you invest in creating two packages spares me the effort required to mentally disentangle unrelated matters raised in a single message. It means that I can more easily file each message in an appropriate folder. And then there's the issue of scope again. The two messages might properly belong in different newsgroups or might have been best sent to slightly different sets of email recipients. Messages are cheap; attention is precious. There's a limited fund of attention available for the messages you write. Conserve it with thoughtful packaging.

Using Thread Hierarchy to Clarify Discussion

Newsgroups and other threaded discussion systems grow inverted trees of messages and responses. Although the tools usually enforce no policy as to how these trees grow, groups can create their own policies to achieve several kinds of information-management goals.

One useful strategy, often neglected, is to use thread hierarchy as a tool to clarify a discussion. For example, Figure 4-2 shows a snapshot of one of my public discussions. The thread entitled "news hyperlink puzzle" described a Netscape newsreader bug, offered two test cases and a hypothesis, and invited participants to try the tests and comment on the hypothesis.

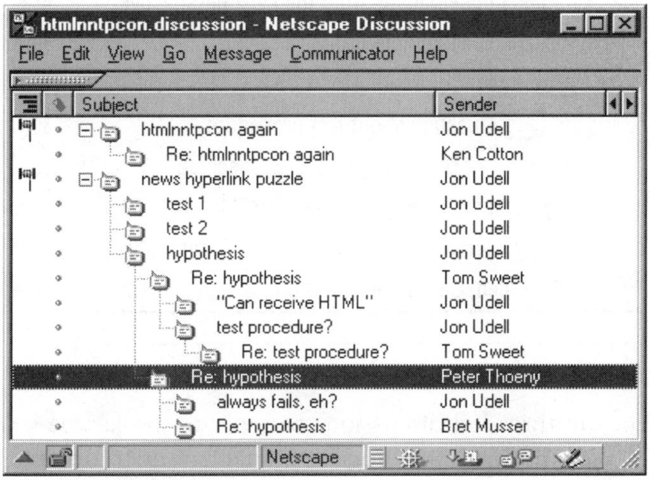

Figure 4-2. Newsgroup hierarchy

At the moment this snapshot was taken, here's what had emerged:

- Tom reported that he could not confirm the hypothesis. He also raised a tangential issue about Communicator's default HTML setting.

- Peter reported that his test also refuted the hypothesis.

- Bret, who was not running Communicator and so could neither confirm nor deny the hypothesis, contributed an observation about "test 1" from the perspective of the Lynx browser.

How much of the sense of that discussion emerges from an inspection of this picture? Almost none. Now suppose the picture instead looked like Figure 4-3.

Here you can see exactly what's going on. The outline view does what each level of a layered information system should do. It tells its own story, summarizes the next layer, and helps the reader decide how—or even whether—to explore the next layer. Note that most of the effect here results from rewritten titles. There are just two structural changes. Tom's reply is divided into its two logical components—the refutation and a tangential query. That move enables the outline structure to clarify follow-on discussion of both matters. And Bret's reply now attaches to "test 2" where it logically belongs. That move is subtle but worthwhile. There's

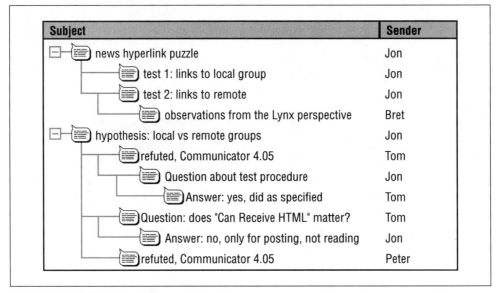

Figure 4-3. A self-explanatory message subtree

a strong tendency in threaded discussions to reply to the last message in a series. Often, though, your reply should logically attach farther up the tree—perhaps even to several different nodes.

Does casual business communication merit this kind of effort? I think so. Why bother to collaborate online if you're not serious about the value of the information you give and receive? Habits of effective titling and layering, once acquired, cost little time and add enormous value to a discussion.

Use Lightweight Threads to Move from Discussion to Consensus

Discussion can be wonderful, but at some point decisions have to be made, actions taken, deadlines met. Some commercial groupware systems claim to be able to help drive discussion toward consensus, but you might want to consider a simpler, cheaper, and less formal approach. Suppose at the beginning of a project you create a thread with this structure:

Project X

Discussion

— Issue 1

— Issue 2

Decisions

I call this kind of thread a *lightweight newsgroup* because anyone can create one. There's none of the administrative overhead normally required to launch a newsgroup, advertise its existence, and make sure everyone who ought to subscribe does. A thread intended as a lightweight newsgroup can simply appear in the flow of an existing well-known newsgroup.

The top-level message, entitled "project X," explains the policy for this thread. The second-level messages, entitled "discussion" and "decisions," are just structural placeholders. Under "discussion," the messages "issue 1" and "issue 2" introduce two matters that are open for discussion. As the top-level policy statement explains, all discussion of each issue should begin at level 4—that is, as a reply to "issue 1" or "issue 2." Each level 4 reply is considered to be a top-level posting in a discussion of the issue named at level 3; additional structures attach to these nodes in the normal way.

What about the "decisions" node? The group leader, who probably also wrote the policy statement and is the authoritative decision-maker for the group, will post a reply under the "decisions" thread for each issue that is decided.

This protocol is fundamentally not much different from what typically goes on in conference rooms. An agenda is set; debate ensues; decisions are recorded. In a newsgroup you give up face-to-face contact—or voice contact, when some participants are on the speaker phone. You gain the ability to collaborate on an equal basis from anywhere, at any time, with full access to all your information sources and no pressure to shoot from the hip. It's true that the messaging tools can't enforce the rules of engagement. Nothing prevents an unauthorized posting to the "decisions" node. Is that a problem? I don't think so. In real conference rooms, people don't usually leap to the whiteboard and scribble rogue decisions. Should that ever happen, there's always the eraser—in NNTP terms, the message-canceling function (see the following tip). From this perspective a newsgroup is nothing more, and nothing less, than a whiteboard that isn't bound by time and space and that produces a permanent, searchable transcript.

 You can use your newsreader to cancel messages—but only those that you yourself have posted. More specifically, your newsreader must be configured to transmit the same email address in the `From:` header as appears on the message you want to cancel. Once you cancel a message, it's gone from the server. However, if the message has been replicated to a local message store, using the offline features of the Microsoft or Netscape newsreaders, the local copy will remain.

Netscape Collabra procedure: Edit → Cancel Message.

Outlook Express procedure: Compose → Cancel Message.

Use Thread Hierarchy to Organize Documentation

I began developing the NNTP examples for this book in a newsgroup—readable by the world, writable only by me—where I documented how to make best use of the collaborative features of the Microsoft and Netscape newsreaders. Figure 4-4 shows an early snapshot of that newsgroup.

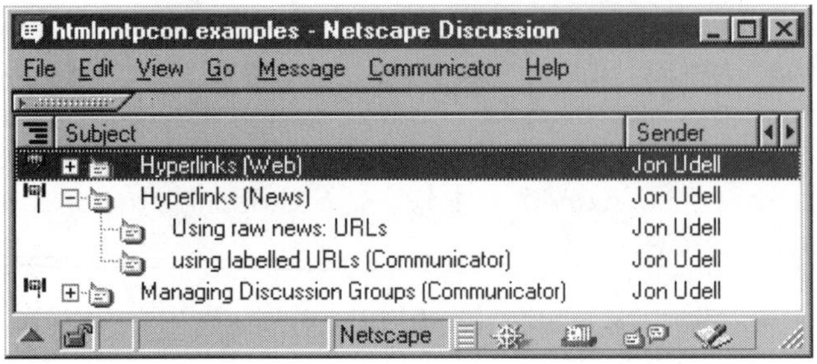

Figure 4-4. Publishing documentation in a newsgroup

It's a simple structure—just a set of topics, each of which expands to reveal a set of examples. Since I'm the only one who can post to the group, I can guarantee that the structure stays clean and orderly. This approach isn't going to replace conventional web publishing. But it's good enough for many purposes, including this one. It's something that anyone with a newsgroup password can do. And because it's newsgroup-based, there's another advantage that you don't get with conventional web publishing. When I add new examples, or modify existing ones (by canceling and reposting), your newsreader will flag the changes as unread messages and direct your attention to them. Web archives have to work hard to achieve this effect; newsgroups do it automatically.

Each message in this newsgroup was an HTML document. As Figure 4-5 shows, these messages were good examples of how HTML-friendly newsgroups can be used not only for discussion, but also as a way to explain and demonstrate things using words and pictures.

Using Messages to Conduct Polls

In groupware contexts, information management doesn't just mean doing a better job of organizing mailing list or newsgroup discussions. It also means using these communication tools creatively to add structure to otherwise free-form interactions. Polling to discover a group's consensus on an issue is, as we'll see in this section, something you can weave into the flow of email or newsgroup messaging.

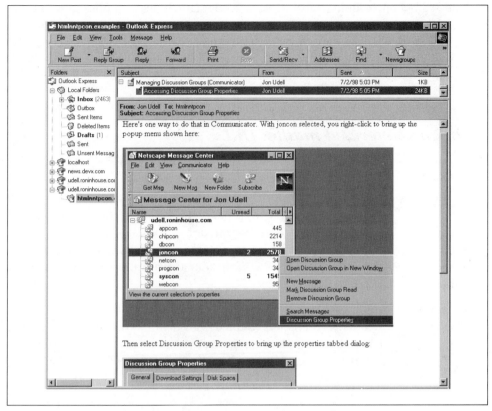

Figure 4-5. A page of documentation published in a newsgroup

How often have you sent out a message asking people's opinions about some topic, waded through dozens of responses, and at the end of the process still not been sure what the consensus opinion was? In this section, we'll look at two ways to turn an email query or a newsgroup posting into a mini-application that conducts a poll.

The first method relies on a special kind of mailto: URL that anyone can include in an email message or newsgroup posting. It also relies on simple client-side email filtering, a feature that's available in many popular mailreaders, including Netscape Messenger, Microsoft Outlook Express, and Qualcomm Eudora.

The second method assumes that there's a web-based polling application running in your groupware environment. I'll illustrate the concept using a Java servlet that implements a very simple kind of web-based polling (see Chapter 10, *Groupware Servlets*), but the same idea would apply to any polling application that expresses votes as URLs that can be sent as email or posted to a newsgroup.

In both cases, the strategy is the same. Much of the information we consume reaches us in the form of messages. Effective groupware recognizes the primacy of the messaging environment and seeks to populate it with applications. Admittedly, mail and news messages offer few degrees of freedom, but they can include URLs, and those URLs can link not only to documents but also to applications. The trick is to take a flexible and pragmatic view of what an "application" can be in this context.

Method 1: Message-Based Polling with Parameterized mailto: URLs

It's commonly known that a mailto: URL on a web page (or in a newsgroup posting or email message) will, when clicked, launch an instance of the Netscape or Microsoft message composer and put the email address encoded in the link into the To: field of a new message. On a web page, the HTML syntax looks like this: `<a href="mailto:udell@monad.net">contact Jon</a>`. In a newsgroup posting or email message, you can simply write *mailto:udell@monad.net*; the Netscape and Microsoft mailreaders will both autoactivate the URL and render it clickable.

Less commonly known is that the link can also carry other header fields, notably the Subject: header. This technique, coupled with mail filtering, enables users of Netscape Messenger or Microsoft Outlook Express to create simple but useful polling applications. This HTML fragment is the frontend of a survey application:

```
<h1>Udell Airways Hub Preference Survey</h1>

<p>We currently use Newark as our hub, but we must now decide between
Boston and LaGuardia. We'd like your feedback.

<p><a href="mailto:udell@monad.net?subject=HubBoston">I prefer Boston</a>
<p><a href="mailto:udell@monad.net?subject=HubLaGuardia">I prefer LaGuardia</a>
```

Notice that the mail address isn't something like *survey@udellairways.com*. This airline is a low-budget operation. It doesn't have its own domain name or mail server, and it's too cheap even to buy an extra mail drop. So the proprietor's own personal email account at his ISP will handle the survey.

Now here's the backend of the application:

- Two inbox folders entitled "Boston" and "LaGuardia"
- A mail filter that says: "If the Subject: contains HubBoston, then move to folder "'Boston'"
- A similar filter for the LaGuardia option

This trivial solution nonetheless solves two important problems: it counts the responses in each category (because mailboxes count messages in folders), and it enables review of the comments sent with each response. This ability to combine numeric and textual analysis of a data set is powerful. It's surprising and delightful to find such a minimal solution. Figure 4-6 shows how to set up the Boston filter in the dialog box invoked by Messenger's Edit → Mail Filters → New.

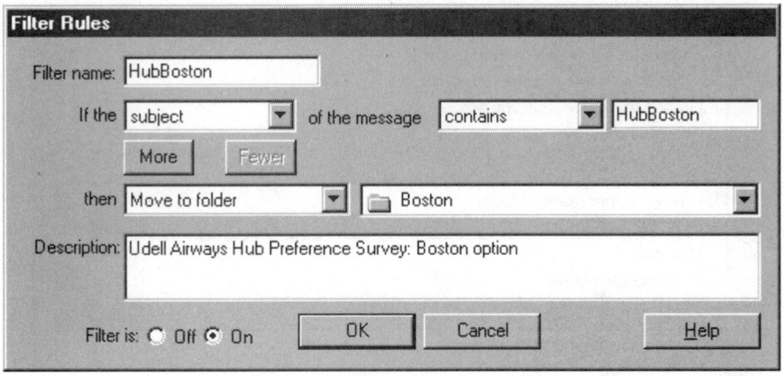

Figure 4-6. Mail filtering in Netscape Messenger

Note that you have to create the Boston folder first in order to be able to select it in the filter dialog. Also note that you don't have to use the GUI dialog. The mail filters are recorded in a text file, which on my machine is called *c:\Program Files\ Netscape\Users\jon\Mail\rules.dat.* Here's the text equivalent of the Boston rule:

```
name="HubBoston"
enabled="yes"

description="Udell Airways Hub Preference Survey: Boston option"
type="1"
action="Move to folder"
actionValue="Inbox.sbd/HubBoston"
condition=" (subject,contains,HubBoston)"
```

It's actually easier to use the GUI in this case, but for complex jobs it's nice to know that you can write the rules directly.

In Outlook Express, you access the filters from Tools → Inbox Assistant → Add. Here too, you have to create the target folder first. Then you can specify the rule, as shown in Figure 4-7.

The advantages of this approach are twofold. First, it's something anyone can do. If you have a web page, you can post parameterized mailto: URLs there. If not, you can still include such URLs in email messages or newsgroup postings. Second, it combines numeric and textual analysis. When you conduct this survey, the anecdotal responses from people are often at least as significant as the numbers of responses in each category. The filters do double duty. They count responses— again, just because folders count the number of items they contain—and they also make it easy to review the messages routed into each folder.

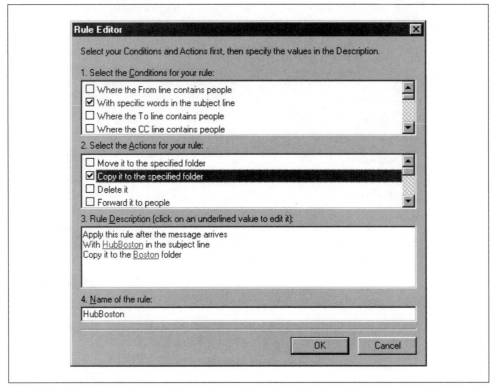

Figure 4-7. Mail filtering in Outlook Express

Method 2: Message-based Polling Using a Polling Application's Web API

One of the main themes running through this book is the notion that web sites, and the applications that run on them (e.g., CGI scripts, Java servlets), have a dual nature. From the perspective of a person running a browser, a web site is an interactive application. We think of a URL as an address that produces a web page. From the perspective of a script—specifically, a web-client script that programmatically uses the HTTP protocol—a web site is a software component. In this case the same URL acts like a function call, possibly parameterized, which yields a well-defined result. When you use a web site or one of its applications this way, it's useful to think of it as implementing an application programming interface (API).

A few years ago I wrote a Java servlet called *Polls* (*http://udell.roninhouse.com/download/Polls.zip*). Like *GroupCal*, a group-calendar servlet that we'll see in Chapter 10, *Polls* makes a Java data structure readable and writable by browsers (or by HTTP-aware scripts). The details aren't important here. What matters is only the web API that *Polls* presents to browsers or scripts.

Here is a URL that creates a new poll, called Picnic99, with three choices for the date of a company picnic:

```
http://host/Polls?name=Picnic99&1=Sat+June+12&2=Sat+June+19&3=Sun+June+20
```

Here is a URL that records a vote for the June 20 date:

```
http://host/Polls?name=Picnic99&vote=Sun+June+20
```

And here is a URL that asks for a tally of votes:

```
http://host/Polls?name=Picnic99&tally=
```

With the *Polls* servlet running in your environment, you can create a poll by plugging the first of the previous three URLs into your browser. The servlet responds with a web page that announces: "Poll Picnic99 created." Users of the poll can vote using the second URL; in this case the servlet responds with a page that announces: "Vote received." Finally, you can view results using the third URL; the servlet emits an HTML table that lists the choices and number of votes for each choice.

This mechanism works easily for users, who need only click on URLs that appear in email or newsgroup messages. But it's not so convenient for a poll creator. To make a new poll, you have to compose and issue the long and complex URL that tells the *Polls* servlet to create a new poll object with the set of choices you specify. Then you have to write the URLs that users will click to vote for each of the choices or to view the tally. Nobody's going to want to type all this stuff, and nobody should have to. The mechanism can be packaged up more neatly. Suppose, for example, that a user who wants to create a new poll can fill out a form like the one shown in Figure 4-8.

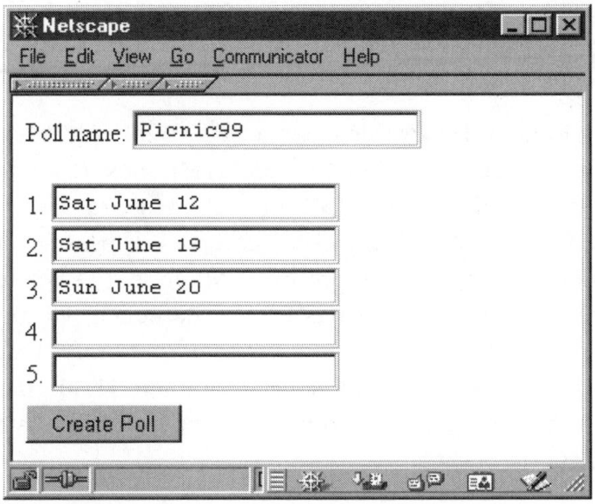

Figure 4-8. Web form to create a poll

The user of the form types in the name of a new poll and up to five choices. The handler for this form—a Perl script that uses methods we'll explore in great detail in Part II—constructs the URL that creates the poll, and transmits it to the server that is hosting the *Polls* servlet. Again, we'll see how this kind of thing works in Part II. For now, it's enough to note that when the script uses the servlet's web API in this way, the servlet creates a new poll called Picnic99, with slots to record votes for the three dates.

Next, the script manufactures URLs used to operate the poll. And these URLs are, in fact, the output of the script, as shown in Example 4-1:

Example 4-1. URLs Manufactured by the Poll-Creating Script

```
Here are the URLs for voting in the Picnic99 poll:

Choice: Sat June 12
<http://host/Polls?name=Picnic99&vote=Sat+June+12>

Choice: Sat June 19
<http://host/Polls?name=Picnic99&vote=Sat+June+19>

Choice: Sun Jun 20
<http://host/Polls?name=Picnic99&vote=Sun+June+20>

Here is the URL for viewing the tally:

<http://host/Polls?name=Picnic99&tally=>
```

You can paste this text into an email message that you send to the group that you want to poll. Or, if there's a newsgroup frequented by the members of that group, you can copy the output into a message that you post to that newsgroup. Either way, by email push or newsgroup pull, you present the group with a web API to the polling application. And you present it in a context that reduces the desired input to clicks on hyperlinks, which will be autoactivated in either a mailreader or a newsreader.

What about really long URLs? In this case, as we've already seen, URL autoactivation in a plain-text message can break, so an HTML message is the best approach. Unfortunately, you can't just take HTML output, which a script such as this one might generate, and paste it into a freshly composed message. Even though you can set your message composer to work in HTML mode, HTML text that you paste into the composer won't be rendered as HTML. Rather, it will be flattened into its textual representation. The solution, shown in Part II (see Example 6-13), is to have the script both compose and transmit a complete HTML message comprising a special header (`Content-Type: text/html` or `Content-Type: multipart/ related`) and an HTML body.

To sum up: this approach relies on the fact that a set of URLs can create a formless, transportable interface to a web application. It's true that HTML-aware mailreaders and newsreaders support full-blown HTML forms, and you can mail or post such forms. But empowering end users to build and distribute such forms is a tall order. In any case, for a quick poll like this one, an HTML form might be overkill. Formless URL-driven data entry is a lightweight, practical alternative.

Ask Not What the IT Department Can Do for Us

We like to imagine that IT departments manage information. In fact they manage very little of the information that flows through a modern company. People, communicating with one another, create most of the raw materials of the knowledge base that every company wishes it could capture and use. The painful truth, unfortunately, is that the IT department cannot deliver applications that will reliably channel all this free-flowing communication. Collaboration is inherently fluid and will not survive if forced into a strict rows-and-columns data-management discipline.

Much of what we collectively know is expressed in the form of messages—email conversations, forum discussions. We create this body of information all the time, every day, message by message. As individuals and in groups, we need to understand why and how good communication habits are not merely a matter of etiquette but, equally important, a way to collectively transform information into knowledge.

When a group relies on electronic messaging, every mistitled or misdirected message, and every poorly organized discussion, is a small act of sabotage. Conversely, every message that is carefully packaged and properly targeted, and every well-organized discussion, adds to the sum of the group's knowledge.

So ask not what the IT department can do for us. Ask, instead, what we can do for ourselves. We use the Internet's standard communication tools to enact what we do as groups. The value of the message bases that we create isn't an IT responsibility; it's ours. Groups that collaborate most effectively will be those that understand the common-sense principles outlined in the last few chapters and strive to make messages carry more signal and less noise.

II

Groupware Docbases

A discussion server creates a kind of document database, or *docbase*, that can store a wealth of semistructured information. But Internet messaging tools—mailreaders and newsreaders—use fixed-function message templates. In this part, we explore how to build web docbases that aren't bound by fixed templates. We'll see how to activate the groupware features latent in web docbases, and we'll develop a complete system to create, publish, and search them.

5

Docbases as Groupware Applications

The pillars of Internet groupware are email, news, and the Web. Each comprises a server application, a client application, a protocol spoken between the two, and finally a data store. The Internet owes much of its dramatic success to the simplicity of these elements. Protocols are expressed as human-readable ASCII text. So are data stores. Simple rules define the protocols and data stores. Those rules guarantee predictable and regular structure. That makes server and client applications relatively easy to build and maintain.

To make this concrete, look at the protocol that a newsreader uses to post a message to a news server as shown in Example 5-1.

Example 5-1. Posting a Message to an NNTP Server

```
$ telnet localhost 119
200 localhost Netscape-Collabra/3.51 11202 NNTP ready
mode reader
200 localhost Netscape-Collabra/3.51 11202 NNRP ready (posting ok).
post
340 Ok
Newsgroups: test
Subject: test
From: udell@monad.net

This is the body of a sample message.
.
240 Article posted
```

I've illustrated this protocol using *telnet*, a command-line application that opens a TCP/IP socket to a server, sends lines of ASCII text to it, and receives lines of ASCII text in return. Internet veterans know that many socket-based Internet servers can be "driven by hand" in this way, just as a news server can. And they know that Internet client applications, behind their pretty graphical faces, send and receive the same kinds of ASCII texts. If I connect my newsreader to a news server and use a network analyzer to watch the packets exchanged between the two, I'll see the same sequence of commands and responses.

Programmers who write communicating programs can do so more easily, and more effectively, when they themselves can read and write the protocols those programs must use. Programmers can write lots of these communicating programs, quickly and cheaply, because almost any programming language—including many script languages—can produce and consume text-based protocols. Programmers can debug these communicating programs readily because, once again, the programmers themselves can easily produce the inputs and interpret the outputs. These facts account for much of the Internet's power, flexibility, reach, and resilience.

All this is old news to Internet veterans, but to a generation indoctrinated in the Microsoft vision of distributed computing, it was a revelation. "Distributed computing is hard," we were told. "Let us figure out how to do it and then give you the tools you'll need." Those tools always involved proprietary APIs, packaged in proprietary system components that in turn spoke inscrutable binary protocols to other proprietary system components.

The Essential Simplicity of Internet Software

What Internet old-timers knew all along, and what Microsoft and everyone else found out a few years ago when the Web went mainstream, is that distributed computing is actually not so hard. Protocols that people can easily read and write are one major simplification. Another is data stores that people can easily read and write. Like Internet protocols, Internet data stores are utterly simple. Example 5-2, for example, shows the data file produced by the NNTP transaction we saw in Example 5-1.

Example 5-2. Contents of an NNTP Message

```
Path: localhost!not-for-mail
From: Jon Udell <udell@monad.net>
Newsgroups: test
Subject: sample message
Date: Tue, 06 Apr 1999 22:20:56 -0400
Message-ID: <35760488.F61E274@monad.net>
NNTP-Posting-Host: localhost
Mime-Version: 1.0
Content-Type: text/plain; charset=us-ascii
Content-Transfer-Encoding: 7bit
X-Mailer: Mozilla 4.5 [en] (WinNT; I)


This is the body of a sample message.
```

In this case, since the news server was Netscape Collabra Server, running on my deskside Windows NT Server, the file's name is *C:\Netscape\SuiteSpot\news-udell\ spool\test\376*. The file divides into two parts: a set of headers and a message body. The rules governing the headers are defined in RFC 1036, entitled "Standard for Interchange of USENET Messages." But you don't need to read RFC 1036 to get a pretty good idea of what these headers do. The `Newsgroups:` header, for example, which we specified in the posting, tells us this message was posted to a newsgroup called *test*. The `Message-ID:` header, which the news server generated, identifies this message uniquely among all messages posted to this news server.

A collection of these files, in a tree of subdirectories, is the news server's primary message database. It's a good example of an Internet-style data store, or document database, or what I'll call throughout this book a *docbase*. I use the term broadly to mean ASCII texts structured according to some rules. For the news message shown in Example 5-2, RFC 1036 defines the rules. Internet email messages look a lot like news messages; RFC 822 defines their rules.

A collection of mail or news messages is an example of a data store that holds *semistructured* information. What's that? It's data that's both structured, because message headers define key dimensions such as author, subject, and date, and unstructured, because message bodies contain free-form text.

A collection of web pages doesn't necessarily hold the same kind of semistructured data. Web pages aren't required to carry headers. Nor are they required to exhibit more complex structures that can be expressed in XML. But you can choose to impose these kinds of rules on a collection of web pages. When you do that, web pages also become containers of semistructured data, and collections of them become docbases.

Semistructured Data

Semistructured data is at the heart of all groupware. Its free-form aspect is crucial, because we communicate mainly using sentences and paragraphs (and nowadays, hyperlinks), not rows and columns. Its structured aspect is likewise crucial, because without any constraints, all that free-form stuff loses much of its potential value.

Dealing with semistructured data requires a special discipline. Practitioners stand with one foot in the world of publishing and another in the world of conventional data management. Much of the remainder of this book shows how, and why, to become that kind of practitioner. We'll develop tools and techniques to produce, transform, and deliver docbases, because by doing so, we can make those docbases into groupware applications.

Sometimes we'll reuse and extend Internet-style protocols and data formats, and sometimes we'll invent new ones. Often we'll stick with a data-management philosophy that views structured text files, stored in hierarchical file systems, as good enough for many practical purposes. Not always, because SQL and object-oriented techniques matter too, and where they do, we'll use them. In this section, though, we'll focus on an important class of applications for which text-file-based data-management is appropriate and effective.

How Docbases Are Groupware Applications

Docbases can function as groupware applications in quite a few different ways. To see what I mean, we'll look at the docbases that were available on the *BYTE* web site and explore how each of them exhibited different kinds of groupware properties. Table 5-1 characterizes these docbases in terms of their size (number of documents), collaborative breadth (number of authors), reach (number of readers), and scope (public or private). It also introduces some terms that need explanation.

The *repository format* defines a docbase's raw data store. For mail and news, that's usually something like Example 5-2. For a web docbase it's often a markup language—Standard Generalized Markup Language (SGML), XML, or perhaps simply HTML.

The *input tool* moves content into the repository. It might be a text editor, or an export filter, or a web form coupled with a scripted handler.

The *delivery format* is the data store that a server application uses to deliver a docbase to a client application.

When repository and delivery formats differ, a *transformation tool* bridges the gap between them. This is usually true for web docbases but not always. In the case of the *BYTE Magazine* archive, for example, a non-HTML repository format was transformed into an HTML delivery format. But in the case of the Virtual Press Room, a docbase that contained a collection of press releases, the repository format was already deliverable HTML, so no transformation was needed. In later chapters we'll see fresh examples of each of these approaches and explore when and why one or the other makes sense.

Finally, the *viewing tool* is the client application that reads and displays the delivery format. Here that means either a web browser or a newsreader, though as Part I discussed, and as we'll see in later chapters, the viewing tool can sometimes also be a mailreader.

Table 5-1. Varieties of Docbases

	Magazine Archive ·	Virtual Press Room (Private)	Virtual Press Room (Public)	News-groups (Public)	Web Mirror of Public News-groups	Private News-groups
# of Docs	10,000	5,000	2,500	8,000	8,000	4,000
# of Authors	tens	hundreds	hundreds	thou-sands	thou-sands	tens
# of Readers	millions	tens	millions	tens of thou-sands	tens of thou-sands	tens
Repository Format	home-grown markup	HTML	HTML	RFC 1036	RFC 1036	RFC 1036
Input Tool	text editor	web form	web form	news-reader	none	news-reader
Delivery Format	HTML	HTML	HTML	RFC 1036	HTML	RFC 1036
Transform-ation Tool	Epsilon Extension Language (EEL) program	none for docu-ments; Perl script used to generate naviga-tional indexes	none for docu-ments; Perl script used to generate naviga-tional indexes	none	Perl script	none
Viewing Tool	browser	browser	browser	news-reader	browser	news-reader
Restricted Access?	no	yes	no	no	no	yes

Groupware Aspects of the BYTE Magazine Docbase

The *BYTE Magazine* docbase presented all of the magazine's text and images. From the outset, I knew that I wanted to build some kind of repository and use some kind of transformation tool to convert content stored in that repository into deliverable web pages. What motivated that design, at first, was mainly a concern about efficiency. I supposed that an online version of *BYTE* would interest a lot of people. It did. Over three years, it attracted more than 3 million readers and eventually up to 10,000 a day. My goal was to provide a rich and comprehensive technical reference libary, but one that would respond quickly under heavy load, even over the slow dialup links that were the only means of access for many international users.

The technique I adopted, which I call *dynamic generation of statically served pages*, generates HTML pages from a markup-language repository. Because the pages were served statically, there was none of the peformance overhead of a so-called "database-driven" site. Throughout the life of this docbase, a 32MB 150MHz server, laughably antique by today's standards, pumped out archive pages at an ever-increasing rate with no sign of strain.

Yet because the pages were generated dynamically, the docbase enjoyed much of the flexibility that we expect from a database-driven site. In fact, it was database-driven, although not in the conventional sense. The repository was its database. It wasn't a real-time or relational or transactional database, but it didn't need to be. It only needed to package the content using a predictable and regular structure. Given that structure, a transformation tool, which I called a *translator* and which people in the SGML/XML world tend to call *processing software,* could generate the deliverable pages.

Although my first concern was efficiency, it soon became clear that this method was enormously flexible. With each iteration of the translator, I found new ways to draw out groupware features that were latent in repository. These features were, conceptually, ways to manage the relationships among various groups, and I thought of them as *bindings.* As it evolved, the docbase created a series of bindings involving authors, readers, subscribers (a subset of readers), vendors, and advertisers (a subset of vendors). It connected readers to authors by way of a feedback mechanism that evolved from a standard mailto: link into a context-sensitive form, generated on demand for each article, that routed comments to the team responsible for that article. It connected readers to vendors by way of a referral mechanism that transformed references to companies, products, and product categories into appropriate links to a partner site that processed and relayed requests for information. It connected advertisers to readers indirectly by way of a mapping between content categories and ad categories—so that an IBM DB2 ad, for example, could selectively bind to database-related articles. The never released final version connected advertisers more directly to subscribers, so that an IBM DB2 ad could selectively bind to pages viewed by subscribers who had registered a preference for database articles.

The BYTE Docbase Translator

Had I started the *BYTE* docbase in 1999, rather than 1995, I'd have used XML to define the repository format and implemented the translator in Perl, using the

XML::Parser module that connects Perl to an XML parser called *expat*.* But in 1995 there was no XML or *XML::Parser*, and I was only beginning to learn about Perl. So I made up my own simple markup language (see Example 5-4) and used a programmable text editor to process it into web pages. The text editor was Lugaru's Epsilon, an Emacs workalike to which I've been hopelessly addicted for many years. The programming language was Epsilon Extension Language (EEL), an embedded C-like interpreter with powerful regular-expression support.

Think of the repository as source code, the translator as a compiler, and the deliverable HTML pages as object code. It took about 45 minutes to "compile" the 10,000-page magazine docbase, but a complete rebuild was only necessary when we needed to propagate a change—which might be a new standard page template or a new embedded function linked to some standard element of a page—across the entire docbase. Otherwise, only an incremental rebuild was needed. Once a new month's content was stored correctly in the repository, the incremental rebuild took just a few minutes.

This approach entails the same trade-offs that govern compiled versus interpreted software. If there had been very frequent inflow of new content, and if the docbase had to absorb and reflect that content in real-time, I'd have needed a system that was database-driven in the conventional sense. It's neither easier, nor harder, to build that kind of system. When you do, you shift work from a compiler, which feeds a statically served site, to a runtime system that implements a dynamically served site. Which approach is best? That depends on a host of docbase variables: the ratio of structured to free-form content, the refresh frequency, the kinds of dynamic features required in the generated HTML, the usage level, the transactional load.

People tend to assume that a dynamically served docbase is intrinsically better than a statically served docbase, because it's backed by a "real" database. But there's an important middle ground. A richly structured and rigorously maintained repository, coupled with smart processing software, can—for a certain class of applications—deliver the best of both worlds. This approach can combine the intelligence of a dynamically served docbase with the low overhead and high performance of a statically served docbase. Groupware applications are often good candidates for this treatment. They tend to be text heavy and semistructured, without strong real-time or transactional requirements.

A lot of useful applications fall into this category, and we'll see more examples of dynamically generated and statically served docbases in later chapters. But we'll

---

* I'd also have written a Document Type Definition (DTD) to formally describe the repository format and used a *validating parser*, which *XML::Parser* isn't, to ensure conformance with the DTD. We'll see an example of this in Chapter 9, *Conferencing Applications*.

also dynamically generate pages where it makes sense to do so, and we'll sometimes mix the two styles. Ultimately what matters are the ends, not the means.

My EEL-based translator is now obsolete. I mainly use Perl and its *XML::Parser*
module to transform docbases. But since I am going to show you some ways that
my EEL translator turned the magazine docbase into a groupware application, and
since it did the same kinds of things that XML-oriented text-processing software
does, let's look at a fragment of the EEL code. Example 5-3 shows a function
called *doBio()*.

Example 5-3. Text Processing with Epsilon's EEL

```
doBio()
  {
  char sTmp[250];      // alloc space for mailto: URL
  bufnum = bufBI;      // switch to buffer containing contents of <bio> tag
  point = 0;           // go to start of buffer
  if (size() > 0)      // test that <bio> tag wasn't empty.
    {
    killTag();         // remove <bio> tag
    point = 0;         // go to start of buffer
    sprintf(sTmp,"<a href=%cmailto:#1%c>#1</a>",0x22,0x22);  // make replacement
    string_replace(RE_MAILURL,sTmp,REGEX);       // look for email address,
                                                 // regex-replace with mailto: URL
    point = 0;                      // go to start of buffer
    stuff("<hr><em><strong>");      // insert styling
    point = size();                 // go to end of buffer
    stuff("</strong></em>");        // insert styling
    bufnum = bufFinal;              // switch to output accumulator
    grab_buffer(bufBI);             // insert contents of <bio> tag
    }
  }
```

This function was called when the translator had encountered a **<bio>** tag, which
might contain text such as: "Jon Udell, executive editor for New Media, can be
reached at jon@byte.com." The purpose of *doBio()* was twofold. Its first job was to
wrap HTML styles around the contents of the **<bio>** region of an article. And in
retrospect, it did that poorly. When you see HTML fragments interspersed with
code, as in Example 5-3, it's usually a sign of a missed opportunity to templatize
an HTML generator. Templates are easy to make and easy to process, and they
help you visualize and modify your page designs. I've since learned that lesson,
and you'll see lots of examples throughout this book of processing scripts that
merge content into templates as they generate HTML pages.

The second job of **doBio()** was to do what the message-authoring tools we discussed in Part I do when they encounter an implied URL—namely, activate that
URL. In this case, that meant transforming *jon@byte.com* into the clickable link
<a href="mailto:jon@byte.com">jon@byte.com</a>. If you're familiar
with regular expressions and text processing, this kind of transformation should

seem utterly ordinary. Indeed it is. Yet in the context of processing software that reads a docbase repository and writes a deliverable docbase, it can be used to add subtle but powerful groupware features to the docbase.

Leveraging Context in the BYTE Docbases

To see how a translator can create groupware, let's first ask again why it should. Why, after all, did the magazine archive exist online in the first place? We wanted to offer a service to readers, we wanted to keep up with the times, we wanted to market our product. And yes, because the Web is an advertising-driven publishing medium and because our product was the kind of content that plays well in that medium, we aimed for advertising revenue too. Many businesses, of course, aren't as naturally content-rich as ours was, so ad revenue doesn't figure into the equation. But for all businesses, there is another reason to be online. Web content, in almost any form, creates groupware opportunities. By that I mean that it creates possibilities to connect internal groups (product development, support, marketing, and other teams) with external groups (existing customers, prospective customers, business partners). These connections can be expressed, through the medium of a docbase, in small details. Suppose, for example, that the HTML rendering of *jon@byte.com* were instead:

```
<a href="mailto:jon@byte.com?subject=Article+Feedback|August+1998|Web+Project|\
Distributed+HTTP">jon@byte.com</a>
```

Here the translator adds extra value to the docbase. It doesn't just activate an implied URL, to make it easier for a reader to send me email. It also uses its knowledge of the context in which that implied URL appears to help the reader send me a much smarter piece of email. How? As it parses the repository, the translator can easily remember contextual clues, such as the issue date or the magazine section of an article. Using the parameterized mailto: trick that we saw in Chapter 4, *Information-Management Strategies for Groupware Users*, it can use this information to spare the reader the trouble of specifying the context that provoked the sending of the message. This also ensures that every message from this source—that is, from any <bio> region in the docbase—will announce its originating context. The recipient might then use a client-side mail filter, as shown in Chapter 4, to manage messages from that source, organizing them (and counting them) by magazine issue ("August 1998") or by magazine section ("Web Project").

This kind of detail is, individually, not earthshaking. But when there are dozens or hundreds of contributors to a docbase, and thousands or even millions of users, the details add up. The docbase is, among other things, a tool that facilitates interactions between its contributors and its users. Enriching the context that surrounds one of those interactions yields a small reward for a small effort. But enriching the context of all the interactions yields a much larger reward for the same small effort.

Leveraging Context in Other Kinds of Docbases

It's uniquely the mission of a trade magazine to use content to mediate between subscribers and vendors. What about other kinds of businesses? Every corporate web site can and should do more than just publish information about its products and services. Those docbases can become groupware applications that connect the teams that create the products and services to the customers who use them. Such connections ought to be bidirectional, and they ought to help to define and enhance relationships among groups within and across the firewall.

Consider, for example, the publication of a user manual online. That's something that many companies already do or want to do. Typical rationales might be that an online manual is a cheap alternative to a printed manual or that it enables electronic updates to the printed manual. In groupware terms, though, a docbase can do much more. It needn't merely dispense information. It can also help the provider of the docbase learn how people use that information—and more importantly, how they use the product that the manual describes. How? By using the docbase translator to add various kinds of context-sensitive intelligence, or *instrumentation*, to the deliverable HTML pages that it generates.

One important use for this kind of instrumentation is to enable context-sensitive feedback. Your documentation probably divides into functional areas, and you may assign different writers and editors to those areas. There is probably also an implied relationship between each of these areas and product development, marketing, or sales teams. A page of a docbase can (and should) "know" to which area it belongs. When it does, it can collect feedback in an intelligent manner—feedback that's aware of its page of origin, of the functional area to which the page belongs, and of the teams responsible for that area. And it can route questions and comments to appropriate teams, ideally using references to roles that refer indirectly to people and groups, rather than hardcoded email addresses.

This may sound complicated and hard, but it really isn't. Suppose you manufacture a bread machine, and the XML repository from which you generate its manual looks like this:

```
<docbase name="BreadMaker Operations Manual" product="BreadMaker" >

<chapter number="3" name="Cleaning and maintaining your BreadMaker"
                category="maintenance">

<section name="First-time cleaning" model="1A">
<p>....</p>
</section>

<section name="First-time cleaning" model="2B">
<p>....</p>
```

```
</section>

</chapter>
</docbase>
```

Note the databaselike nature of this repository. There are, for example, two parallel instances of the "First-time cleaning" section, because different models require different methods. Which section will appear in the docbase? The translator selects the right one for the version of the docbase that it generates.

Now let's suppose the convention in this docbase is that section headings are followed by clickable feedback icons. When it forms the address of an icon's link, the translator stuffs in every scrap of potentially useful contextual information that it can:

```
<a href="/cgi-bin/feedback?docbase=BreadMaker+Operations+Manual&
  product=BreadMaker&chapter=3&model=1A&
  section=First-time+cleaning&category=maintenance">
  <img src="/img/feedback.gif"></a>
```

Creating this instrumentation was easy. What's it good for? That's up to the *feedback* script that runs when a user clicks the link. It might vary the feedback-collecting form that it presents to the user according to the originating docbase, the product it describes, or the category (e.g., **maintenance**) associated with the originating page. It can embed all the contextual clues in the form it generates so that the form's handler can use them to track the feedback, route it to appropriate teams, and store it. The appropriate place to store it might be in a database to support numeric analysis of feedback by product or category, or it might be in another docbase to support review of the anecdotal responses collected by the form.

The BYTE Docbase: From Markup to HTML

To see a more detailed example of the kinds of implied functionality that a translator can extract from a repository, let's look at how a fragment of the *BYTE* repository was converted into its corresponding web page. Example 5-4 shows how my August 1998 *BYTE* column would have looked, had I then relied (as I do now) on XML as a representation language.

Example 5-4. BYTE Docbase Repository Fragment

```
<article>
<section>Web Project</section>

<category>distributed_computing</category>

<keywords>web programming, distributed computing, http</keywords>

<head>Distributed HTTP Now!</head>
```

Example 5-4. BYTE Docbase Repository Fragment (continued)

```
<deck>
Peer-to-peer Web computing is the future. Why not start
exploring the possibilities now?
</deck>

<byline>Jon Udell</byline>

<text>
The more I work with dhttp, the more I'm convinced that it
represents the right way to integrate web/Internet technologies with
the mainstream Windows desktop. Something like a dhttp service, I'm
arguing, ought to be running everywhere. It defines a new platform.

... see <a href="#fig1">figure 1</a> for details ...

... the module <tt>Engine::Server</tt> ...

... <a href="http://www.netscape.com">http://www.netscape.com</a> ...

... Reader Service Number: 1027
</text>

<illustration>
<a name="fig1"/>
<title>Dhttp Architecture</title>
<image>1998-08-wpj-01.gif</image>
<caption>
The dhttp system comprises an engine that hosts one or more
pluggable applications, each with its own ODBC connection.
</caption>
</illustration>

<sidebar>
<section>Web Project</section>

<category>distributed_computing</category>

<keywords>data replication, distributed computing</keywords>

<head>Data replication with DHTTP</head>

<text>...</text>

</sidebar>

<bio>
Jon Udell is BYTE's executive editor for new media. He can
be reached at jon@byte.com.
</bio>

</article>
```

This XML example revises in minor respects the format I actually used. Most notably, my homegrown markup language didn't require each opening tag (e.g., <head>) to be paired with a closing tag (e.g., </head>. Why not? The parser that read the original format aimed to simplify the coding rules for the repository. At the time, I thought that made life easier for the repository maintainer, by reducing keystrokes. But it was a bad bargain, because my homegrown parser never did the kind of robust error checking that XML parsers do. The convenience of fewer keystrokes was more than offset by the burden of finding and correcting errors. It would be a worse bargain today. With the advent of XML as a way to represent markup language and of freely available XML parsers to process such markup, it's foolish to waste time writing parsing code. Let the XML parser do that grunt work for you. Spend your time on what really matters—writing the parser-enabled processing software that adds value to docbases.

We'll pretend that this repository had been XML, ignore the parsing step that XML would have made trivial, and focus on what's still relevant today—namely, the groupware features that the translator injected into the docbase. For a simple but complete example of an XML-enabled docbase translator, see Chapter 9, which shows how a real XML repository (the contents of this book) was translated by an *XML::Parser* script into a docbase (an HTML archive with feedback instrumentation).

Note how the repository format in Example 5-4 freely intermixes XML tags such as <subhead> and <illustration> with HTML tags such as <tt> and <a href>. To an XML parser, everything here looks like well-formed XML. But as we'll see in Chapter 9, well-formed XML can coincide with HTML. In this example, the translator can choose to interpret the non-HTML tags one way and the HTML tags another. For example, an <illustration> tag told the translator to emit a series of HTML tags defining a new region of the generated docbase page. However, the <text> tag told the translator to pass everything until the closing </text> tag— typically, a mixture of text and HTML—to a routine that specialized in converting that repository element into its corresponding output.

What might that routine do? Usually, it just passed the text and HTML through to the generated docbase page. In our case, this stuff was manufactured by an export filter that converted Quark pages into HTML extracts. But sometimes, as we'll see shortly, the routine translated a text pattern into a link, thus adding a dynamic feature to the docbase.

Translator results for a BYTE docbase page

Figure 5-1 shows the docbase page that the translator would have generated from the repository fragment shown in Example 5-4.

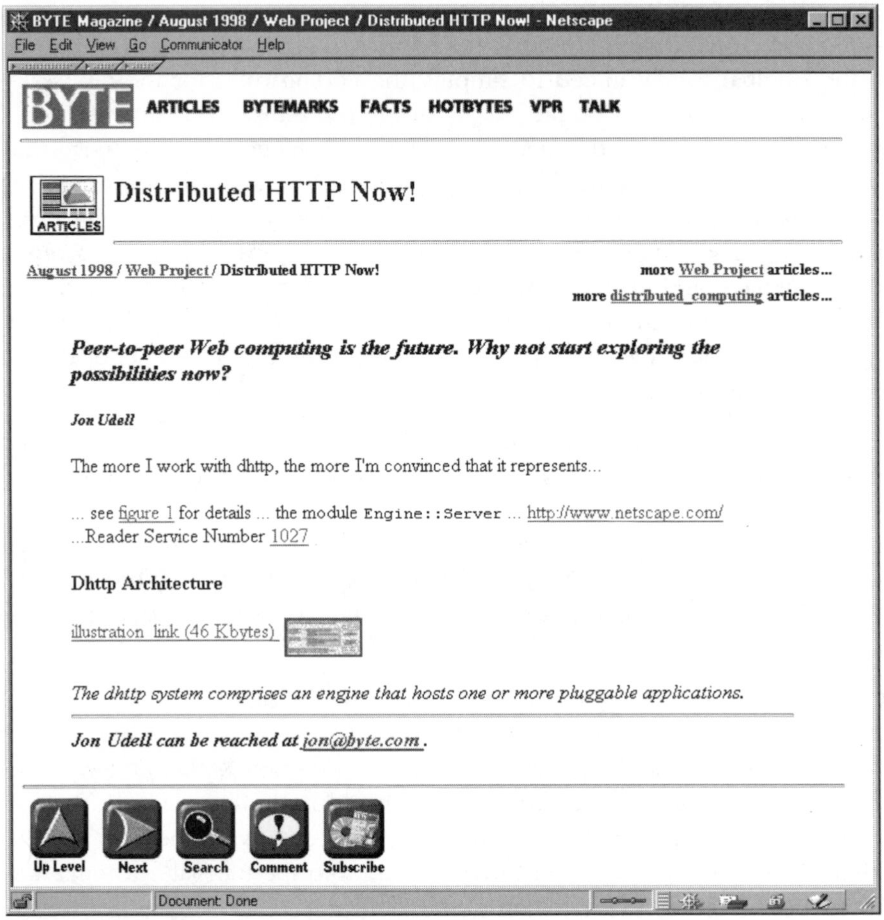

Figure 5-1. Translator output: a generated docbase page

This page is rich with instrumentation. Let's review some of the features the translator has added to the docbase.

Structured title. Using its knowledge of the current article, the translator created a composite title based on the pattern PUBLICATION NAME / ISSUE DATE / SECTION / TITLE and wrote it out as the HTML document title—that's the contents of the <title> .. </title> region, which renders as the text of the browser's window titlebar.

This fielded format is a simple technique that turns out to have remarkably many uses. It brands the page as belonging to the *BYTE* archive, tells the age (August

1998)* and type (Web Project) of the article, and announces its title. In Chapter 8, *Organizing Search Results*, we'll see how this method helps a search-results filter work intelligently. Briefly, all search engines report hits using two items: a URL and the HTML document title. The database-like nature of this composite title enables the search-results filter to organize found stories by age and type, not just by relevance.

There's more. The translator also wrote a mapping file that correlated URLs with document titles. An entry in that file looked like this:

```
/art/9808/sec11/art1/art1.htm | August 1998 | Web Project | Distributed HTTP
```

This file enabled the log-processing filter to work intelligently. It looked up the URL for each entry in the daily web server log, mapped that URL to its composite title, parsed the title into its constituent fields, and used those fields to organize usage reports. One report ranked usage by issue, another by section. These reports helped answer questions like "What are the most popular three issues online?" and "Which sections of the magazine consistently attract the most readers over time?" So the structured titles became a way to help a group of authors and editors gauge the effect of their work on a group of online readers.

Tree-navigation widget. Here's the same structured title that appears in the browser's titlebar, but in this context, it's clickable. A user can jump up one level to a summary page for this month's Web Project section or up two levels to the table of contents for the August 1998 issue.

There's another reason to recapitulate the titlebar here. Before the translator did that, we used to engage in this dialogue several times a month:

User: "Why don't you include the dates of the articles?"

Webmaster: "We do. The date is part of the HTML document title. It appears in the browser's window title bar."

User: "Gosh, you're right! Sorry, I don't know why I didn't look there."

Eventually it dawned on me that nobody looks there. For most people, the document title doesn't seem to belong to the page in the same way that the document's body does. To me, the date in the window's titlebar was obvious, but no matter. The customer is always right.

Of course, the customer would be out of luck if fixing this meant visiting and editing 10,000 pages. Fortunately, the translator already did that routinely and was in a position to know what addresses these links should point to. It took just a few

---

* Alert readers may wonder about the source of the issue date, which doesn't appear in the markup shown in Example 5-4. The name of the markup-language file encoded that information.

lines of code and a rebuild to add this tree-navigation widget and make some users happier.

Section and category "more like this" pages. The translator knew, because it parsed the `<section>` tag, that this article belonged to the Web Project section. It also knew, because it parsed the `<category>` tag, that the article belonged to the `distributed_computing` category. It therefore inserted "more like this" links to appropriate section and category pages.

Where did those pages come from? The translator built them too. It was already processing all the information needed to construct these views of the docbase. Materializing them as the HTML pages behind "more like this" links was straight-forward.

In groupware terms, this feature created bindings between views of the docbase and subgroups of the readership interested in those views. A follower of the Web Project column could easily find more such columns; a reader intrigued by distrib-uted computing could find other material in that category.

Autoactivated URL with referral tracking. Initially the translator just recognized patterns like *http://www.netscape.com/* and turned them into patterns like `<a href="http://www.netscape.com/">http://www.netscape.com/</a>`—thus activating the implied link. How? It's a regular-expression search-and-replace oper-ation. Example 5-3 shows how that was done in EEL. In Chapter 6, *Docbase Input Techniques*, we'll see an example of the same thing in Perl.

A later version of the translator modified the link addresses to look like this:

```
<a href="/refer.pl?url=http://www.netscape.com/&issue=1998-08&
   section=Web+Project&title=Distributed+HTTP">http://www.netscape.com/</a>
```

The script named *refer.pl* logged each use of the link, then issued a redirection to the specified URL. Why? It's easy to track referrals and costs virtually nothing. You might never need to harvest the data, but then again, you might. Why foreclose the option? Referral data measures the affinity of the users of a docbase for the sites mentioned in the docbase. When you report additional context, as shown here, you can track that affinity in a highly granular way.

Interface to partner site. Traditionally, in the trade magazine business, company and product references were accompanied by numbers that also appeared on the blown-in postcards, or *bingo cards,* that readers could use to request product liter-ature from companies. Magazines outsourced the handling of these bingo cards to agencies that tallied the data and produced the mailing labels used by the target companies to fulfill literature requests. Nowadays, as you'd expect, this process is moving online. To modernize its bingo-card system, *BYTE* partnered with Info-Xpress, a company that provides online reader service for a number of magazines.

Thanks to the translator, *BYTE's* interface to InfoXpress was particularly effective. Other sites rely on a generic referral to an InfoXpress subsite. There, users have to enter the number of an item, or drill down through issue, category, or company/ product pages, in order to reach the page on which to make a specific literature request. Our implementation led directly to that page, because the translator used the contextual information at its disposal to transform the reader service number into a URL that looked like this:

```
<a href="http://www.infotracker.com/byte?issue=1998-08&rsn=1027">1027</a>
```

What if an article didn't contain a reader service number? In many cases, the translator could still create an appropriate link to the partner site, based on the value of the article's category tag. These links led to category pages on the partner site. An article that listed a flock of printer manufacturers, without individual request codes, might say: "Click *here* to request more information about printers." The address behind the link might be:

```
http://www.infotracker.com/byte?issue=1998-08&category=printers
```

The translator produced this kind of link when it spotted an instance of the standard "Products Mentioned" element and when it was also in possession of an appropriate category term (from the `<category>` or `<keywords>` tags).

The end result was another kind of binding. In the context of product-related articles, the site connected readers, as directly as possible, to the vendors of those products. The interface to the partner site was expressed not as a single generic link but as thousands of context-sensitive links.

Note that the markup language shown in Example 5-4 does not define a reader service element. It wasn't necessary. The source text already exhibited a perfectly regular pattern matching the Perl regular expression:

```
/Reader Service Number: (\d+)/i
```

Sure, I could have required the repository maintainer to do this:

```
Reader Service Number: <rsn>1072</rsn>
```

But that might be overkill. When data naturally exhibits a regular pattern that you can exploit in a simple and reliable way, you can impose fewer requirements on the people who create and maintain a repository. If a tool writes the repository, this isn't an issue. It can create arbitrarily rich markup. But sometimes it makes sense for people to create markup directly. In those cases, the less the better.

Thumbnail illustrations. The tag `<image>1998-08-wpj-01.gif</image>` referred to a full-size GIF image. But what the translator emitted, instead, was a reference to a thumbnail version of the full-size image. Why? Users, many of whom accessed the site from marginal networks, told me that they preferred this method. It's another use of the layering strategy discussed in Chapter 3, *Intranet*

Collaboration with NNTP and HTML. A thumbnail reveals enough about an image to help a user decide whether it's worth the time needed to download it. The size of the image in bytes also helps the user make that decision. So the translator reported that too. To streamline display of the thumbnail, it extracted its width and height (from bytes 7–10 of the thumbnail GIF) and tucked these values into the WIDTH and HEIGHT attributes of the generated <img src> tag, so that a browser could frame a thumbnail and continue rendering the page without interruption.

What about the full-size images? The translator could have simply linked the thumbnail's <img src> tag to the full image. But that would have presented the image devoid of context. Instead the translator fabricated a new container page for each full-size image. There, along with the image, it recapitulated the standard top and bottom toolbars, the tree-navigation widget (one level deeper, in this case), and the title and caption of the image. Then it linked the thumbnail to this container page.

These were small details. But they improved the layered presentation of the site and sped up page delivery. As a result, more users engaged with the site's content. That meant all the groupware bindings built into the site worked a little more effectively than they otherwise would have.

Automatic mailto: link activation. Email addresses in the <bio> region were made into active *mailto:* links. Back then, the parameterized *mailto:* trick I mentioned earlier wasn't widely supported, so the translator didn't add any extra context to the messages originating from these links.

There was another way to deliver intelligent feedback, though. The *Comment* button was instrumented with contextual information that was sent to a comment-form generator.

Up link. It seems obvious that every node of a hierarchical docbase should provide a link to its parent. And yet for the longest time, I neglected to do that. Why? I figured that people could rely on the browser's *Go Back* button. Having climbed down the tree, they could climb back up. But that's a flawed assumption. Tree traversal is only one way people reach the pages of a docbase and, in many cases, not the dominant way. Referrals from local or remote search engines, or from other people, bring users directly into the middle of your docbase.

In those cases, *Go Back* takes people right back to where they came from. You, however, probably want to encourage them to stay and look around. That means your docbase has to be richly interconnected.

The *Up* link is one of the pathways that can turn a random visit into a memorable session. You should exploit the icon's <alt> text to maximum advantage here, as everywhere. Initially we used the stock phrase "Up Level." But the translator knew more about the parent of a particular page than that. It knew that a parent was

"Aug 1998 Web Project Table of Contents" or "Aug 1998 Table of Contents"—so we added these richer descriptions to the `<alt>` tag.

Next link. In this docbase, each article comprises one main story and zero or more subarticles, or sidebars. These elements are presented as a series connected with *Prev* and *Next* buttons. The use of these buttons is context-sensitive. The example in Figure 5-1 is the first in a series of two—that is, it's a main story that has one sidebar. So the translator includes the *Next* link and omits the *Prev* link. When it generates the sidebar, it includes a *Prev* link and omits the *Next* link. For middle elements in a series longer than two, the translator includes both *Prev* and *Next* links.

Chapter 7, *Docbase Navigation,* shows how to build this kind of navigational machinery into a generated docbase. It's another detail, but the cumulative effect of these kinds of details is to engage more users more deeply with a site's content. That makes all the site's groupware bindings more effective.

Comment link. The address behind this link looked something like this:

```
/comment.pl?issue=1998-08&section=Web%20Project&title=Distributed%20HTTP
```

Given these parameters, the comment script could tailor a feedback form just for this article. That form, in turn, embedded the parameters in hidden fields so that the next script, which handled the form, could assign the comments about this article to appropriate slots in a data store.

The handler also did just what I suggested our hypothetical online bread-machine manual ought to do. It routed feedback (as email) to groups of editors, based on attributes of the article from which a feedback form was generated. And it did so indirectly, mapping magazine sections (e.g., `Reviews`) to roles (e.g., `review-editors`) expressed as lists of email addresses.

Groupware Aspects of the BYTE Virtual Press Room

The Virtual Press Room (VPR) was a docbase built by vendors and their public relations representatives. It enabled these groups to transmit press releases electronically, rather than by fax or snail mail, to the editorial group. These documents, in aggregate, record the entire history of the high-tech industry. Although there are services that collect and publish this material, such as PR Newswire (*http://www.prnewswire.com/*), their scopes are broad. Every trade magazine has its own editorial group, its own readership, and its own natural affinity with the vendor community. The Virtual Press Room created BYTE-specific bindings among these groups.

As Table 5-1 shows, the VPR was an example of a docbase whose repository format coincided with its delivery format. That format was simply HTML, written by the script that handled the VPR's input form. In Chapter 6, we'll see how this kind of script can receive semistructured information, validate it, enable users to preview the docbase page to be built from it, and finally store that page. Associated with the VPR were some other scripts. One built the pages that navigated the part of the docbase that was published on the site. In Chapter 7, we'll look at ways to build navigational systems that support both sequential and random modes of access to a docbase along multiple dimensions. Another script watched for new entries to the docbase, summarized them, and routed them to editors. We'll see an example of this kind of notification system in Chapter 12, *Authentication and Authorization Techniques.*

Let's review how the VPR created bindings among vendors, editors, and readers.

Single Point of Contact to a Group

Press releases that target editors at trade magazines are not only numerous, they are highly duplicated. When it's unclear who should receive a press release, the tendency is to broadcast it to everyone. That's expensive for the sender and annoying to recipients. The Virtual Press Room brokered these communications, presenting all editors with a daily summary of new releases.

For vendors, the VPR created a group communication space that worked as the conferencing spaces that we discussed in Part I can work. It freed contributors from the obligation to identify correct recipients or to limit the scope of their messages. Any editor on staff might, for unpredictable reasons, want to follow up on any particular press release. In a group communication space, these serendipitous connections can happen.

Simultaneous Push/Pull

In the daily or weekly summaries emailed to editors by the script that monitored the VPR, new entries appeared as clickable titles. A recipient could scan a batch of new entries and, if interested in one of them, click through to its docbase page.

This aspect of the VPR echoes another theme from Part I. In group communication, it may be appropriate to push messages at people to make sure they know about some item of information. But such messages need not necessarily tell the whole story. A headline or title is often the right way to announce that more information is available, provided that the announcement empowers the recipient to pull the whole story.

Layered Presentation

The email summaries of new VPR entries worked like list server digests. This technique echoes another Part I theme. In groupware environments, people are saturated with message traffic. Like a docbase, your inbox ought to layer the information it presents to you. At the top level, you'd like to see as few messages as possible. You'd like those messages to show what's important and hide the rest.

The VPR cut down on message traffic by collapsing a day's or week's worth of entries into a single digest message. And it layered that message by presenting only clickable headlines. Each headline contained just enough information to enable a recipient to decide whether or not to click through to the next level—product name, company name, category, summary.

Electronic Storage and Retrieval

Trade magazine editors receive truly frightening quantities of press literature every day. When an item relates to a current assignment, it will be plucked from the pile and used. But what if it relates to a future assignment? The odds that a press release will be remembered, searched for, and found two months after its arrival are very slim. Indexed by company, product, and date, and also full-text searchable, the VPR docbase took care of the filing that busy editors had no time for.

Scoped Collaboration

The VPR docbase lived mostly in private web space, visible only to editors. But submitters could opt, for a fee, to move their announcements to public web space, where they were integrated into the *BYTE* site's navigation and search systems.

As we saw in Part I, it's not enough merely to create differently scoped zones of communication. Groupware should also enable communication to flow among these zones, crossing boundaries when it's appropriate to do so.

Groupware Aspects of the BYTE Public and Private Newsgroups

The public newsgroups connected the editorial staff to its worldwide readership—or more accurately, to a self-selected group of subscribers and nonsubscribers who shared an interest in the subjects explored in the magazine and discussed in the newsgroups. Such an online community may seem uniquely relevant to a magazine, which by definition serves as the focal point for a well-defined interest group. But as we saw in Part I, an online community makes sense for almost any business. Your customers can help one another make the best use of your products if you provide a venue for that interaction. What they say to each other about your strengths and weaknesses may give you more or different insight than what they say to you.

The *BYTE* public web forums were a web reflection of the NNTP newsgroups. Why mirror the newsgroups into web space? As we discussed in Part I, many potential participants aren't familiar with, or comfortable with, NNTP-based discussion. And some are blocked by their corporate firewalls from connecting to foreign news servers. To maximize the reach of the discussions, I supported both news and web modes of access. What emerged was a two-tiered pattern of usage. Most of the 1,500 daily users preferred the web mode; this group read and posted relatively little. Only about 150 visitors each day preferred their newsreaders, but these folks read and posted a lot.

I draw two lessons from this experience. First, there should be more than one way to do things. Larry Wall applied this rule to the design of Perl, because he knows that different cognitive sets require different tools and frameworks. The same rule applies to Internet groupware. People often need to arrive at the same ends by different means. The other lesson is that Internet protocols and data stores are highly interchangeable. NNTP newsgroups, web forums, Notes discussion databases, and listservs are more alike than they are different. Any flavor of server can be made to speak the protocol of any flavor of client. Likewise any data store can be morphed into any other.

Finally, the private newsgroups, as we saw in Part I, supported collaboration among editors who worked in five locations on two continents, sometimes from their offices via the corporate WAN, sometimes from their homes or from hotel rooms by way of the Internet. Secured with SSL, indexed for full-text search, and carved up into concentric scopes, this docbase was a key intranet asset.

6

Docbase Input Techniques

It's time to shift gears, roll up our sleeves, and start building docbases. Our first example will be a web docbase that works like the *BYTE* Virtual Press Room did. In this chapter, we'll look at ways to capture and store docbase records. In Chapter 7, *Docbase Navigation*, we'll explore how to generate sets of pages that enable users to navigate a docbase. By the end of the two chapters, we'll have created a system that you can use to manage monthly status reports, service bulletins, analyst reports, or any template-driven, semistructured documents.

What I'll call the Docbase system includes a family of Perl modules. *Docbase::Input*, featured in this chapter, collects, validates, previews, and stores docbase records. *Docbase::Indexer* and *Docbase::Navigate*, which we'll encounter in Chapter 7, support indexing and navigation of docbase records. These modules are driven by other Perl scripts, some general and some tailored to each instance of the Docbase system. Also associated with each instance are templates that govern the form used to collect its records and define the repository format used to store the records. Finally, each instance uses a standardized directory structure.

Is the Docbase system something you can apply directly with little modification, or is it just a way of illustrating techniques that you'll need to adapt heavily to your purposes? Both. With minor adaptations, mostly involving templates, you can use it to create a variety of docbases that gather, organize, and present sets of semistructured records. In this sense, the Docbase system is reusable.

On another level, what's reusable are the ideas and techniques it embodies. The pattern is: XML storage, mapped to Perl data structures, managed by Perl modules, delivered as HTML pages or SMTP/NNTP messages. We'll see variations on this theme throughout this book, solving lots of different kinds of development problems. In this sense, the Docbase system is intended to serve as an extended example of a way of problem solving that I find almost infinitely fruitful.

An Overview of the Docbase System

The Docbase system uses several kinds of templates, each with its own processor. A form template, processed by a CGI script using the *formGen()* method of *Docbase::Input*, becomes the data-entry form used to collect records. A record template, processed by the *_previewDoc()* and *_writeDoc()* methods of *Docbase::Input*, yields a record in an HTML (or HTML/XML) repository format. We'll focus on these steps in this chapter, and in the next, we'll see how *Docbase::Indexer* and *Docbase::Navigate* transform the stored records into a navigable docbase that can be delivered two ways—dynamically or statically.

An instance of the Docbase system—that is, a collection of service bulletins or analyst reports—uses a set of standard parts. Each instance also customizes some parts. See Appendix A, *Example Software*, for details about acquiring and setting up the Docbase system. If you're inclined to do that, now would be a good time.

Standard Parts Common to Every Instance of the Docbase System

Every Docbase instance relies on a set of standard Perl modules:

Docbase::Docbase
> System-wide constants and methods

Docbase::Input
> Input validation, storage

Docbase::Indexer
> Build page sets for navigation

Docbase::Navigate
> Support for sequential navigation

In addition to these modules, every instance uses these standard Perl scripts:

formgen.pl
> Generate docbase input forms

final-submit.pl
> Receive and record validated input

doc-nav.pl
> Dynamic page display

doc-view.pl
> Dynamic page display

Customized Parts Unique to Each Instance of the Docbase System

For a docbase called ProductAnalysis, whose records store analyst reports, here are the pieces that live in the cgi-bin directory (e.g., */web/cgi-bin/Docbase/ ProductAnalysis*):

form-template.htm
> Template used by *formgen.pl* to generate input form

docbase-template.htm
> Template used by *submit.pl* to store validated record

dynamic-navigation-template.htm
> Template used by *Docbase::Navigate* to present navigational controls in the dynamic version

static-navigation-template.htm
> Template used by *Docbase::Indexer* to present navigational controls in the static version

submit.pl
> Script to validate and store a record

./seqinfo
> Subdirectory for sequence info used in navigation

Anatomy of a Docbase Record

Docbase records are semistructured. Each has parts that correspond roughly to the header and the body of an email message. The header fields of a record contain values that are typically compact—for example, names or dates. These values often belong to *controlled vocabularies*—for example, names of companies, products, or authors. Header fields provide the hooks we'll use in Chapter 7 to build navigational indexes for docbases and in Chapter 8, *Organizing Search Results*, to organize search results.

The body fields of a docbase contain free-form text. They often exhibit patterns— for example, URLs—that provide hooks for the kinds of instrumentation we saw in Chapter 5, *Docbases as Groupware Applications*. The body fields are subject to full-text search, as are header fields. But unlike header fields, they don't provide hooks for building navigational indexes.

In this chapter, we'll focus on a Docbase instance called ProductAnalysis. Its records are reports, written by industry analysts, that assess high-tech products. The creation of a record is a shared responsibility. A manager assigns a report to an analyst, specifying some of the header fields. These manager-specified header fields are as follows.

- Analyst's name

- Date of assignment

- Due date for report

- Name of company

- Name of product (optional, may be supplied by analyst)

There are four analyst-supplied body fields: the report title, a summary of the report (a sentence or paragraph), the full report (many paragraphs), and a chunk of contact information (names, phone numbers, email and web addresses).

Data-collection Strategies

The header fields of a docbase record are conventionally database-like. The body fields are typically just blobs of text. Here are some guidelines to help you build and manage collections of semistructured records:

Not too many fields

When you can make the form short, you should. Users find large flocks of input fields intimidating. From the implementor's perspective, each field involves one more bit of template, validation, and indexing overhead. In Figure 6-2 we'll see how you can override input fields with preassigned values. That's an excellent way to streamline and simplify a form.

Multivalued fields

Collecting contact information can be a chore. Email address, phone number (home? work? both?), fax number, postal address (U.S.? International?)—it can be a real headache to shoehorn all this data into fields. But do you really need to? For years the Virtual Press Room successfully used the method we'll also see at work here: a single contact field, accommodating free-form text, coupled with backend validation that looks for patterns that signify required elements. It's not hard to pick out web addresses, email addresses, and phone numbers.

What if you need to find a particular value that isn't explicitly fielded? It's true that you can't issue an SQL query like `select * from docbase where areacode like '707%'`. However, the record template that governs the ProductAnalysis docbase yields XML-formatted records, so we can search for things inside fields that hold free-form text. In practice, that's often good enough. If finding records where the area code is 707 is a frequent operation, you should make the phone number a distinct header field, then index the docbase on that field using methods detailed in the next two chapters. But if that kind of search only happens once in a blue moon, you might do better to spare yourself (and your users) the overhead of dealing with one more explicit field.

Simple formatting

It's tempting to invite users to format what they write using HTML tags. For this class of docbase, though, I think it's wise to resist that temptation. The *Docbase::Input* module creates effective and readable reports using only the HTML styles that each page inherits from the record template. Within a field, it converts double newlines to paragraph (<p>) tags, then remaining newlines to <br> tags. When users supply paragraph-oriented rather than line-oriented input—as will happen when they paste in material from a word processor—this works out surprisingly well for paragraphs, subheads, and lists.

Of course, you can do better than this. It's easy, for example, to define a stripped-down markup language for subheads, lists, and emphasis. Or you can pass through only these HTML tags while blocking all others. Or you can pass through all the HTML tags, on the theory that only those who know how to use them will even bother to try. If you find that any of these policies doesn't work well, you can easily try another. But don't try to outthink your users or overdesign the system. You can put a lot of effort into building features that deliver no real benefit or that make matters even worse by opening cans of worms best left tightly sealed. Measure the success of a docbase solely in terms of its ability to connect users and information. The Virtual Press Room ran for years, collecting documents from people who told me they found the application self-explanatory and easy to use. You can't argue with simple solutions that work well.

A Docbase Form Template

A user creates a Docbase record by means of a web form. The form isn't served statically, though. It's generated on the fly from a template. After all that discussion in the last chapter about the virtues of dynamically generated but statically served pages, why should we generate this form? The technique helps us to constrain inputs, enforce controlled vocabularies, and divide the responsibility for completing different parts of the form among different people.

Example 6-1 shows the template for the ProductAnalysis input form.

Example 6-1. ProductAnalysis Input Form Template

```
<html>
<head>
<title>Product Analysis Report Form</title>
</head>

<body>

<center><b>Product Analysis Report Form</b></center>

<form method="post" action="!ACTION!">
```

Example 6-1. ProductAnalysis Input Form Template (continued)

```
<table cellpadding="4">

<tr>
<td align="right"><b>Assignment Date</b></td>
<td align="left">|assigndate|</td>
</tr>

<tr>
<td align="right"><b>Due Date</b></td>
<td align="left">~duedate~</td>
</tr>

<tr>
<td align="right"><b>Analyst</b></td>
<td align="left">~analyst~</td>
</tr>

<tr>
<td align="right"><b>Company</b></td>
<td align="left">~company~</td>
</tr>

<tr>
<td align="right"><b>Product</b></td>
<td align="left">~product~</td>
</tr>

<tr>
<td align="right"><b>Title</b></td>
<td align="left"><input name="title" size="40"></td>
</tr>

<tr>
<td align="right"><b>Summary</b></td>
<td align="left"><textarea name="summary" rows="2" cols="50"
wrap="virtual"></textarea></td>
</tr>

<tr>
<td align="right"><b>Full report</b></td>
<td align="left"><textarea name="fulltext" rows="3" cols="50"
wrap="virtual"></textarea></td>
</tr>

<tr>
<td align="right"><b>Contact info</b></td>
<td align="left"><textarea name="contact" rows="3" cols="50"
wrap="virtual"></textarea></td>
</tr>

</table>

<p><center><input type="submit" value="submit"></center></p>
```

Example 6-1. ProductAnalysis Input Form Template (continued)

```
</form>
</body>
</html>
```

I wrote this template by hand, but you could also produce it using an HTML editor. Either way, the crucial idea here is to separate the concerns of a designer, who worries about the form's content and appearance, from the concerns of an implementer, who wires the form to a scripted handler. In this scenario, the form's author and its implementer need only share a common vocabulary of markers, or replaceable elements, that invoke special functions when the template is processed to produce an actual HTML form.

There are three kinds of replaceable elements. The code that processes the template looks for patterns that match these marked elements and replaces them as described in Table 6-1.

Table 6-1. Docbase Input Template: Marked Elements and Replacements

Pattern	Replacement
`!ACTION!`	The CGI path to this docbase's instance of *submit.pl*—for example, */cgi-bin/Docbase/ProductAnalysis/submit.pl*.
`|function-name|`	The result of a Perl function, mapped to `function-name`. For example, `|assigndate|` might map to the Perl function *getDate()*, which might return the value 1999-04-12. On the form this element renders not as an input field, but rather as a computed static value. In order to transmit this value to the form's handler, the form generator also tacks on a hidden field, for example, `<input type="hidden" name="assigndate" value="1999-04-12">`.
`~variable-name~`	The script that generates the form can override this slot with a supplied constant. For example, a manager who assigns a report on Internet Explorer 5.0 can use the form generator to replace *~product~* with the static text `Internet Explorer 5.0`. As in the case of a computed value, this preassigned value appears as static text on the surface of the form. The form generator also adds a hidden field, which transmits the value to the form's handler. By default, when a slot isn't overridden in this way, the form generator replaces *~product~* with the HTML code for an input box, like this: `<input name="product" size="40">`.

Using the Docbase Form Generator

The form generator, *formgen.pl*, runs as a CGI script. It requires at least one argument, which tells the generator which instance of Docbase to use. For example, the CGI call:

```
/cgi-bin/Docbase/formgen.pl?app=ProductAnalysis
```

produces the form shown in Figure 6-1.

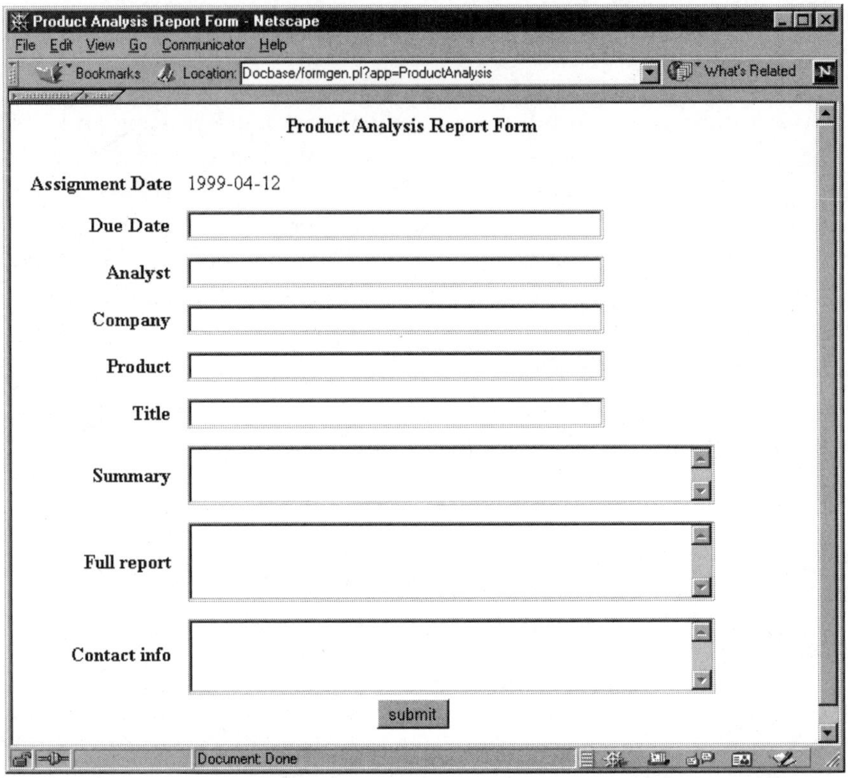

Figure 6-1. Default ProductAnalysis input form

The assignment date, overridden by the |*assigndate*| marker, appears as static text. All other fields are open for input. However, this CGI call:

```
/cgi-bin/Docbase/formgen.pl?app=ProductAnalysis&duedate=1999-05-01&
    analyst=Jon%20Udell&company=Netscape&product=Collabra%20Server%204.0
```

produces the form shown in Figure 6-2.

Here, the generator, using the services of the *Docbase::Input* module, has overridden every replaceable marker with a computed or preassigned value. The analyst who completes this form needs to fill in only four of the fields: `Title`, `Summary`, `Full Report`, and `Contact Info`.

The form generator, *formgen.pl*, appears in Example 6-2. It's brief, because most of the work is done by two modules: *TinyCGI* and *Docbase::Input*.

TinyCGI, which I'll use often, is a minimalistic CGI library. In it I've collected the four simple routines that are at the heart of all CGI programming—*printHeader()* to emit the all-important `Content-type:` header, *readParse()* to gather variables

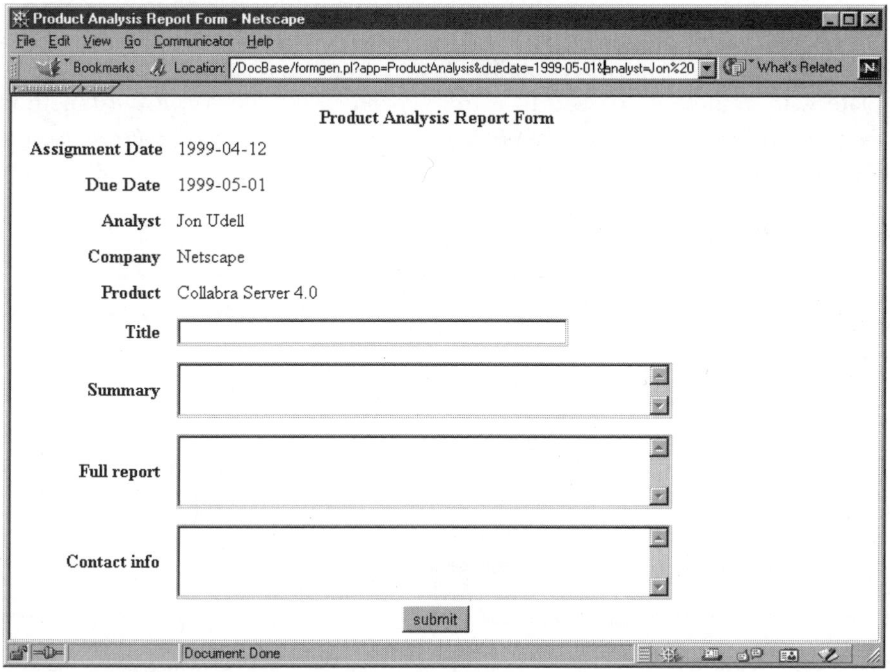

Figure 6-2. Customized ProductAnalysis input form

Example 6-2. The Docbase Form Generator

```perl
#!/usr/bin/perl -w

use strict;

use TinyCGI;                     # load basic CGI services
my $tc = TinyCGI->new();
print $tc->printHeader();
my $vars = $tc->readParse(); # get form variables into hashref

use Docbase::Input;
my $di =                         # set up for this docbase
  Docbase::Input->new($vars->{app});

$di->formGen($vars);             # pass form-variable hashref to form generator
```

from *GET* and *POST* transactions and put them into a Perl hashtable, *escape()* to encode data for HTTP transmission, and *unescape()* to reverse the effects of *escape()*. There's nothing new here; *TinyCGI* simply repackages, for efficiency and convenience, the 1 percent of Perl's standard *CGI* module that I use 99 percent of the time.

Generating an Input Form

As we've seen, the generated form varies according to arguments passed to *formgen.pl*. *Docbase::Input* accomplishes that by matching markers in the form template with arguments passed to it from *formgen.pl*. The *formGen()* method of *Docbase::Input*, shown in Example 6-3, is a typical example of a Perl-based template processor.

Example 6-3. The formGen Method

```
sub formGen                        # merge form template with form variables
  {
  my ($self,$vars) = @_;
  my $app = $self->{app};
  my $form =                       # create the template's name
    "$cgi_absolute/$app/form-template.htm";

  open(F,$form) or print "cannot open form template $form";

  while (<F>)                       # for each line of form template
    {
    if ( m/(!ACTION!)/ )           # rewrite form action
      {
      s#$1#$cgi_relative/$app/submit.pl#;
      }
    if ( m#</form># )              # tack on $app for next script's use
      {
      print "<input type=\"hidden\" name=\"app\" value=\"$app\">\n";
      }
    if ( m/\|(\w+)\|/ )            # perform builtin function
      {
      my $fn = $1;                 # grab function's name
      s/\|$1\|/&{$builtins{$fn}}/e;  # call function, replace marker with value
      }
    if ( m/~(\w+)~/ )              # handle form variables that can be overridden
      {
      my $var = $1;                # grab variable's name
      my $val = $vars->{$var};     # access corresponding hashtable slot
      if (defined $val)            # if slot nonempty, print value on form
                                   # and pass along in hidden variable
        {
        s/~$var~/$val <input type=\"hidden\" name=\"$var\" value=\"$val\">/;
        }
      else                         # turn other form variables into input boxes
        {
        s/~$var~/<input name=$var size=40>/;
        }
      }
    print $_;                      # emit the line
    }
  }
```

The drill is simple: read a line at a time, look for matches, do substitutions. In this example the $vars hashtable, which contains CGI name/value pairs received from

TinyCGI, affords a concise way to map between those pairs and corresponding names that may or may not appear in the form. Perl's `s///e` idiom likewise affords a concise way to convert a name that appears in the form into the result of a Perl function mapped to that name.

It's trivial to build templates and Perl-based template processors, but the technique is very powerful. That's why we'll use it often.

Receiving and Validating Docbase Records

The *Docbase::Input* module will automatically preview input received from a form's handler. We'll see how that works shortly. But validating the fields of a record is the responsibility of each Docbase instance. That's done by customizing the handler for each instance. The handler is always called *submit.pl*. For the ProductAnalysis docbase, the customized handler—shown in Example 6-4—is stored as */web/cgi-bin/Docbase/ProductAnalysis/submit.pl*.

Example 6-4. The ProductAnalysis Version of submit.pl

```perl
#!/usr/bin/perl -w

##########################################################
# boilerplate for every docbase
##########################################################

use strict;
use Docbase::Input;
use TinyCGI;

my $tc = TinyCGI->new();
my $vars = $tc->readParse();                    # collect CGI args
print $tc->printHeader;                          # start emitting page

my $app = $vars->{app};
my $di = Docbase::Input->new($app);

foreach my $key (keys %$vars)                    # basic cleanup of input text
  {
  $vars->{$key} = $di->cleanseInput($vars->{$key});
  }

my ($warnings,$errors) = docbase_validate();    # validate input

$di->processInput($vars,$warnings,$errors);      # process input and warnings/errors

##########################################################
# custom validation tailored for each docbase
##########################################################
```

Example 6-4. The ProductAnalysis Version of submit.pl (continued)

```perl
sub docbase_validate
  {
  my (@warnings) = ();
  my (@errors) = ();
  my $mailpat = $di->getMailPat;
                                              # accumulate warnings

  unless ( $vars->{'contact'} =~ m#$mailpat# ) # email address wanted
    {
    push (@warnings,"<b>contact</b> does not appear to contain an email address ");
    }

  unless ( $vars->{'contact'} =~ m#\d{3,4}# )   # phone number wanted
    {
    push (@warnings,"<b>contact</b> does not appear to contain a phone number ");
    }

                                              # accumulate errors

  foreach my $key (keys %$vars)
    {
    if (! defined $vars->{$key})              # all fields must be non-empty
      {
      push (@errors,'<b>' . $key . '</b> is empty, but required');
      }
    if ( $vars->{$key} =~ /<.+>/ )            # no HTML tags allowed
      {
      push (@errors, '<b>' . $key . '</b> must not contain HTML tags');
      }
    }
    return (\@warnings,\@errors);
  }
```

The first half of this handler is a boilerplate that's the same for every Docbase instance. To tailor it for a new instance, you write a version of *docbase_validate()* that enforces rules specific to this instance, classifies problems as either errors or warnings, and returns these as a pair of lists.

Input Cleanup

Docbase users don't normally compose lengthy text in the HTML form. Typically, they paste in text created by a word processor. That text sometimes includes character codes that you'll want to convert. For example, some Macintosh programs represent a single quote as \xD5. The *cleanseInput()* method of *Docbase::Indexer* turns that into the ASCII single quote, \x27. It's just a set of search-and-replace operations, like this:

```perl
sub cleanseInput
  {
  my ($self, $s) = @_;
```

```
$s =~ s/\x00/ /g;
$s =~ s/\xd1/--/g;
$s =~ s/\xd2/"/g;
$s =~ s/\xd3/"/g;
$s =~ s/\xd5/'/g;
$s =~ s/\x81/Æ/g;
return $s;
}
```

You can easily extend this method to handle other conversions as the need arises.

Validation

The *docbase_validate()* function implements a crucial but often overlooked principle: handlers should parse forms completely and always report all errors and omissions. Failure to do this is endemic on the Web, and it drives users crazy. There's nothing worse than bouncing off a server once to discover that your password is too short, then again to find out that your password includes an invalid character, then again to learn that, oh by the way, the company field that you had left blank is actually required. A form handler sees all the data you send, every time you send it. Why not look at all the data and respond intelligently and completely every time?

To do that, make two lists—one for warnings, one for errors. A warning raises an issue that the user can choose to either address or ignore; these are reported in the Optional Changes section of the preview. In this example, absence of an email address in the contact field triggers a warning. An error raises an issue that the user must deal with; these are reported under the heading Required Changes. In this example, any field that is empty, or that contains an HTML tag, triggers an error.

The *docbase_validate()* function accumulates warnings and errors, then returns the two lists. Note how the Perl idiom for doing that requires you to pass a reference to each of the sublists, rather than the sublists themselves. The latter method won't cause an obvious error, but it will mash the two sublists into a single list, and you'll lose the distinction between warnings and errors. Note also the two idioms for checking variables. To check a specific variable, bind a test to a slot in the hashtable. To check all variables, do that binding inside a loop that iterates over the whole hashtable.

The *submit.pl* script passes the form variables, and the lists of warnings and errors, to the *processInput()* method of the *Docbase::Input* module, shown in Example 6-5.

Example 6-5. The processInput Method

```
sub processInput
  {
  my ($self,$vars,$warnings,$errors) = @_;

  my $warn_count = scalar(@$warnings);   # count warnings
  my $err_count = scalar(@$errors);      # count errors

  if ( $err_count > 0 )                       # mention required changes
    {
    if ( $warn_count > 0 )                    # also mention optional changes
      {
      _doWarnings($self->{app},$warn_count,$warnings);
      }
    print "<p><b>$self->{app}: Required changes: </b>\n";
    my ($i, $c);
    for $i (1..$err_count)
      {
      print "<br>" . ++$c  . ') ' . $errors->[$i-1];
      }
    print "<p>Please use your browser's Go Back button ";
    print "to rewind and fix the required changes.";
    }
  elsif ( $warn_count > 0)                   # mention optional changes
    {
    _doWarnings($self->{app},$warn_count,$warnings);
    print "<p>You can go back and make these optional changes. ";
    print "Or, if what you see below is OK, you can submit it.";
    print $self->_previewDoc($vars);      # preview
    }
  else
    {
    print $self->_previewDoc($vars);      # preview
    }
  }
```

There are three possible outcomes. If there were errors, these are reported (along with warnings, if any) on a Required Changes page that advises the user to go back and correct them.

If there were only warnings, these are reported on an Optional Changes page that also includes a preview of the record. Here, the user has a choice: go back and fix what caused the warnings, or submit the previewed record as is.

Finally, if there were no errors or warnings, only the previewed record appears. The user can submit it or, if something needs changing, can rewind and make those changes.

Previewing Docbase Records

In any system that transforms raw input into HTML pages, it's crucial to show the user a preview of the page exactly as it will finally appear. Although each Docbase instance provides its own input-validation script, all instances share a common previewing service provided by *Docbase::Input*. Its *_previewDoc()* method interpolates user-supplied input into the docbase template, activates mailto: and http:// URLs found in the input, and then shows the user what the final docbase record will look like when actually stored and then rendered as an HTML page. Figure 6-3 shows what a preview looks like when the validation script found warnings but no errors.

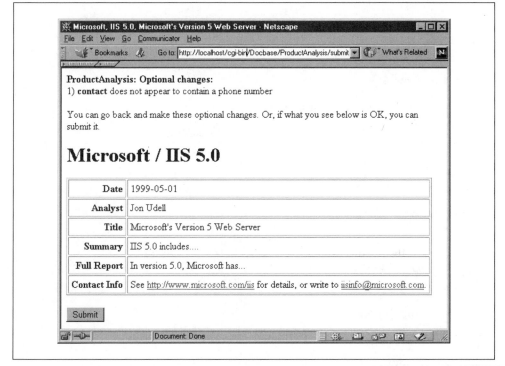

Figure 6-3. Docbase record preview, with optional changes

The preview contains two versions of the record. One appears on the preview form. The other is encoded as a set of hidden variables within the form, ready to be passed along to the handler that will store them if the user presses the *Submit* button. As shown in Example 6-6, the *_previewDoc()* method wires the preview form to *final-submit.pl*, a standard component that's used, unmodified, by every Docbase instance.

Example 6-6. The _previewDoc Method

```
sub _previewDoc
  {
  my ($self,$vars) = @_;
  my $app = $self->{app};
  my $cgi_absolute = $self->{docbase_cgi_absolute};
```

Example 6-6. The _previewDoc Method (continued)

```
my $cgi_relative = $self->{docbase_cgi_relative};
my $preview = '';
$preview .=  "<form method=post action=$cgi_relative/final-submit.pl>";

foreach my $key (keys %$vars)      # pass along hidden vars to next script
  {
  my $value = $tc->escape($vars->{$key});
  $preview .= sprintf("<input type=\"hidden\" name=\"$key\" \
    value=\"%s\">",$value);
  }

my $db_template =                  # make template name
    "$cgi_absolute/$app/docbase-template.htm";

(! -e $db_template)
  {
  $preview = "cannot find docbase template $db_template";
  }
else                               # interpolate values into template
  {
  $preview .= _fillTemplate($db_template,$vars);
  $preview .= "<p><input type=submit value=Submit>";
  $preview .=  "</form>";
  }
return $preview;
}
```

To interpolate the form variables it received from *submit.pl* into the record template, *_previewDoc()* calls another *Docbase::Input()* method, *_fillTemplate()*, shown in Example 6-7.

Example 6-7. The _fillTemplate Method

```
sub _fillTemplate                  # interpolate values into template
  {
  my ($template,$vars) =  @_;
  my $result = '';
  if (! open (F, "$template"))
    {  return "cannot open display template $template";  }
  while (<F>)
    {
    foreach my $key (keys %$vars)
      {
      my $val = $vars->{$key};     # extract value from hashref
      $val = $tc->unescape($val);  # reverse URL encoding if any
      $val =~ s/\n/<br>/g;         # HTML-ize newlines
      s#\[$key\]#$val#;            # replace marker with value
      }
    $result .= _activateUrls($_); # autoactivate URLs
    }
  close F;
  return $result;
  }
```

Here's another template processor that, like the *formGen()* method, exploits a relationship between two namespaces. One is the keys of the $vars hashtable; these are the names of the CGI variables transmitted via the form. The other is the set of bracketed names in the template. The *_fillTemplate()* method maps between these namespaces without needing to know specifically what they contain.

Note how the http:// URLs and email addresses mentioned in the input have been converted, in Figure 6-3, into active links. That means that in the preview context the user not only can verify content, spelling, and style, but also can try the links to make sure that they work correctly. Given regular expressions that match web and email addresses, it's straightforward to convert these into clickable links. The *_activateURLs()* method, called by *_fillTemplate()*, does that transformation like this:

```
sub _activateUrls  # auto-active email and web addresses
  {
  my ($s) = @_;
  $s =~ s/($http_pat)/<a href=\"$1\">$1<\/a>/g;
  $s =~ s/($mail_pat)/<a href=\"mailto:$1\">$1<\/a>/g;
  return $s;
  }
```

Storing Docbase Records

In the Docbase system described here and in Chapter 7, the repository format coincides with the delivery format. The same set of HTML pages serves both purposes. This differs from the *BYTE Magazine* docbase we explored in Chapter 5; in that case, a translator read the repository format and wrote deliverable pages.

Why use one versus the other? The *BYTE* docbase had a fairly complex format but was batch-oriented and maintained by a single production expert who exported material from QuarkXPress and then massaged it to meet a detailed repository specification. There was no need to preview individual pages or validate input interactively, and although a tool could have provided these features, it would have been costly to build and maintain.

The Virtual Press Room, by contrast, had a relatively simple format and was built interactively by many untrained users. These users required an authoring tool that did validate and preview the information they supplied. Because the format was simple, that tool was cheap to build and maintain. Since the preview pages had to be produced immediately, it was convenient to just store them as is.

In the Docbase system, the deliverable HTML pages can be XML pages too, if you format the docbase template as XML. When the two formats coincide, HTML pages are much more manageable than they otherwise would be. The Virtual Press Room was, like the *BYTE* docbase, a pre-XML-era invention. Had I built it in 1999 rather than 1995, I'd have exploited XML, as I'll demonstrate here.

When a user enters a new record in the ProductAnalysis docbase, *Docbase::Input()*
interpolates the validated input into the same docbase template used for the preview. That template might be plain HTML, perhaps augmented with CSS styling.
But as Example 6-8 shows, it can also conform to the rules for *well-formed XML.*
As we'll see again in Chapter 9, *Conferencing Applications,* those rules are minimal. In this case, they simply require that all tags must be closed and all attributes
quoted.

Example 6-8. An HTML/XML Docbase Record Template

```
<html>
<head>
<meta name="company" content="[company]"/>
<meta name="product" content="[product]"/>
<meta name="analyst" content="[analyst]"/>
<meta name="duedate" content="[duedate]"/>
<title>[company], [product], [title]</title>
<link rel="stylesheet" type="text/css" href="../../../Docbase/ProductAnalysis/style.
css"/>
</head>
<body>

<!-- navcontrols --> <!-- navigation controls go here -->

<h1>[company] / [product]</h1>

<table border="1" cellpadding="4">

<tr>
<td align="right" valign="top" class="label">Date</td>
<td align="left" class="duedate">[duedate]</td>
</tr>

<tr>
<td align="right" valign="top" class="label">Analyst</td>
<td align="left" class="analyst">[analyst]</td>
</tr>

<tr>
<td align="right" valign="top" class="label">Title</td>
<td align="left" class="title">[title]</td>
</tr>

<tr>
<td align="right" valign="top" class="label">Summary</td>
<td align="left" class="summary">[summary]</td>
</tr>

<tr>
<td align="right" valign="top" class="label">Full Report</td>
<td align="left" class="fulltext">[fulltext]</td>
</tr>
```

Example 6-8. An HTML/XML Docbase Record Template (continued)

```
<tr>
<td align="right" valign="top" class="label">Contact Info</td>
<td align="left" class="contact">[contact]</td>
</tr>

</table>

</body>
</html>
```

This template is used twice—first to create the preview, as we've already seen, and again to create the final record stored in the docbase.

The combination of HTML, CSS, and XML shown here is a transitional strategy. You could, instead, write a pure XML template like this:

```
<company>[company]</company>
<product>[product]</product>
<analyst>[analyst]</analyst>
```

The problem with this approach is that, for most browsers, you'll end up with a repository format that doesn't coincide with a delivery format. Internet Explorer 5.0 can associate XML tags with CSS or extensible stylesheet language (XSL) styles and thus render a page of XML as it would render a page of HTML. So can the beta version of Navigator 5.0. But this is a new capability that's not yet universally deployed and won't be for a while. So in practice, to support the installed base of browsers, you'd need another step to translate between repository and delivery formats.

The middle-ground approach shown in Example 6-8, which we'll see again in Chapter 9, makes ordinary CSS `class` attributes do double duty. In the presence of a CSS style sheet, these attributes exert stylistic control over the docbase record. That control can be as detailed as your tagging will support—you could even assign a unique style to each field of the record. What's more, styles obey inheritance rules, so styles assigned to a class attached to the `<body>` tag, or to a `<table>` tag, will ripple down through these structures unless explicitly overridden at lower levels. Well, in theory that's what happens. In practice neither the Netscape nor the Microsoft browser currently implements all of CSS1, and you'll run into the usual headaches when you try to figure out which features, and combinations of features, work reliably in both.

Another Use for CSS Tags

Flaky CSS implementations don't detract at all from another role played by the `class` attribute. It is, fundamentally, a selector that operates on a document and returns a subset of its elements. Normally it's a CSS-aware application (e.g., your browser) that does the selection in order to apply a style. But any other application can use the selectors too. Suppose you want to create a view of the docbase that presents report summaries containing a search term. In SQL terms, you'd like to issue the query:

```
select summary from docbase where summary like '%LDAP%'
```

Example 6-9 demonstrates a filter, called *xml-grep*, that reads one of the HTML/CSS/XML files in this docbase and performs the same query.

Example 6-9. A Docbase Query Based on CSS Tags

```
#   usage: xml-grep FILENAME TAG PATTERN
# example: xml-grep 000127.htm summary LDAP

use XML::Parser;

my $xml = new XML::Parser (Style => 'Stream');

$xml->parsefile($ARGV[0]);          # parse the file

sub StartTag {}                     # not needed here

sub EndTag {}                       # not needed here

sub Text
  {
  my $expat = shift;
  if  (
      $expat->current_element eq 'td'       and  # table cell
      $_{class}                eq $ARGV[1]  and  # of class 'summary'
      m/$ARGV[2]/                                # matching LDAP
      )
    {   print "$_{class}: $_\n";    }            # found a hit
  }
```

This script expects three arguments: a filename, a class attribute, and a search string. It's a whole lot slower than *grep*. But it's more flexible, because it will match, for example, either of these patterns:

```
<td class="summary" width="20%">...</td>

<td valign="top" class="summary" align="left" colspan="2">...</td>
```

What's more, this approach can deal with inheritance in the same way that CSS display processors do. For example, the **analyst** field might not always be immediately contained within a cell of an HTML table. Suppose that inside that cell, the name is wrapped up in link syntax, like this:

```
<td class="analyst"><a href="mailto:jon@udell.roninhouse.com">
Jon Udell</a></td>
```

We can still capture my name like this:

```
if  (
    $expat->within_element('td')              and  # inside a table cell
    $last_seen_class_attr         eq $ARGV[1] and  # class="analyst"
    m/$ARGV[2]/                                     # match "Jon Udell"
    )
```

If we saved the value of the last-seen `class` attribute as `$last_seen_class_`
`attr`, then this fragment—which runs in the context of the `<a href>` tag—will
succeed. A line-oriented *grep* can't do this. But an XML query that understands the
hierarchy of an attributed docbase can find things that are nested in other things.
Several formal query languages are proposed for XML, notably XQL (*http://www.*
w3.org/TandS/QL/QL98/pp/xql.html) and XML-QL (*http://www.w3.org/TR/NOTE-*
xml-ql/). Even without a general-purpose XML query language, though, you can
see that it's not hard to write parser-enabled code to do simple queries.

Transforming Docbase Records

The XML nature of the docbase records created by the template in Example 6-8
solves another important problem too. When I managed the Virtual Press Room, I
sometimes had to make wholesale changes to the docbase. That was never a
problem with the *BYTE* docbase, because its "object code" was routinely "compiled" from its "source code." But the VPR's "object code" *was* its "source code,"
and there was no "compiler" in the same sense.

Because the VPR's HTML pages were machine written, they exhibited regular patterns that Perl scripts could latch onto and use to make systematic transformations. But the pages weren't trivially rewritable. Creating those scripts was feasible
but was a time-consuming and ultimately wasteful exercise. XML means never having to waste your time writing custom parsing code.

Docbases need to evolve. Inevitably you'll run into situations that require wholesale rewriting of a set of records. The XML discipline makes that kind of rewrite
vastly simpler than it otherwise would be. That's a huge bonus for a manager of
semistructured information.

Using HTML <meta> Tags

HTML's `<meta>` tag has for years provided a way to make the header of a web
page behave much like the header of an email or news message. You can use the
`<meta>` tag to tuck a set of name/value pairs into a document header. In the long
run, XML may obsolete this way of maintaining a structured header inside a web
page. But for the near future, it's a really useful technique. Like email headers,
these kinds of web-page headers are easy to parse and manipulate, using a variety of tools. Because the `<meta>` tags in Example 6-1 are well-formed XML, any
XML parser can work with them. But as we'll see in the next chapter, sometimes

that can be overkill. It's faster and easier to deal with a simple pattern like this one using Perl's native regular-expression engine.

In Chapter 7, we'll use the meta-tagged header in the docbase record to build indexes that enable several modes of navigation. In Chapter 8, we'll see how full-text indexers can automatically recognize the meta-tagged header and use it to support field-level as well as full-text search of the docbase. That's a powerful capability, but one that's seldom used. Why? It requires a tagging discipline that many web archives lack. By doing that tagging automatically, the Docbase system creates potential value. A smart navigational system is one way to actualize that potential; a smart search system is another.

Note that some of the fields defined in Example 6-8 with <meta> tags duplicate fields governed by CSS class attributes. Why do it both ways? Sometimes you just need to scan for indexable fields, as we'll be doing in the next chapter, and then it's handy to have a nice neat header tucked into the top of every docbase record. Sometimes you need to do a wholesale transformation of the docbase, in which case you'll want to deal with XML elements rather than simple text patterns. There's more than one way to do it!

Mechanics of Docbase Record Storage

Now let's see how a record, having been previewed and submitted by a user, enters the docbase. The preview is hardwired to a common script, *final-submit.pl*, shown in Example 6-10.

Example 6-10. The final-submit.pl Script

```
#!/usr/bin/perl -w

use strict;
use TinyCGI;
my $tc = TinyCGI->new();
print $tc->printHeader;
my $vars = $tc->readParse();

use Docbase::Docbase;
my $db = Docbase::Docbase->new($vars->{app});

use Docbase::Input;
my $di = Docbase::Input->new($db);

$di->writeDoc($vars);
```

It's brief, needing only to pass a hashtable of CGI variables to the *Docbase::Input* method *writeDoc()*, shown in Example 6-11.

Example 6-11. The writeDoc Method

```
sub writeDoc
  {
  my ($self,$vars) = @_;
  my $app = $self->{app};
  my $cgi_absolute = $self->{docbase_cgi_absolute};
  my $web_absolute = $self->{docbase_web_absolute};

  my $db_template =                            # make template name
    "$cgi_absolute/$app/docbase-template.htm";

  my $content .=                               # interpolate vars into template
    _fillTemplate($db_template,$vars);

  my $docnum =                                 # get next record number
    _nextFilenum("$web_absolute/$app/docs","htm");

  my $docfile =                                # make record's filename
    "$web_absolute/$app/docs/$docnum.htm";

  if ( open(F,">$docfile") )
    {
    print F $content;                          # store record
    close F;
    print "<br>Done. Your reference number is $docnum\n";
    }
  else
    {
    print "<p>cannot open docfile $docfile";
    }
  }
```

The *writeDoc()* method is also brief. It uses *_fillTemplate()* again to interpolate form variables into the record template, asks for the next available record number, creates a file named for that record number, and writes the record to the file.

Assigning Reports to Analysts

I've said that the responsibility for a record in the ProductAnalysis docbase is shared between a manager who assigns a report and an analyst who writes it. Let's explore how that can work. It makes sense to bring email into the loop, because the act of making an assignment is best expressed in a push medium. When you assign a report to me, you don't want to wait for me to check the work schedule posted somewhere on the intranet; you want to notify me right away. That notification, expressed as a URL, can link me straight to a partly completed report form, as shown in Figure 6-2.

A plain ASCII message, as shown in Example 6-12, can transmit the URL that links to that form.

Example 6-12. Plain-text Message Assigning a Report to an Analyst

```
To: jon@udell.roninhouse.com
From: sally@udell.roninhouse.com
Subject: Collabra Server report due 1999-05-01

<http://udell.roninhouse.com/cgi-bin/Docbase/formgen.pl?
     app=ProductAnalysis&duedate=1999-05-01&analyst=Jon%20Udell&
     company=Netscape&product=Collabra%20Server%204.0>

Jon, I think the new groupware server is called
Collabra Server 4.0. Could you please verify
that and fill in the correct name on the report?
```

Here we're relying on the ability of the recipient's mailreader to autoactivate the URL—that is, render it as a clickable link. We're also assuming that the recipient is, or can be, connected to the server that generates the form.

Do I really expect the research manager to compose a message like this? No. It's better if she can use a simple application to help compose that message. Ideally, that application presents a dynamically generated form that manages controlled vocabularies. The form should list analysts, companies, and products and offer ways to extend those lists. In Chapter 15, *Distributed HTTP*, we'll explore ways to connect this kind of form to a conventional database, using *namespace completion* to scope database queries and limit the number of items included in the generated HTML `<select>` statements. Here let's just assume a mechanism that enables the research manager to produce the form shown in Figure 6-4.

The handler for this form will interpolate values into a message template in order to construct the assignment message shown in Example 6-12, then transmit that email message. How? It could launch a command-line mailer—*sendmail* or an equivalent such as Software.com's postmail. Or it could use a Perl module, such as *Net::SMTP*.

The URL contained in the message shown in Example 6-12 can get pretty long and complex. From the recipient's point of view it looks awkward, and if it gets broken in transit into two or more lines, autoactivation will fail. As we saw in Chapter 4, *Information-Management Strategies for Groupware Users*, it's helpful to wrap angle brackets around URLs that you want mailreaders or newsreaders to make clickable. Better yet, you can send an HTML-formatted message that wraps the URL in a descriptive label: "Click here to submit your report."

Let's recap the whole scenario. To assign a report, the research manager clicks a link, which invokes a Web script, which—using database-integration techniques I'll demonstrate in Chapter 15—generates the form shown in Figure 6-4. She specifies a `duedate`, an `analyst`, and a `company` but leaves the `product` field open. In the `comments` field, she describes the product to be assessed and asks the analyst to supply the correct product name when filing the report. The handler for this

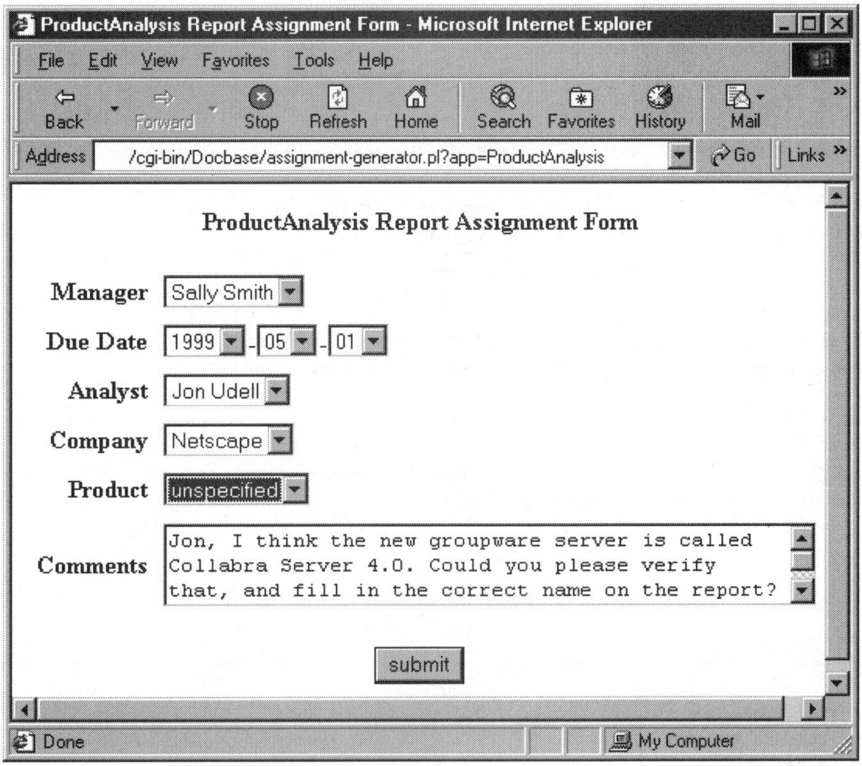

Figure 6-4. The manager's report-assignment form

form interpolates form variables into a template to produce an assignment message.

The analyst, on receiving the message, moves it to a Reports Due folder for use on the due date. On that date, he clicks the URL to produce the form that will collect the completed report. Because the product field is not preassigned in this case, it appears as an open input field on the form rather than as a static value.

If it seems as if templates and form generators are multiplying like rabbits, well, they are. These things, connected in series, create the Web equivalent of the Unix pipeline—a flexible way to assemble simple parts into custom applications. Example 6-13 shows a script that handles the form shown in Figure 6-4, processes it using a template (which is included with the script, following the __DATA__ directive), and sends an HTML email message containing a link that, when clicked, will produce the form used to collect the assignment.

Example 6-13. Handler for the Manager's Report-Assignment Form

```
use TinyCGI;
my $tc = TinyCGI->new;
my $vars = $tc->readParse();          # get form variables
print $tc->printHeader;               # emit HTTP header

use Group::SimpleGroup;               # load directory module (see Chapter 11)

my $g =                               # access analyst group
    Group::SimpleGroup->new('analysts','analysts');

                                      # look up email addresses

my $analyst_email    = $g->getProperty($vars->{analyst},'email');
my $manager_email    = $g->getProperty($vars->{manager},'email');

use Net::SMTP;                        # load SMTP module

my $smtp =                            # connect to mail server
    Net::SMTP->new('udell.roninhouse.com');

if (! defined $smtp)
  {
  print "cannot connect to mail server";
  return;
  }

$smtp->mail($analyst_email);          # address the message
$smtp->to($analyst_email);
$smtp->data();

while (<DATA>)                        # read assignment-form template
  {
  s/ANALYST_EMAIL/$analyst_email/;    # swap in analyst's email address
  s/MANAGER_EMAIL/$manager_email/;    # swap in manager's email address
  s/%(\w+)%/$vars->{$1}/g;            # swap %markers% for matching CGI vars
  $smtp->datasend($_);               # send the line
  }

$smtp->dataend();
$smtp->quit();

print "OK, assignment sent";


__DATA__
To: %analyst% <ANALYST_EMAIL>
From: %manager% <MANAGER_EMAIL>
Subject: Report on %company% (%product%) due on
%year%-%month%-%day%
Content-type: text/html
Content-transfer-encoding: 7bit
```

Example 6-13. Handler for the Manager's Report-Assignment Form (continued)

```
<html><body>
<p>Your report on Company: %company%, Product: %product% is due on
%year%-%month%-%day%.

<p>Click <a href="http://udell.roninhouse.com/cgi-bin/Docbase/form-gen.pl?
app=ProductAnalysis&duedate=%year%-%month%-%day%&analyst=%analyst%&company=%company%
&product=%product%">here</a> for the report submission form.

<p>Comments: %comments%
</body></html>
```

This script uses two Perl modules that we haven't seen yet. *Group::SimpleGroup* looks up email addresses in a simple directory. It's one of a family of three directory modules that we'll build in Chapter 11, *Membership Services*. This one stores names and addresses in a Perl hashtable that's externalized as an ASCII file. Another works with LDAP directories, and a third with the NT accounts database.

The other new module is *Net::SMTP*. As Example 6-13 shows, it makes quick work of connecting to a mail server and sending a message.

Docbase Input in Perspective

Data entry is the linchpin of every information system. It's obvious that to reap the benefits of an accounting package or a human resources package, you have to pump in all the required data in the required formats. With groupware, it's not so obvious what these required formats should be. The messaging tools at the heart of groupware do impose minimum requirements. You can't send an email message (or post a newsgroup message) that doesn't have From:, Date:, and Subject: headers. These fields alone enable an important class of applications— the email, listserv, and newsgroup archives that collectively form a vast fund of web-accessible knowledge.

The next step, though, is a big one. None of the standard email headers will tag a message as a status report or as a status report for project XYZ. Classifying messages in these ways would be a great benefit. Web docbases such as the one we've seen in this chapter occupy a middle ground between email and databases. They're semistructured like email but extensible like databases.

Since email dominates the groupware landscape, the push/pull mechanism I've shown here is a useful way to recruit people to build a web docbase. If I mail you a link to a form generator, you're much likelier to use that form than if I tell you to find the form's URL yourself on the intranet site. Do whatever you can to make docbase input frictionless for your users. But capture as much structure as you can. Every piece of regular structure you can impose on the records will compound the value of a docbase in many ways.

7

Docbase Navigation

Docbases are rich with implied interconnectedness. For example, a report about Internet Explorer in the ProductAnalysis docbase might prompt a reader to explore the docbase along several dimensions:

- More reports about Internet Explorer

- The previous report about Internet Explorer

- More reports by the author of this report

- The next report by the author of this report

- More reports about Microsoft products

- More reports due around the same time as this one

In the relational database discipline, we satisfy the "More reports about..." kind of request with an SQL query, such as:

```
select * from docbase where product = 'Internet Explorer'
```

To handle a "Next report by author..." kind of request, we fetch and then navigate within a result set. These mechanisms enable users to explore the interconnectedness of a data set. But they don't reveal it explicitly. That's our goal in this chapter.

I've said that a docbase marries two disciplines: data management and publishing. From a data-management perspective, it might be enough to just bolt a web interface onto standard database query mechanisms. But a docbase isn't just a database; it's a hypertextual publication. The interface to that publication is distributed across every page of the docbase. A docbase works best when every piece of its distributed interface answers two basic questions: "Where am I?" and "Where can I go from here?"

The answers to these questions can take many shapes and styles. In the *BYTE Magazine* docbase described in Chapter 5, *Docbases as Groupware Applications*, one answer to "Where am I?" was "In the August 1998 issue of *BYTE*." Another was "At the end of the series of elements belonging to the Web Project section."

There were many answers to "Where can I go from here?"

- The previous element
- The parent element
- The section-level table of contents
- The issue-level table of contents
- More Web Project articles
- More distributed computing articles

In the *BYTE Magazine* docbase, the "More like this" links were, in effect, precomputed queries, as were the *Next* and *Prev* links. As I explained in Chapter 5, the system relied on dynamic generation of statically served pages. The *Docbase::Indexer* module I'll demonstrate in this chapter takes a similar approach. It augments docbase records with two complementary sets of navigational controls. What I'll call *tabbed indexes* generalize the notion of "More like this" for any of the header fields of a docbase. And *sequential indexes* implement "Next" and "Previous" for header fields. Both sets of controls explicitly connect each record to related records, along multiple dimensions.

Although you can achieve all these effects by dynamically generating statically served pages, we'll find as we go along that a little server-side assistance can really help matters. I'll show two ways to create these navigational controls, one dynamic and one static. The dynamic method, which entails less indexing overhead and not much runtime overhead, is my preferred solution. However, it requires an HTTP server, and sometimes one isn't available. The static method, which requires no HTTP server but incurs a lot of indexing and storage overhead, can be useful in special situations. For example, you might want to deliver a docbase of service bulletins to field personnel who use CD-ROM-equipped laptops. In that case, it's handy to be able to deploy a docbase that runs straight off the CD-ROM, relying on only the file:// protocol that browsers use to interact with file-based data stores.

It's helpful to think in terms of a continuum. At one end are files containing HTML pages (or XML pages) that browsers can render directly. At the other end are server-side processes that generate these pages. An application can live at any point along that continuum. Its distance from the endpoints isn't a measure of rightness or wrongness but only of appropriateness. If your users need to run a docbase straight off a CD-ROM, and you don't want to configure their laptops with local HTTP servers, then a static docbase is an appropriate solution. Alternatively, as we'll see in Chapter 15, *Distributed HTTP*, you may conclude that you want to equip your users with local HTTP service, in which case a dynamic docbase can be an appropriate solution. A groupware developer who can do things more than one way will be best prepared to come up with the right solution to any given problem.

Introducing the Docbase Navigational Controls

The Docbase system implements both tabbed-index and sequential controls. The ProductAnalysis record shown in Figure 7-1 includes a top-of-page toolbar that presents these controls.

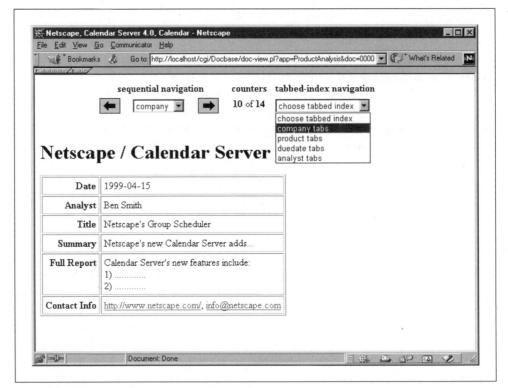

Figure 7-1. The Docbase navigational controls

The toolbar in Figure 7-1 comprises three elements. Let's briefly consider what each of them does.

Sequential Controls

When you click the arrows, you move forward and backward in the data set. The dropdown list between the arrows announces the current index, which defines what it means to go forward and backward. The same dropdown list enables you

to switch to another index. In Figure 7-1, for example, the current index is
`company`. As the `<alt>` tag would announce if your cursor drifted over the right
arrow, clicking there means "Next record by company." The resulting page, in this
case, would be a report about another Netscape product, Messaging Server.

If you switch indexes, the right arrow means something different. For example,
Figure 7-2 shows the same record but with the `analyst` index in effect.

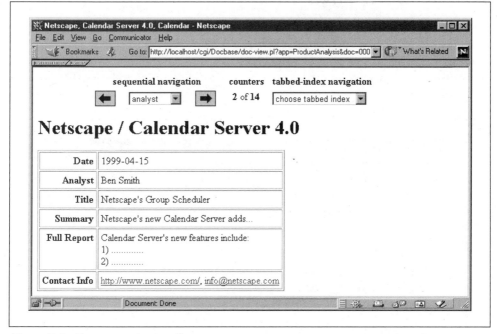

Figure 7-2. Alternate index in effect

In Figure 7-2, the right arrow's `<alt>` tag would pop up the message "Next record
by analyst." Clicking the arrow would produce a report by Ben Smith about Soft-
ware.com's Post.Office.

Sequential indexes enable users to explore local context. When you're browsing in
a library, it's often handy to scan the books surrounding the one you've found on
a shelf. The same principle applies here. The sequential controls make possible
the serendipitous discovery of records that are "near" the current record, relative to
each of the indexes.

Counters

The counters announce your position in the current index and the number of
records in the docbase. When you switch indexes, the position counter adjusts

itself accordingly. The Calendar Server report, for example, is tenth in the `company` index, but second in the `analyst` index.

Why bother with counters? They're probably not essential. But when you're exploring a shelf, it's nice to know how long the shelf is and where your current position is relative to the beginning and the end of the shelf.

Tabbed-Index Controls

The sequential controls implement a localized version of the "More like this" idea. They lead to similar records but operate in a very narrow scope. The *tabbed-index controls* expand the scope of "More like this." In Figure 7-1, the tabbed-index selector is ready to select the option *company tabs.* Figure 7-3 shows the outcome of that selection.

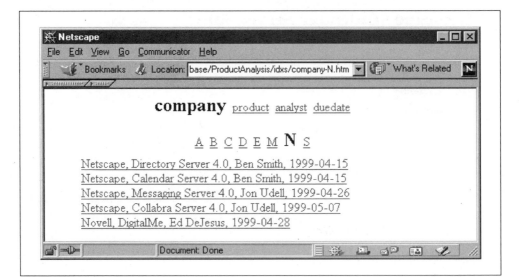

Figure 7-3. A tabbed-index page

The page shown in Figure 7-3 lists reports about products from companies whose names begin with *N*—in this case, Netscape and Novell. See how the *N* tab is emphasized? The transition from Figure 7-1 to Figure 7-3 is context-preserving. For each tabbed index that a record links to, the Docbase system knows which tab on the link's destination page corresponds to the record displayed on the link's source page.

This notion of context preservation is a crucial aspect of web design. We'll see later on how *Docbase::Navigate* achieves this effect. For now, just consider the alternative. It would be easier to connect each docbase record to the tabbed indexes in the same standard way—for example, by wiring the `company` choice on every tabbed-index selector to the index page for the first (e.g., the *A*) tab. What's wrong with that approach? Can't a user who lands on the *A* page just click once to get to the *N* page? Yes. Delivering the *N* page without loss of context is a small detail, one that many web designs overlook. But those small details add up. You have to work harder to make a web navigation system do the right thing, and once you start to think in these terms, you'll uncover more and more right things. Take care of these details. People may not notice, but that's OK. The goal is to make docbases transparently useful.

The tabbed-index pages built by *Docbase::Indexer* maintain two levels of context, using a pair of tabbed controls. In Figure 7-3, one indicates that we are looking at *N* companies and leads to similar pages for products from companies whose names begin with *A*, *B*, and so on. Why not the whole alphabet? As we'll see later, the data set is sparse. There aren't yet enough records to fully populate this tabbed index, so *Docbase::Indexer* includes only those tabs for which records exist. This is another one of those small details that many web designs overlook.

The other tabbed index tells us we're looking at a **company**-ordered list of reports. And it leads to similar pages that list reports other ways. For example, clicking the **analyst** link in Figure 7-3 leads to the page shown in Figure 7-4.

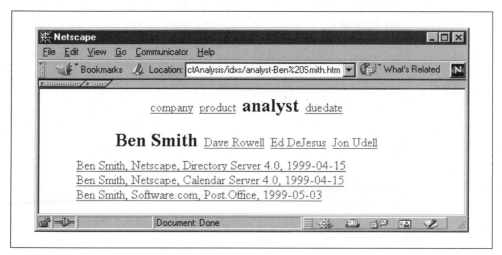

Figure 7-4. An alternate tabbed-index page

The first tab row looks as it did in Figure 7-3, though adjusted to indicate that **analyst** is the current index. But the second tab row takes a different form. Here the tabs are the full names of the analysts who file reports to this docbase. Why? Context again. When an index contains a small set of values, there's room on the screen to show more of each of them. As we discussed in Part I, each level in a layered information system should say as much as it comfortably can about the next level, so users know as much as possible about what that next click will yield.

This chapter will show, in great detail, how to create these navigational controls from a collection of docbase records. We'll see a lot of Perl code and examine some fairly complex Perl data structures. But before we dive in, let's take a moment to reflect some more on why these controls are useful, why it might make sense to create them using the Perl modules we'll build in this chapter, and what all this can mean to a groupware developer trying to manage semistructured information.

Zen and the Art of Docbase Maintenance

One of the themes winding its way through this section is a text-file-oriented approach to managing semistructured data. I'm not wedded to this approach, and in later chapters we'll see applications that use both object-oriented and relational data stores. But I've found text-oriented methods to be appropriate for many practical purposes. These are, after all, the methods used by Internet applications—mail, news, and the Web—that have connected more people to more information than anyone a few years ago dreamed possible.

Let's explore this notion of appropriate technology. Later in this chapter, we'll see an example of a Perl function called *getSeqInfo()* (part of the *Docbase::Navigate* module in Example 7-16) that looks up a piece of an index by reading in a small text file. Shouldn't that be done, instead, as an SQL query against a "real" database? Certainly it could be done that way. Whether it should, though, is another matter. Often we're too easily swayed by a technological imperative that urges us to use the biggest available hammer to drive every nail. When a different tool is appropriate for a job, it makes sense to use it. Perl's unparalleled strengths in two key realms—text processing and data structure wrangling—make it eminently appropriate for many of the challenges that confront a groupware developer.

Groupware applications rarely fail because their developers pick the wrong database engines. They fail, instead, because they don't solve problems that really matter to people, in ways that people find convenient. To prove the worth of an application, you have to get it into people's hands quickly, improve it continuously, and watch the outcome closely. Requirements that you couldn't have anticipated—among them, storage requirements—will emerge. But groupware isn't online transaction processing. The make-or-break issues aren't likely to be the number of transactions per second that you can pump through the system or the nature of its concurrency controls. What matters most is fluid integration of structured and semistructured data. Achieving that requires rapid prototyping not only of code, but also of data structures.

For the same reason that it makes sense to prototype code using a scripting language, it makes sense to prototype data structures by externalizing the in-memory objects of a scripting language. If you later need to upgrade a primordial text-file-based and Perl-managed data store, you can. Nothing fundamental to your application should need to change. The *getSeqInfo()* function, for example, could continue to present the same API to the modules that use it. Only its implementation would need to change—from a file system lookup to a DataBase Management (DBM) lookup, or an SQL lookup, or perhaps an object-database lookup.

None of these alternatives will turn out to have mattered, though, if you end up ditching the application for reasons unrelated to the performance or capabilities of its storage engine. The application might fail because it addresses the wrong group, or the right group in the wrong way, or because it sets the data-entry threshold too high, or because people just don't see a reason to use it, or for any number of other reasons.

If the application does succeed, you may want to upgrade its data store. But only if you have to! Nowadays we often find ourselves shipping the prototype—that is, delivering a Perl or Visual Basic solution—because there turns out to be no need to recast a solution in a compiled language. The same principle can apply in the data realm. The simplest possible data store—for example, Perl hashtables externalized to text files—will help you get a solution up and running quickly. And who knows? You might find yourself shipping the prototype because the simplest solution turns out to be effective and appropriate.

In this chapter, we'll build a pair of Perl modules, *Docbase::Indexer* and *Docbase::Navigate*, which together implement the tabbed-index and sequential controls we saw earlier in this chapter. These modules expect a set of meta-tagged records like those created by the *Docbase::Input* module we explored in Chapter 6, *Docbase Input Techniques*. *Docbase::Indexer* reads these records and writes a collection of tabbed-index pages plus some extra index information to support sequential navigation.

Is this an appropriate data-management solution? Reasonable people may differ. On the one hand, Perl arguably ought not to be doing so much of the indexing work that might otherwise be handled by a database engine. On the other hand, the simple indexing required for this application is well within Perl's comfort zone. Either way, the real point is to give you a practical feel for how to express a semi-structured data store as a richly interconnected web docbase. The principles that govern the expression of a data store, which I'll illustrate here using an XML repository and Perl modules, can apply more broadly to any data store and any programming language.

We'll proceed in phases. Starting with the dynamic version, we'll build the tabbed-index pages, then tackle sequential navigation. Finally, we'll reprise these themes for the static version. Along the way, we'll explore ways you can use Perl to process text and wrangle data structures. These are basic skills, that, once mastered, prepare a groupware developer to meet a wide range of challenges.

Implementing HTML Tabbed Indexes

Let's start with a more complete definition of a tabbed index. It's a software widget that emulates an old-fashioned address book. The labels on the tabs can be letters of the alphabet, subject titles, or symbols. Each tab leads to a page that groups like elements—all reports that were written by Jon Udell, or that pertain to Microsoft, or that were due in August 1998.

Any implementation of a tabbed index in HTML exemplifies a pattern that I call *repeat and vary*. The element that repeats is a row of labeled links that I'll call *active tabs*. The element that varies is the treatment applied to the *current tab*— that is, the single item that is not a link and whose nonlinked status signifies the current location in the data set.

In Figure 7-3, the current tabs are *company* and *N*. Together they signify that the page lists reports about products from companies whose names begin with *N*. Figure 7-5 shows what happens when you click the *M* tab. To signal the transition to the *M* state, the tabbed index undergoes two changes. The *N* tab gains link status and joins the rest of the active tabs. The *M* tab leaves the set of active tabs, loses link status, and takes on the big, bold style that signifies the current tab.

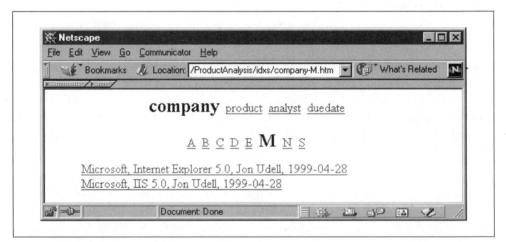

Figure 7-5. Tabbed index by company, after transition to the M page

What makes this seem magical is a kind of figure-and-ground effect. The set of active tabs not involved in the transition forms a constant background for the *N* -> *M* exchange. Because the background doesn't vary, the transition doesn't appear to be a page swap. The tab row appears to be a single active widget, though it's really an illusion created by a sequence of frames. As in motion-picture animation, the illusion depends on subtle change from frame to frame.

The Web abounds with examples of what I call *false tabbed indexes*. One type, shown in Figure 7-6, uses only a single row of tabs.

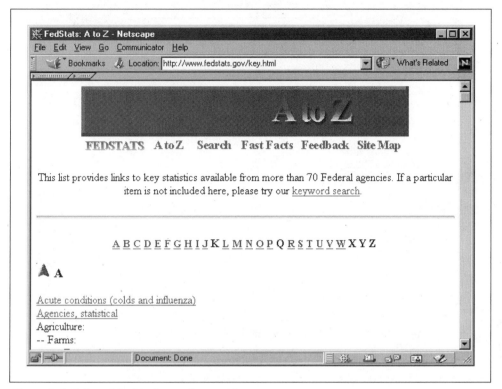

Figure 7-6. False tabbed index: only one tab row

When you jump to a tabbed region (such as the *M* tab in Figure 7-6) you lose the tabbed index, as shown in Figure 7-7. You have to use the *Up* link (the upward-pointing arrow), or the browser's *Go Back* button, to rewind before jumping to another section*.

Another kind of false tabbed index does reproduce the tab rows once per indexed chunk but fails to differentiate the current tab from the active tabs. The page shown in Figure 7-8 was produced by clicking the *P* tab.

In this context, every link on the tab row is a meaningful choice *except* the *P* tab. Because the tab row repeats but does not vary, it offers a meaningless *P* tab, which, when clicked, does nothing.

False tabbed indexes miss out on the best answers to the two basic navigational questions: "Where am I?" and "Where can I go from here?" A true tabbed index

---

* While this book was in production, I noticed that this false tabbed index had become a true one that repeats, and varies, correctly!

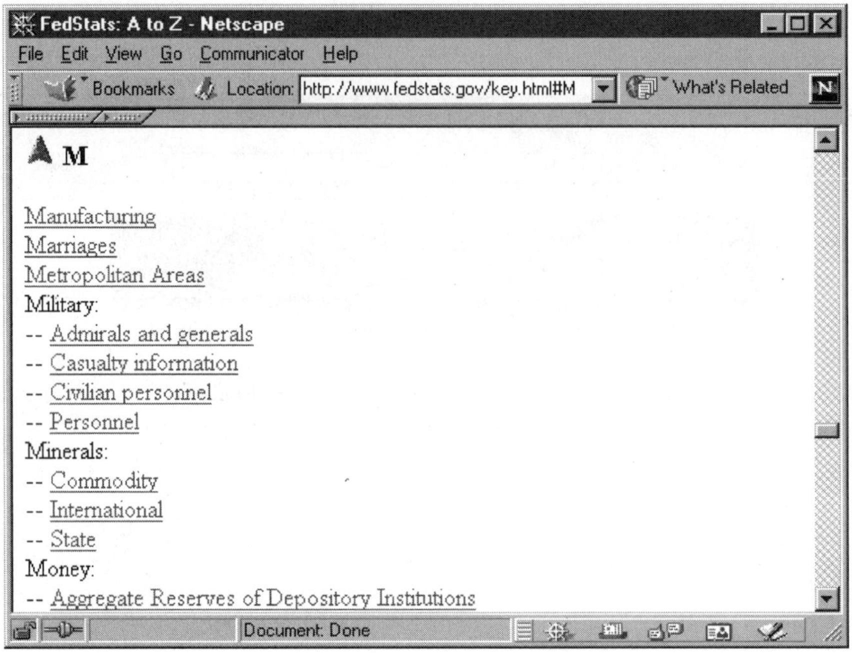

Figure 7-7. False tabbed index: nowhere to go but up

answers both effectively. The answer to "Where am I?" is "On the current tab." The answer to "Where can I go from here?" is "To any active tab."

It's not surprising to see so many false tabbed indexes on the Web. Hand-coding 26 instances of a tab row, each slightly different from the next, is a daunting chore. True, you can build a page of these widgets and then reuse it. But how will that template page handle the situation shown in Figure 7-3: two correlated levels of context, the second of which entails a sparse, but evolving, subset of the 26 possible alphabetic tabs? It's simply unfeasible to maintain these kinds of index pages by hand. This is a job for a script, so let's go to work.

Gathering the Metadata

The values that will populate the tabbed-index pages are tucked into <meta> tags in the header of each docbase record. Let's start with a function to retrieve a set of <meta> tag values from a docbase record. Since the records are stored in XML format, we could use Perl's (or another) XML parser to read in a record, break it into its constituent parts, and pick out the metadata values. But there's more than one way to do it, and in this case, that's not the easiest way. It's faster and simpler to use a Perl regular expression to match a pattern and isolate the values we need.

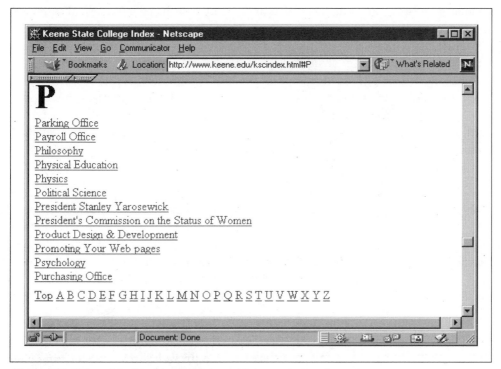

Figure 7-8. False tabbed index: repetition without variation

Example 7-1 shows the *getMetadata()* method in *Docbase::Docbase()*, which does that.

Example 7-1. Retrieving Metadata from a Docbase Record

```
sub getMetadata
  {
  my ($self, $doc) = @_;                    # $doc: /web/Docbase/docs/000014.htm

  my %record = ();                          # create empty hashtable

  open(F, $doc)                             # open the record
    or print "cannot open metadata $doc $!";

  while (<F>)                               # for each line of the record
    {
    last if ( m#</head>#i );                # until end of HTML header
    if ( m#<meta name=\"$indexname\" content=\"([^\"]+)\"#i )  # if found
      {
      $record{$indexname} = $1;             # add name/value pair to hashtable
      }
    }
  close F;
  return \%record;                          # return reference to hashtable
  }
```

Regular-expression aficionados will rightly point out that the pattern that recognizes <meta> tag names and values could be a lot more inclusive. For example, this code will miss <meta name="company"> for extra white space, <meta name=company> for lack of quotes, and <meta content="..." name="..."> for attribute order. Should the pattern generalize to accept some or all of these variations? There are two schools of thought. One holds that applications should emit strictly but accept liberally. Here, that would mean we'd observe a strict standard when writing <meta> tags but would allow some looseness when reading them. Why? Much of the resilience of the Internet flows from the fact that its communicating parts adhere to this philosophy.

The other school of thought holds that when you tolerate sloppiness, you create more of it. The example usually cited is the modern browser, bloated with so-called "bozo-correction" code that will accept anything that remotely resembles HTML, even when ill formed and ambiguous. XML parsers, in reaction to this stance, are very picky about what they accept. In this case the extra white space isn't a problem, but the unquoted attribute will stop any XML parser dead in its tracks.

Both arguments have merit, and there's no cut-and-dried answer. I recommend that you use an XML format even when, as in this case, you wind up relying on a simpler method of parsing. But you might also want to follow a stricter discipline than XML requires. For example, XML allows you to write the attributes of a tag in any order. But just because you can do something more than one way doesn't mean that you should. People don't write these docbase records, the *Docbase::Input* module does, and it will write them the same way every time. Assume that, and you can match <meta> tags with a very simple regular expression. Assume otherwise, and that regular expression gets a lot more complicated. You could account for different attribute orderings, but why bother? Life's too short to waste time making tools more flexible than they need to be. The endgame, after all, is to use those tools to get working groupware applications into people's hands.

You call *getMetadata()* with a docbase record's fully qualified pathname. It returns a reference to a hashtable whose keys are the <meta> tag names, and values are drawn from the <meta> tag's content attribute. If you pass *getMetadata()* the pathname of the record shown in Figure 7-1, that hashtable will look like this:

```
$metadata =
  {
  'company' => 'Netscape',
  'product' => 'Calendar Server 4.0',
  'analyst' => 'Ben Smith',
  }
```

Looping over the records of the docbase produces a collection of these per-record hashtables:

```
opendir(DIR, $docdir) or print "cannot open docdir $docdir $!\n";
my @docs = grep ( /htm/, readdir(DIR) );
my $master = {};
foreach my $doc (@docs)
    { $master->{$doc} = $self->getMetadata("$docdir/$doc"); }
```

The resulting structure, in $master, looks like this:

```
$master =
   {
   '000127.htm',
     {company =>'Netscape', product => 'Calendar Server',},
   '000128.htm',
     {company =>'Microsoft', product => 'Internet Explorer 5.0',},
   };
```

Building the Core Index Structure

Now we want to transform the $master hashtable into a richer structure. For each index (that is, each docbase header field), this new structure will bind a (possibly sparse) set of tab values to the subset of records governed by each tab. The index defines the primary ordering within each subset.

The method that accomplishes this transformation, *buildIndexStructures()*, appears in Example 7-2. It's a complex transformation, which does a lot of different things all at once, so we'll explicate it step by step.

Example 7-2. The buildIndexStructures Method

```
sub buildIndexStructures
  {
  my $self = shift;
  my $docdir = $self->{docdir};                    # docbase path
  my $tabHoHoLoL = $self->{tabHoHoLoL};            # master data structure
  my @indexed_fields =                             # get list of indexed fields
    @{$self->{indexed_fields}};

  opendir(DIR, $docdir) or print "cannot open docdir $docdir $!\n";
  my @docs = grep ( /htm/, readdir(DIR) );
  foreach my $doc (@docs)                          # for each docbase record
    {
    my $record =                                   # extract metadata
      $self->getMetadata("$docdir/$doc");
    foreach my $index (keys %$record)              # for each metadata (index) name
      {
      my $tabstruct = $tabHoHoLoL->{$index};       # tabstruct for this index

      my $tab =                                    # compute tab for this value
        &{$self->{tab_functions}->{$index}}($record->{$index});
```

Example 7-2. The buildIndexStructures Method (continued)

```
    if ( ! defined $tabstruct->{$tab} )       # if new tab for this index's tabstruct
      { $tabstruct->{$tab} = [];   }          # then initialize a listref for it

    $doc =~ s/[^\d\-]+//g;                     # strip pathname to bare docnum

    my $rec =                                 # build new entry for this record
      [$doc,"$record->{$index}",$self->_getNonKeyValues($index,$record)];

    my $LoL = $tabstruct->{$tab};             # get list-of-lists for this tab

    push ( @{$LoL}, $rec );                    # add entry to list
    }
  }

foreach my $index (keys %$tabHoHoLoL)         # for each index
  {
  my $sort_specs = $self->{sort_specs};       # hashtable of sort specs
  my $sortdir = $sort_specs->{$index};        # the sort spec for this index
  my $tabstruct = $tabHoHoLoL->{$index};         # the tabstruct for this index
  foreach my $tab (keys %$tabstruct)          # for each tab
    {
    my $LoL = $tabstruct->{$tab};             # get list-of-lists
    my @temp = sort                           # sort
      {
      if ( $sortdir eq 'ascending' )
        { return $a->[1] cmp $b->[1]  || $b->[0] cmp $a->[0] }
      else
        { return $b->[1] cmp $a->[1]  || $b->[0] cmp $a->[0] }
      } @$LoL;
    $tabstruct->{$tab} = \@temp;              # replace LoL with sorted result
    }

  my @sorted_tabs = ($sortdir eq 'ascending')  # sort tabs according to spec
    ?          sort keys %$tabstruct
    : reverse sort keys %$tabstruct;
  $self->{tabsortHoL}->{$index} = \@sorted_tabs;
  }
}
```

This routine iterates over the complete docbase and builds two structures. In the main structure, shown in Example 7-3, each index has a sparse set of tabs, each of which contains a set of ordered records.

Example 7-3. Example of Ordered Records

```
$tabHoHoLoL =
  {
  'company' =>
    {
    'N', [
        ['000127','Netscape','Calendar Server 4.0','Ben Smith'],
        ['000123','Netscape','Directory Server 4.0', 'Jon Udell']
```

Example 7-3. Example of Ordered Records (continued)

```
      ],
  'M', [
      ['000128','Microsoft','Internet Explorer 5.0','Jon Udell'],
      ['000124','Microsoft','IIS 5.0','Ed DeJesus'],
      ],
  },
  'product' => {...},
  'analyst' => {...},
  }
};
```

In the second structure, shown in Example 7-4, each index has an ordered set of tabs.

Example 7-4. Example of Ordered Tabs

```
$tabsortHoL =
  {
  'company' => ['A', 'C', 'M', 'N'],
  'product' => ['O', 'E', 'I', 'C'],
  'analyst' => [...],
  }
```

In Perlspeak the structure in Example 7-3 is an HoHoLoL—that is, a hash-of-hashes-of-lists-of-lists. Working from the outside in, the enclosing hashtable's keys are the index names, and its values are hashtables. Each of the nested hashtable's keys are tab values extracted from the set of values governed by the controlling index. Each of the nested hashtable's values are lists of the records governed by the controlling tab. Finally, each of these records is a list of metadata values.

We've already seen how to extract metadata from docbase records. What *buildIndexStructures()* does with each of those records, though, takes a bit of explaining. Let's start with the line that computes a tab for the current index of the current record:

```
$tab = &{$self->{tab_functions}->{$index}}($record->{$index}); # compute tab
```

We'll start in the middle of this expression and work outward. $self->{tab_functions} is a reference to a hashtable that looks like this:

```
{
'company' , $tabFnFirstChar,
'product' , $tabFnFirstChar,
'analyst' , $tabFnAll,
'duedate' , $tabFnFirstSevenChars,
};
```

When $index is company, $self->{tab_functions}->{$index} evaluates to $tabFnFirstChar—which is a reference to an anonymous function defined in the following code.

```
my $tabFnFirstChar =
    sub { my ($tab) = @_; return substr($tab,0,1) };
```

So the expression `&{$self->{tab_functions}->{$index}}` is equivalent to `&{$tabFnFirstChar}`—in other words, a function call. And since `$record->{$index}` extracts the current metadata value—say, `Netscape`—the effective function call is `&{$tabFnFirstChar}('Netscape')`.

Note how `$tab_functions` expands the idea of a tab to be any function computable on an index value. In our example the first character is appropriate for `company` and `product` indexes, the whole name for `analyst`, and the first seven characters (year and month) for `duedate`. Other functions will make sense for other indexes.

This approach means that a tabbed-index system can evolve along with its underlying data set. Consider the `duedate` index. After a year, each tab row will be 12 items long. But after three years, rows of 36 monthly tabs will have become unwieldy. Swapping *tabFnFirstSevenChars* for *tabFnFirstFourChars* will reduce the tab row to a manageable three yearly tabs.

Accumulating Tab Sets for Each Index

For each tab, we ask whether a corresponding key exists in the current index's interior hashtable:

```
if ( ! defined $tabstruct->{$tab} )
```

For example, is there an *N* key in the hashtable belonging to the `company` key in the master hashtable? If not, we create that key and initialize its value to be a reference to an empty list:

```
$tabstruct->{$tab} = []
```

Next, we build the interior list that holds the metadata for this record, relative to the current index. That list, which will display on the tabbed-index page, is made up of three parts:

The record number
This is the bare name of the record's file minus its extension.

The primary sort key
This is the value for the current index's slot in the current metadata record. If the index is `company`, it might be `Netscape`.

The remaining values
These are the other values that, along with the primary key, will form the link that appears on the tabbed-index page.

The *_getNonKeyValues()* method, which returns a list of values that excludes the primary key, relies on a list, stored in *Docbase::Indexer*'s `$self->{indexed_` `fields`}, which serves two purposes. First, it enumerates which indexes to build, as we'll see when we run the indexing script. Second, it defines the order in which fields appear on tabbed-index pages. Example 7-5 shows how that second use of the indexed-fields list comes into play.

Example 7-5. Completing a Tabbed-Index Record Using an Ordered Enumeration

```
sub _getNonKeyValues
  {
  my ($self,$special_key, $record) = @_;
  my @return_list = ();
  foreach my $key (@{$self->{indexed_fields}})
    {
    if ( $key ne $special_key )
      {
      push ( @return_list, $record->{$key} );
      }
    }
  return @return_list;
  }
```

Why can't this routine just iterate over the keys of the `$record` hashtable, using `foreach my $key (keys %$record){...}`? When you enumerate the keys of a hashtable, they won't come out in any particular order unless you control the enumeration with a list.

Finally, we form a reference to a list made up of the record number, the primary key, and the remaining values. And we add that list reference to the current tab's list-of-lists (LoL, for short).

Sorting the Records and Tabs

Once the structure shown in Example 7-3 has been built, we traverse it and sort each of the LoLs. Although the *buildIndexStructures* routine shown in Example 7-2 inlines the sorting code for reasons of efficiency, an equivalent and more readable version might look like this:

```
@temp = sort sort_fn @$LoL;

sub sort_fn = { return $a->[1] cmp $b->[1]; }
```

Here it's easier to see what's happening. When you interpose a user-defined function between Perl's *sort* operator and the list you want sorted, your function gets called once per comparison. The values it should compare show up automatically as $a and $b. This fragment compares the first element of each list—that is, the company name for the **company** index, the analyst name for the **analyst** index, and so on. For a descending sort, you'd swap the locations of $a and $b.

To sort on multiple keys, you can tie multiple comparisons together with the || operator. (I found this recipe in O'Reilly's indispensable *Perl Cookbook* by Tom

Christiansen and Nathan Torkington.) In our case, when the primary key matches, we want to do a reverse sort by record number. That way, records that share a primary key will appear newest first within the region defined by the primary key. Since the record number is the zeroth element of each list, here's how to do that:

```
return $a->[1] cmp $b->[1] || $b->[0] cmp $a->[0];
```

Example 7-2 uses this construct twice—once for an ascending sort by primary key and once for a descending sort. Why not segregate this sorting code into a separate function? You can, but the inline version shown in Example 7-2 is almost twice as fast. Function call overhead is fairly expensive in Perl. Normally that's not a huge concern, but in tight inner loops like this one, it can really pay off to inline a function.

Finally, we also sort the keys of each index's HoLoL to create per-index ordered lists of tabs. We save these lists in the instance variable `$self->{tabsortHoL}` and use them to generate tab rows.

Both sorting operations refer to the instance variable `$self->{sort_specs}`, a hashtable that defines the sort order for each index.

```
$sort_specs = {
'company' , 'ascending',
'product' , 'ascending',
'analyst' , 'ascending',
'duedate' , 'descending',
}
```

When `$index` is company, for example, `$sort_specs->{$index}` specifies an ascending sort. We apply that ordering first to the LoLs attached to each of the tabs in each index's hashtable, then to the tabs themselves.

To SQL or not to SQL?

In the Docbase system, records appear in a primary order governed by the current index (say, company) and a secondary order that is reverse chronological. It's as if we said:

```
select * from docbase order by company, age desc
```

Each record's age is encoded in its filename, by virtue of the fact that these are numbered sequentially. As a practical matter, the age of a docbase record is almost always one of the orderings that you'd like an indexing system to provide. Here it's always present as the default secondary ordering.

What about a tertiary ordering? Suppose you want to present the docbase equivalent of:

```
select * from from docbase order by company, product, age desc
```

The Docbase system doesn't do a tertiary sort. And while it could be made to perform fancier orderings of data, I'm not sure that would make sense. At that point you're taking Perl outside its comfort zone. A scripting language that's tuned for rapid development of data-wrangling logic—such as Perl or, if you prefer, Python, REXX, or another alternative—works best within its sweet spot. At the fringes of that zone, you'll reap diminishing returns.

The question is not whether Perl can emulate SQL but rather at what point the cost of that effort outweighs the benefit. When you use Perl within its comfort zone, the benefits, vis à vis an alternative SQL-oriented data-management discipline, include the following.

Low overhead. SQL's overhead includes the initial cost of acquiring and installing an engine and the ongoing administrative effort required to use it. There are lots of situations that require SQL (see Chapter 15) and others where object-style data management makes the most sense (see Chapter 10, *Groupware Servlets*). But when you don't need the declarative querying, and transactional controls that SQL offers, you may not need the overhead of SQL.

Flexible schema. A docbase record is just a bag of fields. The schema that governs a docbase is just a convention shared by the input template, its processing script, and the indexing module. This means that any record can be a variant record that adds special fields for special purposes.

For example, the Virtual Press Room docbase sometimes needed to tag certain press releases that announced products nominated for awards at trade shows. During these periods, I added an extra input field to the form—for example, `SpringComdex98`. There was no need to propagate this mutation across the entire docbase. Clusters of variant records governed by these special-purpose tags can co-exist peacefully with normal records. This flexibility makes data prototyping quick and easy.

"Good-enough" indexing. The Docbase system aims for a modest goal. It's a way to handle sets of semistructured records like those found in your email or newsgroup folders but with customized, user-defined fields. Your mailreader probably doesn't support a query like:

```
select author, date from folder where date > #1999-04-15# and author =
    'Ben Smith'
```

But then, it doesn't really need to. We manage our inboxes pretty effectively just by using the canned views they support—sort by author, by date, and so on. These modes are good enough for our information-rich local message stores, and they're good enough for a lot of simple docbases too.

Constructing the Tabbed-Index Pages

Now let's traverse the index structure and write the tabbed-index pages. The *buildTabbedIndexes()* method, shown in Example 7-6, does most of that work.

Example 7-6. The buildTabbedIndexes Method

```perl
sub buildTabbedIndexes
  {
  my ($self) = @_;
  my $tabstyle = $self->{tabstyle};        # single-page or multipage?
  my $navstyle = $self->{navstyle};        # dynamic or static?
  my $idxdir = $self->{idxdir};            # absolute path of index pages
  my $idxref = $self->{idxref};            # web-relative path of index pages
  my $sort_specs = $self->{sort_specs};    # sort specs for each field
  my @indexed_fields =                     # list of indexed fields
    @{$self->{indexed_fields}};
  my $tabHoHoLoL = $self->{tabHoHoLoL};    # main index structure

  my $path = ( $navstyle eq 'dynamic' )    # dynamic or static delivery?
    ? $idxref                              # Web-server-relative path
    : "."    ;                             # file-system-relative path

  foreach my $current_index (@indexed_fields)
    {
    my $major_tab_row = "<center>";

    foreach my $index (@indexed_fields)    # for each index (e.g. company)
      {
      my @sorted_tabs = @{$self->{tabsortHoL}->{$index}};

      my $firsttab =                       # remember first tab
        $tc->escape($sorted_tabs[0]);

      if ($index eq $current_index)        # current tab
        {
        $major_tab_row .=
          " <strong><font size=+2>$index</font></strong> ";
        }
      else                                 # active tab
        {
        if ($tabstyle eq 'single')         # single-tab major row
          {
          $major_tab_row .=
            " <a href=\"$path/$index.htm\">$index</a> ";
          }
        else                               # multitab major row
          {
          $major_tab_row .=
            " <a href=\"$path/$index-$firsttab.htm\">$index</a> ";
          }
        }
      }
    }
```

Example 7-6. The buildTabbedIndexes Method (continued)

```
    $major_tab_row .= "</center><blockquote>";

  if ($tabstyle eq 'single')               # if single-page mode, create the page
     {
     my $fname = "$idxdir/$current_index.htm";
     open(FS,">$fname") or die "cannot open current index $fname $!";
     print FS $major_tab_row;
     }


   my @sorted_tabs = @{$self->{tabsortHoL}->{$current_index}};

   foreach my $current_tab (@sorted_tabs)  # minor tab row and records
     {
     my $minor_tab_row = $self->_makeMinorTabRow($current_tab,$current_index,
          \@sorted_tabs);
     my $tab_records = $self->_enumerateRecords($current_tab,$current_index);

     if ($tabstyle eq 'multi')             # make a new page
        {
        my $fname = "$idxdir/$current_index-$current_tab.htm";
        open(FM,">$fname") or die "cannot open current index $fname $!";
        print FM $major_tab_row;
        print FM $minor_tab_row;
        print FM $tab_records;
        close FM;
        }
     else                                  # add to current page
        {
        print FS $minor_tab_row;
        print FS $tab_records;
        }
     }

  if ($tabstyle eq 'single')               # pad bottom of page
     {
     print FS "<pre>";
     for (0..50) { print FS "\n"; }
     print FS "</pre>";
     close FS ;
     }
   }
 }
```

Single-page and multipage tabbed indexes

The *buildTabbedIndexes()* method starts by looking at the instance variable `$self->{tabstyle}`. It controls whether the second-level tab rows, and their associated records, will be grouped onto a single page or spread across multiple pages. The example we saw in Figure 7-3 illustrates the *multipage* style. In the company index, the *A* company records are listed in a file called *company-A.htm*, the *B* records in *company-B.htm*, and so on. Alternatively, in the *single-page* style shown in Figure 7-9, all the company records appear in the file *company.htm*.

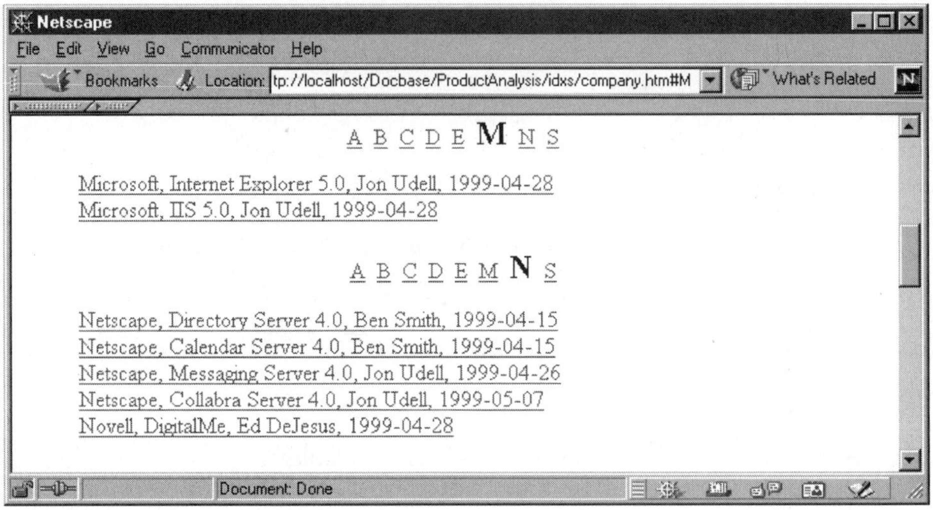

Figure 7-9. The single-page tabbed-index style

Why, in the single-page case, do we pad the bottom of the page with white space? This ensures that every clickable link will yield a visible result—namely, that the row corresponding to that link will snap to the top of the browser's window. Without the padding, a tab row that's less than a screenful distant from the bottom of the page won't react when its tab is clicked. This is another one of the tiny details that add up to create consistent and predictable behavior. Every time you create a link, you create an expectation that some behavior will result from clicking it. A design that frustrates that expectation—for example, the meaningless *P* tab in Figure 7-8—subtly undermines the user's confidence in the whole system. A user interface is really an illusion, one that depends heavily on consistency of behavior. Do everything you can to perfect that illusion.

Why use the single-page style at all? A new docbase tends to be sparsely populated. The *buildIndexStructures()* routine won't create an empty tab, but it will create tabs that have just one or two entries. These look pretty lonely on pages of their own. Moreover, when the data set is very small, there's no reason not to pack it all onto a single page so the user can scan everything at once.

Early in the life cycle of a docbase, when there are not many records, it makes sense to display all of them on a single index page. That way the user can scan the whole data set, as well as navigate by chunks. When the index page gets too big for quick downloading and comfortable scanning, you can switch to the multipage method. We saw earlier how to reduce the size of individual tab values as the number of values grows. Here's another way in which a docbase's navigational system can evolve as the docbase grows.

Emitting the tabbed-index pages

buildTabbedIndexes() loops over all the indexes defined in the instance variable `$self->{indexed_fields}`. It starts by building the major tab row for the current index. To do that, we capture the first element of the sorted list of tab values as `$firsttab`. Why? In the multipage style, the names of the index pages include tab values—for example, *company-N.htm*. Suppose that a tab row has **analyst** as its current tab and **company** as an active tab. We can't blindly link that active tab to the name *company-A.htm*, because in a sparse data set, that page might not exist. Instead we want to link each active tab to the *first available* page in the indicated set. The first element of the sorted tabs gives us the ability to form that page's name. Note that we call *escape()* on the tab's value. The reason is that we're creating an HTML link address, so we need to ensure that **Jon Udell** will be written as **Jon%20Udell**.

Armed with `$firsttab`, we can emit the major tab row for the current index. If the name of the index we're building matches the current tab, then we apply font styling but don't create an HTML hyperlink. Otherwise, we do create a hyperlink, whose address is a filename that varies according to the mode. In single-page mode, it's just the bare index name, for example, *company.htm*. In multipage mode, it's a combination of that name and the first tab in the set; for example, *company-A.htm*.

Next we loop through the ordered set of tabs. For each, we create a minor tab row using the helper routine *_makeMinorTabRow()*, shown in Example 7-7.

Example 7-7. The _makeMinorTabRow Method

```
sub _makeMinorTabRow
  {
  my ($self,$current_tab,$current_index,$listref) = @_;
  my @indexed_fields = $self->{indexed_fields};
  my $target = $tc->escape($current_tab);                # escape the target name
  my $tabIndex =                                          # begin HTML fragment
    "\n<p><center><a name=\"$target\">";
  my $path = ( $self->{navstyle} eq 'dynamic' )          # if dynamic version
    ? $self->{idxref}                                     # URLs start with this
    : "."    ;                                            # else with this

  foreach my $tab (@$listref)
    {
    my $subtab = $tc->escape($tab);                       # escape the tab name
    if ($current_tab ne $tab)                             # active tab
      {
```

Example 7-7. The _makeMinorTabRow Method (continued)

```
    if ($self->{tabstyle} eq 'single')                    # single-page style
      { $tabIndex .= " <a href=\"#$subtab\">$tab</a> ";}
    else                                                  # multipage style
      { $tabIndex .= " <a href=\"$path/$current_index-$subtab.htm\">\
      $tab</a> ";}
    }
  else                                                    # current tab
    { $tabIndex .= " <strong><font size=+2>$tab</font></strong> ";  }
  }
return $tabIndex . "</center><br>\n";
}
```

As with the major tab row, the minor tab row adapts to the prevailing style—either single-page or multipage. It also adapts to the prevailing mode of the system—that is, dynamic or static.

The records governed by each minor tab row are written by *_enumerateRecords()*, shown in Example 7-8.

Example 7-8. The _enumerateRecords Method

```
sub _enumerateRecords
  {
  my ($self,$current_tab,$current_index) = @_;
  my $app = $self->{app};
  my $cgi = $self->{db}->{docbase_cgi_relative};
  my $tabHoHoLoL = $self->{tabHoHoLoL};
  my $return_val = '';
  foreach my $rowref (@{$tabHoHoLoL->{$current_index}->{$current_tab}})
    {
    my $docnum   = $rowref->[0];                        # extract record number
    my $path = ( $self->{navstyle} eq 'dynamic' )       # form mode-appropriate URL
      ? "$cgi/doc-view.pl?app=$app&doc=$docnum&index=$current_index"
      : "../seq/f-$docnum-$current_index.htm" ;
    my @row = @$rowref;
    shift @row;                                         # remove record number
    push(@{$self->{idxHoL}->{$current_index}}, $docnum); # save record number
    $return_val .=                                      # construct HTML fragment
      "<br><a href=\"$path\">" . join(', ',@row) . "</a>" ;
    }
  return $return_val;
  }
```

The *_enumerateRecords()* method walks the list of records for the current index and current tab. It wraps link syntax around each record's fields, excluding the record number stored in the first field of each record. Here too, the link address varies according to the mode of the system—dynamic or static. It also builds a new data structure in *Docbase::Indexer*'s instance variable $self->{idxHoL}. This structure is a hash-of-lists that stores, for each index, an ordered list of record numbers, as shown in Example 7-9.

Example 7-9. Per-index Lists of Ordered Record Numbers

```
$self->{idxHoL} = {
  {'company', ('000127','000104','000113')},
  {'product', ('000104','000127','000113')},
}
```

These ordered lists are the basis of the sequential controls that we'll add later. For now, let's focus on just the tabbed-index controls. We want each of the links written by *_enumerateRecords()* to invoke a page that, like the one shown in Figure 7-1, includes a tabbed-index selector. And we want that selector to work in a context-preserving way. So, for example, if the link goes to a record whose product field is `Calendar Server 4.0`, then selecting `company` on the tabbed-index dropdown list should lead to a tabbed-index page that meets two criteria. On its major tab row, `company` should be the current tab. On its minor tab row, *N* (for Netscape) should be the current tab.

What addresses should *_enumerateRecords()* assign to these links? That depends on whether we're using the static or the dynamic approach. In the former case, it's the address of an HTML page; we'll see later how to build those pages. In the latter case, it's a CGI call that looks like this:

```
/cgi-bin/Docbase/doc-view.pl?app=ProductAnalysis&index=company&doc=000123
```

The script *doc-view.pl*, using the services of the *Docbase::Navigate* module, combines the static HTML page containing the raw docbase record with a dynamically generated tabbed-index selector. Let's see how that's done.

Dynamically Generating the Context-Sensitive Tabbed-Index Selector

We'll start with a template for the tabbed-index selector. Here's the basic skeleton:

```
<form name=Index>
<select name=idx onChange="gotoTabbedIndex(idx.options[idx.selectedIndex].
value);">
<option value=choose>choose tabbed index</option>
<OPTION VALUE=company>company tabs</option>
<OPTION VALUE=product>product tabs</option>
<OPTION VALUE=duedate>duedate tabs</option>
<OPTION VALUE=analyst>analyst tabs</option>
</select>
</form>
```

You can add any desired HTML flesh to this skeleton. For example, in Figure 7-1 the tabbed-index selector appears in a cell of a table.

To streamline the selector, we wire it to the JavaScript onChange event. That way, we don't need to include another widget—for example, a *Go* button to perform the switch to the selected index page.

The **onChange** event needs a JavaScript handler, which we're calling *gotoTabbed-Index()*, so we'll need to include it in the template as well:

```
function gotoTabbedIndex(index)
  {
  if (index != 'choose')
    {
    url = "DOCBASE_WEB/DOCBASE_APP/idxs/" + index + ".htm";
    location = url;
    }
  }
```

The *doc-view.pl* script, its companion script *doc-nav.pl*, and their supporting module *Docbase::Navigate*, mainly concern themselves with sequential navigation. In the next section, we'll see in more detail how these pieces work. Briefly, *Docbase::Navigate::fillNavigationTemplate()* reads an HTML/JavaScript template, which includes the parts we've seen here to support the tabbed-index control, plus other parts that support the sequential controls. It interpolates values into the template. Then, it interpolates *that* result into the raw docbase record to produce a generated HTML page that includes the navigational controls.

Where do the controls go on the page? The docbase template we saw back in Chapter 6 (Example 6-1) includes a placeholder (the HTML comment `<!-- navcontrols -->`) for this dynamically generated element.

For the tabbed-index selector, *fillNavigationTemplate()* makes the substitutions shown in Table 7-1.

Table 7-1. Navigation Template: Substitutions for the Tabbed-Index Selector

Marker	Description
DOCBASE_WEB	The HTTP root for the target index page; e.g., Docbase
DOCBASE_APP	The Docbase subdirectory for the target index page; e.g., ProductAnalysis
OPTION VALUE=...	A new <OPTION> tag whose <VALUE> attribute names the appropriate index page; e.g., *company.htm* (single-page mode) or *company-N.htm* (multipage mode)

In multipage mode, the appropriate target for the jump is the page that preserves the context of the current record. To figure that out, *Docbase::Docbase* provides the *makeContextTabs()* method, shown in Example 7-10.

Example 7-10. The makeContextTabs() Method

```
sub makeContextTabs
  {
  my ($self,$doc) = @_;
  my $metadata =                                      # extract metadata
    $self->getMetadata("$self->{docbase_web_absolute}/$self->{app}/docs/
        $doc.htm");
```

Example 7-10. The makeContextTabs() Method (continued)

```
my $tab_fns = $self->getDefaultValue('tab_functions');  # acquire tab functions

my $tabs = {};

foreach my $key (keys %$metadata)
  {
  my $idx_fn = $tab_fns->{$key};                        # get tab function
  $tabs->{$key} =                                       # apply tab function
    $tc->escape(&{$idx_fn}($metadata->{$key}));
  }

return $tabs;
}
```

makeContextTabs() uses some of the machinery that we've already seen. It calls *getMetadata()* to read the current record's header into a hashtable. Then it grabs the `tab_functions` hashtable that maps indexed fields to the functions that convert their values into tab values. Then it applies those functions to produce another hashtable that maps from fields to the corresponding tab values for the current record, like this:

```
$tabs = {
'company' => 'company-N',
'analyst' => 'Ben%20Smith',
'product' => 'product-C',
}
```

With this information in hand, the substitutions applied to the template's <OPTION> tags can yield the correct results:

```
if ($self->{tabstyle} eq 'multi')
  { s/<OPTION VALUE=(\w+)/<option value=$1-$tabs->{$1}/; }
else
  { s/<OPTION VALUE=(\w+)/<option value=$1/; }
```

Implementing Sequential Navigation

Our docbase records now provide one answer to "Where can I go from here?"—you can go to any of the tabbed indexes. But they don't say anything about "Where am I?" beyond the plain facts evident in the records themselves. There's no notion of sequence. It's true that you can get to the next or previous record in the **company** index by way of its tabbed-index page. That is, you can go to the **company** tabbed-index page for the current record, then select its predecessor or successor. But that's far more cumbersome than the sequential controls we saw in Figure 7-1. There, another answer to "Where am I?" is "In the company (or analyst, or product...) index." And another answer to "Where can I go from here?" is "To the next (or previous) company (or analyst, or product...)."

What's needed, then, is a way to map from a record number to its predecessor or successor, relative to any of the indexes. The first step was to save the sequences of record numbers that were only implicit in the structures we built for the tabbed-index controls. We accomplished that in *_enumerateRecords()*, which, as we saw in Example 7-8, walks the tab structures and builds a new structure with ordered lists of record numbers for each index.

These ordered lists are necessary, but not sufficient, for the sequential controls. For each record, we need the record number of its predecessor (if any) and its successor (if any), relative to each index. While we're at it, let's capture the record's position in each index and the count of records in each index; we'll need these items to display the counters shown in Figure 7-1.

Conceptually, we need a structure built on the pattern `INDEX,POSITION,MAX,PREV,NEXT`. For record 13, the report on Calendar Server, it might look as shown in Example 7-11.

Example 7-11. Sequence Information for a Docbase Record

```
company,10,14,000014,000005
product,2,14,000009,000003
analyst,2,14,000014,000002
duedate,14,14,000014,
```

This structure says, for example, that record 13 is 10th in the **company** index, where it's preceded by record 14 and followed by record 5. In the **duedate** index, it's also preceded by record 14 but has no successor—it's last in that index.

Suppose each record has a small companion file that stores just this information. Then, links in a dynamic navigation system can use a simple CGI component to look up their destination records in this structure. That's just how *Docbase::Navigate* works, as we'll see shortly. A static navigation system that relies only on precomputed web pages is also possible, though more complicated. We'll see how that's done later. First, let's capture the per-record sequence structures. The *buildSequenceStructures()* routine, shown in Example 7-12, does the job.

Example 7-12. Capturing Per-Record Sequence Info

```
sub buildSequenceStructures
  {
  my $self = shift;
  my $app = $self->{app};
  my @indexed_fields = @{$self->{indexed_fields}};
  foreach my $index (@indexed_fields)
    {
    my @idx = @{$self->{idxHoL}->{$index}};        # grab index saved earlier
    my $max = $#idx;
    my $lim = $max + 1;
    foreach my $i ( 0 .. $max )                     # for each record
```

Example 7-12. Capturing Per-Record Sequence Info (continued)

```
    {
    my $prev = ($i == 0)    ? ''   : $idx[$i-1];    # look up predecessor
    my $next = ($i == $max) ? ''   : $idx[$i+1];    # and successor
    $self->{seqHoH}->{$index}->{$idx[$i]} =         # save sequence tuple
      $i+1 . ",$lim,$prev,$next";
    }
  }

  foreach my $doc (@{$self->{idxHoL}->{$indexed_fields[0]}})
    {
    my $seqinfo = "$self->{docbase_cgi_absolute}/$app/seqinfo/$doc";
    open (F, ">$seqinfo") or die "cannot create seqinfo $seqinfo $!";
    foreach my $index (@indexed_fields)
      {
      print F                                       # write sequence tuple
        "$index,$self->{seqHoH}->{$index}->{$doc}\n";
      }
    close F;
    }

  }
```

This routine iterates, once per index, over the ordered lists of record numbers we saved during the *_enumerateRecords()* step. It builds another hashtable, stored in the instance variable $self->{seqHoH}, that holds per-index POS, MAX, PREV, NEXT tuples, like this:

```
  {
  'company' =>
    {
    '000013' => '10,14,000014,000015',
    '000012' => '....',
    }
  'product' =>
    {...},
  }
```

This structure gives us random access to the per-index tuples for each record number. Now we can iterate over the record numbers, grab the per-index tuples for each, and write sequence information into each record's companion file.

Dynamically Generating the Sequential Controls

To complete the dynamically generated solution, let's double back and see how *doc-view.pl*, *doc-nav.pl*, and *Docbase::Navigate* exploit the sequential index information we've just created. Example 7-13 shows the complete template for the controls. Each docbase has an instance of this template named *dynamic-navigation-template.btm*.

Example 7-13. HTML/JavaScript Template for Navigational Controls

```
<script language=javascript>
function setIndex(index)
  {
  url = "DOCBASE_CGI/doc-view.pl?app=THISAPP&doc=THISDOC&index=" + index;
  location = url;
  }

function gotoTabbedIndex(index)
  {
  if (index != 'choose')
    {
    url = "DOCBASE_WEB/DOCBASE_APP/idxs/" + index + ".htm";
    location = url;
    }
  }
</script>

<center>
<table width=500>
<tr>
<td colspan=3 align=center><b>sequential navigation</t></td>
<td align=center><b>counters</b></td>
<td align=left><b>tabbed-index navigation</b></td>
</tr>
<tr>
<td valign=top align=right width=32>
PREVDOC
</td>
<td valign=top align=center>
<form name=Sequence>
<select name=seq onChange="setIndex(seq.options[seq.selectedIndex].text);">
<OPTION>company
<OPTION>product
<OPTION>duedate
<OPTION>analyst
</select>
</form>
</td>
<td valign=top align=left width=32>
NEXTDOC
</td>
<td align=center valign=top><b>THISPOS</b> of <b>MAXPOS</b></td>
<td align=left valign=top>
<form name=Index>
<select name=idx onChange="gotoTabbedIndex(idx.options[idx.selectedIndex].value);">
<option value=choose>choose tabbed index</option>
<OPTION VALUE=company>company tabs</option>
<OPTION VALUE=product>product tabs</option>
<OPTION VALUE=duedate>duedate tabs</option>
<OPTION VALUE=analyst>analyst tabs</option>
</select>
</form>
```

Example 7-13. HTML/JavaScript Template for Navigational Controls (continued)

```
</td>
</tr>
</table>
</center>
```

Names in all caps are the ones that the template processor (see the *fillNavigationTemplate()* method in Example 7-16) looks for. Here's a rundown of what gets replaced, why, and how.

THISAPP and THISDOC

These are markers for the current Docbase application and the current record. Replacements might be "ProductAnalysis" and "000127." These are CGI parameters used in a call to *doc-view.pl*, the same script that we saw *_enumerateRecords()* encode in the addresses of the links it generates.

Here, *doc-view.pl* appears in the JavaScript function *setIndex()*, which is wired to the sequential-index selector. When you switch from the company index to the product index, the dropdown list's onChange handler fires. It redirects the browser to a page produced by *doc-view.pl*. That page displays the same record as the current page but in the new navigational context determined by the index name passed to *setIndex()*.

As shown in Example 7-14, *doc-view.pl* uses two services provided by the *Docbase::Navigate* module. The *getSeqInfo()* method looks up the sequence information for the current record and index. The *fillNavigationTemplate()* method interpolates that information into the template shown in Example 7-13 to create a cluster of navigational controls. It then interpolates the controls into the docbase record, to generate an HTML page that combines the raw record with the controls.

Example 7-14. Sequential Navigation: the doc-view.pl Script

```perl
#!/usr/bin/perl -w

use strict;
use TinyCGI;
my $tc = TinyCGI->new;
print $tc->printHeader;
my $vars = $tc->readParse();             # acquire CGI vars

my $app = $vars->{app};                  # which docbase
my $doc = $vars->{doc};                  # which record
my $idx = $vars->{index};                # which index

use Docbase::Docbase;                    # initialize docbase
my $db = Docbase::Docbase->new($app);
my $docbase_cgi_relative = $db->{docbase_cgi_relative};
```

Example 7-14. Sequential Navigation: the doc-view.pl Script (continued)

```
use Docbase::Navigate;
my $dn = Docbase::Navigate->new($db);          # initialize navigation module

my ($pos,$maxpos,$prev,$next) =                # get sequence info for record
  $dn->getSeqInfo($doc,$idx);



$dn->fillNavigationTemplate($doc,$idx,$pos,$maxpos,$prev,$next);
```

NEXTDOC and PREVDOC

These markers are replaced by links that encode CGI calls to *doc-view*'s companion script, *doc-nav.pl*. For record 13, NEXTDOC might turn into:

```
/cgi-bin/Docbase/doc-nav.
pl?app=ProductAnalysis&direction=next&doc=13&index=company
```

The *doc-nav.pl* script, shown in Example 7-15, uses *getSeqInfo()* twice. First, like *doc-view.pl*, it looks up the predecessor and successor of the current record. Then, if the next record was requested, it calls *getSeqInfo()* again, passing the successor's record number and retrieving the successor's navigational context. That context enables *fillNavigationTemplate()* to build a successor page that combines the next record with its correct navigational controls.

Example 7-15. Sequential Navigation: the doc-nav.pl Script

```
#!/usr/bin/perl -w

use strict;
use TinyCGI;
my $tc = TinyCGI->new;
print $tc->printHeader;
my $vars = $tc->readParse();

my $app = $vars->{app};
my $doc = $vars->{doc};
my $idx = $vars->{index};
my $dir = $vars->{direction};

use Docbase::Docbase;
my $db = Docbase::Docbase->new($app);

use Docbase::Navigate;
my $dn = Docbase::Navigate->new($db);

my ($pos,$maxpos,$prev,$next) = $dn->getSeqInfo($doc,$idx);

if ($dir eq 'next')
  { $doc = $next; }
else
  { $doc = $prev; }
```

Example 7-15. Sequential Navigation: the doc-nav.pl Script (continued)

```
($pos,$maxpos,$prev,$next) = $dn->getSeqInfo($doc,$idx);

$dn->fillNavigationTemplate($doc,$idx,$pos,$maxpos,$prev,$next);
```

Note that *doc-view.pl* and *doc-nav.pl* work in a complementary manner. The former, wired to the **onChange** event of the sequential-index selector, changes the index while holding the record number constant. The latter, wired to the *next* and *prev* arrows, changes the record number while holding the index constant.

<OPTION>indexname

These aren't special markers, they're the normal HTML **<OPTION>** tags that comprise the sequential-index picklist. But in this context we choose to interpret them as template markers too. Why? We want index selection to be sticky. When you move from a record in the **product** index to its successor, you want the new page's selector to default to the **product** index, not the first option in the list. That stickiness is another way of preserving context. It's also what tells the user which sequential index is current. As shown in the *Docbase::Navigate* module (Example 7-16), we can achieve this effect with a simple transformation:

```
if ($self->{tabstyle} eq 'multi')
  { s/<OPTION VALUE=(\w+)/<option value=$1-$tabs->{$1}/; }
```

<OPTION VALUE=indexname>

Here's the part of the template that governs the tabbed-index selector. We saw, at the end of the last section, how that works. Note that the template processor is relying on two different patterns—**<OPTION>indexname** and **<OPTION VALUE= indexname>**—to distinguish between the sequential-index selector and the tabbed-index selector. What if we needed to match a third selector too? Have we exhausted the patterns available without inventing new, non-HTML syntax? Nope. There's still **<Option>indexname** or **<Option VALUE=indexname>** or **<OPTION> indexname**. The template and its processor are a matched pair of components. When you control both, you can widen the interface between them at will.

The Docbase::Navigate Module

The last piece of the dynamically generated solution is *Docbase::Navigate*, the module shared by *doc-view.pl* and *doc-nav.pl*. We've already seen how its methods—*getSeqInfo()*, *makeContextTabs()*, and *fillNavigationTemplate()*—are used. Example 7-16, which presents the complete module, shows these methods.

Example 7-16. Docbase::Navigate

```
use strict;
package Docbase::Navigate;
```

Example 7-16. Docbase::Navigate (continued)

```perl
use TinyCGI;
my $tc = TinyCGI->new();

sub new
  {
  my ($pkg,$db) = @_;
  my $self =
    {
    'db'        => $db,
    'app'       => $db->{app},
    'tabstyle'  => $db->getDefaultValue('tabstyle'),
    };
  bless $self,$pkg;
  return $self;
  }

sub getSeqInfo
  {
  my ($self,$doc,$index) = @_;
  my $app = $self->{app};
  my $db = $self->{db};
  my $seqinfo = "$db->{docbase_cgi_absolute}/$app/seqinfo/$doc";
  open(F,"$seqinfo") or print "cannot open seq $seqinfo";
  while (<F>)
    {
    chomp;
    my ($thisindex,$pos,$maxpos,$prev,$next) = split(/,/);
    if ($thisindex eq $index)
      {
      return ($pos,$maxpos,$prev,$next);
      }
    }
  close F;
  }

sub makeContextTabs
  {
  my ($self,$doc) = @_;
  my $db = $self->{db};
  my $metadata =
    $self->{db}->getMetadata("$db->{docbase_web_absolute}/$db->{app}/docs/
        $doc.htm");

  my $tab_fns = $db->getDefaultValue('tab_functions');

  my $tabs = {};

  foreach my $key (keys %$metadata)
    {
    my $idx_fn = $tab_fns->{$key};
    $tabs->{$key} = $tc->escape(&{$idx_fn}($metadata->{$key}));
    }
```

Example 7-16. Docbase::Navigate (continued)

```perl
    return $tabs;
    }


sub fillNavigationTemplate
  {
  my ($self,$doc,$index,$pos,$maxpos,$prev,$next) = @_;
  my $app = $self->{app};
  my $db = $self->{db};

  my $tabs = $self->makeContextTabs($doc);

  my ($prevlink,$nextlink);

  if ($prev eq '')
    { $prevlink = ''; }
  else
    {
    $prevlink = "<a href=\"$db->{docbase_cgi_relative}/doc-nav.pl?
        app=$app&doc=\$doc&direction=prev&index=$index\">
        <img src=\"$db->{docbase_web_relative}/img/prev.gif\"
        border=0 alt=\"Prev record by $index\"></a>";
    }

  if ($next eq '')
    { $nextlink = ''; }
  else
    {
    $nextlink = "<a href=\"$db->{docbase_cgi_relative}/doc-nav.pl?
        app=$app&doc=$doc&direction=next&index=$index\">
        <img src=\"$db->{docbase_web_relative}/img/next.gif\"
        border=0 alt=\"Next record by $index\"></a>";
    }

  open (DOC, "$db->{docbase_web_absolute}/$app/docs/$doc.htm") or
    print "cannot open doc $db->{docbase_web_absolute}/$app/docs/$doc.htm";

  while (<DOC>)                         # emit docbase record
    {
    if ( m#<!-- navcontrols -->#  )     # emit nav controls
      {
      open (NAV, "$db->{docbase_cgi_absolute}/$app/dynamic-navigation-
          template.htm") or
        print "cannot open nav template";
      while (<NAV>)                     # interpolate into nav template
        {
        my $thispos = $pos;             # sequential controls
        s/DOCBASE_CGI/$db->{docbase_cgi_relative}/;
        s/DOCBASE_WEB/$db->{docbase_web_relative}/;
        s/DOCBASE_APP/$self->{app}/;
        s/THISPOS/<b>$thispos<\/b>/;
        s/MAXPOS/<b>$maxpos<\/b>/;
```

Example 7-16. Docbase::Navigate (continued)

```
        s/THISAPP/$app/;
        s/THISDOC/$doc/;
        s/NEXTDOC/$nextlink/;
        s/PREVDOC/$prevlink/;
        s/<OPTION>$index/<option selected>$index/;

                                    # tabbed-index controls
        if ($self->{tabstyle} eq 'multi')
          { s/<OPTION VALUE=(\w+)/<option value=$1-$tabs->{$1}/;   }
        else
          { s/<OPTION VALUE=(\w+)/<option value=$1/; }

        print $_;
        }
      close NAV;
      }
    else                                # emit normal line of docbase record
      { print $_;  }
    }
  close DOC;
  }

1;
```

A Static Implementation of the Navigational Controls

The display shown in Figure 7-10 contains the same docbase record and navigational controls as in Figure 7-1 but requires no server-side assistance.

The strategy here relies on massive precomputation of HTML/JavaScript pages. It also uses HTML frames to coordinate relationships among generated pages.

The frame-based approach confers a slight user-interface advantage over the single-window display of Figure 7-1. There the controls had to appear at the top of the page in order to occupy a constant location on-screen. But top-of-page screen space is a precious commodity, and the controls chew up a lot of it. What really belongs at the top isn't the controls, arguably, but rather the record's title. It contains the most salient fields of the docbase and deserves top billing. With a frameset, as shown in Figure 7-10, we can free up the top of the page for this purpose and lock the controls to a constant bottom-of-page location.

The static solution relies on the same kinds of methods we've already seen. There's a per-docbase template, in this case *static-navigation-template.htm*, and a template processor, in this case a *Docbase::Indexer* method called *buildStatic-Controls()*. Per-record and per-index, it writes a pair of files. The first, a frameset page, marries the raw docbase record to its controls, as in the following code.

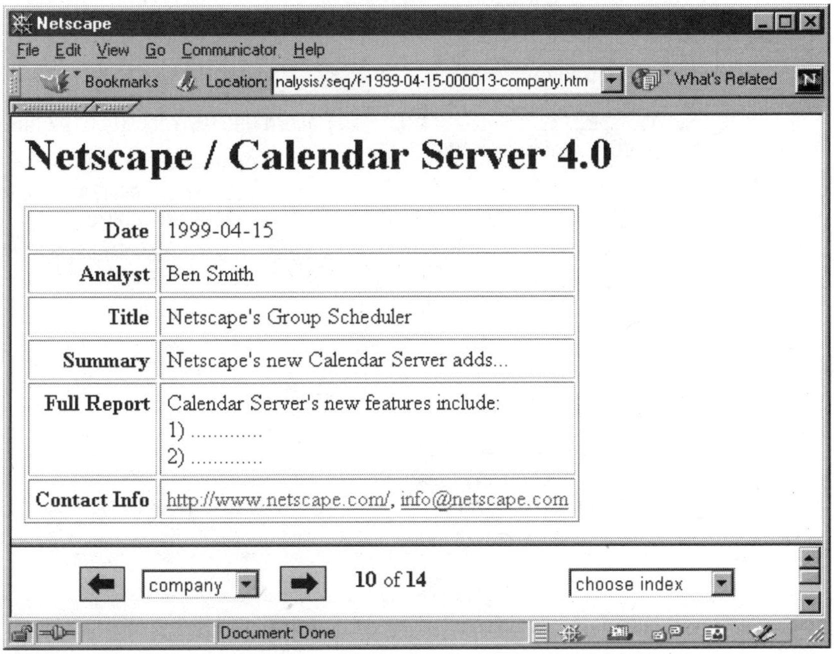

Figure 7-10. Static version of docbase navigation controls

```
<frameset rows=90%,*>
<frame src=../docs/000013.htm>
<frame src=./000013-product.htm>
</frameset>
```

The second file—in this example, *000013-product.htm*—contains the controls generated for a specific record, relative to a specific index. Client-side JavaScript code generated into those controls works the same way it did in the dynamic solution. Figure 7-11 shows how the parts fit together.

This solution shifts nearly the whole computational load to compile-time page production. It requires no CGI scripts and indeed no web server—you can run this docbase from a hard disk or CD-ROM. It's really efficient at runtime too, because we've done away with all the runtime lookups. The current state of the sequential index selector, which was computed on the fly from CGI parameters in the dynamic solution, is now hardwired into each controls page. Likewise, the context-sensitive tabbed-index selector, whose link targets were looked up at runtime, is now hardwired into each controls page.

Apparently we can retire the server, keep all desired behaviors, and even optimize away runtime lookups. It sounds too good to be true, and of course it is. We've traded a little bit of work at runtime for a massive amount of work at compile time. A 100-record docbase with four indexes will occupy 900 files—100 for

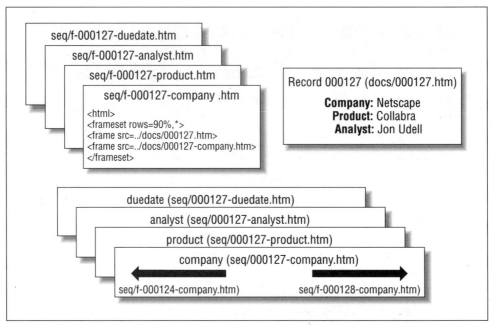

Figure 7-11. Schematic view of frame-based static navigation

the raw records, 400 for the frameset pages, and 400 for the controls pages. That's not counting another 100 or so for tabbed-index pages the exact number depending on the nature of the tabs for each index and the sparseness of the data.

Is this crazy? Not necessarily. Unix and NT filesystems can handle huge sets of small files pretty well. The Web mirror of the *BYTE* public newsgroups ran a variant of this frame-oriented navigation system for years, on a Linux server, without any trouble. In an era of dirt-cheap 6GB hard disks, you can probably afford the overhead of large collections of little files.

Even if all these files don't create a capacity problem, though, they'll surely bog down the indexer for any good-sized data set. The frame-based approach probably only makes sense when you need to deploy a standalone docbase that requires only a browser for viewing. When you find yourself in situations like that, though, it's nice to know how to do things more than one way.

Using Docbase::Indexer

Example 7-17 shows a script that uses the services of *Docbase::Indexer* to build both static and dynamic navigational controls for the ProductAnalysis docbase.

Example 7-17. A Docbase::Indexer Driver Script

```perl
#! perl -w

use strict;

my $app = "ProductAnalysis";

my @indexed_fields = ('company','product','analyst','duedate');

use Docbase::Docbase;
my $db = Docbase::Docbase->new($app);

use Docbase::Indexer;

my $di = Docbase::Indexer->new($db,\@indexed_fields);

$di->buildIndexStructures;

$di->buildTabbedIndexes;

$di->buildSequenceStructures;

$di->buildStaticControls;      # optional, only for static version
```

You could arrange to run this script after each record is added to the docbase. More likely, you'll want to schedule it to run periodically by using a *crontab* entry on a Unix-like system or an AT command on NT.

Docbase Navigation in Perspective

In this chapter we've seen how to derive two complementary sets of navigational controls from a meta-tagged docbase. Tabbed indexes use metadata to shelve documents in flexible ways that can evolve as the data set grows. Sequential indexes enable users who've found an interesting shelf to scan backward and forward along its length.

We've explored these techniques in painstaking detail because, as I've said, the details matter enormously. There are really only two ways we find information in online systems—by navigation and by search. Many online systems are, to my way of thinking, sadly inadequate in both respects. Richly interconnected, multimode navigation, such as we've seen here, makes it a lot easier to find things. As a groupware developer, you should think of this as one way to reward users for the time they spend building docbases. People who know they'll be able to find things are motivated to put things in. Whether the motivation is enlightened self-interest or the greater good doesn't much matter; it's the results that count.

Intelligent search results are another way to reward users who contribute to docbases. In the next chapter, we'll see how to elaborate the results produced by any search engine into value-added views of a set of underlying docbases.

8

Organizing Search Results

Search implementations often begin with the question: "What's the best (or cheapest, or easiest-to-use) search engine? This quest for the One True Search Engine is, I think, misguided. Search engines are more alike than they are different. You plug in a search term, you get back a list of URLs. In this chapter, we'll focus on the much neglected art of *organizing* that list of URLs in useful ways.

Webmasters who obsess about the design of their standard web pages often invest little or no effort in the design of their search-results pages. By design I don't simply mean the kinds of template alterations that stamp a site-branded style onto the default Excite or Verity or Microsoft result pages. And I don't mean just ordering results by relevance, which begs the question: relevant to whom and for what? Rather, I mean a deep reorganization of the result set, which both reflects and adapts to the underlying information architecture of one or more docbases. Search engines can't do this for you. Most aren't intrinsically programmable; those that are (such as the Microsoft Index Server) still can't easily do the kinds of data wrangling required to get the job done well. And yet the task isn't really hard at all, if you build docbases with an eye toward search integration and if you understand how web components work.

We began developing this notion of web components in Chapter 6, *Docbase Input Techniques*, and Chapter 7, *Docbase Navigation*. There, we saw how sets of CGI-based template/processor pairs, connected in series, create the Web equivalent of the Unix pipeline. But there's a larger story to tell about components in the Web environment, and that theme will play out in this chapter and throughout the rest of this book. Let's call the things we built in Chapter 6 and Chapter 7 *microcomponents*. Now we'll shift our attention to *macrocomponents*. These can include search engines, docbases, or any other kind of application that exports a *Web API*.

We first encountered this term back in Chapter 4, *Information-Management Strategies for Groupware Users*, when I showed how the Polls servlet's Web API enables formless data entry using URLs sent in mail messages. In this chapter, we'll first discover and then exploit the Web APIs presented by docbases and by search engines. When you understand properly how these two kinds of macrocomponents work, you can effectively organize search results drawn from any combination of docbases by any search engine.

Is this groupware? Yes, if you construe the term broadly, as I do, to mean a variety of ways to connect people to each other and to information. In Chapter 5, *Docbases as Groupware Applications*, we saw how a navigational system can express *bindings* among groups of users and classes of documents. A search system should work the same way and not just within an individual docbase but across sets of them.

A Docbase's Web API

A docbase is one kind of macrocomponent. What are its APIs, and how can we manipulate them? One API to a docbase, so obvious that we tend to overlook it, is the namespace. Consider a random URL from the ProductAnalysis docbase: */Docbase/ProductAnalysis/docs/000127.htm*. This access handle contains important clues about the document it points to:

The general type

It's a member of the Docbase family. That fact alone distinguishes the kinds of documents likely to be found here from the more informal documents you'd expect to find in, say, a newsgroup.

The specific type

The ProductAnalysis docbase stores a particular kind of structured report, related to a particular business process. When scanning search results drawn from multiple docbases, you might use that fact to zero in on, or conversely to pass over, documents of this type.

The relative age

The single filename *000127.htm* doesn't say anything about the age of the document it contains. A set of such names, though, carries information about the order in which the documents were added to the docbase. We used that information to impose a secondary ordering on the index pages. We can use the same strategy on search pages.

This is, admittedly, an implied API. The docbase doesn't really have a `documentAge` property or a corresponding *getDocumentAge()* method. But it's so straightforward to create such methods that I'll claim poetic license and just pretend that these implied APIs really exist.

URL Namespace Reengineering

Although the URL namespaces built by the Docbase system convey the relative age of records, they don't encode their absolute age. That would be valuable, and it's easy to do. Suppose we tweak *Docbase::Input* so that it generates record numbers like 1999-04-15-000127 rather than simply 000127. That's a trivial change that affects none of the input processing or the sequential- and tabbed-index processing. To all these processes, record numbers (and their corresponding filenames) are just opaque tokens that happen to sort by age. The new format preserves that property but makes the names more useful. Now we can read off a document's creation date directly from its name, whether or not a docbase's structured header carries a `creation date` field. We can arrange sets of records in yearly, monthly, or daily groupings. More subtly, the relationship between the two components of the name—date and sequence number—carries information about the rate at which the docbase is growing.

A URL like *http://host/Docbase/ProductAnalysis/docs/1999-04-15-000127.htm* is admittedly long and hard to type. As we saw in Part I, users are best advised to manipulate it using cut-and-paste or drag-and-drop. They should also enclose it in angle brackets for email transmission, to prevent breakage. These strategies help matters, but admittedly a long name trades away some convenience in exchange for descriptive power. On balance I think the advantages of a more richly descriptive name outweigh the disadvantages of untypeability and possible breakage.

Issues in URL Namespace Design

Some sites take pains to hide URLs behind "friendly" labels. One university's faculty directory uses a JavaScript `onMouseOver` handler to prettify the link addresses displayed in the browser's status window. For a link labeled *Home page for John Doe*, with an address of */directories/faculty/es/JohnDoe.html*, the status window's display echoes "Home page for John Doe." This effort is misguided for several reasons. Recapitulating the link's label in the status bar is redundant. Worse, it reduces the total amount of information available at this level of the system. The information-rich address is now completely hidden. That raw address, presumed unfriendly by the webmaster, actually tells us quite a bit about the document that it points to:

- It's part of a directory, as distinct from other kinds of docbases on the site.

- It's part of a faculty directory, as distinct from the parallel docbase whose records describe administrative personnel.

- It refers to a member of the environmental science department, as distinct from computer science or English.

Admittedly `es` is a cryptic departmental tag. And in the context in which I found that page, it happened to be an unnecessary clue, because the directory entries were already grouped by department. But consider what happens when John Doe's home page appears as a search result. Now `es` is a vital clue as to the document's type and purpose. An intelligent search-results filter can exploit that clue to integrate this document into a collection of search results.

That filter won't care whether the department ID is `es` or `environmental_ science`. Of course, people who encounter the URL would prefer the latter. Why was `es` used? Almost certainly because the directory was built manually, by a webmaster who quite understandably did not want to type out `environmental_ science` or `psychology`. Were the directory a Docbase-style application, these longer departmental names could be maintained as a controlled vocabulary and automatically interpolated into the docbase's namespace.

A Search Engine's Web API

We'll talk about three different search engines in this chapter—Excite, *SWISH-E*, and Microsoft Index Server. Each packages its functionality in a different way. The Excite engine is command-line driven but wrapped in a layer of Perl that is written by a web application that you use to customize your web interface to Excite. *SWISH-E* is a plain command-line program. To integrate it into your site, you have to script your own wrapper around it or use one of the canned wrappers available for it. Microsoft Index Server, unlike the other two, has no command-line interface. It's a Dynamic-Link Library (DLL) that works closely with Internet Information Server. To customize its web interface, you write proprietary scripts and templates.

Once integrated into a site, though, these engines are more alike than different. And, crucially for our purposes here, they're all plug-compatible with one another. How can that be? Indexing strategies and query languages aside, every search engine returns a set of URLs in response to a query. One way or another, you are guaranteed to be able to intercept and process that set of URLs. In some cases, you can wrap your own scripts around the engine itself or around the default scripts that come with it. If that's not possible, because (as with Microsoft Index Server) the engine runs as a deeply intertwined extension of a web server, you can still wrap it using a web-client script.

Web-Client Scripting

You can write web-client scripts in Perl, Python, Java, or any other language that can send a URL to a server and fetch its output. The URL might be the address of a page or, more interestingly in many cases, the equivalent of a submitted form, expressed as a CGI call with arguments. Here, for example, is one way to use Perl to search AltaVista for "Jon Udell":

```
use LWP::Simple;
print get "http://www.altavista.com/cgi-bin/query?pg=q&kl=XX&q=%22jon+udell%22";
```

The implications of this little nugget are just astonishing. In effect, every web site is a scriptable component, and the Web as a whole is a vast library of such components. You can invoke these invidually from any scripting language that can issue HTTP requests and interpret the responses.

What's more, you can join components to achieve novel effects. For example, I've used Yahoo! and AltaVista in combination to measure the "mindshare" of web sites in specific categories. To do that, I wrote a Perl script that uses Yahoo!'s namespace API to unroll the subdirectories under a node of the Yahoo! directory tree, yielding a consolidated list of URLs belonging to some category, such as */Science/Nanotechnology/*. Then the script feeds that list of URLs, one at a time, to AltaVista, using its CGI API to ask, for each site, how many other pages in the AltaVista index refer to that site. The ranked list of these citation counts measures what I call the web mindshare of the sites.

Yahoo! wasn't designed to produce an unrolled list of sites in a category, but its web API can be made to do it. Likewise, AltaVista wasn't designed to count references to each of the sites in such a list, but its web API can be made to do it. These two macrocomponents, driven remotely by a 100-line Perl script (see *http:// www.byte.com/features/1999/03/udellmindshare.html*), can be joined to create a new application that measures web mindshare.

This is heady stuff, and we'll see a lot more of it in chapters to come. For now, let's just notice that web search engines can be yoked to applications in a number of ways. Because one of those ways necessarily exposes a web API, search engines are guaranteed to be able to plug their results into applications that add value to those results.

In this chapter, I'll develop such an application. It comprises a family of Perl modules that abstract two kinds of macrocomponents: docbases and search engines. These modules embody a method of classifying and organizing search results that generalizes to any docbase and to any search engine.

Multiple Engines, Multiple Docbases

A groupware system will often involve docbases of varying types. In this chapter, we'll assume that the analysts who file reports to the ProductAnalysis docbase also collaborate in a searchable private newsgroup. A search for some term, say LDAP, should return results from both the docbase and the newsgroup. It should also organize the results from these different sources according to some normalized schema, so that, for example, reports filed by Jon Udell and newsgroup postings from Jon Udell will cluster together in a *by author* view of the search results.

Groupware systems may also involve multiple search engines. This might be because, over time, you switch from one engine to another. Or it might be because you run engines in parallel. The *BYTE* site, for example, comprised three primary docbases: the magazine archive, the public conferences, and the Virtual Press Room. These three docbases were searchable separately or in combination using either of two engines: Excite and *SWISH*. Why two engines? We found them to be complementary and neither alone to be sufficient. Figure 8-1 shows what the search page looked like for this multisearch-engine, multidocbase system.

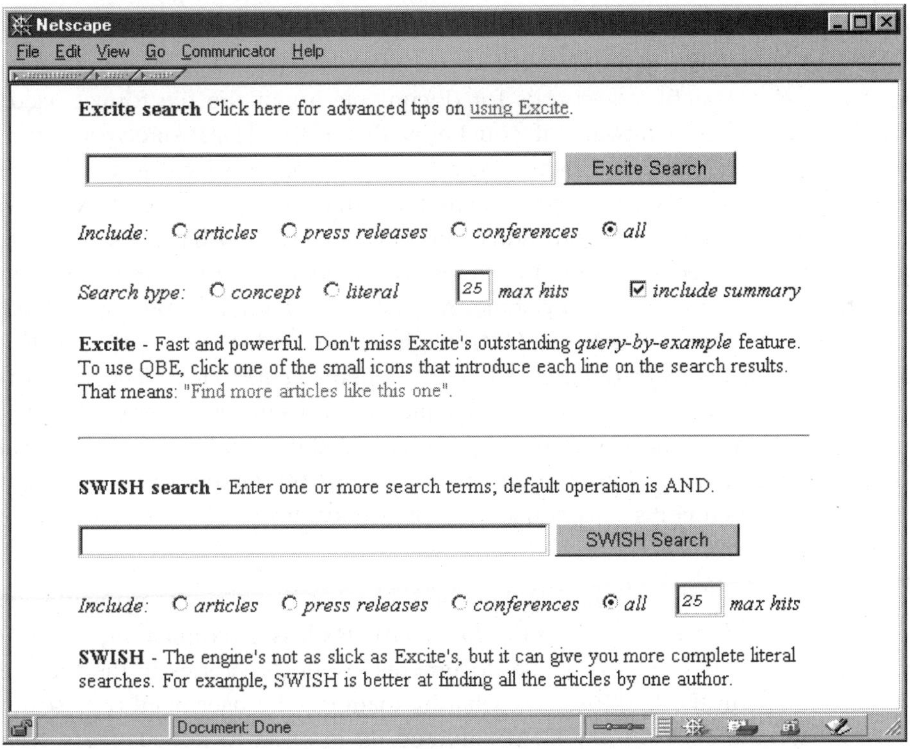

Figure 8-1. A multiengine, multidocbase search form

Excite Versus SWISH

Why use Excite? It's free, and it's also very powerful. Excite grew out of an academic research project. Its inventors knew that, from a formal library science perspective, search is an exacting discipline. They studied the use of academic search systems and learned that the average search expression involved about a dozen terms. At the same time they studied web search systems and found that the typical search expression involved only one or two terms. How, they wondered, could the complex queries needed for effective search be compressed into the simple queries that web users are willing and able to perform? Their answer was the Excite search engine. Its ingenious *concept search* feature enables every search hit to launch, with just a mouse click, a follow-on search that looks for "more articles like this one."* The follow-on search uses just a single term—the document ID associated with each search hit. Excite stores a statistical profile for each indexed document. In aggregate these profiles map out a kind of conceptual space, within which each document is surrounded by a set of neighbors. When you perform a "more like this" search, based on any search hit, Excite returns that document's conceptual neighbors.

Excite's concept search delivers the crucial benefit of serendipity. That is, it helps you to find things that you didn't know you were looking for. Let's say, for example, that you're searching a corpus for documents about the file format used by LDAP-based directory software. If you know that LDIF (LDAP directory information file) is the relevant acronym, you're in great shape. That's just the sort of unusual and highly discriminatory search term that gets good results with most search engines. But what if you didn't know about LDIF? What if the very existence of a thing called LDIF was the thing you needed to discover? Here's where *Excite*'s concept search can really shine. A concept search based on any of the hits produced by an initial search for *LDAP* might return a document called *LDIF file format*—even if this latter document doesn't contain *LDAP*! How? The match isn't based solely on the seed term *LDAP* but rather on a cluster of terms that *Excite* judged significant in the document that launched the follow-on concept search. Shared terms such as *X.500* or *organizational unit* or *distinguished name* could bring the two documents into conceptual proximity, even when they don't share the seed term *LDAP*.

A related benefit of this method is that users can get good results no matter what seed term they choose. For example, *directory* is far less discriminating than *LDAP* and might on the first pass produce documents about directories in the filesystem sense as well as in the LDAP sense. It hardly matters. The user need only scan the first result set and click on any LDAP-oriented hit in order to refocus the search in the LDAP direction.

If Excite's so wonderful—and it is—then why did I bother with *SWISH*? There's more than one way to do it. Sometimes a directed walk through conceptual space is just the ticket. Sometimes, though, you really do want to search for the literal term *LDIF*. In these cases, I found *SWISH* to be more effective than Excite, even

---

* The "more like this" feature isn't unique to Excite. Other search engines that can do this include Verity's Topic and Thunderstone's Texis.

when Excite ran in its literal mode. Moreover, for any large corpus, no single search tool will work best for every query. Finally, Excite doesn't support fielded search based on `<meta>` tags. In this chapter we'll use a rewrite of the original *SWISH*, called *SWISH-E*, which adds this invaluable feature.

Of course *SWISH* and Excite aren't the only choices. There are a variety of non-commercial and commercial tools available; see *http://www.searchtools.com/* for an overview of the field. The question isn't which tool is best but rather which tool—or combination of tools—meets your requirements. And that answer may evolve as your requirements do. So let's look at how a groupware system can flexibly connect a range of search tools to a range of docbases.

Exploiting URL Namespaces and Doctitle Namespaces

We've seen how a docbase's URL namespace can encode a lot of information that can enable both programs and people to categorize the subsets of that namespace that search engines return. There's also a complementary namespace that can carry an additional information load. The `<TITLE>` tag enclosed by an HTML document's `<HEAD>` is an invaluable but often underutilized resource. Text placed there doesn't appear in a web page. It becomes the title of the window in which the browser displays the page. As I mentioned in Chapter 5, you may be disappointed if you rely on the window title to display information that is essential to users. I've found that people don't regard the window title as part of a web page, so you have to recapitulate it in the body of web pages in order to get people to notice it. But while this *doctitle namespace* may not be very interesting to people, it's enormously useful to search-results scripts. Figure 8-2 shows what a search-results page looked like on the *BYTE* site.

The result set draws from three different docbases, but everything fits into a common abstract pattern:

```
DATE
   TYPE SUBTYPE TITLE
   ABSTRACT
```

When you control both the search engine and the docbase, you can always achieve this effect. The question is: With how much effort? Careful design of the URL and doctitle namespaces will yield search results that integrate easily and comfortably into this kind of structure. The trick is to ensure that the two namespaces, in combination, can map as completely as possible to the abstract markers—that is, `DATE`, `TYPE`, `SUBTYPE`, and so on.

In this case, the search-results structure requires a creation date for each result. You can't just rely on the file's modification date that some search tools can report.

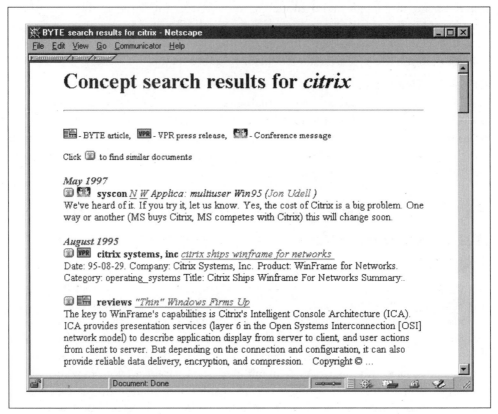

Figure 8-2. Multidocbase search results

For our purposes here, the creation date must be fixed—we want the age of the document, not a last-modified date that changes when someone edits the file or when a filter program transforms the entire docbase.

However, as is typical when you try to map multiple docbases into a common results architecture, the notion of a creation date is open to interpretation. In this example, for documents in the magazine archive, it really means issue date—that is, the month in which the article appeared, not the month in which it was written. For conference messages and press releases, the creation date really means what it says—but it also says less than it could. For records of these two types, the creation date is known not merely to the month, but to the day. Because daily grouping of results didn't map cleanly across all three docbases and because monthly aggregation was simpler yet sufficient, I took the latter approach.

Where did the creation date come from? That depended on the docbase. For magazine articles and press releases, it was included in each record's HTML document title. The URL */art/9704/sec6/art1.htm*, for example, corresponded to the doctitle *BYTE / April 1997 / Cover Story / Cheaper Computing*. Likewise, the URL */vpr/*

000439.htm corresponded to the doctitle *VPR / Citrix / WinFrame for Networks / 95-08-29*. For each docbase, the set of doctitles formed a kind of virtual database. Knowing the schema of that database, the search-results script could pick out fields and use them to structure a results page. Note that the date appears twice for hits from the magazine archive—as the URL component *9704* and the doctitle component April 1997. That's OK; there's more than one way to do it. It doesn't matter which of these namespaces carries the marker you need, so long as at least one of them does.

It's useful to think of the URL and doctitle namespaces as complementary. For example, when we made creation date part of every Docbase URL, we took some of the pressure off the doctitle namespace. If the doctitles don't need to display creation date, they can instead display some other useful dimension—say, author. It's the union of the namespaces that matters to a search-results script, and you can use them in combination to carry the maximum information load.

When URL and Doctitle Namespaces Don't Suffice

You want to cram as much as possible into the URL and doctitle namespaces, because these are what you get back "for free" from search engines. But inevitably, there will be missing pieces. Consider the newsgroup results in Figure 8-2. There's clearly a value that will map well to creation date—namely, the posting date of each newsgroup message. However, that value appears neither in the document's URL nor in its document title. In fact, documents in the primary conferencing docbase had no HTML document titles, because they weren't HTML documents; they were newsgroup messages that carried their fielded information in NNTP headers.

In these cases, you have to dig out the information another way. How? That depends on the nature of the docbase—whether it resides remotely on a server you don't control or locally on a server you do control, whether you have access to the server's file system, and possibly other factors.

Note that the newsgroup search results in Figure 8-2 presented two links. The *N* link's address was a news:// URL such as *news://dev4.byte.com/358C707B. ED39B9C1@aol.com*, and the *W* link pointed to a mirrored web page such as *http://dev4.byte.com/syscon/02137.html*. Given this mirrored-docbase situation, there were many possible ways to get hold of a creation date for a newsgroup search result.

One solution would have been to reengineer the doctitle namespace in the web mirror of the newsgroup, just as was done for the other docbases, and then point the indexers at that web mirror rather than the NNTP server's spool directory.

Another solution, and the one I in fact used in this case, relied on access to the NNTP server's spool directory. In that namespace, a reference to a news message looked like */syscon/1793*—that is, a directory corresponding to the newsgroup named *syscon*, and a numbered file containing the message. The search-results script used this reference to open the message file, absorb its NNTP headers, and parse the `Date:` field.

There are lots of ways to skin the cat, but it's always best when you don't have to. Use the URL and doctitle namespaces for all they're worth.

An Implementation Plan

Given these ideas about a search-results structure, and its relationship to a URL namespace and a doctitle namespace, let's plan and then implement a multidoc-base, multiengine search system. We'll start with the ProductAnalysis docbase that we've been working on for several chapters. To that we'll add a second data component—an NNTP conferencing system that, we'll suppose, is a less formal, less structured complement to the ProductAnalysis docbase. In its newsgroups, analysts can gather source materials, discuss work in progress, and share email that merits the attention of the group. In Chapter 13, *Deploying NNTP Discussion Servers*, we'll look at how to set up this kind of NNTP-based intranet conferencing system. For now, we need only concern ourselves with the data store: a bunch of files that begin with the headers `Newsgroups:`, `From:`, `Date:`, and `Subject:`.

To begin, let's enumerate the abstract markers we'll use to organize search results, and map out the relationships between these markers and each of our two docbases (see Table 8-1).

Table 8-1. Mapping Docbase Elements to Abstract Markers

ProductAnalysis Docbase Elements	Abstract Markers	NNTP Conference Elements
Docbase	Type	conference
ProductAnalysis	Subtype	newsgroup
creation date	Date	date
analyst	Author	from
title	Title	subject
{summary}	Summary	{summary}
company		
product		

Only two mappings come for free. It's quite clear which docbase elements should map to the abstract markers `DATE` and `AUTHOR`. A third mapping—to `SUMMARY`—would also be straightforward, but as the curly braces are meant to indicate, that element isn't defined as an explicit element in either docbase. That's not an insurmountable problem, but it means we'll have to do a bit of extra work to support this mapping.

I've arranged the columns in a way that implies further mappings, but I haven't yet finalized them. To see why not, we need to mock up a few different search-results screens and explore how the abstract markers interact with real data. Suppose the plan is this:

```
DATE
        TYPE  SUBTYPE  TITLE  AUTHOR  SUMMARY
```

Table 8-2 shows a search-results screen based on that plan.

Table 8-2. Search-Results Plan, Version 1

May 1998

TYPE	SUBTYPE	TITLE	AUTHOR	SUMMARY
PA	Microsoft	IE 5.0	Jon Udell	Version 5 features...
CON	analyst.contacts	Did you try Tim	Jon Udell	Tim's the LDAP guru...
PA	Netscape	Directory Server	Ben Smith	The latest rev...
CON	analyst.sources	LDIF spec	Jon Udell	The LDIF format...

In this example, the mappings to the **TYPE** marker are PA, a label (or icon) that denotes a record from the ProductAnalysis docbase, and CON, which signifies a conference message. Already we're in a bit of conceptual trouble. Recall that ProductAnalysis is a member of the Docbase family. So perhaps we should use the **TYPE** marker DOC, for Docbase, and demote the instance name ProductAnalysis to the **SUBTYPE** position. That would map more comfortably to the conference component, where the **TYPE** marker is CON, and newsgroup names occupy the **SUBTYPE** slot. Table 8-3 shows another version based on that idea:

Table 8-3. Search-Results Plan, Version 2

May 1998

TYPE	SUBTYPE	TITLE	AUTHOR	SUMMARY
DOC	ProductAnalysis	Microsoft, IE 5.0	Jon Udell	Version 5 features...
CON	analyst.contacts	Did you try Tim	Jon Udell	Tim's the LDAP guru...
DOC	ProductAnalysis	Netscape, Directory Server	Ben Smith	The latest rev...
CON	analyst.sources	LDIF spec	Jon Udell	The LDIF format...

This solution maps **TYPE** and **SUBTYPE** nicely, but what's going on with **TITLE**? In version 1, we ignored the **TITLE** element of the ProductAnalysis record and mapped **COMPANY** to the abstract **SUBTYPE**, then **PRODUCT** to the abstract **TITLE**. In version 2, we've again ignored the specific TITLE and mapped the COMPANY/ PRODUCT cluster to TITLE. These efforts reflect a sense that, although COMPANY and PRODUCT occupy a lonely position at the bottom of column 1 in Table 8-1, lacking an obvious mapping to column 2, they are nonetheless highly salient features of their data set and therefore should play a prominent role here. For the same reason, the COMPANY/PRODUCT cluster usurps the role of TITLE in the display template for the ProductAnalysis docbase (see Example 6-8).

What if we add a second SUBTYPE and promote COMPANY to the role of SUBTYPE2? That yields the structure shown in Table 8-4.

Table 8-4. Search-Results Plan, Version 3

May 1998

TYPE	SUBTYPE1	SUBTYPE2	TITLE	AUTHOR	SUMMARY
DOC	ProductAnalysis	Microsoft	IE 5.0 / New version of IE	Jon Udell	Version 5 features...
CON	analyst	contacts	Did you try Tim	Jon Udell	Tim's the LDAP guru...
DOC	ProductAnalysis	Netscape	Directory Server / New directory server	Ben Smith	The latest rev...
CON	analyst	sources	LDIF spec	Jon Udell	The LDIF format...

This is certainly a credible solution. On the ProductAnalysis side, we've found a home for COMPANY and kept PRODUCT in the abstract TITLE slot. What's more, we've found a home for the specific TITLE as well—in a PRODUCT/TITLE cluster that maps to the abstract TITLE. On the conference side, we've unpacked the structured newsgroup names to create a very clean and natural SUBTYPE1/ SUBTYPE2 mapping.

Finalizing the Search-Results Design

Should we use version 3? It's purely a judgement call, but even though this version arguably delivers the best and most complete mapping, I'm going to vote for a modified version 1. Here are my reasons:

Get to the point quickly.

Version 3's mappings may be elegant, but they chew up a lot of precious screen real estate. In a search-results display, datatype indicators provide useful clues as to the sources of information. These clues help users decide which links to follow, but other factors weigh more heavily in those decisions. Version 1 gets to the point more quickly.

Don't multiply categories unnecessarily.

Version 3's TYPE/SUBTYPE1/SUBTYPE2 structure seems to work out well for the two docbases we're considering here, but two is a pretty small sample. I'm not sure that other docbases we might want to plug in will be able to comfortably fill this structure.

Be flexible about category definitions.

It's true that version 1 fails to make a strong analogy between ProductAnalysis as a member of the Docbase family and *analyst.contacts* as an instance of NNTP conferencing. On the other hand, the apparently unlikely PRODUCT <-> NEWSGROUP mapping seems quite strong. The SUBTYPE marker can mean "one of the set of reports about Microsoft products" or "one of the set of messages posted to *analyst.contacts.*" Both meanings are appropriate and useful.

This process of analogy making is subtle and elusive. It's also vital when you're trying to build an information system that makes best possible use of diverse data sources. How do you learn to do it? For me the best guide is Douglas Hofstadter's *Fluid Concepts and Creative Analogies*. It's not about information architecture at all, but Hofstadter's insights into how we make and use analogies should be profoundly useful to every information architect.

Let's implement version 1, then, but with a few changes suggested by our exploration of alternatives. We'll steal version 3's idea of using a PRODUCT/TITLE cluster to integrate the specific TITLE from the ProductAnalysis docbase. And we'll represent TYPE using labeled icons. The icon's pictures will indicate general types (Docbase, Conference), and their labels will denote specific types (the ProductAnalysis docbase, the analyst newsgroup). Figure 8-3 shows a refined version of the finished design.

Generating the Results Display

Before we build a test data set, let's make sure we understand where all the data will come from. Table 8-5 shows an inventory of the required pieces.

Table 8-5. Extracting Docbase Elements from Search Results

	ProductAnalysis Docbase	Conference Docbase
DATE	element of URL	*NNTP* Date: *header*
TYPE	element of URL	element of URL
SUBTYPE	element of URL	element of URL
TITLE	HTML document title	*NNTP* Subject: *header*
AUTHOR	HTML document title	*NNTP* From: *header*
SUMMARY	CSS-tagged region of source document	region of source document

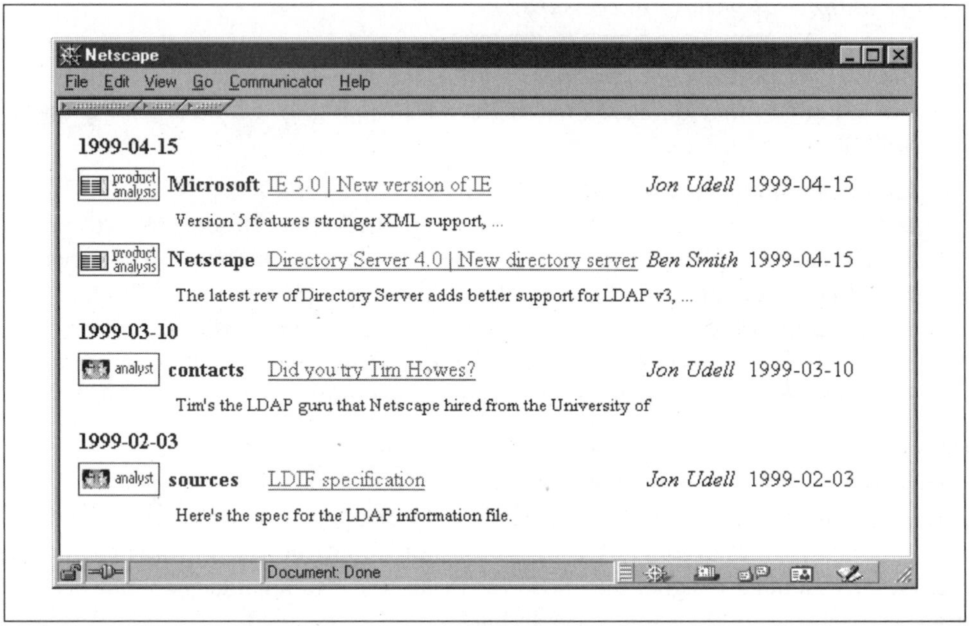

Figure 8-3. Finished design for search-results display

An element shown in boldface will be part of the results returned by any search engine, either as a piece of the URL or the document title. Note that for the ProductAnalysis docbase, whose URLs we are automatically generating, we have reengineered the namespace to include an extra element—the date. That gave us the latitude to reformat the doctitle as COMPANY/PRODUCT/TITLE so that we can include the specific TITLE in the abstract TITLE slot in accord with the final design.

An italicized item may or may not be directly available, depending on the search engine. Excite and *SWISH* return none of these items. The Microsoft Index Server, however, can perform queries based on *custom properties* including HTML <meta> tags and NNTP headers. As we'll see, it can also return the values of custom properties as part of the result set. So we'll need a two-tiered strategy. When an engine can natively supply these elements, we'll want to take advantage of that. But since many don't, we'll need a fallback method.

The simplest approach to digging out values not present in the URL or doctitle namespaces will be to resolve URLs to files, peek into those files at runtime, and parse out the needed information. On the HTML side, the only field that will require this treatment is SUMMARY. In Chapter 6, we set up the record template for the ProductAnalysis docbase using a CSS class attribute to identify the SUMMARY field. So we know it will be easy to pick out using an XML parser or, ideally, just a regular expression.

On the conference side, nearly everything we want will have to be looked up. The NNTP headers are easy to recognize. However, there is no **SUMMARY** field, so we'll need to define the region of the message that will play this role. Again we'll try the simplest thing first: we'll grab a few hundred characters following the double newline that separates the message header from the message body. When news messages are plain text, this method will suffice. When news messages are HTML, things get trickier. The format of the HTML part of the message varies depending on the newsreader that created it and on whether the HTML content was attached or composed inline. There's also the question of how a mechanically extracted fragment of an HTML message will interact with the context that surrounds it in an HTML search-results page. Should you throw away the HTML tags? Convert < and > to the HTML entities < and >? Either solution, if needed, will be easy to implement.

Note that you can make fields that require this extra work optional on the search form. That way, when a user asks for a concise display, the results processor can skip this extra step and compose a results page using only the values present in the URL and doctitle namespaces.

Processing Search Results

Now let's build the Perl modules that implement these ideas. The data structure that's central to this family of modules is a list-of-hashes (LoH), as shown in Example 8-1.

Example 8-1. Using an LoH to Map Abstract Markers to Search-Result Elements

```
my $LoH = [
{
'TYPE'    => 'Docbase-ProductAnalysis',
'TITLE'   => 'Directory Server 4.0 | New directory server',
'URL'     => '/cgi-bin/Docbase/doc-view.pl?app=ProductAnalysis&index=company&doc=1999-
04-15-000014',
'AUTHOR'  => 'Ben Smith',
'SUBTYPE' => 'Netscape',
'PATH'    => ' /web/Docbase/ProductAnalysis/docs/1999-04-15-000014.htm ',
'SUMMARY' => 'The latest rev of Directory Server adds better support for LDAP v3, ...
',
'DATE'    => '1999-04-15'
},
{
'TYPE'    => 'conference-analyst',
'TITLE'   => 'LDIF specification',
'URL'     => 'news://localhost/<364DB8E0.36CA8FE6@top.monad.net>',
'AUTHOR'  => 'Jon Udell',
'SUBTYPE' => 'sources',
'PATH'    => '/netscape/suitespot/news-udell/spool/analyst/sources/27',
```

Example 8-1. Using an LoH to Map Abstract Markers to Search-Result Elements (continued)

```
'SUMMARY' => 'Here\'s the spec for the LDAP information file.,
'DATE'    => '1999-02-03'
},
];
```

This LoH forms an interface between any set of docbases and any set of indexers. To plug in a search engine, we'll need to map actual search results into an instance of this structure. In the case of *SWISH-E*, for example, a search for LDAP might produce this output:

```
1000 /web/Docbase/ProductAnalysis/docs/1999-04-15-000014.htm "Netscape |
     Directory Server 4.0 | New directory server" 1006
 619 /netscape/suitespot/news-udell/spool/analyst/sources/1 "1" 584
 516 /netscape/suitespot/news-udell/spool/analyst/contacts/1 "1" 649
 232 /web/Docbase/ProductAnalysis/docs/1999-04-15-000007.htm "Microsoft |
     IE 5.0 | New version of IE" 1461
```

The pattern for each hit is:

```
RELEVANCE  PATHNAME  DOCTITLE  SIZE
```

The `PATHNAME` isn't a URL; it's a filesystem path. Since a web server's namespace typically won't match that of the filesystem, you might need to transform it into the virtual path that will fill the URL slot of the results structure. Or perhaps, as shown in Example 8-1, into a CGI call, if the document should be served dynamically. We'll also use the pathname to extract the fields that can't be read directly from the pathnames and doctitles. Note that for NNTP results, the doctitle is just the filename, which doesn't carry any useful information.

Testing the Design with Sample Data

Before we populate our LoH with real search results, let's run the mock-up through a template to find out how the design works with sample data. To do that, we'll use a new Perl module, *Search::SearchResults*, and feed it the LoH shown in Example 8-1 like this:

```
my $sr = Search::SearchResults->new($LoH,'DATE','desc','SUBTYPE','asc');
print $sr->Results();
```

We'll explore *Search::SearchResults* and its supporting modules in more detail shortly. Here, just note that we're handing the module's constructor the same $LoH that I wrote, by hand, for Example 8-1. This is an example of what I mean by data prototyping in Perl. The hand-built LoH cleaves our application into two independently testable parts. One part runs the structure through templates to create finished HTML search-results pages. We'll develop that first. Then we'll double back and work on the guts of the problem: transforming raw search results into the LoH.

The module constructor makes no reference to any specific docbase or any specific engine. The results LoH will be populated by two families of modules, one specializing in docbases, another in search engines. All we need to convert the LoH into a finished display is a template to run it through. Where does the template come from? Its name derives from the second argument to the *Search::SearchResults* constructor. In this case, the name becomes *search-template-date.htm*, which contains:

```
<tr><td colspan=4><img src="/img/~TYPE~.gif"></td></tr>
<tr>
<td><b>~SUBTYPE~</b></td><td><a href="~URL~">~TITLE~</a></td><td>~AUTHOR~</td>\
<td><i>~DATE~</i></td>
</tr>
<tr>
<td></td>
<td colspan=3><font size=-1>  ~SUMMARY~</font></td>
</tr>
```

The result is the same display we saw in Figure 8-3. The major grouping is by DATE in descending order. Within each DATE grouping, SUBTYPE appears in ascending order.

Variations on the Display Template

It's quite easy to stamp out variations on the theme. If we use a different template, the outcome of `Search::SearchResults->new('TYPE', 'asc', 'AUTHOR', 'asc')` is shown in Figure 8-4.

Here the major grouping is TYPE in ascending order (based on the values Conference-Analyst and Docbase-ProductAnalysis), and the minor grouping is AUTHOR in ascending order.

In these templates, the first column in the HTML table corresponds to the primary sort key. As did the tabbed-index generator discussed in the last chapter, the search-results processor achieves double ordering by using multiple comparisons in a code block interpolated between Perl's sort operator and the results list.

The Search::SearchResults Module

The module shown in Example 8-2 accepts an unordered LoH and major/minor sort specifications. It orders the LoH according to the sort specs, derives a template name from the major order, and pours the LoH through the template to produce a final HTML search-results page.

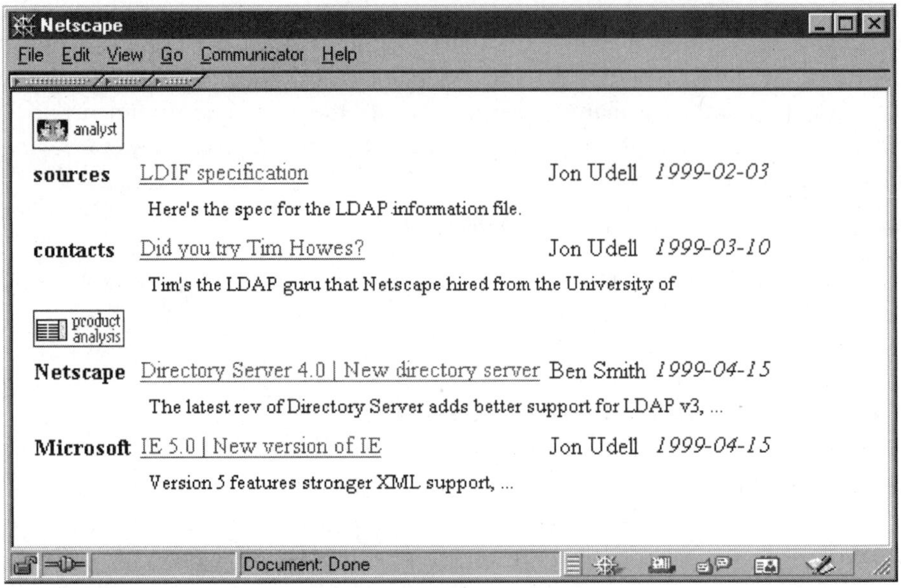

Figure 8-4. Search results by TYPE, AUTHOR

Example 8-2. The Search::SearchResults Module

```perl
#!/usr/bin/perl -w

use strict;

package Search::SearchResults;

my $template_root = "/web/cgi-bin/Docbase";

sub new
  {
  my ($pkg,$rawresults,$major_tab,$major_tab_order,$minor_tab,$minor_tab_order)
      = @_;

  my $self =
    {
    'major_tab'         => $major_tab,
    'major_tab_order'   => $major_tab_order,
    'template_location' => "$template_root/search-template-$major_tab.htm",
    'minor_tab'         => $minor_tab,
    'minor_tab_order'   => $minor_tab_order,
    'boundary'          => undef,
    'rawresults'        => $rawresults,
    'orderedresults'    => undef,
    'tablebegin'        => "<table cellpadding=1>",
    };
  bless $self,$pkg;
```

Example 8-2. The Search::SearchResults Module (continued)

```perl
    $self->loadTemplate;
    $self->orderResults;
    return $self;
    }

sub orderResults
  {
  my $self = shift;
  my $major = $self->{major_tab};
  my $major_order = $self->{major_tab_order};

  my $minor = $self->{minor_tab};
  my $minor_order = $self->{minor_tab_order};

  my @rawresults = @{$self->{rawresults}};

  my @orderedresults = sort
    {
    if ( $major_order eq 'asc' )
      {
      return $a->{$major} cmp $b->{$major}  ||
        (  ( $minor_order eq 'asc' )
          ? $a->{$minor} cmp $b->{$minor}
          : $b->{$minor} cmp $a->{$minor}  )
      }
    else
      {
      return $b->{$major} cmp $a->{$major}  ||
        (  ( $minor_order eq 'asc' )
          ? $a->{$minor} cmp $b->{$minor}
          : $b->{$minor} cmp $a->{$minor} )
      }
    } @rawresults;
  $self->{orderedresults} = \@orderedresults;
  }

sub Results
  {
  my $self = shift;
  my $major_tab = $self->{major_tab};
  my $LoH = $self->{orderedresults};
  my $oldtab = '';
  my $results = $self->{tablebegin};
  foreach my $href (@{$LoH})
    {
    my $newtab = $href->{$major_tab};
    if ($oldtab ne $newtab)
      {
      $oldtab = $newtab;
      my $boundary = $self->{boundary};
      $boundary =~ s/~$major_tab~/$newtab/;
      $results .= "$boundary\n";
```

Example 8-2. The Search::SearchResults Module (continued)

```
      }
   my $template = $self->{template};
   foreach my $key (keys %$href)
      {   $template =~ s/~$key~/$href->{$key}/g; }
   $results .= $template;
      }
  $results .= "</table>";
  return $results;
   }

sub loadTemplate
  {
  my $self = shift;
  my $template_location = $self->{template_location};
  open (TEMPLATE,"$template_location")
     or print "cannot open sr template $template_location $!\n";
  $self->{boundary} = <TEMPLATE>;
  while (<TEMPLATE>)
     { $self->{template} .= $_; }
  close TEMPLATE;
  }

1;
```

Plugging in SWISH-E

It's time to plug in a real search engine. We'll start with *SWISH-E*, which is freely available in source form from *http://sunsite.berkeley.edu/SWISH-E/*. It's a Unix-style program that compiles, most comfortably, in a GNU environment. What if you want to use *SWISH-E* on Windows NT? There are a variety of solutions:

Port SWISH-E to Win32.

> If you're more ambitious than I am, you could convert the program into a Win32 console application.

Build a Win32 version of SWISH-E.

> This isn't the same thing as a native port. Rather, it's a build that uses a Win32-based GNU environment. Several of these are freely available. I've used MingW32 (*http://programming.ccp14.ac.uk/mingw32/~janjaap/mingw32/index.html*) successfully with *SWISH-E*.

Find a SWISH-E Win32 binary.

> I found a Win32 *SWISH-E* binary at *http://www.geocities.com/CapeCanaveral/Lab/1652/software.html*. I'm sure there are others elsewhere.

Buy a copy of WebSite Pro.

> If you're using this NT-based web server from O'Reilly & Associates, it includes a version of *SWISH-E*.

Run SWISH-E on Unix.

SWISH-E will compile and run effortlessly on a Unix system. How does that help you use it in an NT environment? Think in terms of clustered components. Let's say your primary web server is NT-based and that it supports Active-Server-Pages- or Cold-Fusion-based applications. That doesn't mean your search system has to run on the primary server. It's delightfully easy to build a web site as a loosely coupled cluster of servers, bound together with file sharing and URLs.

For example, if your NT server exports Network File System (NFS) drives, a Linux-based indexer can mount the NT drives in order to index them. Or, since NFS isn't standard with NT, you can go the other route. NT can mount Linux drives exported by Samba as Windows-style Server Message Block (SMB) shares. Then you can copy the NT-based content to the Linux server. Either way, the Linux-based *SWISH-E* indexer can now index the content. The same Linux *SWISH-E*, under the control of an Apache-based Perl script, can search the content and return results to browsers.

Note that although the indexer and search engine may live on the Linux server, there is no need to serve found documents from that server. The search-results script already has to translate the pathname returned by the searcher into a URL. It's trivial to redirect hits produced by a search server at *search.yoursite.com* to a primary document server at *www.yoursite.com*. Why would you want to do that? It's a form of load balancing. And you may want the pageviews produced by the search engine to show up in the same log file, and in the same format, as pageviews produced by the site's navigation system.

The point is that web APIs make it easy to build heterogenous clusters. As a result, you can avail yourself of the widest possible selection of tools. Lots of useful tools born in the Unix environment run best there. Sometimes it's less trouble to host them on a Unix box than to port them to NT. The reverse holds true as well: a Unix-oriented site or intranet can profit by having an NT box as a member of its cluster. Thanks to URL middleware, you really *can* have the best of both worlds!

Running the SWISH-E Indexer

SWISH stands for Simple Web Indexing System for Humans, and, while not the world's fanciest or most powerful search tool, *SWISH-E* is admirably simple to use. To index files, you just point it at a bunch of directories and let it rip. For our two-docbase example, here's the *SWISH-E* configuration file:

```
IndexDir /web/Docbase/ProductAnalysis/docs
IndexDir /netscape/suitespot/news-udell/spool/analyst
```

If the configuration file is called *swish-e.conf,* here's the indexing command:

```
swish-e -f index.swish -c swish-e.conf
```

The indexer walks each root recursively, so we'll pick up *analyst/contacts* and *analyst/sources.* The resulting index is named *index.swish.*

There are more elaborate ways to run the indexer. You can restrict it to certain classes of files, such as *.htm* or *.html*—though we wouldn't want to do that here, because we'd miss the numerically named conference messages. Or you can exclude classes of directories, so that if the pathname component */img/* denotes *GIF* or *JPEG* files, the indexer can skip those. *SWISH-E* can also build field indexes based on <meta> tags. To activate that feature, add a directive like this to *SWISH-E*:

```
MetaNames company product analyst duedate
```

After reindexing with this directive in effect, there are now two ways to search. The command:

```
swish-e -f index.swish -w Microsoft
```

returns documents whose HTML bodies contain "Microsoft." However, the command:

```
swish-e -f index.swish -w "company=Microsoft"
```

returns only documents that contain <META NAME="company" CONTENT= "Microsoft">. Users of the ProductAnalysis docbase will greatly appreciate this capability. There's a huge difference between the diffuse set of documents that merely mention Microsoft and the more focused set that is actually *about* Microsoft products.

If fielded search is such a powerful technique, why is it so seldom deployed? It requires a data-preparation discipline that many sites lack. A key advantage of a Docbase-like system is that it automates data preparation and delivers consistent, well-formed <meta> tags.

Note that *SWISH-E* is quite literal in its parsing of <meta> tags. It will match <meta name="company" content="Microsoft">, because it doesn't care about the case of the tag or its attributes. But it won't match <META NAME=company CONTENT=Microsoft>, because it expects the attributes to be quoted. As we saw in Chapter 6, the *Docbase::Input* module does quote <meta> tag attributes.

Classifying SWISH-E Results

Let's load a batch of search results into a Perl variable. We can do that the plain old-fashioned way, using *backtick evaluation* of a search command to capture its output:

```
$search_results = `swish-e -f index.swish -w ldap`;
```

Here's what ends up in `$search_results`:

```
# Swish-e format 1.3
#
# Saved as: index.swish
# DocumentProperties: Enabled
# Search words: ldap
# Number of hits: 4
668 /web/Docbase/ProductAnalysis/docs/1999-04-15-000006.htm "Microsoft |\
  IIS 5.0 | IIS 5.0" 1266
601 /web/Docbase/ProductAnalysis/docs/1999-04-15-000014.htm "Netscape |\
  Directory Server 4.0 | Directory Server" 1312
360 /netscape/suitespot/news-udell/spool/analyst/sources/27 "27" 584
311 /netscape/suitespot/news-udell/spool/analyst/contacts/142 "142" 662
```

The SWISH Search Driver

We need to classify these results relative to the abstract structure we've defined, populate an instance of that structure, and pass it to *Search::SearchResults* in order to produce a web page that displays the results. Example 8-3 shows a search script that does that.

Example 8-3. A SWISH Search Driver

```
#! /usr/bin/perl -w

use strict;
use Search::SearchResults;
use Search::SwishClassifier;

my $results = `swish-e -f index.swish -w ldap`;  # run the search

my $sc = Search::SwishClassifier->new();           # instantiate a classifer

$sc->classify($results);                           # classify results

my $LoH = $sc->getResults();                       # fetch results

$sr = Search::SearchResults->new                   # format results
    ($LoH,'DATE','desc','SUBTYPE','asc');

print $sr->Results();                              # print results
```

We've seen how *Search::SearchResults* works. How does *Search::SwishClassifier* produce the list-of-hashes that it passes to *Search::SearchResults*? The answer turns out to be an interesting case study in object-oriented Perl, combining inheritance with polymorphism.

To understand why both approaches are needed, consider what *Search::SwishClassifier* has to do. It receives a batch of results from the *SWISH-E* searcher. For each result, it has to map specific values (e.g., `Netscape`) to the abstract markers (e.g., SUBTYPE) required by *Search::SearchResults*. It builds a hash of these mappings and accumulates these hashes in a list.

The Classifier Family Tree

Parallel versions of this module for other engines (e.g., *Search::ExciteClassifier* or *Search::MicrosoftIndexClassifier*) would need to do exactly the same tasks, so it makes sense for each of these engine-specific classifiers to inherit from a base class, *Search::Classifier*, shown in Example 8-4.

Example 8-4. Base Class for Classifier Modules

```
package Search::Classifier;

use strict;

my $LoH = [];

sub new
  {
  my ($pkg) = @_;
  my $self = {};
  bless $self,$pkg;
  return $self;
  }

sub getResults        # return my LoH
  {
  my $self = shift;
  return $LoH;
  }

sub addResult         # accumulate into my LoH
  {
  my ($self,$hash) = @_;
  push (@{$LoH},$hash);
  }

1;
```

The *Search::Classifier* module is nothing more than a private list-of-hashes variable, an *addResult()* method that adds a hash to the LoH, and a *getResults()* method that returns the LoH. The *SWISH-E* search script uses the specific module *Search::SwishClassifier*, but when it calls `$sc->getResults()`, no implementation of *getResults()* is found. Perl therefore climbs up the inheritance chain, finds *getResults()* in the base class, and invokes that method. The same will hold true for scripts that process MS Index Server's, Excite's, or any other engine's results.

An engine-specific classifier will inherit bookkeeping capability from an engine-neutral superclass.

Classifiers and Mappers

But there's another dimension to this problem. The results that *Search::SwishClassifier* sees come from multiple docbases. So while it is necessarily engine-specific, it must also be docbase-neutral. In the current example, it has to recognize hits on the ProductAnalysis docbase and hits on the analyst newsgroups. The code that does that recognition needs to be docbase-specific but engine-neutral. That means it should be packaged by docbase rather than by engine.

We'll write a mapping module for each of the two docbases we've built so far. *Search::ProductAnalysisMapper* will know how to map search hits on the Product-Analysis docbase into the abstract LoH. Likewise, *Search::ConferenceMapper* will know how to map hits on newsgroups into that abstract structure. Because these modules will be called by all the Classifiers, they can't depend on anything engine-specific. A ProductAnalysis hit produced by *SWISH-E* differs from the same one produced by another engine but also shares something in common. What differs is the way in which each engine formats the pathname and the doctitle. But the pathname and doctitle themselves are the same. There are really two kinds of recognition that need to occur, according to the division of labor shown in Table 8-6:

Table 8-6. Responsibilities of Mappers and Classifiers

Per-Docbase Mappers	Per-Engine Classifiers
Can identify that a raw search hit is of its own type, regardless of the engine that supplies the hit	Can identify the pathname and doctitle in a raw search hit, regardless of the hit's docbase of origin
Given a pathname and doctitle, can map these to the abstract LoH and return an instance of that structure	Can invite each Mapper to process each pathname and doctitle
	Can add an entry to its unordered SearchResults structure

Figure 8-5 depicts the relationships among Classifiers, sets of search results, and Mappers.

Figure 8-6 shows the transactions between a Classifier and a set of Mappers for an individual search result.

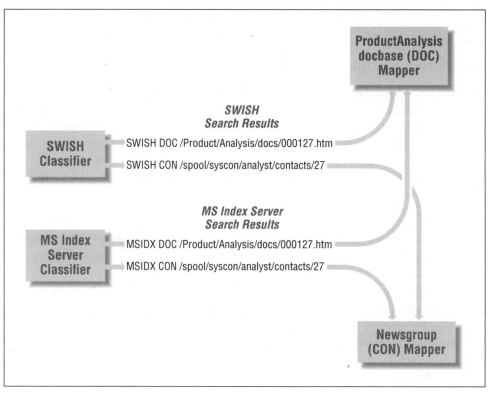

Figure 8-5. Classifiers, search results, and Mappers

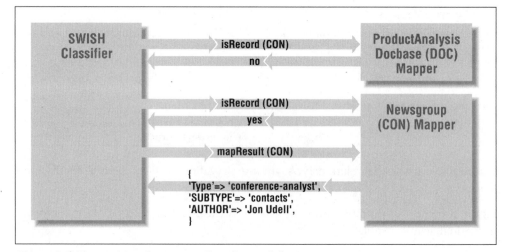

Figure 8-6. Transactions between a Classifier and the Mappers

Inheritance and Polymorphism

Should the Mappers inherit from a base Mapper class that abstracts their common behavior? That sounds reasonable, but let's first write a Mapper to see how it interacts with the Classifiers. Example 8-5 presents *Search::ProductAnalysisMapper*.

Example 8-5. The Mapper for ProductAnalysis Records

```perl
#! /usr/bin/perl -w

use strict;

package Search::ProductAnalysisMapper;

my $app = "ProductAnalysis";
my $docbase_type = "Docbase-$app";

use Docbase::Docbase;
my $db = Docbase::Docbase->new($app);


my $basepath     = "$db->{docbase_web_absolute}/$app/docs/";
my $indexed_fields = $db->getDefaultValue('indexed_fields');
my $cgi_prefix = "http://hostname" .  "$db->{docbase_cgi_relative}";

sub new
  {
  my ($pkg) = @_;
  my $self = {'type' => 'ProductAnalysis'};
  bless $self,$pkg;
  return $self;
  }

sub isRecord                       # look for my docbase signature
  {
  my ($self,$record) = @_;
  return ( $record =~ m#($basepath)# );
  }

sub mapResult                      # map pathname, doctitle into LoH
  {
  my ($self,$pathname,$doctitle) = @_;
  my $result = {};
  $result = fieldsFromPathname($result,$pathname);
  $result = fieldsFromDoctitle($result,$doctitle);
  $result = fieldsViaPathname($result,$pathname);
  $result = fieldsFromDocbase($result);
  return $result;
  }

sub fieldsFromDoctitle             # extract info from doctitle
  {
  my ($result,$doctitle) = @_;
```

Example 8-5. The Mapper for ProductAnalysis Records (continued)

```perl
  my ($company, $product, $title) = split(/    \|  /,$doctitle);
  $result->{SUBTYPE} = $company;
  $result->{TITLE} = "$product | $title";
  return $result;
  }

sub fieldsFromPathname                    # extract info from pathname
  {
  my ($result,$pathname) = @_;
  $pathname =~ m#($basepath)(.{10,10})#;
  $result->{DATE} = $2;
  $result->{PATH} = $pathname;
  return $result;
  }

sub fieldsViaPathname                     # extract info from file
  {
  my ($result,$pathname) = @_;
  my $metafields = $db->getMetadata($pathname);
  $result->{AUTHOR} = $metafields->{analyst};
  open(F,$pathname) or die "cannot open $pathname $!";
  my $summary = '';
  while (<F>)
    {
    if ( m#<td align=\"left\" class=\"summary\">([^<]+)</td>#i )
      {
      $summary = $1;
      last;
      }
    }
  close F;
  $result->{SUMMARY} = $summary;
  return $result;
  }

sub fieldsFromDocbase                     # supply docbase-specific info
  {
  my $result = shift;
  $result->{TYPE} = $docbase_type;
  $result->{PATH} =~ m#docs/([^\.]+)#;
  my $recnum = $1;
  $result->{URL}  =
      "$cgi_prefix/doc-view.pl?app=$app&index=$indexed_fields->[0]&doc=$recnum";
  return $result;
  }

1;
```

Anatomy of a Mapper

The $basepath variable captures the invariant essence of the docbase. No matter which engine indexed a given record, the search result will contain this pattern.

Well, that's not quite true. The basepath may vary from engine to engine depending on whether, or at what point, it converts a filesystem-oriented path into a web-server-oriented path. But we can safely assume that we can synchronize our Mappers on one or the other of these styles. It won't matter which, because in either case the Mapper will form the final URL.

The *isRecord()* method answers the question: "Does this raw search result contain the docbase signature of my class?" The *mapResult()* method receives a pathname and a doctitle that, it assumes, pertain to its own class. It performs a series of docbase-specific steps to map its arguments into an instance of the SearchResults structure. Note how each of these steps—*fieldsFromPathname()*, *fieldsFromDoctitle()*, *fieldsViaDoctitle()*—both receives and hands back a hashtable. Each of these methods specializes in a different data source. The hashtable grows incrementally as it's passed from one data-source expert to the next. Note also how *fieldsViaPathname()*, responsible for those things that can't be found directly in the pathname or the doctitle, calls *Docbase::Docbase::getMetadata()* to fill the AUTHOR slot. When all the data-source experts have run, *mapResult()* returns the completed hashtable.

What, if anything, might *Search::ProductAnalysisMapper* inherit from a hypothetical base class called *Search::Mapper*? The Mapper for newsgroups is shown in Example 8-6. Let's see what commonality emerges.

Example 8-6. The Mapper for Newsgroup Search Results

```
use strict;

package Search::ConferenceMapper;

my $docbase_type = 'conference-analyst';

my $newshost = 'hostname';

my %months = (
'Jan','01',
'Feb','02',
'Mar','03',
'Apr','04',
'May','05',
'Jun','06',
'Jul','07',
'Aug','08',
'Sep','09',
'Oct','10',
'Nov','11',
'Dec','12',
);

my $basepath = '/netscape/suitespot/news-udell/spool/analyst';
```

Example 8-6. The Mapper for Newsgroup Search Results (continued)

```perl
sub new
  {
  my ($pkg) = @_;
  my $self = {'type' => 'Conference'};
  bless $self,$pkg;
  return $self;
  }

sub isRecord
  {
  my ($self,$record) = @_;
  return ( $record =~ m#($basepath)# );
  }

sub mapResult
  {
  my ($self,$pathname,$doctitle) = @_;
  my $result = {};
  $result = fieldsFromPathname($result,$pathname);
  $result = fieldsFromDoctitle($result,$doctitle);
  $result = fieldsViaPathname($result,$pathname);
  $result = fieldsFromDocbase($result);
  return $result;
  }

sub fieldsFromDoctitle
  {
  my ($result,$doctitle) = @_;
  return $result;
  }

sub fieldsFromPathname
  {
  my ($result,$pathname) = @_;
  $pathname =~ m#($basepath)/(\w+)/(\d+)#;
  $result->{PATH} = "$1/$2/$3";
  $result->{SUBTYPE} = "$2";
  return $result;
  }

sub fieldsViaPathname
  {
  my ($result,$pathname) = @_;
  open (F, $pathname) or die "cannot open pathname $pathname $!";
  while (<F>)
    {
    last if ( m#^\n#);            # end of headers

    if ( m#(Subject: )(.+)# )    # Subject: Classifiers and mappers
      {   $result->{TITLE} = $2; }

    if ( m#(Date: )(.+)# )       # Tue, 04 Aug 1998 13:00:49 -0400
      {
```

Example 8-6. The Mapper for Newsgroup Search Results (continued)

```
    my $date = $2;
    $date =~ m#[^\d]+(\d{2,2})\s+(\w+)\s+(\d+)#;
    $result->{DATE} = "$3-$months{$2}-$1";
    }

  if ( m#(From: )(.+)# )        # From: Jon Udell <udell@monad.net>
    {
    my $author = $2;
    $author =~ s#\s+<[^>]+>##;
    $result->{AUTHOR} = $author;
    }

  if ( m#(Message-ID: )(.+)# )
    {
    my $msgid = "news://$newshost/$2";
    $result->{URL} = $msgid;
    }
  }
$result->{SUMMARY} = <F>;
close F;
return $result;
}

sub fieldsFromDocbase
  {
  my $result = shift;
  $result->{TYPE} = $docbase_type;
  return $result;
  }

1;
```

Again *isRecord()* identifies the docbase signature, and *mapResult()* calls a series of data-source experts—minus *fieldsFromDoctitle()*, since conference messages aren't HTML documents—and returns a completed hash. But these data-source experts differ from the others in exactly the ways that define the differences between the two docbases. Can we boost *isRecord()* and *mapResult()* into a superclass? Nope. They only make sense in the context of their own modules' data and methods. Nevertheless, it's significant that these identically named methods exist in both Mappers. To see why, we need to look at one of the specific Classifiers.

A Specific Classifier

Example 8-7 shows *Search::SwishClassifier*, the member of the Classifier family that specializes in *SWISH*.

Example 8-7. The Classifier for SWISH-E Results

```
package Search::SwishClassifier;

use Search::Classifier;
```

Example 8-7. The Classifier for SWISH-E Results (continued)

```perl
@ISA = ('Search::Classifier');

use strict;

use Search::ConferenceMapper;
my $con = Search::ConferenceMapper->new();

use Search::ProductAnalysisMapper;
my $pa = Search::ProductAnalysisMapper->new();

sub new
  {
  my ($pkg) = @_;
  my $self =  {};
  bless $self,$pkg;
  return $self;
  }

sub classify
  {
  my ($self,$results) = @_;
  my @resultlist = split (/\n/,$results);
  foreach my $raw_result (@resultlist)             # for each search result
    {
    foreach my $obj ($pa, $con)                    # for each Mapper
      {
      if ( $obj->isRecord($raw_result) )           # ask Mapper to claim result
        {
        print STDERR "Found: $obj->{type}\n";
        $raw_result =~ m#(\d+)([^\"]+)(\")([^\"]+)#; # parse path and doctitle
        my $pathname = $2;
        my $doctitle = $4;
        my $href =                                 # hand path/doctitle
           $obj->mapResult($pathname,$doctitle);   # to Mapper
        $self->addResult($href);                   # add hashtable to
        }                                          # unordered LoH
      }
    }
  }

1;
```

Anatomy of a Classifier

Search::SwishClassifier creates a Mapper for each kind of docbase. For each search hit, it invites each of these Mappers to claim the hit as its own. When a Mapper does claim a hit, *Search::SwishClassifier* extracts the pathname and the doctitle. Then it asks the Mapper to map this pair of values into an abstract result instance. Finally, it calls `$self->addResult()` to add that instance to the unordered LoH that its base class, *Search::Classifier*, is accumulating.

This isn't inheritance; it's just polymorphism. If Java rather than Perl were the implementation language, we could expect to see something like this:

```
public interface Mapper
  {
  public boolean isRecord (String searchResult );
  public Hashtable mapResult (String pathname, String doctitle);
  ...
```

Then, each Mapper would begin like this:

```
public class ConferenceMapper implements Mapper
  {
  public ConferenceMapper() {}
  ...
```

It's fascinating to see how you can get exactly the same effect in Perl. Well, OK, not quite exactly. The Perl modules don't know that they implement the Mapper interface, so the compiler can't warn you if you deviate from it. But it's not hard to pretend that the interface really exists, and when you do, things work out just fine.

Plugging in the Microsoft Index Server

Included with the freely available NT 4.0 Option Pack, the Microsoft Index Server is a powerful and feature-packed search tool. It's also convenient, because it largely automates the indexing process. When installed, it registers with NT to receive filesystem change alerts and indexes on demand when the directories that it monitors change. That's really helpful, especially for volatile docbases such as newsgroups that can acquire new content hourly. Even for archival docbases, it's convenient not to have to do manual updates or to write scripts to automate scheduled updates. The simplest way to use Index Server is to mark your web server's virtual root as indexable. To be more selective, turn off indexing at the root and enable it only for specific docbases. A docbase doesn't have to reside in the web tree. If you define a virtual root for a docbase that you want to index, the corresponding physical path can be on any local or LAN-attached drive. Or you can specify a URL and use the indexer in web-spider mode. Figure 8-7 shows the setup for our analyst newsgroups.

The virtual root */analyst* maps to the Microsoft NNTP spool directory *nntpfile*\ *root**analyst*. If we set up another root for the ProductAnalysis docbase, then run the indexer, the *Property* pane in Index Server's management console will look like Figure 8-8.

Working with Index Server Custom Properties

Figure 8-8 shows that there's a set of properties for each of our docbases. Index Server has very cleverly mapped NNTP headers from the newsgroups into

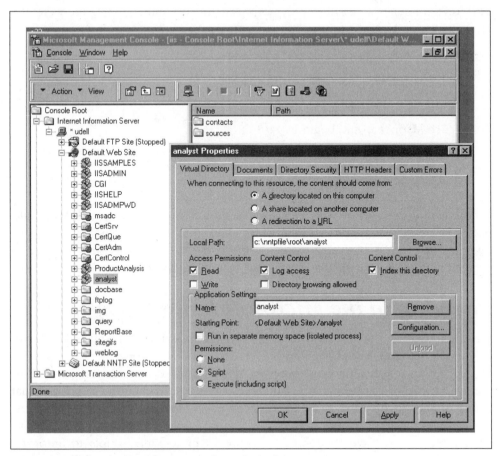

Figure 8-7. Index Server: Selecting a subtree for indexing

properties like `MsgFrom` and `NewsSubject`, and `<meta>` tags from the HTML docbase into properties like `analyst` and `company`. Note, however, that the newsgroup mappings only work in conjunction with the Microsoft NNTP service. Index Server's filter DLLs, which encapsulate per-docbase knowledge of custom fields, trigger on file extensions. The MS NNTP service, which stores news messages using names like *1000000.nws*, plays into this strategy. But if you point Index Server at a standard *INN* spool directory or at a Collabra Server spool directory, it won't recognize any custom properties.

To perform a query that uses these properties, or any query for that matter, you need a trio of related files: a form, a control file, and a results template. Example 8-8 shows a bare-bones search form, which we'll call *query.htm*.

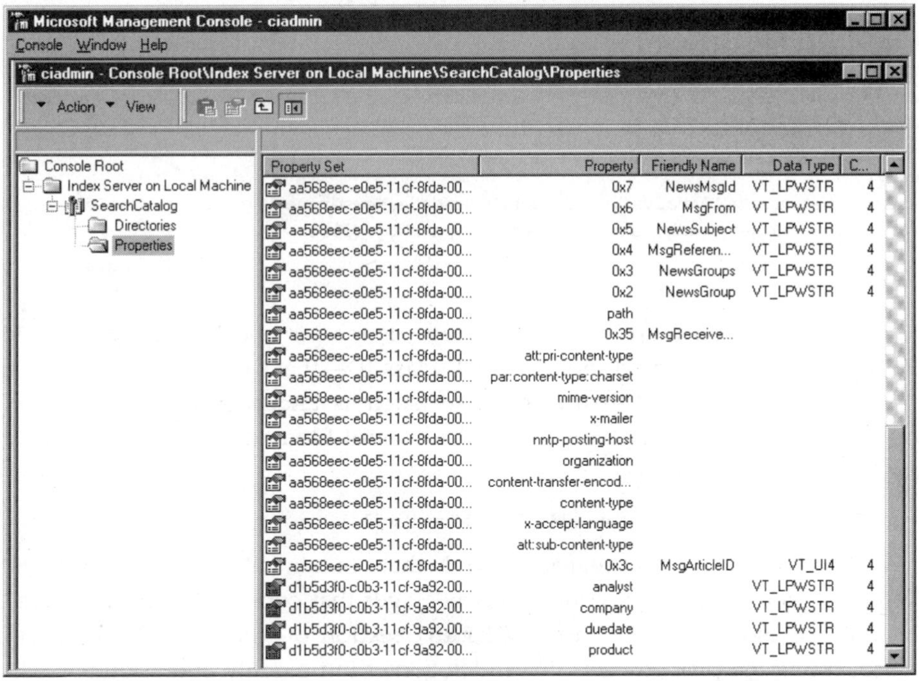

Figure 8-8. Index Server custom properties

Example 8-8. A Basic Index Server Search Form

```
<html><body>

<form action="query.idq" method="get">

<p>Enter your query:
<br><input type="text" name="cirestriction" size="40">
<br><input type="submit" value="go">

<input type="hidden" name="ciscope" value="/">
<input type="hidden" name="cimaxrecordsperpage" value="100">
<input type="hidden" name="templatename" value="query">
<input type="hidden" name="cisort" value="rank[d]">
<input type="hidden" name="htmlqueryform" value="query.htm">
</form>

</body></html>
```

The form names a control file, *query.idq*, which invokes an Internet Services API (ISAPI) DLL to run the search. Example 8-9 shows a simple version of that file.

Example 8-9. A Basic Index Server Control File

```
[Names]
PAanalyst( DBTYPE_WSTR|DBTYPE_BYREF) = d1b5d3f0-c0b3-11cf-9a92-00a0c908dbf1 analyst
PAcompany( DBTYPE_WSTR|DBTYPE_BYREF) = d1b5d3f0-c0b3-11cf-9a92-00a0c908dbf1 company
PAproduct( DBTYPE_WSTR|DBTYPE_BYREF) = d1b5d3f0-c0b3-11cf-9a92-00a0c908dbf1 product
PAduedate( DBTYPE_WSTR|DBTYPE_BYREF) = d1b5d3f0-c0b3-11cf-9a92-00a0c908dbf1 duedate

[Query]
CiColumns=PAcompany,PAanalyst,PAproduct,PAduedate,NewsGroup,MsgFrom,NewsMsgId,
NewsDate,NewsSubject,rank,characterization,vpath,DocTitle

CiTemplate=query.htx
```

The [Names] section maps the <meta> tags defined in the ProductAnalysis docbase to a Component Object Model (COM) class ID—that's the nasty-looking string
of 32 hex characters—and thence to aliases such as PAcompany. These aliases, in
turn, appear in the [Query] section of the control file and enable you to issue a
query like:

```
(@PAanalyst "Jon Udell") or (@MsgFrom "Jon Udell")
```

This query asks for ProductAnalysis records that contain <META NAME="analyst"
CONTENT="Jon Udell"> or conference messages that contain From: Jon Udell.
Why doesn't MsgFrom apear in the [Names] section of *query.idq*? NNTP proper-
ties are among the property sets that Index Server intrinsically understands.

The third query-related file, named *query.htx* in the control file, is the results template. Example 8-10 shows a minimal *query.htx*.

Example 8-10. A Basic Index Server Results Template

```
<%begindetail%>
<p>Url: <%vpath%>
<br>Title: <%DocTitle%>
<br>Newsgroup: <%NewsGroup%>
<br>NewsSubject: <%NewsSubject%>
<br>NewsDate: <%NewsDate%>
<br>NewsMsgId: <%NewsMsgId%>
<br>MsgFrom: <%MsgFrom%>
<br>Company: <%PAcompany%>
<br>Product: <%PAproduct%>
<br>Analyst: <%PAanalyst%>
<br>Duedate: <%PAduedate%>
<%enddetail%>
```

Now the CiColumns section of the control file comes into play. Custom properties can interpolate into the results page if you mention them in the template file.
However, if you run a query against our two docbases using this *query.htm/query.*
idq/query.htx combination, you'll be puzzled to find that only the intrinsic NNTP
properties appear in the output, not the HTML <meta> tag properties. The query

(@PAanalyst "Jon Udell") will find the right set of records, and the result page will include values for `<%vpath%>` (the URL) and `<%DocTitle%>`, but `<%PAanalyst%>` will be blank.

Dealing with Cached Properties

Index Server has a notion of *cached properties*, and it will only interpolate values into properties that are cached. To make `<%PAanalyst%>` appear in the output, you have to follow this procedure:

Cache the property.
In the Index Server's management console, select each custom property you want to cache, right-click it, choose *Properties*, and configure it as shown in Figure 8-9.

Commit these changes.
To do that, right-click the catalog's Properties folder, and select *Commit Changes*.

Stop Index Server and restart it.
This shouldn't be necessary, according to the documentation, but it is.

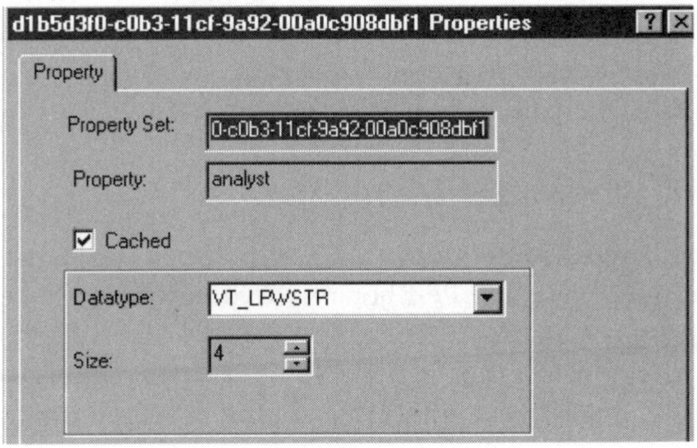

Figure 8-9. Caching Index Server custom properties

Now both the intrinsic NNTP properties and our own user-defined Product-Analysis properties will receive interpolated values in the search-results page.

Using the .htx Template Language

Index Server's query system is flexible, but not flexible enough to accommodate the multidocbase architecture we've designed in this chapter. Although the *.htx* template is programmable, there are limits to what it can do. Here's how you can

attack the problem of mapping results to the kind of abstract structure we've
defined for our SearchResults module:

```
<% if NewsMsgId eq "" %>     <!-- it's a ProductAnalysis record -->
   <br>   TYPE: Docbase-ProductAnalysis
   <br>SUBTYPE: <%PAcompany%>
   <br> AUTHOR: <%PAanalyst%>
<% else %>                   <!-- it's a conference record -->
   <br>   TYPE: Conference-analyst
   <br>SUBTYPE: <%Newsgroup%>
   <br> AUTHOR: <%MsgFrom%>
<% endif %>
```

This sort of works, because Index Server's aggressive approach to custom properties gives the template language access to almost everything that it needs. We'll be
in trouble, though, if we need to dig down for something that isn't available as a
property. For example, in the ProductAnalysis docbase, we could map SUMMARY to
<%Characterization%>. Index Server loads that property with the first few hun-
dred characters from each document. But in fact, this docbase affords a more pre-
cise mapping—to the CSS-tagged summary section of each record. The *.htx*
template language can't go after that data. There's another limitation, too. Note
how the query form in Example 8-8 assigns the value rank[d] to the hidden variable CiSort. That tells Index Server to sort results in descending order by relevance. Quite conveniently, we could change that to NewsDate[d] to sort
conference records by date. But there's no way to accommodate the date style of
the ProductAnalysis docbase. Nor, for that matter, can the *.htx* template language
extract the date from the pathname that includes it.

Querying the Result Set Using SQL

An Active Server Pages (ASP) script can manipulate Index Server query results
much more effectively. Like the Perl library we've developed, a server-based ASP
script can parse the pathname, extract the date from it, and dig into individual
result files to retrieve values not exportable as custom properties. Most interestingly, it affords a much more powerful sorting solution than the one we've
devised. Because Index Server comes with what's called an *OLE DB provider*, its
result set can emulate an SQL result set. So the ASP script can simply say:

```
select * from recordset, order by author, subtype, date desc
```

That's pretty hot stuff! If Index Server were the only search engine that mattered to
you, there would be no need to bother with the library we've developed here. But
suppose you do want the best of both worlds—the comprehensive field indexing
of Index Server and the concept search of Excite. Is there a way to integrate Index
Server into what we've built so far, without building a complete ASP-based system
in parallel? Sure. The simplest approach would be to capture its output using a

new Classifier module, *Search::MicrosoftIndexClassifier*, which would extract the pathname and doctitle from each record and then reuse the existing Mappers.

Integrating Index Server into the SearchResults System

In the case of *SWISH-E*, the search driver runs the search engine, captures the result as a string, and passes that to *Search::SwishClassifier*. Index Server's engine, however, is a DLL that you access indirectly by way of *.idq* or *.asp* files. What to do? Black-box the whole thing. The information left on the browser's command line is the key to this puzzle:

```
http://localhost/msidx/query.idq?cirestriction=%28%40PAanalyst+%22Jon+Udell%22%29
&ciscope=%2F&cimaxrecordsperpage=100&templatename=query&cisort=rank%5Bd%5D
&htmlqueryform=query.htm
```

Any URL-aware programming language can use this web interface to treat Index Server as a component. In Java and Python, web-client capability is built into the standard kit. In Perl, you can use the Library for WWW access in Perl (LWP) module to programmatically fetch URLs. Whatever the method, it's a simple matter to capture Index Server's output so that we can feed it into our search-results kit. To produce record-per-line output analogous to what *SWISH-E* and Excite emit, we can rewrite the *.htx* template like this:

```
<%begindetail%>
<Url><%vpath%><Title><%DocTitle%><Newsgroup><%NewsGroup%><NewsSubject>
    <%NewsSubject%><NewsDate><%NewsDate%><NewsMsgId><%NewsMsgId%><MsgFrom>
    <%MsgFrom%><Company><%PAcompany%><Product><%PAproduct%><Analyst>
    <%PAanalyst%><Duedate><%PAduedate%>
<%enddetail%>
```

This template produces output that's meaningless to humans but that's just right for a *Search::MicrosoftIndexClassifier* that wants to parse results a line at a time. Elements like <Url> would be poor choices if the results page were intended for human consumption. Browsers see these elements as bogus HTML and don't render them. But for a page that's only used by a robotic search-results processor, they're fine.

Exploiting Index Server's Aggressive Indexing of Custom Properties

Since the Mappers can already produce the abstract SearchResults structure using pathnames and document titles from their respective docbases, we could stop right here. But it seems a shame to throw away all the work that Index Server has already done. Why revisit the docbases to look up fields that Index Server has already found? Instead, let's expand the interface that the Mappers implement. To the methods *isRecord()* and *mapResult()*, we'll add the method *mapFullySpecified-Results()*. This per-docbase method will receive a delimited record, pick out the items that pertain to itself, and map them. Here's the ProductAnalysisMapper version:

```
sub mapFullySpecifiedResults
  {
  my ($result,$spec) = @_;

  if ( $spec =~ m#(<Url>)([^<]+)# )
    { $result = fieldsFromPathname($result,$2);}

  if ( $spec =~ m#(<Title>)([^<]+)# )
    { $result = fieldsFromDoctitle($result,$2); }

  if ( $spec =~ m#(<Analyst>)([^<]+)# )
    { $result->{AUTHOR} = $2; }

  $result = fieldsFromDocbase($result);

  return $result;
  }
```

Note that it simply reuses the *fieldsFromPathname()* and *fieldsFromDoctitle()* routines, passing along the values for pathname and doctitle that it receives from *Search::MicrosoftIndexClassifier*. It fills the AUTHOR slot with the value of the analyst <meta> tag, thus avoiding the need to peek into the docbase record as the standard *fieldsViaPathname()* method must do.

The ConferenceMapper version of this method works similarly:

```
sub mapFullySpecifiedResults
  {
  my ($result,$spec) = @_;
  if ( $spec =~ m#(<Url>)([^<]+)# )
    {   $result->{PATH} = $2; }
  if ( $spec =~ m#(<Newsgroup>)([^<]+)# )
    {   $result->{SUBTYPE} = $2; }
  if ( $spec =~ m#(<NewsSubject>)([^<]+)# )
    {   $result->{TITLE} = $2; }
  if ( $spec =~ m#(<NewsDate>)([^<]+)# )
    {   $result->{DATE} = $2; }
  if ( $spec =~ m#(<MsgFrom>)([^<]+)# )
    {   $result->{AUTHOR} = $2; }
  $result = fieldsFromDocbase($result);
  return $result;
  }
```

It gets everything it needs from the pathname plus the NNTP headers transmitted by way of Index Server-specific custom properties. Note that there is nothing Index Server specific about this behavior. Any engine that can supply a complete set of field values in response to a search can use *mapFullySpecifiedResults()* to bypass the fallback mechanism that digs the values out of their original docbase records. Note also how the field-at-a-time parsing of the fully specified record into a hashtable-based accumulator isolates the Mapper from any dependency on the order or composition of the record. If we add a third docbase that exports its own set of custom fields, we only need to ensure that none of them conflict with existing fields. Recognition of the new fields will be encapsulated in the new docbase's Mapper. Neither it nor the existing Mappers will care whether any given field exists, and no Mapper will care where any of its fields appear in the record.

Using the optimized Mappers

Example 8-11 shows a new Classifier, *Search::MicrosoftIndexClassifier.*

Example 8-11. A Different Kind of Classifier

```
package MicrosoftIndexClassifier;
use Classifier;

use ConferenceMapper;
my $con = ConferenceMapper->new();

use ProductAnalysisMapper;
my $pa = ProductAnalysisMapper->new();

@ISA = ('Classifier');

sub new
  {
  my ($pkg) = @_;
  my $self =  {};
  bless $self,$pkg;
  return $self;
  }

sub classify
  {
  my ($self,$results) = @_;
  my @resultlist = split (/\n/,$results);
  foreach (@resultlist)
    {
    foreach $obj ($pa, $con)
      {
      if ( $obj->isRecord($_) )
        {
        my $href = $obj->mapFullySpecifiedResults($_);
        $self->addResult($href);
        }
      }
    }
  }

1;
```

It's a tad simpler than *SwishClassifier*, because it doesn't need to parse out each record's pathname and doctitle. It just hands the whole delimited record—a super-set of all the elements in each docbase—to the Mappers.

Docbase Search in Perspective

Effective search isn't only, or even mostly, a matter of choosing the "right" search engine. Use whatever comes to hand. Use multiple engines, even. It's not the engines alone that deliver high-quality search results. What matters more is the instrumentation you build into the data sets that you index and into the filters that use the instrumentation to intelligently organize raw search results.

Don't neglect field indexing. It's a powerful technique that's rarely applied. There's a world of difference between a document that mentions IBM and a document that is of type `PressRelease` and whose subject company is IBM.

Remember that the metadata strategy outlined in Chapter 6 works for you in several ways. It enables the kinds of navigational tools we saw in Chapter 7, and it also enables the kinds of smart search results we've seen in this chapter. Of course `<meta>` tags are just one form of useful metadata. You could equally well keep the same information in an SQL database.

Even if you don't store and use extra fields, don't neglect the two most basic forms of docbase metadata: URLs and HTML document titles. Search engines always return these two elements. Apply a disciplined standard to both namespaces, and you'll be able to do a much better than average job of organizing search results.

III

Groupware Applications and Services

Internet services are, by their very nature, scriptable components that can be combined in novel ways. This part shows how to build custom groupware solutions—a collaborative document-review system, a helpdesk, a group calendar, a subscriber-oriented docbase notification system—based on HTTP, NNTP, SMTP, and LDAP services. Discussion plays a key role in several of these solutions, and the part concludes with a tutorial on setting up and using NNTP discussion servers.

9

Conferencing Applications

As we saw in Part I, conferencing supports modes of collaboration that email handles poorly. But NNTP servers aren't just bulletin boards that people can post messages to. They also provide *discussion services* that custom groupware applications can exploit in useful ways. In this chapter, we'll see how you can use an NNTP server as a component that adds discussion features to two different kinds of groupware applications.

The first example connects an XML docbase—namely, the manuscript of this book—to a newsgroup. It enables a group of reviewers to comment on the chapters, subsections, and paragraphs in the book. We'll use the NNTP API, along with the docbase's web API, to implement this notion of a *reviewable docbase*. At the same time, we'll learn how to write an application that uses an XML parser to read an XML repository, and transform it into deliverable web pages. The second example adds a discussion component to a helpdesk application. The primary data store will be an SQL database; it receives trouble reports by way of a web form. But that form's handler also echoes the trouble reports into a newsgroup, so that users and IT staff can discuss them. Here we'll also use the NNTP API to reorganize the newsgroup, moving trouble tickets and their associated discussion from an *open* to a *closed* status.

Both applications show that an NNTP discussion need not be an unstructured free-for-all. You can create a framework that ties discussion to the elements of a docbase or to rows in an SQL database. These uses of NNTP may surprise you. But they flow naturally from the Internet model of programmable macrocomponents.

Example 1: A Reviewable Docbase

The online bookstore Amazon.com enables readers to review books by posting comments to the web site. Of course, all books, including this one, undergo thorough review before they ever reach the reading public. Why not use Internet groupware to support that review process? Given tagged sources that comprise a book—or indeed any structured docbase—here's a recipe for building a reviewable docbase with a discussion component.

Generate a Newsgroup Framework

Figure 9-1 shows part of a newsgroup framework, based on a draft of this book and generated by a Perl script we'll analyze shortly. The `Subject:` headers of the messages in the newsgroup correspond to chapter and subsection titles extracted from the docbase. The outline structure of the newsgroup also corresponds to that of the book. Message bodies contain pointers—that is, URLs—that lead to their respective docbase sections. This setup alone can serve as a simple framework for a discussion tied to the docbase. But it also sets the stage for a more sophisticated application based on a specially instrumented version of the docbase.

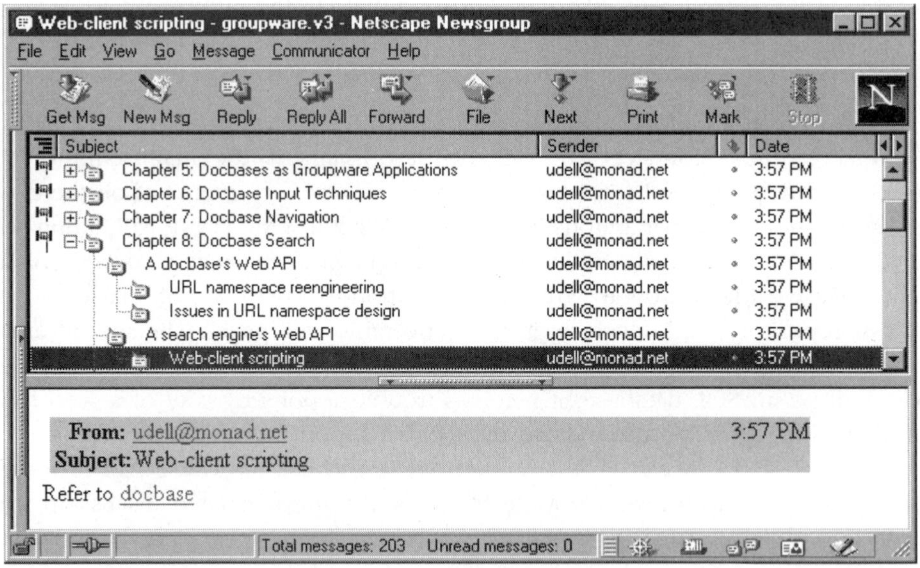

Figure 9-1. A newsgroup framework for a reviewable docbase

As we'll see, the script that processes the book's XML repository into deliverable HTML pages also builds this newsgroup's framework.

Instrument the Deliverable Version of the Docbase

Figure 9-2 illustrates the fragment of the docbase that's the destination of the *Refer to docbase* link in Figure 9-1. Note how each paragraph ends with a hyperlinked sequence number. These numbers are, in themselves, really useful. They enable reviewers to talk about "element 994" rather than "the fourth paragraph after the heading 'web-client scripting' in Chapter 8." In an XML repository, every element's end tag must be explicitly declared. That makes it easy for processing software to do something when it encounters an end tag—for example, to emit an element number.

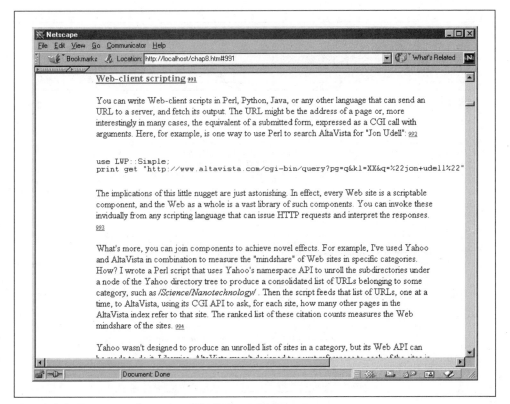

Figure 9-2. Fragment of a reviewable docbase

It's handy to be able to refer to numbered paragraphs. What's most interesting, though, is the link wrapped around the numbers shown in Figure 9-2. Here's an example of such a link:

```
/comment.pl?docbase=groupware.v3&chapnum=8&elt=994&id=925155710_156
    &fragment=Chapter+8,+Section+Web-client+scripting,+Para+994,+What%27s+more,
    +you+can+join+components+to+achieve+novel
```

The script invoked by this URL produces a form that quotes element 994 and solicits comments about it.

Generate a Feedback Form from a Template

The *comment.pl* script mentioned in the previous URL does more of the same kinds of things we've seen already: it reads a form template, replaces markers in the template with corresponding CGI arguments, encodes those arguments in hidden variables for downstream use, and emits the modified template as the HTML form shown in Figure 9-3.

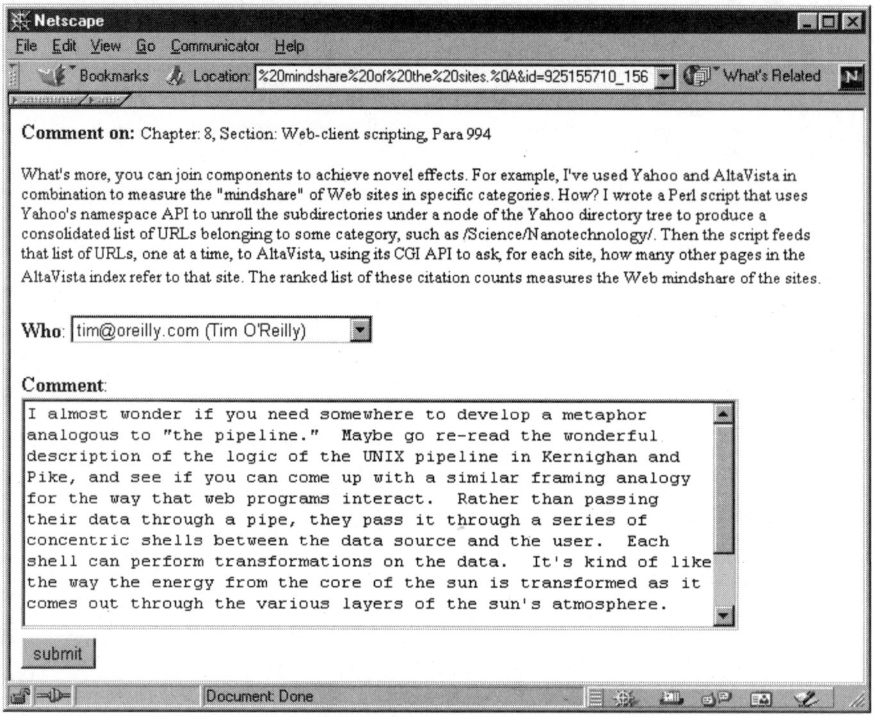

Figure 9-3. The docbase comment form

This form echoes the docbase element to which the comment will apply. The reviewer selects his or her name from a list, types a comment, and submits the form.

Inject Comments Issuing from the Docbase Feedback Form into the NNTP Discussion Framework

The handler for the comment form constructs an NNTP message that includes the chapter number, the NNTP message ID of the newsgroup message to which the comment should attach as a response, the reviewer's name, the text being commented upon, and the comment itself. Figure 9-4 shows the state of the newsgroup after a comment has been posted.

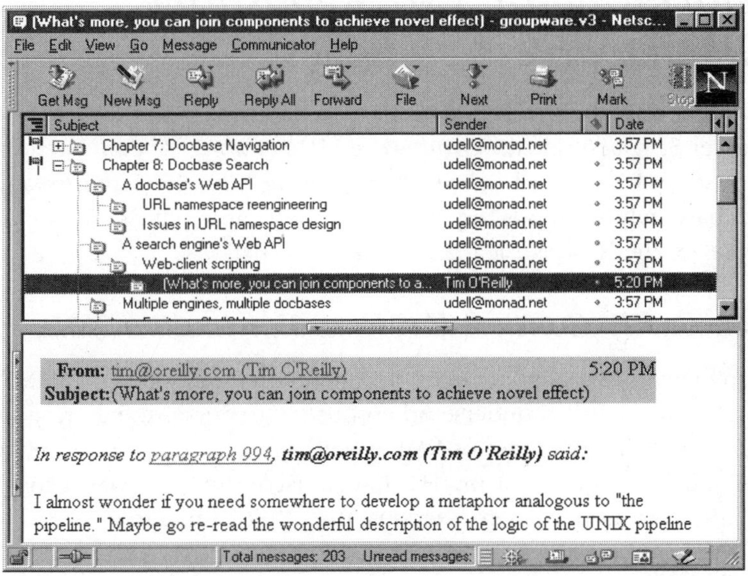

Figure 9-4. Discussion framework with attached comments

A comment posted automatically from the form attaches neatly to its appropriate spot in the framework. Note, though, that users can also comment on a docbase section by replying directly to its corresponding placeholder message in the framework, without using the docbase's comment form. That means they can violate the outline by posting new top-level messages or attaching responses to incorrect placeholders.

Should the outline be more tightly controlled? It could be. Chapter 13, *Deploying NNTP Discussion Servers*, shows how newsgroup authentication works. You could use these techniques to ensure that a newsgroup would accept postings only from a web-based agent and never from an interactive user. Should you? That depends. Document review typically involves small teams of collaborators. Often the best policy may be to provide a framework that organizes the discussion while still allowing communication to flow freely. I'd recommend trying that approach first. The point, after all, is to encourage discussion. You want people to be free to respond to one another's comments.

Now that you've seen the application, let's explore how it works. To do that, we need to follow two intertwined threads. In one, we'll use an XML-parser-based script to read XML sources and write HTML pages. In the other, we'll link those generated pages to a hybrid application that has a web frontend and an NNTP backend. We'll tackle the XML part first.

Transforming an XML Repository into Reviewable Web Pages

I began writing this book in HTML, then switched midstream to XML. Using terms from Chapter 5, *Docbases as Groupware Applications*, I converted a docbase whose repository format and delivery format were both the same stream of HTML into a docbase whose repository format is XML and whose delivery format is HTML. Here are the lessons I learned when I did that.

You Can Easily Convert HTML to Equivalent XML

XML doesn't have to involve complex document type definitions (DTDs) written in weird syntax that's hard to understand and use. Of course, there are good reasons to use DTDs, but the inventors of XML wisely chose to make them optional. As a result, the initial conversion of my HTML manuscript to XML was a trivial exercise that took just a few hours. There were just three rules I had to apply:

- Close all tags.
- Quote all attributes.
- Escape ampersands.

I used keystroke macros in my text editor to add end tags to `<p>`, `<li>`, and `<img>` elements. To close an empty tag such as `<img>`—that is, a tag that has no content other than its attributes—you need only precede the trailing angle bracket with a forward slash, like this:

```
<img src="fig2.gif"/>
```

I also used search-and-replace to escape the ampersand (&), which in XML is written as `&amp;`. This applies to invidual ampersands as well as those that introduce HTML entities such as `&lt;` and `&gt;`, which represent < and >.

This XML-ized flavor of HTML now has its own acronym: XHTML (Extensible HyperText Markup Language, *http://www.w3.org/TR/xhtml1/*). And there are XML editors, including SoftQuad's XMetaL (*http://www.softquad.com/*) and the W3C's test-bed browser, *Amaya* (*http://www.w3c.org/amaya/*), that support XHTML. You can use these to convert HTML to its equivalent XHTML or to write XHTML directly.

XML Means No More Custom Parsing Code

The docbase applications we've seen thus far required trivial kinds of parsing. If you only need to extract `<meta>` tag information from a docbase, as does *Docbase::Docbase::getMetadata()* in Chapter 6, *Docbase Input Techniques*, it's probably overkill to use an XML parser. Simple Perl scripts work well for simple parsing problems. But to add the feedback mechanisms we're building here requires a deeper and more complete understanding of the docbase's structure.

If you find yourself writing code to parse complex structures, you should rethink your approach. XML parsers that can do this for you are freely available (see, for example, *http://www.xml.com/*). These parsers won't write your application for you. It's up to your code to do something useful with the tags, attributes, and text chunks recognized by the parser. But the recognition itself can and should reside in an off-the-shelf component that you plug into your application

Perl's XML::Parser Module Is Really Useful

Parsers based on C and Java were available long before Perl's *XML::Parser* module was. They worked well, but I wasn't very productive with these tools. When you add value to an XML repository, what matters most is rapid development and capable text processing. These are of course two of the outstanding qualities of Perl. The advent of a Perl-based XML parser rewrote the productivity equation for me.

XML and HTML Can Fruitfully Coincide

One of the exciting things about XML is that you can invent your own tags. So you can, for example, replace HTML's meager set of six header tags—`<h1>` through `<h6>`—with meaningful names like `<section>`, `<chapter>`, and `<figure>`. But just because you can doesn't mean you have to. In an HTML-oriented world, you'll need to convert these logical constructs into the kinds of tags that browsers can render. Standards that address this problem include Document Style Semantics and Specification Language (DSSSL) and—the current favorite—Extensible Stylesheet Language (XSL). Even when tools that work with these standards become widespread and standard, they might be overkill for simple applications. Consider this approach:

```
<h1 class="chapter">Conferencing Applications</h1>
...
<p class="figure-title">Figure 9-1: ....</p>
```

These are HTML constructs augmented with CSS attributes. But if the docbase containing these constructs passes muster when you run it through an XML parser—as it will if you close all tags, quote all attributes, and escape ampersands—then it is also by definition an XML docbase. In this situation, you can merge the repository and delivery formats or diverge them.

In the merged case, the "XMLness" of the docbase ensures that you can search it or transform it, while its "HTMLness" means that browsers need no XML-to-HTML translation in order to render the docbase. CSS tags that provide purely structural markers when you work with the XML aspect of the docbase double as stylistic markers when you work with its HTML aspect.

In the diverged case, the "XMLness" of the docbase is a springboard from which to launch enhanced renderings. These can retain the "HTMLness" (and "CSSness") of the repository while adding the kinds of features that should be derived from the docbase rather than encoded in it.

For example, it was straightforward to generate a table of contents from this book's repository and to cross-link the headers in the generated table of contents with the headers in the generated chapters. It was also straightforward to number the chapters and figures during the translation from repository to delivery format. Figure 9-5 shows the table-of-contents view of this book side by side with a piece of a chapter.

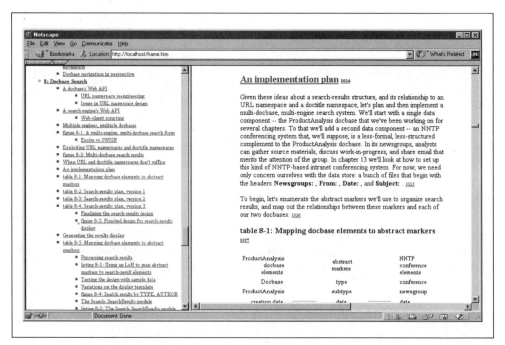

Figure 9-5. Generated table of contents

The two panes are linked in both directions. Clicking a link in the table-of-contents pane synchronizes the chapter pane to the indicated chapter and section. Clicking a chapter heading or subheading does the same thing to the table-of-contents pane. A script can do this cross-linking because even though the book's source is "only" HTML/CSS, it is also XML, structured so that it's easy to pick out chapter headings, listings, and figures. The same code uses this information again to build the newsgroup outline, which is just another view of the table of contents shown in the left pane of Figure 9-5.

A Transitional Approach to XML Authoring Has Near-term Value

This way of combining HTML, CSS, and XML is a transitional strategy. I hope it won't be needed once browsers that render XML directly (subject to CSS or XSL styles) have become widespread and standard, along with tools that help us write XML. But even in "Internet time" these developments sometimes take longer than we'd like. Meanwhile it can be useful to leverage the ability of today's browser's to directly render XML-ized HTML.

In order to build a reviewable docbase from XML sources, somebody has to produce those XML sources. In the case of this book, that somebody was me. As I've already mentioned, it was a short hop from the HTML stream I began with to the XML stream I switched to midway through the book. Of course, I've been writing in tagged-text formats for years. People who haven't, and who depend on WYSI-WYG HTML text editors, can use one of the emerging breed of XHTML editors.

Remember, too, that you can sometimes control docbase inputs using an XML-ized input template. Because the Docbase system can do that, it's an example of an XML authoring application that can reliably produce well-formed and valid XML, using the *Docbase::Input* module we saw in Chapter 6.

DTDs Don't Have to Be Complex

Even though it's easy for me to write *well-formed XML* using just a text editor, what I produce this way isn't always *valid XML*. What's the difference between well-formed XML and valid XML? Well-formed XML merely conforms to syntactic rules: all tags properly closed, all attributes quoted. Valid XML is well-formed XML that also conforms to a DTD that spells out the elements and structures that can appear in a document. Example 9-1 shows the DTD that I used for this book.

Example 9-1. An HTML/CSS-oriented Document Type Definition

```
<!DOCTYPE GroupwareBook [

<!ELEMENT GroupwareBook
  (h1 | h2 | h3 | h4 | h5 | p | ul | ol | table | div)+>

<!ELEMENT table   (tr | th)+>
<!ELEMENT tr      (td)+>
<!ELEMENT th      (td)+>
```

Example 9-1. An HTML/CSS-oriented Document Type Definition (continued)

```
<!ELEMENT ul        (ul | li | a)+>
<!ELEMENT ol        (ol | li | a)+>
<!ELEMENT img       EMPTY>
<!ELEMENT a         (#PCDATA)>
<!ELEMENT hr        EMPTY>
<!ELEMENT td        (#PCDATA | img | a | ul | br | b | u |\
   i | center | p | blockquote | tt | hr)*>
<!ELEMENT p         (#PCDATA | i | u | b | span | center | a | tt)*>
<!ELEMENT li        (#PCDATA | a | p | b | span | tt | i)*>
<!ELEMENT h1        (#PCDATA | a)*>
<!ELEMENT h2        (#PCDATA | a | tt)*>
<!ELEMENT h3        (#PCDATA | a)*>
<!ELEMENT h4        (#PCDATA | a)*>
<!ELEMENT h5        (#PCDATA | a)*>
<!ELEMENT i         (#PCDATA | a | p)*>
<!ELEMENT center    (#PCDATA | p | a | table)*>
<!ELEMENT br        (#PCDATA | a)*>
<!ELEMENT tt        (#PCDATA | a)*>
<!ELEMENT u         (#PCDATA | a)*>
<!ELEMENT blockquote (#PCDATA | a | i)*>
<!ELEMENT b         (#PCDATA | a)*>
<!ELEMENT div       (#PCDATA | p | a | b | table | ul)*>
<!ELEMENT span      (#PCDATA | a)*>

<!ATTLIST h1
    class (chapter) #REQUIRED
>


<!ATTLIST p
    class ( listing-title  |
            figure-title   |
            table-title    |
            footnote       |
            quotation      |
            UsageTipTitle  |
            UsageTip
            ) #IMPLIED
>


<!ATTLIST a
    href CDATA #IMPLIED
    name CDATA #IMPLIED
>


<!ATTLIST hr
    width CDATA #IMPLIED
>


<!ATTLIST table
    class         (inline-image) #IMPLIED
    border        CDATA #IMPLIED
    cellspacing   CDATA #IMPLIED
    cellpadding   CDATA #IMPLIED
```

Example 9-1. An HTML/CSS-oriented Document Type Definition (continued)

```
    cols          CDATA #IMPLIED
    width         CDATA #IMPLIED
>

<!ATTLIST td
    align         CDATA #IMPLIED
    valign        CDATA #IMPLIED
    colspan       CDATA #IMPLIED
>

<!ATTLIST div
    class       ( inline-code      |
                  inline-listing   |
                  inline-table     |
                  UsageTip
                )  #REQUIRED
    align       CDATA #IMPLIED
>

<!ATTLIST img
    src       CDATA #REQUIRED
>

<!ATTLIST span
    class ( footnote|
           UsageTip
           )        #REQUIRED
>


]>
```

This DTD specifies the (quite small) subset of HTML that I used in this book. Because I'd already written part of the book when I switched to XML, the DTD wasn't a prescription but rather a codification of the HTML idioms that I had already chosen to use. This seemingly backward approach might horrify an SGML purist, but it should delight an XML zealot. The whole *raison d'etre* of XML, after all, is to bridge two very different cultures: the primordial tag soup of HTML and the structural rigor of SGML. Even though I'm highly attuned to structured-text disciplines, I had always been intimidated by the thought of creating a DTD from scratch. In practice it wasn't a bad idea to just start writing, using whatever HTML idioms came easily to hand, and then discover and refine the DTD that was implicit in my usage of HTML.

The DTD's DOCTYPE is GroupwareBook. That means a document that is an instance of this DTD will have this structure:

```
<GroupwareBook>
... the book ...
</GroupwareBook>
```

The first ELEMENT declaration lists the top-level HTML tags that can appear within the outermost tag pair. The remaining ELEMENT declarations list each of the HTML tags in the book and define the elements (if any) that can nest within them.

The structure defined by this DTD is very flat, nothing like the rich structures defined by SGML DTDs such as DocBook (*http://www.oasis-open.org/docbook/*) and Text Encoding Initiative (TEI) (*http://www.uic.edu/orgs/tei/*). These DTDs are excellent tools, and you should certainly consider using them when starting a major new documentation project. But what if you're sitting on a pile of existing HTML and have users who are writing more of it every day? A simple, flat DTD such as this one can be the path of least resistance to a version of the HTML that you can manage using parser-based software.

The ATTLIST declarations enumerate each attribute that's used in the book. Again there's nothing complicated here, though the DTD does enforce some simple rules. For example, the <div> tag's class attribute is required. Further, the value of that attribute must be one of the listed options.

Using a validating parser

Perl's *XML::Parser* is not a validating XML parser. It checks only for well-formedness, not for conformance to a DTD. But there are plenty of validating parsers around. I started with DataChannel's DXP, a Java-based validating parser that has now evolved into XJ Parser, a freely available tool jointly developed by Microsoft and DataChannel (*http://www.datachannel.com/*). More recently I've used MSXML, a component that's built into Internet Explorer. I use these validating parsers to keep my book's XML sources in line with its DTD and use *XML::Parser* for the script that transforms those well-formed and valid XML files into a reviewable docbase.

Why does validity matter? Well-formed XML isn't always what you think it is. For example, the DXP parser showed me at one point that I had a <div> tag in Chapter 2, *Public Online Communities*, whose matching </div> tag didn't occur until Chapter 7, *Docbase Navigation*. Clearly I had intended to write a matched tag pair in each chapter. To a nonvalidating parser, though, two wrongs can make a right. Without consulting a DTD, it can't know that a <div> tag—as I meant to use it—shouldn't contain whole chapters or subheads. Consider this fragment that omits a </div>:

```
...
</p>
<!-- </div> This tag accidentally omitted -->

<h3>Groups need privacy too</h3>
...
```

Here's how the MSXML parser handles that situation:

```
Element content is invalid according to the DTD/Schema.
Expecting: #PCDATA, p, a, b, table, ul.
 845 5 <h3>Groups need privacy too</h3>
```

The `<h3>` is invalid because, absent a `</div>`, the still-open `<div>` would contain an `h3`—which the DTD says it cannot. When the parser sees an element that the DTD won't permit in the current context, it tells you what would have been allowed. It flags the line and column of the erroneous element and echoes the text on that line.

Although you need to install Internet Explorer to get MSXML, you don't need to use it within the browser. You can also run the parser from the command line on Windows 95/98/NT, as Example 9-2 shows.

Example 9-2. Using the MSXML Parser from the Windows Command Line

```
var doc = new ActiveXObject("microsoft.xmldom");
doc.load("book.xml");
if (doc.parseError != "")
        {
        WScript.echo(doc.parseError.reason, doc.parseError.line,
                doc.parseError.linepos, doc.parseError.srcText);
        }
```

If this code lives in a file called *validate.js*, you can use the Windows Scripting Host (*http://msdn.microsoft.com/scripting/default.htm?/scripting/windowshost/*) to run this script from the Win95/98 or NT command line like this:

```
cscript validate.js
```

Managing document structure: declarative versus procedural methods

If you're retrofitting a DTD to an HTML stream, as I was, you can use a validating parser to incrementally develop the DTD. When you start from scratch, no element is allowed until you declare it and define the context in which it can appear. Should `<h1 class="chapter">` be valid inside a `<div>` element? In standard HTML it is. In my DTD it isn't, because I reserved `<div>` exclusively as a container for figures and listings. Neither is plain `<h1>` valid. I reserve it exclusively for chapter heads, and its `ATTLIST` declaration in the DTD requires a `class` attribute.

Example 9-1 is full of compromises. A pure XML approach might use `<figure-title>` rather than `<div class="figure-title">`. In that case, the DTD could enforce a more complete definition of a figure, for example:

```
<!ELEMENT figure (figure-title, figure-body, figure-caption)>
```

But how are you going to display this construct? For the current installed base of browsers, you'd have to write parser-based code to translate these elements into

HTML, possibly augmented with CSS. Both 5.x browsers can now associate XML constructs directly with CSS styles but at the time of writing (summer 1999) this remains an experimental capability. When it matures, and when these browsers substantially displace the 3.x/4.x browsers, a pure XML approach will become possible. Until then, a hybrid HTML/CSS/XML strategy can help you weather the transition.

There are trade-offs, to be sure. In the hybrid case, the DTD can't enforce the previous definition of a figure. At best, it can enforce an enumeration of the attributes used with the <div> element and constrain where that element may appear and what it may contain. It's possible to enforce a richer definition of a figure. But you can't do it declaratively with the DTD. You have to do it procedurally, in a parser-based application.

Which approach is best? Neither is inherently right or wrong. This book isn't a particularly complex document, so it made sense to trade structure-declaring power for rendering convenience. This trade-off can also make sense for lots of routine business documents, such as those you can create and manage using the Docbase system we explored in Chapters 6 and 7. If I were writing a Boeing 777 manual, on the other hand, I'd want to trade rendering convenience for all the declarative power that the DTD could possibly provide. What's great about XML is that you can locate an application of it anywere along a continuum. Some applications profit by adding a bit of rigor to HTML, some by using the maximum amount of rigor that XML can provide. XML embraces both approaches and everything in between.

Final Observations on the Transitional HTML/CSS/XML Approach

Here are some final points to keep in mind about the transitional strategy I've sketched here.

You can idealize the installed base

The CSS-oriented approach aims squarely at the installed base of 4.x browsers. In that context, the XML-to-HTML translation affords an opportunity to smooth over differences between the Microsoft and Netscape implementations of CSS1. For example, I tagged listings using <div class="inline-listing"> and defined this CSS style:

```
div.inline-listing
        {
        font-family: courier;
        font-size: 10pt;
        white-space: pre;   /* MSIE doesn't do this */
        }
```

But it only works in Communicator. MSIE doesn't honor the request to treat white-space in a preformatted fashion.* One solution would have been to use the `<pre>` tag in the HTML/XML source, making both browsers preserve white space in listings. But I didn't want a temporary quirk of one browser to force me to use a soon-to-be-obselete tag, and I didn't want to have to revisit the XML source and alter those tags when the quirk eventually went away. So instead I tweaked the HTML generator to wrap a `<pre>..</pre>` tag pair around `<div class="inline-listing">..</div>`. This isn't a perfect solution. But it enables me to mark up the text as if `white-space: pre` were supported by both browsers. Once it is, I can remove the `<pre>..</pre>` from the processing script and rely on CSS.

XML-ized HTML is a lot more valuable than plain HTML

No one yet knows for sure how XML rendering is ultimately going to work. By the summer of 1999, browser support for XSL and document object models was a work in progress. XML parsers, however, were widely available. No matter which way the wind blows, you'll be better prepared if your documents are well formed and valid. Think of it as insurance. Even if in the short term you rely on HTML/CSS-based presentation services, you'll know that you can mechanically transform content—if it's well-formed and valid XML—when it comes time to exploit next-generation technologies.

DTDs can't do everything

Tim Bray, coeditor of the XML specification, points out that there are always going to be limits to the structural rules that you can enforce declaratively using a DTD. For example, a Docbase application might want to constrain the set of values allowed in a `<meta>` tag, such as `<META NAME="company" CONTENT="Microsoft">`, based on a database lookup. Clearly you won't want to enumerate an entire database column in a DTD declaration. A parser-based application is going to have to do the lookup in order to validate this kind of document.

Instrumenting a Docbase for Collaborative Review

To transform an XML repository into an HTML docbase with an NNTP discussion component, you need to do the following three things.

---

* In fairness, despite this glitch, MSIE is on the whole a far better implementation of CSS than Communicator. Netscape embraced CSS late and reluctantly and has been playing catch-up.

Insert link targets into the docbase

Links in the discussion area point back to these targets, as do links in the web-based table of contents.

Insert comment links into the docbase

These links invoke the comment form, or rather the script that generates that form. The links encode the information that the script needs to produce an NNTP message that will bind to the right spot in the newsgroup and that will point back to the right spot in the docbase.

Create the initial discussion framework

The docbase's headers (h1..h6) define the desired structure. To populate the newsgroup accordingly, you generate a set of NNTP messages whose `Message-ID:` and `References:` headers correspond to that structure; then load those messages using one of several techniques. Let's consider each of these three steps in more detail.

Inserting Link Targets into the Docbase

We want to translate `<p>` or `<li>` into `<a name="252"><p>` or `<a name="1124"><li>` so that comments posted regarding these elements can point back to the right spot in the text.

Although the final solution I'll present uses Perl's *XML::Parser*, the examples in Example 9-3 and Example 9-4 use two other parsers, one driven by Java and one by JavaScript. Why? There's more than one way to do it, and that can come in handy when you're stuck. For example, when I started working with XML, I'd rather have used Perl, but the *XML::Parser* module wasn't quite ready at the time. No matter. At the end of the day, a component is just a component. What matters is getting the job done, not which programming language you use. There isn't One True Language for the successful developer of Internet groupware. This book includes examples of Perl, Java, JavaScript, Visual Basic, SQL, and C. If I had eschewed XML because I couldn't (at the time) write parser-based Perl scripts, I would have been cutting off my nose to spite my face. Value resides in components, not in programming languages.

There are macrocomponents—the clients and servers that make up the mail/news/Web trio—and there are microcomponents that can bind the macrocomponents into useful new configurations. Keep an open mind and a well-stocked toolkit. Microcomponents such as XML parsers and NNTP interface modules come in many varieties. When you need one that doesn't happen to come in your favorite flavor, try a different flavor. If you're a Perl programmer, but the component you need happens to come in only the Python or Java flavor, it may be quicker to learn the little bit of Python or Java you'll need to use that component than to reinvent it in Perl. That's particularly true in web environments where, as we've seen, parts can easily combine. In the case of my first reviewable-docbase builder, for example, links inserted into the generated docbase by a Java program invoked CGI scripts written in Perl.

Example 9-3 shows a Java-based solution to the problem of instrumenting a docbase with link targets. It uses the DataChannel/Microsoft XJ Parser.

Example 9-3. Inserting Link Targets Using the DataChannel/Microsoft XJ Parser

```java
import java.util.*;
import java.io.*;
import java.net.*;
import com.datachannel.xml.om.*;

public class parseXML
{

static int element = 0;

public final static void main(String argv[])
    {
    String myURL = "book.xml";

    boolean caseSensitive = false;
    boolean validating = true;
    boolean preserveWhiteSpaces = false;
    Document doc = new Document();
    try
        {
        doc.load(myURL);
        traverse( (IXMLDOMNode) doc.getDocumentElement());
        }
    catch (Exception e)
        {
        e.printStackTrace();
        }
    }

public static void traverse (IXMLDOMNode node)
    {
    XMLDOMNamedNodeMap attrMap = (XMLDOMNamedNodeMap) node.getAttributes();

    XMLDOMNodeList childList = (XMLDOMNodeList)node.getChildNodes();

    if ( node.getNodeType() == node.ELEMENT_NODE )
        {
        if ( node.getNodeName().equals("p") ||
            node.getNodeName().equals("li") )
            {
            System.out.print( "<a name=\"" + element++ + "\">");
            }
        System.out.print( "<" + node.getNodeName() );
        IXMLDOMNode attr = attrMap.nextNode();
```

Example 9-3. Inserting Link Targets Using the DataChannel/Microsoft XJ Parser (continued)

```
        while ( attr != null )
            {
            System.out.print ( " " + attr.getNodeName() + "=\"" +
                                attr.getNodeValue() + "\"");
            attr = attrMap.nextNode();
            }
        System.out.println(">");
        }
    else if ( ( node.getNodeType() == node.TEXT_NODE ) )
        {
        System.out.println(node.getNodeValue());
        }
    else if ( ( node.getNodeType() == node.ENTITY_NODE ) )
        {
        System.out.print ( node.getNodeValue() );
        }
    else
        {
        System.out.println ( "\nnode: " + node.getNodeType()) ;
        }

    IXMLDOMNode child = childList.nextNode() ;
    while ( child != null )
        {
        traverse(child);
        child = childList.nextNode();
        }

    if ( node.getNodeType() == node.ELEMENT_NODE )  // close the element
        {
        System.out.println("</" + node.getNodeName() + ">");
        }
    }

}
```

This Java program begins by reading the whole XML document into an in-memory tree. Then it traverses that tree, emitting element tags, attributes, and contents. It applies just one transformation to the XML source, prepending link targets to the elements that are the reviewable chunks of the docbase. In this example, these are paragraphs and list items. The code emits the XML tags themselves and all the attributes that come with each tag. Why? Remember that we're depending on this XML to be HTML/CSS as well. This book, for example, uses CSS-enhanced tags like `<h1 class="chapter">` and `<p class="figure-title">`. The transformed docbase has to preserve the tags with their attributes so that a browser can render the output as HTML, governed by CSS styles.

Let's look at another way to do it. Example 9-4 inserts link targets using JavaScript to drive the MSXML parser. And in this example, the script is embedded in a web page.

Example 9-4. Inserting Element Anchors Using MSXML in an ASP Script

```jscript
<%@ language = "jscript"%>

<%
var element = 1;

var doc = Server.CreateObject("microsoft.xmldom");

doc.load("c:\\web\\book.xml");

if (doc.parseError != "")
    {
    Response.write(
        doc.parseError.reason + "," +
        doc.parseError.line + "," +
        doc.parseError.linepos + "," +
        doc.parseError.srcText);
    }

traverse(doc.documentElement);

function traverse(node)
    {
    if (node.nodeTypeString == "element")
        {
        doStartTag(node);
        if (node.childNodes.length != null)
            {
            var i;
            for (i = 0; i < node.childNodes.length; i++)
                {
                traverse(node.childNodes.item(i));
                }
            }
        doEndTag(node);
        }
    else if (node.nodeTypeString == "text")
        {
        Response.write(node.nodeValue);
        }
    else if (node.nodeTypeString == "entity")
        {
        Response.write(node.nodeValue);
        }
    else
        Response.write ("node: " + node.nodeType);
    }

function doStartTag(node)
    {
    if (
        (node.nodeName == 'p')        ||
        (node.nodeName == 'li')
```

Example 9-4. Inserting Element Anchors Using MSXML in an ASP Script (continued)

```
        )
        {
        Response.write( '<a name="' + element++ + '">\n');
        }
    Response.write("<" + node.nodeName);
    doAttrs(node);
    Response.write(">\n");
    }

function doEndTag(node)
    {
    Response.write("</" + node.nodeName + ">");
    }


function doAttrs(node)
    {
    if  ( node.attributes.length > 0 )
        {
        var i;
        for (i = 0; i < node.attributes.length; i++)
            {
            Response.write( " " + node.attributes.item(i).nodeName + "=" +
                        node.attributes.item(i).nodeValue);
            }
        }
    }

%>
```

Because this script runs in the Active Server Pages environment, it can do XML-to-HTML conversion on the fly. This is useful, but since on-the-fly conversion can be a slow process for a large document, the technique I actually used for this book instead generates HTML pages that are statically served, or just read into a browser using the file:// protocol

Inserting Comment Links into the Docbase

Comment links are the numbered links at the end of each paragraph and list element, as shown in Figure 9-2. The text of each link is the same sequence number encoded in the link targets we just made. The address lurking behind those few digits, though, includes all sorts of instrumentation:

The NNTP message ID associated with the element's controlling header

The fourth paragraph under an <h2> header, for example, will encode that header's message ID so that a comment posted by way of that paragraph's comment link will nest under the NNTP message that represents that header.

The URL for the element

> For this book, I processed the whole set of chapters as a single XML stream. But since it would be inconvenient to view the book as a single HTML document, I carved the HTML output into per-chapter chunks. So if paragraph 253 occurs in Chapter 7, its URL—for Version 2 of the draft—would be */groupware/ v2/chap7.htm#253.*

The complete text of the element

> The comment form quotes this text so that reviewers can refer to it as they compose their comments. That form's handler, which constructs and posts the NNTP message that is the comment, uses a leading fragment of the text as the `Subject:` header of the message.

When you click on the comment link, these items enable a CGI script to generate a form that quotes the section heading and paragraph from the book, collects comments about it, and posts a message containing all this information to the reviewers' newsgroup. As we'll see shortly, there's an alternate implementation in which clicking the link launches a mail message that works in a similar way.

Creating the Discussion Framework

Controlling NNTP message and reference IDs is the key to this step. Newsreaders don't transmit message IDs when they post. It's normally the server's job to create those IDs. It assigns a unique ID, such as *35E6C779.961DE7D1@monad.net.* But if you create a message that includes a `Message-ID:` header, the news server will honor that ID so long as it doesn't conflict with any existing messages. Since you can't use a newsreader to transmit such a message, how do you send it? We saw in Chapter 5 how to use *telnet* to drive an NNTP server "by hand." There are several ways to automate the posting of a news message. Standard *INN* and most derived implementations—including Netscape's Collabra Server, but not Microsoft's NNTP Service—come with a command-line tool called *inews.* Given a file called *msg.txt* containing a set of NNTP headers and a message body, you can post a message like this:

```
inews -h msg.txt
```

A hybrid Web/NNTP application might use a CGI Perl script to pipe the data to an instance of *inews,* as shown in this Perl fragment:

```
open (INEWS, " | inews -h") or die "cannot open pipe to inews $!";
print INEWS $msg;
```

If you lack the *inews* tool, you can use one of a number of NNTP client modules. These are available for Perl, Python, Java, and doubtless many other languages that can use TCP/IP sockets. For Perl programmers, the hardest part is deciding which module to use. There are at least three available on the Comprehensive Perl Archive Network (CPAN, *http://www.cpan.org/): Net::NNTP, LWP* (which is nominally a web client but which also handles NNTP), and *NNTPClient*. Example 9-5 shows how to post a message using *Net::NNTP*.

Example 9-5. Posting a Message Using Net::NNTP

```
use Net::NNTP;

my $nntp = Net::NNTP->new('localhost');

my @msg = (
"Newsgroups: groupware.v3\n",
"Subject: (What\'s more, you can join components...\n",
"From: udell@monad.net\n",
"Message-ID: <925327035_159@local>\n",
"References: <925327035_158@local>\n",
"\n",
"I almost wonder if you need somewhere to develop a metaphor\n",
"analogous to \"the pipeline.\" Maybe go reread the wonderful...\n",
);

$nntp->post(@msg);
```

Newsgroup hierarchy arises from `References:` headers. This header, which is optional, can contain one or more message IDs. Newsreaders use this information to create hierarchical views of newsgroups. In our example, we want each message representing an `<h1>` docbase tag to omit the `References:` header. These chapter names will form the top level of the tree. Messages corresponding to all other docbase `<hn>` tags should carry a `References:` header that is the message ID of the closest ancestral (that is: `<hn-1>`) tag. A series of `<h2>` tags, for example, should all refer back to the nearest preceding `<h1>`; an `<h3>` following one of those `<h2>` tags should refer back to that `<h2>`. If the message ID of that `<h2>` is `<925327035_158@local>`, then the message shown in Example 9-5 will become a reply to it.

How should we form the message IDs? It's a good idea to incorporate a timestamp so that this batch of autogenerated messages won't conflict with any others. Since it only takes a second to generate the batch, the timestamp alone won't guarantee uniqueness. So we'll tack a sequence number onto the end of each ID. That yields IDs like the ones shown in Example 9-5.

Generating a Reviewable Docbase Using Perl and XML::Parser

I started with the Java DXP parser but switched immediately to Perl's *XML::Parser* when it became available. You can use *XML::Parser* in a variety of modes, or "styles." For example, the Tree style builds a complete in-memory representation of parsed XML content, which your script can then navigate and transform. The Stream style, which I'll demonstrate here, doesn't build an in-memory tree. Instead, it calls handlers, registered by your script, for three events—recognition of the beginning of a tag, of a tag's content, or of the end of a tag. Here's the skeleton of an *XML::Parser* script that uses the Stream style:

```perl
#! perl -w

use strict;
use XML::Parser;

my $xml = new XML::Parser (Style => 'Stream');

$xml->parsefile("book.xml");

sub StartTag {}

sub Text {}

sub EndTag {}
```

The work of transforming this book's XML source into a reviewable docbase is divided among the three handlers, *StartTag()*, *Text()*, and *EndTag()*. Let's walk through these one at a time.

The StartTag() handler

The parser calls *StartTag()* (see Example 9-6) when it recognizes a tag, passing the tag name explicitly, and a hash representation of the attributes in Perl's default hash, %_. What's that? It was news to me too. I was familiar with $_, Perl's default scalar, which magically stores the current line in a file-reading loop, or the current list element in a **foreach** loop. And I knew about @_, the default list that holds subroutine arguments. But I never suspected there might also be a default hash. Live and learn!

Example 9-6. The StartTag Handler

```perl
sub StartTag
  {
  my ($expat,$element) = @_;

  if (withinCommentableElement($expat,$element) )
    {
    print DOCBASE $_;
    return;
    }

  $comment_chars = "";

  if ( isPreformattedElement ($element) )    # work around broken CSS in MSIE
    {   print DOCBASE "\n<pre>"; }

  if ( $element  eq 'h1'    )                # new chapter
    {
```

Example 9-6. The StartTag Handler (continued)

```
    $counters->{chapter}++;                         # update counters
    $counters->{figure}  = 0;
    $counters->{listing} = 0;
    $counters->{table}   = 0;
                                                    # start new HTML output file
    open (DOCBASE, ">./docbase/chap$counters->{chapter}.htm")
        or die "cannot chap$counters->{chapter}.htm";

    print DOCBASE <<EOT;                             # emit boilerplate
<head>
<link rel="stylesheet" type="text/css" href="chap-style.css">
</head>
<body>
EOT
    }

  $tocListTags = '';

  if ( my $hdr = isHeader ($element) )          # do table-of-contents outline
    {
    $newTocLev = $hdr;
    $lastHdrElt = $element;
    $tocPreamble = "<a name=\"$counters->{element}\">\
<a href=\"chap$counters->{chapter}.htm#$counters->{element}\"\
 target=\"chap\">\n";
    if ($newTocLev > $tocStack[-1])
        {
        $tocListTags .= "<ul>\n";
        push (@tocStack, $newTocLev);
        }
    else
        {
        while ($tocStack[-1] > $newTocLev )
            {
            $oldTocLev = pop @tocStack;
            $tocListTags .= "</ul>\n";
            }
        }
    }

  if ( isCommentableElement ($element) )    # emit tag with jump target
    {
    print DOCBASE "\n<a name=$counters->{element}>$_\n";
    }
  else                                       # emit plain tag
    {
    print DOCBASE "$_";
    }
  }
```

StartTag() begins by calling *withinCommentableElement()*, a routine that tests whether the current element is contained within any of those to which comment links can attach.

```
sub withinCommentableElement
  {
  my ($expat,$element) = @_;
  my $within = 0;
  foreach my $elt ('p','li','h1','h2','h3','h4','h5')
    {
    if ( $expat->within_element($elt) )
      {
      $within = 1;
      }
    }
  return $within;
  }
```

Why do we need this routine? We want to accumulate complete paragraphs, list items, or headings for the quote that will be included in each comment link. Suppose a paragraph contains a `<span>...</span>`. We don't want the *StartTag()* invocation that handles that tag to clear `$comment_chars`, the variable that's accumulating the paragraph that contains this element. So if *withinCommentable-Element()* succeeds, *StartTag* just echoes the tag and returns.

When a new chapter appears in the stream, *StartTag()* increments the chapter counter, resets the figure and listing counters, and begins a new output file for that chapter's generated HTML.

When a header appears, *StartTag()* records the HTML list syntax (`<ul>` tags) for the table of contents so that headers will indent properly. It also records link targets for these table-of-contents entries, so the links wrapped around the corresponding headers in the generated web page can jump to the right spot in the table of contents.

Finally, it writes the header tag to the generated web page. To headers, paragraphs, and list items—those elements that participate in the commenting system—it prepends link targets. The headers in the generated web pages, and the references in newsgroup messages, point to these targets in the docbase.

The Text() handler

The parser sends all the characters it finds between matched pairs of start and end tags to the *Text()* routine, shown in Example 9-7.

Example 9-7. The Text() Handler

```
sub Text
  {
  my ($expat) = @_;
  my $chars = $_;

  $comment_chars .= $chars;                            # save text for use by Endtag
```

Example 9-7. The Text() Handler (continued)

```
  if ($expat->current_element() eq 'h1')          # if new chapter
    {
    $chars = "Chapter $counters->{chapter}: " . $chars; # announce its number
    }

  if ( my $level = isHeader ($expat->current_element) ) # if header
    {
    my ($prev) = $level-1;                          # compute parent level
    $prev = "h" . $prev;                            # form parent h tag
    $msg_id++;                                       # update msg_id counter
    my $s_msg_id = $timestamp . "_" . $msg_id;      # form message id
    $current_header = $chars;                        # remember current header's text
    $lastHdrs{$expat->current_element} = $s_msg_id;     # remember governing ID
    $lastHdrId = $s_msg_id;                          # remember last ID
    my $s_ref_id = "";
    if ($expat->current_element ne 'h1')            # if not an h1
      {   $s_ref_id = $lastHdrs{$prev} }            # make a References: header
    make_nntp_msg ( $s_msg_id, $s_ref_id,           # add an entry to nntp load file
      $counters->{chapter},$current_header);
    }

  if ( my $type = isFigureOrListingOrTable ($expat->current_element) )
    {
    $current_figttl = $chars;
    $counters->{$type}++;
    print DOCBASE "$type $counters->{chapter}-$counters->{$type}: ";
    }

  if ( isHeader ($expat->current_element))          # if header
    {
    my $elt = $counters->{element};
    my $cnum = ($expat->current_element() eq 'h1')
          ? "$counters->{chapter}: "
          : '';
    print TOC                                       # write table-of-contents entry
      "$tocListTags $tocPreamble <li>\
<span class=\"lev$newTocLev\">$cnum $_</span></li></a>\n";

    print DOCBASE                                    # write HTML doc fragment
      "<a href=\"toc.htm#$elt\" target=\"toc\">$chars</a>";
    }
  else
    { print DOCBASE $chars; }

  }
```

Note that this routine also runs in what you might think of as the interstitial spaces of the XML stream. For example:

```
    <p>some text</p>  <- Text receives "some text"
                      <- Text receives two newlines
    <p>more text</p>  <- Text receives "more text"
```

Why does the parser report the newlines in this apparent no-man's land? Because there's always an enclosing scope. There has to be an outermost tag pair—which could be `<html>..</html>` or `<GroupwareBook>..</GroupwareBook>`—enclosing the whole stream. So there really is no interstitial space.

Note how characters accumulate in `$comment_chars()`, the variable that will ultimately produce the quoted version of each element that appears on the comment form. Like *StartTag()*, *Text()* may be called within an `<li>` or `<p>` tag pair. This happens, for example, when the parser sees an inline element such as `<span>` or `<strong>`. So the *Text()* routine uses `$comment_chars` to accumulate characters across multiple calls. *StartTag()*, as we've seen, resets `$comment_chars` to the empty string.

When *Text()* encounters an HTML header—that is, an element in the set `h1..h6`—it builds an entry in a file of NNTP messages that will be used to populate the newsgroup. It forms a message ID from the timestamp taken at the beginning of the run, plus a message counter. The characters received from the parser—that is, the contents of the header—go into the variable `$current_header`. It will later be used by the *EndTag()* routine to complete the table-of-contents entry for this element. The *Text()* routine also passes `$current_header()` to the *make_nntp_msg()* routine for use as the `Subject:` header of the NNTP message. *make_nntp_msg()* also receives the message ID created for this element. And for headers other than the top-level `<h1>`, it receives another message ID for use in the `References:` header. The *Text()* routine finds this ID in the `%lastHdrs` hashtable, which it also maintains. In the case of an `<h3>` header, for example, it looks up `$lastHdrs{h2}` to find the ID of the `<h3>`'s parent.

The *Text()* routine could post NNTP messages as it creates them, but instead it just builds a file that looks like Example 9-8:

Example 9-8. An NNTP Load File to Create the Discussion Framework

```
From: udell@monad.net
Message-ID: <925224566_151@local>
Subject: Chapter 8: Docbase Search
Newsgroups: groupware.v3
Content-type: text/html

Refer to <a href="http://localhost/.//chap8.htm#969">docbase</a>

From: udell@monad.net
Message-ID: <925224566_152@local>
Subject: A docbase's Web API
Newsgroups: groupware.v3
References: <925224566_151@local>
Content-type: text/html

Refer to <a href="http://localhost/.//chap8.htm#973">docbase</a>
```

Example 9-8. An NNTP Load File to Create the Discussion Framework (continued)

```
From: udell@monad.net
Message-ID: <925224566_153@local>
Subject: URL namespace reengineering
Newsgroups: groupware.v3
References: <925224566_152@local>
Content-type: text/html

Refer to <a href="http://localhost/.//chap8.htm#978">docbase</a>
```

Why a standalone file of messages? It enables pipelined processing. For example, the first version of this generator was written in Java, and the NNTP loader was written in Perl. When I rebuilt the generator in Perl, there was no need to change the loader. The Perl generator only had to target the same interface—the file format shown in Example 9-8—as the Java version had. The loader itself, shown in Example 9-9, is very simple.

Example 9-9. An NNTP Message Loader

```
use Net::NNTP;

$nntp = Net::NNTP->new('localhost');

my @msg = ();

open(F,"nntp_msgs") or die "cannot open nntp_msgs $!";
while (<F>)
  {
  push (@msg,$_);
  if ( m/^Refer to/ )
    {
    if (! $nntp->post($msg)) { die "cannot post" }
    @msg = ();
    }
  }
close F;
```

The *Text()* routine also takes care of autonumbering figures and listings by trapping elements of these types and inserting formatted numbers into two output streams—the table of contents and the docbase itself. Finally, it emits the characters received from the parser—wrapping a table-of-contents link around header text to create the other half of the table-of-contents/chapter cross-linkage.

The EndTag handler

The *EndTag()* routine (Example 9-10) adds the instrumented comment link to each commentable element. The link's address encodes the information that the form-generating script passes to its handler, which in turn posts the comment to the news server using *Net::NNTP*. By the time the parser calls *EndTag()*, all this information is available. Before emitting a `</p>` or `</li>` tag, it writes a link whose text is just an element number, but whose address is a muscular CGI call that passes the docbase name, chapter number, element number, the NNTP message ID for this element's governing header, and the complete text of the element for quoting purposes. Finally, **EndTag()** increments the element counter.

Example 9-10. The EndTag() Handler

```
sub EndTag
  {
  my ($expat,$element) = @_;

  if ( withinCommentableElement($expat,$element) )
    {
    print DOCBASE $_;
    return;
    }

  if ( isCommentableElement($element) )                # need to add comment link
    {
    my $escaped_current_header =                       # escape current header
      escape ($current_header);

    my $encoded_chars = escape($comment_chars);        # escape current element

    if ($protocol eq 'mail')                           # email version
      {
      $comment_chars = "Chapter: $counters->{chapter}, Section:
          $escaped_current_header, Para $counters->{element}: [$comment_chars]";
      print DOCBASE "\n<span class=\"eltnum\">
          <a href=\"mailto:udell\@monad.net?subject=groupware.$version,
          $escaped_current_header&body=$encoded_chars\">" .
          $counters->{element} . "</a></span>";
      }
    else                                               # nntp version
      {
      $comment_chars = "Chapter: $counters->{chapter}, Section: $current_header,
          Para $counters->{element}<p>$comment_chars";
      print DOCBASE "\n<span class=\"eltnum\">
          <a href=\"http://$server/$cgi_path/comment.pl?
          docbase=groupware.$version&chapnum=$counters->{chapter}&
          elt=$counters->{element}&fragment=$encoded_chars&
          id=$lastHdrId\">" . $counters->{element} . "</a></span>";
      }
    }

  if ( my $type = isFigureOrListingOrTable($element) ) # update table-of-contents
    {
    my $tocElt = "<a name=\"$counters->{element}\"><a href=\"chap$counters->
        {chapter}.htm#$counters->{element}\" target=\"chap\"><li>
      $type $counters->{chapter}-$counters->{$type}: $current_figttl</li></a>\n";
    }

  print DOCBASE $_;                                    # emit tag
```

Example 9-10. The EndTag() Handler (continued)

```
if ( isPreformattedElement ($element) )                    # CSS workaround
   {    print DOCBASE "</pre>"; }

if ( isCommentableElement ($element) )                     # update element counter
   {    $counters->{element}++; }

}
```

Uses and Limits of the Docbase Review Application

From the perspective of a user—that is, a docbase author or reviewer—there are two parallel interfaces to the docbase. You can start with the generated HTML table of contents, cross-linked with the HTML chapters (see Figure 9-5). Or you can subscribe to the newsgroup, where commentary intersperses with another view of the table of contents (see Figure 9-4).

The relationship between these two views of the docbase is admittedly a bit tricky. For example, to what URL should the comment handler refer you when you submit your comment? There are various possibilities:

- Back to your point of origin in the docbase

- To the newsgroup's top-level view

- To the newsgroup at the location of the header governing the commented-upon element

- To the newsgroup at the location of the posted comment

The last option might seem best, since the posted comment includes a backlink to its origin in the docbase. Unfortunately both the Microsoft and Netscape newsreaders handle the transition from web space to news space poorly, as we saw in Part I. Neither establishes the desired context in which to view related comments. So the best we can do by way of newsgroup referral is to go to the newsgroup itself, using a URL like *news://hostname/groupware.v3*. Since this maneuver results in severe loss of context, it's probably best to go with the first option—transfer of control back to the docbase at the comment's point of origin. Arguably this is better anyway, since a reviewer who has posted a comment may be more inclined to keep on reading and commenting than to take a wandering detour through the marginalia.

At some point, when the review process moves from initial feedback to collaborative discussion, the focus might shift to the newsgroup. To use it most effectively, participants should subscribe to the group when it's first created and mark all messages—that is, the autogenerated framework corresponding to the docbase's outline—as read. In the Netscape Collabra newsreader, do this: Message → Mark → All Read. In Microsoft Outlook Express, do this: Edit → Mark all as Read. This action ensures that subsequently posted comments will stand out from the framework, since newsreaders highlight unread messages. You can also restrict the view to only the unread messages. In Collabra, use View → Messages → Unread; in Outlook Express, use View → Current View → Unread.

Once you've read a comment, the unread-message views will no longer include it. How can you isolate comments once you've read them? Since all comment postings will be newer than the framework postings, a reverse date view of the newsgroup will bring them to the top of the list. You can also categorize comments by sorting on the `Author:` field.

Postings can come from two sources. The comment form invoked from the docbase is a useful way to seed the discussion with initial comments. Once these are bound to the correct spot in the framework, additional newsreader-initiated discussion can grow around them, as normal NNTP response subtrees. This mode of collaboration does, of course, raise interesting sociological questions. Who will have access to the docbase and to the newsgroup? Should some users be given posting rights to the newsgroup, others only reading rights, others no access at all? For a small and tightly knit team of authors and reviewers, the simplest access policy is probably best—and is certainly easiest. That policy might be to use HTTP basic authentication to protect the docbase and NNTP's *authinfo* mechanism to protect the newsgroup. Note that for comments that originate from the docbase, there's a kind of single-sign-on effect. Since a CGI script posts the comment, a user need only log on to the web server.

An Alternate, Email-based Comment Mechanism

Even with tight access controls, a newsgroup may be too public a venue for the kinds of collaboration that need to occur. Authors can have thin skin; reviewers must often deliver criticism; sometimes the review process works better using private channels of communication rather than a shared bulletin board. Fortunately there's always .more than one way to do Internet groupware. Why not an email option? This turns out to be a simple matter. The end-tag handler shown in Example 9-10 has two modes: news and email. They're identical except for the address behind each comment link. In email mode, the address is a parameterized mailto: URL that uses the *&body=* trick we saw in Chapter 4, *Information-Management Strategies for Groupware Users*, to launch an instance of the message

composer that's preaddressed and preloaded with the chapter, section, and text of
the target element. Figure 9-6 shows how this can work.

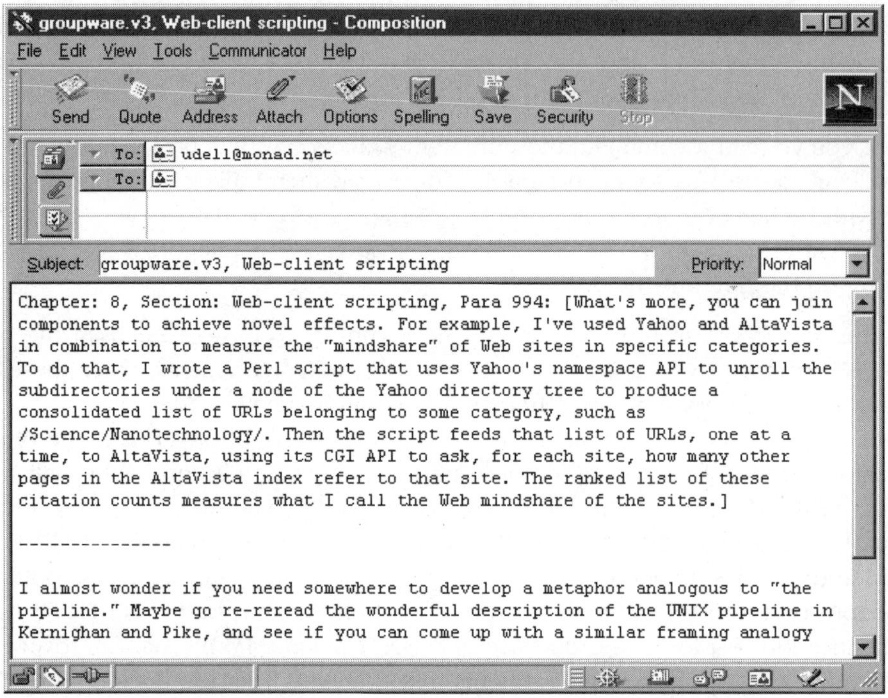

Figure 9-6. An email-based comment mechanism

Ideally the message would be in HTML format so that the quoted text could be
styled—for example, in a smaller font and a different color. Unfortunately current
mail composers cannot override the `Content-Type:` header in order to force the
message into HTML mode.

This email technique offers benefits beyond private communication. Most notably,
it requires no news server or web server. The comment form is handled entirely
by the client. Users can even compose and send comments while offline.

If you configure the docbase to use the file:// protocol instead of http://, the docbase can be viewed offline too. This approach also does away with the need to
configure web-server (and news-server) security. You can just email an instrumented docbase to one or more reviewers and receive comments as return email.
If the comment messages are addressed to a list, this approach can even mimic the
collaborative environment of the newsgroup.

Example 2: A Conferencing-Enabled Helpdesk Application

Despite the lengthy XML detour, this chapter is really about conference-enabled groupware. We've seen how to inject a docbase outline into an NNTP newsgroup, where it can serve as a framework for discussion and review. Now let's try a variation on the theme. HelpDesk is a hybrid web/NNTP application that uses web techniques to populate and view a database of trouble tickets and uses a newsgroup to add a conferencing dimension to that database. Figure 9-7 shows the form used to open a trouble ticket.

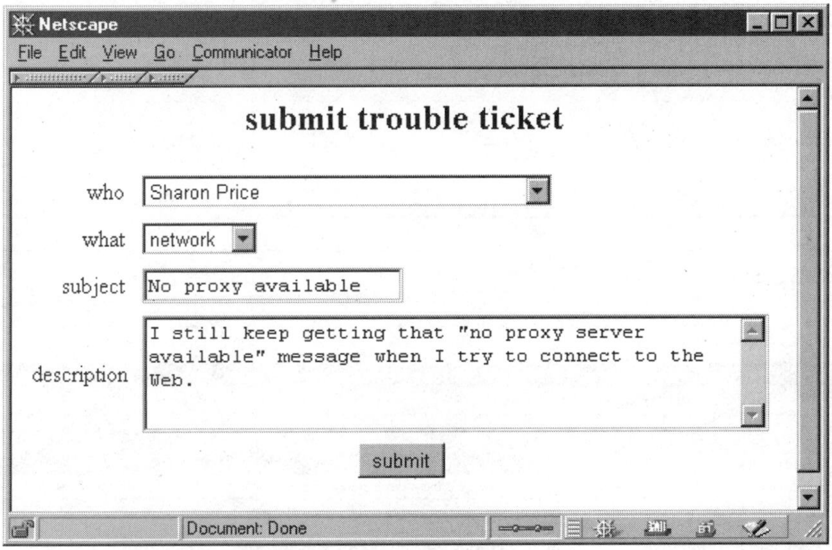

Figure 9-7. Opening a trouble ticket

The form's handler creates a record in an SQL database, which can be inspected using the web-based viewer shown in Figure 9-8.

How does the form handler connect to the SQL database? It could use any of a number of conventional web-to-database techniques. We'll look at one way to do web-to-SQL integration in Chapter 15, *Distributed HTTP*. At issue here is how to use an NNTP server as a discussion component. We've already seen how a web form's handler can inject messages into a newsgroup to create a framework for discussion. HelpDesk does that too. Figure 9-9 shows the newsgroup view that corresponds to the database shown in Figure 9-8.

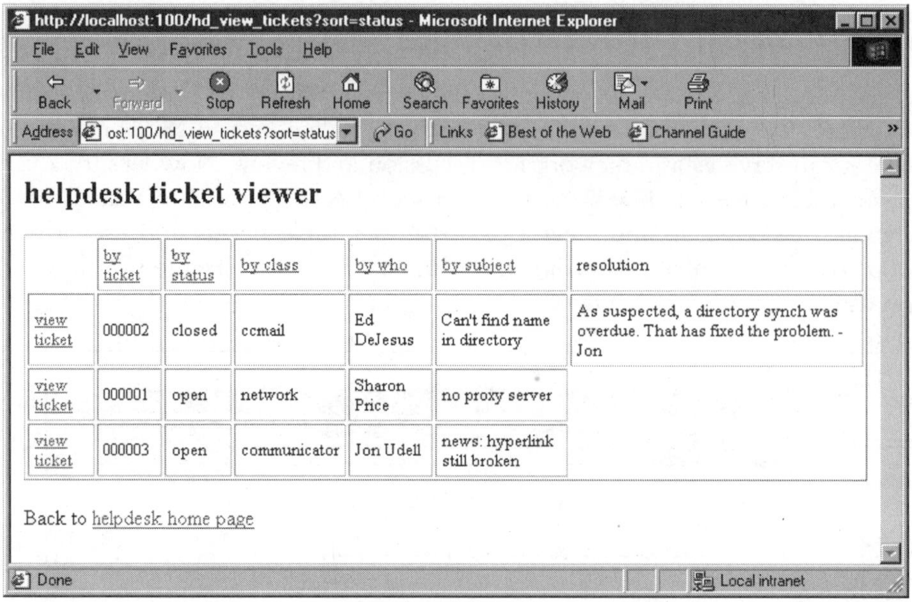

Figure 9-8. Viewing the ticket database

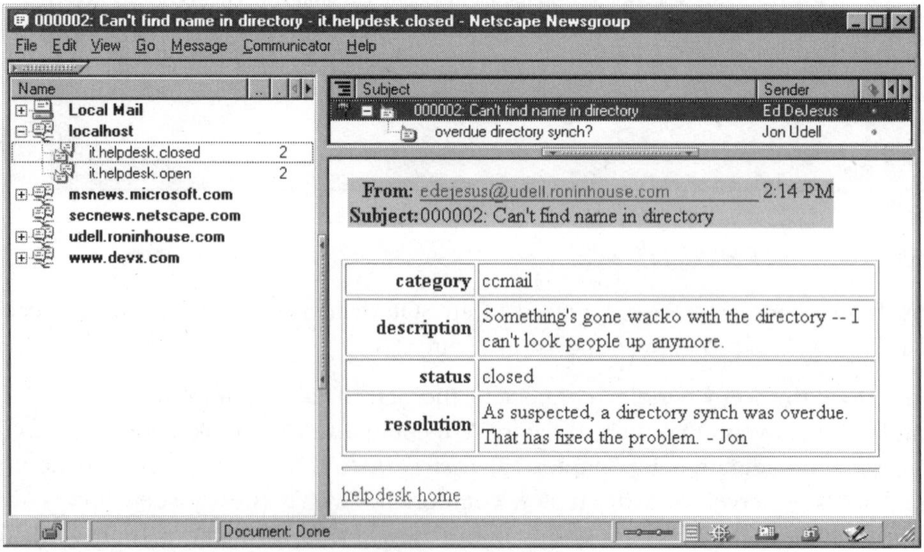

Figure 9-9. Newsgroup view of the HelpDesk database

There are two newsgroups—one for open tickets, one for closed tickets. The form handler posts new tickets to the open group; we'll see presently how they move to the closed group. As does the reviewable docbase, HelpDesk allows free-form discussion to grow around the framework. The idea here is that the IT staff needn't be solely responsible for handling reported problems. Users can and should help one another. A lot of the answers that IT staff are called on to provide are already part of the knowledge base of the user community, but that knowledge doesn't manifest itself to the community. Capturing questions and answers in a newsgroup could produce the equivalent of a Frequently Asked Questions file purely as a by-product of the kinds of everyday interactions that normally occur. Consider also the way in which a news server natively supports the upload and download of binary files. The solution to many an IT problem involves distributing an updated driver or patched software application. A private news server makes it easy to transfer these files and—just as important—to document and discuss their installation, use, and consequences.

Advanced Newsgroup Scripting

Let's think through what this application requires. The open/closed status of the trouble tickets implies an aspect of workflow: tickets begin in the open state, then can move to the closed state. And as shown in Figure 9-8, a closed ticket adds an explanation of how the problem was resolved. The Web component of HelpDesk can easily transform the database's representation of a ticket using SQL statements. But what about the NNTP component? We'd like it to reflect the changes made to the database. That will require three capabilities:

Rewriting messages
Since the framework messages include all the database fields, they should change when the database changes.

Moving messages
In the NNTP context the best way to reflect an open-to-closed transition would be not only to rewrite the affected message, but also to move it from the open group to the closed group.

Moving response subtrees
What if a framework message has grown a subtree of responses? When the parent message moves, so should its children.

As it turns out, all these capabilities are within reach. NNTP wasn't designed for these purposes, but it's an Internet-style application with a socket-based command set and a structured-text data store. Those properties make it extremely flexible. Let's explore how to implement the three requirements listed earlier.

Step 1: Rewriting Messages

We don't think twice about editing a web page. You make a change and presto! The next time somebody asks to view the page (subject to browser caching, of course) the altered page appears. If you mainly interact with replicated Usenet newsgroups, you probably don't think of newsgroup messages as changeable in the same way that web pages are. In that context, it would make no sense to rewrite one copy of a replicated message. But it's a completely different story on a dedicated conference server. There, messages are singular and unique, just like web pages. If you locate an NNTP message in its spool directory and edit the message body, the altered result will appear the next time a newsreader requests the message—subject to the same caching that affects browsers.

Of course, you have to find the message in order to edit it. As it sits in the spool directory, the message is just a numbered file. Trouble ticket 17, for example, might correspond to the file */spool/it/helpdesk/open/43*. (That's true for standard *INN* and for most derivatives, including Collabra Server. With the Microsoft NNTP service, the name will instead be something like *F300000.nws*.) Why isn't the file named 17 too? The news server allocates numbers for all messages in a newsgroup—both the program-generated ones and the user-written ones. If discussion has been lively, ticket 17's corresponding file will carry a higher number. How can we discover that number? The newsgroup is a kind of docbase. The ticket number is a controlled field of that docbase. We need only scan the docbase for the record that contains **Subject: 000017**. Example 9-11 shows how that can work.

Example 9-11. Locating a Trouble Ticket in the Newsgroup

```perl
sub getFilenumFromTicknum
  {
  my ($ticknum,$group) = @_;
  opendir(D, "$newsroot/$group");
  my @files = readdir(D);                           # read news spool
  closedir(D);
  foreach my $file (@files)
    {
    next if ( ($file eq '.') or ($file eq '..') );
    if ( ! open (MSG, "$newsroot/$group/$file") )    # open message
      {
      print "cannot open $newsroot/$group/$file $!";
      return;
      }
    while (<MSG>)                                     # scan for ticket
      {                                              # number
      if (  (m#^Subject: (\d{6,6})#) and ($1 eq $ticknum) )
        {
        close MSG;
        return $file;
        }
```

Example 9-11. Locating a Trouble Ticket in the Newsgroup (continued)

```
    }
  close MSG;
  }
return -1;  # shouldn't happen
}
```

To rewrite the message in place, you need only read it in and write it back out with changes—for example, changing the contents of the `Status` field (a table cell in the message body) from open to closed and adding some text to the `Resolution` field.

Rewriting messages in situ

In fact HelpDesk does this rewriting *en passant*, because it also deletes the message from the closed group and reposts it to the open group. It's worth noting, though, that you can rewrite messages in place. You can even extend that capability to newsgroup users. How? Schedule a process to periodically scan a newsgroup and append this kind of URL to all new messages:

```
<http://yourhost.com/cgi-bin/editmsg.pl?newsgroup=talk&filenum=43>
```

The scanning process knows that a message is new if it doesn't see a pattern like this. It knows the message's newsgroup and filename because it enumerates each message during the scan. Using this information, it can instrument the message base for *in situ* editing. The editing script, when invoked from one of these links, can read the message, present its text to the user in a web form, and write back the altered message to the news spool. Note that the script should withhold the message headers, allow the user to edit only the message body, then recombine the original headers with the new body.

Step 2: Moving a Message

The NNTP protocol doesn't include a *move-message* command, but you can build one using two existing commands: *cancel* and *post*. Example 9-12 shows the raw protocol used to cancel an NNTP message.

Example 9-12. Posting an NNTP Cancel Message

```
> telnet localhost 119
200 udell. Netscape-Collabra/3.51 11202 NNTP ready
mode reader
200 udell. Netscape-Collabra/3.51 11202 NNRP ready (posting ok).
post
340 Ok
From: edejesus@udell.roninhouse.com
Newsgroups: it.helpdesk.open
Subject: cancel cmsg <12345@localhost>
Control: cancel <12345@localhost>
```

Example 9-12. Posting an NNTP Cancel Message (continued)

```
This message was canceled by HelpDesk
.
240 Article posted
```

A weak form of security governs this operation. You can't just match the ID of the message you want to cancel. You also have to match the email address that appears in the `From:` header of that message. That's why in general you can use your newsreader to cancel only your own messages. (The procedure, by the way, is Edit → Cancel Message in Netscape Collabra and Compose → Cancel Message in MS Outlook Express.) It's a weak form of protection, because it's trivial to forge an identity in a mail/news client and thus transmit any email address with a cancel posting. Still, it's not useless. If you autopost a discussion framework using an administrator's email address, then no user can inadvertently cancel any of the framework messages.

To move a message from the open group to the closed group involves the following steps:

1. Locate and save a copy of the message file. We've already seen how to track down the file that contains the message representing ticket 17.

2. Extract the `Message-ID:` and `From:` headers from the message. Here's a function that can match and return any NNTP header:

```perl
sub getHeaderFromNNTPMessage
  {
  my ($msg,$group,$header) = @_;
  if (! open(MSG,"$newsroot/$group/$msg") )
    {
    print "cannot open $newsroot/$group/$msg $!";
    return;
    }
  while (<MSG>)
    {
    if ( m#^$header: (.+)# )
      {
      close MSG;
      return $1;
      }
    }
  close MSG;
  return -1;
  }
```

And here's a call to that function:

```perl
my $msgid = getHeaderFromNNTPMessage($msgfile,'open',"Message-ID");
```

3. Create a cancel message based on this information. Example 9-5 shows how to do that using *Net::NNTP*.

4. Post the cancel message. Use one of the techniques mentioned earlier—see, for example, Example 9-12.

5. Create a new message based on the canceled one. Change its `Newsgroups:` header from open to closed. Eliminate the `Message-ID:` header, because the news server will reject the posting if it sees an already-used ID but will create a new ID if you supply none.

6. Make other changes as needed. For the HelpDesk example, we're revising the message as we move it. So we'll also rewrite the `Status` and `Resolution` fields in the message body.

7. Post the new message to the closed group. Example 9-5 shows how to do that using *Net::NNTP*.

Step 3: Moving a Subtree

If the message that you move has attached responses, the following steps will move them along with it:

1. Record the Message-ID of the parent in the old newsgroup. After canceling it and reposting it to the new group, locate and record its new ID. Why not just assign these IDs as we did in the docbase review app? You could. But since you're going to have to look up the IDs of all user-posted messages, it's probably simpler to use the same method everywhere.

2. Scan the newsgroup for messages whose References: header mentions the old ID of the parent message. These are the responses that need to be canceled and reposted.

3. For each of these messages, post a new version. In the new version, replace the ID in the `References:` header with the new ID of the former parent. Eliminate the server-supplied headers `Message-ID:` and `NNTP-Posting-Host:`. Post the altered message to its new location.

4. For each reposted child message, post a cancel message. The `Message-ID:` header should refer to the child's original message ID in the old group.

HelpDesk's Ticket-Closing Function

Example 9-13 shows HelpDesk's ticket-closing function, which performs all three operations: it rewrites a message, moves it, and moves an attached response subtree.

This function runs in the context of a *dhttp plug-in*—that is, a service provided by the Perl-based web server that I call *dhttp*. I'll explain how that works in Chapter 15, but for now, just think of this function as part of a CGI script. It differs only in minor details from an equivalent CGI script that might run under

Apache or an ASP script under IIS. Those differences, which involve how the function receives CGI command-line arguments and how it connects to an SQL database, don't affect the meat of this routine. The point of Example 9-13 is to show one way to follow the NNTP recipes given earlier.

Example 9-13. HelpDesk's Ticket-Closing Function

```perl
sub do_hd_close_ticket_handler
  {
  my ($args) = @_;
  my ($argref) = getArgs($args);
  my ($ticknum) = unescape($$argref{ticknum});
  my ($resolution) = unescape($$argref{resolution});
  my ($msgfile) = getFilenumFromTicknum($ticknum,'open');
  if (! open(TICKET_TO_CLOSE,"$newsroot/open/$msgfile") )
    {
    print "cannot open $newsroot/open/$msgfile $!";
    return;
    }
  my @msg = ();
  my @refs = ();
  while (<TICKET_TO_CLOSE>)                # scan/convert the message
    {
    if ( m#Message-ID: (<[^>]+>)# )        # save list of msgs referencing
      {                                    # this one
      @refs = getFilenumsReferencingId($1,'open');
      }
    if ( m#^NNTP-Posting-Host:# )  {}      # eliminate this header
    else                                   # rewrite the message
      {
      s#it\.helpdesk\.open#it\.helpdesk\.closed#;
      s#<b>resolution</td><td></td>#<b>resolution</td><td>$resolution</td>#;
      s#<b>status</td><td>open</td>#<b>status</td><td>closed</td>#;
      s#name=\"status\" value=\"open\"#name=\"status\" value=\"closed\"#;
      push (@msg,$_);
      }
    }
  close TICKET_TO_CLOSE;                   # if not closed, server cannot cancel

  if (! $nntp->post(@msg) )                # post converted message
    {                                      # to closed group
    print "cannot post open msg to closed";
    return;
    }
  my ($closed_msg) =                       # get filename of newly posted message
    getFilenumFromTicknum($ticknum,'closed');

  my $closed_id =                          # get ID of newly posted message
    getHeaderFromNNTPMessage($closed_msg,'closed',"Message-ID");

  my $st1 =                                # update ticket status in SQL db
    "update hd set status = \'closed\' where ticknum = \'$ticknum\'";
  if (! dbSqlReturnStatus($main::hd_dbh,$st1) )
```

Example 9-13. HelpDesk's Ticket-Closing Function (continued)

```
    {
    print "cannot update ticket status";
    return;
    }

  my $st2 =                               # update ticket ID in SQL db
    "update hd set msgid = \'$closed_id\' where ticknum = \'$ticknum\'";
  if (! dbSqlReturnStatus($main::hd_dbh,$st2) )
    {
    print "cannot update ticket msg_id";
    return;
    }

  $resolution = prepareForDb($resolution);
  my $st3 =                               # update resolution in SQL db
    "update hd set resolution = \'$resolution\' where ticknum = \'$ticknum\'";
  if (! dbSqlReturnStatus($main::hd_dbh,$st3) )
    {
    print "cannot update ticket resolution";
    return;
    }

  my $child = "";
  foreach $child (@refs)                  # repost children of closed msg
    {
    my @child = '';
    if (! open(CHILD_TO_CLOSE,"$newsroot/open/$child") )
      {
      print "cannot open $newsroot/open/$child $!";
      return;
      }
    while (<CHILD_TO_CLOSE>)              # scan/convert message to be
      {                                  # canceled/moved
      if    ( m#Message-ID: (<[^>]+>)# )      {} # server creates this header
      elsif ( m#Lines: (<[^>]+>)# )           {} # and this one
      elsif ( m#NNTP-Posting-Host: # )        {} # and this one
      elsif ( m#References: (.+)# )      # we control the References: header
        {
        push(@child , "References: $closed_id\n");
        }
      else                               # and the Newsgroup: header
        {
        s#it\.helpdesk\.open#it\.helpdesk\.closed#;
        push(@child, $_);
        }
      }
    close CHILD_TO_CLOSE;
    if (! $nntp->post(@child) )
      {
      print "cannot post child to close";
      return;
      }
    }
```

Example 9-13. HelpDesk's Ticket-Closing Function (continued)

```
push(@refs,$msgfile);                     # add original open ticket

my $cancel_msg = "";
foreach $cancel_msg (sort @refs)        # create and post cancel messages
  {
  my $msg_id = getHeaderFromNNTPMessage($cancel_msg,'open',"Message-ID");
  my $from = getHeaderFromNNTPMessage($cancel_msg,'open',"From");
  my (@msg) = ();
  push (@msg, "From: $from\n");
  push (@msg, "Control: cancel $msg_id\n");
  push (@msg, "Newsgroups: it.helpdesk.open\n");
  push (@msg, "Subject: cmsg cancel $msg_id\n");
  push (@msg, "\n");
  push (@msg, "This message was cancelled from the helpdesk.\n");
  if (! $nntp->post(@msg) )
    {
    print "cannot cancel msg from open group";
    return;
    }
  }

print httpStandardHeader;
print "OK, $ticknum is closed.";
print "<p>Go to <a href=/hd_home>helpdesk home page</a>";
}
```

What happens to the internal structure of a subtree when you move it? It gets flattened, because a parent ID found anywhere in a child's References: header triggers a reposting of the child as a first-level response to the reposted parent. In fact, a child may only indirectly refer to the parent but directly refer to an intervening child. It's possible to transitively chase references and re-create the complete hierarchy of the original subtree. But I'm not sure it's worth the trouble.

Uses and Limitations of HelpDesk

HelpDesk's biggest problem is that it lacks a single, coherent user interface. The Web and news views refer to each other using URLs, but they're only weakly coupled. Most users would likely prefer tighter integration. The following are some ways to achieve that effect:

A Web-based conferencing system

> Using this approach, you could park the database viewer in one HTML frame and the conference component in another. Then you could use JavaScript to synchronize these two views—for example, by binding navigation of the database to navigation of the discussion (and vice versa).

A Java-based newsreader

> This solution would retain the NNTP server as a backend but replace the newsreader with a Java applet. Here, too, it would be possible—though

tricky—to synchronize the database view and the conference view using Java-Script.

A scriptable browser-based discussion widget

The kinds of user-interface controls that make today's newsreaders more attractive than web-based alternatives—notably, collapsible trees, sortable views, and rich-text message composers—could become first-class scriptable browser widgets. At that point there might be no need for a standalone newsreader or, for that matter, a mailreader.

A componentized newsreader

Alternatively, instead of moving the newsreader's rich UI into the browser, why not make the standalone newsreader a scriptable component? As I'll point out again in the epilogue to this book, it's odd that the Internet messaging clients—mailreaders and newsreaders—aren't programmable in the same ways that browsers are.

Whatever emerges, the key point is that conferencing ought to be a service that any application can profitably use. NNTP conferencing isn't the only possible component, but it's capable, universally deployed, and a lot more adaptable than you might think.

10

Groupware Servlets

In Part I and Part II we saw how the core Internet client applications—mail, news, and web—can singly and in combination enable a group to create, share, catalog, and find documents that form the basis of collaborative work. Here in Part III, we've begun to explore ways to extend the core services, using the Web's CGI and namespace APIs and the NNTP API to create customized groupware. We'll do more of this in later chapters, because the core Internet services—and in particular, web servers—are amazingly versatile components. But conventional web servers are really just specialized file servers that have been outfitted with a mechanism—the CGI gateway—to launch external programs. In this chapter we'll focus on an alternative mechanism that's more naturally attuned to the delivery of network services. Java servlets present the same kinds of web APIs as do conventional CGI scripts. They're inherently fast, reliable, lightweight, and threaded, and they can capably manage the kinds of complex data structures that groupware services typically involve. For all these reasons, servlets belong in every groupware developer's toolkit.

We'll look at two groupware servlets: *Polls* and *GroupCal. Polls,* which we saw briefly in Chapter 4, *Information-Management Strategies for Groupware Users,* is a URL-driven survey tool that you can use to quantify the sense of a group regarding some question or issue. *GroupCal* is a shared bulletin board that presents free-form data in a calendar format. Writing these two servlets convinced me that Java's best use, at least for now, is server side, not client side. The current buzz surrounding Java application servers such as Sun's NetDynamics (*http://www. netdynamics.com*) and IBM's WebSphere (*http://www.software.ibm.com/ webservers/appserv/*) supports that view. So before we look at some simple ways to deliver servlet-based groupware, let's consider why Java is so effective in this role.

Why Server-Side Java Matters

If you search for calendar software in the utilities area of URLs:*http://www. developer.com/* and similar sites, you'll find lots of Java applets that create graphical displays of calendar data. From this perspective, the user interface of my *GroupCal* servlet, which is just dynamically generated HTML and a smidgen of JavaScript, seems primitive. It's nothing like the GUI applications and components that Java can create. But is that the best use of Java?

The Web has created a universal standard client—namely, the HTML/JavaScript browser. It's fashionable to sneer at the humble browser, but it remains the workhorse of the Web. The network services that matter—ordering books, reserving airline tickets, tracking packages—are delivered using HTML, not applets. And for good reason. When Southwest Airlines sells you a ticket, it doesn't want to have to ask you to upgrade your browser or wait for a downloadable component. It just wants to send you an electronic form that will work well enough in any browser, over any kind of network connection. The Web's basic client/server mechanism isn't broken and never really needed a client-side-Java fix. Innovative, high-quality graphical user interfaces certainly do matter. But Dynamic HyperText Markup Language (DHTML) may prove to be a more practical means to that end than Java.

Java's early emergence as a browser-based portable GUI was a red herring. The job that Java is best qualified for isn't to reinvent the browser, but rather to feed it more of the kinds of services that it is already well positioned to consume. If you view Java as a toolkit for the construction of network services, its features appear in a very different light than if you view Java as a way to deploy portable and graphical client-side applications. The following are some of the reasons Java is attractive for server-side use.

Safe Memory

Buffer overruns create a whole class of pernicious Internet security holes. An oddly constructed email message, for example, may cause a certain Internet Message Access Protocol (IMAP) server to overflow a statically allocated buffer, which in turn can enable an attacker to gain control of that host. Recognizing the danger, thoughtful developers work hard to combat it. The Apache Group, for example, has devoted much effort to ensure that the Apache web server's data structures grow dynamically and won't cause buffer overruns. You can of course implement safe memory in C or C++, but it requires great diligence and above-average skill. In Java, safe memory is just an aspect of the language. You don't have to do anything special to take advantage of it.

As network services proliferate, the number of programmers involved in creating them will grow. Not all of these programmers will be able to write memory-safe C or C++ programs. Java can help offset the security risks that come with new network services. What about Visual Basic? It's true that VB programs are memory-safe. But VB alone is not very useful. As a provider of network services, it relies heavily on packaged components written, for the most part, in C++. The memory safety of these components will vary according to the skills and inclinations of the programmers who build them.

Simple and Portable Multithreading

Network services need to handle lots of concurrent requests and respond quickly to all of them. Multithreaded software isn't the whole answer to this problem, but it's a key ingredient of many solutions. Java's thread model is simple and accessible. Again this means that a new wave of developers will be able to exploit a capability that was formerly available only to a more elite group. The tricky problem of thread synchronization, for example, becomes very simple in Java, as we'll see in this chapter.

The portability of multithreaded Java software plays an important role here too. The platform on which network services run needn't be a monolithic superserver. Web APIs can stitch together a cluster of commodity servers. That cluster can be compact, tightly coupled, and homogeneous, or it can be far-flung, loosely coupled, and diverse. Either way, Java's portable multithreading can help you build responsive network services.

Network Awareness

Java's Remote Method Invocation (RMI) provides an elegant way to build distributed software. RMI was invented because JavaSoft saw a need for a simple, lightweight alternative to object request broker (ORB) technologies such as the Object Management Group's common object request broker architecture (CORBA) and Microsoft's distributed component object model (DCOM). With CORBA and DCOM, building a distributed version of even the simplest "Hello, world" program is—without specialized tools—a daunting exercise. In an all-Java environment, RMI can simplify this chore.

But even RMI can be overkill. The applications that inhabit the Internet groupware environment are, after all, just good old-fashioned socket clients and socket servers. Java has excellent facilities for interacting with, and implementing, socket-oriented applications. And its URL classes, *java.net.URL* and *java.net.URLConnection*, make it very easy for Java clients to use HTTP-based services. We'll see later in this chapter how it might make sense for a servlet, which is a provider of HTTP-based services, to also be a consumer of other HTTP-based services.

Java Object Storage

When we use web technology to connect server applications to data, we tend to think in terms of SQL databases and relational data. Java servlets can do that, using the Java Database Connectivity (JDBC) APIs, just as Perl or other kinds of CGI scripts can, using various kinds of SQL adaptors. But servlets can also manage object data. How? Using *serialization*, a Java program can write in-memory Java objects to disk storage and reconstitute those objects when reading them back into memory. JavaSoft introduced serialization in Version 1.1 of the Java Development Kit (JDK) to support RMI, which required the ability to send serialized objects over network connections. But you can also serialize Java objects to files, and that means you can create and use very simple object databases.

The servlets we'll explore in this chapter do just that. They are both, in essence, just web APIs to in-memory Java objects that are made persistent using serialization. These objects aren't constrained by SQL's tabular row-and-column format. Like Perl, Java has hashtables and lists, and can combine these to make arbitrarily complex structures—such as the hashes-of-hashes-of-lists (HoHoLs) or lists-of-hashes (LoHs) that we found to be so useful in earlier chapters. Groupware needs these kinds of data structures because it has to model what people really do, and that's messy. Relationships among people, tasks, events, and resources are complex and fluid. Forcing these organic structures into the Procrustean bed of normalized relational tables can be a painful and unproductive exercise. Object storage can model webs of relationships much more directly than SQL databases can.

The basic object persistence exploited by *Polls* and *GroupCal* isn't an exclusive capability of Java. Perl CGI scripts using modules such as *Data::Dumper* can achieve similar results. But Java currently offers a better upgrade path to real object database technology. Why would you need that? There's a limit to the amount of object storage that you can manage in memory and serialize *en masse* to disk. An object database, such as ObjectDesign's ObjectStore (*http://www.odi. com/*) or POET Software's POET (*http://www.poet.com/*), creates a kind of object cache, mapping between in-memory structures and disk storage as needed. You don't need to change your Java code to gain this benefit, because these products can work transparently with your existing hashtables (*java.util.Hashtable* objects) and lists (*java.util.Vector* objects). They also provide transaction controls and search capabilities.

Groupware needs object storage. Java servlets can manage simple object stores. And because object database vendors are creating Java bindings to their products, servlets can be easily (sometimes transparently) upgraded to industrial-strength object storage.

Servlet Efficiency

A servlet runs in the context of a host that may be a conventional web server, a Java-based web server, or a Java-based application server. In all these cases, the host keeps a Java virtual machine always running, with servlets loaded and ready to respond to requests. To achieve this effect with scripting languages such as Perl or Python, you need special and server-specific adaptations of these languages. *mod_perl* (*http://perl.apache.org/*) binds Perl into the Apache web server and caches Perl code so that scripts run with almost no startup delay. *mod_python* does the same thing for Python under Apache. ISAPI Perl and PerlEx (*http://www. activestate.com/*) likewise adapt Win32 Perl for low-latency invocation under the control of Win32 web servers such as Microsoft's IIS.

The servlet programming model is attractive because it's a standard way to do what these various script-engine adaptors achieve by very different means. *mod_ perl*, for example, is a powerful technology that I use and recommend. But it's a discipline unto itself, with a learning curve that even seasoned Perl CGI programmers must climb. Because of the way *mod_perl* embeds Perl in Apache, for example, you have to be very careful not to contaminate the Perl global namespace visible to all instances of the Apache daemon. In the servlet realm, servlets are more effectively isolated from one another, because a servlet's scope ends at its package boundary and because each servlet runs on its own separate thread of execution. And once you learn this drill, it's pretty much the same from one servlet host to the next. Servlets mostly keep the "write once, run anywhere" promise.

How much does this thread-based dispatching enhance the efficiency of servlets? That depends on several things. A Java implementation for Solaris or Win32, where Java threads can map directly to native operating system threads, may run threaded servlets more efficiently than a Java implementation for a version of Unix that has to provide its own pseudothread mechanism. However, it's not clear that the native-thread approach always wins out over the pseudothread approach. In either case, another key factor is the load placed on the servlet host. The thread-per-request model works pretty well, but it isn't infinitely scalable.

At very high levels of traffic, the overhead required to create a thread for each request becomes a real burden. That situation calls for a *thread-pool* model in which the server manages a fixed-size pool of request-handling threads. Should you worry? Not unless you plan to deploy servlets on a very busy public server. On an intranet server that handles hundreds of requests per day, or even on an Internet server that handles thousands, the thread-per-request model is good enough.

Java performance

Java servlets don't raise the same concerns about Java performance as do Java applets and GUI applications. I ran *GroupCal* in the standard JDK virtual machine

(VM) for several years; its performance was never an issue. Servlets persist, so they don't suffer from the download-and-activate lag that plagues Java applets. Nor do servlets have to push through layers of Java GUI code in order then to push through more layers of native operating system GUI code. Servlets operate behind the scenes, using network- and data-access procotols, providing network-based services that interact with other services and with browsers. In this middleware environment, the performance of interpreted Java looks pretty good.

Even though the performance of unassisted Java may be acceptable for your servlet, faster is always better. When I compiled *GroupCal* to a native Win32 binary, using Asymetrix's SuperCede compiler, the resulting servlet was indeed noticeably faster, especially for calendar searches. SuperCede was acquired in early 1999 by Instantiations (*http://www.instantiations.com/*) and, sadly, discontinued. Although other native-code Java compilers are available, including Instantiations' JOVE and Tower Technology's TowerJ (*http://www.towerj.com/*), these are high-end commercial products beyond the reach of most intranet groupware developers. The techniques that SuperCede pioneered will, let's hope, emerge in more affordable commercial products or in open-source products.

The native-code approach is vastly more convenient for a servlet than for an applet. The SuperCede product bound the native-code programs that it compiled to a special Java VM. It's no problem to run a specialized VM on a server. Browsers don't know or care; they only consume services provided by the servlets running in that VM. For client-side Java, the story is very different. A client that wants to run a native-code applet must first acquire its supporting VM. This requirement largely negates the zero-footprint benefit of client-side Java.

Flexible Servlet-Hosting Options

Pure Java-based web servers are one way to host servlets. Sun's Java Web Server (JWS, *http://www.sun.com/software/jwebserver/*), a commercial product, was the first servlet host I used. Open-source Java Web servers include *Jetty* (*http://www.mortbay.com/software/Jetty.html*), *Jigsaw* (*http://www.w3.org/Jigsaw/*), and *Acme.Serve* (*http://www.acme.com/*).

You can also host servlets using conventional web servers. Sun's Java Servlet Development Kit (JSDK) includes an adaptor that enables the Netscape, Microsoft, and Apache web servers to host servlets. (The JSDK also comes with *servletrunner*, a stripped-down servlet host that you can use to exercise servlets in a standalone fashion.) A free adaptor for Netscape's web servers is Gefion Software's WAICool-Runner (*http://www.gefionsoftware.com/*). Commercial adaptors for various web servers are available from Live Software (JRun, *http://www.livesoft.com/*), and other vendors. O'Reilly & Associates' WebSite Pro includes servlet support.

Should you use a Java-based web server or a conventional web server to host servlets? That depends on what kind of web server you prefer. Sun's JWS, for example, is a full-featured web server. It has a complete authentication model that can restrict access to URLs based on user and group permissions; it comes with a GUI administration and monitoring tool that runs as a Java applet; it can establish SSL-secured sessions with browsers. JWS is a fine general-purpose web server. But, if like many people, you're already committed to Apache, IIS, or another conventional web server, you don't need to switch to JWS or another Java web server just to host servlets. Servlet-hosting adaptors enable you to leverage what you already have while adding servlets to the arsenal of tools that you can use to create groupware applications.

A servlet host can also be a pure application server. For example, I like to run servlets under the control of *Acme.Serve*, because it's so easy to control the services provided by this small and simple Java web server. Its file-serving capability is just another servlet, which you can easily disable. In that configuration *Acme. Serve* responds only to the URLs handled by the servlets you attach to it. Contrast this with JWS, which, because it's a full-fledged web server that installs all sorts of default behaviors, creates a whole new set of potential security risks that need to be analyzed and doors that need to be locked.

The Polls Servlet

As we saw in Chapter 4, the *Polls* servlet presents a simple web API used to create a new instance of a poll, cast votes, and view the tally. Table 10-1 illustrates the Polls API.

Table 10-1. The Polls Servlet's Web API

Action	URL
Create a new poll	*/Polls?name=Picnic99&1=Sat+June+12&2=Sat+June+19&3=Sun+June+20*
Cast a vote	*/Polls?name=Picnic99&vote=Sun+June+20*
View the tally	*/Polls?name=Picnic99&tally=*

At the heart of *Polls* is a Java hash-of-hashes (HoH)—that is, a Java *Hashtable* whose keys are the names of poll instances (such as Picnic99) and whose values are hashtables. The keys of each interior hashtable are the names of the choices in that poll (e.g., "Sat June 19"), and the values count the votes for each of these choices. Table 10-2 depicts these structures.

Table 10-2. The Polls Servlet's Central Data Structure

Key: poll name	Value: Hashtable	
Picnic99	key: choice name	value: vote count
	Sat June 12	12
	Sat June 19	5
	Sun June 20	14
Preferred HMO	Tufts	3
	Matthew Thornton	11
	Harvard Pilgrim	7

In Perl, as in Java, it's easy to create this kind of HoH. But a Perl CGI script can't so easily meet the following requirements:

- Retain the object in memory across multiple invocations of the script.

- Protect the object from concurrent use by multiple clients.

- Retrieve the object from disk at start-up and keep the in-memory version synched with the on-disk version as updates occur.

Larry Wall likes to say that Perl aims to makes easy things easy and hard things possible. These hard things, though, are easy in Java. (But as we'll see, Java can also make some easy things hard.) When the servlet host starts up *Polls*, its instance data (the HoH) persists across calls to the servlet. A conventional Perl CGI script has to refresh its in-memory objects on each invocation, by querying a database or accessing some other kind of disk-based storage. An Apache *mod_perl* script, always resident in memory, nevertheless can't safely use shared Perl data structures, because there's no simple way to synchronize access to them from concurrent Apache child processes.

Making the Hard Things Easy

In Java, protecting the *Polls* object from multiple concurrent voters is as easy as adding the *synchronized* keyword to the declaration of the servlet's *vote()* method. Example 10-1 shows how that can work.

Example 10-1. The Polls Servlet's vote() Method

```
private synchronized void vote ( Hashtable hParams, HttpServletResponse res )
    throws IOException
    {
    Hashtable hPoll = (Hashtable) Polls.get ( getPollName(hParams) );
    Integer voteTally = (Integer) hPoll.get ( getVoteName(hParams) );
    int tally = voteTally.intValue();
    tally++;
    hPoll.put ( getVoteName(hParams), new Integer (tally) );
    PrintStream out = new PrintStream(res.getOutputStream());
```

Example 10-1. The Polls Servlet's vote() Method (continued)

```
System.out.println ( "Vote received. Poll: " + getPollName(hParams) +
                                  "Vote: " + getVoteName(hParams) );
    }
```

Each time you issue a request to a servlet, its host calls the servlet's *service()* method, passing two arguments. The first, an *HttpServletRequest* object, contains the CGI-style parameters passed by way of an HTTP *GET* request, plus the HTTP headers included with the request. The second, an *HttpServletResponse* object, is used by the servlet to modify the HTTP headers sent back to the client. When *Polls' service()* method sees the parameter *vote=Sun+June+20*, it calls the *vote()* method to increment the counter for that item. What if two requests come in at the same time? The servlet runs on a thread, and that thread blocks (has to wait) while executing a method guarded by the *synchronized* keyword. This technique can very easily coordinate requests to update a shared data structure.

Saving and restoring the object are trivial tasks, too, thanks to Java serialization. Java's *Hashtable* object implements the *Serializable* interface. That means you can simply open a *FileOutputStream*, hook an *ObjectOutputStream* to it, and call *writeObject()* to save it to disk, as shown in Example 10-2.

Example 10-2. Serializing the Polls Object to a File

```
private synchronized void saveObjects()
    {
    try
        {
        FileOutputStream   f = new FileOutputStream("polls.obj");
        ObjectOutputStream o = new ObjectOutputStream(f);
        o.writeObject(Polls);
        o.flush();
        o.close();
        }
    catch (IOException e)
        { System.out.println(e); }
    }
```

The *service()* method calls *saveObjects()* right after it calls *vote()*. It does this only to make a permanent record of the *Polls* object, so the servlet can reconstitute it after a restart. Once it loads the object file at start-up, though, it never refers to it. Votes are written to, and tallies read from, the servlet's own live in-memory *Polls* object. The servlet is literally just a web API to that object.

Loading the *Polls* object at start-up is equally simple, as shown in Example 10-3.

Example 10-3. Reading the Polls Object at Start-up

```
private void loadObjects()
    {
    try
```

Example 10-3. Reading the Polls Object at Start-up (continued)

```
        {
        FileInputStream   f = new FileInputStream("polls.obj");
        ObjectInputStream o = new ObjectInputStream(f);
        Polls = (Hashtable) o.readObject();
        o.close();
        }
    catch (IOException e)
        {  System.out.println(e); }
    catch (ClassNotFoundException e)
        {  System.out.println(e);  }
    }
```

After *loadObjects()* runs, the *Polls* object that was written out using *saveObjects()* is reconstituted as a live Java *Hashtable*.

Making the Easy Things Hard

This is nifty stuff. But even as it makes some hard things easy, Java makes some easy things hard. For example, the *vote()* method goes to a lot of trouble to bridge the chasm that divides primitive Java types (i.e., *int*) from their object counterparts (i.e., *Integer*). The keys and values of a Java *Hashtable* have to be objects, not primitive types. But you can't increment an *Integer*, so the *vote()* method has to unpack the *Integer*, increment its corresponding *int*, and then repackage it as an *Integer* to store it back in the *Hashtable*, as shown in Example 10-1. In Perl, these gymnastics would reduce to a simple statement like:

```
$hash{$key}++;
```

Then there's the problem of sorting the results of each poll. In Perl, you can sort the keys of a hashtable by their corresponding values like this:

```
@sorted_keys = sort { $hash{$b} <=> $hash{$a} } keys %hash;
```

For a *Polls* hashtable this yields, in **@sorted_keys**, a list of the choices ordered by the number of votes for each choice. You can then print a tally, from most popular choice to least, like this:

```
foreach $choice (@sorted_keys)
    { print "$choice: $hash{$choice}\n"; }
```

These kinds of quick, powerful data wrangling idioms aren't built into the basic Java toolkit. There are plenty of freely available libraries that you can use to sort and rearrange Java objects, but even something as basic as an ordered collection isn't part of the core language. The lesson is that Java giveth but also taketh away. Servlets are a great way to paste a web API onto dynamic, thread-safe, persistent, object-database compatible data structures. But servlets have to work harder to manipulate those live structures than do Perl scripts.

The GroupCal Servlet

As we saw in Part I, we tend to ask more of email than it can deliver. Conferencing can help restore email to its realm of appropriate use while providing an alternate venue for groupthink activities. But newsgroups, too, have their limits. A private newsgroup is a great place to share drafts of work in progress or to discuss travel plans. You don't want to go there, though, to find out whether Bob turned in the report that was due yesterday or to find out who's going to be at the conference next week.

These kinds of things belong in a calendar. Unfortunately, Internet calendaring isn't yet as standard or as universal as the core mail/news/Web services. Netscape and Microsoft both offer calendar servers—but they're quite different creatures. Netscape's Calendar Server works only with Communicator's Calendar client. Likewise, the calendaring features of Microsoft's Exchange Server, though exportable to web clients, work best with the Exchange client. The standard Internet client doesn't yet include a calendar client that can interoperate with mature, open, standard, and multiply implemented calendar servers.

Internet Engineering Task Force (IETF) committees are working to define a framework for standard Internet calendaring and scheduling (see *http://www.ietf.org/html.charters/calsch-charter.html*). Works in progress include iCalendar, a MIME type specialized to represent things like people, appointments, and todo items; and Calendar Access Protocol (CAP), which will enable diverse calendar clients and servers to interoperate. But it's early days for iCalendar/CAP products. We can only hope that the next generation of standard Internet clients will support these formats and protocols.

In the meantime, there are web-based calendar applications popping up all over the place. The *GroupCal* servlet belongs to this genre. It doesn't tackle the scheduling problem at all; it's just a shared bulletin board with a simple web API that both people and programs can use. Daily information pertaining to a user or a group is represented as chunk of plain text or HTML. Browsers and scripts can view, edit, and search the calendar.

GroupCal could doubtless be extended to support the features that today's proprietary calendar products tout and that tomorrow's open Internet-based products will also support: meeting scheduling, resource allocation, reminders, and the like. But that's a wheel that I'm not going to try to reinvent. For our purposes here, I'll use *GroupCal* to make two points about the role any calendar service ought to play in an Internet groupware architecture. First, a calendar service should double as an application and a component. It should do useful things right out of the box, but since group dynamics are complex and subtle, it should also be fully programmable. *GroupCal* is, just because it's a Java servlet with a web API. Second, a calendar service should exploit a flexible, object-oriented data model. Java servlets can naturally create and use simple object stores and can transparently upgrade to industrial-strength object databases.

GroupCal's HTML Interface

From a user's perspective, *GroupCal* is a typical Web-based calendar viewer and editor. The main screen is shown in Figure 10-1.

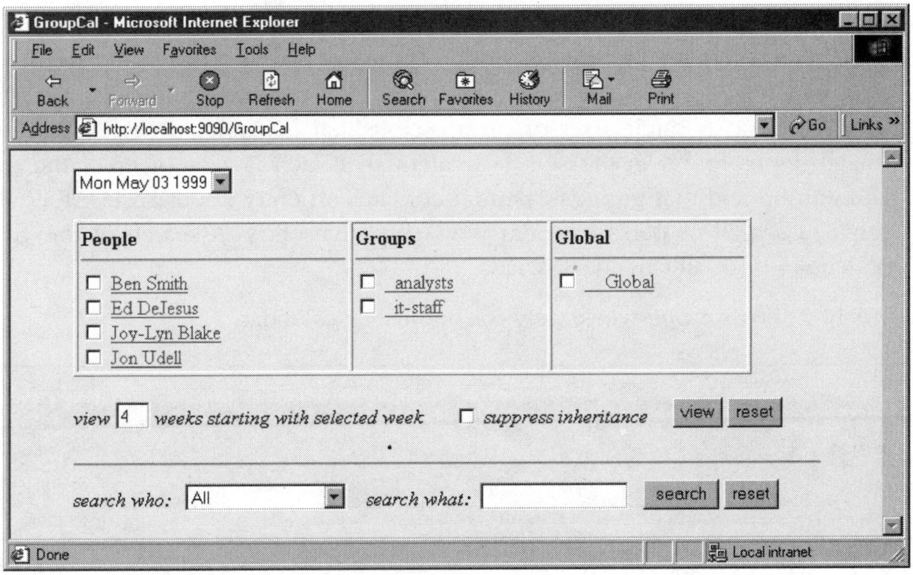

Figure 10-1. GroupCal's main screen

From this screen, you can do the following things:

Select a week.

> *GroupCal* defaults to the week that contains the current day; you can use the weeks picklist to select another week.

Select one or more users or groups to view.

> *GroupCal* maintains a calendar for each user and for each group. It also maintains a set of mappings among users and groups. If Ed belongs to the *analysts* group, then all views of his calendar will inherit entries from that group calendar. There can be multiple inheritance, in the sense that Ed can belong to two groups—*analysts* and *it-staff*—and inherit entries from both of these group calendars into his personal calendar. In addition, all users inherit from the global calendar. Entries made there, for company holidays, birthdays, or other events of general interest, will appear on everyone's personal calendar regardless of group membership.

View calendars.

The viewing screen (see Figure 10-2) presents the set of calendars selected (checked) on the main screen. Each calendar view begins with the current week and extends for the number of weeks specified in the *View n weeks* input field. By default each calendar view extends for four weeks.

Edit a calendar for the current week.

Clicking any hyperlinked name invokes the edit screen (see Figure 10-3). There you can add or modify calendar entries for the selected user or group.

Search calendars.

The search function returns calendar entries containing the search term you specify. By default it searches all calendars. You can use the picklist to restrict the search to a single user or group. Note that a restricted search will only match terms found in the selected calendar. If Ben is a member of the *analysts* group and that group's calendar contains an entry about an LDAP conference, a search of Ben's calendar won't find that entry. A search of the group calendar, or of all calendars, will.

Figure 10-2 shows a one-week view for one user's calendar.

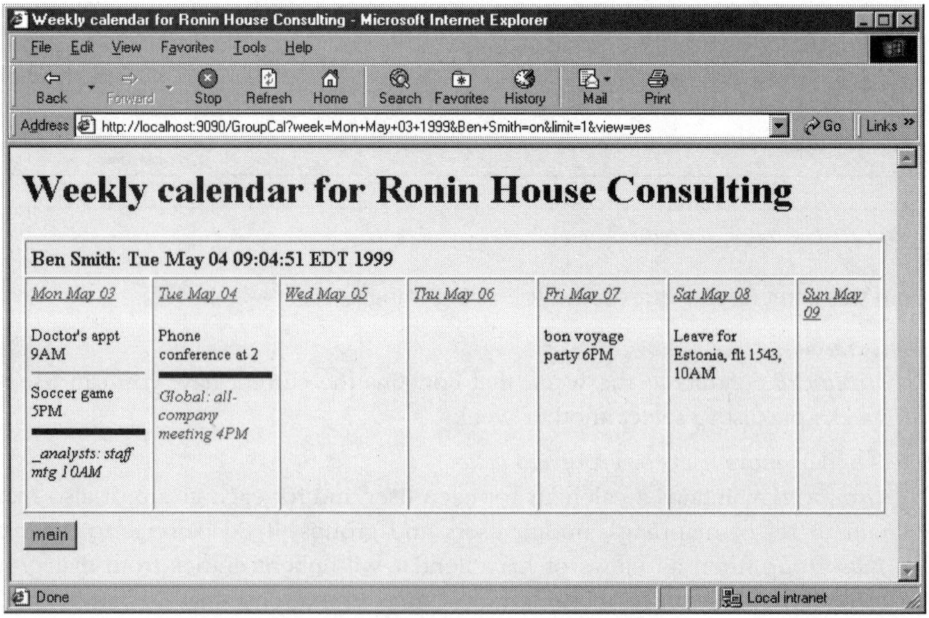

Figure 10-2. GroupCal's view screen

Note how entries from groups—*analysts* and *Global*—merge with personal entries.

Figure 10-3 shows the edit screen.

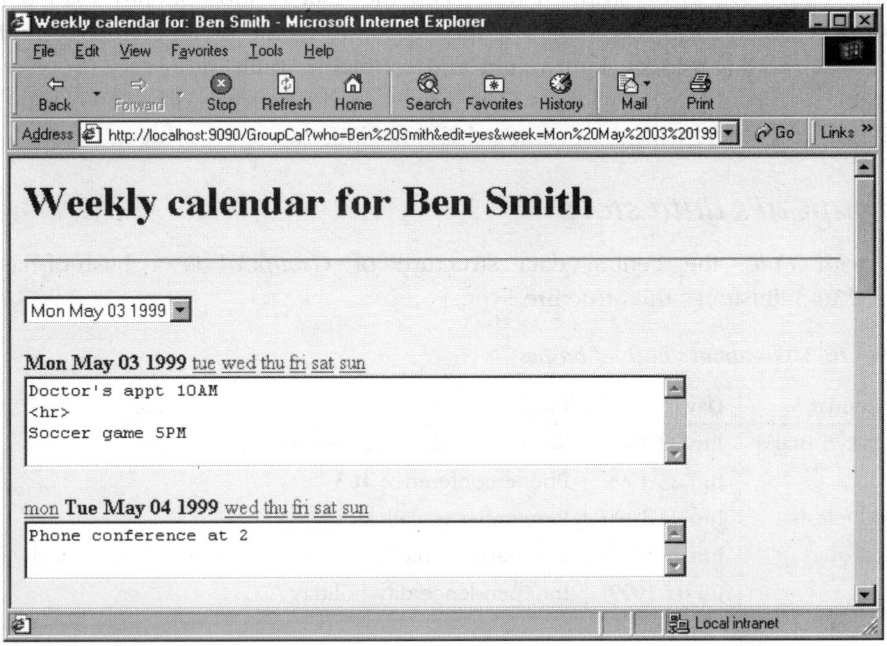

Figure 10-3. GroupCal's edit screen

The weeks picklist defaults to the main screen's selected week. You can change it in order to edit any other week on Ben's calendar. Daily entries are just chunks of plain text or HTML. There's no requirement to use HTML, but an entry more complex than a phrase or two will display more nicely if you do.

Should users write HTML?

GroupCal's HTML policy differs from the one we enforced in the ProductAnalysis docbase. There, we assumed that users should not be allowed to fuss with HTML, and we implemented some simple translations—converting newlines to `<p>` and `<hr>` tags, converting URLs into hyperlinks—to make that unnecessary. Why allow HTML in *GroupCal* entries? Partly because the users for whom I originally wrote this application enjoyed trying out a few simple HTML tags. But mainly because *GroupCal* is written in Java, which is nowhere near as effective as Perl for text-transformation work.

There are freely available regular-expression libraries for Java, and the translations implemented for the ProductAnalysis docbase could be carried over to *GroupCal* as well. The problem is a bit more complicated, though, because the calendar isn't a write-once-then-read-only docbase; it's a fully rewritable data store. That would require a two-way translation. HTML tags added to the input supplied in an entry field would have to be stripped out when the data is subsequently loaded back into an entry field for re-editing. The ideal solution would be an HTML (or preferably, XML) editing widget, lightweight and scriptable, built into every browser just as the basic HTML form widgets (text boxes, radio buttons, dropdown lists) are. Unfortunately there isn't yet a standard HTML/XML data-entry widget.

GroupCal's data store

As with *Polls*, the central data structure of *GroupCal* is a hash-of-hashes. Table 10-3 illustrates this structure.

Table 10-3. GroupCal's hash-of-hashes

Calendar	Day	Entry
Joy-Lyn Blake	Jun 22 1999	Write monthly status report
	Jun 23 1999	Phone conference at 3
Ed DeJesus	Jun 24 1999	Remember to call Aldo
Global	Jun 20 1999	Company picnic
	Jul 04 1999	Independence day holiday

The data structure is sparsely populated—that is, the per-user and per-group hash-tables contain key/value pairs only for days for which calendar entries have been made. That sparseness, along with the relatively compact format that Java uses to represent this data, enables *GroupCal* to manage a set of calendars entirely in memory. Like *Polls*, it writes updates to a disk file, but only for safekeeping. All read and write operations on calendars use the in-memory hashtables. Why? It's fast, easy, and effective. One of the delightful aspects of Java is that it contains everything you need to create a simple object store. As we saw in the case of *Polls*, you can do that using synchronization and serialization.

However, synchronization alone can't fully protect *GroupCal*'s data. It's true that by synchronizing its *update()* method, we can ensure that any thread calling that method will block if another thread is executing the same method. But the fact that updates are serialized inside the servlet, and can't make a mess out of the hashtables, doesn't necessarily mean updates are serialized from the perspective of the calendar users. Why not? Suppose you fetch a week of my calendar into an edit screen in your browser, then I fetch a week into mine. When we both click our respective *submit* buttons, the possible outcomes are as follows:

No conflict

> If we fetched different weeks, or even if we fetched the same week but modified entries for different days within that same week, everything's OK. First your edits are applied, then mine, or vice versa.

Conflict

If we fetched the same week and modified an entry for the same day, there's a problem. Buffered in a form inside each of our browsers was the same original version of that day's entry, which we have each changed in a different way. Whoever submits the form last, wins.

There's nothing Java-specific or even web-specific about this dilemma. It's just a classic problem that arises when a database record is buffered simultaneously on multiple clients. To solve this problem, *GroupCal* could maintain a list of locked calendar records and refuse to edit any locked records. Or it could always allow revisions but keep a complete version history for each record. It needn't be costly to do that. Since records are rarely edited, the data structure will remain sparse. This is a handy technique, especially if you enable users to drill down into the version history to see who changed what and when. *GroupCal* doesn't support that feature, but the task-tracking application we'll see in Chapter 15, *Distributed HTTP*, does.

Before implementing a record-locking or versioning mechanism, though, you might want to step back and consider the bigger picture. We're only in this apparent fix, after all, because *GroupCal* allows every user to edit every calendar. Some groups will think this policy is fine, but others won't. In that case, no record-locking protocol will suffice. You may not want some users to even see, never mind edit, other calendars. If that's so, see Chapter 11, *Membership Services*, and Chapter 12, *Authentication and Authorization Techniques*, for a discussion of membership systems and access-control techniques.

From simple serialization to object databases

I said earlier that synchronization and serialization can combine to create lightweight databases of Java objects. We've seen how synchronization protects the integrity of the hashtables that *Polls* and *GroupCal* manage, by guaranteeing that only one thread at a time can execute an update method. Like *Polls*, *GroupCal* synchronizes its *update()* method, which uses serialization to save in-memory hashtables to disk.

Although *GroupCal*'s *update()* method could serialize the master HoH, as does *Polls*, it instead serializes individual per-user calendar objects. This makes no difference to the *update()* method, which only knows that it's been given some kind of serializable object. Why the more granular approach? It's more efficient, because it saves only an individual calendar touched by an update, not the whole set of calendars. In practice, though, saving the whole set isn't as problematic as you might think. Thanks to sparse storage, *GroupCal* object files grow slowly. Web latency—that is, the time it takes to send a request to a web server and receive a response—more than offsets the time needed to serialize months' worth of calendar data for a dozen users.

Another reason to serialize on a per-user basis is that each individual calendar then becomes a discrete and potentially mobile object. Suppose I need to use my calendar on an untethered notebook PC that can't connect to the calendar server. I can detach my calendar, copy that file to my notebook, and use a local instance of *GroupCal* to interact with it. We'll see more of this local-web-server approach in Chapter 15.

Despite the surprising efficiency of simple serialization, there's a limit to the amount of data that you can manage in a memory-resident data structure. With sparse data and lots of memory, you might be able to get away with this approach for a long time. And while you can, you'll enjoy the twin benefits of simplicity and high performance. But it would be nice to know that if your application scales up dramatically, as Internet-based applications are wont to do, a more robust storage mechanism will be available. Happily, that's so. Commercial object databases now come with bindings to Java. That means that an in-memory Java object, such as a *Hashtable*, can be a window onto disk storage. An application that uses that object can access its parts just as though they were present in memory, because, for the most part, they are. When a referenced part isn't already available, the object database automatically pages it in.

How does an application acquire this enhanced object storage? The details vary depending on the particular object database you use. In the case of Object Design's ObjectStore, the Java binding kit comes with alternate, persistence-enabled versions of Java storage classes such as *Hashtable* and *Vector*. An *OSHashtable*, for example, is the ObjectStore version of Java's *Hashtable*. *OSHashtable* has the same interface as *Hashtable*, and the two can be used interchangeably.

To create a persistence-enabled *GroupCal*, you make a new root object in an ObjectStore database and associate that root with the *OSHashtable* object that represents *GroupCal*'s collection of calendars. Now all references to that object—gets, puts, enumerations—refer without any modification to persistent objects that live in the ObjectStore database. You do have to wrap begin-transaction and end-transaction calls around all references to persistent objects. There's a trade-off here between transaction granularity and simplicity. An easy solution is to bracket the servlet's main *service()* routine with a single pair of transaction calls.

In this scenario, memory is no longer an issue. A persistence-enabled *GroupCal* can handle 10,000 calendars as easily as 10. And its data store can be managed using the transactional controls and querying capabilities of the database engine.

Why groupware needs objects

In the case of *GroupCal*, is object database technology just a solution in search of a problem? After all, its structures are simple and regular. With the exception of the daily entries—which are text fields of variable length and unlimited size—there is nothing that you couldn't model equally well in any conventional SQL database. I'll admit that in its present form, *GroupCal*'s use of object storage is perhaps gratuitous. But I chose the technique because I envisioned features that would push the limits of SQL and exploit the strengths of object storage.

Consider how group scheduling might benefit from this approach. Mark Drummond, CTO of TimeDance.com, describes his company's web-based group scheduler as follows:

> What we're doing, in essence, is bolting a bulletin board to an event. In our approach, an event is an object (in a fairly technical sense). In a traditional approach, an event is an entry in a database. Without a start time, there's no way that the event can be put into the DB. With the event-as-object approach, there are a number of nice benefits. We can collect constraints on acceptable values for various parameters of the event. For instance, we can collect constraints on the start time of an event. "Any day next week" might work for you; "Not Friday" is a constraint that I bring to bear; and "Not Tuesday morning" is requested by someone else.
>
> The event's start time now has a set of constraints on it and it's possible to add value to the users' lives by putting some "constraint satisfaction machinery" around the information to help them make better decisions. The bulletin board attached to each event is a catch-all mechanism that allows the users to share information that would otherwise be forced out of band, into email or voicemail.*

TimeDance models these events using server-side Java objects, which are then mapped into an SQL data store. My hunch is that over time this object-to-relational mapping will matter less. Object-oriented applications will increasingly rely on object data stores.

There's an XML angle here as well. An XML file is really just a textual representation of object data. Browsers are learning to map that data into their document object models. At the same time, object databases are evolving XML bindings that will, in theory, simplify the work of middle-tier groupware components.† In its current form, *GroupCal* uses procedural logic to express Java objects as HTML. That doesn't change when it's backed by an object database—it still has to externalize objects as HTML. But as object databases begin to make XML persistent, the boundaries between XML data structures and Java data structures (or those of other object-oriented languages) will begin to blur. Middle-tier components can

---

* Private correspondence, quoted with permission.

† Early examples of this new breed of XML data server were POET Software's Content Management Suite (*http://www.poet.com/*) and Object Design's eXcelon (*http://www.odi.com/*).

get out of the business of mapping from live data objects to presentation services, data-exchange formats, and storage, and focus more on what it is they actually *do* with that data.

This notion of a calendar service as a middle-tier component, isolated from presentation and storage issues, is crucial. Java servlets are well suited to this role because they're inherently efficient, as we've seen. They're also inherently programmable. Just because it presents a web API, a servlet can be driven by a scripted web client. The inverse is also possible. A servlet can itself be a web client with respect to other URL-accessible services. This ability to simultaneously provide and consume HTTP-based services enables a simple yet powerful approach to middle-tier development. We'll explore some of the possibilities here and go more deeply into the subject in Chapter 15.

GroupCal as a Web Component

Suppose we did outfit *GroupCal* with meeting and task objects. Since these things are more objectlike than relational, XML might be a good way to represent them. An XML-capable object database could serve up this data; XSL presentation services could render it in a browser; DHTML scripting could support interactive viewing and editing.

This is all very exciting but slightly ahead of the curve in terms of the installed base. Netscape is playing a catch-up game with XML; browser support for XSL is still experimental; the Microsoft and Netscape DHTML technologies are quite different. For the time being, web applications that manage complex data objects within a calendar framework rely on server-side production of HTML. This approach is time-honored (as Internet time goes, that is) but still really useful.

As we saw with the Microsoft Index Server (Chapter 8, *Organizing Search Results*), one way to work with a software component that exports a web API is to treat it as a black box accessible only through that API. Anything that a user can do by way of a browser, a web-client script can do by manipulating URLs. This duality, inherent in all web software, can often enable startlingly simple solutions to seemingly hard problems.

Importing Data into GroupCal Using its Web API

When I first deployed *GroupCal*, a colleague asked if he could import data from his personal information manager (PIM) into *GroupCal*. My first response was: no way! But on reflection I saw that this was actually an easy thing to do. To load data into *GroupCal*, a web-client script need only issue a series of HTTP requests like this:

```
/GroupCal?who=Jon+Udell&update=append&Fri+Jun+19+1999=remember+to+call+mom
```

GroupCal already had an implied import capability, just by virtue of the fact that it could accept data from browsers. The program itself didn't need any new import-related features. All that was needed was a web-client script that could issue a set of URLs, and one converter per PIM. The job of a converter is to morph calendar data extracted from the PIM into the set of URLs that is *GroupCal*'s *de facto* import format.

To illustrate this idea, we can use any calendar product that exports an accessible format. Here, for example, are a couple of calendar entries in comma-separated variable (CVS) format, similar to what Netscape's Calendar can export:

```
"Jon Udell","06-19-1999","09:00","09:15","15","Remember to call mom"
"Jon Udell","06-19-1999","14:30","15:00","30","Staff mtg"
```

Example 10-4 shows a Perl script that loads these entries into *GroupCal*.

Example 10-4. A GroupCal Import Script

```perl
#! /usr/bin/perl -w

use strict;

use LWP;
use Date::Manip;
use TinyCGI;

my $tc = TinyCGI->new();

&Date_Init("TZ=EST");                               # initialize Date package

my $user = "Jon+Udell";

open (F, "import.csv")                              # open import file
  or die "cannot open import file $!";

my $headers = <F>;
my $field = "\"([^\"]+)\"";                         # define field pattern
while (<F>)
  {
  m#$field,$field,$field,$field,$field,$field#;     # match fields
  my ($date, $entry) = ($2,$6);                     # extract date and entry
  $date =~ m#(\d+)-(\d+)-(\d+)#;                     # extract date fields
  my ($mm, $dd, $yyyy) = ($1, $2, $3);              # save date fields
  my $weekday =
    $Date::Manip::Week[&Date_DayOfWeek($mm,$dd,$yyyy)-1];   # get weekday
  my $month    = $Date::Manip::Month[$mm-1];        # get month
  $month    = substr($month,0,3);                   # format month
  $weekday  = substr($weekday,0,3);                 # format weekday
  $date     = "$weekday+$month+$dd+$yyyy";          # construct date
  $entry = '<hr>' . $entry;                         # format entry
  my $url = sprintf                                 # format URL
    ("http://localhost:9090/GroupCal?who=%s&update=replace&%s=%s\n",
```

Example 10-4. A GroupCal Import Script (continued)

```
   $user, $date, $tc->escape($entry) );
  pokeCal($url);                                       # transmit URL
  }

sub pokeCal
  {
  my ($url) = @_;
  my $ua = new LWP::UserAgent;

  my $request = new HTTP::Request 'GET';               # new Request object

  $request->header                                     # set credentials
    ('Authorization', "Basic QWxhZGRpbjpvcGVuIHNlc2FtZQ==");

  $request->url($url);                                 # set URL

  print my $response = $ua->request($request);         # transmit request
  }
```

Perl's *LWP* module provides the HTTP client services needed to access *GroupCal.* In Chapter 8 we saw how you can write a one-line URL-fetcher using *LWP::Simple.* Why not do that here? Because *GroupCal* implements HTTP basic authentication, the importer shown in Example 10-4 has to transmit login credentials along with its HTTP requests. That's more than *LWP::Simple* alone can do, so the script also taps *LWP::UserAgent* and *HTTP::Request.* We're taking a shortcut by hardcoding the MIME-encoded user/password pair required by *GroupCal*'s authentication scheme. A more robust version might prompt the user for these credentials, then use Perl's *MIME::Base64* module to encode them into the form required by HTTP basic authentication.

The *GroupCal* import script uses another Perl module that we haven't encountered yet. *Date::Manip* provides a mechanism to convert from MM-DD-YYYY format to *GroupCal*'s "Fri Jun 19 1999" style. Finally, *TinyCGI* provides the *escape()* function that translates characters not allowed in URLs (e.g., the double quote) into an alternate form (e.g., %22).

It's a snap to construct *GroupCal* URLs for each record in the CSV export file. The *update=append* part of the URL tells *GroupCal* to append this data to the specified entry rather than replacing it, as does the alternate *update=replace* form used by *GroupCal*'s interactive edit form.

Exporting Data from GroupCal Using its Web API

If *GroupCal*'s web API can import data from a CSV export file, can it also export to another calendar? Sure. Again the work is mostly already done. *GroupCal*'s viewer emits neatly structured HTML pages that are a snap to parse using simple regular expressions. There is a potential conflict between *GroupCal*-written HTML, which creates a table cell for each daily entry, and user-written HTML, which could be used to nest a table within an entry's cell. Distinguishing between system-generated and user-written HTML tables could be tricky. Fortunately we can cheat by wiring *GroupCal* to emit distinctive table syntax. Since *GroupCal* assumes a dumb HTML viewer, not a smart XML/XSL viewer, we can recruit our old friend the CSS **class** attribute for this job. Here's a fragment of generated HTML that shows how the **class** attribute can distinguish a *GroupCal*-written table cell from a user-written table cell:

```
<td class="gcEntry">
...
</td><!-- end gcEntry -->
```

It's not really necessary to use the **class** attribute here. Any arbitrary attribute can play the same role. The **class** attribute is legal HTML, though, which matters if you ever need to validate against an HTML DTD. And as we've seen, it doubles as a hook for CSS styles. While we're at it, let's have *GroupCal* emit each of these special tags between newline boundaries. That makes no difference to browsers but a world of difference to the line-oriented export script shown in Example 10-5. When you can work both sides of the street as we're doing here, it makes sense to adjust web APIs for the convenience of scripts that use them.

To vary the example, let's use the vCalendar format (see *http://www.imc.org/pdi/ vcal-10.txt*), a standard that's used in a number of calendar products. The script in Example 10-5 reads a *GroupCal* web page and writes a vCalendar import file that any vCalendar-aware application can read.

Example 10-5. A GroupCal Export Script

```perl
#! /usr/bin/perl -w

use strict;
use Date::Manip;

&Date_Init("TZ=EST");

open (F, "groupcal.html") or die "cannot open $!";    # open saved GroupCal page
print "BEGIN:VCALENDAR\n";                             # begin vCalendar file
while (<F>)
  {
  if ( m#<td class=\"gcEntry\"# )                      # match GroupCal entry
    {
    m/(\w{3})\+(\w{3})\+(\d{2})\+(\d{4})[#\w]*>(\w{3}) (\w{3}) (\d{2})/;
    my $date = &DateCalc("$6 $7 $4");                  # extract date
    my $yyyy = substr($date,0,4);
    my $mm = substr($date,4,2);
    my $dd = substr($date,6,2);
    $date = "$yyyy$mm$dd";                             # reconstruct date
    my $dtstart = $date . 'T100000Z';                  # fabricate an appt time
    my $dtend = $date . 'T101500Z';
```

Example 10-5. A GroupCal Export Script (continued)

```
    my $entry = "";
    while (<F>)                                    # read in the entry
      {
      chomp;
      last if ( m#</td><!-- end gcEntry -->#  );
      $entry .= $_;
      }
    if ( $entry ne '' )
      {
      $entry =~ s/<[^>]+>/ /g;                     # de-HTMLize the entry
      print <<"EOT";                               # emit vCalendar event
BEGIN:VEVENT
DTSTART:$dtstart
DTEND:$dtend
SUMMARY:$entry
DESCRIPTION:$entry
END:VEVENT
EOT
      }
    }
  }

print "END:VCALENDAR\n";                           # close vCalendar file
```

As is typical of such transformations, the mapping isn't a perfect one. The SUMMARY field, which appears in Netscape Calendar's daily, weekly, and monthly views as the title of each entry, is limited to a short string of characters. The DESCRIPTION field doesn't truncate, but users have to drill down into an entry to view it. The compromise solution here is to put each *GroupCal* entry in both places.

Since Calendar doesn't render HTML tags, this filter eliminates them. Finally, since a vCalendar entry isn't valid without start and end times, the import script pretends that each *GroupCal* entry is a 6 A.M. appointment.

If *GroupCal* really wanted to be a group scheduler and todo list manager, rather than just a shared bulletin board organized in a time-based fashion, it would need some new data structures. We'd like these structures to display in *GroupCal* entries but not as part of the free-form editable data. Managing appointment or todo data inside *GroupCal* would require a major change to the servlet. But if such data is managed in another web component, we can easily hook that component's display and editing features into *GroupCal*'s existing framework. Let's see how that can work.

Connecting a Task Database to GroupCal

We'll assume there's an SQL-based task database managed primarily by some other application. The task database contains the data shown in the following table.

User	Project	Task	Due	Done
Jon Udell	1	1	4/30/1999	NULL
Joy-Lyn Blake	2	1	5/1/1999	NULL
Jon Udell	2	2	4/20/1999	5/1/1999
Jon Udell	3	1	5/6/1999	NULL
Jon Udell	3	2	5/6/1999	5/6/1999

We'd like to integrate *GroupCal* with that task database by injecting task data into its calendar views. For example, each daily calendar entry could document the tasks due on the current day for the selected user. Today's calendar entry could summarize all pending tasks. Each pending task appearing in a calendar entry could also include a link that, when clicked, moves the task from a pending to a completed state. In this way, *GroupCal* can both view and modify the task database.

An obvious solution would be to use Java's JDBC classes to connect the servlet to the SQL task database. But just because you can do that doesn't mean that you have to. In this case, we'll also assume that the task-database manager exports a higher-level web API than *GroupCal* can use. Suppose, for example, that the task-database manager supports the API shown in Table 10-4.

Table 10-4. The Task-Database Manager's Web API

Action	URL
Query for tasks due on today's date (i.e., the date argument is today's date)	*/todo_view?user=Jon+Udell&date=Mon+May+04+1999*
Query for tasks due on a different date (i.e., the date argument isn't today's date)	*/todo_view?user=Jon+Udell&date=Mon+May+04+1999*
Mark a pending task as done	*/todo_mark_done?user=Jon+Udell&project=1&task=2*

When the date argument is today's date, the task-database manager answers the *todo_view* URL with an HTML-formatted table of all tasks due on or before today, highlighting past-due tasks in red. When the date argument isn't today's date, it answers with a table of just the tasks due on that date. Finally, the *todo_mark_done* URL moves the specified task from pending to completed status.

Figure 10-4 shows a weekly calendar view that uses this web API to include task information.

How do the HTML-formatted SQL results returned by the task-database manager appear in the calendar? *GroupCal* uses Java-style web-client programming to fetch them. Example 10-6 shows how that can work.

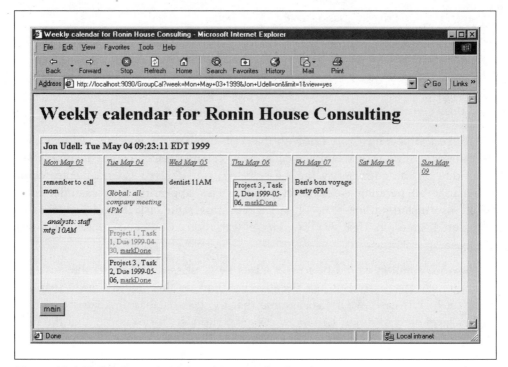

Figure 10-4. Task information injected into a calendar view

Example 10-6. Servlet as Web Client

```
public static String getTodo (  HttpServletRequest req,
                                String who, String key, String sAuth )
  throws MalformedURLException
  {
  String sAuthHeader = req.getHeader("AUTHORIZATION");  // capture auth header
  String sCredentials = sAuthHeader.substring(6,sAuthHeader.length());
  String compare_date = key.substring(4,key.length());
  String sRet = "";
  try {                                                 // form "todo server" URL
    URL url = new URL("http://todohost/todo_view?user=" +
        GroupCalUtil.encode(who) + "&date=" +
        GroupCalUtil.encode(compare_date));
    URLConnection c = url.openConnection();
    c.setRequestProperty("Authorization", sCredentials); // pass credentials
    InputStreamReader in = new InputStreamReader (c.getInputStream () );
    BufferedReader buf = new BufferedReader (in);
    String s = "";
    while (true)
      {
      s = buf.readLine();
      if ( s == null ) break;
        sRet += s;
      }
```

Example 10-6. Servlet as Web Client (continued)

```
   in.close();
   }
catch ( IOException e )
  { sRet = "<p>todo server unavailable";  }
return sRet;
}
```

GroupCal calls this method once per calendar entry, passing the date for that entry. Won't that be slow? That depends on how the task-database manager's web API is implemented. An effective web-to-SQL adaptor can answer a flock of HTTP requests in short order. If invoking SQL queries on a per-calendar-entry basis proves unwieldy, then batch the requests into a single query and unpack its results inside the servlet.

In this kind of distributed setup, where should the authorization for the *mark-Done* function reside? Not in *GroupCal*. Although it uses HTTP authentication to protect calendars, *GroupCal* isn't the primary manager of the task database. That responsibility lies with the "todo server." *GroupCal* can, as shown in Example 10-6, pass along the credentials that it received.

Groupware Servlets in Perspective

Java application servers and multitier development are hot topics at the moment, for good reasons. Client-side Java may or may not someday supplant the native Windows, Unix, and Macintosh GUIs, but server-side Java is well suited to the delivery of network services into the standard HTML/JavaScript client. In the middle-tier environment, the servlet architecture makes it straightforward to build portable, reliable, and responsive services that export and use web APIs and manage complex object data.

For groupware developers, servlets are an essential item in a well-stocked toolkit. You can deploy them on high-end commercial platforms, but as we've seen in this chapter, you can also create simple groupware servlets using nothing but the JDK and a bit of imagination.

11

Membership Services

Groupware requires ways to define users and groups, test for membership in groups, and manage users' preferences and group affiliations. In this chapter we'll explore these issues while developing a notification system that alerts a group of subscribers to docbase updates. We'll also build a family of group membership modules that share a common interface but talk to different data stores.

Internet groupware presents special opportunities and challenges, because it can encompass scopes as narrow as a few individuals and as broad as the entire wired planet. To build groupware applications for these environments, you'll need various kinds of directory services. A directory can model human resources, such as users and groups, and other resources, such as a computers, printers, networks, and offices. Applications that consult a directory don't have to create their own directory information or provide their own tools to manage it. And yet the world is full of applications that do just that. Why? Even within companies there has never been a single dominant standard for directory service. Of course, there are plenty of standards, including Unix's */etc/passwd* and */etc/group*, NetWare 3's bindery, NetWare 4's NetWare Directory Service (NDS), NT's Security Accounts Manager (SAM) database, the Windows 2000 Active Directory, the VINES StreetTalk service, and many others.

From the perspective of a LAN-based groupware application—cc:Mail, for example—there were three choices:

Use the native services

> Define a directory in terms of a least-common-denominator subset of the native directories on all supported platforms, then implement that directory on each platform.

Use a metadirectory

Banyan's Enterprise Network Services (ENS) for NetWare was one of the first notable examples of a metadirectory. When Novell introduced NetWare 4, there was no way for NetWare 3 customers to use the new global directory service without upgrading to Version 4. Sensing correctly that a lot of companies wouldn't want to do that, Banyan adapted StreetTalk to work as a wide-area synchronization service for the NetWare 3 bindery and brought the highly regarded StreetTalk API to the NetWare environment for use by groupware applications. History repeats itself. Now Entevo (*http://www.entevo.com/*) has built an Active Directory service for NDS and legacy NT domains.

Use a proprietary directory

It was a lot of work to use native directories, and the least-common-denominator constraint was severe. Many attributes of individuals and groups that might matter to a groupware application—a person's photograph, a group's organizational role—couldn't be stored in conventional network operating system (NOS) directories. So most groupware applications provided their own directory services. If you were lucky, an application came with a synchronization tool so that you could jump-start the creation of the proprietary groupware directory by filling it with basic information—perhaps just lists of users and groups—drawn from a native directory.

The Case for Internet Directory Services

The rise of the Internet made an already hard problem a lot harder. Large internal corporate directories manage tens of thousands or, in a few cases, hundreds of thousands of users. These are big numbers, but they pale in comparison to the throngs that may interact with corporate web sites. At BYTE, for example, the internal network served only 100 users, but the web site attracted over 3 million in its first three years. It's true that these visitors weren't known to the site as members of a group. But a subscriber-access version of the site, which I built and was ready to deploy when the magazine was discontinued, did test for membership in a group of over 300,000 subscribers. More than three orders of magnitude separated the 100-user staff directory from the 300,000-user subscriber directory.

In the past, we have simply called the latter kind of directory a customer database and managed it with SQL. That will continue to make sense for transactional data—orders, billing, and the like. But Internet groupware creates new opportunities—most notably in the realm of customer service. Given the choice, many people would prefer to resolve a billing problem by email, rather than by calling an 800 number. Email isn't nearly as available as the telephone, but it's headed there fast. As email drives toward universal adoption, the management of customer email addresses is going to look more like a directory problem and less like a conventional database problem. Why? Groupware is about relationships more than it is about transactions. A directory, which is a species of object database, is a good way to define and manage relationships. Communication tools such as mail and conferencing applications work in the context of relationships, so they're naturally attuned to directories. Groupware applications built on top of these tools (or their underlying protocols) likewise are natural users of directories. A person's membership in the customer service group, and relationship to a group of customers, are two equally important facts that interactive email users and groupware applications alike should be able to look up in a directory.

The Internet does provide a rudimentary kind of directory in the form of the Domain Name System (DNS), which maps between IP addresses (192.172.248.100) and names *(udell.roninhouse.com)*. But the DNS wan't designed as a general-purpose directory. More recently, Lightweight Directory Access Protocol (LDAP) has emerged as the standard for accessing full-featured, Internet-oriented directory services. Netscape deserves much credit for popularizing LDAP, which began as a University of Michigan project that aimed to streamline and simplify the Open Systems Interconnect (OSI) X.500 standard. The influence of X.500 pervades Lotus Notes, NetWare's NDS, Active Directory, several large-scale commercial email systems, and the public-key infrastructure that supports the digital certificates exchanged between browsers and web servers when they establish secure (SSL-encrypted) sessions. What makes LDAP special is that it's fast becoming the lingua franca of directories. Nearly every major vendor of network software has endorsed LDAP and is building products that work with it.

The LDAP Consensus

One of the first tangible outcomes of the LDAP consensus appeared in the Netscape and Microsoft 4.x browsers. Although many users still don't realize it, both products' email address books—along with the browsers themselves—are LDAP clients. That wouldn't have meant much if there were no LDAP servers to talk to. Fortunately all the major web-based email directories—including Four11, Switchboard, and WhoWhatWhere—immediately adapted their services to respond to LDAP queries. Suddenly, for the first time, you could ask the Internet—straight from your mail client—for Jon Udell's email address, as shown in Figure 11-1.

Internet novices found this unremarkable. Hadn't the Internet always worked this way? Well, no, actually it hadn't. Given the politics and inertia that had long plagued Internet-directory efforts, it was a pleasant surprise when the pieces came together as quickly and easily as they did in 1997.

Internet enthusiasts like to say that it's easier to adapt technologies proven on a global scale for use on local networks than to adapt LAN technologies for global use. In terms of scalability and interoperability that's true, but companies will for some time continue to rely on LAN-based file, print, and directory services. Here

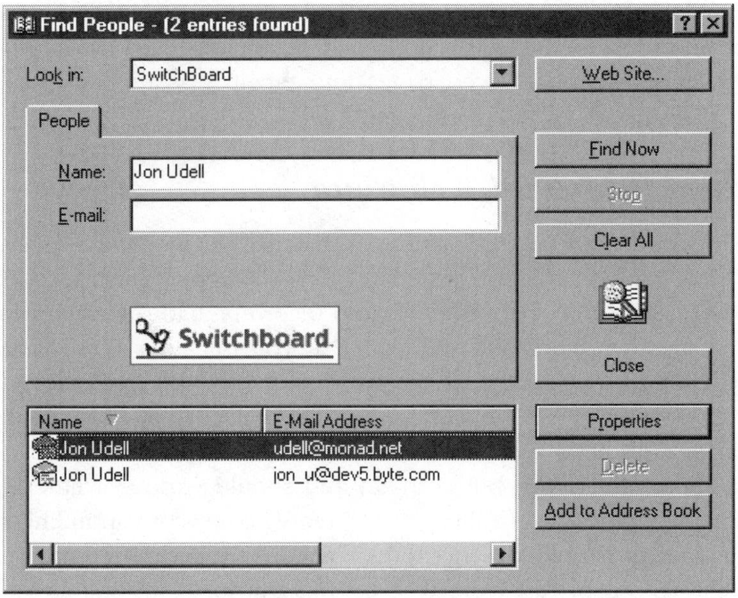

Figure 11-1. Looking up an email address in Outlook Express

too the influence of LDAP is strong. Novell's X.500-derived NDS will be accessible to LDAP clients. Microsoft executed an abrupt about-face when it abandoned plans for a proprietary directory service and decided to build NT 5's Active Directory on the LDAP model. But unlike the Internet, where LDAP could rush unopposed into a directory services vacuum, LAN directories are entrenched and will change much more slowly. Groupware developers will have to work both sides of the street for some time to come. The strategies I'll discuss in this chapter, and the techniques I'll demonstrate, assume eventual widespread use of LDAP both locally and globally. But they also assume a long and gradual transition to LDAP.

A Subscriber-Based Notification System

For now, let's put LDAP and Active Directory on the back burner and build a simple notification system based on group membership. Notification enables groupware systems to find a middle ground between push and pull technologies. To use an HTTP or NNTP docbase, a user has to actively pull information from it. People are busy, though, and the cornucopia of information sources to which the browser gives access is overwhelming. Many useful docbases languish because, as their creators like to complain, "Nobody checks them." To combat this problem, an old method, email, was given a new name: push technology. Docbases can use email updates to reach out and touch their users. To do this most effectively, you should strike a balance between push and pull. For example, to showcase the improved

HTML rendering in the Navigator 3.0 mailreader, Netscape launched a campaign called InBox Direct, which delivered web pages from participating sites into subscribers' email inboxes. This was a good way to make a point about HTML email, but wholesale replication of web pages into email inboxes can create a lot of clutter.

The Hybrid Push/Pull Technique

There is a hybrid solution that strikes a balance between the push and pull extremes. The PointCast system, the first of a new breed of push technologies that supplanted email with special protocols and receivers, had the right idea. A PointCast feed pushes headlines and summaries at you but links these items to more detailed documents that you can—at your discretion—pull from the Web. This is just good old-fashioned information layering and packaging, something newspapers and magazines have done for hundreds of years. You can't put everything on the front page or the cover, but you can and should expose a little bit of every item there and link each headline or summary to its corresponding document. Docbase managers should do this too. It doesn't require a PointCast or Active Desktop channel. Email can work well for this purpose, so long as you properly layer and package what you transmit.

Let's apply this idea in a notification system for the ProductAnalysis docbase. Subscribers to the docbase will receive email updates that summarize and link to newly added reports, as shown in Figure 11-2.

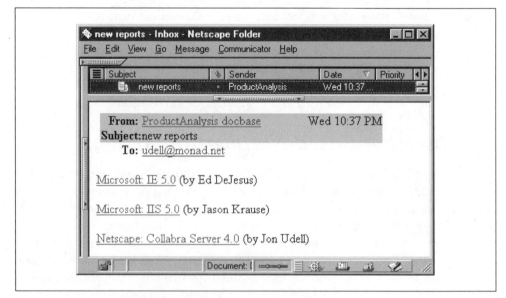

Figure 11-2. An email update from the ProductAnalysis notifier

Two strategies limit the demands this notifier places on its subscribers. First, it sends just one message per update cycle. The message lists all the new reports that appeared in that cycle. Second, it associates each subscriber with a list of companies and includes only reports pertaining to companies on that list.

Directory Options for the Docbase Notifier

What role should a directory play in this application? We could use it to define the group of subscribers, to store their email addresses, and perhaps even to store their lists of preferred companies. On an intranet it would make sense to use an NOS directory for this purpose if it already enumerates all potential subscribers. Ideally you'd reuse that list of names and just assign a subset of them to the subscribers group. This approach works especially well when you can tie the web component of the application to the NOS directory. In an NT environment running Microsoft's IIS web server, for example, HTTP authentication relies on the same user and group permissions that govern the regular filesystem. Since the emailed updates link back to web-based reports, it's very convenient to be able to send URLs to people who, by virtue of their membership in an NOS-defined group, are precisely the ones whose NOS credentials give them access to those files.

On a large intranet, though, and certainly on the Internet, the NOS directory probably isn't the way to go. Some intranets are bound together with global directories such as StreetTalk or NDS, but most aren't. There's no global directory on the Internet, so HTTP and NNTP have evolved their own ways of defining users and groups. Unix-based web servers, for example, have traditionally supported *.htpasswd* and *.htgroup* files that parallel the native NOS */etc/passwd* and */etc/group*. Why? It's not a good idea to define users of public services in the same way that you define users of the internal network. Segregating these two populations from each other is a basic tenet of computer security.

Internal and External Populations

Unfortunately neither the Microsoft approach, which joins the two populations, nor the Unix way, which divides them, is really practical in its pure form. TCP/IP knows no boundaries. It wants to connect everything to everything, and we want that too. It's not enough to deploy public services on the Internet and private services on the intranet. We want to use the Internet as an extension of our intranets, so that docbases and applications that we use in our offices are equally available to us when we're working at home or on the road. And we want to let transient collaborators use these docbases and applications too. So Internet services wind up being neither purely public nor purely private but an awkward mixture of both.

Netscape's SuiteSpot servers offer one interesting solution to this problem. If you define users and groups in Netscape's LDAP-based Directory Server, the web, mail, news, and calendar servers can all share a common directory. That directory can stand apart from the native NOS directory, but it doesn't have to. In Windows NT environments you can arrange to synchronize the LDAP and NOS directories. If Netscape's Enterprise Server were the web engine, you'd get the same effect as with IIS: URLs sent to members of the group of subscribers could be governed by permissions defined in terms of that same group. What if, instead of Enterprise Server, you wanted to use a more popular server such as Apache or IIS? You'd need to empower your web-based applications to do the LDAP lookups themselves. That's doable, as we'll see shortly.

If your application is going to have to look up user and group information, does it matter whether it finds that information in a directory or in some other kind of database? The application doesn't really care. It's a question of what makes administrative sense. If your NOS directory already lists the email addresses of the users to whom you want to send updates, then use it—directly if you can or else indirectly by means of replication. If most or all of the users are outside your company, then you'll probably wind up listing them in a conventional database. What about the lists of companies? With X.500-derived directories such as NDS, Street-Talk, and Netscape's Directory Server, you can attach new attributes to directory entries; with conventional NOS directories, you can't. But just because you can store these kinds of user preferences in a directory doesn't mean that you should. In principle it makes sense to centralize user-related data. In practice, depending on the nature and quantity of that data, it may not.

A Simple Perl-based Group Directory

Enough theory. Let's build a simple directory, get the notifier up and running, and then explore some alternate directory modules. Build a directory? That may sound strange, but it turns out that you can provide the basic ingredients—the ability to associate a user with a group, get and set user entries with simple or complex attributes, and test for a user's membership in a group—in just a few lines of Perl, as shown in Example 11-1.

Example 11-1. Group::SimpleGroup, a Minimal User Directory Module

```
package Group::SimpleGroup;

use strict;
no strict 'refs';
use Data::Dumper;

my $root = "/subscribers";

sub new
```

Example 11-1. Group::SimpleGroup, a Minimal User Directory Module (continued)

```perl
  {
  my ($pkg,$group_db,$group_name) = @_;
  do "$root/$group_db";
  my $self =
    {
    'group_object'        =>  ${$group_name},
    'group_db'            =>  $group_db,
    'group_name'          =>  $group_name,
    };
  bless $self,$pkg;
  return $self;
  }

sub members
  {
  my ($self) = @_;
  return keys %{$self->{group_object}};
  }

sub isMember
  {
  my ($self,$member) = @_;
  return ( defined $self->{group_object}->{$member} ) ? 1 : 0 ;
  }

sub setMember
  {
  my ($self,$member) = @_;
  $self->{group_object}->{$member} = {};
  }

sub getMember
  {
  my ($self,$member) = @_;
  return $self->{group_object}->{$member};
  }

sub setProperty
  {
  my ($self,$member,$prop_name,$prop_val) = @_;
  $self->{group_object}->{$member}->{$prop_name} = $prop_val;
  }

sub getProperty
  {
  my ($self,$member,$prop_name) = @_;
  return $self->{group_object}->{$member}->{$prop_name};
  }

sub dumpGroup
  {
  my ($self) = @_;
  print Dumper($self->{group_object});
  }
```

Example 11-1. Group::SimpleGroup, a Minimal User Directory Module (continued)

```
sub saveGroup
  {
  my ($self) = @_;
  my $dump = Data::Dumper->new([$self->{group_object}],
                               [$self->{group_name}]);
  my $db = "$root/$self->{group_db}";
  open (F,  ">$db") or die "cannot create $db $!";
  print F $dump->Dump;
  close F;
  }

1;
```

Group::SimpleGroup manages a file of Perl data structures in ASCII form; the file might look like this:

```
$subscribers =
  {
  'joe' =>
    {
    'email' => 'joe@udell.roninhouse.com',
    'phone' =>
      {
      'number' => '555-1212',
      'ext'    => '374',
      },
    },
  'sharon' =>
    {
    'email' => 'sharon@udell.roninhouse.com',
    'phone' =>
      {
      'number' => '555-1234',
      'ext'    => '393',
      }
    },
  };
```

You can create the file using a text editor or by means of scripts that make *Group::SimpleGroup* calls. As we've seen before, Perl enables you to compose nested data structures directly. Example 11-2 shows how to create a new entry for user Ringo, add an email property to the entry, fetch Ringo's email address, list the contents of the directory, and save the directory.

Example 11-2. Using the Group::SimpleGroup Module

```
use Group::SimpleGroup;

my $d =                                      # load the subscribers directory
  Group::SimpleGroup->new("subscriber_db", "subscribers");

$d->setMember("ringo");                      # create user ringo
```

Example 11-2. Using the Group::SimpleGroup Module (continued)

```
$d->setProperty("ringo",                       # set ringo's email address
  "email","ringo\@udell.roninhouse.com");

my $email = $d->getProperty("ringo","email");  # get ringo's email address

$d->dumpGroup();                               # print out the subscriber
                                               # directory
$d->saveGroup();                               # rewrite the subscriber_db file
```

The text file written by *saveGroup()* is simultaneously code and data. When you create an instance of *Group::SimpleGroup*, the module's constructor loads the file whose name you pass to it and interprets it as though it were a script—which it is—using Perl's *do* statement. The result is a live in-memory representation of the data structure described in the file. That structure is a hashtable that lists members of a group and defines their properties. Its name, in this example, is $subscribers. The constructor receives the text of that name ("subscribers"), forms a symbolic reference (${"subscribers"}), and stores that reference in the instance variable $self->{group}. If you alter the structure with *setMember()* and *setProperty()* calls and then call *saveGroup()*, Perl's *Data::Dumper* module externalizes it again as as text. The first argument to Dumper->new() names the file that receives the ASCII version of the structure, and the second argument names the variable ($subscribers) that appears on the left hand of the assignment statement written by *saveGroup()*.

A Data-Prototyping Strategy

This technique is to the realm of data management what scripting is to the world of programming: a way to get prototypes up and running in minutes or hours rather than days or weeks. Even if you plan eventually to use a directory, or an SQL or object database, it can be very useful to deploy a first version of your application on this kind of data-store prototype. Data structures need to evolve as rapidly and fluidly as code does, but industrial-strength data-management tools don't allow the kind of freehand data modeling that can really speed up initial development.

Sometimes the prototype is all that you need. I once ran a notification system for 50 users based on the methods shown here. It wasn't a scalable solution, but it didn't need to be. Managing relatively static membership and subscription data in a text file was an appropriate solution for that application and that group of users. Similar opportunities abound for groupware developers. Try the simplest thing that could possibly work, get something up and running, and let usage determine your next steps. If you've built the wrong application, it's doomed anyway. There's no reason to waste effort preparing for a scale-up that won't ever happen; cut your losses and try another tack. If you've built the right application, you can always swap out a simple-minded data store for a more robust one, if and when the need arises.

Anatomy of the Docbase Update Notifier

The notifier shown in Example 11-3 draws on three data sources:

A directory

> The *Group::SimpleGroup* module defines the group of subscribers and lists their email addresses.

A docbase

> The notifier tracks the records in the ProductAnalysis docbase and issues updates when new records appear.

An SQL database

> One of the tables in this database, *cmp_docs*, associates docbase reports with the companies about which they're written. Another table, *cmp_users*, maps subscribers to companies. We'll assume these and related tables exist, are managed by another application, and are also used elsewhere. For example, the assignment mechanism described in Chapter 6, *Docbase Input Techniques*, would use a *company* table in this database to populate the corresponding picklist in the report-assignment form. A database-backed web application would enable subscribers to define and update their own lists of subscribed companies.

Example 11-3 shows the docbase update notifer.

Example 11-3. The ProductAnalysis Notifier

```
use strict;

use Docbase::Docbase;
use Group::SimpleGroup;
use Net::SMTP;
use DBI;

# docbase setup
my $db = Docbase::Docbase->new('ProductAnalysis');

# directory setup
my $sg = Group::SimpleGroup->new('subscriber_db','subscribers');

# mail setup
my $smtp = Net::SMTP->new('smtp.udell.roninhouse.com');

# db setup
my $dbh = DBI->connect('DBI:ODBC:SUBS','','')
  or die ("connect, $DBI::errstr");
$dbh->{RaiseError} = 1;
```

Example 11-3. The ProductAnalysis Notifier (continued)

```perl
# other setudoc dhp
my $docdir    = "$db->{docbase_web_absolute}/$db->{app}/docs";
my $highwater = getHighwater();
my $hostname  = 'udell.roninhouse.com';


my (@docs) = reverse sort <$doc_dir/*.*>;      # load doc list
setHighwater($docs[0]);                        # remember highwater mark
my $metadata = {};                             # initialize metadata cache
loadDocsByCompany();                           # load metadata cache and SQL table
sendMessages();                                # issue update messages

# fini
$dbh->disconnect;
$smtp->quit;

sub loadDocsByCompany
  {
  my $st = "delete from cmp_docs";             # empty out the table
  dbSqlExecute($dbh,$st);
  foreach my $doc (@docs)                      # enumerate docbase
    {
    $doc =~ m#(\d{6,6})#;                       # isolate sequence number
    if ($1 gt $highwater)                      # compare to highwater mark
      {
      my $metarecord = $db->getMetadata($doc);  # get metadata for doc
      $metadata->{$doc} = $metarecord;          # save it
      my $company = $metarecord->{company};     # extract company name
      my $st = "insert into cmp_docs (cmp,doc) values ('$company','$doc')";
      dbSqlExecute($dbh,$st);                   # load a row of cmp_docs
      }
    }
  }


sub sendMessages
  {
  my $st = "select distinct cmp_users.user,cmp_docs.doc \
      from cmp_docs,cmp_users where cmp_docs.cmp = cmp_users.cmp";
  my $allrows = dbSqlReturnAllRows($dbh,$st);
  my $messages = {};
  foreach my $row (@$allrows)
    {
    my ($user,$doc) = @$row;
    $user = allTrim($user);
    $doc = allTrim($doc);
    my $url = $doc;
    my $email = $sg->getProperty($user,'email');
    push (@{$messages->{$email}}, "<a href=\"http://$hostname/$url\">\
      $metadata->{$doc}->{company}: $metadata->{$doc}->{product} \
      (by $metadata->{$doc}{analyst})</a>");
    }

  foreach my $email (keys %$messages)
    {
```

Example 11-3. The ProductAnalysis Notifier (continued)

```
    $smtp->mail($email);
    $smtp->to($email');
    $smtp->data();
    $smtp->datasend("To: $email\n");
    $smtp->datasend("From: notifier\n");
    $smtp->datasend("Subject: new ProductAnalysis reports\n");
    $smtp->datasend("Content-type: text/html\n");
    $smtp->datasend("\n");
    $smtp->datasend( join ("<p>",@{$messages->{$email}}));
    $smtp->dataend();
    }
  }

sub allTrim
  {
  my ($s) = @_;
  $s =~ s/^\s+//;
  $s =~ s/\s+$//;
  return $s;
  }

sub getHighwater
  {
  open (F,"highwater") or die "cannot create highwater $!";
  my $hw = <F>;
  $hw =~ m#(\d{6,6})#;                      # isolate sequence number
  close F;
  return $1;                                # return sequence number
  }

sub setHighwater
  {
  my ($highwater) = @_;
  open (F,">highwater") or die "cannot create highwater $!";
  print F $highwater;
  close F;
  }

sub dbSqlExecute
  {
  my ($dbh,$st) = @_;
  my $sth = $dbh->prepare($st) or die ("prepare, $DBI::errstr");
  my $rv = $sth->execute or die ("execute, $DBI::errstr");
  $sth->finish;
  }

sub dbSqlReturnAllRows
  {
  my ($dbh,$st) = @_;
  my $sth = $dbh->prepare($st) or die ("prepare, $DBI::errstr");
  my $rv = $sth->execute or die ("execute, $DBI::errstr");
  my $allrows = $sth->fetchall_arrayref;
```

Example 11-3. The ProductAnalysis Notifier (continued)

```
$sth->finish;
return $allrows;
}
```

The modules used by the notifier are as follows:

Docbase::Docbase

A docbase is a collection of meta-tagged HTML files. The notifier uses *Docbase::Docbase::getMetadata()* to extract the structured header from each docbase record.

Group::SimpleGroup

The notifier uses this module to look up email addresses in a simple text-file-based directory. Later in this chapter, we'll build two alternate directory modules, one for Windows NT domains and one for LDAP directories.

DBI (a CPAN module)

Perl's universal database interface works on the Windows Open Database Connectivity (ODBC) model. A driver manager, *DBI*, accepts plug-in modules for individual databases—*DBD::Oracle*, *DBD::Solid*, and so on. One of these plug-ins, *DBD::ODBC*, adapts *DBI* for use with any data source that accepts ODBC connections. As a result, the notifier—or any Perl *DBI* application—will work the same way on a Unix system running the Solid database as on a Win32 system running Oracle. You can even use ODBC and the Microsoft Jet engine to control a Microsoft Access database. This technique, which bypasses Access and manages a *.MDB* file directly, is very convenient for standalone development in Win32 environments. It's also surprisingly effective for low-intensity production use—see Chapter 15, *Distributed HTTP*, for details.

Net::SMTP (a CPAN module)

Another of the modules in Perl's LibNet family, *Net::SMTP* is a simple and effective way to send Internet mail messages programmatically. Why not just use a command-line mailer? You can if you like, but the availability and behavior of such tools varies from system to system. On Windows, there is no standard Internet mailer. The advantage of *Net::SMTP* is that it assumes only a TCP/IP connection, and it works the same way everywhere.

The notifier begins by loading and configuring each of its supporting modules. In this example, the *DBI* constructor names an ODBC data source that happens to refer to a *.MDB* file. In an Oracle environment, the connection call might look like `DBI->connect("DBI::Oracle:","user","password")`. The *Net::SMTP* constructor names the mail server that will relay messages to subscribers. The *Group::SimpleGroup* constructor names the file that lists subscribers and their email addresses. The *Docbase::Docbase* constructor names the docbase whose records the notifier is tracking.

The notifier stores a high-water mark—that is, the name of the most recent doc-base record from the last update cycle—in a file called *highwater*. *getHighwater()* fetches that name into a variable. The array @docs receives a reverse-sorted list of docbase records. *setHighwater()* stores the first element of that list—the most recent record for the current update cycle—as the new high-water mark. The variable $metadata, initially an empty hashtable, will store the metadata extracted from each record in the current cycle's update set.

Implementing Attribute-Based Docbase Subscription

loadDocsByCompany() populates the two data structures used by the *sendMessages()* function. One of these is the metadata cache, $metadata. The other is the SQL table *cmp_docs*, which maps between company names and doc-base records. *loadDocsByCompany()* begins by emptying the *cmp_docs* table. Then, for each record, it updates $metadata with the results of a call to *getMetadata()*. At the same time it inserts a company-to-docname mapping into the *cmp_docs* table. Since the records appear in reverse order, *loadDocsByCompany()* can halt when it sees the record that matches the old high-water mark. Figure 11-3 illustrates the data structures in play at this point and the desired set of notification lists.

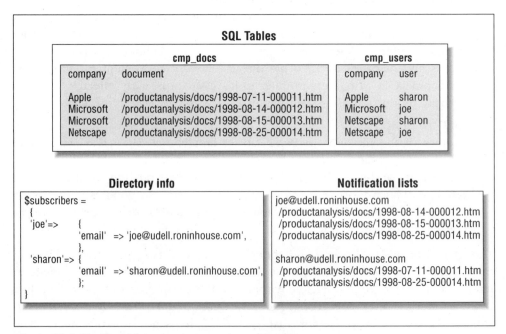

Figure 11-3. Notifier's data structures and resulting lists

sendMessages() begins by combining two SQL tables—*cmp_docs*, which was just built, and *cmp_users*, which is separately managed—to create a result set that expresses the docbase records to be included in each subscriber's update message.

An Alternate, Non-SQL Approach to Attribute-Based Subscription

The `SELECT DISTINCT` statement is one way to map subscribers to docbase records, but suppose that the subscription lists were stored in a directory rather than an SQL database. That might make sense if the subscription were considered to be part of an employee's organizational role and if the definitions of those roles were maintained in an LDAP directory.

In that case you could still transfer the data from LDAP to SQL in order to be able to execute the same `SELECT DISTINCT` statement. But once you've pulled the lists out of the directory, you wouldn't have to feed them to SQL. You could just combine the structures directly in Perl. Here's an alternate version of *loadDocsByCompany()* that puts the docname-to-company mappings in a hash-table rather than an SQL table:

```
sub loadDocsByCompany
  {
  my (@docs,$highwater) = @_;
  $docs_by_company = {};
  foreach $doc (@docs)
    {
    last if ( $doc eq $highwater);
    my $metarecord = $db->getMetadata($doc);
    my $company = $metarecord->{company};
    push ( @{$docs_by_company->{$company}}, $doc);
    }
  return $docs_by_company;
  }
```

This function produces a hashtable whose keys are company names and whose values are lists of docbase records. Given this mapping, here's a function to combine it with the per-user lists of subscribed companies:

```
sub getDocsByPerson
  {
  my ($docs_by_company) = @_;
  my $docs_by_person = {};
  my ($companies,$company);
  foreach $person ( $sg->members )              # e.g., 'Joe'
    {
    $companies =                                # e.g., [Netscape,Adobe]
        $sg->getProperty($person,'companies');
    foreach $company (@$companies)             # e.g., 'Adobe'
      { push ( @{$docs_by_person->{$person}}, @{$docs_by_company->{$company}}); }
```

```
    }
    return $docs_by_person;
    }
```

For each subscriber in the group, `$companies` gets that person's list of preferred companies. Since we're using the Perl-based *Group::SimpleGroup* here, the value returned from the *members()* method is a native Perl list. If another kind of directory stored the list in comma-separated variable format, Perl's split function could turn that into a list like this:

```
    my @list = split(',' , "Netscape, Adobe")
```

The structure produced this way is actually a bit more refined than what `SELECT DISTINCT` yields. It you refer back to Example 11-3, you'll see that the *sendMessages()* routine still has to massage the SQL result set, using a hashtable to condense multiple rows of per-user data into single per-user lists.

Working with Users and Groups in the NT Accounts Database

Suppose the notifier runs on an NT-based intranet, all the subscribers are listed in the NT domain's Security Accounts Manager (SAM) directory, and the `FullName` slot of each user's directory entry includes an email address as well as a first and last name. In this situation it makes sense to define the group of subscribers using NT's User Manager and then let the notifier consult the NT directory in order to enumerate subscribers and fetch their email addresses.

As usual there's more than one way to do it. You can manipulate the necessary Win32 APIs from a number of scripting languages, including Visual Basic, Python, and Perl. Hooking directly into the low-level Win32 APIs used to query the directory is, however, a wholly NT-centric approach. What if you'd also like to be able to work with a Novell NDS directory or an LDAP directory? Happily Microsoft has provided Active Directory Services Interface (ADSI), a component that works with all three of these directories—and potentially others as well. ADSI will be included as a standard component of Windows 2000. Until then, it's (freely) available separately at *http://www.microsoft.com/windows/server/Technical/directory/adsilinks.asp.*

ADSI works on the ODBC model. It's a driver manager that provides a generalized interface to data sources—in this case, directories—and that accepts pluggable drivers that adapt it to a range of specific data sources. As its name implies, ADSI's eventual purpose is to connect applications to Microsoft's own Active Directory. Since that product won't be widely deployed anytime soon, ADSI's immediate role is to encourage the development of directory-aware applications that will be compatible with Active Directory.

Example 11-4 shows *Group::NTGroup*, which supports the same interface as *Group::SimpleGroup* but which connects to an NT domain instead of a Perl-managed data structure. It's written in Perl, which means our notifier can use it interchangeably with *Group::SimpleGroup*. But since ADSI runs as an OLE automation server, any OLE-aware scripting languages can use it. ADSI services are also available to those languages that can embed in ASP web pages—including VBScript, JavaScript, Python, and Perl.

Example 11-4. Group::NTGroup, a Simple NT-Oriented Group Directory

```perl
package Group::NTGroup;
use strict;
use Win32::OLE;

sub new
  {
  my ($pkg,$domain,$group_name) = @_;
  my $self =
    {
    'domain' => $domain,
    'group'  => Win32::OLE->GetObject("WinNT://$domain/$group_name,Group"),
    };
  bless $self,$pkg;
  return $self;
  }

sub members
  {
  my ($self) = @_;
  my @members = ();
  my $group = $self->{group};
  my $m = $group->Members();
  foreach my $member (in $m)
    {   push (@members, $member->{Name}); }
  return @members;
  }

sub isMember
  {
  my ($self,$member) = @_;
  return grep  ( /^$member$/, $self->members ) ? 1 : 0;
  }

sub setMember
  {
  my ($self,$member) = @_;

  if (! $self->existsUser($member) )         # if user doesn't exist
    {
    my $dn = "WinNT://$self->{domain}";
    my $d = Win32::OLE->GetObject($dn);
    my $u = $d->Create("user",$member);      # create user
    $u->SetInfo;
    }
```

Example 11-4. Group::NTGroup, a Simple NT-Oriented Group Directory (continued)

```perl
  my $group = $self->{group};                  # then add to group
  $group->add("WinNT://$self->{domain}/$member");
  $group->SetInfo;
  }

sub getMember
  {
  my ($self,$member) = @_;
  my $dn = "WinNT://$self->{domain}/$member";
  $member = Win32::OLE->GetObject($dn);
  $member->GetInfo;
  my $member_hash = {};
  for (1..$member->{PropertyCount})
    {
    my $prop = $member->Next;
    $member_hash->{$prop->Name} = $member->Get($prop->Name);
    }
  return $member_hash;
  }

sub delMember
  {
  my ($self,$member) = @_;
  my $group = $self->{group};
  $group->remove("WinNT://$self->{domain}/$member");
  $group->SetInfo;
  }

sub setProperty
  {
  my ($self,$member,$prop_name,$prop_val) = @_;
  my $dn = "WinNT://$self->{domain}/$member";
  $member = Win32::OLE->GetObject($dn);
  $member->GetInfo;
  $member->Put($prop_name,$prop_val);
  $member->SetInfo;
  }

sub getProperty
  {
  my ($self,$member,$prop_name) = @_;
  my $dn = "WinNT://$self->{domain}/$member";
  $member = Win32::OLE->GetObject($dn);
  $member->GetInfo;
  return $member->Get($prop_name);
  }

sub existsUser
  {
  my ($self,$member) = @_;
  my $dn = "WinNT://$self->{domain}/$member,User";
  my $u = Win32::OLE->GetObject($dn);
  return (defined $u) ? 1 : 0;
  }
```

Example 11-4. Group::NTGroup, a Simple NT-Oriented Group Directory (continued)

```
sub dumpGroup
  {
  my ($self) = @_;
  my $group_hash = {};
  foreach my $member ($self->members)
    { $group_hash->{$member} = $self->getMember($member); }
  return $group_hash;
  }

1;
```

Group::NTGroup's constructor shows how you tap into ADSI. The parameter you pass to *GetObject()*, called an AdsPath, has two components. The leading part, which can be *WinNT://*, or *NDS://*, or *LDAP://*, selects the directory provider that will satisfy all subsequent requests to the object created by this call. The trailing part of the AdsPath names the location in a directory tree to which the object will refer.

In a Novell environment, you'd initialize the module with an AdsPath like *NDS:// RONIN/o=RoninHouse/cn=Subscribers.* In an LDAP context, it would look similar: *LDAP://RoninHouse.com/o=RoninHouse/cn=Subscribers.*

An ADSI group object answers the *Members()* method call with a handle to an OLE collection of its members. In VBScript you can enumerate that collection like this:

```
set group   = GetObject("WinNT://UDELL/Subscribers")
set members = group.Members

for each user in members
        Wscript.echo user.name
next
```

As you can see in Example 11-4, Win32 Perl supports the same idiom. Perl wizards unfamiliar with Win32 Perl may not recognize the construct (in $m), which isn't part of Perl's standard repertoire. It's a Win32 extension added to the ActiveState version of Win32 Perl so that scripts can navigate OLE collections.

To operate on other parts of the directory, you call *GetObject()* with different AdsPath strings. For example, the *getMember()* method calls GetObject("WinNT:// DOMAIN/USERNAME") to get a handle to a user object so it can work with that user's directory entry.

We can't get and set arbitrary properties here; the module only works with the schema that governs the directory it's talking to. NDS, Active Directory, and others are extensible, but NT domains aren't. In this case the notifier can't get and set an email attribute because there isn't one. But there are a couple of fields available for its use. As I mentioned, one solution would be to always append an email address to the `FullName` field, for example: `Jon Udell <udell@monad.net>`. Alternatively, you could tuck an email address into the `Description` slot of the NT directory entry.

Working with Users and Groups Using LDAP

LDAP is becoming the de facto standard way to access directory services. ADSI, which we used earlier to access the NT accounts database, can also talk to LDAP servers. But ADSI is a Windows-only component. In this section we'll develop a third variation on our directory module theme, *Group::LdapGroup*.

I've used two different LDAP modules for Perl. One is Netscape's *PerLDAP* (*http:// www.mozilla.org/directory*), made freely available in conjunction with the open-source release of Netscape's Directory SDK. The other is a CPAN module, *Net::LDAP*. Which is best? As usual, it depends. *PerLDAP* binds to libraries included with the Netscape Directory SDK. That's a good thing if, for example, you need to use LDAP on encrypted channels, since *PerLDAP* can use the SSL capability of the Directory SDK. But Perl modules that depend on C-based libraries tend to be harder to build and deploy than Perl modules made of nothing but Perl, such as *Net::LDAP*. It's a "100% pure Perl" solution, a convenience for which you trade SSL support.

The module shown in Example 11-5 uses *Net::LDAP*, which is appropriate for our docbase notifier. This kind of application runs autonomously, behind the firewall, and doesn't really need to secure its connection to the directory server. If you build an access-controlled docbase, as we'll do in the next chapter, you might or might not want to use *PerLDAP* to encrypt LDAP sessions. Again, it depends. If users connect directly to a directory server over the Internet and that server contains private information, you'll want to encrypt those sessions. But if users connect to a web server or application server via SSL and thence to a directory server that's colocated with the web server behind the firewall, then SSL between those two servers might not be necessary.

You can connect to an LDAP server using ADSI, a Perl module, or some other method. But once you're connected, what are you going to tell it to do? LDAP itself is a pretty solid standard, but directory servers can and do differ. Each server has its own schema for users, groups, and other directory objects. So while the module in Example 11-5 will run on any platform, it's specific to one directory server—Netscape's—and would need to be adapted to work with another LDAP server. A more ambitious version of this module would abstract the differences among a variety of different directory servers.

Example 11-5. The Group::LdapGroup Module for Netscape Directory Server

```perl
package Group::LdapGroup;
use strict;

use Net::LDAP;

sub new
  {
  my ($pkg,$host,$port,$base,$group_name,$authdn,$authpw) = @_;
  my $self =
    {
    'base'               => $base,
    'group_name'         => $group_name,
    'ldap'               => Net::LDAP->new($host,port=>$port),
    'member_attr'        => 'uniquemember',
    'user_object_class'  => ["top","person","organizationalPerson",
    };                      "inetOrgPerson"],
  bless $self,$pkg;
  $self->{ldap}->bind ( dn => $authdn, password => $authpw );
  return $self;
  }


sub members
  {
  my ($self) = @_;
  my $msg = $self->{ldap}->search(
      base   => $self->{base},
      filter => "(cn=$self->{group_name})",
      );
  my $result = $msg->as_struct;
  my $members = $result->{(keys %$result)[0]}->{$self->{member_attr}};
  return $members;
  }

sub isMember
  {
  my ($self,$member) = @_;
  return grep  ( /uid=$member,$self->{base}/, @{$self->members} ) ? 1 : 0;
  }

sub setMember
  {
  my ($self,$member) = @_;

  if ( ! $self->existsUser($member) )          # if user doesn't exist
    {
    $self->{ldap}->add (                       # create user
        dn   => "uid=$member,$self->{base}",
        attr => [ 'cn'  => [$member],
                  'sn'  => $member,
                  'objectclass' => $self->{user_object_class},
                ]
        );
    }
```

Example 11-5. The Group::LdapGroup Module for Netscape Directory Server (continued)

```perl
  my $members = $self->members;

  if ( ! grep ( /uid=$member/, @{$members} )  )
    {
    push ( @{$members},                          # add user to list
      "uid=$member,$self->{base}" );
    my $result = $self->{ldap}->modify(          # update group
        dn => "cn=$self->{group_name},$self->{base}",
        replace => { $self->{member_attr} => $members });
    $result->code &&
      warn "failed to update group membership: ", $result->error ;
    }
  }

sub getMember
  {
  my ($self,$member) = @_;
  my $msg = $self->findPerson($member);
  return $msg->as_struct;
  }

sub setProperty
  {
  my ($self,$member,$prop_name,$prop_val) = @_;
  my $msg = $self->findPerson($member);
  my $result = $self->{ldap}->modify(
      dn => "uid=$member,$self->{base}",
      replace => { $prop_name => $prop_val });
  $result->code &&
      warn "failed to set member property: ", $result->error ;
  }

sub getProperty
  {
  my ($self,$member,$prop_name) = @_;
  my $msg = $self->findPerson($member);
  my $struct = $msg->as_struct;
  my $key = (keys %$struct)[0];
  return $struct->{$key}->{$prop_name}->[0];
  }

sub existsUser
  {
  my ($self,$member) = @_;
  my $msg = $self->findPerson($member);
  return $msg->count;
  }

sub dumpGroup
  {
  my ($self) = @_;
  my $member_hash = {};
```

Example 11-5. The Group::LdapGroup Module for Netscape Directory Server (continued)

```
    foreach my $member (@{$self->members})
      {
      $member =~ m#uid=([^,]+)#;
      $member_hash->{$member} = $self->getMember($1);
      }
    return $member_hash;
    }

sub findPerson
  {
  my ($self,$member) = @_;
  return $self->{ldap}->search (
        base   => $self->{base},
        filter => "(uid=$member)" );
  }

1;
```

Group Membership in Perspective

A directory of users and groups, and an API to search and update that directory, is central to all groupware applications. What should that directory be? That depends on a lot of things: the scope of your application, the kinds of user/group data you need to store, and the availability of existing directories. Ideally you want to use existing directories, not create new ones. In practice, until LDAP pervades LANs and intranets, you'll find yourself in a transitional zone, working with a mixed bag of application-specific directories and NOS directories. A thin abstraction layer that isolates your groupware applications from these various directory APIs is one strategy that will help you weather the transition.

12

Authentication and Authorization Techniques

In the last chapter, we built a simple update notifier. It's based on the push/pull technique. Each message summarizes new docbase records and includes links that point back to the complete records. If those documents are intended for use only by subscribers, you'll need to enforce some kind of access control.

In this chapter, we'll look at ways to control access to both statically served and dynamically served documents, using either the Apache or Microsoft IIS web servers. We'll also explore how to combine simple user-based access control with a more sophisticated attribute-based approach that's sensitive not only to who is requesting a document, but also to what's in the document.

We should define some terms before proceeding. By *authentication* I mean proving a user's identity, typically by looking up a name/password combination in a directory. By *authorization* I mean proving that an authenticated user is allowed to access some protected resource.

HTTP Basic Authentication

Available with every web server, HTTP basic authentication is a very simple protocol. When a browser asks for a protected resource, the server sends back an authentication header instead, like this:

```
HTTP/1.0 401 Unauthorized
WWW-Authenticate: Basic realm=subscribers
```

The browser reacts to this message by presenting its standard login dialog to the user, accepting a name and password, then retrying its original request but with the addition of this header:

```
Authorization: Basic QWxhZGRpbjpvcGVuIHNlc2FtZQ==
```

The gobbledygook is a Base64-encoded representation of credentials in the form `username:password`. When the server receives the `Authorization:` header, it decodes the credentials, in this case yielding `Aladdin:open sesame`.

If the server determines that user *Aladdin*, with the password `open sesame`, is authorized to access the resource named in the original request—which might be an HTML file or a CGI script—then it releases that resource. Otherwise, typically, it reissues the authentication challenge so the user can try to log in again.

This technique provides a weak form of security. It's weak because login credentials travel as cleartext—that is, unencrypted. Anyone with a strategically placed packet sniffer—and nowadays, that includes a lot of kids who have too much time on their hands and who think of computer espionage as a recreational sport—can capture your users' passwords with alarming ease. You can strengthen basic authentication dramatically by using SSL to encrypt the credentials—along with the rest of the data that passes between the browser and the server. Chapter 13, *Deploying NNTP Discussion Servers*, shows how to use SSL to encrypt NNTP sessions; the same procedure applies to HTTP sessions too.

Shared Account Versus Individual Accounts

Ideally your authenticated docbase can leverage a preexisting directory of users and groups. If not, you'll have to create some kind of directory, perhaps using one of the methods we saw in the last chapter. In either case, the simplest kind of authentication for a group involves a single account shared by everyone in the group.

The shared-account method is convenient. But when you map a whole group onto one individual, you lose the ability to deal with anyone as an individual. If someone leaves the group, you can't revoke that person's access—you have to modify the shared account and alert everyone in the group to the change.

The alternative is to bite the administrative bullet and create user accounts for everyone. Then you can segregate users into groups and regulate access to resources using group accounts.

What's the best approach? As usual, it depends on all sorts of factors. On intranets or public sites that only require casual security for fairly small groups, the lazy shared-account method may be good enough. When security needs to be more stringent or when groups get larger, it may be necessary to assign and manage individual accounts. Until LAN-based and Internet-oriented directory services converge, the management of individual and group identities is going to be an unavoidably vexing problem.

Basic Authentication for Apache

To implemented shared-account authentication in Apache, start by creating a user account and assigning a password to that account. You can do that with the *htpasswd* tool, like this:

```
htpasswd -c subscribers subscriber
```

This command prompts for a password and when you supply one, it creates a file called *subscribers* containing a single record for a user named *subscriber,* along with an encrypted version of the password you type in.

To control access to all the files in a directory, you need to associate the user account with a web subtree. In Apache, you do that in the server's configuration file (either *access.conf* or the master file *httpd.conf*) like this:

```
<Directory /web/Docbase/ProductAnalysis/docs>
AuthType Basic
AuthName subscribers
AuthUserFile /secure/subscribers
require user valid-user
</Directory>
```

Group Authentication in Apache

You can define a group of subscribers by listing names in a file, like this:

```
subscribers: ed joe sharon
```

If that group definition is stored in the file */secure/groups*, you can use the following configuration directives to permit only group members:

```
<Directory /web/Docbase/ProductAnalysis/docs>
AuthType Basic
AuthName subscribers
AuthUserFile /secure/subscribers
AuthGroupFile /secure/groups
require group subscribers
</Directory>
```

In this case, you have to define the group in */secure/groups* and also list all the individual subscribers and their passwords in */secure/subscribers.*

Managing Larger Groups in Apache

If there are hundreds or thousand of users, you can speed things up dramatically by storing the names and passwords in a DBM database, which is a disk-based hashtable of name/value pairs. Apache comes with a Perl script, *dbmmanage*, that you can use to add names and cleartext passwords to a DBM file of names and encrypted passwords. You configure Apache to use that database as shown in the following code.

```
<Directory /web/Docbase/ProductAnalysis/docs>
AuthType Basic
AuthDBMUserFile /secure/subscribers
require user valid-user
</Directory>
```

In this case, the subscriber database lives in a pair of files called *subscribers.dir* (the DBM index) and *subscribers.pag* (the DBM data). The `AuthDBMUserFile` directive requires a supporting Apache module, *mod_auth_dbm*, which isn't compiled and linked in to a default build of Apache. To add the module, edit the *Configuration* file in Apache's *src* directory, uncomment the line that refers to *mod_auth_dbm*, and then rebuild Apache like this:

```
$ ./Configure
$ make
```

If you want to use an SQL database instead of a DBM file and you've configured Apache to use *mod_perl*, you can use the Perl module *Apache::AuthenDBI* (available on CPAN). This approach won't make lookups any faster than the DBM method, but it's more flexible. DBM libraries don't support record locking, so if you want to handle updates cleanly, you'll want to use an SQL engine. There are quite a few Apache modules that deal with authentication and authorization; in addition to CPAN, see *http://www.apache.org/* for Apache modules and *http://perl. apache.org/* for Apache/Perl modules.

Basic Authentication for IIS

With IIS, start by denying the anonymous user's permission to read the subtree you want to protect. On a standalone server named *UDELL* or in a domain of the same name, that anonymous account by default is *IUSR_UDELL*. Normally the anonymous user can read the entire web subtree, either because you've granted read permission for that account or because it belongs to a group that has read permission. To revoke read permission, locate the folder you want to protect (e.g., */web/Docbase/ProductAnalysis/docs*) in the Windows Explorer, do right-click → Properties → Security → Permissions, and remove the anonymous user. While you're there, add the name of the account to which you do want to grant access. Be sure to click *Replace Permissions on Subdirectories* if you want to apply these changes to the whole subtree.

You also need to tell IIS that it's OK to use basic authentication when the anonymous user's credentials fail—as will happen now that you've revoked that user's permission to read the subtree. In IIS 4, you do this in the Microsoft Management Console (MMC). Find the virtual root corresponding to the directory you want to protect—or one of its parents, if you want basic authentication to be available more broadly on this server—and do right-click → Properties → Directory Security → Anonymous Access and Authentication Control → Edit. Check the *Basic*

Authentication box. If need be, you can use its associated *Edit* button to specify an authenticating domain controller instead of the default, which is the local server's directory.

This second step—configuring IIS to use basic authentication for files that the anonymous user doesn't have permission to read—is crucial but easy to forget. If you do forget, IIS behaves very strangely when you try to access protected pages. It prompts for credentials but accepts none—not even those of the administrator.

Managing Larger Groups in IIS

To grant access to groups listed in the NT directory, follow the same procedure, but grant permission to a group account rather than an individual user account. Things get trickier when the group gets too big for the local server or the domain controller to handle or when you don't want your authenticated population to overlap with the domain population.

Solutions to this problem typically involve an Internet Services API (ISAPI) filter, which is the IIS analog to an Apache module. I'm not aware of a freely available filter that's equivalent to Apache's *AuthenDBI.* A low-end commercial product is *DAF* (dynamic authentication filter, *http://www.dafweb.com/*), which authenticates users against names and passwords stored in an ODBC database. A high-end commercial product is Microsoft's Site Server (*http://www.microsoft.com/siteserver/*), which includes a Personalization and Membership Service that maps between Site Server's LDAP service and NT's domain directory. Alternatively, you can create your own authentication filter; we'll see a trivial example of that later in this chapter.

Protecting Scripts in Apache

The techniques we've seen so far can protect statically served files and would work for the static version of the docbase viewer we developed in Chapter 7, *Docbase Navigation.* What about the other viewer that relies on a server-side script to dish out pages dynamically? In that case you'd need to protect the directory from which the script runs or perhaps the script itself. Here's a CGI URL that produces a record from the ProductAnalysis docbase:

```
/cgi-bin/Docbase/doc-view.pl?app=ProductAnalysis&
    index=company&doc=1999-03-14-000027.htm
```

In Apache you can protect that script like this:

```
<Directory /web/cgi-bin/Docbase>
AuthType Basic
AuthDBMUserFile /secure/subscribers
require user valid-user
</Directory>
```

Since Apache's notion of access control is directory oriented, though, this setup restricts access to all the docbases accessible by way of */cgi-bin/Docbase* scripts. If you need a more granular approach, you can instead do this:

```
<Directory /web/cgi-bin/Docbase/ProductAnalysis>
```

The problem with this method is that you'll need to locate a copy of *doc-view.pl*, or at least a wrapper that would refer to a common instance of *doc-view.pl*, in each docbase's CGI subdirectory.

Protecting Scripts in IIS

To protect a script in IIS, find the script file in the Explorer, revoke the anonymous user's permission to read the script file, and grant the desired user or group permission. That's not all, though. You also have to find the script file in the MMC, do right-click → Properties → File Security → Anonymous Access and Authentication Control → Edit, and uncheck *Allow Anonymous Access*. Otherwise, the anonymous user will try to read the script file in order to execute it, and that access will fail before any further authentication can occur.

Unlike Apache's approach to access control, IIS' can be file oriented as well as directory oriented. That means you can store differently authenticated scripts in a common directory. But you still can't use a single script protected in this way to serve multiple docbases to different audiences. Conventional HTTP authentication, whether it's applied to statically served files or to scripts that serve files dynamically, is an all-or-none game. Either you can see a file, or you can't. Either you can run a script, or you can't.

Attribute-Based Access

Let's up the ante. Suppose we don't merely want to allow an undifferentiated group of subscribers to access the ProductAnalysis docbase. Suppose, instead, we want to restrict access based on a relationship between an attribute of a docbase record and an attribute of a subscriber record. Protections applied to directories, files, or scripts won't suffice.

In the last chapter, we built a notifier that alerts subscribers when a docbase receives new reports about companies in which the docbase subscribers have registered an interest. If we want to use conventional authentication techniques to deny access to reports about companies other than those a subscriber has signed up for, we'd have to materialize nodes in filesystem space for each company, locate HTML files (or file-serving scripts) at each node, and bind a user or group authorization method to each node. You might be able to make this work, but it would be crazy to try—the administrative burden would crush you.

The problem isn't *how* authentication is done. Whether you're using basic authentication or a cookie, as we'll see later in this chapter, or even a client-side digital ID, the problem is that standard authorization only allows or denies a file or script. It can't make access-control decisions based on attributes of documents. Authorization is tightly coupled to the filesystem. We've got to break that coupling in order to be able to apply basic authentication in a more granular way.

An Authenticating Script for Apache

We'll start by observing that web servers aren't the only things that can issue `Authorization:` headers. Scripts can do that too. Example 12-1 is a simple Perl script that challenges for a name and password, just as an authenticating web server does.

Example 12-1. Scripting the Name/Password Challenge

```
use MIME::Base64;

if ( ! defined $ENV{HTTP_AUTHORIZATION} )    # if no Authorization: header
  {
  print "HTTP/1.0 401 Authentication\n";     # issue authorization challenge
  print "WWW-Authenticate: Basic realm=\"subscribers\"\n\n";
  return;
  }

print "HTTP/1.0 200 Ok\n";                      # needed for ISAPI Perl or mod_perl
print "Content-type: text/html\n\n";            # the standard header
$ENV{HTTP_AUTHORIZATION} =~ m/Basic (.+)/i;     # get MIME-encoded credentials
print "Hello " . decode_base64($1);             # print "Hello Aladdin:open sesame"
```

We've introduced another CPAN module here. *MIME::Base64* converts back and forth between plain text and the Base64 encoding used by the HTTP basic authentication protocol. If you put this code in a file called *auth.pl*, put that file into the */cgi-bin* directory of an Apache web server, and ask your browser to fetch */cgi-bin/auth.pl*, you'll provoke an authentication dialog. Type in the credentials *Aladdin* and `open sesame` and you'll get the reponse `Hello Aladdin:open sesame`.

If that doesn't work, define the symbol `SECURITY_HOLE_PASS_AUTHORIZATION` and rebuild Apache. What? Open a security hole? Well, here's what the Apache source code says about allowing scripts to see the `Authorization:` header:

```
/*
 * You really don't want to disable this check, since it leaves you
 * wide open to CGIs stealing passwords and people viewing them
 * in the environment with "ps -e".  But, if you must...
 */
```

On an Apache server that hosts multiple CGI-capable sites, it's probably a good idea to hold `Authorization:` headers close to the vest. Apache wisely defaults to this behavior. But if you run your own Apache server on a dedicated machine that you control, it's reasonable to pass the `Authorization:` header through to your scripts. IIS, by the way, always does so.

Here's how this protocol works. The initial request sends no `Authorization:` header, so the script responds with a challenge, then exits. Why does it exit? The code following the credentials check is protected. When the browser retries the request, the script sees an `Authorization:` header and the protected code runs.

Clearly we need to do more than just check for the presence of an `Authorization:` header. We'll want to look up the credentials somewhere and decide whether to authenticate the user. Having done so, the protected code will be in a position to do more. It could, for example, look up the value of the company field in a requested docbase record and compare that with the list of companies subscribed to by the authenticated user. But before we build that piece, let's look at why this script won't work the same way in IIS and how to fix that.

An Authenticating Script for IIS

As far as Apache is concerned, the script shown in Example 12-1 has nothing to do with any of the authentication and authorization schemes that Apache may be using. The script itself, in other words, is unprotected. There's no directive in *httpd.conf* that names */cgi-bin* as a protected directory, so there's no trigger that causes Apache to issue an authentication challenge. When a user tries to run the script, it acts autonomously to provide its own authentication and authorization.

If you try the same thing with IIS, though, you'll find that the script behaves differently. The browser can't log in with any random credentials, as in the Apache case. It can only authenticate with the credentials of a real user listed in the server's local domain or in the domain to which the server belongs.

This behavior is arguably a bug. Even though the script isn't declared to IIS as a protected resource, IIS—seeing the incoming `Authorization:` header—steps in and decides to authenticate the credentials against the NT domain. Only a valid domain user—albeit *any* user!—can pass. It's not clear what resource IIS thinks it is protecting when it does this. The behavior might be OK if you want to write a script that uses generic domain authentication but then provides its own custom authorization—such as the documents-by-subscribed-company rule that we want to enforce. But it's not OK if you need to support subscribers who aren't domain users. Are you out of luck in this case? No, but you can't solve this problem in Perl (at least not yet). You'll have to fire up a compiler and build a simple ISAPI filter.

A Pass-Through ISAPI Authentication Filter

Web servers process requests in phases—user authentication, HTTP header processing, URL-to-filename mapping. Each phase creates the opportunity for a server extension—which can be a Netscape Server API (NSAPI) plug-in, or an Apache module, or an ISAPI filter—to alter the server's behavior in some useful way. In this case we need to hook into the user authentication phase. Microsoft's Visual C++ compiler makes that very easy to do, because it includes a wizard that knows about the phases of IIS request processing and can generate the framework for a filter that deals with one or more of these phases. To create a custom authentication handler, start the MS Developer Studio and do File → New → Projects → ISAPI Extension Wizard. Check the *Generate a Filter Object* box, uncheck *Generate a Server Extension Object*, and then complete the ensuing dialog box, as shown in Figure 12-1.

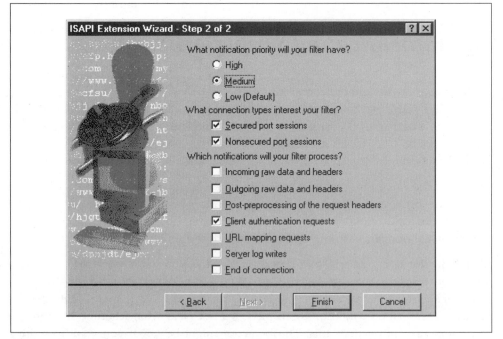

Figure 12-1. Generating the framework for an ISAPI filter

Example 12-2 shows our completed authentication filter. It's mostly boilerplate code written by the wizard. The four lines in the body of the *CMod_ authFilter::onAuthentication()* method are the only human contribution to this filter.

Example 12-2. A Pass-Through Isapi Authentication Filter

```cpp
// MOD_AUTH.CPP - Implementation file for your Internet Server
//    mod_auth Filter

#include "stdafx.h"
#include "mod_auth.h"

CWinApp theApp;

CMod_authFilter theFilter;

CMod_authFilter::CMod_authFilter() {}

CMod_authFilter::~CMod_authFilter() {}

BOOL CMod_authFilter::GetFilterVersion(PHTTP_FILTER_VERSION pVer)
{
  // Call default implementation for initialization
  CHttpFilter::GetFilterVersion(pVer);

  // Clear the flags set by base class
  pVer->dwFlags &= ~SF_NOTIFY_ORDER_MASK;

  // Set the flags we are interested in
  pVer->dwFlags |= SF_NOTIFY_ORDER_LOW | SF_NOTIFY_SECURE_PORT |
                   SF_NOTIFY_NONSECURE_PORT |
                   SF_NOTIFY_AUTHENTICATION | SF_NOTIFY_END_OF_NET_SESSION;

  // Load description string
  TCHAR sz[SF_MAX_FILTER_DESC_LEN+1];
  ISAPIVERIFY(::LoadString(AfxGetResourceHandle(),
      IDS_FILTER, sz, SF_MAX_FILTER_DESC_LEN));
  _tcscpy(pVer->lpszFilterDesc, sz);
  return TRUE;
}

DWORD CMod_authFilter::OnAuthentication(CHttpFilterContext* pCtxt,
  PHTTP_FILTER_AUTHENT pAuthent)
{
  strcpy(pAuthent->pszUser,"nobody");      // become user nobody
  pAuthent->cbUserBuff = strlen(pAuthent->pszUser);
  strcpy(pAuthent->pszPassword,"nobody"); // with password nobody
  pAuthent->cbPasswordBuff = strlen(pAuthent->pszPassword);
  return SF_STATUS_REQ_NEXT_NOTIFICATION;
}

// Do not edit the following lines, which are needed by ClassWizard.
#if 0
BEGIN_MESSAGE_MAP(CMod_authFilter, CHttpFilter)
  //{{AFX_MSG_MAP(CMod_authFilter)
  //}}AFX_MSG_MAP
END_MESSAGE_MAP()
#endif  // 0
```

The *onAuthentication()* method reaches into a structure in which IIS has recorded the name and password collected from the user and changes those credentials to `nobody:nobody`. Why? If user *nobody* is a valid (albeit weakly privileged) local or domain user, authentication will succeed. This wouldn't be very useful if it meant that you had to map all external users to user *nobody*. In that case, you'd only reproduce the existing anonymous user mechanism. Fortunately the original credentials are still sitting untouched in the `Authorization:` header, where our *auth.pl* script expects to find them. Weird? I guess so, but that's how IIS works. You can simultaneously be `nobody:nobody` to IIS and `Aladdin:open sesame` to a groupware application. Products like DAF and, on a grander scale, Microsoft's own Site Server rely on this same method: a real NT account acts as a proxy for a set of external accounts.

To install this filter, right-click the web server's icon in the MMC, select Properties → ISAPI Filters, and give the name of the filter—for example, *mod_auth.dll*

An Attribute-Based Authorization Script

Now we can proceed, in a portable manner, to build an access-control application that correlates docbase attributes with user attributes. Example 12-3 focuses on the part of the solution that compares a docbase attribute to a database of subscriptions.

Example 12-3. Authorizing Users by a Docbase Attribute

```
use strict;

use DBI;

my $dbh = DBI->connect('DBI:Solid:Subscriptions','dba','dba') # connect to subs db
  or die ("connect, $DBI::errstr");

my $http_authorization_header = $ENV{HTTP_AUTHORIZATION};    # extract auth header

sub isBasicAuthUserForCompany
  {
  my ($http_authorization, $dbh) = @_;
  $http_authorization_header = m/Basic (.+)/i;               # isolate credentials
  my $http_authorization = $1;
  my ($user, $password) = split (':', $1);                   # get name/pw
  my ($st) =                                                 # make query
   "select count(*) from cmp_users where cmp = '$company' and user = '$user'";
  return (
        isAuthenticated($user,$password) and                 # authenticate (not shown)
        dbSqlReturnValue ($dbh, $st)                         # authorize
        );
  }

sub dbSqlReturnValue
  {
```

Example 12-3. Authorizing Users by a Docbase Attribute (continued)

```
my ($dbh,$st) = @_;
my $sth = $dbh->prepare($st);   # prepare sql
my $value;
$sth->execute;                  # execute sql
$sth->bind_col(1, \$value);     # bind result to value
$sth->finish;                   # finish sql
return $value;
}
```

In this fragment, `$http_authorization` gets the value of the CGI environment variable `$ENV{HTTP_AUTHORIZATION}`. This is the `Authorization:` header sent from a browser in response to a prior challenge issued by this (or another) script. We'll assume that `$company` was extracted from a docbase record, using our old friend *Docbase::Docbase::getMetadata()*. `$dbh` is a handle to the database that contains the *cmp_users* table.

The *isBasicAuthUserForCompany()* function does two checks. It sends the name/password credentials to *isAuthenticated()* for authentication (look ahead to Example 12-4 to see how that's done), and it looks up the user/company pair in *cmp_users* for authorization. We're using Perl's *DBI* interface here, so the database could be any of those supported by a *DBD* module. This code will run under Unix/Apache or NT/IIS, because Perl's *DBI* and *DBD* modules are available in both environments.

For an NT-based intranet application, we could dispense with the ISAPI filter and let NT authenticate the user against its directory. We could then use *Group::NTGroup::isMember()* to test whether that user was a member of the *subscribers* group, but even that won't be necessary if we assume that only authorized subscribers are listed in the database.

On an NT-based system that serves a nonlocal population of users, though, we'll need to use the filter and provide a version of *isAuthenticated()* that does some form of directory- or database-style authentication. The same holds true for a system based on Apache, Netscape, or any other server that is directory-independent in the Unix style rather than directory-integrated in the NT style.

Scripted Authentication Using Netscape Directory Server

Suppose we're using the Netscape Directory Server. It stores passwords in one of three ways: as cleartext, encrypted with the Unix *crypt()* function, or encrypted using Secure Hash Algorithm (*SHA*). Here's how the server represents an SHA-encrypted password as an attribute of a user object:

```
{SHA}W8r/fyL/UzygmbNAjq2HbA67qac=
```

The gobbledygook after {SHA} is another Base64-encoded value. It decodes to a 20-byte SHA hash. We can extract that value in hexadecimal form like this:

```
use MIME::Base64;
print unpack('H*', decode_base64('W8r/fyL/UzygmbNAjq2HbA67qac='));
```

The result is '5bcaff7f22ff533ca099b3408ead876c0ebba9a7', which is the hexadecimal representation of the SHA hash value of the password open sesame.

Like Unix's *crypt()*, SHA is a one-way hashing function. When you assign a password in Directory Server, it applies the one-way hash to the cleartext password to produce an encrypted password, which it stores in a user object in the directory. When a browser, mailreader, or newsreader tries to authenticate to a Directory Server–based application—such as Netscape's web, mail or news server—the sequence of events is as follows:

The client sends a name and password to the provider of the service it's requesting.
We'll call this provider the *application server*, to distinguish it from the directory server. This client-to-application-server connection can be a cleartext channel or it can be SSL-encrypted. In either case the application server ultimately gets hold of a cleartext password.

The application server looks up the user in Directory Server and retrieves the encrypted password.
Again this channel may be cleartext or SSL-encrypted.

The application server compares the two sets of credentials.
It applies SHA to the cleartext password received from the user to produce an encrypted password. Then it compares that encrypted password with the one retrieved from Directory Server. If the two match, the application server accepts the credentials as authentic.

Although the hash algorithm itself is thought to be irreversible, which means that there is no way to recover a cleartext password from its hashed counterpart, all the usual caveats apply. We like to say that this kind of scheme authenticates a user, but really it just authenticates a set of credentials that may or may not have issued from that user. If I leave my browser logged in to a protected site and you walk up to my PC and start fetching pages, the cached credentials will still look just fine to the application server. Of course, the jig is up if I allow my cleartext password to travel over an unencrypted connection and you capture it with a sniffer. The jig may or may not be up if you gain access to my directory server and capture encrypted passwords. The passwords, even though encrypted, are vulnerable to brute-force dictionary attacks. For this reason the cryptographically ideal password is a long string of gobbledygook. Unfortunately that kind of password is worse than useless to the poor human who is supposed to use it, who can't memorize a long string of gobbledygook and who will have to write it down on a scrap of paper and stick it to a keyboard or monitor. This dilemma is the Scylla and Charybdis of computer security, and there's no simple way to navigate through it.

Bearing these caveats in mind, we can write a script that uses Directory Server in the same way that Netscape's SuiteSpot servers do. We've already seen how to fetch attributes of a user object by using *Group::LdapGroup*. Here's a fragment that fetches Aladdin's SHA-encrypted password:

```
use Group::LdapGroup;

my $g = Group::LdapGroup->new("ldap.roninhouse.com",389,
        "o=RoninHouse","subscribers","uid=admin,o=RoninHouse",
        "admin_password");
print $g->getProperty("Aladdin","userpassword");
```

If we've received a password from a user who purports to be Aladdin, we SHA-encrypt the cleartext password and compare it to the encrypted one:

```
use MIME::Base64;
use SHA;

my $sha = new SHA;
$sha->add("open sesame");
my $digest = $sha->digest();                # compute digest
my $password =                              # look up password in directory
  $g->getProperty("Aladdin","userpassword");
$password =~ s/(SHA{([^}]+)/;               # isolate password in $1
if ( $1 eq encode_base64($digest) )         # compare
        { print "Authenticated"; }
else
        { print "Not authenticated"; }
```

An Authorizing Docbase Viewer

Now let's put the pieces together. Example 12-4 shows how an authorizing version of a docbase viewer, such as the *doc-view.pl* script we saw in Chapter 7, can restrict access to a docbase based on a combination of group membership and attribute-based subscription. It enforces the following requirements:

- The user can be authenticated to a directory server.

- The user is a member of the *subscribers* group.

- The **company** field of the requested document matches one of the subscribed-to companies listed for that user in the subscription database.

In addition to illustrating these mechanisms, Example 12-4 shows how it's possible to integrate the Perl technologies we've seen already into the Active Server Pages environment.

Example 12-4. An ASP Version of the Authorizing Viewer

```
<%@ language = PerlScript%>

<%
use Group::LdapGroup;
use MIME::Base64;
use SHA;
use Docbase::Docbase;

my $g = Group::LdapGroup->new("ldap.roninhouse.com",389,"o=RoninHouse.com",
        "ProductAnalysisSubscribers","uid=admin,o=RoninHouse.com","admin_passwd");

my $doc = $Request->{doc}->{Item};              # retrieve CGI var
                                                # for document
my $dbh = $Application->Contents->dbhandle;     # acquire db handle

my $db = Docbase::Docbase->new('ProductAnalysis');  # initialize docbase
my $metarecord = $db->getMetadata("$docroot/$doc"); # look up metadata for doc
my $company = $metarecord->{company};           # extract company field

my $deny_message  = "";

my $basic_auth_obj =                            # get basic auth header object
   $Request->ServerVariables(HTTP_AUTHORIZATION);

my $basic_auth  = $basic_auth_obj->{Item};      # extract header from object

if ( ! isBasicAuthUserForCompany($company) )    # can't authorize user
  {                                             # for company
  $Response->{Status} ="401 $deny_message";     # say why not in status header
  $Response->AddHeader("WWW-Authenticate",      # and issue auth challenge
       "Basic realm=ProductAnalysisSubscribers");
  }
else
  {
  $Response->write("Authorized");               # success
  #—code to display record goes here— # show the authorized record
  }

sub isBasicAuthUserForCompany
  {
  my ($company) = @_;

  if ( $basic_auth eq '' )                      # if no auth credentials
    {
    $deny_message = "NoCredentials\n";          # fail for that reason
    return 0;
    }

  $basic_auth =~ m/Basic (.+)/i;                # isolate MIME-encoded credentials
                                                # in $1
  my ($user, $typed_password) =                 # extract user:password
    split(':',decode_base64($1));
```

Example 12-4. An ASP Version of the Authorizing Viewer (continued)

```
    if (! isAuthenticated ($g, $user, $typed_password) ) # if password bad
      {
      $deny_message = "BadPassword";                # fail for that reason
      return 0;
      }

    if (! $g->isMember($user) )                    # if user not member of this group
      {
      $deny_message = "NotMember";                 # fail for that reason
      return 0 ;
      }

    return isSubscribedToCompany ($user, $company); # test subscription
    }

sub isAuthenticated
  {
  my ($g,$user, $typed_password) = @_;

  my $sha = new SHA;                              # create new SHA object

  $sha->add($typed_password);                     # load in password typed by user

  my $digest = $sha->digest();                    # hash it

  my $computed_encrypted_password =               # MIME-encode it
    encode_base64($digest);

  chomp $computed_encrypted_password;             # trim newline added by encoder

  my ($stored_encrypted_password) =               # look up password
      $g->getProperty($user,"userpassword");

  $stored_encrypted_password =~ s/{SHA}//;        # isolate password

  return                                          # return comparison
      ( $computed_encrypted_password eq $stored_encrypted_password );
  }

sub isSubscribedToCompany
  {
  my ($user, $company) = @_;

  if ( $company eq '' )                           # no company found in
    {                                             # requested doc
    $deny_message = "NoCompanySpecified";         # fail for that reason
    return 0;
    }

  $user = alltrim($user);
  my $st =
    "select count(*) from cmp_users where cmp = '$company' and user = '$user'";
  my $rs = $dbh->Execute($st);                    # execute sql
  my $count = $rs->Fields(0)->value;              # extract company name
```

Example 12-4. An ASP Version of the Authorizing Viewer (continued)

```
if (! $count)                                # user not subscribed to company
  {
  $deny_message = "NotSubscribedToCompany";  # fail for that reason
  return 0;
  }

return 1;
  }


%>
```

This example expands on the fragment shown in Example 12-3, combining database-oriented subscription lookup with directory-oriented user lookup. And, just to show that it's possible, I've switched from a portable Perl implementation to an ASP-specific setup. Although Example 12-4 is written in Perl, it runs in the ASP environment under IIS or another NT server that supports Active Server Pages. Where the earlier example used *DBI* to connect to a database, this example uses an ActiveX Data Objects database (ADODB) object.

Where does that ADODB object come from? It's not shown in Example 12-4 because it's part of the Active Server Pages environment. The *global.asa* file that governs the authorizing script's */cgi-bin* directory contains the following setup code:

```
<SCRIPT LANGUAGE=VBScript RUNAT=Server>
sub Application_OnStart
Set Conn = Server.CreateObject("ADODB.Connection")
Conn.Open "Subscribers"
Set Application("dbhandle") = Conn
end sub
</SCRIPT>
```

In addition to its method of attribute-based authentication, this script illustrates one way to cache a database connection. The *Server.CreateObject()* call happens just once, producing a database connection that's tucked into a slot of the ASP Application object. Each time the authorizing script runs, it fetches a handle to that connection from the persistent Application object. Could we cache a connection to the LDAP directory as well? Not with the current version of *Group::LdapGroup*. But a version of that module that used ADSI could do so by stashing an ADSI handle into the ASP Application object, just as we're doing with the ADOBD object shown here.

It's fascinating to see how PerlScript, the version of Win32 Perl that plugs into the ASP environment, can wield all the Perl modules we've seen so far while simultaneously tapping into the facilities of the ASP environment. What would Example 12-4 look like if written in the generic Perl style of the earlier Example 12-1? Not much different. I'd have used *TinyCGI* to fetch the CGI variables instead of ASP's Request object, and *DBI* to connect to the database. The resulting script would be a more general solution that could run under NT/IIS or Unix/Apache. However, you'd need to cache the database connection differently in each of these environments. ActiveState's PerlEx (*http://www.activestate.com/*) is one way to do that for NT/IIS; *mod_perl* (*http://perl.apache.org/*) and *Apache::DBI* (a CPAN module) combine to create one solution for Unix/Apache; the *dhttp* system we'll explore in Chapter 15, *Distributed HTTP*, solves the problem in another way for either environment. For the kinds of scripts that you need to write to support custom groupware, portability often has little to do with the script language itself. What matters more is the environment in which the script runs and the components available to it.

There's no file-oriented access control here; our authorizing script is the sole arbiter of access to the docbase. It follows that you can't locate the docbase in a public web directory, since users then can bypass the access script and scoop up the files directly. If you locate the docbase somewhere that's script accessible but not web-visible, you can guarantee that the script is the only way to reach it and that the script's access-control logic will always apply.

Using Cookies to Authorize Access

Although cookies have become a major Internet *cause célèbre*, there really isn't much difference between name/password-based and cookie-based authorization. In both cases, the browser transmits credentials to the server by way of an HTTP header—it's either `HTTP_AUTHORIZATION` or `HTTP_COOKIE`. In both cases, security is weak when credentials travel over an unencrypted connection and much stronger when the data is encrypted with SSL. In both cases, authentication can persist so that users need not repeatedly assert their identities. The chief advantage of the cookie method is also its worst public-relations problem: cookies persist across browser sessions. (With basic authentication, credentials persist only during a session.) A cookie enables a server to recognize a user and authorize access automatically, without any input from the user. In order to do that, cookie data has to live on your hard disk. We'll review what that data is, how it gets onto your hard disk, and how it can be used. But first let's frame this volatile issue with a few observations:

Any form of authentication does away with anonymity.
Large areas of the Internet are open to anonymous use and will likely remain so. Groupware, though, is about relationships, and relationships are based on identity. If you choose to participate in a groupware application—on a public Internet site that serves 300,000 magazine subscribers or on an intranet server that hosts a team of a dozen collaborators—you must be willing to identify yourself. From this perspective it makes no difference whether you announce

your identity by way of an HTTP_AUTHORIZATION header or an HTTP_COOKIE header.

Privacy depends on honor and trust.

When you give up your anonymity, you also lose absolute control of your privacy. All your actions and behavior in an authenticated realm can be monitored. At issue is whether, or to what degree, you actually are monitored and how the information collected about you will be used. Ideally an authenticated service should invite you to specify what you will allow it to remember about you, explain how what it remembers will help you, and state whether that information will be released and, if so, to whom and on what terms. Users who participate in authenticated services place their trust in these kinds of agreements. Providers of authenticated services have to honor the terms of these agreements. Again, though, this has nothing to do with cookies. The issue is authentication itself and its implications, not the means of authentication.

Offer multiple means of authentication.

Despite these arguments, a lot of people just plain hate the idea of cookies. Why fight that? If someone thinks that a cookie is a kind of virus (it isn't), you're not likely to be able to change that perception, and there's really no reason to try. Offer basic authentication as an alternative. We'll see shortly how you can use both methods in parallel.

Setting a Cookie

Here's a generic Perl fragment that sets a cookie:

```
print "Content-type: text/html\n";
print "Set-Cookie:
            ProductAnalysisSubscriber=Aladdin%00926515678%00192.168.1;
            path=/cgi-bin; expires=Wed, 11-May-2000 00:00:00 GMT\n\n";
```

Or to continue with ASP-based PerlScript as in Example 12-4:

```
$Response->AddHeader("Set-Cookie",
        ProductAnalysisSubscriber=Aladdin%00926515678%00192.168.1;
        path=/cgi-bin; expires=Wed, 11-May-2000 00:00:00 GMT\n\n";
```

On a Windows machine, when user *Jon* is logged in and the web server is localhost, Internet Explorer records that information in the file *c:\WINNT\Profiles\Jon\Cookies\jon@localhost.txt*.

On the same Windows machine, Communicator adds the following line to *c:\program files\Netscape\users\jon\cookies.txt*:

```
localhost  FALSE  /  cgi-bin  FALSE  958035600  ProductAnalysisSubscriber
    Aladdin%00926515678%00192.168.1
```

Table 12-1 lists the elements of this cookie.

Table 12-1. Anatomy of a Cookie

Element	Description
localhost	Which domain or specific server created and can read back the cookie? Use DOMAIN=.DomainName.com if multiple servers in a domain need to read the cookie.
FALSE	Can all machines in the server's domain read the cookie? Defaults to FALSE. Only a single server can read it. Note that regardless of this setting, no server outside the cookie's domain of origin can read it.
/cgi-bin	For which set of URLs will the browser send the cookie? In this case, only for scripts run from */cgi-bin*. Defaults to /.
FALSE	Will your browser send its cookie only in secure mode? Defaults to FALSE. Your browser will send a cookie in both secure (SSL) and nonsecure modes.
958035600	The cookie expiration date, expressed as the number of seconds since January 1970.
ProductAnalysis-Subscriber	The name of the cookie.
Aladdin %00926515678%0019 2.168.1	The value of the cookie. In this case, the concatenation of the username *Aladdin*, a timestamp, and an IP subnet address.

What to Put in a Cookie and for How Long

Cookies often work hand in hand with basic authentication, since you only want to plant a cookie on a browser once you've authenticated the user of that browser. What credentials should the cookie store? You could put a username/password combination in a cookie, but that's usually not a good idea. If `Aladdin:open sesame` authenticates Aladdin to a central directory, an unattended browser or stolen cookie file could be really bad news. Instead, the cookie value shown in Table 12-1—a username/timestamp/subnet combination—merely remembers that user *Aladdin* successfully authenticated to the ProductAnalysis docbase from the stated subnet at the stated time.

What if you did store real credentials in the cookie but encrypted them? This only offers a marginal benefit. It's true that someone who steals a cookie file is unlikely to be able to decode the value. But if the thief knows or can guess what resource the cookie authorizes access to, there is no need to decode anything. To the authorizing application, the cookie value is just an opaque token that it will match against some stored value. Remember: authentication doesn't prove identity; it only proves that something on the other end of the wire is sending the credentials that you associate with an identity.

How can you authenticate and authorize with this username/timestamp/subnet cookie value? One approach is as follows:

1. Use basic authentication to prove Aladdin's identity by means of a directory lookup, as in Example 12-4.

2. Combine Aladdin's name with a timestamp and subnet address to create a cookie value.

3. Store the value in a database.

4. Set a cookie containing that same value.

Then, amend the authorizing script to test for either basic authentication or cookie authentication:

```
if (
    isCookieAuthUserForCompany ( $cookie, $company            )  or
    isBasicAuthUserForCompany  ( $user, $password, $company )
)
```

If *isCookieAuthUserForCompany()* finds a cookie named `ProductAnalysis-Subscriber`, and if it finds that cookie's value in the database, it authorizes access—subject to the company-subscription test, that is.

If *isCookieAuthUserForCompany()* finds no cookie named `ProductAnalysis-Subscriber`, it fails and *isBasicAuthUserForCompany()* springs into action. If it authenticates the given username/password, it creates a cookie value, stores it in the database, sends the cookie back to the browser, and authorizes access—again subject to the subscription test.

How exactly this should work is a matter of policy. You might, for example, want to ask users whether or not they want your system to remember them. You might want to send cookies only to browsers on known subnets, so that colleagues working on borrowed laptops or from Internet cafes won't leave access tokens lying around where they shouldn't.

The database used in this approach creates an audit trail. If it shows that Aladdin authenticated from a subnet where Aladdin wasn't, or on a date when Aladdin didn't, you've got some security analysis to do and some evidence to work with.

When the cookie expires, Aladdin can acquire a new one by reauthenticating with his name/password. What expiration date should you choose when you set the cookie? As usual, it depends. You're trading risk for convenience. The risk is that a cookie-configured browser that automatically accesses a protected docbase will fall into the wrong hands. The convenience is that when that browser is in the right hands, its user has easier access to the docbase. Further complicating matters, in this case, is the subscription aspect of authorization. If a subscription to a docbase expires, access will be refused no matter what the cookie says. There really isn't a right answer here. A cookie is just a tool that you can use when it's appropriate to do so.

13

Deploying NNTP Discussion Servers

Conferencing, the core groupware application, works most effectively across a range of collaborative scopes. Chapter 4, *Information-Management Strategies for Groupware Users*, shows why it's useful to deploy conferencing at departmental, corporate, and global scopes. Now we'll explore how to do that.

Traditionally, the setup and administration of news servers was a black art practiced exclusively by the wizards who run newsfeeds for large companies and Internet service providers. It's true that managing a full Usenet feed is a complex task and an ongoing challenge. But when you run a standalone news server that doesn't need to connect to the Usenet and doesn't need to expire articles, things get a whole lot simpler. In this mode, an NNTP server works as a dedicated conferencing system. Deployed on a LAN, an intranet, an extranet, or the Internet, it can provide discussion services to anyone running a standard Internet client.

Let's define a deployment scenario. Earlier examples in this book have revolved around a team of analysts who write and publish reports. Let's locate these analysts in a fictitious company—the Ronin Group—that requires the following modes of conferencing:

The analysts' think tank
> This set of newsgroups will be a place for analysts to discuss work in progress and share research data. Some of this information needs to be hidden, not only from the world at large, but also from participants in other internal newsgroups.

The sales lounge
> This set of newsgroups serves the people who market and sell the Ronin Group's reports. They can't be allowed to read the private deliberations of the analysts. Conversely the analysts don't want to be exposed to the scheming and plotting that goes on in the sales lounge.

The company water cooler

Although the nature of the business puts the sales force and the analysts into a somewhat adversarial relationship, it also requires these groups to find ways to collaborate. To this end, the virtual water cooler—a set of newsgroups visible to every Ronin Group employee—serves the same social function as the real water cooler in the Ronin Group's main office. There's no formal agenda or protocol. It's just a place for networking, in the social sense of the word. Chance encounters and spontaneous remarks are welcome and can trigger the kinds of serendipitous connections that make this social activity an important business function.

What's wrong with the real water cooler? There aren't many opportunities to gather there. The Ronin Group operates primary satellite offices in five cities on two continents, plus a number of field sales offices. Several analysts work from their homes. Everyone's traveling a lot. Face time is valuable but scarce. The flow of social interaction needs to be ongoing; it can't all be compressed into those few moments when everyone can be together.

Also visible in the companywide scope are the *it.helpdesk* groups (see Chapter 9, *Conferencing Applications*). All Ronin Group employees use a common suite of software applications and share the same network infrastructure. The IT staff has its hands full just trying to keep all this stuff up and running— there's little time to spare for training and hand-holding. The *it.helpdesk* groups recycle questions and answers into a community knowledge base. And they ease the IT staff's support burden. More capable users can directly assist less capable ones, and when they do so they create a document trail for others to follow.

The public conferences

Here visitors to the Ronin Group's site can meet to discuss issues and trends. Why support public conferences? The Ronin Group sees both a marketing and a research benefit. From a marketing perspective, the company likes to place itself at the center of an online community regarded for high-quality networking. From a research perspective, that networking is as valuable to the analysts as it is to the site visitors. It keeps the analysts' ears to the ground; it puts them in touch with people who apply the products and technologies about which the Ronin Group reports.

Ad hoc focus groups

Since the Ronin Group competes with other providers of the same kinds of reports, it can't afford to expend too much of its intellectual capital in the public groups or engage in discussion that veers into proprietary areas. Internet-accessible but access-restricted focus groups are a place for private collaboration with business partners, freelance employees, and customers.

Administratively, these are just like the groups restricted to salespeople and analysts, except that they can also include nonstaffers.

Like the virtual water cooler, these ad hoc newsgroups help compensate for scarce face time. Anyone who's been to a focus group or a retreat knows that parting promises to stay in touch are rarely kept. Often that's because these temporary groups have no reason not to dissolve. Sometimes, though, collaboration would precede and/or follow the gathering if there were a mechanism to support it. Private conferencing is a great way to facilitate the run-up to a meeting. An agenda can be posted and discussed, initial sparring can occur, and trial balloons can be floated, so that less of the precious face time need be spent on these preliminaries. Likewise private conferencing can support the postmortem phase. Decisions can be posted and discussed; consensus can be adjusted and refined. You can use email for this purpose, and people do, but a threaded discussion that creates a central, searchable, and web-accessible transcript is a much more effective tool for the job.

News Server Alternatives

Now for the nuts and bolts. We'll explore how to use three different news servers—the standard Unix *INN*, Microsoft's NNTP service, and Netscape's Collabra Server—to support these conferencing scenarios. We'll also look at how one proprietary groupware server—Microsoft's Exchange Server 5.5—can support NNTP conferencing.

I include *INN* because it's so widely available nowadays—every Linux CD comes with a copy of it. There are a lot of Linux machines popping up in organizations nowadays, and even the most modest of these systems—say, a 16MB 486 that no longer pushes Microsoft Office at an acceptable rate—can under Linux quite capably deliver local NNTP service. Setup can be surprisingly painless, as is administration when you factor out the complexity of Usenet replication. The biggest drawback to *INN* is that it lacks SSL support. If you're lucky enough to be using a virtual private network (VPN), that may not matter. VPN traffic is encrypted in the network transport layer, so that individual applications such as web and news servers need not provide their own encryption. Nor does *INN*'s lack of SSL support matter for public newsgroups that you want to make available to all comers.

If you don't have a VPN and you do want to conduct confidential and access-restricted discussions across the Internet, you'll need a modern *INN* derivative with SSL support. Both the Microsoft and Netscape news servers meet this requirement. Either of these is also a good choice if you lack in-house Unix expertise, since both can run on Windows NT. People who know how to deploy other kinds of services on NT will find these servers straightforward to set up and manage.

It's true that the SSL-specific aspects of news server administration are complex and can be intimidating. But that's an SSL thing, not an NNTP thing. It's tricky to create and install the server certificates (a.k.a. digital IDs) needed to run a news server in SSL mode. It's even trickier to create and deploy client-side certificates as an alternative to basic or cookie authentication. But the same procedures govern secure web or mail servers. The battle is simply to grasp how the Microsoft and Netscape server suites deal with SSL and public-key infrastructure (PKI) matters. Once you know how to set up and operate a secure web server, you know most of what you need to set up and operate a secure news server—and vice versa.

Note that no matter which server you choose, you'll be able to take advantage of HTML messaging. This sometimes surprises people. With all the snazzy new features in the Netscape and Microsoft newsreaders—automatic encoding of attachments, inline images, tables, rich text, and hyperlinks—it's easy to suppose that some kind of backend support must be required. Not so. An HTML news message is a clump of ASCII headers and a body made of lines of ASCII data—just like any other news message. Interpretation of the HTML is the newsreader's job. When HTML-aware newsreaders see the header `Content-Type: text/html`, they render the message body as HTML. But the server doesn't know or care what's in the body of an HTML message.

Deploying INN on Linux

The latest version of *INN* is available at *http://www.isc.org/*, so you can always grab the source and build your own *INN* if you really want to. But Linux distributions come with a prebuilt *INN* that you can just install and use. For example, if you ask the Red Hat installer to include *INN*, Linux will boot up with a news server running and ready for use.

There are a lot more moving parts in *INN* than you'll need to run local discussions. It's a complex beast and has grown more so over time. In addition to the server itself, *innd*, there are: *inndstart*, which launches the server; *nnrpd*, which is started once per connection to handle conversations between newsreaders and the main server; *innwatch*, which monitors the server; and a handful of other helpers. There are also news-related *crontab* entries for scheduled replication and expiration tasks.

If you're setting up a Usenet node, you'll need to understand and work with many of *INN*'s components. To find out how, see O'Reilly & Associates' *Managing Usenet* by Henry Spencer and David Lawrence. For light-duty local conferencing, though, you don't need to worry about most of that machinery. I'll focus here on just the minimum setup.

Start by editing the configuration file called *inn.conf*—on my Red Hat system, it's
/etc/news/inn.conf—and name your company or department in the
organization: field. If you don't, all messages posted to your server will carry
the header:

```
Organization: A poorly installed InterNetNews site
```

In the same file, add your fully qualified domain name (e.g. *udell.roninhouse.com*)
to the **pathname:** field.

Then edit *expire.ctl*, the expiration policy. The default setup includes the line:

```
*:A:1:10:never
```

That says: "Keep all (A) articles from any site (*) for one (1) to ten (10) days, and
never purge articles." To shut off expiration, change the line to:

```
*:A:never:never:never
```

Connecting to INN and Creating Newsgroups

To verify that *INN* is working, try connecting to it using your newsreader or just by
pointing *telnet* at port 119. If you don't get a response, look for clues in the system message log—*/var/log/messages* on my system. Then check the *INN* FAQ files.
The section called "Reasons why *INN* isn't starting" covers the most common cases.
These FAQ files are on the Red Hat CD, but if you don't have them locally, check
the Usenet group *news.nntp.software* or search the Web. One of the most common problems is that the server, running as user *news*, can't access a file that
you've edited and rewritten while logged in as *root*. You can run *inncheck* to find
these kinds of permission glitches. If that was indeed the problem, you can use:

```
$ chown news:news filename
```

to restablish *news* as the owner and group for *filename*.

Once you've got *INN* up and running, use the *ctlinnd* command to create your
own newsgroups, for example:

```
$ ctlinnd newgroup public
Ok
$ ctlinnd newgroup watercooler
Ok
$ ctlinnd newgroup thinktank
Ok
$ ctlinnd newgroup saleslounge
Ok
```

The names of these groups imply their intended scopes: *public* for discussion
involving Ronin Group staff and the outside world; *watercooler* for internal but
companywide discussion; *thinktank* for exclusive use by analysts; *saleslounge* for
the sales force.

Controlling Access to Scoped Newsgroups in INN

You enforce scoping in the configuration file called *nnrp.access*, which might look like this:

```
*:RP:analyst:bigideas:thinktank.*,watercooler.*,public.*
*:RP:sales:bigbucks:saleslounge.*,watercooler.*,public.*
*:RP:::public.*
```

The five fields of an *nnrp.access* entry are: permitted hosts, permissions (Read, Post), username, password, and affected groups. The first line of this example says: "Newsreaders connecting from any host (*) can read and post (RP) to *thinktank*, *watercooler* and *public*, after authenticating as user *analyst* and typing the password `bigideas`." The second line is like the first, but the user is *sales*, the password is `bigbucks`, and the exclusive group is *saleslounge* rather than *thinktank*. The third line says: "Anybody (*) can read and post (RP), without authenticating, in the *public* group." The rules have to be ordered from most restrictive to least restrictive; that's why the *public* rule comes last.

nnrp.access can be tricky, so it's a good idea to verify what each class of user can do. The *telnet* transcript shown in Example 13-1 shows that only the *public* group is open to nonuthenticated users. After authenticating as user *analyst*, both *watercooler* (the companywide group) and *thinktank* (the analysts-only group) are available.

Example 13-1. Testing INN Access Controls

```
telnet localhost 119
200 InterNetNews server INN 1.7.2 08-Dec-1997 ready
mode reader
200 InterNetNews NNRP server INN 1.7.2 08-Dec-1997 ready (posting ok).
list
215 Newsgroups in form "group high low flags".
public 0000000001 0000000001 y
.
group thinktank
411 No such group
authinfo user analyst
381 PASS required
authinfo pass bigideas
281 Ok
list
215 Newsgroups in form "group high low flags".
public 0000000001 0000000001 y
watercooler 0000000000 0000000001 y
thinktank 0000000000 0000000001 y
```

That's the basic setup for *INN*. If you're going to deploy *INN*-based discussions on an Internet-visible server, you should look carefully at how your version of *INN* works and consider disabling unneeded—and potentially dangerous—behavior. For example, the version of *INN* shown in these examples automatically starts up a replication daemon called *innfeed*, governed by a configuration file (*innfeed.conf*) that names some default replication partners. To be on the safe side and ensure that nothing will leak from your server to the outside world, it's probably a good idea to shut down that daemon and/or remove those replication partners from the configuration file.

If your discussion service is isolated on a LAN or intranet, there's less reason to worry about information leakage. In this environment, a Linux-based *INN* server can transform an aging PC from a boat anchor into a really useful collaborative resource.

Deploying the Microsoft NNTP Service

The Microsoft NNTP service that's included in the freely available NT 4.0 Option Pack (*http://www.microsoft.com/ntserver/nts/downloads/recommended/nt4optpk/default.asp*) is an underappreciated jewel. It requires NT Server 4.0 with Service Pack 3 and also requires MSIE Version 4.01 or newer.

You can include the NNTP service in an initial installation of the Option Pack or add it later, but either way it's not one of the default options. To install it, you'll have to expand the list of IIS subcomponents presented by the Option Pack installer and explicitly choose the NNTP option.

This product isn't a full-blown news server. ISPs and others who want to use Microsoft software to run NT-based newsfeeds need the more capable NNTP server included in the Microsoft Commercial Internet Services (MCIS) product. But the Option Pack server is ideal for standalone use, especially when your authentication needs dovetail with NT domain security.

You manage the service by way of the Microsoft Management Console (MMC)—though as with IIS you also use the Windows Explorer to adjust directory permissions, and User Manager to create users and groups. To create a new newsgroup, right-click the NNTP server icon in the MMC, select Properties → Groups → Create New Newsgroup, and add your groups. We'll want to enforce the same set of scopes: *public, watercooler, thinktank,* and *saleslounge*. Assuming that internal users are already listed in the NT domain database, you can do the following:

Create the NT group RoninGroupUsers.
> Populate it with the analysts, the salespeople, and everyone else who should participate in companywide discussion around the watercooler.

Create the NT groups RoninGroupAnalysts and RoninGroupSales.
> Populate these with analysts and salespeople, respectively.

Set permissions.
> For each of the three newsgroups—*watercooler, thinktank, saleslounge*—find the corresponding folder in the Explorer. In the case of *thinktank*, that might

be *c:\nntpfile\root\thinktank.* For each folder, revoke permission from *Everyone* and grant Change permission to the NT group that will have exclusive use of that newsgroup.

That's the basic setup. The *public* group remains world-accessible because you haven't revoked *Everyone*'s permission to its newsgroup folder. The three restricted groups map to NT groups. An attempt to access any of those groups provokes an authentication challenge. Only valid NT credentials will work, and an authenticated user will get the right kind of access—both analysts and salespeople can use the *watercooler*, only analysts the *thinktank*, only salespeople the *saleslounge.*

Controlling the Visibility of Newsgroups in MS NNTP

Although the setup we've just described will work, it isn't ideal. When you mix unrestricted and restricted groups, there's a problem with the visibility of restricted groups. Ideally all users not only should be denied access to unauthorized groups, but also should be prevented even from finding out that such groups exist. The basic setup doesn't hide unauthorized groups. This can create a confusing situation in which users who only intend to access an unrestricted group are nevertheless shown—and prompted to authenticate to—the restricted ones.

What to do? There is a way to hide these groups from nonauthenticating users. Start by creating a virtual directory for each restricted group, as shown in Figure 13-1. This applies to a single group, such as *thinktank*, or a hierarchy, such as *thinktank.planning, thinktank.contacts*, and so on.

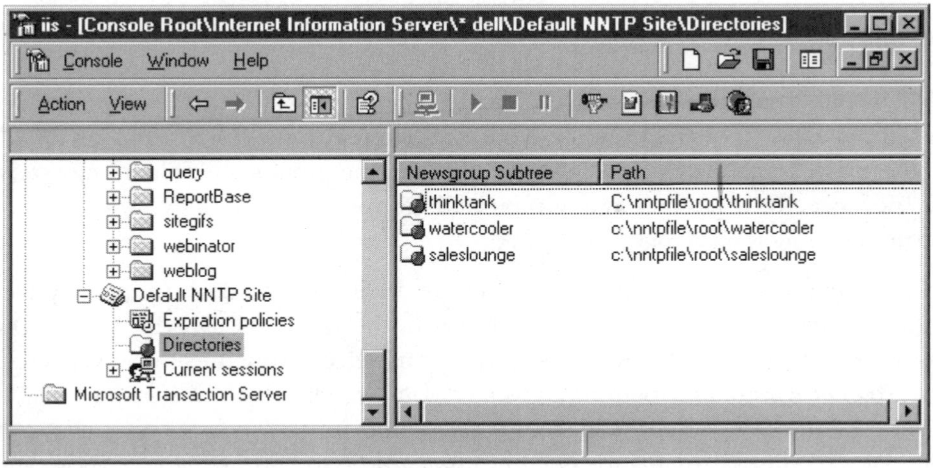

Figure 13-1. Microsoft NNTP virtual directories

From the directories icon under the NNTP server icon in the MMC, do right-click → New → Virtual Directory. Map the virtual newsgroup to its actual location in the file system—for example, map *thinktank* to *c:\nntpfile\root\thinktank*.

Now select that virtual newsgroup's icon, do right-click → Properties, and check *Restrict Newsgroup Visibility*, as shown in Figure 13-2.

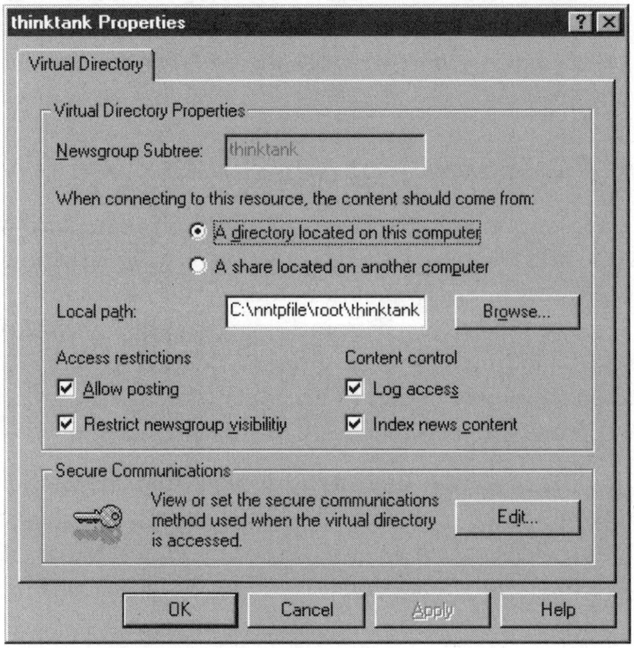

Figure 13-2. Restricting newsgroup visibility

Follow this procedure for each of the restricted groups, and these groups will never appear to a casual visitor to your site. However, they won't appear to your authorized internal users either. Why not? When the groups are hidden, newsreaders never see or try to access any protected groups; therefore, they never provoke an authentication challenge.

The solution is to have internal users set their newsreaders to preemptively authenticate. Both the Microsoft and Netscape newsreaders can do this. In Outlook Express, right-click the news-server icon, select Properties → Server, check the *Log On Using* radio button, and enter your credentials. In Netscape Collabra, right-click the news-server icon, select *Newsgroup Server Properties*, and check the box labeled *Always ask me for my user name and password*. Now you know what these obscure settings are for!

When internal users preemptively authenticate and external users don't, different classes of users see different views of the news server. This is crucial not only for reasons of security, but also because this kind of scoping helps shield internal users from information overload. If all the internal groups are visible company-wide, people will get overwhelmed with irrelevant chatter and the sheer complexity of the newsgroup hierarchy, and may react by avoiding the whole system. If, on the other hand, you arrange so that each authenticated user sees a minimal set of companywide groups, plus a minimal set of role-specific groups, the system is much less intimidating. If you can leverage NT domain security, it's really easy to tailor different views of the discussion space. It's also easy—and very useful—to form ad hoc discussion zones that cross departmental boundaries or even include contractors and other company outsiders to whom you issue temporary credentials.

Finally, note that if you run an all Microsoft shop, or more specifically if every internal newsreader is Outlook Express, you can leverage another aspect of NT domain security—Windows NT challenge/response (formerly NTLM, or NT LAN Manager) authentication. It's a name/password protocol that, unlike NNTP's *authinfo* mechanism, encrypts credentials (but not session data) on the wire. This is better than using *authinfo* to send cleartext names and passwords, not as strong as SSL, and worth doing if your situation permits. To use this method, right-click the NNTP server icon, select Properties → Directory Security → Password Authentication Method → Edit, and uncheck both *Allow Anonymous* and *Basic Authentication*. This same procedure applies to virtual web directories defined under IIS, by the way.

Protecting MS NNTP Newsgroups with SSL

Even if your newsreader population is all Microsoft, challenge/response authentication encrypts only credentials, not session data. That's not strong enough for Ronin Group analysts who want to hold secure private discussions in an Internet-accessible *thinktank* newsgroup. So let's see how to beef up either of the name/password schemes—*authinfo* or challenge/response—using secure sockets. If you've ever set up a secure web server, you'll find this procedure familiar. (If you haven't, consider this your introduction to both subjects.) You start by generating a public-key/private-key pair for the news server. Under NT 4.0, you do that with a tool called Key Manager. It's accessible from many places in the MMC; one way to get to it is from the properties page of a virtual directory (Properties → Secure Communications → Edit → Key Manager). This is the tool you use to create the server certificate that enables your news server to run securely.

Start by doing Key → Create New Key. Specify a file in which to save the generated file, and fill in the forms. In the Common Name field, use the DNS name of your NNTP server. When you're finished, Key Manager creates a file that looks like this:

```
Webmaster: udell@roninhouse.com
Phone: 555-555-5555
Server: Microsoft Key Manager for IIS Version 4.0

Common-name: news.roninhouse.com
Organization Unit: Ronin House
Organization: Ronin Group
Locality: Keene
State: New Hampshire
Country: US

-----BEGIN NEW CERTIFICATE REQUEST-----
MIIBwTCCASoCAQAwgYAxCzAJBgNVBAYTAlVTMRYwFAYDVQQIEw1OZXcgSGFtcHNo
aXJlMQ4wDAYDVQQHEwVLZWVuZTEUMBIGA1UEChMLUm9uaW4gR3JvdXAxFDASBgNV
BAsTC1JvbmluIEhvdXNlMR0wGwYDVQQDExR1ZGVsbC5yb25pbmhvdXNlLmNvbTCB
nzANBgkqhkiG9w0BAQEFAAOBjQAwgYkCgYEA3wxkWJXM32nZue66eLZG8OSE3FN6
igfJrZRxwvy96LuoAUEab22NRbBe8VqQN/nt9P9VVPbE8ZOi1HKCzj55XXDGnoQq
xUdz+aLXU9iq8jjFFqYew7DGZx3h1iBVKv8guMtgo2XVQwHiZPT79owMXBhR2yml
S+EDEhoz42Yi04ECAwEAAaAAMA0GCSqGSIb3DQEBBAUAA4GBAL7HT+hIblhERASE
ZWC6tP1u6YwsXV+mnBVXo+iwmNpYeFmKMWwhzr0s7ue0PpfhF7eTZxKrxmBAYJVT
rDosPCpinJ165e8WUrvLjwyV4ODsKL17fzCIdmkgHRtCHV1WIf0u4lU1wxjrYHKq
QAjP9UzR+IAoieTJSkLI/F/Q4CBN
-----END NEW CERTIFICATE REQUEST-----
```

The ASCII gobbledygook in this example is a certificate request. What's that? When a newsreader connects to a secure news server, it receives the server's public key and uses it to encrypt a temporary key that the client and server agree to use for the rest of the session. However, the client won't accept the server's public key (a.k.a. *server certificate* or *digital ID*) unless it has been digitally signed by a third party—a certificate authority (CA) that is one of the certificate-signing entities that the client is configured to trust. So the administrator of the to-be-secured server has to get the generated public key signed by a CA. To do that, you present the CA with a certificate request such as the one shown earlier.

Which CA? Here's where the best strategy for a private news server may differ from what makes sense for a public web site. If you're running a public site that takes credit-card orders from anyone who shows up, you'll want to make things as easy as possible for customers. That means you'll want to use a commercial CA, such as VeriSign (*http://www.verisign.com/*) or Thawte (*http://www.thawte.com/*), for two reasons. First, the Microsoft and Netscape browsers are preconfigured to accept certificates signed by these authorities. Second, customers know that sites presenting such certificates are reputable in the eyes of the CA—that is, the site operators have submitted documents proving that they run legitimate businesses and have paid the CA to verify those documents. To give customers this convenience and peace of mind, site operators must spend not only money but also time and effort—the process entails a lot of paperwork and delay.

Self-Signing a Server Certificate Using MS Certificate Server

You could get a commercial CA to sign your private news server's certificate. The benefit would be automatic recognition of the server; the drawback would be expense of time, money, and effort. An attractive alternative is to become your own private CA and mint your own server certificates. The NT 4.0 Option Pack's Certificate Server can do just that and rather easily, too.

If you've installed Certificate Server, you can sign your own certificate. Start by loading the URL *http://YourServer/CertSrv/CertEnroll/default.htm*. Click the link labeled *Process a Certificate Request*. An HTML form asks for the ASCII gobbledy-gook (a.k.a. certificate request) that you just saved. Open that file, grab the text, paste it into the form, and submit the form.

The server responds with a signed certificate and prompts you to download it to a file. Do that. Now return to Key Manager. select Key → Install Key Certificate and select the file you just saved. If all went well, Key Manager will inform you that the key is complete and ready to be used by the server that generated it, as shown in Figure 13-3.

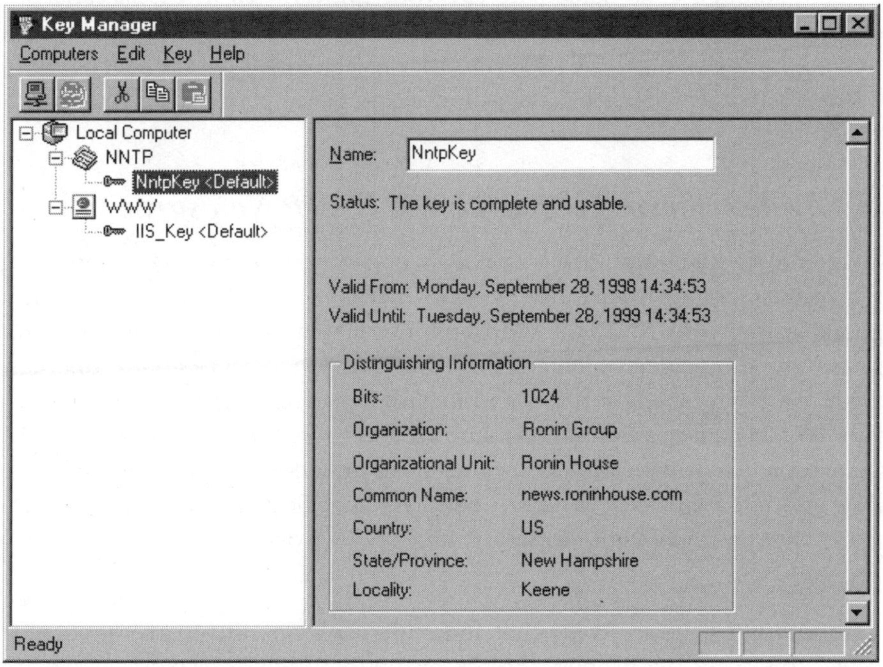

Figure 13-3. Valid certificate for a secure news server

Once you've installed the server certificate, it can accept SSL connections on port 563 and regular connections on port 119. Note carefully: the Microsoft NNTP service, unlike Netscape's Collabra Server, listens to both ports at the same time. That means that although an analyst who authenticates to the *thinktank* newsgroup on port 563 will indeed get an encrypted session, another analyst can authenticate to the same newsgroup on port 119 and send credentials in the clear. What to do? Go to the MMC properties page for each virtual directory (see Figure 13-2), do right-click → Properties → Secure Communications → Edit, and check the *Require Secure Channel* box. Now these restricted groups won't answer on port 119.

This was pretty easy, but we've introduced a new complication. The Ronin Group's population of browsers/newsreaders won't automatically recognize server certificates that are self-signed by the Ronin Group certificate authority. This isn't a showstopper. Both the Microsoft and Netscape clients will, when presented with a server certificate signed by an untrusted authority, offer to add that CA to their list of trusted CAs. Users need only click through a series of dialogs in order to view information about the CA and decide how broadly to trust it. This can be a one-time-only procedure—per browser—if you tell your users to trust the internal CA broadly and indefinitely. But the procedure is still confusing to people who have never gone through it, so make sure everyone knows what to expect, and be prepared to answer lots of questions. If all this seems like too much hassle, you can always go the commercial CA route in order to eliminate this CA acceptance step. One way or another, SSL is a hassle—but if you value your privacy, it's worth the trouble.

Using Index Server to Search MS NNTP Newsgroups

In Chapter 8, *Organizing Search Results*, we saw how to manage a mixed set of search results coming from Index Server—that is, some hits from an HTML docbase and some from NNTP newsgroups. Recall that Index Server automatically maps newsgroup headers, such as `From:` and `Subject:`, to custom properties that you can name in queries, sort on, and include in search-results templates. When a news server becomes a community knowledge base, these kinds of fielded queries—in conjunction with full-text search—can enhance its value tremendously. A typical question might be: "Where's that LDIF specification that Ed posted awhile ago?" To answer it, you could form this Index Server query:

```
(@MsgFrom Ed) and LDIF
```

Of course you'd have to know that Index Server maps the `From:` field of news messages to the custom property `MsgFrom` and that `@MsgFrom` binds a search term to that field. Most users won't know that, so you'll want to package up the NNTP-specific search idioms into a form backed by a canned query (a *.IDQ/.HTX* pair) or perhaps an ASP script. You'll also need to tell users where to find that search form, since it lives in web space rather than NNTP space. As we'll see, Collabra

Server achieves a much tighter—albeit proprietary—integration of search into the NNTP realm.

Fielded search is handy, but if you can't spare the time to implement it, you needn't feel too guilty. Much of the benefit of fielded search can be available directly through the newsreader. For example, to find that LDIF spec from Ed, you might just need to go to *thinktank.specifications* and sort the view by sender. If Ed wrote a good title, it will be easy to pick out the LDIF article from among the cluster of postings from Ed.

Are you out of luck if Ed posted the spec to *thinktank.misc*? Not really. Full-text search can overcome this misclassification and will find a document even when it's in the wrong place. You should set up a meaningful newsgroup hierarchy, get everyone to agree on what belongs where, and try to abide by that policy. But everyone's busy; information flows through the organization at a relentless rate; knowledge-management guidelines will often be ignored. That's OK. You'd rather Ed post the LDIF spec to *thinktank.misc* than leave it on his own hard disk. At least the information's in the system somewhere. It's best to define what the right places are and put things in their right places, but when that doesn't happen, search offers a safety net.

Searching MS NNTP newsgroups securely

When you start up Index Server on a machine that has both IIS and the NNTP service running, it expects to index content in virtual directories defined by both services. You can verify that a newsgroup will be indexed by right-clicking its virtual directory and checking its properties page. Alternatively you can enable indexing at the root of the news server by checking the *Index News Content* box on its Properties → Home Directory page. But this kind of sweeping policy can be dangerous, especially if your server hosts a mixture of public and private newsgroups. It's probably best to specify explicitly which news subtrees to include in the index.

Suppose there is discussion of LDAP in the *public* newsgroup, which anyone can read, and in the *thinktank*, which only analysts can read. What happens when someone does a search for LDAP against an index that includes both unrestricted and restricted groups? It depends on whether or not you require authentication for the search form and its supporting *.IDQ* file or script. If you don't, then anyone who searches for LDAP will stumble across some amount of unauthorized information. How much depends on what your search handler does with the results. If it only reports URLs, then the search will reveal two things that it shouldn't: the fact that the newsgroup containing the found messages exists and the fact that it has material matching the search term. It's more likely, though, that it will report the author, the subject, and a summary of the message. Clearly that's a bad information leak, so you'll want to authenticate all searches. You can do that by disallowing anonymous access to pages and scripts that perform searches and by setting appropriate NTFS permissions on those files. That way, users will have to authenticate in order to search. A salesperson who does a search won't even see a hit on a *thinktank* message.

There are several complications here. First, realize that any search script can access the index. It won't help to authenticate *search1.htm* if, elsewhere on the server, there's an unprotected *search2.htm* lying around. You'll need to make sure that you lock down every search script. This is a serious concern. You'd rather that the rule were to show only what's explicitly permitted, rather than to hide only what's explicitly denied.

The second problem has to do with public access. Let's assume that you do nail down the permissions on all the search-related pages and scripts. Site visitors who can freely read and post to the *public* newsgroup will be surprised by an authentication challenge when they try to search. To work around this problem, you can segregate the restricted and unrestricted content into two different Index Server catalogs. Use a nonauthenticating script to enable site visitors to search public areas and an authenticating script to enable internal users to search private areas.

This still isn't perfect, though, because internal users also want to search the public areas, and now they'll need to search twice to cover the gamut of documents. One solution is to duplicate the public content in the private catalog. Another is to keep the catalogs distinct. Use a frontend script to search both catalogs, and authenticate only when necessary. Admittedly that's a lot of work. In this respect Collabra Server is a more appealing solution. Its NNTP-based search technology deals with newsgroup permissions in a unified and finely granular way.

Deploying Netscape's Collabra Server

Collabra Server runs on a number of Unix platforms and Windows NT. It shares a common administration server with Netscape's other SuiteSpot servers: Enterprise (Web), Messaging (mail), Calendar, and Directory. If you download the Collabra Server evaluation kit from the Netscape site (*http://www.netscape.com/download*) and install it on a machine that has no other SuiteSpot servers running, you'll end up with both Collabra Server and Administration Server running. Administration Server's responsibilities include managing users, groups, keys, and certificates. Its installer asks what kind of directory service you want to use. If you're running Directory Server, choose that. If not, you can use a local LDAP directory. All the SuiteSpot servers will be able to talk to that local directory, but you won't be able to create your own directory-aware applications, as we did in Chapter 11, *Membership Services*. Figure 13-4 shows the Administration Server's main screen, with both Directory Server and Collabra Server installed and running.

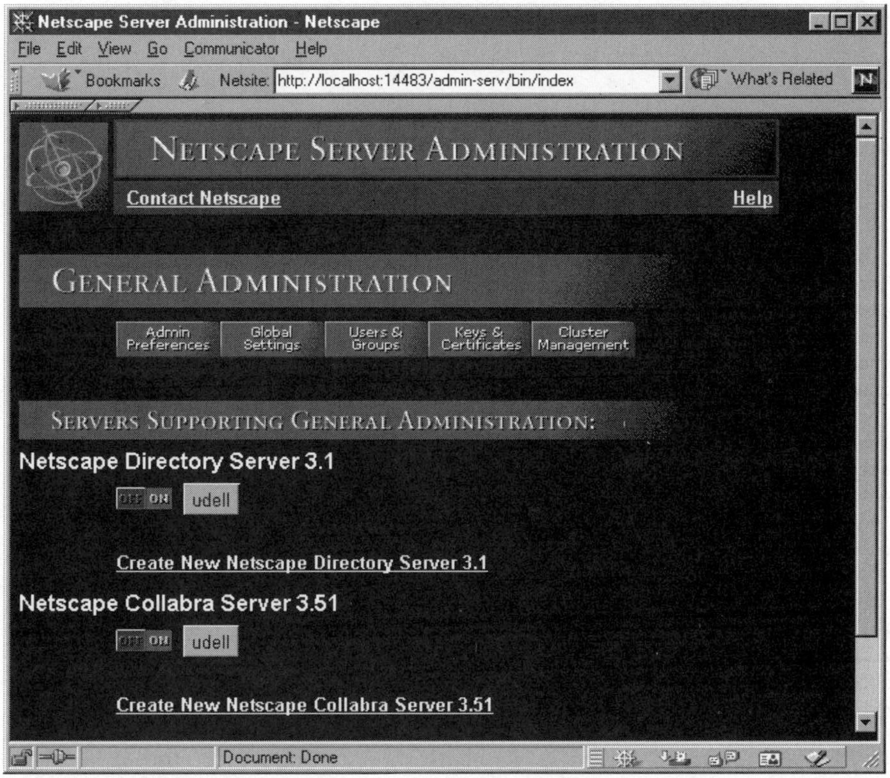

Figure 13-4. Administration Server, managing Directory Server and Collabra Server

Creating Users and Groups in Collabra Server

SuiteSpot server administration is web-based. You access the Administration Server on a port that it selects randomly when it installs—in this example, 14483. All communication paths can be SSL-encrypted. You can run Administration Server in SSL mode, requiring browsers to establish secure connections to it. You can run Directory Server in SSL mode, so that all LDAP connections to it—from any of the SuiteSpot servers or from your own LDAP-aware applications—must be encrypted. Finally, you can run Collabra Server itself in SSL mode, as we'll see, so that news-reader-to-news-server traffic will be encrypted.

You can create users and groups interactively from the Users and Groups tab of Administration Server's main screen. A faster and easier method, if you're running Directory Server, is to create an LDIF load file and add entries directly. Example 13-2 shows a sample load file that defines users and groups for our Ronin Group example.

Example 13-2. An LDIF Load File

```
dn: uid=Ed,o=RoninGroup
cn: Ed
sn: DeJesus
objectclass: top
objectclass: person
objectclass: organizationalPerson
objectclass: inetOrgPerson
userpassword: {SHA}W8r/fyL/UzygmbNAjq2HbA67qac=

dn: cn=RoninGroupUsers,o=RoninGroup
objectclass: top
objectclass: groupOfUniqueNames
cn: RoninGroupUsers
uniquemember: uid=Ed,o=RoninGroup
uniquemember: uid=Sally,o=RoninGroup

dn: cn=RoninGroupAnalysts,o=RoninGroup
objectclass: top
objectclass: groupOfUniqueNames
cn: RoninGroupAnalysts
uniquemember: uid=Ed,o=RoninGroup

dn: cn=RoninGroupSales,o=RoninGroup
objectclass: top
objectclass: groupOfUniqueNames
cn: RoninGroupSales
uniquemember: uid=Sally,o=RoninGroup
```

To add these entries, click the *Directory Server* button on the Administration Server's main screen and select Database Management → Add Entries. Type the name of the load file and the admin password you assigned when you installed Directory Server, then click *OK* to load the entries. Note that you can preassign SHA-encrypted passwords; see Chapter 12, *Authentication and Authorization Techniques*, for examples of how to do this encryption.

Creating Discussion Scopes in Collabra Server

To carve out the discussion scopes, click the *Collabra Server* button on the Administration Server's main screen and select Discussion Groups → Manage Discussion Groups → OK to invoke the Discussion Group Manager shown in Figure 13-5.

To control visibility and access, select the root newsgroup and select Access Control Rules → Edit. On the ensuing screen, select *Authenticated Users/Groups Only* and click *OK*. Now, on the access-control screen for the root newsgroup, set *Allow Role Of:* to (Deny). At this point, you've configured the server to be able to do authentication, but you've denied authenticated users all privileges in the root newsgroup and any new newsgroups you create under it. Why the blanket denial?

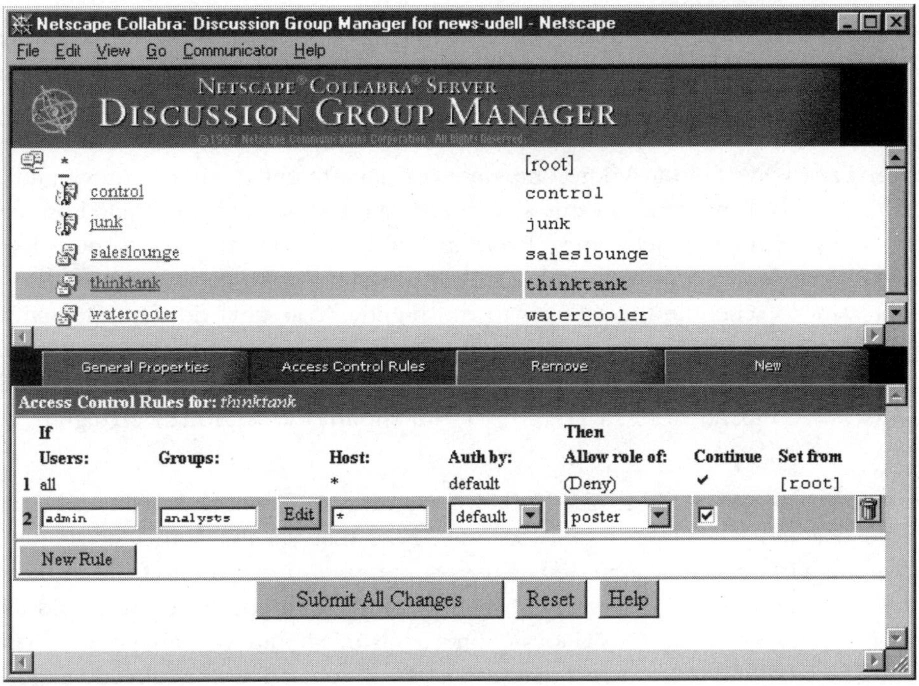

Figure 13-5. Defining discussion scopes in Collabra Server

In terms of Collabra Server privileges, it's easier to giveth than to taketh away. This scheme ensures that as you create newsgroups, you can grant precisely the permissions that you want them to have.

Next, select the root group and click the *New* tab to create a new newsgroup. Use Access Control Rules → New Rule to override the permissions inherited from the root. Figure 13-5 shows the situation after creating *watercooler*, *thinktank*, and *saleslounge*. The second access-control rule for *thinktank* says that members of the group *analysts* can read and post to that group; nobody else can. The *Continue* box is checked, which means that newsgroup hierarchy created under *thinktank* will inherit this rule. Using the same procedure, you can associate the group *sales* with the *saleslounge* newsgroup, and the umbrella group *users* with the *watercooler* newsgroup.

Now Collabra Server is set up to authenticate according to these rules, but it won't do so until you turn on access control. To do that, click the *Access Control* tab on Collabra Server's main admin screen. Turn access control on and check *Require Authentication on First Connect*. Stop and restart the server to apply these changes.

Other Configuration Tasks for Collabra Server

To disable expiration, click the *Expiration* tab and select Edit → Never Expire Arti-cles. To index the newsgroups, select Discussion Groups → Full Text Indexing. Type any name (e.g., **my-indexer**) into the Index Identifier: field and click *OK*. Now select Server Preferences → Technical Settings and set the Organization: field to your company's (or department's) name. You can adjust the frequency of indexing on this screen too, but the choices are limited, ranging from every 15 minutes to hourly. Even an hourly indexer run gets to be a lot of work for the server, so unless you absolutely require up-to-the-hour indexes, you might want to schedule the indexer to run nightly. You can't do that interactively in the Administration Server. You'll need to edit the file */netscape/suitespot/config/ newstime.conf.* To index at 4 A.M., change the entry in *newstime.conf* for the *indexsend* command from AtInterval 60 (hourly) to AtHour 4 (nightly at 4 A.M.).

Now you're almost ready to go, but if you're running Collabra Server on NT and you've enabled NT's TCP/IP port security, note that it's not sufficient simply to leave port 119 open. Collabra Server uses some extra ports to talk to itself. If you don't open these too, the server will seem to work until you try to post, and then it will squawk about an "NNTPlocalconnect" error. Should you abandon NT port security? I wouldn't recommend that, especially if your NT box is directly exposed to the Internet. Instead, add these extra ports to the ones that NT permits, using Control Panel → Network → Protocols → TCP/IP → Properties → Advanced → Enable Security → Configure. Collabra Server uses the first two available ports after the reserved range 1–1024. On my NT box it takes 1027 and 1028. You can check Collabra Server's log (Reports → View Server Log) to verify which pair it's using. While you're at it, open up another pair of ports—the ones that the built-in search server uses. The rule for these is 5000 + (2 * Collabra Server port). In other words, if you're running Collabra Server on port 119, then the first search server port is 5238, and the second is 5239.

Note that although NNTP servers conventionally run on port 119, and *INN* has to, its modern derivatives can run on any port you specify. Likewise, the Microsoft and Netscape newsreaders can connect to NNTP servers on any port. Why does this matter? If you offer a public discussion area on port 119, some people won't be able to get to it, because their corporate firewalls don't allow traffic on that port. One of the arguments in favor of web-based conferencing is that it can reach more people than NNTP conferencing can, since firewalls almost universally per-mit traffic on the HTTP port 80. But this isn't really an application issue—web

---

* Not all of Collabra Server is configurable from the GUI admin screens, just as not all of the MS NNTP service is. In the former case, you edit text files, Unix-style. In the latter case, you poke around in the NT registry.

service versus NNTP service. It's a port issue—80 versus 119. If you can't reach everyone you need to on 119, try running your NNTP server on port 80.

Advertising Newsgroups to Users

Running news service on a nonstandard port may confuse users. Even when you're running on the standard port 119, it can be difficult to get people to find and use newsgroups. How can you advertise the discussion service to users? There's a hard way and an easy way. The hard way involves explaining the following procedure:

1. Launch the newsreader.
2. Add a new host to the list of hosts to which it subscribes.
3. Specify the NNTP port on that host, if nonstandard.
4. Select the new host and view its list of offered newsgroups.
5. Subscribe to one or more groups.

Here's the easy way: publish a URL like *news://udell.roninhouse.com/public* on a web page. Or, if you're using a nonstandard port, *news://udell.roninhouse.com:80/public*. Both the Netscape and Microsoft browsers will automatically perform all the steps shown earlier when referred to this kind of URL. It's a great way to avoid not just one long-winded explanation but several. That's because the procedure for manually attaching to a news server and subscribing to its groups differs between the Microsoft and Netscape newsreaders.

A web page that presents a set of these quick-start news URLs is also an opportunity to define the purpose of each newsgroup that you offer. Who's invited to contribute and why? Should HTML be used freely, sparingly, or never? Are attachments permitted? Is the group searchable, and if so, how? Lotus Notes has an excellent feature called the *policy document*—it's a special record in every Notes database that answers these kinds of questions. You can likewise begin every NNTP newsgroup with a posting that serves as a policy document, but it's also a good idea to provide a summary web page that lists all the newsgroups you're offering, spells out the policies for each, and gives quick-start access to the groups. Note that if you publicize an SSL-protected newsgroup in this way, you need to use *snews://* instead of *news://*.

Securing Collabra Server Newsgroups

The Netscape counterpart to Microsoft's Key Manager is a command-line tool called *sec-key*, which lives in */netscape/suitespot/bin/admin/admin/bin*. Run it to generate a key pair; save the resulting certificate signing request (CSR) in a file; submit the CSR to a certificate authority (again, this can be your own CA or a commercial one); and save the signed certificate issued by the CA in another file. Then, from Administration Server's main screen, select Keys & Certificates → Request Certificate, complete the form shown in Figure 13-6, and submit it.

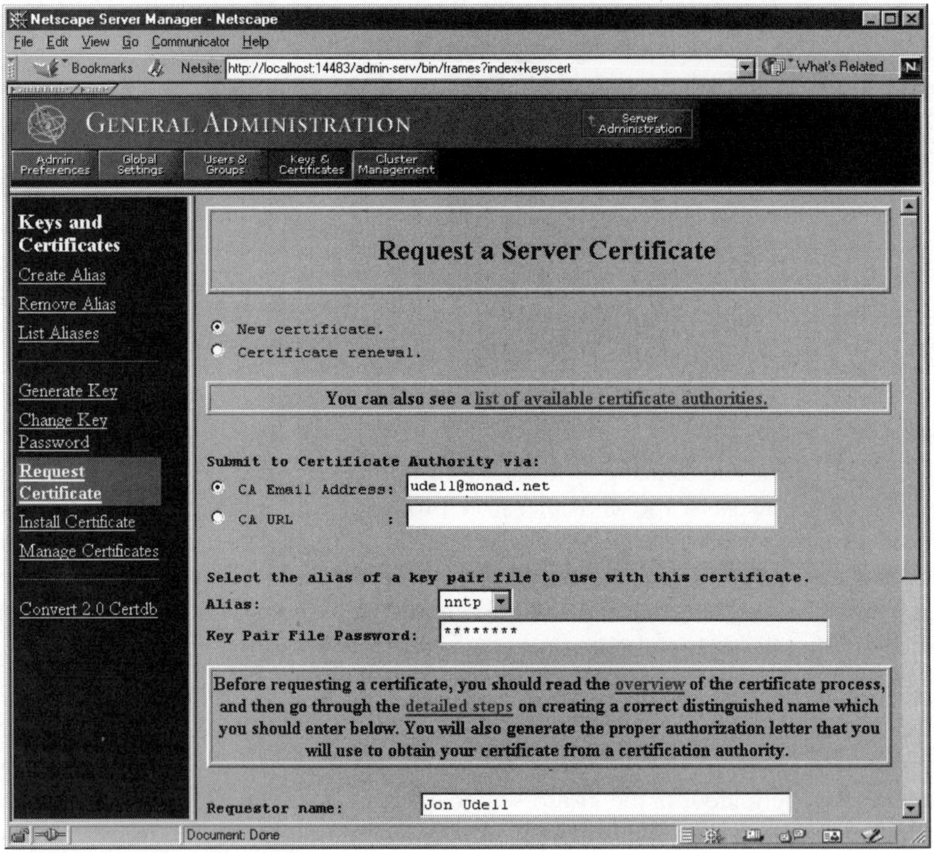

Figure 13-6. Requesting a server certificate in Collabra Server

If you elect to mail the request, the Administration Server prints it to the screen and saves it to a file. Depending on how your CA works, you can cut the text from the screen and paste it into the CA's request-processing form or mail the CSR to the CA. When the CA sends back a signed certificate by one or another of these means, save it in a file. Then, back in the Administration Server, select Keys & Certificates → Install Certificate, paste the contents of the file into the form, and submit it. Review the information on the ensuing screen, then click *Add Certificate* to install your new server certificate. Finally, restart the Administration Server and all its dependent services to complete the procedure.

Now you can enable SSL encryption in Collabra Server. Go to the Collabra Server admin screen and select Encryption → Activate Connection Security → On. The default port changes from 119 to 563, which is the standard port for secure NNTP. Click *OK*, then shut down and restart Collabra Server to bring it back up in secure mode. Note that you can no longer restart Collabra Server by way of web-based administration. You have to be at the server's console so that you can type the password that protects the server's private key; Netscape's security policy regards that password as sacrosanct and will not allow it to travel over a wire. Remember, finally, to add the secure NNTP port to any local, router, or firewall filters that need to know about it.

Searching Collabra Server Newsgroups

For Netscape clients only, Collabra Server offers a really slick integrated search capability. From the Message Center select Edit → Search Messages to invoke the search dialog shown in Figure 13-7.

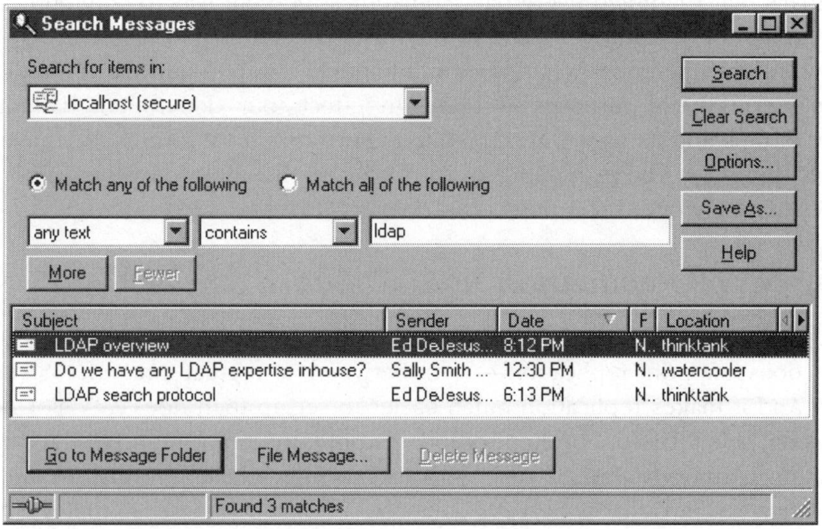

Figure 13-7. Searching newsgroups in Collabra

From the list of mail folders and news servers, choose the Collabra Server instance that you want to search—in this example, it's `localhost(secure)`, a secure instance of Collabra Server running on my local machine. You can restrict searches to the `Sender:`, `Subject:`, or `Date:` fields or choose `any text` for a full-text search. In this example, I've authenticated to the server as user *Ed*, a member of the *analysts* group. In response to a search for LDAP, I'm shown Ed's postings in *thinktank* and Sally's postings in *watercooler*, because I have access to both areas. But if I authenticate as Sally, a member of *sales*, only Sally's LDAP posting will appear, because members of that group can access *watercooler* and *saleslounge* but not *thinktank*.

Collabra Server's search mechanism is clean, simple, and effective—provided, of course, that your users are all running Netscape clients. Netscape hoped that the NNTP protocol extensions that support Collabra Server's search feature would be adopted more widely, but so far that hasn't happened. What can you do if you're not playing to a homogeneous audience of Netscape clients? Remember that NNTP newsgroups are just docbases—that is, text files with headers. You can index them with any web indexing tool just as you index web pages. Of course, you'd have to do extra work to filter search results according to the permissions held by an authenticated user performing a search.

Searchable private newsgroups are an incredible resource. The old adage applies, though: you get out of it what you put into it. As a member of a three-person development team, I habitually posted many of the key project-related web pages and emails that I handled every day. Sometimes the goal was to communicate this information to my team in a centralized way; sometimes it was just to save it for my own future reference. Whatever the immediate motive, our team's newsgroups always served both purposes at once. In effect, our department had its own Usenet forums and its own Deja.com-like memory of those forums. If you've never worked this way, you're missing out on one of the most powerful productivity benefits that networked computers can deliver.

Using NNTP Replication with Collabra Server

Although we're not concerned in this book with conventional newsfeeds, Collabra Server does support replication—even between a regular and an SSL-enabled server. And it makes replication much easier to set up than does *INN*. For non-SSL replication, select Discussion Replication → Configure Replication Host and name a replication partner. In the SSL case, you also need to make sure that the necessary CA certificate is in Collabra Server's database of trusted signers, so that the replication process will be able to accept the server certificate presented by a replication partner. You use the admin server's Keys & Certificates → Install Certificate function to tell Collabra Server to trust a CA that it doesn't already trust. Like browsers, Collabra Server trusts a number of commercial CAs by default, so if you use one of them, this extra step isn't necessary.

NNTP replication is powerful stuff, and it remains useful—even in today's wired world—as a way to push data around on marginal networks. For example, suppose that some of the Ronin Group's satellite offices are served by skinny and slow Internet pipes. When newsgroups are used to exchange not only text messages, but also large binary attachments—images, Acrobat *.PDF* files, software updates—direct interactive use of a single server in the central office can be painful. In this situation, store-and-forward technology still has an important role to play. The existence of the Usenet proves that NNTP can move more data in this way than any individual company is likely to require. Collabra Server domesticates *INN*'s newsfeed mechanism into something that an average network administrator can comfortably handle.

Deploying the MS Exchange NNTP Service

Proprietary groupware systems, including Lotus Notes, Microsoft Exchange, Novell GroupWise, and SoftArc FirstClass, are all converging on Internet groupware standards. At the same time, there's another kind of convergence within the realm of Internet groupware standards. The NNTP threaded-discussion protocol and the IMAP email standard are becoming two different ways to do the kinds of conferencing described in this book. Here, we'll briefly explore how Exchange handles both NNTP discussions and IMAP public folders.

Microsoft Exchange has always supported the notion of a public folder—that is, a piece of your private message store that you can share with a selected group of collaborators. Even before there was an Exchange Server, earlier Microsoft mail products implemented public folders in terms of shared directories on a file server. More recently Exchange Server gained the ability to replicate between NNTP newsgroups and public folders, so that Exchange clients could read and participate in newsgroups by way of public folders, without requiring a separate newsreader. Exchange Server 5.5 went further. It added an NNTP service so that public folders can look, to a newsreader, just like normal NNTP newsgroups.

If you're just looking for a native NNTP service, Exchange Server would be massive overkill. On the other hand, if your company has standardized on Exchange for internal email, and perhaps also for Internet email, the NNTP interface is an interesting way to combine Internet-style and proprietary groupware.

Collaboration among Heterogeneous Clients

Figure 13-8 shows how the Ronin Group's newsgroup hierarchy appears to an internal user running Microsoft Outlook 98.

Figure 13-9 shows the same hierarchy seen as NNTP newsgroups by the Outlook Express client (which could as easily be another IMAP mailreader and/or NNTP newsreader).

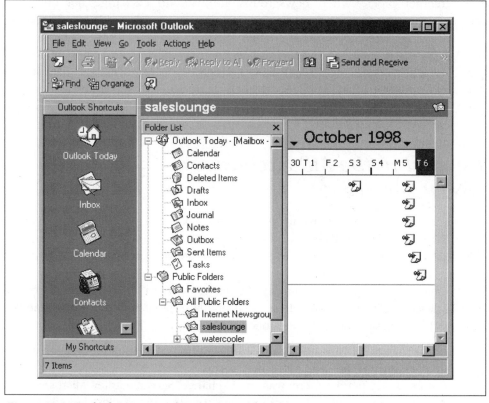

Figure 13-8. Outlook 98's view of Exchange public folders

Note that the discussion hierarchy appears twice in Figure 13-9. The icon labeled Exchange (NNTP) is an NNTP connection to the Exchange NNTP service. The icon labeled Exchange (IMAP) is something quite different and yet oddly similar—an IMAP connection to Exchange's IMAP interface. Like the NNTP service, the IMAP service presents an Internet-style API to clients while, under the covers, connecting those clients to the same message store that native Exchange clients talk to. This is useful because, like the NNTP interface, it opens Exchange to standard Internet clients.

Internet-style Groupware APIs

If newsreaders can talk to Exchange using the NNTP and IMAP protocols, other programs can too. For example, the conferencing-based applications we saw in Chapter 9—a helpdesk, a document-review system—can now be deployed to a population of Outlook users connected to an Exchange Server. These scripted, socket-based applications are easy to build and are more general than equivalents written using Messaging API (MAPI), the native lingo of Microsoft mail products. It's true that there's a rich assortment of components that encapsulate MAPI for

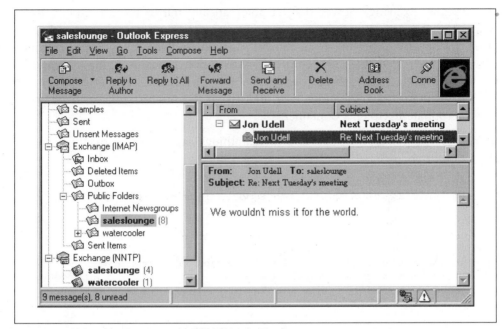

Figure 13-9. The native NNTP view of Exchange public folders

Visual Basic programs and OLE automation controllers. Even so, it's hard to beat the simplicity and generality of the native Internet methods.

Creating and Publishing Exchange Public Folders

Exchange Server is a Swiss Army knife that can do all sorts of things: it's a mail server, a multiprotocol message switch, an LDAP directory server, and more. One thing it can't do, though, is create public folders. That's the prerogative of an Exchange client such as Outlook 98. To create a public folder in Outlook 98, right-click the All Public Folders icon and select *New Folder.* Who can see, read, and post to that folder? That's determined by the server administrator. The root public folder carries a rich set of permissions for both anonymous and authenticated users; these inherit but can be overridden. A public folder created in this way does not automatically appear as part of the NNTP newsgroup hierarchy, though. To make that happen, use the Server Administrator, select Tools → Newsgroup Hierarchies → Add, and select the public folders that you want to export as newsgroups.

Exchange offers excellent user-level control over newsgroup visibility and access but less seamless mapping of domain groups than with the Microsoft NNTP service. To set up our standard Ronin Group scopes using the Exchange Administrator, double-click each public folder, click *Client Permissions,* and specify an appropriate role. For a public newsgroup, assign the role of Author to the anonymous user. That makes the newsgroup visible and gives everyone Read and Post permissions. Exchange Server doesn't automatically mirror the NT groups *users*, *sales*, and *analysts*, but you can create *Recipients Containers* corresponding to these groups by exporting from the NT domain and importing into Exchange. Then, for the *watercooler* newsgroup, deny the anonymous user all access and let all users read and post (that is, assign the role of Author). For *saleslounge* and *thinktank*, deny the anonymous user and assign the Author role to members of the appropriate Recipients Container.

Here's a *telnet* transcript that verifies that things are set up correctly from the NNTP client perspective:

```
telnet exchange.yourhost.com 119
200 Microsoft Exchange Internet News Service Version 5.5.1960.6 (posting allowed)
list
215 list follows
public 0 1 y                     # anonymous users get public access
.

authinfo user ed                 # ed is a RoninGroup analyst
381 more authentication required
authinfo pass *******
281 authentication accepted
list
215 list follows                 # he gets everything except saleslounge
watercooler 1 1 y
thinktank 0 1 y
public 0 1 y
.
```

IMAP Public Folders Versus NNTP Newsgroups

IMAP public folders are still relatively new. Many Internet mail users continue to rely on Post Office Protocol 3 (POP3) to fetch mail from remote servers and use mailreaders such as Outlook Express, Netscape Messenger, and Eudora to organize and manage that mail locally. There are some serious drawbacks to POP3. If you use more than one client machine, which is your canonical message store? There can't be one. At best, you can configure your POP clients not to delete messages from the server after fetching them. That way, you can maintain a complete set of incoming messages on your laptop and on your desktop machine. But you can't synchronize the management of those two message stores. If you move messages into a subfolder on one machine, you'd have to repeat that same set of actions on the other machine to keep things in sync—and that's just not practical.

Then there's the problem of outbound mail. It's useful to echo outbound messages to the Sent folder on your client so that you can reconstruct both ends of conversations. But which Sent folder? In the multiclient-machine scenario, you have to cc all outbound messages to yourself to make them appear in the inbound message streams on all your clients. Then you have to filter or manually file all of these extra inbound messages.

With IMAP, you get a canonical server-based message store. When you create a folder or move a message to a folder, it happens on the server. When you connect to the server from any client, you'll see the same view of that canonical folder structure as you would from any other client. Doesn't POP still surpass IMAP when you want to read and compose messages offline? It's true that a local message store is an automatic consequence of using POP. But IMAP clients can also replicate the server-based message store to your local machine, where it's available for offline use just as with POP. Both Netscape Messenger and Microsoft Outlook Express can do this kind of IMAP replication.

A server-based message store does not, by itself, dramatically rewrite the groupware equation. But the addition of shared folders does. Most of the rationale for deploying NNTP stems from the need to transcend the boundaries of interpersonal mail and move some kinds of collaboration into a shared space. If you can publish an IMAP folder, control who has access to it, post HTML messages to it, and read and reply to the messages in a threaded manner, is this really any different from an NNTP newsgroup? Nope. It's possible that this way of using IMAP will supplant the way of using NNTP that I advocate in this book. IMAP's client-side control of folder structure will work to its advantage in the long run, enabling users to organize their collaborative spaces without the help of server administrators.

IV

Advanced Internet Groupware

Today's Internet tools and services can support groupware activities more effectively than most people realize. But they also promise more than they deliver. This part explores how to use the ideas underlying all Internet software—simple protocols, pipelined components, structured text—to solve advanced groupware problems. We'll see how to automate the testing of web-based groupware and how to aggregate services on behalf of groups. In the final chapter, we'll explore ways that scripted HTTP services, distributed to users' workstations, can tackle problems such as offline use of applications and data replication.

14

Automating Internet Components

The Internet groupware services—HTTP, SMTP, and NNTP—manifest themselves to users as browsers, mailreaders, and newsreaders. Because these same services can be driven by scripts that speak simple ASCII request/response protocols over TCP/IP sockets, interactive and batch modes are two sides of the same coin.

We've already seen a number of examples of this duality. In Chapter 8, *Organizing Search Results*, we used web-client scripting to intercept and process the output of the Microsoft Index Server. In Chapter 9, *Conferencing Applications*, we used a news server as a discussion component and a mail server as a message dispatcher. In Chapter 10, *Groupware Servlets*, we saw another kind of duality—a Java servlet both provided a web API, used by other programs to import and export calendar data, and consumed a web API provided by a "todo" server.

We think of the Internet as a library of documents, but it's also a library of software components. Some are *microcomponents*, like the Perl modules that you'll download from CPAN if you decide to try out some of the examples in this book. Others are *macrocomponents* such as AltaVista, Yahoo!, or any Internet (or intranet) site that offers services accessible to browsers and scripts alike by way of a web API. Web sites are scriptable components just because they *are* web sites. And they're made of microcomponents and macrocomponents that can exploit a rich assortment of other components, both local and remote, to do their work. The Internet makes distributed, component-based computing not just easy, but almost automatic—like breathing.

The Object Web and Internet Groupware

Industry pundits have long predicted the advent of an *object Web*, a global network of distributed software objects. "The network is the computer," said Sun Microsystems' chairman and CEO Scott McNealy. Depending on whom you talked to, the technology that would make that vision real was Java, or CORBA, or DCOM, or directory services. As it turns out, none of these technologies has yet fundamentally altered what the Internet could already do pretty well—namely, connect people to other people and to data using simple, easy-to-understand protocols.

What does all this mean to you as a developer of Internet and intranet groupware applications? Two things. First, you should aggressively exploit the existing library of Internet-based components. Second, you should realize that your own applications are also components, use them as such, and look for easy ways to make them more useful in that role.

The methods I advocate in this book will seem, to some people, radical in their reliance on homegrown, scripted software. Why glue together Internet components with scripts when you could buy a shrink-wrapped commercial package that will simply provide the groupware solution you need? If you can do that, you should. There's nothing noble about doing it yourself, and where effective alternatives exist, it's foolish to try.

Reasonable people will differ about the extent to which commercial groupware solutions do, in fact, exist. Most would agree, though, that Lotus Notes and Microsoft Exchange don't solve all your groupware problems right out of the box. They've got to be customized, because group communication is wildly idiosyncratic. There's no such thing as a turnkey groupware system. No matter what, you're going to have to write some code if you want to make groupware work in your organization.

If you buy that argument, then try this one. The object Web isn't waiting for next-generation technologies to arrive. It's already happening, embodied in the best practices surrounding existing Internet tools and applications. The Internet way of building software has become the *de facto* standard, and it challenges the old "build versus buy" equation. Conventional wisdom says that you shouldn't build your own applications and components, because they'll be slow, unreliable, and nonreusable. In fact, although homegrown solutions *can* suffer these ills, they need not. The same best practices that brought us the object Web, ahead of schedule and below the radar screen, can help you build, automate, test, monitor, and manage groupware solutions.

Using Web APIs as Automation Interfaces

A standard web application is necessarily automatable. By "standard web application" I mean a server-based program that collects input from, and displays results in, an HTML/JavaScript browser. It's fashionable nowadays to sneer at this basic model of web computing and to regard it as a poor first approximation of what newer browsers can do more gracefully using Java or dynamic HTML.

Java and/or DHTML may in fact usher in an era of more GUI-like web applications with capabilities—like drag-and-drop—that are beyond the scope of the standard HTML widget set and JavaScript object model. But the last web applications to exploit these capabilities will be the ones that most people rely on most of the time for most of the useful services that the Web offers: search, online shopping, airline reservations. Very few of these kinds of applications require drag-and-drop. Arguably none of them do. What they do require is what first-generation CGI technology has been delivering effectively for about four years: zero-install electronic forms connected to middle-tier logic and backend databases.

Public web-based services stick with this model because it's simple and universal. Unless there are compelling reasons not to, your web-based groupware applications should stick with it too, and not only for reasons of simplicity and universality. Every application written to this model is at once interactive and scriptable. The implications of that fact are profound and far-reaching, and they take time to sink in.

My moment of epiphany came when I worked for a large publishing corporation with many divisional web sites. There was a corporate mandate to present the individual sites as a single coherent megasite, but no one could agree on how to aggregate all the content or unify the many different search mechanisms. Driving home from a meeting at which an IT executive had opined that multisite search was an eight-man-month, hundred-thousand-dollar problem, I suddenly saw that it was really a four-hour, zero-dollar problem that I could solve that very evening. How? All the necessary components were already deployed and web-accessible. The individual sites were periodically scanned and indexed by the public search engines. Some of those engines support advanced search pages that can be used to restrict search to pages drawn from specific sites. On AltaVista, for example, you can issue the following query:

```
host:udell.roninhouse.com and groupware
```

This query returns only pages on udell.roninhouse.com (my own server) that mention groupware. Similarly, for that set of divisional web sites, AltaVista had already done the necessary aggregation, and it already enabled a sophisticated user to search our sites! Documenting how to do that interactively, using AltaVista's query syntax, was one solution to the problem. Much more compelling, though, was the solution I actually delivered the next morning. It was simply a form, hosted on my site, that listed the divisional sites. I wired the form to a script that created an advanced AltaVista query, shipped it to the AltaVista site, and reorganized and displayed the results.

How did that metasearch script work? We've already seen the basic ingredients. A web-client library (such as Perl's LWP) transmits URL-formatted requests to target sites and fetches web pages in response. A script analyzes the resulting web pages, using regular expressions to match patterns and rearrange the output. (We'll see several examples of this procedure later in this chapter.) I call this technique *pipelining the Web*, because it most resembles the good old-fashioned Unix pipeline.

Pipelining the Web

One of Unix's greatest sources of power and flexibility is its notion of a pipeline of text-based components. To count the number of Apache daemons currently running on my Red Hat Linux system, for example, I don't need a *count-apache-daemons* command, because I can just type:

```
ps aux | grep httpd | wc -l
```

In other words: list all processes, restrict the list to lines containing *httpd*, then count those lines. If you find yourself using this idiom often, you can package it into an alias called *count-apache-daemons*, which you can then use in shell scripts indistinguishably from the native commands *ps*, *grep*, and *wc*. With just these two simple ideas—scripts and a pipeline to connect them—Unix invented lightweight software components and rapid application development.

The Unix way reigned supreme during the era of text-based computing. Then the rise of the graphical user interface threatened to make it obsolete. In the GUI model, programs received input as a stream of user-interface events—mouseclicks and keystrokes—and produced output by manipulating a bitmapped window display. For most people, the benefits of this new approach far outweighed the drawbacks. The prime benefit—what people really mean when they talk about "point-and-click ease of use"—is discoverability. All of the functions of a GUI-based system can be discovered by exploring its toolbars, menu trees, and dialog boxes. The chief drawback—what Unix veterans curse when they find themselves managing NT systems—is that there often isn't any way to automate those functions.

The notion of web applications as scriptable components is especially deep and powerful, because it addresses two completely different problems, both longstanding: how to make distributed computing easy enough for routine use and how to use graphical applications as pipelined components in the manner of *ps*, *grep*, and *wc*.

The web model radically simplified the programming of an important subset of the GUI widget set—namely, the widgets used in electronic forms. An easy way to create and use listboxes, radio buttons, and text-input fields was part of the story, but that in itself wasn't new. For over a decade, from Hypercard's debut in the mid-'80s through the many incarnations of Visual Basic, there have been scripting tools that could hide the arduous details of GUI programming—things like mouse-hit detection and event-loop management.

What the web model brought to the party was a simple, text-based, language-neutral interface to the GUI. People could easily read and write the descriptions that drove web pages and forms, and so could programs written in any script language. In an environment in which those web pages and forms were often built dynamically by CGI programs, the interface to those CGI programs was again text based and language neutral—URLs that could be read and written by people or by scripts written in any language.

Web Interfaces Versus GUI Interfaces

Web APIs are both discoverable and scriptable. They're discoverable because, by interactive use of a web application (such as AltaVista), we can expose the URLs that control its functions. They're scriptable because we can wield those URLs using web-client tools. It's easy to take these properties of web APIs for granted. To put things in perspective, think about what you *can't* do with conventional GUI applications that lack these properties.

Consider a typical GUI application, Windows NT's User Manager. It enables you to point and click your way through a series of dialog boxes but affords no means of automating those actions. Administrators of large domains had to do a whole lot of pointing and clicking until ADSI (see Chapter 11, *Membership Services*) made User Manager's underlying functions available to scripts.

Notice, though, that the kind of automation made possible by ADSI is not achieved by way of User Manager, which remains trapped in its point-and-click world. Instead ADSI provides alternate paths to the underlying functions. Could User Manager itself be scriptable? Yes. A number of Windows applications, notably Word and Excel, expose many of their interactive functions to scripts by way of OLE automation interfaces. But Windows applications don't *automatically* expose automation interfaces to scripts. It takes a lot of extra work to do that.

Thought Experiment: a Web-Style Win32 Application

Imagine a web-style version of User Manager. Why not? There's nothing particularly graphical about this tool. It just displays lists of names, adds and deletes names, and pushes names from one list to another. These functions are well within the capability of server-generated HTML.

As an HTML application, User Manager would present forms to list users, edit their accounts, adjust their group memberships. The HTTP *GET* or *POST* requests issuing from those forms would define User Manager's API. Even if that API weren't explicitly documented, you could discover it by just browsing and using your browser's *View Source* function to inspect each form's widget names and CGI wiring.

This ability to inspect, clone, and modify web forms helps make the Web a 'nearly frictionless environment for software development. If a form uses the HTTP *GET* method, the script name and all its arguments will be left sitting in what we might call the browser's command line—that is, the *Location* window in Navigator or the *Address* window in Internet Explorer. If the form uses the HTTP *POST* method, then only the script name appears on the browser's command line. How do you discover the script's arguments? The form's HTML source contains all their names, so you can look there. Alternatively you can save a copy of the form, change *POST* to *GET*, and then submit it. Now the arguments will appear on the browser's command line.

This version of User Manager wouldn't have to do anything special to expose a discoverable and scriptable API. It would do so just because it was a web application. And it would also exhibit the following useful properties.

Local and remote capability

Many of the NT administrative tools, including User Manager, can use remote procedure call (RPC) technology to connect to remote machines. That means you can use an instance of User Manager running on one machine to manage the user database on another machine. Like an OLE automation interface, this kind of RPC interface is an optional, not intrinsic, feature of a Win32 applicatation. A web-enabled User Manager, built on an HTTP service, would *inherently* support local or remote clients. We'll see examples of this technique in the next chapter.

Bookmarks

Many of NT's admin tools are primarily navigators and editors of specialized information spaces. A web-enabled User Manager would be able to remember and replay paths through its space—the directory—using bookmarks. The tool most in need of this capability isn't User Manager, though. It's RegEdit, the registry editor. Spend a day within earshot of an NT administrator and you'll hear mantras like this chanted repeatedly: "HKEY_LOCAL_MACHINE, System, CurrentControlSet, Services, W3SVC, Parameters..." Once the target key is found and altered (and the machine has been rebooted), the problem may still not be solved. So the administrator must repeat the same mantra and travel the same path to the same registry key for another try. This is nuts! In web mode, you'd bookmark that page after the second or third visit to it.

Pipelining

In a web-style environment, every one of User Manager's dialog boxes would be a page with an address. You could visit those pages interactively, and scripts could visit them programmatically using the very same mechanism. The User Manager page that lists a user's group affiliations, for example, might do so by writing an HTML <SELECT> statement. Knowing this, a script could treat User Manager as a component in a pipeline. It could invoke the page with a web-client call, parse the list of groups in the <SELECT> statement, then pass the list along to the next component in the pipeline—perhaps a report writer. As we'll see shortly, XML-formatted responses can make this procedure simpler and more reliable.

During the run-up to Windows 98, Microsoft fueled speculation that the whole Windows environment would switch over to this web mode of operation. All views of the system would be dynamic web pages rendered by a local HTML engine, and web-style scripting would be the way to automate Windows. That mostly didn't happen, apart from the common view of web and local filespaces provided by the (now deemphasized) Active Desktop. But although Windows hasn't gone that way—at least not yet—it's still a great idea.

XML-RPC: a Next-Generation Web API

Simple, elegant, and useful applications of Internet technology always put a smile on my face. One such application is running at *http://www.mailtothefuture.com/*. It enables you to send mail to yourself (or, actually, anyone) at some future date.

This is an interactive application that, because it's a CGI-based web service, I could with a little effort also use as an HTTP-based reminder component built into a groupware or workflow system of my own devising. To do that, I'd follow the procedures outlined earlier: discover the web API, and write a script to control it.

But the author of MailToTheFuture, Dave Winer, has taken this game to a new level. A pioneer in understanding and applying XML, Dave cooked up a marvelously simple and elegant idea that he calls XML-RPC (see *http://www.scripting. com/frontier5/xml/code/rpc.html*). In a nutshell, it's a way of formalizing the CGI interface to a web-based service using XML to define both the *methods* supported by a service and the *data marshaling* used when communicating with a service.

The architecture of XML-RPC is gloriously simple. A service that supports XML-RPC, such as MailToTheFuture, responds to method calls that are nothing more than HTTP *POST* requests with XML-formatted payloads. For example, to add a new message to your queue at MailToTheFuture, you invoke the method:

```
mailToTheFuture.addMessage(username, password, msgstruct)
```

To use this method, you post an XML-RPC request that expresses that method name and its three parameters. Example 14-1 is a Perl script that illustrates one of the (infinitely many) easy ways to form and transmit such a request. The XML-RPC request appears in literal form following the script's __END__ directive.

Example 14-1. Invoking the mailToTheFuture.addMessage Method from Perl

```perl
#! /usr/bin/perl -w
#
# This script implements the addMessage method at Dave Winer's
# www.MailToTheFuture.com site, using XML-RPC.
#
my $req_data = join('', <DATA>);                    # slurp the XML from __END__ zone

use strict;
use LWP;
my $ua = new LWP::UserAgent;                         # make a user agent
my $req = new HTTP::Request 'POST';                  # make a request

$req->url('http://www.mailtothefuture.com/RPC2');    # set url
$req->header(Host => "yourhost");                     # Host: yourhost
$req->user_agent($ua->agent);                         # User-Agent: libwww-perl/5.36
$req->content_type('text/xml');                      # Content-Type: text/xml
$req->content_length(length($req_data));             # Content-Length: 762
$req->content($req_data);                            # append request data

my $res = $ua->request($req);                        # send the request

if ($res->is_success)
  { print $res->content;   }                         # echo response
else
  { print "Could not transmit request\n"; }

__END__
<?xml version="1.0"?>
<methodCall>
  <methodName>mailToTheFuture.addMessage</methodName>
    <params>
      <param>
        <value>yourname@yourmailhost.com</value>
      </param>
      <param>
        <value>yourpassword</value>
      </param>
      <param>
        <value>
         <struct>
           <member>
             <name>dateTime</name>
             <value>5/23/99; 11:15:00 AM</value>
           </member>
           <member>
             <name>messageBody</name>
             <value>test message body</value>
           </member>
           <member>
             <name>receiverMailAddress</name>
             <value>yourname@yourmailhost.com</value>
           </member>
```

Example 14-1. Invoking the mailToTheFuture.addMessage Method from Perl (continued)

```
      <member>
        <name>subject</name>
        <value>test message subject</value>
      </member>
    </struct>
  </value>
  </param>
  </params>
</methodCall>
```

Anatomy of an XML-RPC Transaction

An XML-RPC request can be as easily read and written by a human as by a program. That's one of the great features of all Internet software: the protocols (HTTP, SMTP, NNTP) are text based and therefore easy to understand and manipulate in any programming language.

Of course, the same thing applies to ordinary web-client scripting. What's special about XML-RPC? Well, consider the response that comes back when you send the wrong password to the MailToTheFuture service using its normal CGI interface:

"Sorry! There was an error: Can't send you the cookie for 'yourname@yourmailhost. com' because the password is incorrect."

You can certainly teach your script to recognize and deal with these kinds of responses, but it's going to be a fragile mechanism. You're relying on free-form text patterns, and when they change, your script will break.

Now consider the response that comes back from MailToTheFuture's XML-RPC interface when you send the wrong password:

```
<?xml version="1.0"?>
<methodResponse>
  <fault>
    <value>
      <struct>
        <member>
          <name>faultCode</name>
          <value>
            <int>4</int>
          </value>
        </member>
        <member>
          <name>faultString</name>
          <value>
            <string>The password is incorrect.</string>
          </value>
        </member>
      </struct>
```

```
    </value>
   </fault>
</methodResponse>
```

Like the request, this response is well formed—and thus automatically parsable—XML. Every XML-RPC service will use this same pattern. It's true that, for each application, you'll need to decide how to handle `faultCode` 4. But you won't need to guess that the output is an example of a `methodResponse` or that its `value` is a `fault` object containing a `struct` made up of a `faultCode` and a `faultString`.

Other XML-Formatted Request/Response Protocols

This notion of a standard, human-readable-and-writable, script-parsable lingo for requests and responses is a lot more in tune with the ecology of the Web than DCOM, CORBA, or RMI. It's all HTTP based, so you get firewall penetration, SSL encryption if you need it, and a wealth of tools that know how to work both the client and server ends of the HTTP protocol.

As you might expect, XML-RPC isn't the only implementation of this idea. Others include Allaire's web Distributed Data Exchange (WDDX, *http://www.wddx.org*) and webMethod's Web Interface Definition Language (WIDL, *http://www.w3.org/TR/NOTE-widl*).

Like XML-RPC, WDDX defines an XML-formatted request/response protocol. The WDDX SDK includes libraries that enable COM, Java, JavaScript, VBScript, Perl, and Cold Fusion applications to serialize complex data structures as WDDX packets and to exchange such packets. This means, for example, that you can take a server-based Cold Fusion array, serialize it as XML, send it to a browser, and unpack it as a VBScript array object used in a browser-based script.

Using webMethod's WIDL, you can encapsulate existing CGI-style services, such as AltaVista's, in an XML interface. The company's B2B Integration Server (see *http://www.webmethods.com/*) uses this technique to create XML-based proxies that wrap clean, consistent, and stable XML packaging around CGI services that are messy, inconsistent, and ever-changing.

What's the downside to this approach? The XML-RPC technique can complement, but not yet replace, standard CGI techniques. When you serve up an HTML form to a browser, it's still going to respond using a conventional HTTP *GET* or *POST*, not an XML-RPC packet. Until the forms mechanism built into standard browsers becomes XML-aware, browser-driven groupware applications will still need to support a conventional HTML forms interface, at least on the input side. In terms of output, though, you're free to intermix HTML for consumption by humans and XML for consumption by robots.

Using Web APIs to Monitor and Test Groupware Applications

In Chapter 12, *Authentication and Authorization Techniques*, we built an access-control mechanism with some fairly complex logic. To read a record in the doc-base, a user has to authenticate, pass a group membership test, and finally pass a subscription test—that is, the company that's the subject of a requested report has to be among the feeds to which the user subscribes. Testing this kind of application is a tedious affair. To do it properly, you have to pretend to be a series of different users—one who fails authentication and one who passes, one who fails group membership and one who passes, one who uses basic authentication and one who accepts cookies. The combinations add up quickly, and it's time-consuming to run through them all. Once the application is deployed, you can let the users be the canaries in the coal mine, sounding the alarm when things go wrong. That's standard procedure for many web applications but far from satisfactory. All too often, people who run into problems don't report them. And really, why should they have to? The systems you build ought to monitor themselves. That sounds like a tall order, but in fact it's easier than you might think. The reason is that HTML-based software is inherently testable in ways that GUI software is not.

"On the Internet, nobody knows you're a dog." So went the caption of an oft-cited cartoon that depicted a dog sitting in front of a browser. More to the point here, an Internet application doesn't know the difference between a human and a robot, and web robots are easy to build. From the application's point of view, a user manifests as a URL request—possibly a CGI call with arguments—that may be accompanied by an HTTP header such as **HTTP_AUTHORIZATION** or **HTTP_COOKIE**. The URL and the HTTP headers are just strings of text that you can encode in a web-client script. Add it all up and you've got the basic ingredients of a powerful quality-assurance testing methodology.

To apply this methodology, start by listing the behaviors that you want to test. In the docbase access-control case, for example, we'll want to verify that access will be correctly denied—with an appropriate explanation—for any of several reasons and that access will be granted only when a request passes all the tests.

We can express the desired behaviors as a set of requests paired with a set of expected responses. Here's a sample request:

```
GET http://localhost/cgi/auth.asp?doc=1998-10-19-000001
Authorization: AWxhZGRpbjpvcGVuIHNlc2FtZQ==
```

Assuming that the credentials encoded in this **Authorization** header (**Aladdin:open sesame**) pass the authentication and group membership tests, but that Aladdin doesn't subscribe to the company newsfeed to which the requested document belongs (e.g., reports about Netscape), here's the expected response:

```
200 NotRegisteredForCompany
Content-Type: text/html
Client-Date: Thu, 22 Oct 1998 21:02:39 GMT
Client-Peer: 127.0.0.1:80

Denied: NotRegisteredForCompany
```

To test an application, build a script around a data structure that records a list of these requests. To discover these, you can drive the application interactively, perform the test cases by hand, and capture their associated URLs. If an authorization or cookie header is involved, you can compose it yourself or alter the backend script to capture it. The responses come for free. You could save them yourself, from a browser, but why not use the script to do that for you? If you number each test case, you can use the script to capture responses in files with corresponding names.

Baseline Mode Versus Test Mode

This method leads to the interesting notion of a dual-mode test script. In baseline mode, it processes a set of requests and creates the corresponding response files. The resulting collection of output files is a snapshot of an application in a known good state. Then, in test mode, the script reprocesses the requests, but now it compares the expected responses that it previously stored with the actual responses that it gets from the application. Any differences between the expected and actual responses mean that something changed.

But what does the change mean? It depends. Variance can occur for all sorts of normal or abnormal reasons. A normal reason might be that you've rewritten an error message, so that even though an application has correctly refused access in a certain situation, that refusal manifests itself differently than it did before. This hypersensitivity might be construed as a problem, but I think of it as an opportunity to review the things I've changed in the course of development. When all the response mismatches are of this type, you can assess the changes since the last baseline at a glance. To silence the complaints, just rerun the baseline to bring it into sync with the current state of the application.

Abnormal reasons for response mismatches include, but are not limited to, software failures. And that's the beauty of this approach. From the perspective of a user who is wrongly denied access, it doesn't matter whether a coding error crept into a CGI script, or an administrative goof invalidated a password, or a directory server died. The application could fail to produce the expected web page for any number of reasons. No matter what the cause, the result looks the same to the test script: an expected response doesn't match an actual response.

You might think that a mismatch must be triggered by a failed byte-for-byte comparison. It can be, but I've found that in many cases a simpler method—just comparing the lengths of the expected and actual responses—does the job. It's intriguing that such a trivial analysis of responses works so well. Of course, that won't be true if program-generated responses contain variable-length elements, such as computed values. Then you might need a smarter response analyzer. Or, as we'll see, you could make the application responsible for emitting codes—in the body of the page, wrapped in HTML comment syntax, or in a customized HTTP header—that the tester would look for.

Testing Sequences of Actions

Testing individual URLs like this is well and good, but a real application often involves sequences of actions, some of which may alter the state of the application's environment. Table 14-1 shows a sample test sequence.

Table 14-1. A Sample Test Sequence

Test	Description
001	Authenticated user clicks change-password link
002	Failed attempt to change password: old and new passwords don't match
003	Failed attempt to change password: invalid character in password
004	Successful attempt to change password
005	Successful docbase access using new password

This sequence isn't repeatable, because it changes the state of the system. At test 1, the user (or the robot tester) presents valid credentials in order to access the change-password form. Test 4 changes the user's password—in a database, or directory, or wherever it's stored—and test 5 uses the new password. We can't repeat the sequence, because the credentials encoded in test 1 are no longer valid. This leads to the idea of test *constructors* and *destructors*—that is, code snippets that run before and after each test. A constructor can put the application's environment into an appropriate state for a given test. Test 1's constructor, for example, could issue a directory or database call to set the test user's password to a specified original value. Alternatively test 5's destructor could do the same thing, undoing the change introduced at test 4. Another good use of destructors is to clean up dummy inputs that are artifacts of the testing process. For example, the only real way to verify that the docbase input system is working is to add a report to a docbase. Since you don't want to contaminate a docbase with these dummy records, you can use a test destructor to delete them.

Don't be fooled by the highbrow terminology; you can do these things very simply. Example 14-2 shows a sample test script called *test-harness* (see Appendix A, *Example Software*, for details).

Example 14-2. The Docbase Test Script

```perl
#! /usr/bin/perl

use strict;
no strict 'refs';

use DBI;
use LWP;
my $ua = new LWP::UserAgent;

my $mode = $ARGV[0];

if ( ($mode ne 'baseline') and ($mode ne 'test') )
  {
  print "Usage: test-harness [baseline | test]\n";
  exit;
  }

print "mode: $mode\n";

my %sequence =                               # enumerate tests
  (
  '000' =>
    {
    'Description'    => 'No-header request fails access to docbase record',
    'Request'        => 'http://localhost/cgi/auth.asp?doc=1998-10-19-000001',
    'HeaderNames'    => [],
    'HeaderValues'   => [],

    },

  '001' =>
    {
    'Description'    => 'Invalid basic-auth user fails access to docbase record',
    'Request'        => 'http://localhost/cgi/auth.asp?doc=1998-10-19-000001',
    'HeaderNames'    => ['Authorization'],
    'HeaderValues'   => ['Basic AWxhZGRpbjpvcGVuIHNlc2FtZQ=='],
    },

  '002' =>
    {
    'Description'    => 'Valid basic-auth user gains access to docbase record',
    'Request'        => 'http://localhost/cgi/auth.asp?doc=1998-10-19-000001',
    'HeaderNames'    => ['Authorization'],
    'HeaderValues'   => ['Basic QWxhZGRpbjpvcGVuIHNlc2FtZQ=='],
    },

  '003' =>
    {
    'Description'    => 'Valid basic-auth user fails feed registration',
    'Request'        => 'http://localhost/cgi/auth.asp?doc=1998-10-19-000001',
    'HeaderNames'    => ['Authorization'],
    'HeaderValues'   => ['Basic QWxhZGRpbjpvcGVuIHNlc2FtZQ=='],
```

Example 14-2. The Docbase Test Script (continued)

```perl
     'Constructor'    => 'unRegisterAladdinForNetscape',
     'Destructor'     => 'reRegisterAladdinForNetscape',
     },

  '004' =>
    {
    'Description'    => 'Valid cookie user gains access to docbase record',
    'Request'        => 'http://localhost/cgi/auth.asp?doc=1998-10-19-000001',
    'HeaderNames'    => ['Cookie'],
    'HeaderValues'   => ['ProductAnalysisSubscriber=
                          Aladdin%000926517024%00192.168.1'],
    },

  '005' =>
    {
    'Description'    => 'Valid cookie user fails feed registration',
    'Request'        => 'http://localhost/cgi/auth.asp?doc=1998-10-19-000001',
    'HeaderNames'    => ['Cookie'],
    'HeaderValues'   => ['ProductAnalysisSubscriber=
                          Aladdin%000926517024%00192.168.1'],
    'Constructor'    => 'unRegisterAladdinForNetscape',
    'Destructor'     => 'reRegisterAladdinForNetscape',
    },
  );


foreach my $testname (sort keys %sequence)
  {
  my $request = new HTTP::Request 'GET';          # make new request
  my $testhash = $sequence{$testname};            # fetch request hash
  print "Test: $testname ($testhash->{Description})\n";
  my $i = scalar ( @{$testhash->{HeaderNames}} );

  while ( $i-- )                                   # add HTTP headers to request
      {
      my $header_name  = $testhash->{HeaderNames}->[$i];
      my $header_value = $testhash->{HeaderValues}->[$i];
      $request->header($header_name => $header_value);
      }

  $request->url($testhash->{Request});            # set request URL

  my $constructor = $testhash->{Constructor};     # try constructor
  if ( defined &{$constructor} )
      {  &{$constructor} }

  my $response = $ua->request($request);          # issue request

  my $response_code = sprintf("%s %s\n", $response->code, $response->message);
  my $response_content .= $response->headers->as_string . "\n";
  $response_content .= $response->content;
  print $response_code;
  $testhash->{ResponseCode} = $response_code;
```

Example 14-2. The Docbase Test Script (continued)

```perl
  my $destructor = $testhash->{Destructor};          # try destructor
  if ( defined &{$destructor} )
      { &{$destructor} }

  my $result_file = $mode . "_" . $testname;         # form result name
  open (F, ">$result_file") or die "cannot create $result_file";
  print F $response_code;
  print F $response_content;
  close F;
  if ($mode eq 'test')                               # compare to baseline
    {
    my @expected_stats = stat( "baseline_" . $testname );
    my $expected_len   = $expected_stats[7];
    my @test_stats     = stat( $result_file );
    my $test_len       = $test_stats[7];
    print "Expected: $expected_len, Got: $test_len\n";
    $testhash->{Outcome} = ($test_len eq $expected_len)
      ? "<font color=green><b>CORRECT</b></font>"
      : "<font color=red><b>ERROR</b></font>";
    }
  print "\n";
  $sequence{$testname} = $testhash;
  }

open(F, ">test.htm");                                # emit HTML results
print F "<table border cellpadding=4>";
print F "<tr><td><b>name</b></td><td><b>description</b></td><td>
        <b>response</b></td><td><b>outcome</b></td></tr>";
foreach my $testname (sort keys %sequence)
  {
  my $testhash = $sequence{$testname};
  print F "<tr><td>$testname</td><td>$testhash->{Description}</td>
          <td><a href=test_$testname>$testhash->{ResponseCode}</a></td>
          <td>$testhash->{Outcome}</td></tr>";
  }
print F "</table>";
close F;

sub unRegisterAladdinForNetscape
  {
  my $dbh = DBI->connect('DBI:ODBC:SUBS','','') or die "DBI::errstr";
  my $st = "update cmp_users set cmp = 'none' where user = 'Aladdin'";
  $dbh->do($st) or die "DBI::errstr";
  $dbh->disconnect;
  }

sub reRegisterAladdinForNetscape
  {
  my $dbh = DBI->connect('DBI:ODBC:SUBS','','') or die "DBI::errstr";
  my $st = "update cmp_users set cmp = 'Netscape' where user = 'Aladdin'";
  $dbh->do($st) or die "DBI::errstr";
  $dbh->disconnect;
  }
```

We want tests 0 and 1 to refuse access for different reasons and test 2 to grant access. To ensure that test 3 correctly refuses access, we use a constructor to set the test user's password to the one that the test will use. It's just a function whose name is tucked into the test's Constructor slot.

The response goes into a file whose name correspond to the test's name. When the test script runs in baseline mode, accumulating expected responses, it creates the file *baseline_003*. When it runs in test mode, it creates the file *test_003* and then compares it with *baseline_003*.

Testing a Complex Authentication Scenario

Each test uses *auth.asp*, the docbase access script we developed in Chapter 12, in a slightly different way. Recall that the steps required to authenticate a user and grant access to a requested docbase record are as follows:

1. Look for credentials. If the user has chosen basic authentication, the credentials will be encoded in the `HTTP_AUTHORIZATION` header. If the user accepted a cookie, the credentials will be encoded in `HTTP_COOKIE`. Either method can work, so try to grab both headers.

2. Try basic authentication. MIME-decode the `Authorization` header to produce a name/password pair. Authenticate these credentials—in this case, by SHA-encrypting the password and comparing it with the encrypted password stored in the user's entry in an LDAP directory. If authentication succeeds, test for membership in the group of users that has permission to read this docbase, using another LDAP lookup. If any of these steps fails, then...

3. Try cookie authentication. Look for the cookie named `ProductAnalysis-Subscriber`. If it exists, look up its value in an SQL database. If that's found, extract the corresponding username and test it for group membership as in the basic-authorization case. Fail if any of these tests fails.

4. Verify company-feed subscription. An authenticated user who is a member of the permitted group must still pass one more test. A request to read a report in this docbase will succeed only if the company that is the subject of this report corresponds to one of the feeds to which the user subscribes. To find out, get the company name from the report's metadata and look for a user/company pair in the feeds database.

There are lots of moving parts here and lots of things that can break. When the robot tester produces a set of test results that match the expected results, we can be fairly certain that each part is doing its job. Note that from the robot's perspective, a correct result can be either a success or a failure from the user's perspective. What's more, the robot may need to differentiate among modes of failure that to the user all look the same. In this case, for example, a mistyped password or an expired or damaged cookie both result in the same thing: a basic authentication challenge. Why? Since the script will always accept a valid name and password, basic authentication is the method of last resort. And since that method requires the script to issue an HTTP 401 header, it can't at the same time use a normal web page to communicate with the user. In both cases, the user will see the same login dialog box. How can the robot differentiate a basic-authentication failure from a cookie-authentication failure? Go back and look at Example 12-4. The script uses the message that follows the 401 status code to announce the reason for issuing the challenge—it's either "BadPassword" or "InvalidCookie."

Reporting Test Results

When the script can tell the user why it's refusing access, it should. So when the group-membership or subscription-feed tests fail, it issues an explanatory web page. Here too, though, it uses the message that follows the 200 status code to announce the reason why it's denying access. The user won't see that message, but the robot will. It can use the status codes and messages that it collects to neatly summarize the test results, as shown in Figure 14-1.

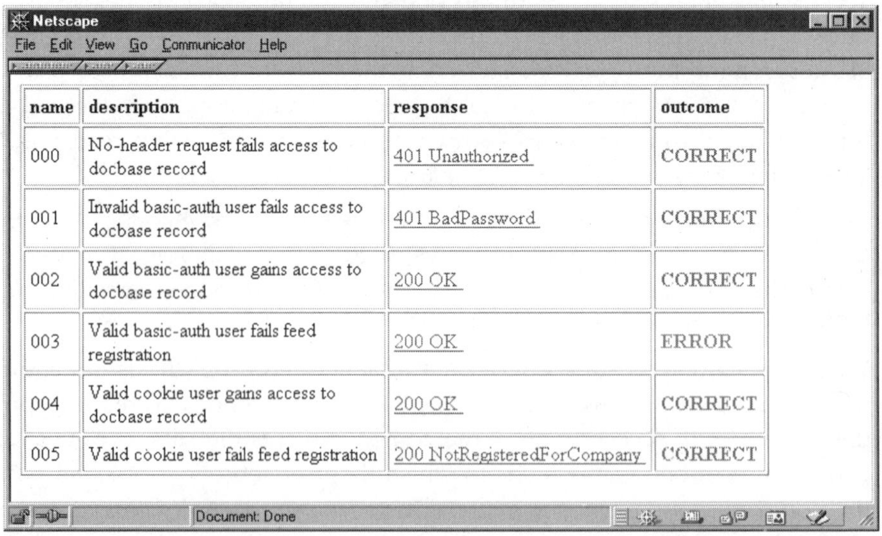

name	description	response	outcome
000	No-header request fails access to docbase record	401 Unauthorized	CORRECT
001	Invalid basic-auth user fails access to docbase record	401 BadPassword	CORRECT
002	Valid basic-auth user gains access to docbase record	200 OK	CORRECT
003	Valid basic-auth user fails feed registration	200 OK	ERROR
004	Valid cookie user gains access to docbase record	200 OK	CORRECT
005	Valid cookie user fails feed registration	200 NotRegisteredForCompany	CORRECT

Figure 14-1. The test script's report

The error reported for test 3 was real. This test ran using an ODBC/Jet connection to an Access database—that is, a *.MDB* file. You wouldn't use that kind of setup in a real multiuser situation, and this error shows why. After test 3's constructor ran, Aladdin should have been unregistered for Netscape-related reports. But *auth.asp* didn't see the effect of the constructor's update, so it erroneously granted access. What caused this problem? The Jet database engine uses separate threads to read and write. Those threads aren't fully synchronized—there's a write delay that makes Jet unsafe for multiuser access. The point here isn't Jet's lack of concurrency controls that it was never designed to have. The point is that the test system reacts properly to an obscure and erroneous condition.

Each hyperlinked status code leads to the full web page that was fetched for that test. Those pages include everything sent back from the server—HTTP headers as well as content. The web model of programming makes it trivial to create this kind of drill-down feature. You should think of every element on every report page as an opportunity to link to another layer of information. Suppose the test script saved versions of each baseline and its associated test runs rather than just overwriting those files. Entries in the Outcome column could summarize that historical data—perhaps by reporting the percentage of all runs that got correct results. The percentage number could link to a detailed report that you'd use to look for patterns and correlations.

From Quality Assurance to Monitoring

We've entered new territory here. What began as a way to ensure that applications work correctly has turned into a way to monitor their availability and measure their performance. When I ran the *BYTE* site, an hourly script tested every one of the services: the static archive, the feedback system, the search systems, the newsgroups and web conference system, the Virtual Press Room, and more. Failures triggered email messages to members of my team and to my pager.

I also used this monitoring technique to keep tabs on two partner sites—one that served ads into our pages and one that handled reader-service links. From time to time we noticed outages in these services. But pinpointing the outages was like trying to find an electrical problem in your car. When you try to show it to the mechanic, you can never make the problem appear. Once I added URLs on these sites to the test script, it was a whole new ball game. With a month of twice-hourly samples in hand, I could prove when and roughly for how long there had been outages. In one case I alerted a site manager to a problem before his own staff had caught up with it.

Aggregating and Repackaging Internet Services

We've talked about using public search engines as components of a custom search application. Let's work through two examples of that idea. The first gathers information from a set of technology news sites. The second trolls a set of public LDAP directories.

A Technology News Metasearcher

The Web nowadays offers more search engines than you can keep track of. Even metasearchers—that is, applications that aggregate multiple search engines—are becoming common. For example, I use a tool called Copernic (*http://www. copernic.com/*) to do parallel searches of AltaVista, Excite, and a number of other engines.

Despite the wealth of searchers and metasearchers, there's always a need for a more customized solution. The analysts at our fictitious Ronin Group, for example, track technology news by subject. The technology news sites, including PR Newswire (*http://www.prnewswire.com/*), Business Wire (*http://www.businesswire. com/*), and Yahoo! (*http://www.yahoo.com/*), deliver lots of fresh technology news. But consider the plight of the Ronin Group's XML analyst. None of the available metasearchers cover all the technology news sites that she'd like to include in her daily search for XML-related news.

What to do? It's straightforward to build a custom metasearcher. You discover the web API for each engine that you want to search, create a URL template, interpolate a search term into that URL template, transmit the URL, and interpret the results.

Discovering the Web APIs

In some cases, you'll find your URL template sitting on the browser's command line after you run a search. For example, when you search CMP's TechWeb site (*http://www.techweb.com*), the following URL appears on the command line:

```
http://www.techweb.com/se/techsearch.cgi?queryText=xml&sorted=true&
    collname=current&publication=All
```

At the PR Newswire site, though, the search form uses the HTTP *POST* method. So the URL template we're looking for isn't on the browser's command line. But it's easy to discover by viewing the form's HTML source. Here's the relevant piece of that form:

```
<FORM ACTION="http://199.230.26.105/fulltext" METHOD="POST">
<INPUT TYPE="text" NAME="SEARCH" SIZE=35 MAXLENGTH=70>
<INPUT NAME="NUMDAYS" TYPE=Radio VALUE="3" CHECKED>
</FORM>
```

That's equivalent to this HTTP *GET* request, which you can formulate and test on the browser's command line:

```
http://199.230.26.105/fulltext?SEARCH=xml&NUMDAYS=3
```

The metasearch strategy

Figure 14-2 illustrates the general strategy for a metasearcher. To each of a set of engines, it sends a query. From each, it receives an HTML page in response. To each of these HTML pages, it applies a regular expression to identify search results and normalize them.

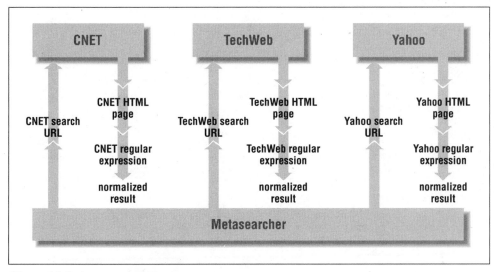

Figure 14-2. A metasearch strategy

To identify the patterns that define search results for each of the target engines, you need to inspect the HTML source of the result pages. Then you write regular expressions to isolate the desired elements. For example, here's a search result from Business Wire:

```
<a href="http://www.businesswire.com/webbox/bw.052599/191451672.htm">
SoftQuad Now Shipping XMetaL 1.0—Setting the Standard for XML Content
Creation</a></b><br>
```

We'd like to capture two pieces of this link: its address and its label—that is, the story's headline. Here's a Perl regular expression that will match this search result:

```
\"(http:[^\"]+)(\">)([^<]+)
```

This expression captures the URL in Perl's special variable $1 and the headline in $3.

Implementing the Newswire module

The Perl module shown in Example 14-3 packages these techniques. Its central data structure is a hash of lists (HoL) whose keys are the names of news sites and whose values are three-element lists. Each list comprises the following.

- A parameterized URL template to drive the search

- A regular expression to match search results

- A hostname to prefix to the resulting link (not always needed)

Example 14-3. A Technology News Metasearcher

```perl
#!/usr/bin/perl -w

use strict;
package NewsWire;
use LWP::Simple;

sub new
  {
  my ($pkg,$search_term) = @_;
  my $self =
    {
    'headlines'      => {},
    'nw_enum'        =>
      {
      'bizwire' =>
        [
        "http://search.businesswire.com/query.html?qm=1&qt=$search_term",
        "\"(http:[^\"]+)(\">)([^<]+)",
        '',
        ],

      'cnet' =>
        [
        "http://www.news.com/Searching/Results/1,18,1,00.html?querystr=
            $search_term&startdate=&lastdate=&numDaysBack=
            03&newsCategory=null&newscomTopics=0",
        "\"(/News/Item/[^\"]+)(\">)([^<]+)</a>, ([^<]+)",
        'http://www.news.com',
        ],

      'yahoo' =>
        [
        "http://search.news.yahoo.com/search/news?n=10&p=$search_term",
        "(http://biz.yahoo.com/[^\"]+)(\">)(.+)</A>",
        '',
        ],

      'infoseek' =>
        [
        "http://infoseek.go.com/Titles?col=NX&sv=IS&lk=noframes&nh=
            10&qt=%2B$search_term%2B&rf=i500sRD&kt=A&ak=news1486",
        "(Content\?[^\"]+)(\">)(.+)</a>",
        'http://infoseek.go.com/',
        ],

      'techweb' =>
        [
```

Example 14-3. A Technology News Metasearcher (continued)

```
            "http://www.techweb.com/se/techsearch.cgi?queryText=$search_term&
                sorted=true&collname=current&publication=WIR&submitbutton=
                Search&from_month=01&from_day=01&from_year=99&to_month=
                $month&to_day=$mday&to_year=$year",
            "(http://www.techweb.com/wire/story/[^\"]+)(\"[^>]+>)(.+)</a>",
            '',
            ],

        'newspage' =>
            [
            "http://www.newspage.com/cgi-bin/np.Search?previous_module=NASearch&
                PreviousSearchPage=NewSearch&offerID=&Query=$search_term&
                NumDays=7&NewSearchSubmitBtn.x=15&NewSearchSubmitBtn.y=5",
            "href=\"(/cgi-bin/NA.GetStory[^>]+)(>)(.+)</A>",
            'http://www.newspage.com',
            ],

        'prnewswire' =>
            [
            "http://199.230.26.105/fulltext?SEARCH=$search_term&NUMDAYS=3",
            "(http://www.prnewswire.com/cgi-bin/stories.pl[^>]+)(>)([^<]+)",
            '',
            ],
        },
    };
    bless $self,$pkg;
    return $self;
    }


sub getNewswire
    {
    my ($self,$newswire) = @_;
    my $search_url = $self->{nw_enum}->{$newswire}->[0];
    my $result_pat = $self->{nw_enum}->{$newswire}->[1];
    my $server_pre = $self->{nw_enum}->{$newswire}->[2];
    print STDERR "search_url: $search_url, $result_pat\n";
    my $raw_results = get $search_url;
    my $count = 0;
    if ( $raw_results eq '' )
        { print STDERR "Error: no response from $newswire\n"; }
    print STDERR "trying $newswire...";
    while ( $raw_results =~ m#$result_pat#g )
        {
        $count++;
        my $url = "$server_pre$1";
        my $headline = "$3 ($newswire)";
        $headline =~ s#<b>##g;
        $headline =~ s#</b>##g;
        if ( $url eq '' )
            { print STDERR "Error: empty URL in $newswire\n"; }
        if ( $headline eq '' )
            { print STDERR "Error: empty headline in $newswire\n"; }
```

Example 14-3. A Technology News Metasearcher (continued)

```
  $self->{headlines}->{$headline} = $url;
  }
if (! $count )
  { print STDERR "Error: $newswire returned nothing\n"; }
else
  { print STDERR "$count results\n"; }
}

sub getAllNewswires
  {
  my ($self) = shift;
  foreach my $nw (sort keys %{$self->{nw_enum}})
    {
    $self->getNewswire($nw);
    }
  }

sub printResults
  {
  my ($self) = shift;
  print "<ul>\n";
  foreach my $headline ( sort keys %{$self->{headlines}} )
    {
    $headline =~ s/^\s+//;
    print "<li><a href=\"$self->{headlines}->{$headline}\">$headline</a> \n";
    }
  print "</ul>\n";
  }

1;
```

Here's a script that uses this module to gather a list of current XML-related news stories:

```
use NewsWire;
my $nw = NewsWire->new("xml");
$nw->getAllNewswires;
$nw->printResults;
```

Some of the output from this script appears in Figure 14-3.

Note that some of the stories are carried by multiple sources. Why not condense these into single entries? You could do that, though it's interesting to see the overlap among the various services. And the degree of repetition is one measure of the importance of a story.

Suppose you want to count the repeated items. The results structure in the *Newswire* module could easily be adapted for that purpose. But the real point here is that even without explicitly adding that capability, the existing HTML output can be further transformed by another stage of a web pipeline. You don't have to anticipate every possible requirement, and build every imaginable feature, into a

Figure 14-3. Technology news metasearch results for an XML query

web component. It's arguably better that you don't, but rather—as is the Unix tradition—just build parts that do simple, well-defined jobs and that can be embedded in a pipeline.

An LDAP Directory Metasearcher

To show that any Internet service can be aggregated and repackaged, we'll switch gears and focus on public LDAP directories. The Netscape and Microsoft mailreaders both include LDAP clients. They come preloaded with the addresses of several public directories, including Bigfoot, Switchboard, and Four11. It's remarkable that you can search these directories in real time as you compose messages, but the feature isn't as useful or well used as it might be. One reason is that it's never clear which directory to search. None are authoritative; any of them might turn up the right answer to a given query.

Searching the directories one after the other is a tedious affair. Suppose you start with Switchboard, and you're looking for me. It's a big Internet, and there are a few different Jon Udells, so if you know I live in New Hampshire, you'll want to start with a restrictive query, and if that fails then broaden it. What if even the broader search fails? You might try Four11, first restrictively and then broadly. It soon adds up to a lot of wasted motion. You'd like to apply the restrictive search to several sites at once and then, if necessary, search all those sites a second time more broadly. You can achieve that effect with a simple form/script pair. Figure 14-4 shows the search form.

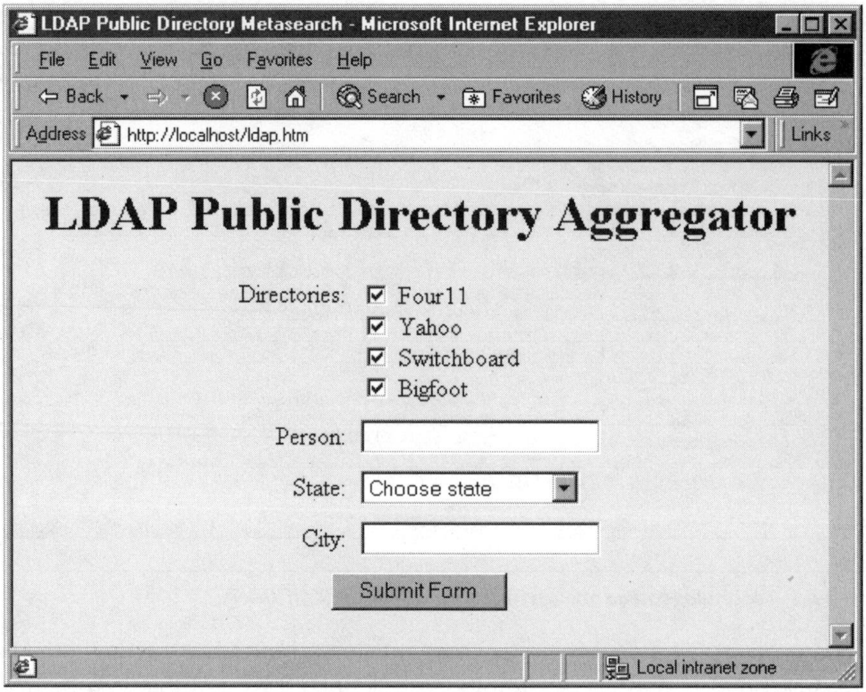

Figure 14-4. Aggregated LDAP search form

Example 14-4 shows the accompanying script.

Example 14-4. Aggregated LDAP Search Script

```perl
use strict;
use TinyCGI;
my $cgi = TinyCGI->new;
print $cgi->printHeader;
my $vars = $cgi->readParse();

use Mozilla::LDAP::Conn;                          # use the PerLDAP module

my %searchroots = (
'ldap.bigfoot.com'       =>   "",
'ldap.four11.com'        =>   "",
'ldap.yahoo.com'         =>   "",
'ldap.switchboard.com'   =>   "o=switchboard,c=us",
);

my @servers = ();
foreach my $server (keys %searchroots)
    {
    if ( $vars->{$server} eq 'on' )               # if LDAP server selected on form
        { push (@servers,$server); }              # add to list to search
    }
```

Example 14-4. Aggregated LDAP Search Script (continued)

```perl
my $person;
if ( $vars->{person} eq '' )                     # by default
    { $person = "cn=*"; }                        # use wildcard for cn
else
    { $person = "cn=$vars->{person}"; }          # else use supplied name

my $state;
if ( $vars->{state} eq 'Choose state')           # by default
    { $state = "st=*"; }                         # use wildcard for state
else
    {
    my ($st1,$st2) = split(',',$vars->{state}); # else value like "NH,New Hampshire"
    $state = "| (st=$st1)(st=$st2)";             # use either part
    }

my $city;
if ( $vars->{city} eq '')                        # by default
    { $city = "l=*"; }                           # use wildcard for location
else
    {
    $city = "l=$vars->{city}";                   # else use supplied name
    }

my $search =                                     # construct the query
  "(& ($person) ($city) ($state) )";

print "<p>search: $search";

print "<pre>";

foreach $server (@servers)
    {
    print "<p>$server: ($searchroots{$server})";

    my $conn =                                   # connect to LDAP server
      Mozilla::LDAP::Conn->new($server,389);

    my $entry =                                  # transmit query
      $conn->search($searchroots{$server}, "subtree", $search);

    while ($entry)                               # enumerate and print results
        {
        $entry->printLDIF();
        $entry = $conn->nextEntry();
        }
    }
```

This method does more than just aggregate search across multiple directories. In an organization with various LDAP clients deployed—the Microsoft and Netscape mailreaders, Eudora, and perhaps others—it provides a common interface to a fielded LDAP search. That interface can hide idiosyncrasies of the various back-end services that would confuse and frustrate users. For example, at one time the st slot in some public LDAP directories used the full state name (e.g., New Hampshire) and in others the abbreviated name (e.g., NH). Users shouldn't need to worry about this kind of thing, and when you repackage services for them, they won't have to. These kinds of operational details can be learned once and then shared with the whole group. There are lots of opportunities to create this kind of Internet groupware, and many benefits flow from doing so.

Consider what happens when an important new LDAP directory becomes available. In the normal course of events, it won't show up in people's address books until the next browser release. If it's an internal directory, that will never happen. Either way there's a procedure for adding a new LDAP directory to the browser's address book, but not many users are likely to discover it. And of course it's a different procedure for every LDAP client, so if you want to document it, you might have to do so three or four times. A centralized lookup service not only gives access to new external and internal directories, it also announces their existence as they come online. Making people aware of information resources is sometimes more than half the battle. Years ago a friend who worked at Lotus told me that he'd sold his car within an hour of posting a notice on an internal Notes database. "That's amazing," I said. "Yeah," he replied, "of course, it took me most of the day to figure out which Notes database to post the ad in."

A deep problem lurks under the surface of that remark. Computer software can't yet organize and classify knowledge, and I'm not betting that we'll see meaningful progress on that front anytime soon. The task requires uniquely human traits—creative synthesis, adaptive logic, flexible analogy making. I don't pretend that the Internet component model I've outlined here relieves us of the burden of organizing and classifying knowledge, because I don't think anything can—or should. But the techniques of aggregation and repackaging create power tools for knowledge management. And since those tools are programmable components, themselves subject to aggregation and repackaging, they can breed new tools. For Internet groupware developers, the challenge and the opportunity is to apply the existing tools and create new ones in order to help networked teams work smarter.

15

Distributed HTTP

When I deployed *GroupCal*, the servlet-based group calendar discussed in Chapter 10, *Groupware Servlets*, most people liked it. But *BYTE's* editor-in-chief complained that it didn't work on airplanes, where he spent a lot of his time. Like all web-based software, GroupCal assumes that its display engine—that is, the browser—connects over a network to an HTTP server.

How hard could it be, I wondered, to run the servlet locally on a disconnected client? Not very hard at all, I found. That discovery prompted me to write a contact manager based on a tiny web server written in Perl. These experiments showed me that web-based groupware—such as a calendar or a contact manager—needn't depend on a network connection to a conventional HTTP server. Such applications, written in Java, Perl, or any other productive, socket-capable language, can also rely on lightweight, local HTTP servers implemented in these same languages. My two prototypes, one in Java and one in Perl, exhibited the following characteristics:

Small footprint
> Both weighed in at under a megabyte, so they could be delivered on a single floppy or by way of a reasonable download. That megabyte included the local web server, the application logic, and the data.

Good performance
> Both ran acceptably under Windows 95 on my aging 486-50, 16MB notebook PC.

Simple configuration
> Both could be installed by just unzipping the contents of a floppy, or equivalent download, into a single directory. One required a single environment variable, the other a single registry entry. That was it.

Simple removal

In both cases, you could just nuke the directory. Remember when that used to work? It still can.

Local/remote transparency

Both ran identically when connected to the Internet and talking to a remote HTTP server, or when disconnected and talking to the local server.

Browser orientation

Both exploited the fact that the universal HTML/JavaScript client that's already on every PC can frontend a vast number of useful applications, most as yet unwritten.

The principle at work here, best articulated in *The Essential Distributed Objects Survival Guide*, by Bob Orfali, Dan Harkey, and Jeri Edwards, is that the client/server architecture of today's Web will inevitably evolve into a peer-to-peer architecture. Many of the nodes of the "intergalactic" network they envision will be able to function as both client and server. I always bought into this vision but didn't see a practical way to apply it. Part of the answer, I think, is that servers needn't be the complex beasts we usually make them out to be. They can in fact be much simpler than the behemoth client applications we routinely inflict on ourselves. In that simplicity lies great power.

A Perl-Based Local Web Server

I started with *tinyhttpd.pl*, a classic Perl gem that implements a simple web server in about 100 lines of code. I threw away the file-serving and CGI-execution parts, leaving just a simple socket server that could accept calls on port 80 and extract data sent using the *GET* or *POST* methods. In normal Perl CGI, a URL like:

```
/sfa_home?cmp_name=Netscape
```

causes the web server to launch the Perl interpreter against the script named *sfa_ home*, which script in turn receives the data:

```
cmp_name=Netscape
```

by one of several means.

High-performance variants such as *mod_perl* and ISAPI Perl keep the Perl interpreter in memory. The same high performance arises when Perl itself implements the web server. This model doesn't make sense for heavily trafficked public sites. But it makes a great deal of sense for a local web server (or a lightly loaded intranet server). In my Perl-based local web server, called *dhttp* (for "distributed HTTP"), the script name in a CGI-style URL becomes a function name with arguments. For example, the server converts:

```
/sfa_home?cmp_name=Netscape
```

into the Perl function call:

```
&do_sfa_home('cmp_name=Netscape')
```

Since the HTTP server is always running, there's no process-creation or interpreter-spawning overhead; the URL frictionlessly becomes a scripted function call. You can see this same principle at work in Zope (*http://www.zope.org/*), a popular Web application server that is both written in Python and extensible using Python.

Platform Capabilities and Application Features

Here are the key things that these frictionless function calls can do in the Win32 desktop environment:

*   Dynamically generate HTML pages and forms
*   Interpolate values into those generated pages and forms
*   Access local (or remote) filesystem, SQL, and OLE resources
*   Issue HTTP redirections

These Perl capabilities, combined with some conventions for using HTML and JavaScript, yielded an application called SFA (which stands for "sales force automation"), shown in Figure 15-1

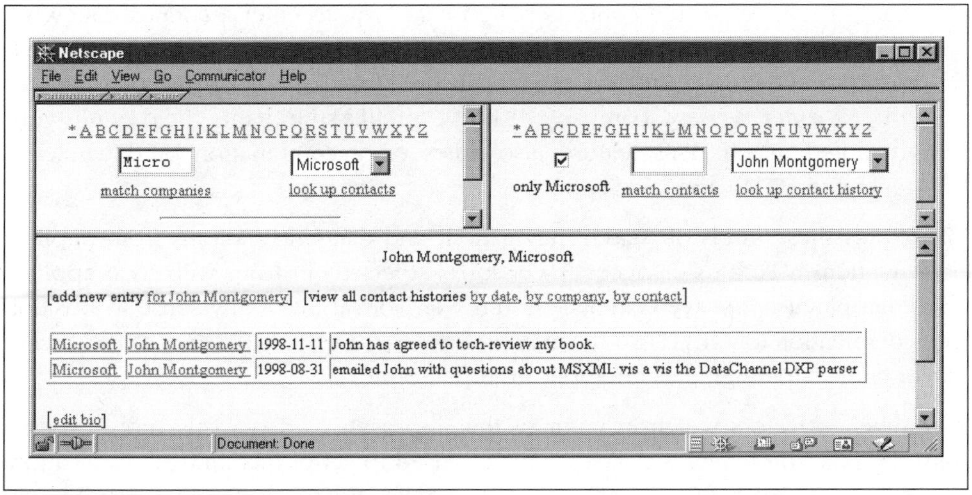

Figure 15-1. A dhttp-based contact manager

I don't pretend you'll want to dump Act in order to use this web-style contact manager. But it does exhibit the following interesting features:

Namespace completion

Type **M** in the *match companies* field and you'll regenerate that pane with a list containing just the companies whose names begin with M. This feature relies on the local server's ability to regenerate a form, using partial input in the *match companies* field to drive an SQL query that builds an HTML `<select>` statement.

Event bubbling

When you look up a company, the contacts picklist adjusts dynamically to display only contacts at the selected company. Then the contact info pane adjusts dynamically to display records for the first name in the contacts picklist. This feature relies on the JavaScript `onLoad` event. When the company pane loads, its `onLoad` handler specifies the URL that loads the contacts pane; likewise, the contacts pane controls the loading of the contact info pane.

Flexible bindings

By default the contacts pane binds to what's selected in the company pane and displays an appropriately labeled checkbox. But if you uncheck that box, then type **J** in the *match contacts* field, and click that link, you'll generate a list of all the J contacts at all companies. This feature relies on a combination of dynamically generated HTML (used to vary the widgets that appear on the form) and dynamically generated JavaScript (used to vary the handlers for those widgets).

Context-sensitive forms

When you select a company for which contacts exist, the contacts pane lists them. If none exist, the contacts pane invites you to enter a contact. Likewise, when you click *match companies* and your input selects one or more companies, the company pane lists them. If none match, the company pane invites you to enter a new company. And it prefills the name field with your attempted match. This feature also relies on a combination of dynamically generated HTML and JavaScript.

We expect these kinds of search, navigation, and data-entry idioms from applications written in FoxPro or Access. We don't expect them from web-style applications that play to pure web clients. Should we? Does it make any sense to position the combination of an HTML/JavaScript browser, ODBC/JET, and a local-web-server-cum-script-engine as an application platform?

A number of factors weigh in favor of this approach. Perl is vastly more capable than the FoxPro or Access dialects typically used to script this kind of application. The resulting application is small and fast. It relies on an existing and familiar client. And it exhibits complete local/remote transparency.

There are also drawbacks. Browsers don't yet offer strong standardized support for data-entry idioms such as accelerator keys and custom field-tabbing. JavaScript implementations can be flaky. The methodology, an intricate tapestry of signals, substitutions, and redirections involving Perl, SQL, HTML, and JavaScript, is complex. However, these techniques aren't exclusive to *dhttp*. They're also useful with a conventional web server running Apache and *mod_perl*, or IIS and ActivePerl. As we explore how *dhttp* works, keep in mind that the techniques also apply more generally to the construction of web-based software. Developing for a local web server is basically the same as developing for a conventional web server. This approach relies on, and extends, familiar skills.

The dhttp System

I've implemented *dhttp* in Perl, but the system is small enough and simple enough at this point so that it could easily be redone in Python or another versatile and socket-aware scripting language. What matters is not the language itself but the strategic position in which a *dhttp* system situates that language. From the perspective of a single *dhttp* node implemented on a standard Windows PC, the script language can transmute local file, SQL, and OLE resources into applications that play to local or remote web clients. In a *dhttp* network the script language is even more radically empowered. Replication of SQL data among the nodes of the network turns out to be a relatively easy problem to solve. Likewise replication of code. When I accomplished both of these things in the same day, I had to stop and take more than a few deep breaths. Could a system so simple really be this powerful? Perhaps so. But let's first consider how a *dhttp* application works in standalone mode.

A Developer's View of the dhttp System

Figure 15-2 shows a high-level view of the *dhttp* architecture.

The engine divides into three modules—the server itself, a set of public utilities, and a set of private utilities. A public utility, in this context, is one that a web client can call by means of a URL. A private utility, on the other hand, is visible only to local *dhttp* components—either the server itself or any of its plug-in apps. An example of a public server utility is *do_engine_serve_file()*. It responds to the URL:

```
/engine_serve_file?app=hd&file=home.htm
```

by dishing out the file *home.htm* from the *dhttp/lib/Apps/hd* subdirectory. The prefix "engine_" tells the server to form a reference to the function *Engine::PubUtils:: do_engine_serve_file()* and then call that function.

An example of a private engine function is *upload_file()*. It handles the HTTP file upload protocol—that is, it can parse data posted from a web form that uses the multipart/formdata encoding and return a list of parts. I wrote *upload_file()* for one particular *dhttp* plug-in but placed it in the package *Engine::PrivUtils* so that other plug-ins could use it too.

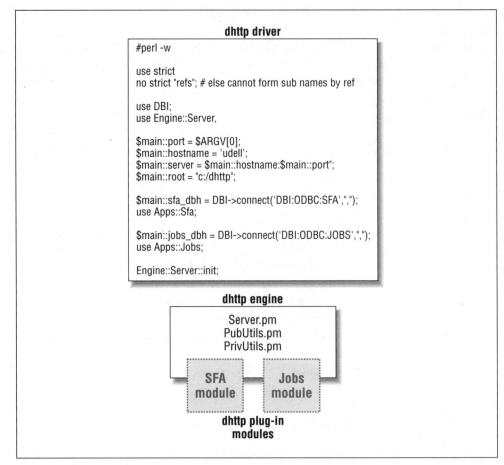

Figure 15-2. dhttp architecture

An instance of *dhttp* hosts one or more plug-in apps, each implemented as a Perl module with its own namespace separate from other apps and from the server. Like the server, each app comprises public (that is, URL-accessible) as well as private functions. But in the case of an app, both kinds of functions are packaged into a single module. How does the engine tell them apart? The prefix "do_" signals that a function is public.

The Core serve_request() Method

Example 15-1 shows the *serve_request* routine at the core of *server.pm*. Running inside a loop that accepts inbound socket connections, it demonstrates two key points. HTTP service stripped to its essentials is a very simple thing. And it's equally simple to connect URLs directly to functions exported by script-language modules.

Example 15-1. The serve_request Method

```perl
sub serve_request
  {
  $_=<NS>;                                 # read first line
  my ($method, $url, $proto) = split;      # GET /sfa_home HTTP/1.0

  my ($args,$headers,$signal,$app,$fn);

  while (<NS>)                             # read the headers
    {
    s/\n|\r//g;                           # trim cr and nl chars
    /^Content-Length: (\S*)/i &&($main::$content_length=$1);   # save Content-Length
    /^Content-Type: (\S*)/i && ($main::$content_type=$1);      # and Content-Type
    /boundary=(.+)/ &&  ($main::http_upload_boundary='--'.$1); # and upload boundary
    length || last;                       # empty line means end of header
    }

  if ( $method eq 'GET' )                 # GET method
    {
    if ($url =~ s /^([^\?]*)\?//)         # args follow the ?
      { $signal = $1; $args = $url; }
    else                                  # no args
      { $signal = $url; $args = ''; }
    }
  else                                    # POST method
    {
    $signal = $url;
    read(NS,$args,$content_length);
    }

  $signal =~ s#/##;                       # remove initial /
  $signal =~ m#([^_]+)#;                  # isolate service name
  $app = $1;

  if ($app eq 'engine')
    { $fn = 'Engine::PubUtils::do_' . $signal; }
  else
    { $fn = 'Apps::' . $app . '::do_' . $signal; }

  if (defined &{$fn})
    { &{$fn}($args); }                    # dispatch the function
  else
    { warn "(engine) undefined function $fn"; }
  }
```

Hello, World with dhttp

To write the classic "Hello, world" application in *dhttp*, you'd create the file */dhttp/lib/Apps/hello.pm* with the following:

```perl
package Apps::hello;
use Engine::PrivUtils;
```

```
sub do_hello_world
   {
   transmit httpStandardHeader;
   transmit "Hello, world";
   }
```

Then in *dhttp/dhttp*, the main driver, add the line:

```
use Apps::hello;
```

Now the server will respond to the URL */hello_world* by calling the function *Apps::hello::do_hello_world()*. Alternately you could create the */dhttp/lib/Apps/hello* subdirectory and place a *hello.html* file in it. In this case, *dhttp* will serve the file in response to the URL */engine_serve_file?app=hello&file=hello.html*.

So where's the beef? A conventional server would just respond to the URL */hello. html*. Why the extra gymnastics to serve a file with *dhttp*? The answer is that while it's possible to make *dhttp* serve static files in the same way that normal web servers do, that's the least interesting of its capabilities. Dynamic pages are *dhttp*'s forte. When you instantiate HTML/JavaScript templates and interpolate database extracts into those templates, you can achieve remarkable effects.

Into the Starting Gate

Conventional web servers, as installed, leave you far short of the starting gate—at least as far as Perl-based web development is concerned. Sure, they tell you how to map Perl to the *cgi-bin* directory, but that's just the first step. What about low-latency script invocation? It's up to you to acquire and integrate the necessary stuff—either ISAPI Perl on Win32 or *mod_perl* on Unix. What about low-latency database connections? Again it's up to you to piece together a solution. On Win32, this might involve ODBC connection pooling in conjunction with ASP/PerlScript or alternatively ActiveState's PerlEx. On Unix, you'll need to figure out *Apache::DBI*.

Only some of the web developers who deploy Perl-based CGI are in a position to exploit low-latency script invocation. Of that subset, still fewer are able to exploit low-latency database connections. With *dhttp* you start with a Perl environment that already solves these two key problems. So while *dhttp* is indeed small and simple and fast, I don't consider it minimal. It includes the essential ingredients that I always need to add to conventional Unix or NT web servers in order to prepare them to do useful work in Perl.

Every developer who uses Perl on a web server should be using it to maximum advantage. For high-intensity applications, *dhttp* doesn't pretend to be a solution. In these cases, you need to create a persistent and database-aware Perl environment—using *mod_perl* or PerlEx. The effort invested to learn how these environments work will be repaid many times over. Where *dhttp* shines is with low-intensity applications. Scads of these could exist, and many more would if the activation threshold for creating them were lower. Scalability isn't the issue in many cases; availability is. Given the right environment, it's easy to spin out lots of useful, lightweight web applications.

Connecting dhttp to SQL Data

A *dhttp* plug-in can create one or more persistent connections to a SQL database. The example in Figure 15-2 uses Perl's universal database connector, *DBI*, along with the *DBD::ODBC* module that maps between *DBI* calls and ODBC data sources. Because *dhttp* is a single-threaded system, it's OK to use the Jet (MS-Access-style) ODBC driver to work with local *.MDB* files, although you can use any data source that comes with an ODBC driver. The advantage of the *DBI* and *DBD::ODBC* approach is that it's fully portable. If you run *dhttp* on a Unix system, you can replace *DBD::ODBC* with, for example, *DBD::Solid* or *DBD::Oracle*.

An alternate method I've used with *dhttp* relies on a Windows-specific Perl module, *Win32::ODBC*. Why sacrifice *DBI*'s portability? The target for *dhttp* isn't conventional server machines but rather the huge population of Windows-based desktop systems. Nowadays, these systems are often overpowered and underutilized. Windows 98 and MS Office can't soak up all the cycles on a 500MHz Pentium-based box. If you want to recruit these machines as nodes of a distributed network, portability between Unix and Win32 may matter less than convenient installation in the Windows environment. In that respect, the *Win32::ODBC* approach is attractive. Its ODBC support runs deeper and wider than does that of *DBD::ODBC*. For example, you can use *Win32::ODBC* to conjure up a data source that hasn't been defined using the ODBC Driver Manager, like this:

```
my $sfa_dbh = new ODBC("DBQ=$root/sfa.mdb;Driver={Microsoft Access Driver (*.
mdb)};");
```

The *DBD::ODBC* method expects that the file *sfa.mdb* has been defined as an ODBC data source. As such, *dhttp* apps that rely on that method depend on registry entries. That in turn creates an extra installation step and complicates deployment of *dhttp*. The *Win32::ODBC* method, which can create a data source on the fly, helps minimize the installation footprint. Ideally you want zero impact on the client machine; that's the beauty of the web software model. That's not possible when you install client components, as *dhttp* does, but it's wise to make those parts as unobtrusive and dependency-free as you can.

If you go the *Win32::ODBC* route, must you give up portability? Nope. It stands to reason that two different Perl ODBC modules will share a lot in common. Abstracting the differences between *DBD::ODBC* and *Win32::ODBC*, for the basic set of SQL functions needed by *dhttp* apps, is quite easy. The following is a *Win32:: ODBC* version of a function that runs an SQL query and returns the result set as a Perl list-of-lists.

```
sub dbSqlReturnAllRows     # Win32::ODBC version
  {
  my ($dbh,$st) = @_;          # input: db handle, and sql statement
  my (@results);
  $dbh->sql($st);
  while ($dbh->FetchRow())
    {
    my (@row) = $dbh->Data($dbh->fieldnames);
    push (@results, \@row);
    }
  return \@results;
  }
```

And here's a *DBD::ODBC* version of the same routine:

```
sub dbSqlReturnAllRows     # DBD::ODBC version
  {
  my ($dbh,$st) = @_;        # input: db handle, and sql statement
  my $sth = $dbh->prepare($st) or die ("prepare, $DBI::errstr");
  $sth->execute or die ("returnAllRows, $DBI::errstr");
  my (@row, @results);
  while (@row = $sth->fetchrow)
    {
    my @data = @row;
    push(@results, \@data);
    }
  $sth->finish;
  return \@results;
  }
```

The *dhttp* apps I've written so far all work in terms of this abstraction layer, so they're portable between *DBI* (which is now available on both Win32 and Unix) and *Win32::ODBC* (which is available only on Windows).

A persistent connection to the database

There are a variety of ways that web-server-based scripting languages can cache database connections. Examples include Apache's *mod_perl* with *Apache::DBI*, IIS with Active Server Pages and any ActiveX script language, and ActiveState's *mod_perl* work-alike, PerlEx. In the *dhttp* system, this notion of a persistent database handle reduces to its bare essentials: a variable in the namespace of the main *dhttp* driver.

That variable, for example, **$sfa_dbh** in Figure 15-2, is set once when the engine loads the plug-in app. Thereafter, methods that make database calls pass this handle to the public engine methods that talk to the database.

How much time does it save to cache the handle? Here's a do-nothing *dhttp* method:

```
sub do_sfa_nothing
  { print httpStandardHeader; }
```

On my machine, a test script can invoke that method in a tight loop at the rate of about 33 calls per second. That's pretty quick, by the way. IIS configured to spawn Perl once per call can do only 10 calls per second. IIS with ISAPI Perl—which eliminates the process-creation cost of spawning Perl—still yields only 22 calls per second. A do-nothing ASP PerlScript function does slightly better at 26 calls per second, but still short of the 33 calls per second I get with *dhttp*.

Now let's connect to a *DBD::ODBC* data source, then disconnect from it:

```
sub do_sfa_connect_disconnect
  {
  my $dbh = DBI->connect("DBI:ODBC:sfa",'','')
       or die ("connect, $DBI::errstr");
  $dbh->disconnect;
  print httpStandardHeader;
  }
```

A test script can only run this method about half as fast as the do-nothing method: at about 17 calls per second. Because they cache database handles at start-up, *dhttp* modules pay the connection penalty once only, at start-up. Now in reality, web applications don't sit in tight loops making database calls, so caching the database handle isn't really going to double perceived performance. But there's no point in repeatedly creating and destroying a resource that need only be created once.

Implementing Data-Bound Widgets

Idioms that we take for granted in conventional client/server database apps—such as data-bound widgets—aren't often found in pure web-style apps. True, you can create these effects with Java applets, ActiveX controls, or DHTML scripts, but these techniques tend to compromise either speed or cross-browser compatibility. A system that exploits a powerful scripting language like Perl can express quite rich behavior in terms of the standard HTML/JavaScript client.

Consider the picklist in the company pane in Figure 15-1 (top left). Here's a fragment of the form template that governs the picklist:

```
<td>
<input name=cmp_complete size=6 value="CMP_COMPLETE"
                onChange="javascript:sfa_company_complete()">
</td>
<td>
<select name=cmp_name onChange="javascript:sfa_company_continue()">
COMPANY_LIST
</select>
</td>
<FONT_SPEC>LIST_TRUNCATED
```

When you send *dhttp* the URL */sfa_company?cmp_name=M*, it decomposes the URL into a function call: `do_sfa_company("cmp_name=M")`. The function reads a form template containing the previous fragment and sends back a transformed version of it. One of the transformations replaces the marker COMPANY_LIST with a set of <OPTION> attributes that complete the <SELECT> tag in the form template. In this case, the completion string assigned to the variable $cmp_name is M, so the list will display just the companies whose names match that prefix. Here's how *do_sfa_company()* transforms the COMPANY_LIST marker:

```
if ( m#COMPANY_LIST# )
  {
  my $prepared_cmp_name = prepareForDb($cmp_name);
  $st = sprintf("select cmp_name from cmp where cmp_name like \'%s\'
       order by cmp_name", $prepared_cmp_name . '%');
  ($truncated,$picklist) = getPicklist($st,$cmp_name);
  $form .= $picklist;
  next;
  }
if ( m#LIST_TRUNCATED# )
  {
  if ($truncated)
    { s/LIST_TRUNCATED/<br>(list truncated at
         $picklist_limit,<br>try narrower selection)/; }
  else
    { s/LIST_TRUNCATED//; }
  next;
  }
```

And here's the *getPicklist()* routine that maps between the SQL statement and the corresponding set of HTML <OPTION> tags:

```
sub getPicklist
  {
  my ($st,$selected) = @_;
  my ($lref) = dbSqlReturnAllRows($sfa_dbh,$st);        # process query into LoL
  my ($rowref, $result);
  my $count = 0;
  foreach $rowref (@$lref)
    {
    last if ( $count++ > $picklist_limit );
    my $key = $$rowref[0];
    $result .= "<option value=\"$key\"";               # begin HTML fragment
    if ($selected eq $key)                             # if current selection
      { $result .= " selected"; }                      # make it selected
    $result .= ">$key</option>\n";
    }
  my @ret = ( ($count > $picklist_limit), $result);
  return @ret;
  }
```

If you call *sfa_do_company()* method without arguments (i.e., using the bare URL */sfa_company*), it dumps the whole company-name column into the picklist—unless there are more than specified in the package variable $picklist_limit. A picklist with hundreds of entries isn't very useful, so if the list exceeds the limit, *getPicklist()* truncates it and reports that it did so. *do_sfa_company()*, as it processes the form template, can do two things with the `LIST_TRUNCATED` marker. If the list is within the limit, it removes the marker. If the list exceeds the limit, it replaces the marker with a message that invites the user to specify a narrower selection.

Namespace Completion

There are two ways to narrow the selection. Both involve namespace completion, a feature that's prized by users of the *Emacs* text editor. The idea is that you can constrain the set of values within some namespace by supplying partial input. In *Emacs*, there are several namespaces subject to completion. When you're looking for a file, *Emacs* completes partial input against the filesystem namespace. It displays a list of only those files or directories that match what you type, and it refines that list as you expand the partial input. You can also complete against the namespace of *Emacs* commands. On the editor's command line, you can type **a?** to enumerate all the commands that start with a and ab? to enumerate the shorter list of commands that start with ab.

The Netscape and Microsoft 4.x browsers do a kind of namespace completion but not as effectively as *Emacs* does. If you've visited the URL */sfa_home*, and the string */sf* is unique within the list of recently viewed URLs, both will complete */sfa_home* as soon as you type */sf.* But what if you've also recently visited the URL */sfa_home?cmp_name=Microsoft?* In that case, both browsers will still complete */sfa_home* as soon as you type */sf.* This behavior is subtly but crucially different from that of *Emacs.* In *Emacs*, the user explicitly asks for namespace completion, provides a completion string, and gets back a view of a namespace that's restricted appropriately. The 4.x browsers don't restrict the list of recently visited URLs according to the completion. If */sfa_home?cmp_name=Microsoft* was the result you wanted, completion of */sfa_home* is a false and useless result. You still have to drop down the list of recently visited URLs, and there it's no easier to pick out */sfa_home?cmp_name=Microsoft* than it would have been without any completion.

Happily this problem was corrected in MSIE 5.0. You can use the Tab key to complete partial input on the browser's command line, and it does correctly narrow the list of recently visited URLs.

While we're on the subject, there's another kind of completion that browsers don't get quite right. Dropdown lists driven by the HTML **SELECT** widget support completion but only on the first letter of input. Although most people don't realize it, in a list of U.S. states you can type **M** to jump directly to the entry for Maine. Even fewer people realize that you can navigate within the M states by continuing to type **M**—for example, after the fourth M you've selected Michigan. Almost nobody realizes that you ought to be able to select Michigan (but cannot) by simply typing **MI**. Do that, and you'll instead land in Idaho.

Implementing namespace completion with dhttp

Within the constraints of the standard HTML/JavaScript client, *do_sfa_company()* tries to accomplish two things: make completion work properly, and gently introduce users to the idea of namespace completion. That's why there are two ways to do completion. The first uses a tabbed index that can perform any first-letter completion with a single click. Because *do_sfa_company()* is a template processor, it's surprisingly easy to create that widget. The form template has a marker, TAB_INDEX. Here's the Perl fragment that converts it into a row of links that do first-letter completion:

```
if ( m#TAB_INDEX# )
  {
  my ($tab);
  $form .= "<a href=\"javascript:sfa_company_index('')\">*</a> "; # wildcard
  foreach $tab ('A'..'Z')
    { $form .= "<a href=\"javascript:sfa_company_index('$tab')\">$tab</a> "; }
  next;
  }
```

Each of the links invokes the JavaScript function, *sfa_company_index()*, which is part of the same form template:

```
function sfa_company_index (tab)
  {
  cmp_name = tab;
  url = getServer() + '/sfa_company?cmp_name=&cmp_name=' + escape(cmp_name);
  parent.frames[0].location = url;
  }
```

Note that there needn't be a form template at all; *do_sfa_company()* could simply emit everything on the fly. It's handy, though, to express the template as a separate file. That way it's easier to prototype and test the pages that will be emitted dynamically and to visualize the relationship between the HTML text and the JavaScript code on those pages.

Namespace completion driven by a tabbed index

The *sfa_company_index()* JavaScript function does three simple things:

- Collects the user's selected first letter

- Forms a URL that incorporates that partial input

- Recycles that URL back into the engine

In this case, the URL reinvokes the *do_sfa_company()* method but qualifies it with an argument that carries the completion letter; for example, */sfa_home?cmp_name=M*. This process can iterate indefinitely; each click on the tabbed index regenerates the picklist for the selected tab. What if the picklist's limit is 50, and there are more than 50 M companies? The second completion mechanism—the input box labeled *match companies*—can now come into play. There you can type **Mi** or **Micro** to restrict the picklist to just the companies whose names match these prefixes.

Namespace completion driven by partial input

Here's the template fragment for the input box:

```
<input name=cmp_complete size=6 value="CMP_COMPLETE"
    onChange="javascript:sfa_company_complete()">
<br><a href="javascript:sfa_company_complete()">match companies</a>
```

There are two ways to invoke the JavaScript function *sfa_company_complete()*. It's the handler for the input box's onChange event, so if a user enters text and tabs to the next widget in the form, completion will run. It's also wired to the *match companies* link. Why the redundancy? For the usual reasons. There's more than one way to do it; different mechanisms make sense to different people; it's easy to accommodate many styles. The onChange event is a subtle and effective way to invoke completion. If you're already typing in the input box, the Tab key is handier than the mouse. A user who knows that the ? key invokes completion in *Emacs* might quickly learn that the Tab key is its analog in a family of *dhttp* apps. Of course, most users of browser-based software aren't hardwired for *Emacs*, and many never even think of using the keyboard for anything besides data entry. So while it's nice to provide a keyboard shortcut for a minority of expert users, you should never omit the prominent clickable link that most people expect.

The form template includes a marker, *CMP_COMPLETE*, which *do_sfa_company()* replaces when it emits the form. The two completion functions share the use of this marker by way of the *cmp_name* argument that each function embeds in the URL it creates and invokes. For tabbed-index completion, loading the selected first letter into the input box documents the new state of the picklist. It's also a bridge to the input-box method. It helps the user to discover that if a value of **M** yields a list of M companies when you click the *match companies* link, a value of **Mi** will yield a shorter list of Mi companies. For input-box completion, the partial string is "sticky"—that is, it persists across regenerations of the frame, so you can see the effects of growing or shrinking the partial input.

Failed namespace completion leads to data entry

What happens if you click (or type) **Q**, but there are no Q companies yet in the database? The app interprets this as a request to add the first Q company, and it replaces the company pane with an input form. Here's how *do_sfa_company()* handles that case:

```
if ( length($picklist) == 0 )        # No companies match completion
    {                                # Invite user to add one.
    transmit httpRedirectHeader
```

```
        ("$server_name/sfa_ave_company?mode=add&cmp_name=$$argref{cmp_name}");
    }
else                                    # One or more companies match
    {                                   # completion. Emit the form.
    transmit httpStandardHeader;
    transmit $form;
    }
```

The application displays in a three-pane frameset, as shown in Figure 15-1. When the top-left company pane produces an empty list, the HTTP redirection sent back to the browser applies to that pane, and the add-company form appears there. The contact or contact-history panes are unaffected as yet. If the the user adds a new company, these panes will synchronize with it by means of the event-bubbling mechanism we'll discuss shortly. If the user decides not to add a new company, though, these panes continue to supply context regarding the most recently selected company and access to functions that add and view contacts and contact histories.

The general strategy here is to build a stateful and context-preserving display from a sequence of inherently stateless HTTP transactions. There are two complementary ways to create the URLs that drive an application and that preserve context across HTTP transaction boundaries. The template processor that emits each piece of the display is one intelligent URL manipulator. The JavaScript code that can be embedded in each piece of the display is another. When these two mechanisms work together, you can achieve really powerful effects.

Polymorphic HTML Widgets

The contacts pane works like the company pane. There's a tabbed index for first-letter completion and an input box for completion of longer bits of partial input. If either of these completion functions produces an empty list of contacts, the add-contact form appears in the contacts pane. The company-name widget in the add-contact form is an example of what I mean by a polymorphic HTML widget. Suppose the initial state is as shown in Figure 15-1. The partial input **Micro** in the company pane has regenerated the picklist to include just matching companies—in this case, the single entry Microsoft. It also regenerated the contacts pane, constraining its picklist to just Microsoft contacts. Because John Montgomery is the selected contact, the contact-history pane displays associated contact records. In this context, if Paul Maritz isn't yet in the database as a Microsoft contact, clicking *P* or typing **Paul** replaces the contacts pane with the add-contact form shown in Figure 15-3.

The *only Microsoft* checkbox shown in Figure 15-1 constrains the list of contacts to those at Microsoft. So the company-name widget on the add-contact form need not, and should not, accept input. It should merely report the company name that

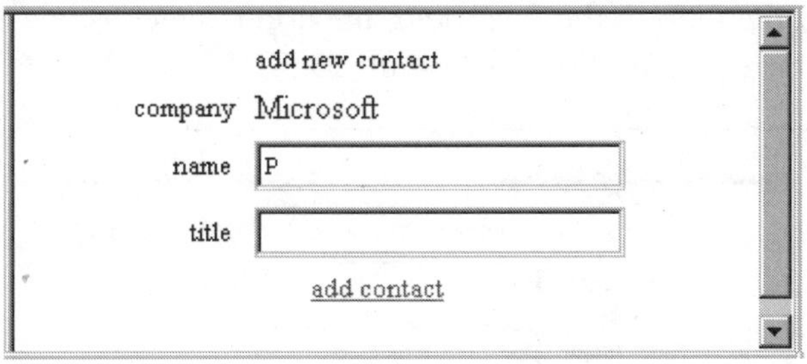

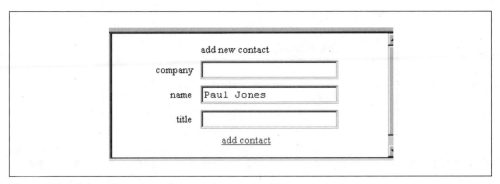

Figure 15-3. The add-contact form, constrained to a selected company

will be included in the new contact record, and it does so by printing the name on the surface of the form.

You can release that constraint by unchecking the checkbox. Why would you? You ought to be able to look up any contact directly, without having to know—and select—that person's company. If the database lists Pauls who are contacts at other, non-Microsoft companies, clicking *P* or typing **Paul** won't produce an add-contact form; it will constrain the contacts picklist to those other Pauls and synchronize the contact-history pane to the first of them.

Now suppose you want create a new contact record for Paul Jones and, at the same time, create a new company record for this Paul's company, JonesWare. After releasing the company constraint, you can invoke an add-contact form by typing **Paul Jones**. If there aren't yet any Paul Joneses in the database, that produces the form shown in Figure 15-4.

Figure 15-4. The add-contact form, unconstrained by company

The contact name carries over from the previous form, but now the company-name widget is an input box. In this case, the user wants to create a company record for JonesWare—but the user might also want to look up an existing company other than the one to which the contacts pane was originally constrained. To support that lookup, completion works here too. Suppose JonesWare already exists in the company table. If you type partial input into the company-name field, perhaps **Jo**, and then tab to the next field, the add-contact form regenerates with a picklist of Jo companies, as shown in Figure 15-5.

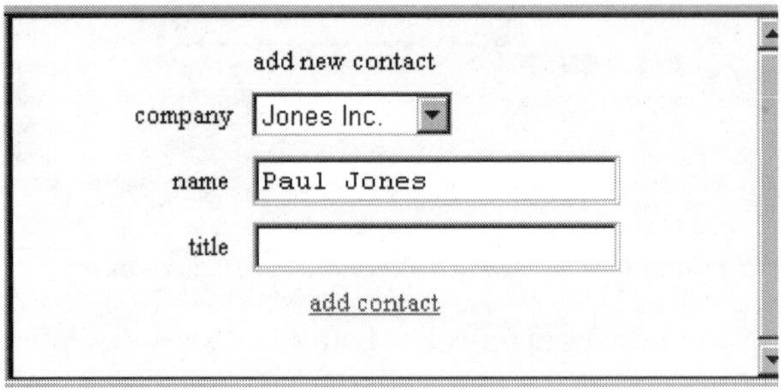

Figure 15-5. The add-contact form, with company-name completion

In this case, the company-name widget has morphed into a picklist that helps the user distinguish between JonesWare and Jones Inc.

What if JonesWare weren't yet in the database? In that case, the user can create a new company record for JonesWare and a new contact record for Paul Jones in a single go, by typing both names into the form shown in Figure 15-4. That's a lot to do all at once, so to give the user a chance to confirm the creation of both records, the form morphs into yet another state. As shown in Figure 15-6, the link's label documents that two operations will occur at once.

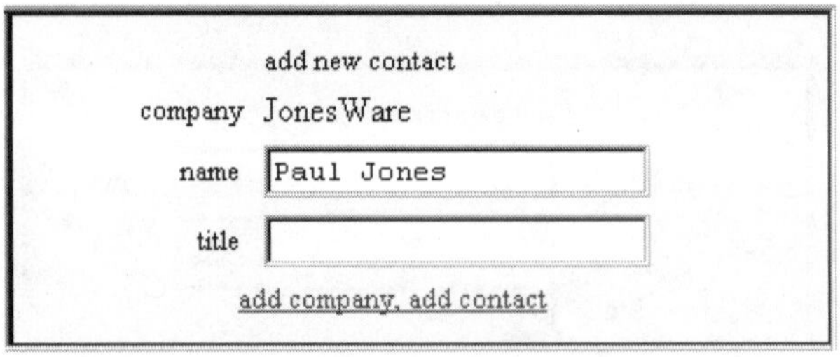

Figure 15-6. The add-contact form, confirming creation of both a company and a contact

So how can a dumb HTML form widget polymorphically adapt itself, depending on context, to appear as a label, an input box, or a picklist? This effect requires collaboration between server-side and client-side code. We already know, in general, how the server-side part works. If the form template contains the marker *COMPANY_WIDGET*, the method that handles the add-contact form—*do_sfa_add_contact()*—can replace that marker with just text or with HTML fragments that specify either an input box or a picklist. A signal encoded in a URL and passed to the method as an argument will supply the contextual clue that governs which flavor of widget to emit.

From the perspective of the JavaScript code in the emitted form, though, there's a problem. The JavaScript function wired to the *add contact* link needs to collect input, weave it into a URL, and send that URL back into the engine. In particular, it needs to get hold of the company name. But since the company-name widget is polymorphic, its value may reside in one of three different JavaScript objects. Table 15-1 lays out the different ways that these objects can extract the value.

Table 15-1. Modes of JavaScript Access to a Polymorphic HTML Widget

Widget Type	Widget Name	Value Accessor
label (value transmitted in hidden field)	`document.sfa_add_contact.cmp_label`	`document.sfa_add_contact.cmp_label.value`
input box	`document.sfa_add_contact.cmp_name`	`document.sfa_add_contact.cmp_name.value`
picklist	`document.sfa_add_contact.cmp_name.options`	`document.sfa_add_contact.cmp_name.options[document.sfa_add_contact.cmp_name.options.selectedIndex].text`

How can the JavaScript function select among these access modes when it builds the URL that it sends back into the engine? It needs a hint from the server-side method that emitted the form. Example 15-2 shows the relevant piece of *do_sfa_add_contact()*.

Example 15-2. Server-Side Setup for Polymorphic HTML Widget

```
if ( m#CMP_WIDGET# )                          # emit company-name widget
{
                                              # case 1
if ($con_restrict eq 'on')                    # widget constrained to
  {                                           # selected company
  $form .= "<input type=hidden name=mode      # tell JavaScript
      value=plain>";                          # the mode is "plain"
  $form .= "<input type=hidden name=cmp_label # pass label in hidden field
      value=\"$cmp_name\">";
  $form .= "$cmp_name";                       # emit label
  }
                                              # case 2
if ( ($con_restrict ne 'on') and              # widget not constrained to company
     ($cmp_name       eq '' )        )        # no partial input supplied
  {
  $form .= "<input type=hidden name=mode      # tell JavaScript the mode
      value=input>";                          # is "input"
  $form .= "<input name=cmp_name              # emit input box
      onChange=sfa_add_contact_continue()>";
  }
```

Example 15-2. Server-Side Setup for Polymorphic HTML Widget (continued)

```
                                              # case 3: name completion
if ( ($con_restrict ne 'on') and             # widget not constrained to company
     ($cmp_name    ne ''  ) and              # partial input supplied
     ($cmp_create  ne 'on')   )              # don't create a new company record
  {
  $form .= "<input type=hidden name=mode     # tell JavaScript the mode is
      value=picklist>";                      # "picklist"
  my $prepared_cmp_name = prepareForDb($cmp_name); # SQL-escape the supplied
                                             # completion value
                                             # construct query
  $st = sprintf("select cmp_name from cmp where
      cmp_name like \'%s\' order by cmp_name",
      $prepared_cmp_name . '%');
  ($truncated,$picklist) = getPicklist($st,'none'); # build the completion list
  $form .= "<select name=cmp_name>";              # emit the picklist
  $form .= $picklist;
  $form .= "</select>";
  }
                                              # case 4
if ($cmp_create eq 'on')                      # do create a new company record
  {
  $form .= "<input type=hidden name=mode      # tell JavaScript the mode is
      value=create>";                         # "create"
  $form .= "<input type=hidden name=cmp_name  # pass the value
      value=$cmp_name>";
  $form .= "$cmp_name";                        # emit the value as a label
  }
}
```

The template processor emits, along with each variant of the polymorphic widget, a signal in the hidden field **mode** that tells the client-side code which variant it has received. Now the client code can select the appropriate syntax to access the widget's value, as shown in Example 15-3.

Example 15-3. Client-Side Setup for Polymorphic HTML Widget

```
function sfa_add_contact_continue ()
  {
  mode = document.sfa_add_contact.mode.value; // identify the mode
  cmp_create = '';

  if  (mode == 'plain')                    // company was a constrained value
    {                                      // name was passed in hidden variable
    cmp_name = document.sfa_add_contact.cmp_label.value;
    }

  if  (mode == 'input')                    // company unrestricted
    {
    cmp_name =
      document.sfa_add_contact.cmp_name.value;  // name is in the input box
    }

  if  (mode == 'picklist')                 // company-name completion
```

Example 15-3. Client-Side Setup for Polymorphic HTML Widget (continued)

```
   {                                       // value is selected item in list
   cmp_name = document.sfa_add_contact.cmp_name.options
       [document.sfa_add_contact.cmp_name.options.selectedIndex].text;
   }

if  (mode == 'create')                   // company record creation
   {
   cmp_create = 'on';                    // tell the handler to create
   cmp_name =                            // the company
     document.sfa_add_contact.cmp_name.value; // name is in the input box
   }

con_name = document.sfa_add_contact.con_name.value;
con_title = document.sfa_add_contact.con_title.value;
url = getServer() + '/sfa_handle_add_contact?cmp_name=' +
     escape(cmp_name) + '&cmp_create=' + escape(cmp_create) +
     '&con_name=' + escape(con_name) + '&con_select=' +
       escape(con_name) + '&con_title=' + escape(con_title);
parent.frames[1].location = url;
   }
```

Polymorphic data-bound HTML widgets in perspective

Is this technique really practical? I'll admit that a complex scenario like this one is challenging to create and maintain. In theory you could specify these kinds of idioms more abstractly and write a code generator that would emit a combination of Perl, HTML, JavaScript, and SQL. In practice I've only done that in limited ways and haven't yet come up with a general solution. Still, it's instructive to see just how much UI richness can be achieved using only the standard basic building blocks of web software.

As always, the trick is to find the sweet spot that's one step short of the point of diminishing returns. Back in Chapter 6, *Docbase Input Techniques*, for example, we saw (in Figure 6-4) a form that a manager can use to generate another form that assigns a project to an analyst. The generated form contains database-driven fields: analyst, vendor, product. For the manager who generates that form, data-bound polymorphic widgets that support namespace completion will be a boon. Because the widgets are bound to database columns, each of the namespaces can be managed as a controlled vocabulary. Because the namespaces support completion, large lists can be segmented dynamically for convenient use in HTML picklists.

Internet groupware, as an information-management discipline, means weaving different kinds of data—email, web pages, SQL tables—into a coherent pattern. Web applications that use data-bound widgets to manage controlled vocabularies are one of the means to that end. Note that none of the polymorphic-HTML techniques we've seen here are specific to *dhttp*. You can do the same things using Perl (or another scripting language) on a conventional web server, and in many cases that's the right way to do it. But a lightweight local web server like *dhttp* can be an attractive option.

The assignment-form generator, after all, is a tiny little application that might be used by only one person—the manager who issues assignment forms. Administrative policy surrounding a departmental or corporate intranet server can impede the deployment and maintenance of these kinds of ad hoc apps. Access to the server can be an issue as well. If the manager travels a lot or works from home without inbound access to the intranet server, local use of the app and its data—even while offline—will be crucial. I don't argue that this approach is a better way to do web software, only that it's a different—and complementary—way to do it.

Event Bubbling

The three-pane viewer is an idea as old as the hills, or at least, as old as Smalltalk-80. Here we're exploring how to build that kind of viewer using standard web tools and methods. The key ingredients are frames—a sometimes dubious feature of HTML that in this case, I argue, is appropriate—and JavaScript handlers for onLoad events. Let's take it from the top, when the plug-in receives the */sfa_home* URL. Example 15-4 shows the *do_sfa_home()* method.

Example 15-4. The do_sfa_home() Method

```
sub do_sfa_home
  {
  my ($args) = @_;
  my ($argref) =   getArgs($args);
  my $cmp_name    = escape(getArgval($$argref{cmp_name}));
  my $con_name    = escape(getArgval($$argref{con_name}));
  my $server_name = makeServerName();
  transmit <<"EOT";
HTTP/1.0 200 OK
Content-type: text/html

<frameset rows=40%,*>
<frameset cols=50%,*>
<frame src="$server_name/sfa_company?cmp_name=$cmp_name&con_name=$con_name">
<frame src="$server_name/engine_null_frame">
</frameset>
<frame src="$server_name/engine_null_frame">
</frameset>
EOT
  }
```

The arguments are optional. When other parts of the app pass arguments to this method, it just hands them along to the company-pane handler, which, in turn, hands them along to the contacts-pane handler. The top-level method's job is just to establish the three-pane frameset and invoke the */sfa_company* URL to paint the company pane. Why doesn't it invoke handlers for the contacts and contact-history panes? Event bubbling takes care of that. The top-level method only needs to clear those panes, which it does using the public method *engine_null_frame()*, which emits an empty HTML body.

When you call the bare URL */sfa_home*, no completion string constrains the company picklist displayed in the company pane. So the whole company table (subject to the specified limit) appears in the picklist. If Apple Computer is the first company in the list, then it's the currently selected item. The form template for the company pane uses that selection, in its **onLoad** handler, to sync the contacts pane accordingly. Example 15-5 shows the **onLoad** handler.

Example 15-5. JavaScript onLoad Handler for the Company Pane

```
function sfa_company_load ()
  {
  cmp_name = document.sfa_company.cmp_name.options
      [document.sfa_company.cmp_name.options.selectedIndex].text;
  con_name = document.sfa_company.con_name.value;
  con_select = document.sfa_company.con_select.value;
  url = getServer() + '/sfa_contacts?cmp_name=' + escape(cmp_name) +
      '&con_name=' + escape(con_name) + '&con_restrict=on';
  parent.frames[1].location = url;
  }
```

When this handler runs, the company-name variable picks up the value **Apple Computer** and weaves it into the */sfa_contacts* URL that it builds.

If Apple Computer contacts are already in the database, the contacts pane repeats the process. The first item of the picklist—let's say, **Steve Jobs**—is the default selection. The **onLoad** handler for the contacts pane extracts that value, and weaves it into the */sfa_history* URL that drives the contact-history pane. The handler for that pane uses the value to constrain the list of entries to just those for Steve Jobs.

What if no Apple Computer contacts were in the database yet? In that case, the *do_sfa_contacts()* method in the server-side code issues a redirection to the *do_sfa_add_contact()* method. It replaces the contacts pane with the form we saw in Figure 15-3 through Figure 15-6. The value **Apple Computer**, which was originally the default picklist selection in the company pane, propagates through and becomes the text of the company-name widget on that form, in its incarnation as a read-only label.

Networked dhttp

When you point a browser at a local instance of *dhttp*, you can pretend that you're running a purely local application. It doesn't matter whether you're online or offline, and this offine capability is one of the unique strengths of the local-web-server technique. But *dhttp* really is an HTTP server, so if you're connected to the office LAN or WAN, your colleagues can use your plug-in apps just the same way you do. In other words, a network of *dhttp* nodes is a peer-to-peer network.

This peer capability is so general that it takes a bit of getting used to. Suppose you and I each run an instance of *dhttp*, and we each maintain our own private database of contacts—mine on machine *my-dhttp*, and yours on machine *your-dhttp*. Table 15-2 shows the matrix of possibilities.

Table 15-2. Peer-Networking Matrix

Operation	Browser	URL
I use my database.	mine	*http://my-dhttp/sfa_home*
I use your database.	mine	*http://your-dhttp/sfa_home*
You use your database.	yours	*http://your-dhttp/sfa_home*
You use my database.	yours	*http://my-dhttp/sfa_home*

Why wouldn't we both simply use another machine, visible to both of us? We could, that's another option. Nothing prevents you from deploying *dhttp* on a conventional shared server. For light-duty intranet applications, its single-threadedness isn't a problem. And sometimes a shared data store makes the most sense.

Won't the use of a central server cripple our ability to use local data and to work offline? Not necessarily. We'll see shortly how to synchronize two or more *dhttp* nodes. But let's assume that in this case, our two data sets are mostly nonoverlapping. You don't need most of my records, and I don't need most of yours, but once in a while we'd like to look at—or even add to—each other's data sets. The symmetrical peer-to-peer model handles this situation without requiring replication of data to a shared server. Couple that with the ability to collect data while offline, and a peer-to-peer system can support some interesting scenarios. Suppose, for example, you detach your laptop from the network, visit a client, and collect some new contact information. On returning to the office, you dock your system, then go to lunch. A coworker in a satellite office elsewhere on the corporate WAN needs a phone number you just entered in your database. What was a portable offline data-collection device an hour ago is now a web server that provides the phone number on request.

Lotus Notes users will point out, rightly, that Notes handles this same scenario—though in a different way. A Notes user would undock, go to the meeting, enter data, return to the office, dock, and replicate with the central Notes server. Another user could then look it up directly on the central server or look it up locally after replicating with the server.

Services and Applications

The *dhttp* model doesn't preclude the Notes approach, but it does blur the boundary between services and applications. A *dhttp* plug-in is an interactive application that I can use on my own machine to enter and view data. But because it's an HTTP-accessible service, it can be available to colleagues on the intranet, or even over the Internet, by way of their browsers. This kind of service can also work silently in the background, feeding information to other services. The desktop machine in my office can be as fully available—to an intranet or, with the right kind of firewall or VPN configuration, to the Internet—as is any nominal server machine.

Does it make sense to run services locally? Well, we live in interesting times. On the one hand, we're in the midst of a return-to-the-mainframe movement—for good reason. PCs have gotten way too complex. A botched Windows registry all too often requires wiping the hard disk clean and reinstalling apps and data. Network computers didn't take off as some people predicted, but the web model—disposable and interchangeable clients, install-free and upgrade-free software, network-based applications—is going strong. From this perspective, the last thing you'd want to do is add another moving part to your PC.

On the other hand, we do continue to want, have, and use PCs. Every month they grow more powerful. Although people lambaste Windows 95/98, the truth is that these systems are quite capable of delivering lightweight services as well as running interactive applications. NT and Linux are both gaining share on the desktop, and of course both these systems are capable servers. So the question arises: are these PCs only to be used to run Microsoft Office applications against file-server-based data and as terminals into which web-based applications are projected? If not—if we're going to continue to have and use local data and apps along with all the server-based stuff—then we'll want to figure out how local and remote computing can work together. A peer-to-peer system can help unite these two realms.

Data Retrieval with dhttp

To illustrate how *dhttp* can work both as an application and a service, let's focus on ways to retrieve SQL data. A typical *dhttp* plug-in uses some kind of data-viewing widget to present dynamic views of SQL data and attach instrumentation to those views. Figure 15-7 shows the viewer used by another plug-in, called Jobs, which tracks assigned tasks.

You can do an ascending or descending sort on any column by clicking the up or down links surrounding the column's title. A menu of functions that apply to each row appears in the first column as a dropdown list. In this case, the *client focus* function constrains the view to only the jobs for the client listed in that row. The

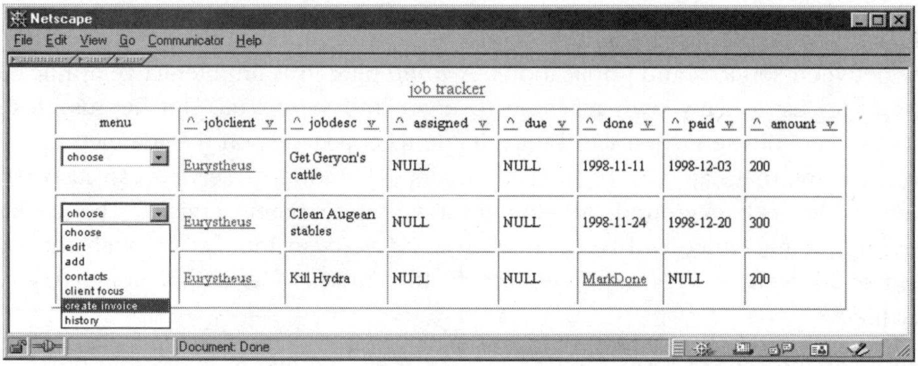

Figure 15-7. Data viewer for the Jobs plug-in

contacts function launches the SFA module, in a separate window, and synchronizes its display to the client listed in that row. The *create invoice* function launches Word and generates an invoice, pulling records from both the SFA and the Jobs databases.

Nothing here is specific to *dhttp*. It's just basic web-to-database integration, relying on server-generated pages. Because the server is local, though, the usual rap against this technique—that it requires repeated round trips to the server—carries less force. In this case, it's a very short round trip. Example 15-6 shows the method that implements the viewer:

Example 15-6. Implementation of the Jobs Data Viewer

```perl
sub viewData
  {
  my ($args) = @_;
  my ($history) = $args->{history};
  my ($user)    = $args->{user};

  my @viewcols = ($history) ? @histcols : @dispcols;
  my $table    = ($history) ? "_jobs"   : "jobs";
  my $cols = ($history) ? $select_cols . ",EDITOR" : $select_cols;

  my $st = sprintf("SELECT $cols FROM $table %s %s %s",
    $args->{constraint},
    $args->{orderby},
    $args->{orderhow},
    );

  my $results = dbSqlReturnAllHashRefs($main::jobs_dbh,$st);

  my $server_name = makeServerName();

  my $data = "";
  my $th = "<tr>";
```

Example 15-6. Implementation of the Jobs Data Viewer (continued)

```
$th .= "<td align=center><$fs>menu</td>";

foreach ( @viewcols )
  {
  $th .= "<td align=center><$fs>";

  amy linkpat = "<a href=$server_name/jobs_home?host=$main::hostname&port=
      $main::port&
      user=$user&orderby=$_&orderhow=ORDERHOW&selectcol=$args->{selectcol}&
      selectval=$args->{selectval}&history=$history>";

  $th .= $linkpat . "^</a>";
  $th =~ s/ORDERHOW/asc/;
  $th .= "  $_  ";
  $th .= $linkpat . "v</a>";
  $th =~ s/ORDERHOW/desc/;
  $th .= "</td>\n";
  }

  $th .= "</tr>\n";

$data .= "<table align=center border cellpadding=4 width=90%>\n";
$data .= $th;

foreach my $row (@$results)
  {
  $data .= "<tr>";

  my $escaped_jobclient = escape($row->{JOBCLIENT});

  $row->{MENU} = makeMenu($user,$row->{JOBCODE},$escaped_jobclient);

  if ($history)
    { $row->{TS} = tsToDate($row->{TS});}

  $row->{JOBCLIENT} = "<a href=\"$server_name/jobs_home?host=$main::hostname&
      port=$main::port&user=$user&cmp=$escaped_jobclient\"
      onClick=\"window.open(\'/sfa_home?cmp_name=$escaped_jobclient\')\">
      $row->{JOBCLIENT}</a>";

  foreach ( @jobdates )
    { $row->{$_} = shortDate($row->{$_}); }

  foreach ( 'MENU', @viewcols )
    { $data .= "<td><$fs>$row->{$_}</td>\n";  }

  $data .= "</tr>\n";
  }
$data .= "</table>";
return $data;
}
```

The *viewData()* method receives SQL WHERE and ORDER BY clauses from *jobs_home()* and composes an SQL query accordingly. As it builds the header and body of the HTML table that it emits, *viewData()* adds links that call */jobs_home* again, with arguments that specify new WHERE and ORDER BY clauses.

Extending the Data Viewer

This technique is simple, concise, and yet very flexible. Every element of the display is a potential hook for a function that generates a new kind of view, and it's trivial to create these new views. Suppose, for example, that you want the client name to link directly to a view in the contacts database. Here's a solution:

```
$row->{jobclient} = "<a href=$server_name/jobs_home?
        user=$user onClick=window.open(\'/sfa_home?cmp_name=" .
        escape($row->{JOBCLIENT}) .
        "\')>$row->{JOBCLIENT}</a>";
```

This snippet turns the client name into a link. The link's address points to the *jobs_home()* method, so clicking it regenerates the view. But at the same time, the onClick handler launches the contact manager in another browser window, calling SFA with the client's name so it will come up displaying the client company along with contacts at that company.

This methodology relies heavily on wrapping methods as URLs, turning scraps of data into URLs, and recycling URLs back into the engine. Coupled with a powerful scripting language like Perl, these techniques confer extraordinary leverage.

Replicating Data

Like all web applications, the Jobs module's API can be used programmatically as well as interactively. We can imagine a web-client script that would replicate data across multiple *dhttp* nodes. It would perform the following steps:

1. Invoke each instance's viewer.

2. Parse the resulting HTML table.

3. Build a master data set.

4. Create and invoke the update URLs needed to transmit the newest version of each record to each node.

That's doable but tedious. Not because it's hard to fetch and parse the data—it's actually trivial to convert an HTML table into lists and hashtables. What's tedious is building the fetch and update URLs. Each plug-in exports its own unique web API, so scripts that use those APIs are hardwired to each plug-in.

What if we were to turn *dhttp* into an SQL server? The public function *do_engine_sql()* shown in Example 15-7 does just that. It accepts a URL-encoded SQL query, and returns a result set formatted as a list-of-lists. Amazingly, in just 25 lines of

Perl, this function transforms a Windows PC into a low-intensity database server. Suddenly the ODBC interface and the Jet engine—components that exist on a vast number of desktop machines—can export SQL capability to local or remote web clients.

Example 15-7. Turning dhttp into a Lightweight SQL Server

```
sub do_engine_sql
  {
  my ($args) = @_;
  my ($argref) = Engine::PrivUtils::getArgs($args);
  my ($st)     = Engine::PrivUtils::unescape($$argref{st});
  my ($conn)   = Engine::PrivUtils::unescape($$argref{conn});
  my ($dbuser) = Engine::PrivUtils::unescape($$argref{dbuser});
  my ($dbpw)   = Engine::PrivUtils::unescape($$argref{dbpw});
  my $dbh = DBI->connect($conn,$dbuser,$dbpw)
  if (! defined $dbh)
    {
    print "$DBI::errstr";
    return;
    }
  my $lref = Engine::PrivUtils::dbSqlReturnAllRows($dbh,$st);
  my @results = ();
  foreach $rowref (@$lref)
    {
    my @row = ();
    foreach my $i (0..scalar(@$rowref))
      {
      if (defined $rowref->[$i])
        { push (@row,$rowref->[$i]); }
      else
        { push (@row,''); }
      }
    $row = join("\x0",@row);
    push(@results,$row);
    }
  Engine::PrivUtils::transmit Engine::PrivUtils::httpStandardHeader;
  Engine::PrivUtils::transmit join("\x1",@results);
  $dbh->disconnect;
  }
```

This method connects to the database belonging to a specified *dhttp* plug-in, runs a query, and returns a package of results. For example, this URL selects all contacts at Microsoft:

```
/engine_sql?app=sfa&st=select+*+from+cmp+where+cmp_name%3d%27Microsoft%27
```

And this URL inserts a record into the Jobs database:

```
/engine_sql?app=jobs&st=insert+into+jobs+(JOBCODE)+values+(jru_12345)
```

A non-**SELECT** statement produces no output, but a **SELECT** statement returns a table as a Perl LoH (list-of-lists). The containing list is delimited by an ASCII 1, and each sublist by an ASCII 0.

We've already seen lots of examples of web-client scripting, so it's not too hard to envision a replication script that issues SQL queries to a set of *dhttp* nodes, amalgamates the results, and then issues the SQL updates that will synchronize the data sets managed by each node. Before we write that script, though, we need to ask and answer some important questions.

What Makes Records Unique?

Let's assume that we'll timestamp every new record. That makes it quite unlikely that records created on two different nodes will collide. (If you're worried about a collision, add more randomness to the ID.) But the record ID ought to carry more information. If a record migrates from my machine to yours, it seems useful to be able to distinguish my contributions to your data set from yours. One solution would be to combine a timestamp with a piece of machine-specific data—for example, the IP address or the machine name. Better, since users can log in from any node and since IP addresses can change, we can combine the timestamp with a user ID.

If you use *dhttp* in standalone mode, that *dhttp* instance can hardcode the user ID, or receive it on the command line, or look it up in a directory. But what about networked *dhttp*? If I add a record to your machine, we want my user ID stamped on that record, not yours. One way to solve this problem is to incorporate the user ID into a standard URL prefix that's part of all the URLs generated by a *dhttp* plug-in. In the Jobs module, for example, every URL starts like this:

```
/jobs_METHOD?host=$host&port=$port&user=$user&...
```

We'll see a little later why *host* and *port* are standard elements of every URL, but for now, we'll just focus on the user ID. By adding this piece to the root URL and then propagating it throughout the plug-in (and the JavaScript functions in the associated HTML templates), so that every URL-generating method recycles this information back into the engine, the application becomes user-specific yet location-independent. Table 15-3 expands on the matrix shown in Table 15-2.

Table 15-3. Peer-Networking Matrix with URL-Embedded User IDs

Operation	Browser	URL
I use my database.	mine	*http://my-dhttp/jobs_home?user=me*
I use your database.	mine	*http://your-dhttp/jobs_home?user=me*
You use your database.	yours	*http://your-dhttp/jobs_home?user=you*
You use my database.	yours	*http://my-dhttp/jobs_home?user=you*

I can add the record whose ID is `jon_911878273` to any node in the network. Unless I'm in two places at once at exactly the same time, the record will be unique throughout the whole network. What's more, each node can differentiate its own records (that is, its users' records) from foreign ones.

What Happens in Case of a Replication Conflict?

It's not hard to identify the superset of unique records in a network of nodes, then fill in the gaps in each node's local data store. But suppose I add record `jon_911878273` to my node, then it propagates to yours, then we both change our copies of it. If our edits don't alter the record ID, the changed record will only replicate to nodes that don't yet have a copy of the record. If our edits do alter the record ID, it'll go everywhere, but as a new record.

The Jobs plug-in tackles this problem by remembering all updates. It records all changes to each record in a shadow table that parallels the master table. Suppose the master table, called *jobs*, looks like this:

Jobcode	Timestamp	Client	Amount
hercules_12345	12345	Eurystheus	200

Now Ben edits the record and changes the amount to 300. The shadow table, called *_jobs*, looks like this:

Jobcode	Timestamp	Client	Amount	Editor
hercules_12345	13999	Eurystheus	300	ben
hercules_12345	12345	Eurystheus	200	jru

Note that the shadow table tacks on an extra field, `editor`, where it stores the ID of the user who made the change. As it adds the change record, the Jobs module also updates the master table, changing its 200 to 300.

The shadow table can now replicate to other nodes, just like the master table. To do that, the replication script just needs to know that it's the timestamp, not the jobcode, that makes records unique within the shadow table.

Since the shadow table exists, why not give users access to it? The Jobs module does this by adding another item to the menu embedded in each row of its display. Labeled *history*, this item reinvokes the viewer with arguments that restrict it to the set of shadow table records for that row's master record. Figure 15-8 shows the history viewer in action, displaying changes to the record for Hercules' cattle-of-Geryon task:

Now we're in a position to write the replication script. It will do the following:

1. Replicate the master table to all nodes.

2. Replicate the shadow table to all nodes.

3. Apply the newest shadow-table record to the corresponding master table on all nodes.

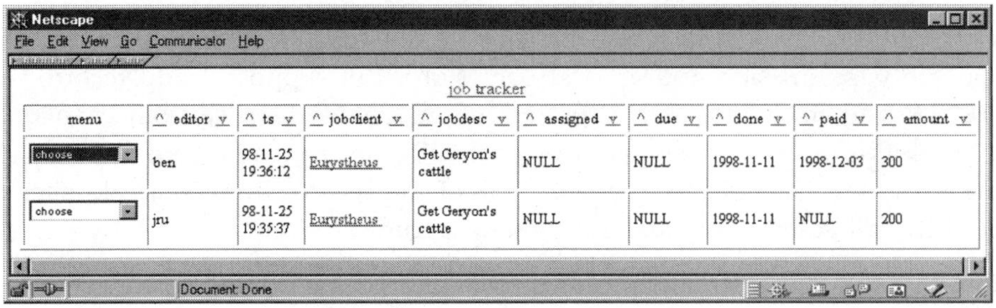

Figure 15-8. Viewing change history

This scheme doesn't prevent replication conflicts, per se. If I edit my copy of a record, and you edit yours, and we replicate, and my copy of the record is newer, then both our master tables get my copy. But we also both get the complete shadow table and can drill down to view the history of changes to each record. Example 15-8 shows a script that will synchronize a Jobs table across two or more *dhttp* nodes.

Example 15-8. Data Replication with dhttp

```perl
#! perl -w

use strict;
no strict 'refs';
use LWP::Simple;
use TinyCGI;

my $tc = TinyCGI->new();

my $hosts =
  {
  jru_nt   =>
    {
    user      => 'jru',
    port      => 9191,
    conn      => 'DBI:ODBC:JOBS',
    dbuser    => '',
    dbpw      => '',
    datedelim => '#',
    },
  jlb_linux   =>
    {
    user      => 'jlb',
    port      => 9191,
    conn      => $tc->escape('DBI:Solid:tcp 1313'),
    dbuser    => 'dba',
    dbpw      => 'dba',
    datedelim => '\'',
```

Example 15-8. Data Replication with dhttp (continued)

```
      },
    };


  my %dbtypes = (
  'JOBCODE',      'S',
  'TS',           'N',
  'JOBCLIENT',    'S',
  'JOBDESC',      'S',
  'ASSIGNED',     'D',
  'DUE',          'D',
  'DONE',         'D',
  'PAID',         'D',
  'AMOUNT',       'N',
  'EDITOR',       'S',
  );

  my @jobfields = qw(JOBCODE TS JOBCLIENT JOBDESC ASSIGNED DUE DONE PAID AMOUNT);
  my @_jobfields = (@jobfields,'EDITOR');

  my %tables = (
  'JOBS', \@jobfields,
  '_JOBS', \@_jobfields,
  );

  fetchTables();                              # phase 1

  synchTables();                              # phase 2

  applyEdits('JOBS');                         # phase 3

  sub fetchTables
    {
    foreach my $host (keys %$hosts)           # for each host in the network
      {
      foreach my $table (keys %tables)        # for each table
        {
        my $keycol = keycol($table);
        my $field_list = $tables{$table};     # get list of fields
        my $fields = join(',',@{$field_list}); # convert to comma-separated string
        my $st =                              # build select statement
          $tc->escape("select " . $fields . " from $table");
        my $port = $hosts->{$host}->{port};
        my $conn = $hosts->{$host}->{conn};
        my $dbuser = $hosts->{$host}->{dbuser};
        my $dbpw = $hosts->{$host}->{dbpw};
        my $url = "http://$host:$port/engine_sql?conn=$conn&dbuser=
            $dbuser&dbpw=$dbpw&st=$st";
        my $result = get $url;
        my @rows = split("\x1",$result);
        foreach my $row (@rows)
          {
```

Example 15-8. Data Replication with dhttp (continued)

```perl
        my @row = split("\x0",$row);
        my $key = $row[$keycol];
        ${$host.$table}->{$key} = $row;
        if (! defined ${'master'.$table}->{$key} )
          {
          ${'master'.$table}->{$key} = $row;
          }
        }
      }
    }
  }


sub synchTables()
  {
  foreach my $host (keys %$hosts)
    {
    foreach my $table (keys %tables)
      {
      foreach my $key (keys %${'master'.$table})
        {
        if (! defined ${$host.$table}->{$key} )        # if master record
          {                                            # not on target host
          my $port =   $hosts->{$host}->{port};
          my $conn =   $hosts->{$host}->{conn};
          my $dbuser = $hosts->{$host}->{dbuser};
          my $dbpw =   $hosts->{$host}->{dbpw};
          my $sql = mkSqlInsert($host,$table,$key);    # make SQL INSERT statment
          $sql = $tc->escape($sql);
          my $url = "http://$host:$port/engine_sql?conn=$conn&dbuser=
                 $dbuser&dbpw=$dbpw&st=$sql";
          get $url;                                    # run SQL statement
          }
        }
      }
    }
  }

sub applyEdits()
  {
  my ($table) = @_;
  my $keycol = keycol($table);
  my @updates = ();

  foreach my $shadowkey (keys %${'master_'.$table})
    {
    my $shadowrow = ${'master_'.$table}->{$shadowkey};
    my (@shadowrow) = split("\x0",$shadowrow);
    my $primarykey = $shadowrow[$keycol];
    my $highwater = ${'shadow'.$table}->{$primarykey};
    if ( (! defined $highwater) or ( $shadowkey > $highwater) )
      {
```

Example 15-8. Data Replication with dhttp (continued)

```perl
        ${'shadow'.$table}->{$primarykey} = $shadowkey;    # newest version
      }
    }

  foreach my $host (keys %$hosts)                          # for each host
    {
    foreach my $primarykey (keys %${'shadow'.$table})
      {
      my $shadowkey = ${'shadow'.$table}->{$primarykey};
      my $newestrow = ${'master_'.$table}->{$shadowkey};
      my $sql =                                            # build SQL update
        mkSqlUpdate($host,$table,$primarykey,$newestrow);
      my $escaped_sql = $tc->escape($sql);
      my $port  = $hosts->{$host}->{port};
      my $conn  = $hosts->{$host}->{conn};
      my $dbuser  = $hosts->{$host}->{dbuser};
      my $dbpw  = $hosts->{$host}->{dbpw};
      my $url = "http://$host:$port/engine_sql?conn=$conn&dbuser=
          $dbuser&dbpw=$dbpw&st=$escaped_sql";
      get $url;                                            # apply newest update
      }
    }


sub mkSqlUpdate
  {
  my ($host,$table,$primarykey,$newestrow) = @_;
  my @rowvals = split("\x0",$newestrow);
  my $colnames = $tables{$table};
  my $where_clause = " where $colnames->[0] = \'$primarykey\'";
  my $set_clause = "";
  my $datedelim = $hosts->{$host}->{datedelim};

  foreach my $i (1..scalar(@$colnames)-1)
    {
    $set_clause .= "$colnames->[$i]=";

    if (! defined($rowvals[$i]) or $rowvals[$i] eq '')
      { $set_clause .= "null,"; }

    else
      {
      if ( $dbtypes{$colnames->[$i]} eq 'D' )
        { $set_clause .= $datedelim . shortDate($rowvals[$i]) . "$datedelim,"; }

      if ($dbtypes{$colnames->[$i]} eq 'N'  )
        { $set_clause .= "$rowvals[$i],"; }

      if ($dbtypes{$colnames->[$i]} eq 'S'  )
        { $set_clause .= "\'" . prepareForDb($rowvals[$i]) . "\',"; }
      }

    }
```

Example 15-8. Data Replication with dhttp (continued)

```perl
  chop $set_clause;
  return "update $table set $set_clause $where_clause";
  }


sub mkSqlInsert
  {
  my ($host,$table,$key) = @_;

  my $datedelim = $hosts->{$host}->{datedelim};
  my $rowref = ${'master'.$table}->{$key};

  my @rowvals = split("\x0",$rowref);

  my $colnames = $tables{$table};

  my $values_clause = '';
  my $columns_clause = '';
  foreach my $i (0..scalar(@$colnames)-1)
    {
    $columns_clause .= "$colnames->[$i],";

    if (! defined($rowvals[$i]) or $rowvals[$i] eq '')
      { $values_clause .= "null,"; }

    else
      {
      if ( $dbtypes{$colnames->[$i]} eq 'D' )
        { $values_clause .= $datedelim . shortDate($rowvals[$i]) . "$datedelim,"; }

      if ($dbtypes{$colnames->[$i]} eq 'N'  )
        { $values_clause .= "$rowvals[$i],";   }

      if ($dbtypes{$colnames->[$i]} eq 'S'  )
        { $values_clause .= "\'" . prepareForDb($rowvals[$i]) . "\',"; }
      }

    }
  chop $columns_clause;
  chop $values_clause;
  return "insert into $table ($columns_clause) values ($values_clause)";
  }


sub shortDate
  {
  my ($date) = @_;
  return (defined $date) ? substr($date,0,10) : 'NULL';
  }

sub keycol
  {
```

Example 15-8. Data Replication with dhttp (continued)

```
my ($table) = @_;
if (substr($table,0,1) eq '_') # shadow table
  { return 1; }
else                            # normal table
  { return 0; }
}


sub prepareForDb
  {
  my ($val) = @_;
  $val =~ s/'+/''/g;
  $val =~ s/^\s+//;
  $val =~ s/\s+$//;
  return $val;
  }
```

The synchronization script proceeds in three phases:

fetchTables

> This phase collects records from two or more nodes. The example shown in Example 15-8 fetches the data into in-memory hashtables. For modest data sets, that's fine. For bigger data sets, you'd need to streamline the procedure. One approach would be to use a tied hash—that is, a Perl hashtable backed by a DBM-style database, such as SDBM, NDBM, or ODBM. Their characteristics differ, but all work like simple object databases, supporting the illusion that a data set of unlimited size can be accessed by way of an in-memory Perl variable. Alternatively you could limit the amount of data fetched by the replicator, by using a timestamp to restrict the result set.

> For each node, the *fetchTables()* routine creates one hashtable per SQL table. It also creates a master hashtable that holds the superset of all the per-node tables.

synchTables

> This routine traverses the master hashtable built by *fetchTables()*. For each record, it checks to see if each per-node hashtable has a copy of the record. If not, it adds the record by sending an SQL *insert* statement to the node.

applyEdits

> This routine traverses shadow tables and builds a superset shadow table. The keys for entries in this table are the master-table record IDs embedded in the shadow records. When *applyEdits()* sees a duplicate shadow record, it checks the timestamp embedded in the record and updates the superset shadow table only when a duplicate is newer. Next, it walks the superset table and builds a list of SQL update statements. Finally, it sends these updates to each node.

Which node runs the replication script? Because *dhttp* is a peer-to-peer system, any node can run it. Or, since the replication script is just a standalone web-client script, another machine—one that isn't part of the *dhttp* peer network—can run it. Peer-to-peer technology is quite flexible. If you and I are attending a convention, we could meet in a conference room, join our notebook PCs with a null 10Base-T cable, and synchronize data that we'd collected offline in meetings. The next day, back in the home office, a central replication service could synchronize both our PCs with a shared server. In the latter case, we might not even need to initiate the replication, since the central server could contact our machines and pull data from them.

Putting dhttp in Perspective

Of course, there are other, less exotic ways to move data. A typical office PC running Windows can easily be a peer file server. A central replication service could simply pull entire database files from a group of machines, sort out their differences, and put them back. The file-oriented approach sacrifices granularity, though. When you grab whole files, you can't ask for just yesterday's records. More generally, it sacrifices all the benefits that flow from a true distributed computing model. A distributed HTTP service is, I'm arguing, as fundamental to a web-centric model of computing as is a browser. Think about what Windows brought to the table back when DOS reigned: large memory, a GUI, device independence. Once developers could assume these services were available—wherever their code ran—there was no looking back. The *dhttp* model brings a new core service to the table—a lightweight, scripted, HTTP-aware service that connects local and remote applications and services to resources on the local machine.

That *dhttp* can serve files is, as we've seen, the least interesting of its capabilities. Products such as Microsoft's Personal Web Server haven't caught on widely as desktop-based applications, because they don't really solve a new problem on the LAN. What made first-generation web servers interesting was the way they made the whole Internet a giant LAN. With peer file sharing, I can already grant you access to files on my disk, so in that respect a local web server is largely redundant.

Of course, the Internet web server soon evolved into something more akin to an object request broker than a file server. Like ORBs, web servers connect clients to methods, which in turn connect to data. This ORB-like quality, along with the simplicity and universality of the HTTP protocol and the web programming model, is what makes the *dhttp* technique useful. Consider the invoice function of the Jobs module. In a standalone context, it's just one of any number of ways to automate Microsoft Word. You could equally well use a Visual Basic for Applications (VBA) macro to clone a Word document from a template, merge ODBC data into it, save it, and print it. In a LAN context, you could export that VBA macro to a group by using DCOM to start a remote instance of Word and then calling the macro in that remote instance. In an Internet/intranet context, you could export it by way of an ASP web page, which could also start a remote instance of Word and call the macro. The third approach is clearly the most general. Done that way, the invoice function will work on the intranet, or the LAN, or on a standalone machine, since an ASP server can run in all three places.

Anywhere, Everwhere Services

At stake here is the ability to carve applications into sets of services that can be deployed anywhere and that will work the same way everywhere. One of the best expressions of this idea is the Forte Application Environment, a high-end toolset for three-tiered software development. A Forte developer writes GUI, business-logic, and data-access services in Transactional Object-Oriented Language (TOOL), the Forte scripting language, without regard to where those services run. When it's time to deploy the application, the developer partitions it, allocating services to machines purely for reasons of convenience and efficiency. To continue with our invoice example, let's suppose that complex business rules attach to the function that generates an invoice. In Forte's system you can locate those rules in a middle-tier service, where they're easier to maintain and update, or you can locate them directly on clients, where they'll run a lot faster because there's no network latency.

The Forte toolkit not only makes services location independent, it abstracts multiple GUIs with a portability layer that's also controlled by the script language. You can write a graphical application once and deploy it to a diverse population of Windows, Unix, and Macintosh workstations. Clearly *dhttp* relies not on a portable native GUI, but on the browser with its universal HTML/JavaScript display model. That works for applications that can comfortably display using only first-generation browser technology, and a premise of this book is that many useful but unwritten applications fall into that category. The HTML/JavaScript client has yet to be exploited to its full capability. To the extent that new applications do exploit it, they target the world's largest installed base of application platforms.

The Next Plateau

Isn't the installed base rapidly evolving? Absolutely. There are at least three models competing to dominate the next stable plateau:

Java

> So far, Java's bid to supplant native GUIs with a portable (and mobile) alternative has mostly failed. You can chalk that up to immaturity of the language

and tools, restrictions imposed by the sandbox security model, computational overhead of the Java virtual machine, or some combination of these and other factors. Whatever the reason, Java to date is far more successful as a provider of network services than as a replacement for the native GUI. That might change in the next few years, or it might not.

ActiveX

The power of ActiveX components is seductive. Microsoft's Developer Network site (*http://msdn.microsoft.com/*) deploys two versions of a tree control that affords navigational access to a vast collection of documents. One version is Java based, the other ActiveX based. If I need to use that site and I happen to be running Communicator, I'll switch to MSIE just so I can use the ActiveX version of the tree control. It's far more effective. It's also Windows-centric. The ActiveX approach isn't yet a practical, portable way to extend the capabilities of all browsers on all platforms. That might change in the next few years, or it might not.

DHTML+DOM+XML+XSL+script

This bubbling cauldron of alphabet soup promises to establish a happy medium. There is, after all, a large middle ground to occupy. The HTML/JavaScript technology, at one end of the spectrum, has done more with a handful of basic GUI widgets than most anyone would have guessed was possible. Complete native GUI capability, at the other end of the spectrum, will always be needed for certain applications, such as visual interfaces to geographic data. But in between these endpoints lie huge numbers of applications that create, edit, navigate, search, and transmit semistructured and structured data. What's needed here is a richer successor to HTML/JavaScript, and that's just what is now evolving. To the extent that this effort succeeds, the kinds of user interface techniques we've seen in this chapter are likely to remain relevant.

Consider the Jobs module's data viewer. I chose to write it using only standard HTML/JavaScript constructs, because today that's the only way to ensure cross-browser portability. One alternate solution that's just appeared—for MSIE 5 only—is to use a combination of XML and XSL. Using MSIE 5 you can, for example, embed an XML "data island" in a web page and associate that chunk of XML with an XSL style sheet that maps the data into what the browser ultimately renders as an HTML table. I can't wait for this approach (or something like it) to become a cross-browser standard and penetrate 95% of the installed base of browsers. It's the appropriate successor to HTML/JavaScript.

When that successor arrives, the need for script-driven template processing, *à la* the HTML/JavaScript user interfaces shown in this chapter, won't go away. If anything, it will intensify. How, for example, will XML get into the web page? Dynamic generation of the page will continue to afford crucial leverage by enabling scripts to select and tailor the data sets handed to the browser for display. Likewise, how does the XSL style sheet get into the web page? Dynamic generation of the page will again continue to afford crucial leverage, by instantiating different versions of XSL style sheets to support dynamically changing requirements. A page generator will matter as much to these next-generation pages as to today's pages. And a local page generator will continue to be a useful complement to a server-based one. It's an enabling service. The more places that it can run, the more it can enable.

Replicating Code

We centralize services in part to cut down on the administrative burden of maintaining distributed services. The zero-footprint, no-install nature of web-based software is one of its most compelling features. But it's not appropriate to centralize everything. Some services ought to run locally because the network connection is intermittent, or because it's more efficient to connect to local resources, or simply because they're personal rather than shared. In these cases code needs to be not merely mobile, like Java, but persistent, like ActiveX. What happens, in a distributed network of peers, when you need to update not only the data stored on each node, but the methods that operate on that data? The *dhttp* environment enables a simple solution to this problem. Example 15-9 shows the public engine function *do_engine_update_sub()*, which enables a *dhttp* node to update one of its plug-ins *in situ* and on the fly.

Example 15-9. dhttp Support for Code Replication

```
sub do_engine_update_sub
  {
  my ($args) = @_;
  my ($argref)  = &Engine::PrivUtils::getArgs($args);
  my ($app)     = &Engine::PrivUtils::unescape($$argref{app});
  my ($subname) = &Engine::PrivUtils::unescape($$argref{subname});
  my ($subcode) = &Engine::PrivUtils::unescape($$argref{subcode});
  my ($module) = '';
  my ($found) = 0;
  open(F,"$main::root/Apps/$app.pm")
    or $main::debug && warn "cannot open $main::root/Apps/$app.pm";

  while (<F>)
    {
    if ( m#^1;# )                 # module ends with 1;
      {
      if (! $found )             # if target sub not yet found
        { $module .= $subcode; }  # emit the new code
      $module .= $_;             # then emit the 1;
      last;                      # then bail out
      }
    if ( m#^sub $subname$# )      # found the target sub
```

Example 15-9. dhttp Support for Code Replication (continued)

```
    {
    $found = 1;
    my $end = 0;                        # not at the end of the target sub yet
    my $line;
    $module .= $subcode;                # emit the new code
    while ( (! $end) and ($line = <F>) )
      {
      if ( ($line =~ m#^sub#) or # found the next sub
           ($line =~ m#^1;# ) )   # found end of module
        {
        $end = 1;                       # signal we're at the end of the replaced sub
        $module .= $line;               # emit next sub's declaration or 1;
        }
      }
    }
  else
    { $module .= $_;  }
  }
close F;
open (F, ">$main::root/Apps/$app.pm"); print F $module; close F;
eval ($module);
}
```

This method receives a URL-encoded Perl function over the HTTP connection, evaluates that function in the namespace of a *dhttp* plug-in, and rewrites the plug-in's source code accordingly. A web-client script can use this method to project a new version of any of the plug-in's methods into any *dhttp* node. The update occurs instantly, without requiring a server restart, because *do_update_sub()* uses Perl's *eval* function to alter the target method *in situ*. It also rewrites the plug-in's source code so that when the server does restart, it uses the new version. Example 15-10 shows how to update the method *do_sfa_foo()* from Version 1 to Version 2.

Example 15-10. Using dhttp Code Replication

```
use Engine::Server;
use Engine::PrivUtils;

$host = 'jon_linux';
$port = 9191;

while (<DATA>)  {$sub .= $_;}

$sub = Engine::PrivUtils::escape($sub);

# first update the method on the target

print Engine::Server::getUrl($host,$port,"/engine_update_sub?app=sfa&
  host=$host&port=$port&subname=do_sfa_foo&subcode=$sub");
```

Example 15-10. Using dhttp Code Replication (continued)

```
# then call the method

print Engine::Server::getUrl($host,$port,"/sfa_foo");

__DATA__
sub do_sfa_foo
  {
  print httpStandardHeader;
  print "foo v2";
  }
```

Assuming that the URL */sfa_foo* originally returned "foo v1," this script updates the method *do_sfa_foo()*, then calls it, producing the output "foo v2."

Scary, isn't it? In fact, much too scary. With very little effort, we've arranged so that any *dhttp* node can expose not only its SQL data, but also its plug-in code, to any HTTP-aware client that wants to rewrite the data or the code. And the code is being executed by a full-strength Perl interpreter. Like any powerful technology, this one's a double-edged sword. Wielded responsibly, it can enable all sorts of useful things. In the wrong hands, it can spell disaster. As with genetic engineering, there are two ways to respond to this dilemma:

Reject the technology.
> You might reasonably conclude that potential risks outweight potential benefits. Peer-to-peer replication of code is inherently uncontrollable, therefore dangerous, therefore to be shunned.

Embrace the technology.
> You might also reasonably conclude that if peer-to-peer replication of code seems too simple and too powerful, then the correct response is to tap into the source of that simplicity and power, analyze the associated risks, and learn how to manage them.

The latter response leads to a discussion of ways to use *dhttp* securely. As we'll see, some of the conventional solutions apply. In addition, the presence of an always running process on each node creates an interesting new opportunity based on the notion of a local HTTP proxy.

Secure dhttp

If you implement local HTTP service using a conventional web server, as of course you can, your security options are as follows:

IP address restriction
> This technique, which all web servers support, can be used to reject all but a specified set of hosts. It's of dubious value when the users you want to

support present different addresses at different times. That can happen when they log in variously from desktop machines behind the firewall or ISP-connected home machines outside the firewall. It can also happen when they log in from desktop machines that receive dynamically allocated IP addresses.

Basic or cookie authentication

Every method in the *dhttp* system is a kind of CGI call. With basic authentication you can require name/password credentials for every call. With cookie authentication you can allow those credentials to persist on client machines across sessions.

SSL encryption

Basic or cookie-style credentials are very weak forms of security when used on a cleartext channel. They're much stronger when the channel is encrypted using SSL. Moreover, an SSL channel encrypts not only credentials, but all data flowing through it.

Encryption is the most attractive solution. How might *dhttp* do that? One option appears to be SSLeay, the open-source implementation of SSL. But the legal issues surrounding the use of SSLeay are complex and unresolved. First, there are the patents that RSA Data Security holds on the encryption algorithms used in SSL ciphers. Because these are U.S. patents, it is a patent violation to use SSLeay inside the U.S. without acquiring RSA's commercial BSAFE library and linking SSLeay with it. Does that mean SSLeay is legal for non-U.S users? Not necessarily. The names of the ciphers, notably RC4, are trademarks, and trademark protections cross all borders. The SSLeay distribution now acknowledges this fact:

RC4 is a trademark of RSA Data Security, so use of this label should perhaps only be used with RSA Data Security's permission.

These issues, compounded by the U.S. government's prohibition on the export of strong cryptography, quite seriously complicate efforts to build tools that use SSL. It's an odd situation. SSL technology is so prevalent, in inexpensive or free browsers and web servers, that people assume SSL itself is inexpensive or free, and that's far from true. A BSAFE license is very expensive. Netscape and Microsoft have amortized the cost of licensing RSA's technology across a large population of browsers and servers. That makes it easy to use SSL in the context of secure browsers and servers. But it's not easy to use SSL in other tools that interoperate with secure browsers and servers.

One solution, on a Windows machine with MSIE installed, is to use MSIE's licensed encryption components—for example, by way of the interface library WININET.DLL. That's not ideal, though, because WININET isn't a cleanly isolated system service like ODBC. It's more like a browser-specific component. If you regard *dhttp* as a system service, you don't want its security mechanism to depend on how the user configures the MSIE advanced preferences, as can happen if you depend on WININET.

Another solution, for a Windows or Unix machine with any browser installed, is to use a version of SSLeay that's linked with RSAREF, a reference implementation of the patented RSA algorithms that RSA makes available for noncommercial use. But SSLeay/RSAREF isn't readily available, it's not easy to build it, and even if you did, it's not completely clear what you are and are not allowed to do with it.

Rethinking the Encrypted Channel

Let's step back for a moment and ask: Why SSL? Largely because that's how browsers do encryption, and we want *dhttp* to work with browsers. For server-to-server communication between *dhttp* nodes, another encryption technology—one unencumbered by patents and other legal issues—might work. To test this idea, I wrapped up a reference implementation of the Blowfish encryption algorithm (see Bruce Schneier's *http://www.counterpane.com/*) in a Perl extension module. How? The details of Perl's extension mechanism are beyond the scope of this book, and in any case I'm far from an expert on the subject. See the Perl documents *perlxs* and *perlxstut* for an introduction to Perl extension modules. Suffice it to say that it's possible to outfit a robust scripting language—in my case Perl, but in yours, perhaps, Python or something else—with symmetric encryption and decryption functions. For example:

```
use Blowfish;

my $key = "*y)==.67Ab,\XsQxa789{%^2";
Blowfish::initialize($key, length($key));

my $cleartext = "Hello, world";

my $ciphertext = Blowfish::encipher($cleartext, length($cleartext));

my $deciphered = Blowfish::decipher($ciphertext,length($ciphertext));
```

Secure Proxying

That's mildly interesting. It gets really interesting when you add the notion of a *dhttp* node that proxies requests on behalf of the local browser. Now we can see why a *dhttp* plug-in, such as the Jobs module, might want to specify a host and port as part of every URL that it generates. Suppose every URL were expressed in terms of the local machine, which handled local requests locally and proxied remote requests. To illustrate this idea, Table 15-4 expands the previous example yet again.

Table 15-4. Peer-Networking Matrix with Local Proxying

Operation	Browser	URL
I use my database.	mine	*http://my-dhttp/jobs_home?host=my-dhttp&user=me*
I use your database.	mine	*http://my-dhttp/jobs_home?host=your-dhttp&user=me*
You use your database.	yours	*http://your-dhttp/jobs_home?host=your-dhttp&user=you*
You use my database	yours	*http://your-dhttp/jobs_home?host=my-dhttp&user=you*

Now when the browser asks for a page from a remote *dhttp* node, it relays the request through the local *dhttp* node, which acts as a proxy server. When the destination is local, the proxy passes the request straight through to the local server. When the destination is remote, it performs the following steps:

1. Encrypt the request.

2. Create a new LWP HTTP request object.

3. Add to that object the HTTP header `Remote-Dhttp`, whose value is the local machine's hostname and port.

4. Send the `Remote-Dhttp` header and the encrypted HTTP request to the remote node.

On the other end, the remote node handles requests from itself in the usual way. When encrypted requests arrive from a remote partner, it decrypts them.

This proxy scheme creates an encrypted browser-to-server channel that doesn't use SSL. Of course, that channel can also be used noninteractively by local processes that communicate with remote nodes. How secure is it? As cryptography guru Bruce Schneier likes to point out, the security of any algorithm depends on the key. Methods of generating, distributing, and using keys are what make or break a cryptosystem. A network of *dhttp* nodes that uses only a single shared key, and that never changes that key, will be cryptographically weak. Even so, it will be more secure than a network of *dhttp* nodes that does no encryption at all. Computer espionage tends to follow the path of least resistance. An unlocked door is far more inviting to an intruder than one that is locked, no matter what the quality of the lock.

dhttp in the Windows Environment

If you buy into the notion that *dhttp* is a service that can usefully enable groupware development, and your target group is—as most are—Windows based, you'll want a more elegant way to run *dhttp* than by launching Perl from the command line at system start-up. One way to hide the *dhttp* process from the user is to use the Windows Scripting Host (WSH). For example, if you rename the main *dhttp* driver from *dhttp* to *dhttp.pls*, then you can run it like this:

```
dhttp.pls
```

In this mode, there's no command console. Instead WSH runs *dhttp*, thanks to the PerlScript layer that enables ActivePerl to plug into WSH. If you package the previous command into a *.CMD* file and refer to that file from the Windows start-up folder, *dhttp* will start silently when Windows starts. Of course, it will run silently too. Messages that went to the default error channel, STDERR, won't appear, so you'll need to log them or—when you want them to appear to an interactive user—convert statements that print to STDERR into statements that use the *WScript->echo()* method.

The real problem here is system shutdown. The *dhttp* server spends nearly all its time blocked on an *accept()* call, waiting for the next incoming connection. As a result, the process that runs *dhttp* can't react to Windows messages. When Windows tries to tell that process that it wants to shut down, there's no response. Windows then invites the user to forcibly terminate the process—and that's hardly the desired effect.

Is there a way to make *dhttp* a true Windows application that can process Windows messages? This amounts to asking if Perl itself can run as a true Windows application rather than as a Win32 console application. Historically Perl has always been easy to embed. In just a few lines of C code you can slave a Perl interpreter to a compiled program. When ActiveState released ActivePerl, the version of Perl that finally merged the core Perl codebase with ActiveState's Win32 enhancements (e.g., ISAPI Perl, *Win32::OLE*, and more), the conventional way to embed Perl wasn't supported. But ActiveState supplied another way: PerlEz, a DLL that a host Win32 application can use to embed Perl.

PerlEz is part of the answer, but there remains the problem of getting at Windows messages. Embedded in a Windows application, *dhttp* still blocks on the *accept()* call in its central request-handling loop. What to do? Run PerlEz, and in turn *dhttp*, on a background thread. That way, the application's primary thread can continue to pump Windows messages, and the application can shut down normally. Example 15-11 presents a minimal solution using Microsoft Foundation Classes (MFC).

Example 15-11. Embedding dhttp Using PerlEz

```
#include "stdafx.h"
#include "resource.h"

#include "dhttp.h"
#include "/ap/lib/core/perlez.h"
```

Example 15-11. Embedding dhttp Using PerlEz (continued)

```
CTheApp NEAR theApp;

UINT PerlEzProc(LPVOID pParam )
  {
  PerlEzCreateOpt("c:\\dhttp\\dhttp","-Ic:\\dhttp\\lib","9191");
  return 0;
  }

CMainWindow::CMainWindow()
  { LoadFrame(IDR_MAINFRAME); }

void CMainWindow::OnPaint()
  {}

void CMainWindow::OnAbout()
  {
  CDialog about(IDD_ABOUTBOX);
  about.DoModal();
  }

BEGIN_MESSAGE_MAP( CMainWindow, CFrameWnd )
  //{{AFX_MSG_MAP( CMainWindow )
  ON_WM_PAINT()
  ON_COMMAND(ID_APP_ABOUT, OnAbout)
  //}}AFX_MSG_MAP
END_MESSAGE_MAP()

BOOL CTheApp::InitInstance()
  {
  m_pMainWnd = new CMainWindow;
  m_pMainWnd->ShowWindow(m_nCmdShow);
  m_pMainWnd->UpdateWindow();

  AfxBeginThread(PerlEzProc,NULL);

  return TRUE;
  }
```

Since the window doesn't display anything, you might simply omit the *ShowWindow()* call and run it invisibly. Alternatively, you might place an OLE control on the canvas and route status messages into that control.

Groupware and dhttp

What, finally, does *dhttp* have to do with groupware? By my definition, groupware encompasses scopes as narrow as three coworkers sharing a LAN and as wide as the entire Internet. Groupware applications, even when they seem to belong in some particular scope, usually end up needing to cross boundaries. Groups evolve, zones of privacy need to be adjusted fluidly, populations of users and machines change constantly. An ActiveX-based solution that works for some particular group may no longer suffice when that group morphs into something else. Internet-style technology holds the promise of true universality. But if it's going to be an appropriate platform for groupware, we'll have to make the most of it.

A ubiquitous TCP/IP network, the Internet protocols, and the browser/mailer/ newsreader are planks of a pretty good platform. These things alone, however, don't add up to the kind of distributed computing system that will fully enable Internet groupware. I don't claim that *dhttp* is the solution, only that it's a sketch of what one important part of the solution might look like. Forte's toolset is wonderful, but it costs a fortune, and it isn't likely to show up on your intranet anytime soon. Lotus Notes is also wonderful, and it costs a lot less than a fortune. It may be the right answer for you, but if so, you're probably not reading this book. If you've gotten this far, it's because you think that Internet protocols, open-source development, and world-class scripting languages are keys that can unlock still more riches than they already have done. And because you think that groupware remains an important undiscovered treasure.

16

Epilogue

It's been four years since I first began the research and development efforts that led me to write this book. That's quite a while, as Internet time goes. A lot has changed since Netscape's products first demonstrated the vision of Internet groupware that continues to inspire me. And yet that vision is, in many ways, still not yet real.

We'll always remember Netscape's browser as the engine that propelled the World Wide Web to the forefront of public awareness and became the first truly universal software client. That was a tremendous achievement, but Netscape's agenda was even more ambitious. What I've been calling the standard Internet client—that is, a suite of applications including a web browser, mailreader, and newsreader—is really a Netscape invention. In Communicator and its clones, the idea was to integrate a bunch of Internet protocols and applications into a common framework. We would use the browser to interact with hypertextual documents and forms-based applications. We would use the messaging tools to interact with people. Eventually the boundaries would blur, and the tools we'd use to produce and consume documents and applications would be the same ones we'd use to communicate with individuals and groups.

Perhaps Internet time isn't what it used to be, now that Netscape is just a division of AOL. The marriage of the standard Internet client's web and messaging components, which was promised in the 4.x browsers, is still not yet consummated. Communicator and Internet Explorer create expectations that they only partly fulfill. Consider, for example, their implementations of NNTP conferencing. Understood properly, this technology is a powerful and accessible way for groups to create, share, and discuss rich hypertextual documents. The Microsoft and Netscape newsreaders are collaborative tools, that, as we saw in Part I, can transform an ordinary NNTP server into a kind of read/write web server.

Without a roadmap such as this book provides, few people are likely to discover the true groupware potential of NNTP. Even with a roadmap, you'll run into vexing obstacles. We saw in Chapter 9, *Conferencing Applications*, for example, that despite NNTP's surprising versatility, it's hard to create a user experience that seamlessly joins web space and news space. Today's Internet client gives us a tantalizing glimpse of what Internet groupware could be and can actually deliver more of the goods than most people realize. But the golden spike that will join the Web to Internet messaging has yet to be driven.

It's inevitable, in my view, that the two realms will merge, although when and how is anybody's guess. For the time being, my strategy is to make the most of the considerable integration that already exists and to further it in every way possible. I'll review, once more, why and how to do so. And then I'll close by suggesting how today's unfinished Internet groupware tools might evolve into tomorrow's Internet groupware platform.

Today's Internet Groupware Opportunities

In Chapter 1, *The Conferencing Dimension*, I argued that discussion is the essential groupware application, distinct from email and complementary to it. If you haven't yet enabled this mode of communication in your company, I urge you to do so now. Do it in the fastest, cheapest, most expedient way. The right answer for you might prove to be a so-called proprietary solution, such as Notes, Exchange, or FirstClass. Or it might be an open Internet-style solution based on NNTP or web conferencing. Either way, what ultimately matters is *that* you empower your people to collaborate this way, not what flavor of software supports the collaboration. It's not even clear what the terms "proprietary" and "open" mean, frankly, now that products like Notes and Exchange aggressively support Internet standards such as IMAP and NNTP.

Conferencing matters because so much of what we collectively know is recorded in the messages that we write and because email-only environments force group communication into unnecessarily narrow channels. We abuse email when we try to make it into a conferencing tool. True conferencing, as I define it in Chapter 1, restores email to its realm of appropriate use and moves group communication into more public spaces where it can best flourish. As we saw in Chapter 2, *Public Online Communities*, conferencing is a cornerstone of the public online community. It can support and energize a web site and enable your company to connect online with customers and partners. The same conferencing technology, deployed on the intranet, can help networked teams collaborate effectively.

Of the many ways to implement conferencing, the Usenet style—NNTP clients talking to NNTP servers—can be the cheapest and easiest, because the clients are already widely deployed. To activate them, you just need an NNTP server, which, as we saw in Chapter 13, *Deploying NNTP Discussion Servers*, can be an inexpensive or free item and is no harder to set up and operate than any other kind of discussion server. If you're not already committed to another solution, I suggest that you give this one a try, particularly if your people are already using the Netscape or Microsoft mailreaders. These products share much in common with their companion newsreaders, notably the message-composing tools through which so much vital message traffic flows. The message composers are landmarks that can help orient users as you teach them about the subtler mail/news synergies that we explored in Chapters 3 and 4.

The Dynamics of Discussion

No matter which conferencing tools you use, effective collaboration doesn't just happen by itself. You have to create the right environment by designing scoped zones that support departmental, companywide, and public discussion. You have to show people when, why, and how to operate within these scopes and move among them. You have to understand and demonstrate the habits of information layering and packaging that amplify the power of the conferencing medium. Even when you can do all these things, realize that it's just plain hard to get to critical mass on an intranet. The Internet's virtual communities are made up of self-selected individuals, drawn from a huge population, who share common interests and a burning desire to collaborate. We don't choose our coworkers, and although we have to collaborate with them, we are not always as enthusiastic about doing so.

To push intranet collaboration over its activation threshold, realize that a conferencing system is just a central repository of semistructured information. When that repository delivers valuable services, such as anywhere, anytime navigation and search, it's just a better filesystem, one that meets the requirements of individuals as well as of groups. Appeals to enlightened self-interest tend to work better than appeals to the common good. Look for ways to make participation in discussions intrinsically rewarding.

Building Web Docbases

A discussion is a species of docbase—that is, a set of documents that share common properties and that store semistructured data. With clever and determined use of the tools that create and view discussions, you can achieve excellent results. But in the Internet realm, message composers work with fixed-function message templates. You can't, for example, add a Company or Project field to an Internet mail or news message. To do that, we shifted gears in Part II and explored how to build web docbases. These can handle the same kinds of semistructured data that we put into messages but don't suffer from the constraints of a fixed-function template.

The template for a web docbase can be anything that you need it to be. You can define its metadata very simply using HTML <meta> tags or more elaborately using XHTML or full-blown XML. In Chapter 6, *Docbase Input Techniques*, we built a system that uses XHTML record templates to help users preview and validate docbase records and that stores records in the same XHTML format. In Chapter 7, *Docbase Navigation*, we extended that system, using the metadata to create navigational views of docbases. In Chapter 11, *Membership Services*, and Chapter 12, *Authentication and Authorization Techniques*, we tapped that metadata again to create subscription and authorization services based not only on group membership, but also on docbase attributes.

Every docbase is potentially a groupware application. It becomes one when you activate *bindings*, latent in the metadata, that connect docbase records to groups and their activities. Every scrap of metadata that you capture and store can pay back rich dividends, and you can mine that metadata in unusual places. In Chapter 8, *Organizing Search Results*, we saw how URLs and HTML doctitles form namespaces that you can fruitfully manage as metadata repositories. We saw, as well, that it's valuable to think of different species of docbases, including newsgroups and web archives, as components that plug into a common information architecture. Using the search mechanisms we explored in Chapter 8, you can define such an architecture abstractly, then adapt it to different kinds of docbases (or search engines). Doing that furthers groupware objectives by adding value to the docbases that you invite users to create.

Integrating Web and Messaging Components

The Netscape and Microsoft mail/news clients aren't as flexible or programmable as their counterpart browsers, and that's a problem for groupware developers who want to leverage and customize these messaging tools. But mail and news servers, like web servers, are wonderfully flexible and programmable components. The underlying protocols—SMPT, NNTP, and HTTP—are simple enough to operate manually, and are therefore well supported by scripting languages such as Perl. A script can access mail, news, or web services almost as easily as an interactive mailreader, newsreader, or browser.

In Part III, we exploited the component nature of Internet services to create hybrid groupware applications. In Chapter 9, for example, we built a reviewable docbase system that joins an XML docbase to an NNTP newsgroup; we used the NNTP API to populate the newsgroup with a discussion framework linked to the docbase; we used conventional CGI techniques to transform comments issuing from the docbase into correlated newsgroup postings. An alternative version of the reviewable docbase idea relied on email instead of a newsgroup, providing a lighter solution requiring no web or NNTP machinery.

These applications surprise some people, but really they shouldn't. Integration of web technology with Internet messaging doesn't happen automatically, but thanks to the profound componentization of the core services, solutions are eminently scriptable.

Applications, Components, and Services

When you build web-based groupware applications, you're also creating componentized, scriptable services. In Chapter 10, *Groupware Servlets*, for example, we saw how a servlet-based group calendar implicitly supports import and export APIs, just because a web-client script can issue the same URLs that browsers do when they read and write calendar data. Servlets, like conventional CGI applications, can be coupled together in a kind of web version of the Unix pipeline. The same servlet that provided web APIs to import and export scripts also consumed a web API provided by a "todo server," using its services to inject todo data into calendar displays.

When web applications are used both interactively and programmatically, it can be helpful to structure their outputs for the convenience not only of browsers, but also of scripts. We saw a simple example of this idea in Chapter 10, when we altered the calendar's HTML output in a way that made no difference to browsers but that simplified script-based parsing of that output. In Chapter 14, *Automating Internet Components*, we saw how to take this idea to the next level, using XML-RPC to define well-structured request/response protocols based on HTTP.

Directory services are another kind of component used by groupware applications. LDAP has emerged as the consensus standard not only in the Internet realm but on the LAN. In Chapter 11 we explored a transitional strategy that creates a common interface to a simple text-file-based directory, to the Windows NT domain database, and to LDAP. Built with Perl, these three directory modules demonstrate another way to componentize services used by groupware applications. In this case, the technique helps isolate applications from a directory services infrastructure that is in transition to LDAP but not yet fully standardized on it.

Data Prototyping and Object Persistence

The simplest of Chapter 11's directory modules merely persists Perl data structures to a text file. I used this example to make a point about data prototyping. Groupware data stores, including directories, need to evolve as quickly as applications do. They also typically need to model complex relationships that can be tedious to express in an LDAP or SQL schema. When you're using a scripting language to prototype an application, it can make sense to prototype the application's data store too, as persistent objects expressed directly in that same scripting language. You may eventually need to migrate to a more robust data store, but only if the application proves out and even then only if transactional load or concurrency issues require that you do.

Java offers particularly nice support for managing web-accessible data structures directly in memory and for serializing them to disk storage as needed. We used this approach in Chapter 10, in servlets that present web APIs to Java objects. If you go this route, you can upgrade from simple Java serialization to a commercial object database that does offer transaction support and concurrency controls.

Advanced Techniques

We've seen a lot of scripting in this book. Too much? I admit there's a tendency to regard some of the cobbled-together solutions I've shown as "just a bunch of scripts." It's true that to integrate the range of components needed to create useful groupware, you're going to have to write scripts. But in Part IV I show that precisely because these scripts use the same methods and protocols as do the core Internet services, they can be not only flexible but also very resilient. The monitoring tool we build in Chapter 14, for example, sees all HTTP services equally, whether they're provided by homegrown scripts or by open-source or commercial applications. In my experience, any nontrivial web site is always built using a mixture of these components. The commercial ones aren't necessarily more (or less) intrinsically reliable than the homegrown ones. No matter what, it's an administrative chore to make sure all the parts are working together smoothly. But when the parts are Internet-style components, that chore is automatable—and rather easily too.

Scripted HTTP services are so useful that, in Chapter 15, *Distributed HTTP*, I explore the idea of deploying them locally, on users' workstations, where they can deliver applications into local or remote browsers and be components used by local or remote processes. This peer-to-peer approach to web computing can attack a range of problems typical of groupware, including support for offline users and data replication.

Next-Generation Internet Groupware

The future of Internet groupware is up for grabs. No matter which way the wind blows, it's clear that web-based applications will play a central role. But I'm not betting that web mail and conferencing will supplant the existing forms of Internet messaging, at least not anytime soon. We live and breathe email, and I don't know anybody who prefers an HTML (or Java) mailreader to a native-GUI mailreader.

Oddly, although most people prefer today's "fat" messaging clients to "thin" HTML alternatives, few have really begun to exploit the capabilities of their fat-client tools. Here are some of the missed opportunities:

Secure mail

The Microsoft and Netscape mailreaders have long supported end-to-end encryption of messages using S/MIME. When was the last time you exchanged encrypted email with someone? It's an odd thing, but people who fret about the strength of the encryption that protects their online credit-card orders think nothing of sending reams of confidential information all around the Internet in the form of cleartext SMTP messages.

Why hasn't S/MIME taken off? Mainly because most people haven't found it worthwhile to acquire the client certificates (digital IDs) that enable this feature, despite the fact that such certificates are inexpensive (*http://www. verisign.com/*) or free (*http://www.thawte.com/*).

Digital signatures

The Microsoft and Netscape mailreaders have also long supported digital signatures. A recent spate of email-borne worms and viruses—first Melissa, then ExploreZip.worm—underscored the need for strong authentication of messages. These attacks weren't more technically adept than countless others, but they were far more socially adept. Receivers of Melissa got mail that seemed to be from people they knew. Receivers of ExploreZip.worm, even more insidiously, got mail that seemed to be from people they knew *in response to messages they had just sent to those people.* In both cases, that mail came from a trusted person's machine but *not* from a trusted person.

A point that was missed in all the debate about renewed virus-checking vigilance is that the habit of digitally signing messages could have thwarted both attacks. I do most of my business, and you probably do a lot of yours, by means of electronic communication—primarily email. In that realm, we're usually represented by nothing more than our email addresses, which are trivial to forge. I can, for example, configure my mailer so that email I send appears to come from Bill Gates, thus defaming Gates (and Microsoft) in personal or public-forum messages.

Digital signatures, which solve this problem by binding the use of an email address to a digital ID backed by a trusted third party, have to date largely been stigmatized as geeky. We need to regard them, instead, as a mark of professionalism. If we're doing business by way of email, you should expect me to stand behind my electronic identity, and I should want to sign my messages so you'll take me seriously. My company, and your company, should be very concerned about either of us unleashing a worm bearing a corporate domain name.

The tools we have aren't perfect. Hardware-assisted signing, with smartcards, is a long-overdue solution to the necessary evil of the digital-ID password. Digital-ID request and installation procedures are still not quite as smooth as they could be. But digitally signed email (and newsgroup conferencing) is workable now and has been for several years.

IMAP

The Microsoft and Netscape mail clients both support IMAP, in principle freeing users from the limitations of POP. Most people, though, still connect to POP servers and can't use IMAP's server-based features. IMAP public folders, which as we saw in Chapter 13 can do everything NNTP newsgroups can do and more, likewise aren't available to most users or well understood by those who could use them.

HTML messaging

The Netscape and Microsoft mail/news clients include HTML message composers that can produce, in a WYSIWYG manner, HTML that expresses everything that Microsoft Word is typically used to express: outline structure, font styles, color, tables, inline images. I wish I had a nickel for every Word document I've received as an email attachment. Such documents, written in HTML, are a fraction of the size of their Word counterparts, and they display instantly in HTML-aware messaging clients.

HTML messaging isn't just about fonts, tables, and images, though. What's really at stake is the production and aggregation of intranet content. We are all prolific consumers of web-based content, and we are all prolific producers of intranet content, but the stuff we read on the Web doesn't look or act like the stuff we write to each other. Today's HTML message composers aren't the final answer, but they're an important step in the right direction.

NNTP conferencing

By the summer of 1999, as I was completing this book, there was a groundswell of interest in online community and particularly in the uses of conferencing on public sites and intranets. There are lots of ways to do conferencing, and as I've said, what's most important is that you do it, not how. It's ironic, though, that a mature solution—NNTP conferencing—is available everywhere but used almost nowhere.

All these technologies have been widely available since the debut of 4.x browsers. But, Internet time notwithstanding, they've progressed little since then. It's a chicken-and-egg problem. Hardly anybody uses the stuff, so there's little incentive for vendors to improve it. Because the stuff isn't improving, users aren't attracted to it. For example, although I routinely sign my own email messages, I've said little about the subject of client certificates in this book. Why? It's hard enough to get people interested in the most basic of the underutilized Internet groupware features, such as conferencing. If you also try to push public-key infrastructure at the same time, you'll have an even harder time making headway.

I'm not sure how we break out of this vicious loop, but I think it's naive to assume that the Web will magically take care of everything. Web users, for example, have shown no interest in acquiring the client certificates that would not only enable signed and encrypted email, but also strongly authenticate their online credit-card purchases.

What's at stake here transcends the tug-of-war between the thin HTML and fat GUI styles of software. Much of the Internet infrastructure that was sketched out in a tremendous rush of innovation a few years ago has failed to mature as expected. I hope this book has shown where that innovation was headed and how the Internet clients that we use every day contain the germs of many groupware ideas and techniques. But where do we go from here?

A Modest Proposal

On the server side, we're in great shape. We've seen how the core Internet services are scriptable components that can be combined and recombined endlessly. Because these services live in the network, they can evolve frictionlessly. Playing to the lowest-common-denominator client, they deliver tremendous value and are creating more every day.

It's the client that worries me. For all its strengths, the standard web client—that is, the HTML/JavaScript browser—falls far short of the rich features built into the (nearly) standard messaging client. Unfortunately, that messaging client isn't a programmable component in the same sense that the browser is. Somehow, these two streams of development have to merge. Messaging is at the center of all groupware activities. We need to be able to deeply customize our messaging environments. There are two ways this can happen:

Enrich the browser's user interface and local data store.

> There's a reason we prefer our fat messaging clients. They're powerful information-management tools, and we need all the power we can get, because message traffic is our lifeblood. It's about time to extend HTML's tired old widget set, and if that happens, messaging widgets—a multipane viewer, a tree control, a rich-text and forms-capable composer—should top the list of desirable new HTML features. Of course, these things should be scriptable by way of a standard Document Object Model (DOM).

> Better UI alone won't solve the problem, though. Browsers today are quite limited in their ability to store and manage local data. A cookie file is hardly

the place to put megabytes of semistructured, searchable message data. Messaging clients use powerful—and proprietary—embedded database engines to manage local message stores. Should this machinery migrate into the browser? Perhaps so. Ideally the proprietary message stores would offer standard DOM bindings so that custom messaging applications built on top of them could be portable.

Componentize the messaging client.

Instead of moving all the rich functionality of the messaging client into the browser, why not bring the browser's programmability into the messaging client? There's almost no limit to what you can achieve with the right set of scriptable components. But in the Internet realm, the messaging client is conspicuously unable to work as a scriptable component. Notes and Exchange developers routinely create custom forms and message types that provide, right in the messaging environment, the flexibility that Internet developers can only achieve in web space.

As in the browser case, this solution should provide an API that insulates scripted applications from the proprietary message store. There are all sorts of groupware services and components that need to be built. If the messaging client becomes a platform for such services and components, it needs to be an open one so that development activities have the best chance of reaching critical mass.

I'd settle for either or both of these solutions. One way or another, I hope we'll end up with an Internet messaging platform that has the ultimate flexibility of the web programming model, plus all the features of the fat messaging clients. That's the platform on which we can build the next generation of Internet groupware.

V

Appendixes

Appendix A, *Example Software*, is a guide to the software components created for this book and is available on my web site (*http://udell.roninhouse.com/*). Appendix B, *Internet RFCs: A Groupware Perspective* traces the groupware technologies discussed in this book to their roots in the Internet Engineering Task Force's Request for Comment (RFC) series of documents.

A

Example Software

Kit for Chapter 4

You can recreate the polling example using any URL-driven polling application. The *Polls* servlet discussed in Chapter 4, *Information-Management Strategies for Groupware Users* (and Chapter 10, *Groupware Servlets*) is just one of many possible ways to do it. The point of the example in Chapter 4 is to show how and why it can be useful to reduce the user interface of a polling application to URLs that can be transmitted in email or newsgroup messages. That said, here are the pieces used in the example given in the book.

The Polls Servlet

To reproduce the example, you'll need the *Polls* servlet (*http://udell.roninhouse. com/examples/Polls.zip*), plus a servlet host in which to run the *Polls* servlet. There are lots of servlet hosts available; see *http://www.servlets.com/resources/urls/ engines.html*. *Polls* and *GroupCal*, the two servlet examples in my book, are primarily set up to work with Jef Poskanzer's Acme.Serve (*http://www.acme.com/ resources/classes/Acme.tar.Z*), an open-source servlet host.

The documentation for the *GroupCal* servlet (*http://udell.roninhouse.com/ examples/GroupCalDoc.htm*) has details on compiling Acme.Serve for Unix or NT. Once you've done that, the setup for *Polls* is as follows:

1. In *Serve.java*:

```
Servlet Polls = new Acme.Serve.Polls();
serve.addServlet( "/Polls", Polls );
```

2. Recompile *Serve.java*

3. Run *Serve.java*:

```
java Acme.Serve.Serve
```

4. Test the *Polls* servlet:

```
http://hostname:9090/Polls?name=Groupware&1=Rules&2=Sucks&3=DontCare
http://hostname:9090/Polls?vote=Rules
http://hostname:9090/Polls?tally=yes
```

The Poll-Creating Form

Here's the HTML used to create the example form:

```
<form method="post" action="/cgi-bin/polls.pl">
<p>Poll name: <input name="pname">
<br>
<br>1. <input name="1">
<br>2. <input name="2">
<br>3. <input name="3">
<br>4. <input name="4">
<br>5. <input name="5">
<p><input type="submit" value="Create Poll">
</form>
```

The Poll-Creating Form's Handler

And here's the script that handles the form. It pokes the poll-creating URL into the *Polls* servlet and responds with a set of pasteable URLs used to operate the poll.

To run the script, you'll need two Perl modules: *TinyCGI* (included with the Docbase kit) and the CPAN LWP module.

```
#! perl -w

use strict;

use TinyCGI;
use LWP::Simple;

my $tc = TinyCGI->new;
my $href = $tc->readParse();
print $tc->printHeader();

my $pname = $href->{pname};
my $host = "http://hostname:9090";
my $url = "$host/Polls?name=$pname";
foreach my $choice (keys %$href)
  {
  next if ( $choice eq 'pname' );
  next if ($href->{$choice} eq '');
  $url .= "&$choice=" . $tc->escape($href->{$choice}) ;
  }

get $url;
```

```
print "<p>---- begin fragment to email or post to newsgroup ------------";
print "<p>Here are the URLs for voting in the poll:<br>";

foreach my $choice (sort { $a <=> $b } keys %$href)
   {
  next if ( $choice eq 'pname' );
  next if ($href->{$choice} eq '');
  print "<p>Poll: $pname, Choice: $href->{$choice}";
  print "<br><$host/Polls?name=$pname&vote=" .
             $tc->escape($href->{$choice}) . ">";
   }

print "<p>Here is the URL for viewing the tally:<br>";
print "<br><$host/Polls?name=$pname&tally=yes>";
print "<p>---- end fragment to email or post to newsgroup ------------";
```

Kits for Chapters 6 and 7

The Docbase kit (*http://udell.roninhouse.com/examples/Docbase-1.0.tar.gz*) includes the family of modules used in Chapter 6, *Docbase Input Techniques*, and Chapter 7, *Docbase Navigation*:

TinyCGI
> Essential CGI functions

Docbase::Docbase
> Common definitions and functions for the Docbase system

Docbase::Input
> Dynamic generation of input forms; previewing; validation; record storage

Docbase::Indexer
> Convert meta-tagged headers into sequential and tabbed-index controls

Docbase::Navigate
> Navigational controls for dynamically viewed Docbases

Contents of the Docbase Kit

The kit also includes a set of templates for the ProductAnalysis docbase illustrated in the book, along with some sample records. Here is the complete list of files included in the kit:

```
MANIFEST
Changes
Makefile.PL
test.pl
Docbase.pm.safe
lib/TinyCGI.pm
lib/Docbase/Docbase.pm
lib/Docbase/Input.pm
```

```
lib/Docbase/Navigate.pm
lib/Docbase/Indexer.pm
cgi/ProductAnalysis/docbase-template.htm
cgi/ProductAnalysis/dynamic-navigation-template.htm
cgi/ProductAnalysis/dynamic-sequence-template.htm
cgi/ProductAnalysis/form-template.htm
cgi/ProductAnalysis/frame-template.htm
cgi/ProductAnalysis/indexer.pl
cgi/ProductAnalysis/seqinfo/seqinfo
cgi/ProductAnalysis/static-sequence-template.htm
cgi/ProductAnalysis/submit.pl
cgi/ProductAnalysis/test.pl
cgi/doc-nav.pl
cgi/doc-view.pl
cgi/final-submit.pl
cgi/formgen.pl
web/ProductAnalysis/docs/1999-06-24-000001.htm
web/ProductAnalysis/docs/1999-06-24-000002.htm
web/ProductAnalysis/idxs/idxs
web/ProductAnalysis/seq/seq
web/ProductAnalysis/style.css
web/img/next.gif
web/img/prev.gif
```

Installing the Docbase Kit

After unzipping and untarring the kit into a scratch directory, you follow the usual procedure for installing a Perl module:

1. *perl Makefile.PL*

2. *make* (*nmake*, for Win32 environments)

3. *make test*

4. *make install*

Step 1: Running the Makefile.PL Script

This script, which builds the makefile used to do the installation, asks for some details about your web server installation:

```
Absolute CGI path (default: /home/httpd/cgi-bin): /web/cgi
Relative CGI path (default: /cgi-bin): /cgi
Absolute Web path (default: /home/httpd/html): /web
Relative Web path (default: )(nothing is ok):
Web server running as user (default: nobody)(Unix only):

Using these values:
cgi_absolute: /web/cgi
cgi_relative: /cgi
web_absolute: /web
web_relative:
webserver running as: nobody
```

```
Are you sure? This makefile will try to install scripts and
templates based on these values. [N,y]:
```

The defaults are those for my Linux system running Apache. In this example, I'm installing on my NT system running IIS. The Docbase system needs to know both the absolute and web-server relative paths to the Web (that is, HTML document) and CGI (that is, script) areas on your server.

In this example, the Docbase-generic scripts will be copied to */web/cgi/Docbase*, and the Docbase-specific scripts will be copied to */web/cgi/Docbase/Product-Analysis*.

Step 2: make (or nmake)

This step assumes that you have a *make* tool on your system, which, in the Win32 world, many people do not. In that case, you can get a free copy of nmake at *ftp://ftp.microsoft.com/Softlib/MSLFILES/nmake15.exe*.

Step 3: make Test (or nmake Test)

This step runs a series of tests that try to validate that your installation went correctly. You should see output like this:

```
1..7
ok 1
Testing TinyCGI
ok 2
Testing Docbase::Docbase
ProductAnalysis.../web/cgi/Docbase...multi...ok 3
N...ok 4
Testing Docbase::Input
ok 5
Testing Docbase::Navigate
ok 6
Testing Docbase::Indexer
ok 7

For further testing, try this URL:

/cgi/Docbase/ProductAnalysis/test.pl

after you have run 'make install'.
```

Part of the test script uses *Docbase::Indexer* to derive tabbed-index pages and sequential navigation controls from the two sample docbase records included with the kit.

The final message indicates that you can use your browser to try out these navigational mechanisms on the sample docbase—ProductAnalysis—that's installed with the kit. But first, you have to complete the installation.

Step 4: make Install (or nmake Install)

This step moves the Perl modules from the scratch directory to their official locations and builds one or more types of documentation, depending on your platform and configuration.

Note that once you've run *make install*, the *perldoc* command is one way to view
the POD (plain old documentation) that's built into a Perl module:

```
C:\>perldoc Docbase::Input
NAME
     Docbase::Input - Generate and process Docbase input forms.

SYNOPSIS
       use strict;

       use TinyCGI;
       my $cgi = TinyCGI->new();
       print $cgi->printHeader;
       my $vars = $cgi->readParse();

       use Docbase::Docbase;
       my $db = Docbase::Docbase->new($vars->{app});

       use Docbase::Input;
       my $di = Docbase::Input->new($db);

       $di->formGen($vars);

AUTHOR
       Jon Udell, udell@monad.net
```

You can also try the test page (*/CGI_RELATIVE/Docbase/ProductAnalysis/test.pl*).
Figure A-1 shows how that page should look in a browser.

Reusing the Docbase Kit

To make a new docbase, you start with the version of *lib/Docbase/Docbase.pm*
that's in your scratch (build) directory. It contains this structure:

```
my $docbase_defaults =
    {
    'ProductAnalysis'    =>
        {
        'tabstyle' => 'multi',
        'navstyle' => 'dynamic',
        'indexed_fields' => ['company','product','analyst','duedate'],
        'tab_functions'   =>
            {
            'company' => $tabFnFirstChar,
            'product' => $tabFnFirstChar,
            'duedate' => $tabFnFirstSevenChars,
            'analyst' => $tabFnAll,
```

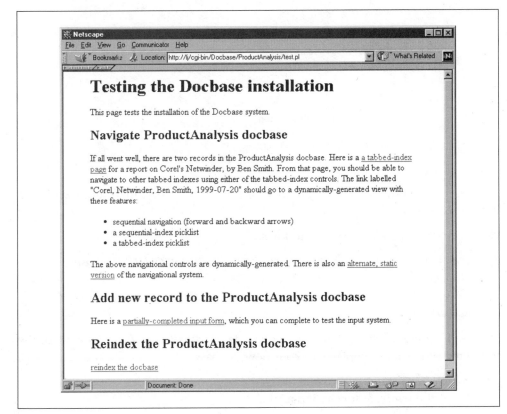

Figure A-1. Docbase installation test page

```
        },
    'sort_specs' =>
        {
        'company' => 'ascending',
        'product' => 'ascending',
        'analyst' => 'ascending',
        'duedate' => 'descending',
        },
    },
'AnotherDocbase'    => {},
};
```

Suppose you want to make a status report docbase, with controlled fields employee, department, and week_of. You might extend $docbase_defaults by adding:

```
'StatusReport'    =>
    {
    'tabstyle' => 'multi',
    'navstyle' => 'dynamic',
    'indexed_fields' => ['department','employee','week_of'],
```

```
'tab_functions'  =>
    {
    'week_of'     => $tabFnFirstSevenChars,
    'employee'    => $tabFnAll,
    'department'  => $tabFnAll,
    },
'sort_specs' =>
    {
    'week_of'     => 'descending',
    'employee'    => 'ascending',
    'department'  => 'ascending'
    }
}
```

Do this to the copy of *Docbase.pm* in your scratch directory, then rerun *make test* and *make install*.

Next, clone two subdirectories as follows:

> *CGI_ABSOLUTE/Docbase/ProductAnalysis* → *CGI_ABSOLUTE/Docbase/ StatusReport*
> *WEB_ABSOLUTE/Docbase/ProductAnalysis* → *WEB_ABSOLUTE/Docbase/ StatusReport*

Delete the contents of *WEB_ABSOLUTE/Docbase/StatusReport/docs*. Then adapt the following scripts and templates to your new docbase:

CGI_ABSOLUTE/form-template.htm
> This is the template for the input form.

CGI_ABSOLUTE/docbase-template.htm
> This is the XML template for the stored record.

CGI_ABSOLUTE/dynamic-navigation-template.htm
> This is the template for the tabbed-index controls.

CGI_ABSOLUTE/dynamic-sequence-template.htm
> This is the template for the sequential controls used by the dynamic version of the viewer.

CGI_ABSOLUTE/submit.pl
> This script validates input, classifies problems as warnings or errors, and invokes the previewer.

CGI_ABSOLUTE/indexer.pl
> This script, which you'll probably want to run on a scheduled basis, updates the navigational indexes. You can omit the *buildStaticControls()* call if you're only using the dynamic viewer.

CGI_ABSOLUTE/static-sequence-template.htm
> This is the template for the sequential controls used by the static version of the viewer. Not needed if you're only using the dynamic viewer.

CGI_ABSOLUTE/frame-template.htm

> This is the template for the framesets that control the static version of the viewer. Also not needed if you're only using the dynamic viewer.

Remember to use `app=StatusReport` in the URLs that operate on this docbase. For example, to add records to the StatusReport docbase, you'd use a URL like this:

```
CGI_RELATIVE/Docbase/formgen.pl?app=StatusReport&employee=Jon+Udell
```

Kit for Chapter 8

The family of modules presented in Chapter 8, *Organizing Search Results*, illustrate ways to organize search results drawn from multiple docbases and produced by multiple search engines:

Search::SearchResults

> Converts an LoH (list-of-hashes) that abstractly represents multidocbase, multi-engine search results into a template-governed HTML display

Search::Classifier

> Parent of a family of Classifiers—each specializing in a particular search engine, each using a set of Mappers to map literal search results into abstract search results

Search::SwishClassifier

> The Classifier that's specific to the *SWISH* search engine

Search::MicrosoftIndexClassifier

> The Classifier that's specific to the Microsoft Index Server

Search::ProductAnalysisMapper

> The Mapper that understands meta-tagged records from the ProductAnalysis docbase

Search::ConferenceMapper

> The Mapper that understands newsgroup postings.

These modules suggest a general strategy for categorizing search results. I haven't packaged them up with an installer, because you'll need to customize them for your search engine, and your document collections. But the modules, along with sample templates, are available in *http://udell.roninhouse.com/examples/ SearchResults.zip.*

Kit for Chapter 9

Example 1: Reviewable Docbases

To re-create the reviewable-docbase example, see *http://udell.roninhouse.com/ examples/ReviewableDocbase.zip* which includes:

- Chapter 1, *The Conferencing Dimension*, in XML-ized HTML format

- CSS style sheets for this chapter, and a table of contents

- A script to transform the XML content into reviewable HTML content

- Apparatus (a CGI form template, a form generator, and a form handler) used for the newsgroup version of the comment mechanism

The script, *reviewable.pl*, expects to read *chap1.xml* and write *chap1.htm*. It runs in one of two modes, governed by the $protocol variable in the script. If you use $protocol = 'mail', each header and paragraph will end with a link that begins an email message commenting on that element of the document.

If you instead use $protocol = 'news', the script will write a file called *nntp_msgs*. This file of NNTP messages defines the skeleton of a newsgroup used for collaborative review of the document. If you're running a local NNTP server (see Chapter 13, *Deploying NNTP Discussion Servers*), you can load these messages into a newsgroup on that server, as shown in Example 9-9.

In the newsgroup version of this application, the links in the generated document will call the script *comment.pl*, which in turn reads and interpolates values into the form template *comment.htm*, which form is in turn handled by *comment-handler. pl*.

Requirement: the Perl XML::Parser module

To run the script, you'll need Perl and the *XML::Parser* module. The build-it-yourself version of *XML::Parser* is on CPAN (*http://www.cpan.org/modules/by-module/XML/*). Users of ActiveState Perl (*http://www.activestate.com/*) who can't or don't want to build *XML::Parser* themselves can install a binary version directly from the ActiveState site, like this:

```
c:\> perl ppm
PPM interactive shell (0.9.5) - type 'help' for available commands.
PPM> install XML-Parser
```

Requirement: an NNTP server

This example requires an NNTP server if you want to use the comment mechanism in newsgroup mode. I've used *INN* (available on every Linux CD, or from *http://www.isc.org/*), Netscape Collabra (see *http://www.netscape.com/download/*), and the MS NNTP Service in the freely available NT 4.0 Option Pack (*http://www. microsoft.com/ntserver/nts/downloads/recommended/nt4optpk/default.asp*).

See Chapter 13 for an overview of setting up these servers. For this example, you'll need to create a newsgroup called *groupware.v3*.

Requirement: the Perl TinyCGI module

The *TinyCGI* module (included with the Docbase kit, *http://udell.roninhouse.com/ examples/Docbase-1.0.tar.gz*).

Requirement: the Perl Net::NNTP module

The CPAN libnet bundle (e.g., *http://www.cpan.org/modules/by-module/NET/libnet-1.0606.tar.gz*) includes *Net::NNTP*.

Note that a smaller, simpler alternative to the libnet bundle is CPAN's NNTPClient (*http://www.cpan.org/modules/by-module/News/*). It's just a single *.pm* file that, unlike the more full-featured *Net::NNTP*, can be easily deployed even on a server that you don't control—for example, if your application needs to run on an ISP's server.

Example 2: HelpDesk

Requirement: an NNTP server

See Example 1 earlier in this appendix. For this example, you'll need two newsgroups: *it.helpdesk.open* and *it.helpdesk.closed*.

Requirement: Net::NNTP

See Example 1 earlier in this appendix.

Requirement: dhttp kit

You'll also need the *dhttp* kit (*http://udell.roninhouse.com/examples/dhttp-v2.tar. gz*). The mini-web server in that kit is the host for the scripts that support the Web parts of the HelpDesk example.

As explained later in this appendix, you install *dhttp* by just unzipping into a subdirectory. In the root of that unzipped archive, you'll find the main *dhttp* driver script, which is called simply *dhttp*.

Requirement: a DBI/DBD data source

The HelpDesk app uses an SQL data store to keep track, in a structured way, of trouble tickets that are also posted to the news server for discussion. Linux and NT examples of the *dhttp* driver script, illustrating two different data-source configurations, are shown in Example A-1 and Example A-2.

Example A-1. Configuring the dhttp Driver for HelpDesk: NT Example

```perl
#! /usr/bin/perl -w

use strict;
no strict 'refs';

use DBI;
use DBD::ODBC;

$main::debug = 0;

$main::port = $ARGV[0];
$main::hostname = 'jon_nt';
$main::server = "$main::hostname:$main::port";
$main::fontspec = "font size=-1";
$main::root = "d:/dhttp/lib/dhttp";

$main::date_delim = "#";        # e.g.: # for ODBC, ' for Solid SQL

use Engine::Server;

$main::hd_dbh = DBI->connect('DBI:ODBC:HD','','')
    or die ("hd_dbh: cannot connect");
use Apps::hd;

Engine::Server::init;
```

Example A-2. Configuring the dhttp Driver for HelpDesk: Linux Example

```perl
#! /usr/bin/perl -w

use strict;
no strict 'refs';

use DBI;
use DBD::Solid;

$main::debug = 0;

$main::port = $ARGV[0];
$main::hostname = 'jon_linux';
$main::server = "$main::hostname:$main::port";
$main::fontspec = "font size=-1";
$main::root = "/home/jon/dhttp/lib/dhttp";

$main::date_delim = "\'";         # e.g.: # for ODBC, ' for Solid SQL

use Engine::Server;

$main::hd_dbh = DBI->connect('DBI:Solid:tcp 1313','dba','dba')
```

Example A-2. Configuring the dhttp Driver for HelpDesk: Linux Example (continued)

```
    or die ("hd_dbh: cannot connect");
use Apps::hd;

Engine::Server::init;
```

The differences are mainly to do with SQL. In this example, I'm using ODBC to talk to a *.MDB* file on NT and the Solid server (*http://www.solidtech.com/*) on Linux. So it's necessary to adjust the DBI connection strings for each of these data sources as well as the delimiter used to form date literals. Had I used Solid on both NT and Linux, I'd have needed to set only the hostname and the path to the root of the *dhttp* installation.

Configuring the Apps::hd module for the HelpDesk app

There's a further bit of configuration in the file *./lib/dhttp/Apps/hd.pm*. Here's the top of that file on my NT machine:

```
    package Apps::hd;

    use Engine::PubUtils;
    use Engine::PrivUtils;

    $newsroot = "c:/nntpfile/root/it/helpdesk";
    $newshost = "jon_nt";

    use Net::NNTP;
    my $nntp = Net::NNTP->new($newshost);

    my $hd_fontspec = "font size=-1";
    my $approot = "Apps/hd";
```

In this case, the news host at 'jon_nt' is the MS NNTP Service, rooted at *c:/ nntpfile/root/it/helpdesk*. On my Linux box, running *INN*, the equivalent lines are:

```
    $newsroot = "/var/spool/news/it/helpdesk";
    $newshost = "jon_linux";
```

Starting the HelpDesk app

With your news server running, you can start *dhttp* on port 9191 (from its home directory) like this:

```
    perl -Ilib/dhttp dhttp 9191
```

Initializing the HelpDesk database

The *hd::do_hd_makedb()* function creates the SQL table used by the HelpDesk application. It assumes that the data source named in the *dhttp* driver script is available. To use *hd::do_hd_makedb()*, go to a browser and issue this URL:

```
    http://host:port/hd_makedb
```

Using the HelpDesk application

To display the home page of the HelpDesk application, go to a browser and issue this URL:

```
http://host:port/hd_home
```

Click *open a new ticket* on the home page to bring up a trouble ticket form. Fill it out and submit it. If things are working properly, you can click *view tickets* on the home page to view the ticket in the SQL database and click *discuss open tickets* to launch your newsreader and view the ticket in a newsgroup.

Kit for Chapter 10

The *GroupCal* servlet kit (*http://udell.roninhouse.com/examples/GroupCal.zip*) includes the Java code for the *GroupCal* servlet, plus HTML templates, configuration files, and documentation (*http://udell.roninhouse.com/GroupCalDoc.htm*) that explains how to run the servlet in either of two hosts: the open-source Acme.Serve or Sun's Java Web Server.

By default, *GroupCal* will not try to inject "todo" information into calendar views, as shown in Chapter 10. If you want to try that, create a service that responds to URLs like:

```
http://SERVER:PORT/todo_view?user="Jon+Udell&date="Thu+Jul+01+1999"
```

The *dhttp* kit includes a plug-in, *todo.pm*, that implements a bare-bones version of such a service, for an ODBC data source.

To use this module, define this SQL table:

```
CREATE TABLE ASSIGNMENTS (PROJECT CHAR(10), TASK INTEGER, DUE DATE,
    DONE DATE, USER CHAR(20));
```

Then populate it with some task data, for example:

```
INSERT INTO ASSIGNMENTS (PROJECT, TASK, DUE, DONE, USER)
    VALUES ('PROJ1', 2, #1999-09-11#, NULL, 'Jon Udell');
```

Then, edit *GroupCalProps.txt* and tell *GroupCal* to look for a todo server:

```
enableTodo=true
```

Finally, restart *GroupCal.*

Kit for Chapter 11

The directory kit (*http://udell.roninhouse.com/examples/Directories.zip*) includes the three modules presented in Chapter 11, *Membership Services: Group:: SimpleGroup, Group::NtGroup,* and *Group::LdapGroup.*

These aren't full-featured modules, just illustrations of a way to abstract different kinds of directory services. The idea is that you can build something simple using the Perl-only module, then scale up to a real directory when (or if) that becomes necessary.

To use *Group::Simple*, you'll need the CPAN Perl module *Data::Dumper*.

To use *Group::NtGroup*, you'll need the Microsoft ADSI kit (see *http://www. microsoft.com/windows/server/Technical/directory/adsilinks.asp*). This module will, therefore, work only on Win32 systems.

To use *Group::LdapGroup*, you'll need the CPAN Perl module *Net::LDAP*. *Group::LdapGroup* is specific to a particular LDAP server—namely, Netscape's. You can get an evaluation copy of that server at *http://download.netscape.com/*.

To use one of these modules, locate it somewhere on Perl's `@INC` path. For example, on my NT box, the possible locations are the current directory, *c:\ActivePerl\ lib*, and *c:\ActivePerl\site\lib*.

Kit for Chapter 12

The ASP-based authorizing view is in *http://udell.roninhouse.com/examples/auth. asp.txt* (remove .txt extension for use), and its *global.asa* file is *http://udell. roninhouse.com/examples/global.asa.txt*.

Requirements for the Authorization Example

To run the script as shown in Chapter 12, *Authentication and Authorization Techniques*, you'll need these modules:

Group::LdapGroup
> From the directory kit (*http://udell.roninhouse.com/examples/Directories.zip*). Since this module requires a specific LDAP server, you might rather use *Group::Simple* instead.

Docbase::Docbase
> From the Docbase kit (*http://udell.roninhouse.com/examples/Docbase-1.0.tar. gz*). The example uses *Docbase::Docbase::getMetadata()* to extract metadata from the ProductAnalysis docbase.

CPAN's MIME::Base64
> The example uses *MIME::Base64::decode_base64()* to decode basic authorization credentials.

CPAN's SHA
> The example uses *SHA::digest()* to encode credentials for comparison with credentials stored in Netscape Directory Server.

Kit for Chapter 14

Quality Assurance Monitoring

The test harness script (*http://udell.roninhouse.com/examples/TestHarness.txt*) relies on these CPAN modules:

DBI

The generic database driver

DBD

A driver for a specific datasource (e.g., *DBD::ODBC*)

LWP

For web-client capability

By default, test-harness is set up to exercise the authorization script (*auth.asp*) from Chapter 12. Its configuration is governed by a hashtable that looks like this:

```
%sequence =
  (
  '000' =>
   {
    'Description'  =>  'No-header request fails access to docbase record',
    'Request'      =>  'http://localhost/cgi/auth.asp?doc=1998-10-19-000001',
    'HeaderNames'  =>  [],
    'HeaderValues' =>  [],
   },
  ...
  '003' =>
   {
    'Description'  =>  'Valid basic-auth user fails feed registration',
    'Request'      =>  'http://localhost/cgi/auth.asp?doc=1998-10-19-000001',
    'HeaderNames'  =>  ['Authorization'],
    'HeaderValues' =>  ['Basic QWxhZGRpbjpvcGVuIHNlc2FtZQ=='],
    'Constructor'  =>  'unRegisterAladdinForNetscape',
    'Destructor'   =>  'reRegisterAladdinForNetscape',
   },
```

To configure test-harness for some other web application, rewrite this hashtable. You might prefer to swap in your own stuff, since the authorizing docbase viewer used here is a bit complex to set up. Specify one or more requests, optionally with HTTP headers and optionally with the names of Constructor and Destructor routines that prepare the environment for a test and clean up after it.

To gather baseline data, run test-harness once in baseline mode, like this:

```
perl test-harness baseline
```

Then run it in test mode, like this:

```
perl test-harness test
```

The results, written to *test.htm* in the current directory, can be viewed in browser.

Technology News Metasearcher

The NewsWire module (*http://udell.roninhouse.com/examples/NewsWire.pm*), which requires CPAN's *LWP*, is configured for a half-dozen technology news sites. Because the URLs used to search these sites tend to evolve, as do the result pages sent back from them, you may need to tweak one or more of the sites enumerated in this module.

You can use a simple driver script (*http://udell.roninhouse.com/examples/nw*) to exercise the *NewsWire* module. To run a metasearch for XML stories, put *NewsWire.pm* and nw in a directory and type:

```
perl nw XML > xml-results.html
```

LDAP Search Aggregation

The LDAP aggregation example includes a CGI script (*http://udell.roninhouse.com/ examples/ldap_aggregator*), which is the handler for an HTML form (*http://udell. roninhouse.com/examples/ldap.html*).

Instead of the *Group::LdapGroup* module in Chapter 11, which uses *Net::LDAP*, this example uses *Mozilla::PerLDAP*, which is available from *http://developer. netscape.com/tech/directory/* or directly from the ActiveState site, if you're running Win32 Perl.

To try this example, install *PerLDAP*, then load the form into a browser and try searching for names. Alternatively, if you've already installed *Net::LDAP*, you might want to convert the script to use that module instead.

Kit for Chapter 15

The *dhttp* kit (*http://udell.roninhouse.com/examples/dhttp-v2.tar.gz*) installs by unzipping into any subdirectory on a Unix or NT box equipped with Perl 5. You'll need CPAN's *DBI* and a *DBD* datasource driver if you want to run the apps I've included with *dhttp* or try your own database-oriented apps. You'll also need CPAN's *Net::NNTP* for the HelpDesk (*hd*) app described in Chapter 9.

The *dhttp* distribution divides into the following three parts.

1: dhttp Top-Level Scripts

./dhttp
> The main driver; starts the engine and load the apps

./code_synch
> Demonstrates code replication

./data_synch
   Demonstrates data replication

2: Engine Components

./lib/dhttp/Engine/Server.pm
   The miniature HTTP server

./lib/dhttp/Engine/PubUtils.pm
   Methods visible both to web clients and internal methods

./lib/dhttp/Engine/PrivUtils.pm
   Methods visible only to internal methods

./lib/dhttp/Engine/edit_file.htm
   A system-level template for the *Engine::PubUtils::do_edit_file()* method

3: Application Components

sfa (a sample contact manager)
   ./lib/dhttp/Apps/sfa.pm
      The *sfa* module

   ./lib/dhttp/Apps/sfa/bios/.
      Subdirectory for bios of contacts

   ./lib/dhttp/Apps/sfa/sfa_company.htm
      Template for the company pane

   ./lib/dhttp/Apps/sfa/sfa_contacts.htm
      Template for the contacts pane

   ./lib/dhttp/Apps/sfa/sfa_multi_history.htm
      Template for the contact-history pane

   ./lib/dhttp/Apps/sfa/sfa_ave_company.htm
      Template for forms to add, edit, or view a company record

   ./lib/dhttp/Apps/sfa/sfa_add_contact.htm
      Template for add-contact form

   ./lib/dhttp/Apps/sfa/sfa_add_history.htm
      Template for add-contact-history form

HelpDesk
   ./lib/dhttp/Apps/hd.pm
      The *hd* module

   ./lib/dhttp/Apps/hd/ticknums/.
      Subdirectory for ticket numbers

./lib/dhttp/Apps/hd/home.htm
> Template for home page

./lib/dhttp/Apps/hd/trouble.htm
> Template for trouble-ticket form

./lib/dhttp/Apps/hd/trouble.msg
> Template for trouble ticket as NNTP message

./lib/dhttp/Apps/hd/close.htm
> Template for ticket-closing form

Jobs

./lib/dhttp/Apps/jobs.pm
> The jobs module

./lib/dhttp/Apps/jobs/jobs_ave_job.htm
> Template forms to add, view, or edit job records

Enabling dhttp Applications

The driver script includes commented-out sections for each of the three applications mentioned above: *sfa*, *hd*, and *jobs*:

```
#$main::sfa_dbh = DBI->connect('DBI:ODBC:SFA','','')
#    or die ("sfa_dbh: cannot connect");
#use Apps::sfa;

#$main::jobs_dbh = DBI->connect('DBI:ODBC:JOBS','','')
#    or die ("jobs_dbh: cannot connect");
#use Apps::jobs;

#$main::hd_dbh = DBI->connect('DBI:ODBC:HD','','')
#    or die ("hd_dbh: cannot connect");
#use Apps::hd;
```

You can enable any or all of these applications. In this example, to enable *sfa*, you'd uncomment the first three lines, assuming (on NT) that the ODBC system data-source name (DSN) SFA corresponds to a working data source, which might simply be a *.MDB* file on the local machine, or else an SQL server on the local or some other machine.

Starting dhttp and Running Plug-ins

After unzipping *dhttp* into a home directory, you start it (on port 9191) like this:

```
perl -Ilib/dhttp dhttp 9191
```

To create the tables needed for the *sfa* plug-in, use a browser to request the URL *http://host:port/sfa_makedb*. To start the *sfa* plug-in, request the URL *http://host:port/sfa_home*. Follow a similar procedure for the jobs plugin: first *http://host:port/jobs_makedb*, then *http://host:port/jobs_home*.

Testing Code Replication

The example in Chapter 15, *Distributed HTTP*, showed how the code_synch script, which is the root directory of the *dhttp* distribution, uses the engine's *do_update_ sub* method to update a method in the *sfa* module. To try this, make sure sfa is running, then adjust the host and port variables in the script and run code_synch.

Testing Data Replication

If you're running two or more instances of the *jobs* plug-in, you can try the data replication example shown in Chapter 15. If, for example, *dhttp* is running on the hosts `jon_linux` and `jon_nt`, each with a live instance of `jobs`, then the `$hosts` structure in data_synch might look like this:

```
my $hosts =
    {
    jon_nt   =>
        {
        port     => 9191,
        conn     => 'DBI:ODBC:JOBS',
        dbuser   => '',
        dbpw     => '',
        datedelim => '#',
        },
    jon_linux  =>
        {
        port     => 9191,
        conn     => $tc->escape('DBI:Solid:tcp 1313'),
        dbuser   => 'dba',
        dbpw     => 'dba',
        datedelim => '\'',
        },
    };
```

When you run data_synch, it visits each of the hosts mentioned in `$hosts` and synchronizes the tables used by the jobs plug-in.

This mechanism depends on a special discipline observed by the `jobs` plug-in. Every URL generated by the module includes three elements: `host`, `port`, and `user`. We'll see why `host` and `port` are needed in the next section on proxying and encryption. Here, let's focus on why *hd* requires the `user` element.

Suppose you're running *dhttp* on the host `your_dhttp`, and I'm running it on `my_ dhttp`. That means that to edit my local database, I'll do this:

```
http://my_dhttp:9191/jobs_home?host=my_dhttp&port=9191&user=jon
```

Likewise, to edit your local database, you'll do this:

```
http://your_dhttp:9191/jobs_home?host=your_dhttp&port=9191&user=you
```

But suppose I need to work, remotely, in your database. In that case, I'll do this:

```
http://your_dhttp:9191/jobs_home?host=your_dhttp&port=9191&user=jon
```

Because `jobs` threads `user=jon` through all subsequent interactions issuing from this URL, my edits in your database are stamped with my name and are distinct from your edits in your database, which are stamped with your name.

Testing Proxying and Encryption

Here's an alternate way for me to edit your *jobs* database:

```
http://my_dhttp:9191/jobs_home?host=your_dhttp&port=9191&user=jon
```

In this case, I point my browser at *my* instance of *dhttp*, not yours. Noticing that the destination host (`your_dhttp`) differs from the source host (`my_dhttp`), the *Engine::Server* module switches into proxying and encryption mode. That is, `my_dhttp` uses web-client calls to relay the browser's HTTP requests, in encrypted form, to `your_dhttp`, which decrypts the requests.

In this mode, the client instance of *dhttp* (proxying for my browser) includes the HTTP header `Remote-Dhttp: my_dhttp:9191` with its requests. When the server instance notices this header, it encrypts its responses and sets the variable `$main::other_hostname`.

To support this mode, a *dhttp* plug-in application has to observe two rules. First, it has to thread the CGI variables `host` and `port` through all of its methods and HTML/JavaScript templates. Second, it has to call *transmit()* instead of *print()*. Here is *Engine::PrivUtils::transmit()*, which decides whether to send plain-text or encrypted responses:

```
sub transmit
    {
    my ($output) = @_;
    if ($main::other_hostname ne '')
        {
        my $cipher = dhttp_encrypt($output,length($output));
        print escape("DHTTPCIPHER$cipher");
        }
    else
        {
        print "$output";
        }
    }
```

Basic Versus Advanced Encryption

The *dhttp* distribution includes only a basic, proof-of-concept form of encryption. It reverses strings, as in the following code.

```
sub dhttp_encrypt
    {
    my ($s) = @_;
    my $rev = reverse($s);
    return $rev;
    }

sub dhttp_decrypt
    {
    my ($s) = @_;
    my $rev = reverse($s);
    return $rev;
    }
```

As mentioned in Chapter 15, you can instead use any symmetrical technique; for example, I have tested this scheme using Blowfish. Even so, the implementation was cryptographically naive. Because *dhttp* encrypts requests and responses a line at a time, it's quite obvious which requests contain known strings like `HTTP/1.0` and `GET /sfa_home`. And there are no provisions for secure key exchange.

The encrypting mode of *dhttp* is really intended only to suggest the possibilities inherent in a model of computing in which HTTP peers are pervasive and act simultaneously as servers and proxies.

B

Internet RFCs: A Groupware Perspective

Since 1969, the loosely organized Internet Engineering Task Force (IETF) has documented the standards that govern the Internet in a format called Request for Comment (RFC). Thirty years later, in August 1999, the series extended to 2,648 RFCs. The Internet groupware technologies discussed in this book are defined, for the most part, in this remarkable collection of documents. This appendix traces the evolution of email, news, the Web, security, directory services, and various metadata initiatives to their roots in the RFC series. You can find the RFCs in many places on the Web including the home page of the IETF (*http://www.ietf.org/*) and, in a more easily navigable and searchable form, at *http://www.faqs.org/*.

The Internet standards process moves slowly, and it surprises some people to learn that many seemingly well-established parts of the Internet's infrastructure—for example, LDAP, IMAP, and S/MIME—are as yet merely proposed standards. Even such stalwarts as Dynamic Host Configuration Protocol (DHCP) and MIME are draft, not yet official standards.

We think of the RFCs as prescriptive, and indeed they're full of legalistic phrases like "an implementation SHALL..." There is even an RFC (2119, Key words for use in RFCs to Indicate Requirement Levels) that defines what RFCs mean by terms like SHALL, SHOULD, and MAY. But in truth the RFCs function not so much as a body of law but rather as a kind of groupware docbase, embedded in a process of ongoing contribution and review. The IETF is, in fact, one of the greatest groupware stories of all time. The Internet is fundamentally a collaborative project, so perhaps we shouldn't be surprised to find that some of its earliest technologies—such as email and news—remain some of the most mature, effective, and flexible groupware tools.

Email: Core Infrastructure

The seminal document that defines the basic plumbing of Internet email is RFC821 (August 1982, Simple Mail Transfer Protocol). It's amazing to think that so much of the world's communication now depends on a protocol in which one machine contacts another and says, in plain ASCII, "Hello, I have mail for Joe, here is the message." It seems too simple, but that's why it works so well.

A series of RFCs from RFC521 (September 1973, Standardizing Network Mail Headers) to RFC822 (August 1982, Standard for the Format of ARPA Internet Text Messages) traces the evolution of mail headers. These headers govern the delivery of Internet mail. More broadly, RFC822 formalizes the notion of a semistructured document that combines a structured header with a free-form body. In mailboxes, listserv archives, and newsgroups, these kinds of documents store vast quantities of intellectual capital.

Note that RFC822 specifies a mechanism for extending the mail header. A formal extension field, defined in a subsequent RFC, can carry extra metadata. For example, RFC2369 (July 1998, The Use of URLs as Meta-Syntax for Core Mail List Commands and their Transport through Message Header Fields) defines how email headers can document listserv commands, as shown in this fragment sent by the Lyris list server:

```
List-Software: Lyris Server version 3.0
List-Subscribe: <mailto:subscribe-perl-xml@lyris.activestate.com>
List-Owner: <mailto:owner-perl-xml@lyris.activestate.com>
X-List-Host: ActiveState Tool Corp. <http://www.activestate.com>
```

The first three headers in this example are what RFC822 calls *extension fields*. These are expected to be defined in another RFC (in this case, RFC2369) and must not begin with "X-". The fourth header is what RFC822 calls a *user-defined field*. These are not defined in another RFC, typically begin with "X-", and may be preempted by published extensions.

This mechanism suggests one way to create Internet-style custom messages. For example, an email or news message about the subject of custom message headers might categorize itself like this:

```
X-MetadataDomain: Internet
X-MetadataCategory: messaging
X-MetadataRefs: RFC822, RFC2369
```

These headers could be used by messaging clients, and by the tools that build and manage message archives, to organize messages using a richer metadata scheme than `Author:`, `Subject:`, `Date:`.

An experimental application that uses these headers should also support—and propose in an RFC—formal variants that could become standard extension fields:

```
MetadataDomain: Internet
MetadataCategory: messaging
MetadataRefs: RFC822, RFC2369
```

Quite a few RFCs define headers that can appear in Internet messages. RFC2076 (February 1997, Common Internet Message Headers) usefully summarizes these various headers.

Email: Fetching and Managing Messages

The POP mechanism is defined in a long series of documents beginning with RFC918 (October 1984, Post Office Protocol) and culminating in RFC1939 (May 1996, Post Office Protocol - Version 3). There is also an obscure companion to RFC1081, RFC1082 (November 1988, Post Office Protocol - Version 3, Extended Service Offerings), that defines a way to use POP for group discussion, in a manner analogous to the IMAP public folder. The author of RFC1082 wrote:

> Since mailers and user agents first crawled out of the primordial ARPAnet, the value of discussion groups have been appreciated (though their implementation has not always been well-understood).

Although never widely implemented, RFC1082 is another illustration of a major theme of this book: the close but problematic relationship between Internet mail and conferencing.

IMAP has also evolved through a long series of documents, from RFC1064 (July 1988, Interactive Mail Access Protocol - Version 2) to RFC2060 (December 1996, Internet Message Access Protocol - Version 4rev1). Confusingly, the expansion of the IMAP acronym changed along the way. Originally intended mainly for online use—that is, while connected to a mail server—IMAP evolved into a superset protocol that also supports disconnected use à la POP.

Because there was some confusion about how an IMAP client locates and gains access to shared mailboxes (public folders) on an IMAP server, RFC2342 (May 1998, IMAP4 Namespace) spells out the mechanism. Said the authors of RFC2342, "This allows a client to avoid much of the manual user configuration that is now necessary when mixing and matching IMAP4 clients and servers."

Email: Semistructured Documents

The notion that messages carry semistructured data is central to this book. RFC934 (January 1985, Proposed Standard for Message Encapsulation) introduces the idea of a message body that is logically divided into regions separated by an "encapsulation boundary." This idea was elaborated in a series of MIME RFCs, from RFC1341 (June 1992, MIME (Multipurpose Internet Mail Extensions) to RFC2045 (November 1996, MIME (Multipurpose Internet Mail Extensions) Part One: Format of Internet Message Bodies).

This series spells out the basic idea of MIME: a `Content-Type:` header can specify that a message body contains structured text, image data, other application-specific data, or a composite of these types.

The author of RFC1049 (March 1988, A Content-Type Header Field for Internet Messages) wrote, "A standardized Content-Type field allows mail reading systems to automatically identify the type of a structured message body and to process it for display accordingly." This idea would become central not only to mailers and newsreaders, which use the `Content-Type:` header to identify and process rich content and attachments, but also to browsers. RFC2046 (November 1996, Multipurpose Internet Mail Extensions (MIME) Part Two: Media Types) extended and revised RFC1049.

RFC2048 (November 1996, Multipurpose Internet Mail Extensions (MIME) Part Four: Registration Procedures) describes rules and procedures for registering new MIME content types.

A series beginning with RFC1872 (December 1995, The MIME Multipart/Related Content-Type) and ending with RFC2387 (August 1998, same title) defines how email programs can format compound documents made of interrelated parts. It suggests the use of the cid: (Content-ID) URL scheme, supported in modern HTML-aware mailreaders, as a way to form intradocument links.

RFC1873 (December 1995, Message/External-Body Content-ID Access Type), a companion to RFC1872, defines the use of a `Content-ID:` header as a mechanism for intradocument references.

To illustrate how this can work, suppose I drag an image into an HTML mail message I'm writing with Netscape Composer. To the recipient, it appears that the image is embedded within the text, like this:

```
As you can see in this picture:

+----------+
| picture  |
+----------+

the graphic is shown inline.
```

If you inspect the body of such a message, you'll see how the MIME multipart/related Content-Type, the cid: protocol, and the `Content-ID:` header interact:

```
Content-Type: multipart/related;
 boundary="------------9F32153EFCC9C5CAFE0BDFE9"


--------------9F32153EFCC9C5CAFE0BDFE9
Content-Type: text/html; charset=us-ascii
Content-Transfer-Encoding: 7bit

<!doctype html public "-//w3c//dtd html 4.0 transitional//en">
<html>
As you can see in this picture:
<p><img SRC="cid:part1.37AF2335.CC7D920@monad.net" ALT=""
BORDER=0 height=62 width=150>
<p>the graphic is shown inline.

--------------9F32153EFCC9C5CAFE0BDFE9
Content-Type: image/jpeg
Content-ID: <part1.37AF2335.CC7D920@monad.net>
Content-Transfer-Encoding: base64
Content-Disposition: inline; filename="C:\TEMP\nsmailN4.jpeg"
```

```
/9j/4AAQSkZJRgABAgEASABIAAD/7QE0UGhvdG9zaG9wIDMuMAA4QklNA+0AAAAAABAASAAA
AAEAAQBIAAAAAQABOEJJTQPzAAAAAAAIAAAAAAAAAA4QklNJxAAAAAAAAoAAQAAAAAAAAC
OEJJTQP1AAAAAABIAC9mZgABAGxmZgAGAAAAAAABAC9mZgABAKGZmgAGAAAAAAABADIAAAAB
AFoAAAAGAAAAAAABADUAAAABAC0AAAAGAAAAAAABOEJJTQP4AAAAAABwAAD//////////////
////////////A+gAAAA//////////////////////////wPoAAAAP//////////
```

Another series, from RFC1523 (September 1993, The text/enriched MIME Content-Type) to RFC1896 (February 1996, same title) documents a predecessor to HTML email. It defines a simple, HTML-like tag language used to format ASCII text messages:

```
<bold>Now</bold> is the time for
<italic>all</italic> good men
```

The mechanism supporting HTML email is described in RFC2110 (March 1997, MIME E-Mail Encapsulation of Aggregate Documents), which was superseded by RFC2557 (March 1999, MIME Encapsulation of Aggregate Documents, such as HTML (MHTML)). Say the authors of RFC2557:

> In order to transfer a complete HTML multimedia document in a single e-mail message, it is necessary to: a) aggregate a text/html root resource and all of the subsidiary resources it references into a single composite message structure, and b) define a means by which URIs in the text/html root can reference subsidiary resources within that composite message structure.

HTML email messages need to be able to refer, by means of hyperlinks, to messages and to parts of messages. The mid: and cid: URL schemes defined in RFC2392 (August 1998, Content-ID and Message-ID Uniform Resource Locators) serve this purpose.

Email: Encryption and Authentication

A series that begins with RFC1040 (January 1988, Privacy Enhancement for Internet Electronic Mail: Part I—Message Encipherment and Authentication Procedures) and culminates in RFC1421 (February 1993, same title) defines protocol extensions and processing procedures used to encrypt and authenticate RFC822 messages. The base64 encoding scheme, used in many Internet protocols to represent binary data using printable ASCII characters, is defined here.

RFC1114 (August 1989, Privacy Enhancement for Internet Electronic Mail: Part II—Certificate-Based Key Management), superseded by RFC1422 (February 1993, same title) defines a public-key infrastructure that supports message encryption and authentication. It does so by interpreting the CCITT 1988 Recommendation X.509 certificate mechanism "to serve the needs of privacy-enhanced mail in the Internet environment."

I sign all my email messages, and when I do they carry the Multipart/Signed `Content-Type:` header defined in RFC1847 (October 1995, Security Multiparts for MIME: Multipart/Signed and Multipart/Encrypted).

RFC1991 (August 1996, PGP Message Exchange Formats) describes the use of PGP to encrypt and authenticate messages. RFC2015 (October 1996, MIME Security with Pretty Good Privacy (PGP)) defines the MIME content types application/pgp-encrypted, application/pgp-signature and application/pgp-keys. It specifies how to use MIME to format messages that are signed and/or encrypted using PGP.

A set of documents including RFC2632 (June 1999, S/MIME Version 3 Certificate Handling), RFC2633 (June 1999, S/MIME Version 3 Message Specification), and RFC2634 (June 1999, Enhanced Security Services for S/MIME) defines Secure/Multipurpose Internet Mail Extensions (S/MIME). This mechanism for encrypting, signing, and ensuring the integrity of messages is supported in the Version 4.x (and later) Netscape and Microsoft mailreaders. RFC2634 proposes optional extensions for:

* Signed receipts
* Security labels
* Secure mailing lists
* Signing certificates

A scheme for authenticated mailbox access is proposed in RFC1731 (December 1994, IMAP4 Authentication Mechanisms) and RFC1734 (December 1994, POP4 AUTHentication Mechanisms). These RFCs also define how clients and servers can agree on a mechanism for encrypting a session.

In the Web realm, RFC2069 (January 1997, An Extension to HTTP : Digest Access Authentication) seeks a middle ground between HTTP authentication, which is simple but vulnerable, and encryption technologies (such as SSL) that are far safer but require a heavy security infrastructure. RFC2095 (IMAP/POP AUTHorize Extension for Simple Challenge/Response) attempts to do the same for IMAP and POP authentication: it defines a way to encrypt just the credentials used in authentication.

"There is a strong desire in the IETF to eliminate the transmission of clear-text passwords over unencrypted channels," say the authors of RFC2595 (June 1999, Using TLS with IMAP, POP3, and ACAP). This RFC governs the use of Transport Layer Security (TLS), SSL's successor, to encrypt connections to IMAP, POP, and Application Configuration Access Protocol (ACAP) servers. Note that the mailreaders bundled with the Microsoft and Netscape 4.x browsers can connect, using SSL, to secure IMAP (and, in the case of Outlook Express, POP) servers.

News Infrastructure

RFC850 (June 1983, Standard for Interchange of USENET Messages), superseded by RFC1036 (December 1987, same title) specifies that USENET (news) messages must be formatted as valid Internet mail messages (RFC822) and must also include—in addition to RFC822's required `Date:` and `From:`—the extension fields `Newsgroups:`, `Subject:`, `Message-ID:`, and `Path:`.

RFC977 (February 1986, Network News Transfer Protocol) spells out the commands sent by NNTP clients to inquire about and fetch articles (news messages), the replication protocol between NNTP servers, and the response codes sent by NNTP servers.

Web: Core Infrastructure

RFC1630 (June 1994, Universal Resource Identifiers in WWW) introduces three fundamental concepts:

Universal Resource Identifier (URI)
> A general-purpose namespace mechanism

Uniform Resource Locator (URL)
> An instance of a URI that is the address of some resource, accessible by means of a protocol such as HTTP or NNTP

Uniform Resource Name (URN)
> An instance of a URI that, unlike a fragile URL, is guaranteed to remain always available

RFC1736 (February 1995, Functional Recommendations for Internet Resource Locators) recommends that URL schemes should be:

- Global in scope

- Readily parseable

- Human readable and writable

- Extensible

RFC1738 (December 1994, Uniform Resource Locators (URL)) describes common URL schemes, including http:, news:, mailto:, and file:. RFC1808 ( June 1995, Relative Uniform Resource Locators) defines the rules for relative URLs that are fully qualified with reference to a stated or implied base URL.

RFC2396 (August 1998, Uniform Resource Identifiers (URI): Generic Syntax) subsumes RFC1738 and RFC1808, defining "a single generic syntax for all URI." A URI, say the authors, "can be further classifed as a name, a locator, or both." It reiterates RFC1630's URI/URL/URN taxonomy: "A URN differs from a URL in that its primary purpose is persistent labeling of a resource with an identifier."

The URL/URN distinction can be misleading. A World Wide Web Consortium (W3C) document entitled "Cool URIs don't change" (*http://www.w3.org/Provider/ Style/URI*) notes astutely:

> Some seem to think that because there is research about namespaces which will be more persistent, that they can be as lax about dangling links as they like as 'URNs will fix all that'. If you are one of these folks, then allow me to disillusion you.

This W3C document suggests a number of ways that you can (and should) design URL namespaces that you'll be able to maintain over time, even as underlying storage and organizational patterns evolve.

RFC1945 (May 1996, Hypertext Transfer Protocol—HTTP/1.0) and its successor, RFC2616 (June 1999, Hypertext Transfer Protocol— HTTP/1.1), document the basic plumbing of the Web. These RFCs describe: how clients connect to servers, issue requests, and optionally authenticate; the basic request types (GET, HEAD, POST); the headers sent by clients and servers; mechanisms for caching and proxying.

RFC2109 (February 1997, HTTP State Management Mechanisms) defines how cookies work. It specifies the syntax and use of the `Set-Cookie:` header that a server uses to plant a cookie on a browser and the `Cookie:` header that a browser uses to send a cookie back to a server.

As discussed earlier in the section "Email: Core Infrastructure", the mechanisms described in RFC2518 (February 1999, HTTP Extensions for Distributed Authoring—WEBDAV) could in theory support a new generation of collaborative tools that would supersede many of the technologies discussed in this book. Unlike HTTP/1.1, which encodes method parameters in HTTP headers, WebDAV requests are formatted in XML. The protocol includes support for locking, getting and setting of properties, defining collections, and copying or moving individual objects or entire subtrees.

Web: HTML

RFC1866 (November 1995, Hypertext Markup Language - 2.0) is the first HTML-related RFC. Says the W3C, "It set the standard for core HTML features based upon current practice in 1994." More recent HTML specifications—for HTML 3.2 and 4.0—are not part of the RFC set but can be found on the W3C site (*http://www.w3c.org/*).

The mechanism described in RFC1867 (November 1995, Form-based File Upload in HTML) remains one of the primary tools used to enable a two-way flow of data in web-based systems. RFC1867 also suggests the idea, later adopted in the HTML standard, that forms can use `ACTION=mailto:` to transmit field data by way of email.

Web: URL Schemes

A series of RFCs document URL schemes based on a variety of protocols. These include:

RFC2255 (December 1996, The LDAP URL Format)
Enables web-style access to LDAP servers. For example, my entry in the Switchboard directory is accessible, from a browser, using the URL:

```
ldap://ldap.switchboard.com/
cn%3DJon%20Udell%2C%20ou%3DZEDHINGL%2C%20o%3Dswitchboard%2C%20c%3DUS
```

RFC2192 (September 1997, IMAP URL Scheme)
Defines an imap: URL scheme that supports web-style references to objects (e.g., messages) that live on IMAP servers.

RFC2368 (July 1998, The mailto URL Scheme)
Extends the mailto: scheme defined in RFC1738, enabling the message composition and filtering techniques that we saw in Chapter 4, *Information-Management Strategies for Groupware Users* and Chapter 9, *Conferencing Applications*.

RFC2384 (August 1998, The POP URL Scheme)
According to RFC2384, "A POP3 mailbox (like an [IMAP4] mailbox) is a network resource, and URLs are a widely supported generalized representation of network resources. A means of specifying a POP3 mailbox as a URL will likely be useful in many programs and protocols."

Finally, here's a bit of web trivia. If you store the following text in a file:

```
<IMG
    SRC="data:image/gif;base64,R0lGODdhMAAwAPAAAAAAAP///ywAAAAAMAAw
    AAAC8IyPqcvt3wCcDkiLc7C0qwyGHhSWpjQu5yqmCYsapyuvUU1vONmOZtfzgFz
    ByTB1OQgxOR0TqBQejhRNzOfkVJ+5YiUqrXF5Y5lKh/DeuNcP5yLWGsEbtLiOSp
    a/TPg7JpJHxyendzWTBfX0cxOnKPjgBzi4diinWGdkF8kjdfnycQZXZeYGejmJl
    ZeGl9i2icVqaNVailT6F5iJ90m6mvuTS4OK05M0vDk0Q4XUtwvKOzrcd3iq9uis
    F81M1OIcR71EewwcLp7tuNNkM3uNna3F2JQFo97Vriy/X14/f1cf5VWzXyym7PH
    hhx4dbgYKAAA7"
    ALT="Larry">
```

and then view the file in a Netscape browser, you'll see a (grainy) picture of Larry Masinter, the author of RFC2397 (August 1998, The "data" URL scheme). Internet Explorer, however, does not support this approach to compound documents in HTML.

Calendaring/Scheduling

RFC2445 (November 1998, Internet Calendaring and Scheduling Core Object Specification (iCalendar)) defines a common format for the exchange of calendaring and scheduling information across the Internet. The Netscape Calendar export example in Chapter 10, *Groupware Servlets*, uses this format.

RFC2446 (November 1998, iCalendar Transport-Independent Interoperability Protocol (iTIP): Scheduling Events, BusyTime, To-dos and Journal Entries) describes how calendaring systems work with calendar objects; it defines verbs such as PUB-LISH, REQUEST, REPLY, COUNTER (that is, to counterpropose an alternate meeting time), and DECLINE-COUNTER (to decline such a counterproposal).

RFC2447 (iCalendar Message-based Interoperability Protocol (iMIP)) defines how to transport calendar objects in email messages using the MIME type text/calendar.

Chat

RFC1459 (May 1993, Internet Relay Chat Protocol) defines IRC channels, message formats, and communication models.

Security

RFC1244 (July 1991, Site Security Handbook) surveys a range of issues that remain paramount concerns for a groupware developer/administrator who straddles the intranet/Internet boundary. RFC1281 (November 1991, Guidelines for the Secure Operation of the Internet), which covers some of the same ground, stresses that "users are individually accountable for their own behavior" and "have a responsibility to employ available security mechanisms and procedures for protecting their own data."

RFC2069 (January 1997, An Extension to HTTP : Digest Access Authentication) defines a mechanism like Windows NT's Challenge/Response protocol. This mechanism enables an HTTP client to authenticate to a server using encrypted rather than cleartext credentials. Although implemented in some web servers, it has never been supported in mainstream browsers.

RFC2617 (June 1999, HTTP Authentication: Basic and Digest Authentication) describes the original HTTP basic authentication scheme and updates RFC2069's description of digest authentication.

Say the authors of RFC2246 (January 1999, The TLS Protocol Version 1.0):

> This document and the TLS protocol itself are based on the SSL 3.0 Protocol Specification as published by Netscape. The differences between this protocol and SSL 3.0 are not dramatic, but they are significant enough that TLS 1.0 and SSL 3.0 do not interoperate (although TLS 1.0 does incorporate a mechanism by which a TLS implementation can back down to SSL 3.0).

For more information on Transport Layer Security (TLS) see *http://www.certicom. com/faqs/tls_ssl_faq.txt*, which describes TLS as "effectively SSL 3.1, made official by the IETF" and which points to a number of related initiatives.

Public Key Infrastructure (PKI)

RFC2459 (January 1999, Internet X.509 Public Key Infrastructure - Certificate and CRL Profile) describes the X.509 v3 certificate format and X.509 v2 Certificate Revocation List (CRL). RFC2510 (March 1999, Internet X.509 Public Key Infrastructure - Certificate Management Protocols) describes PKI management protocols—it is, in effect, a guide to the operation of a Certificate Authority. RFC2511 (March 1999, Internet X.509 Certificate Request Message Format) defines the format of a Certificate Request Message. RFC2527 (March 1999, Internet X.509 Public Key Infrastructure - Certificate Policy and Certification Practices Framework) offers a framework that a Certificate Authority can use to formulate and articulate its policies.

These RFCs govern the infrastructure that supports the secure news servers demonstrated in Chapter 13, *Deploying NNTP Discussion Servers*.

Directory Services

RFC1034 (November 1987, Domain Names - Concepts and Facilities) discusses the architecture of the DNS, and RFC1035 (November 1987, Domain Names— Implementation and Specification) spells out the implementation details.

Recognizing that the DNS is the only truly global Internet directory but that it could never support per-resource URL resolution, RFC2168 (June 1996, Resolution of Uniform Resource Identifiers, Using the Domain Name System) proposes a hybrid approach: a DNS resource record called Naming Authority Pointer (NAPTR) that maps parts of URIs to domain names. The idea is that a URN can refer, through DNS, to a resolver that produces an address.

LDAP's purpose was to lower the "high cost-of-entry" that had prevented the widespread use of X.500-style directory services on the Internet. The core protocol is defined in a series that begins with RFC1487 (July 1993, X.500 Lightweight Directory Access Protocol) and ends with RFC2251 (December 1997, Lightweight Directory Access Protocol (v3)). RFC2252 (December 1997, Lightweight Directory Access Protocol (v3): Attribute Syntax Definitions) defines "the framework for developing schemas for directories accessible via the Lightweight Directory Access Protocol." RFC2254 (December 1997, The String Representation of LDAP Search Filters) defines the LDAP query language illustrated in Chapter 14, *Automating Internet Components.*

Despite LDAP's success, the vision of a consolidated Internet white pages service remains elusive. There are many public LDAP directories, but none are authoritative, and there's no real coordination among them. RFC1684 (August 1994, Introduction to White Pages Services Based on X.500) and RFC2218 (October 1997, A Common Schema for the Internet White Pages Service) explore why and how to create an Internet white pages service.

RFC2307 (March 1998, An Approach for Using LDAP as a Network Information Service) suggests that an LDAP directory can unify the lookup of a number of different kinds of intranet entities, including users and groups, email aliases, IP services, and shared filesystems.

RFC2538 (March 1999, Storing Certificates in the Domain Name System (DNS)) suggests that the DNS can support key-management activities. Say its authors, "Cryptographic public keys are frequently published and their authenticity demonstrated by certificates. A CERT resource record (RR) is defined so that such certificates and related certificate revocation lists can be stored in the Domain Name System (DNS)." RFC2587 (June 1999, Internet X.509 Public Key Infrastructure - LDAPv2 Schema) explores the same idea but for LDAP rather than DNS.

RFC2425 (September 1998, A MIME Content-Type for Directory Information) defines the text/directory MIME type as a container for directory information. No specific directory implementation is assumed. Examples show how to encapsulate directory entries in both LDIF and vCard formats. RFC2426 (September 1998, vCard MIME Directory Profile) defines the "vCard profile," which captures the information that typically appears on a business card. See the Internet Mail Consortium (*http://www/pdi.org/*) for more on vCard.

Metadata and Resource Discovery

RFC1807 (July 1995, A format for Bibliographic Records) defines a fielded text format for exchanging bibliographic records in email messages. Here's part of a sample record:

```
BIB-VERSION:: CS-TR-v2.0
          ID:: OUKS//CS-TR-91-123
       ENTRY:: January 15, 1992
ORGANIZATION:: Oceanview University, Kansas, Computer Science
       TITLE:: The Computerization of Oceanview with High
               Speed Fiber Optics Communication
        TYPE:: Technical Report
    REVISION:: 2, FTP retrieval information added
      AUTHOR:: Finnegan, James A.
```

Instead of defining custom headers, this approach extends the metadata capability of Internet messages by defining a structured payload. If you were to write this kind of RFC nowadays, you'd probaby use XML to define the structure of the payload.

RFC1464 (May 1993, Using the Domain Name System to Store Arbitrary String Attributes) takes another approach to Internet-based storage and retrieval of metadata. This document proposes the use of name=value pairs in the DNS TXT resource record defined in RFC1035. There's more than one way to do things!

RFC1689 (August 1994, A Status Report on Networked Information Retrieval: Tools and Groups) captures the emergence of the Web from a primordial soup of ancestral technologies: Archie, Veronica, gopher, and WAIS.

The experimental RFC2016 (October 1996, Uniform Resource Agents (URAs)) explores the general idea underlying metasearch tools such as the ones discussed in Chapter 14.

Chapter 8, *Organizing Search Results*, points out that metadata-based field indexing is a key complement to full-text indexing. RFC2413 (September 1998, Dublin Core Metadata for Resource Discovery) formalizes a basic metadata scheme that represents the consensus of a team of librarians, researchers, and text-markup experts.

Miscellaneous

Many of the themes in Part I echo recommendations that appear in RFC1855 (October 1995, Netiquette Guidelines). This document discusses one-to-one and one-to-many communication, information layering and packaging, and much more.

After 30 years of nroff-formatted RFCs (see RFC2223, Instructions to RFC Authors, for details), RFC2629 (June 1999, Writing I-Ds and RFCs using XML) proposes to leapfrog into the next-generation markup language, XML. This RFC includes a DTD for writing RFCs. How to view them? "Browsers that support either XSL or Cascading Style Sheets (CSS) are able to view the source file directly. At present, the author doesn't use any of these browsers, instead converting source files to either text or HTML."

Index

About the Author

Jon Udell was *BYTE Magazine*'s executive editor for new media, the architect of the original *www.byte.com*, and author of *Byte*'s Web Project column. He's now an independent Web/Internet consultant and a freelance author whose work appears in a number of print and online publications. His home page is *http://udell.roninhouse.com/*.

Colophon

Our look is the result of reader comments, our own experimentation, and feedback from distribution channels. Distinctive covers complement our distinctive approach to technical topics, breathing personality and life into potentially dry subjects.

The animals on the cover of *Practical Internet Groupware* are seals and sea lions. Seals and sea lions are related; both are marine mammals belonging to the order Pinnipedia. Sea lions, along with fur seals, are members of the eared seal family. Eared seals, as their name implies, have external ears on either side of the head. These ears are covered by a small flap. All other seals, or true seals, lack external ears, having only small, wrinkled openings where their ears would otherwise be. Another principle difference between eared seals and true seals is the functionality of their rear flippers. Eared seals can turn their rear flippers forward in order to move about on land. True seals cannot, and can move on land only by rolling, sliding, or wriggling from place to place. Despite the awkwardness of both seals and sea lions on land, both swim very gracefully using undulating motions of their front flippers. Fish and squid are the main staples of the seal and sea lion diet. These mammals can dive to great depths—up to 2,000 feet in some species—in search of food.

Seals and sea lions have long been hunted for their blubber and their fur. There are eighteen living species of seal and four major species of sea lion still in existence. Some species are endangered or threatened. All are currently protected.

Jeffrey Liggett was the production editor for *Practical Internet Groupware*; Deborah English was the proofreader; Maureen Dempsey, Claire Cloutier LeBlanc, and Abigail Myers provided quality control. Robert Romano and Rhon Porter created the illustrations using Adobe Photoshop 5 and Macromedia FreeHand 8. Chris Maden, Erik Ray, and Mike Sierra provided technical support. Brenda Miller wrote the index.

Edie Freedman designed the cover of this book, using a 19th-century engraving from the Dover Pictorial Archive. Kathleen Wilson produced the cover layout with

QuarkXPress 3.32 using the ITC Garamond font. Whenever possible, our books use RepKover™, a durable and flexible lay-flat binding. If the page count exceeds RepKover's limit, perfect binding is used.

Alicia Cech designed the interior layout based on a series design by Nancy Priest. The inside layout was implemented in FrameMaker 5.5.6 by Mike Sierra. The text and heading fonts are ITC Garamond Light and Garamond Book. This colophon was written by Clairemarie Fisher O'Leary.

How to stay in touch with O'Reilly

1. Visit Our Award-Winning Web Site

http://www.oreilly.com/

★ "Top 100 Sites on the Web" —*PC Magazine*
★ "Top 5% Web sites" —*Point Communications*
★ "3-Star site" —*The McKinley Group*

Our web site contains a library of comprehensive product information (including book excerpts and tables of contents), downloadable software, background articles, interviews with technology leaders, links to relevant sites, book cover art, and more. File us in your Bookmarks or Hotlist!

2. Join Our Email Mailing Lists

New Product Releases

To receive automatic email with brief descriptions of all new O'Reilly products as they are released, send email to:
listproc@online.oreilly.com
Put the following information in the first line of your message (*not* in the Subject field):
subscribe oreilly-news

O'Reilly Events

If you'd also like us to send information about trade show events, special promotions, and other O'Reilly events, send email to:
listproc@online.oreilly.com
Put the following information in the first line of your message (*not* in the Subject field):
subscribe oreilly-events

3. Get Examples from Our Books via FTP

There are two ways to access an archive of example files from our books:

Regular FTP

- ftp to:
  ftp.oreilly.com
  (login: anonymous
  password: your email address)
- Point your web browser to:
  ftp://ftp.oreilly.com/

FTPMAIL

- Send an email message to:
  ftpmail@online.oreilly.com
  (Write "help" in the message body)

4. Contact Us via Email

order@oreilly.com
To place a book or software order online. Good for North American and international customers.

subscriptions@oreilly.com
To place an order for any of our newsletters or periodicals.

books@oreilly.com
General questions about any of our books.

software@oreilly.com
For general questions and product information about our software. Check out O'Reilly Software Online at **http://software.oreilly.com/** for software and technical support information. Registered O'Reilly software users send your questions to: **website-support@oreilly.com**

cs@oreilly.com
For answers to problems regarding your order or our products.

booktech@oreilly.com
For book content technical questions or corrections.

proposals@oreilly.com
To submit new book or software proposals to our editors and product managers.

international@oreilly.com
For information about our international distributors or translation queries. For a list of our distributors outside of North America check out:
http://www.oreilly.com/www/order/country.html

O'Reilly & Associates, Inc.
101 Morris Street, Sebastopol, CA 95472 USA
TEL   707-829-0515 or 800-998-9938
            (6am to 5pm PST)
FAX   707-829-0104

Titles from O'Reilly

WEB

Advanced Perl Programming
Apache: The Definitive Guide,
    2nd Edition
ASP in a Nutshell
Building Your Own Web Conferences
Building Your Own Website™
CGI Programming with Perl
Designing with JavaScript
Dynamic HTML:
    The Definitive Reference
Frontier: The Definitive Guide
HTML: The Definitive Guide,
    3rd Edition
Information Architecture
    for the World Wide Web
JavaScript Pocket Reference
JavaScript: The Definitive Guide,
    3rd Edition
Learning VB Script
Photoshop for the Web
WebMaster in a Nutshell
WebMaster in a Nutshell,
    Deluxe Edition
Web Design in a Nutshell
Web Navigation:
    Designing the User Experience
Web Performance Tuning
Web Security & Commerce
Writing Apache Modules

PERL

Learning Perl, 2nd Edition
Learning Perl for Win32 Systems
Learning Perl/TK
Mastering Algorithms with Perl
Mastering Regular Expressions
Perl5 Pocket Reference, 2nd Edition
Perl Cookbook
Perl in a Nutshell
Perl Resource Kit—UNIX Edition
Perl Resource Kit—Win32 Edition
Perl/TK Pocket Reference
Programming Perl, 2nd Edition
Web Client Programming with Perl

GRAPHICS & MULTIMEDIA

Director in a Nutshell
Encyclopedia of Graphics
    File Formats, 2nd Edition
Lingo in a Nutshell
Photoshop in a Nutshell
QuarkXPress in a Nutshell

USING THE INTERNET

AOL in a Nutshell
Internet in a Nutshell
Smileys
The Whole Internet for Windows95
The Whole Internet:
    The Next Generation
The Whole Internet
    User's Guide & Catalog

JAVA SERIES

Database Programming with
    JDBC and Java
Developing Java Beans
Exploring Java, 2nd Edition
Java AWT Reference
Java Cryptography
Java Distributed Computing
Java Examples in a Nutshell
Java Foundation Classes in a Nutshell
Java Fundamental Classes Reference
Java in a Nutshell, 2nd Edition
Java in a Nutshell, Deluxe Edition
Java I/O
Java Language Reference, 2nd Edition
Java Media Players
Java Native Methods
Java Network Programming
Java Security
Java Servlet Programming
Java Swing
Java Threads
Java Virtual Machine

UNIX

Exploring Expect
GNU Emacs Pocket Reference
Learning GNU Emacs, 2nd Edition
Learning the bash Shell, 2nd Edition
Learning the Korn Shell
Learning the UNIX Operating System,
    4th Edition
Learning the vi Editor, 6th Edition
Linux in a Nutshell
Linux Multimedia Guide
Running Linux, 2nd Edition
SCO UNIX in a Nutshell
sed & awk, 2nd Edition
Tcl/Tk in a Nutshell
Tcl/Tk Pocket Reference
Tcl/Tk Tools
The UNIX CD Bookshelf
UNIX in a Nutshell, System V Edition
UNIX Power Tools, 2nd Edition
Using csh & tsch
Using Samba
vi Editor Pocket Reference
What You Need To Know:
    When You Can't Find Your
    UNIX System Administrator
Writing GNU Emacs Extensions

SONGLINE GUIDES

NetLaw   NetResearch
NetLearning   NetSuccess
NetLessons   NetTravel

SOFTWARE

Building Your Own WebSite™
Building Your Own Web Conference
WebBoard™ 3.0
WebSite Professional™ 2.0
PolyForm™

SYSTEM ADMINISTRATION

Building Internet Firewalls
Computer Security Basics
Cracking DES
DNS and BIND, 3rd Edition
DNS on WindowsNT
Essential System Administration
Essential WindowsNT
    System Administration
Getting Connected:
    The Internet at 56K and Up
Linux Network Administrator's Guide
Managing IP Networks with
    Cisco Routers
Managing Mailing Lists
Managing NFS and NIS
Managing the WindowsNT Registry
Managing Usenet
MCSE: The Core Exams in a Nutshell
MCSE: The Electives in a Nutshell
Networking Personal Computers
    with TCP/IP
Oracle Performance Tuning,
    2nd Edition
Practical UNIX & Internet Security,
    2nd Edition
PGP: Pretty Good Privacy
Protecting Networks with SATAN
sendmail, 2nd Edition
sendmail Desktop Reference
System Performance Tuning
TCP/IP Network Administration,
    2nd Edition
termcap & terminfo
The Networking CD Bookshelf
Using & Managing PPP
Virtual Private Networks
WindowsNT Backup & Restore
WindowsNT Desktop Reference
WindowsNT Event Logging
WindowsNT in a Nutshell
WindowsNT Server 4.0 for
    Netware Administrators
WindowsNT SNMP
WindowsNT TCP/IP Administration
WindowsNT User Administration
Zero Administration for Windows

X WINDOW

Vol. 1: Xlib Programming Manual
Vol. 2: Xlib Reference Manual
Vol. 3M: X Window System
    User's Guide, Motif Edition
Vol. 4M: X Toolkit Intrinsics
    Programming Manual,
    Motif Edition
Vol. 5: X Toolkit Intrinsics
    Reference Manual
Vol. 6A: Motif Programming Manual
Vol. 6B: Motif Reference Manual
Vol. 8 : X Window System
    Administrator's Guide

PROGRAMMING

Access Database Design and
    Programming
Advanced Oracle PL/SQL
    Programming with Packages
Applying RCS and SCCS
BE Developer's Guide
BE Advanced Topics
C++: The Core Language
Checking C Programs with lint
Developing Windows Error Messages
Developing Visual Basic Add-ins
Guide to Writing DCE Applications
High Performance Computing,
    2nd Edition
Inside the Windows 95 File System
Inside the Windows 95 Registry
lex & yacc, 2nd Edition
Linux Device Drivers
Managing Projects with make
Oracle8 Design Tips
Oracle Built-in Packages
Oracle Design
Oracle PL/SQL Programming,
    2nd Edition
Oracle Scripts
Oracle Security
Palm Programming:
    The Developer's Guide
Porting UNIX Software
POSIX Programmer's Guide
POSIX.4: Programming
    for the Real World
Power Programming with RPC
Practical C Programming, 3rd Edition
Practical C++ Programming
Programming Python
Programming with curses
Programming with GNU Software
Pthreads Programming
Python Pocket Reference
Software Portability with imake,
    2nd Edition
UML in a Nutshell
Understanding DCE
UNIX Systems Programming for SVR4
VB/VBA in a Nutshell: The Languages
Win32 Multithreaded Programming
Windows NT File System Internals
Year 2000 in a Nutshell

USING WINDOWS

Excel97 Annoyances
Office97 Annoyances
Outlook Annoyances
Windows Annoyances
Windows98 Annoyances
Windows95 in a Nutshell
Windows98 in a Nutshell
Word97 Annoyances

OTHER TITLES

PalmPilot: The Ultimate Guide
Palm Programming:
    The Developer's Guide

O'REILLY®

TO ORDER: **800-998-9938** • **order@oreilly.com** • **http://www.oreilly.com/**
OUR PRODUCTS ARE AVAILABLE AT A BOOKSTORE OR SOFTWARE STORE NEAR YOU.
FOR INFORMATION: **800-998-9938** • **707-829-0515** • **info@oreilly.com**

International Distributors

UK, EUROPE, MIDDLE EAST AND AFRICA (EXCEPT FRANCE, GERMANY, AUSTRIA, SWITZERLAND, LUXEMBOURG, LIECHTENSTEIN, AND EASTERN EUROPE)

INQUIRIES
O'Reilly UK Limited
4 Castle Street
Farnham
Surrey, GU9 7HS
United Kingdom
Telephone: 44-1252-711776
Fax: 44-1252-734211
Email: josette@oreilly.com

ORDERS
Wiley Distribution Services Ltd.
1 Oldlands Way
Bognor Regis
West Sussex PO22 9SA
United Kingdom
Telephone: 44-1243-779777
Fax: 44-1243-820250
Email: cs-books@wiley.co.uk

FRANCE

ORDERS
GEODIF
61, Bd Saint-Germain
75240 Paris Cedex 05, France
Tel: 33-1-44-41-46-16 (French books)
Tel: 33-1-44-41-11-87 (English books)
Fax: 33-1-44-41-11-44
Email: distribution@eyrolles.com

INQUIRIES
Éditions O'Reilly
18 rue Séguier
75006 Paris, France
Tel: 33-1-40-51-52-30
Fax: 33-1-40-51-52-31
Email: france@editions-oreilly.fr

GERMANY, SWITZERLAND, AUSTRIA, EASTERN EUROPE, LUXEMBOURG, AND LIECHTENSTEIN

INQUIRIES & ORDERS
O'Reilly Verlag
Balthasarstr. 81
D-50670 Köln
Germany
Telephone: 49-221-973160-91
Fax: 49-221-973160-8
Email: anfragen@oreilly.de (inquiries)
Email: order@oreilly.de (orders)

CANADA (FRENCH LANGUAGE BOOKS)
Les Éditions Flammarion ltée
375, Avenue Laurier Ouest
Montréal (Québec) H2V 2K3
Tel: 00-1-514-277-8807
Fax: 00-1-514-278-2085
Email: info@flammarion.qc.ca

HONG KONG
City Discount Subscription Service, Ltd.
Unit D, 3rd Floor, Yan's Tower
27 Wong Chuk Hang Road
Aberdeen, Hong Kong
Tel: 852-2580-3539
Fax: 852-2580-6463
Email: citydis@ppn.com.hk

KOREA
Hanbit Media, Inc.
Sonyoung Bldg. 202
Yeksam-dong 736-36
Kangnam-ku
Seoul, Korea
Tel: 822-554-9610
Fax: 822-556-0363
Email: hant93@chollian.dacom.co.kr

PHILIPPINES
Mutual Books, Inc.
429-D Shaw Boulevard
Mandaluyong City, Metro
Manila, Philippines
Tel: 632-725-7538
Fax: 632-721-3056
Email: mbikikog@mnl.sequel.net

TAIWAN
O'Reilly Taiwan
No. 3, Lane 131
Hang-Chow South Road
Section 1, Taipei, Taiwan
Tel: 886-2-23968990
Fax: 886-2-23968916
Email: taiwan@oreilly.com

CHINA
O'Reilly Beijing
Room 2410
160, FuXingMenNeiDaJie
XiCheng District
Beijing, China PR 100031
Tel: 86-10-86631006
Fax: 86-10-86631007
Email: beijing@oreilly.com

INDIA
Computer Bookshop (India) Pvt. Ltd.
190 Dr. D.N. Road, Fort
Bombay 400 001 India
Tel: 91-22-207-0989
Fax: 91-22-262-3551
Email: cbsbom@giasbm01.vsnl.net.in

JAPAN
O'Reilly Japan, Inc.
Kiyoshige Building 2F
12-Bancho, Sanei-cho
Shinjuku-ku
Tokyo 160-0008 Japan
Tel: 81-3-3356-5227
Fax: 81-3-3356-5261
Email: japan@oreilly.com

ALL OTHER ASIAN COUNTRIES
O'Reilly & Associates, Inc.
101 Morris Street
Sebastopol, CA 95472 USA
Tel: 707-829-0515
Fax: 707-829-0104
Email: order@oreilly.com

AUSTRALIA
WoodsLane Pty., Ltd.
7/5 Vuko Place
Warriewood NSW 2102
Australia
Tel: 61-2-9970-5111
Fax: 61-2-9970-5002
Email: info@woodslane.com.au

NEW ZEALAND
Woodslane New Zealand, Ltd.
21 Cooks Street (P.O. Box 575)
Waganui, New Zealand
Tel: 64-6-347-6543
Fax: 64-6-345-4840
Email: info@woodslane.com.au

LATIN AMERICA
McGraw-Hill Interamericana
Editores, S.A. de C.V.
Cedro No. 512
Col. Atlampa
06450, Mexico, D.F.
Tel: 52-5-547-6777
Fax: 52-5-547-3336
Email: mcgraw-hill@infosel.net.mx

O'REILLY®

TO ORDER: **800-998-9938** • *order@oreilly.com* • *http://www.oreilly.com/*
OUR PRODUCTS ARE AVAILABLE AT A BOOKSTORE OR SOFTWARE STORE NEAR YOU.
FOR INFORMATION: **800-998-9938** • **707-829-0515** • *info@oreilly.com*